CU00922712

TOPOGRAPHY OF LONDON

TOPOGRAPHY
OF LONDON

FACSIMILE OF
JOHN LOCKIE'S
GAZETTEER
1813

LONDON TOPOGRAPHICAL SOCIETY
PUBLICATION No.148
1994

Publication No.148
LONDON TOPOGRAPHICAL SOCIETY
3 Meadway Gate, London NW11 7LA

ISBN 0 902087 39 8

Printed in Great Britain by
Cromwell Press Ltd, Broughton Gifford, Wilts
Bound by Cedric Chivers Ltd, Bristol

INTRODUCTION

In 1985 the London Topographical Society issued an *A to Z of Regency London*. This street atlas proved very popular. The map it featured was Richard Horwood's survey of London, first published in 1792–1799, and revised in 1813. Horwood's huge map consisted of thirty-two sheets and purported to show every building in the metropolis. For large areas of London it supplied all the house numbers, too. Horwood had compiled a sheet index of 1,700 streets, which was woefully inadequate, and for our *A to Z* we commissioned Joseph Wisdom to produce an entirely new index which would include every street Horwood had named on his map. The completed index consisted of approximately 6,000 entries.

John Lockie's gazetteer – the one you are now holding – was published in the same year as Horwood's i.e. 1813. This new index improved on Horwood's hugely. Indeed it has many names that are not in our *A to Z* either, for it includes no less than 10,000 London place names. The first edition of Lockie's gazetteer had appeared in 1810. This 1813 edition contained a new feature – a map engraved by H. Cooper, invaluable since it demonstrated the area he had included in his listing. In 1810 he had announced the imminent publication of an entirely new map which he had himself compiled. Measuring four feet by two feet it would be published by subscription and cost fourteen shillings. 'Of its Copiousness he [Lockie] presumes confidently to assert, that it far exceeds that of any other Plan of London now extant, containing upwards of Two Thousand Places, the Names of which are not to be found in the *large Map of Thirty-Two Sheets, by* HORWOOD. Subscriptions for the above PLAN are received by the Author, at the PHOENIX FIRE-OFFICE, *Lombard Street*.'

Sadly, John Lockie's new map never appeared. It is Cooper's map which reappears in a second printing of the second edition in 1816.

But who was Lockie? Nothing appears to be known about him other than his statement on the title-page that he was employed as an inspector of buildings by the Phoenix Fire Office, the very company which had loaned Horwood £500 to enable him to complete his survey. It is intriguing to speculate whether the two ever met – the struggling, impecunious Horwood whose prodigious efforts undermined his health leading to an early death at forty-five in 1803; and the self-assured Lockie operating in a more rarefied atmosphere. Whether in fact Lockie actually 'went over the whole Metropolis again' for the second edition must always remain a moot point. Clearly his profession would have provided him with the wherewithal to accomplish this remarkable feat.

The real joy of Lockie's *Topography*, beyond any accusations of professional jealousy, lies in its 'user-friendliness.' Not for Lockie the bald grid-references of a modern A–Z street map. He takes the reader by the arm and walks along the street with him, crosses over the way, turns right, and there is the desired road, just past the church. The introduction of street numbering in the latter years of the eighteenth century was, by 1813, almost universal throughout the central area of London, enabling Lockie to give such directions as 'at 52, opposite Brick Lane, quarter of a mile on the left from 65 Shoreditch'; 'at 38, nearly

2

opposite Spital-Square, leading to Long Alley', '6th on the left from 138 Bermondsey Street'; 'between St Saviour's Church and the Thames, entrance by Pepper Alley.' Oxford Street is described as 'running from St. Giles's, where the numbers begin and end 1 and 400, to Tyburn-Turnpike, where there is 245, about a mile and a third in length.' It is not merely streets which are minutely described in the *Topography*; as the subtitle on his title-page proclaims it includes 'the new buildings to the present time.' Lockie indeed inserts a vast range of buildings, from breweries to prisons, and from the Post Office to the Mint.

Lockie really comes into his own with his distinctions between like-named streets. In the index to the *A to Z of Regency London* you will find 39 New Courts, 23 Union Places, and even 5 Queen's Head Courts. To find the New Court you need you may have to turn up 39 map references, turning then 39 times to the map sheets. It is a time-consuming and frustrating exercise. Lockie, however, gives a full description of the topography of each. And only in Lockie is there a virtually full listing of the multitudinous side-courts, back alleys, slum terraces, and blind cul-de-sacs which barely figure on Horwood. This is the real teeming world of Regency London, with names which sound as if culled from the pages of Dickens, still more than a generation away – Unanimous Row, Three Dagger Court, Monster Row, Money-Bag Alley, and Pyed-Horse Yard. There are still sufficient relics of an older London in evidence for almost the last time before Nash, Bazalgette, and above all the railways arrived to sweep away all this trumpery nonsense for ever.

Today it is only possible to walk the streets of Lockie's *Topography* in the mind's eye. Two world wars and massive redevelopment have seen to that. Both Lockie and the Phoenix Fire Assurance Company deserve the thanks of posterity for their heroic endeavours to preserve a moment of time in such a modest form.

David Webb

TOPOGRAPHY OF LONDON

Sam Cash

TOPOGRAPHY

OF

LONDON;

GIVING

A CONCISE LOCAL DESCRIPTION OF,

AND

ACCURATE DIRECTION TO,

EVERY

SQUARE, STREET, LANE, COURT,

DOCK, WHARF, INN, PUBLIC-OFFICE, &c.

IN THE

Metropolis and its Environs,

INCLUDING

The New Buildings to the present Time,

UPON A PLAN NEVER HITHERTO ATTEMPTED.

THE WHOLE

ALPHABETICALLY ARRANGED,

And comprising the Description of more than Three Thousand Places,
the Names of which are not to be found upon any of the
Maps of the present Year.

TAKEN FROM ACTUAL SURVEY,

BY JOHN LOCKIE,

INSPECTOR OF BUILDINGS TO THE PHŒNIX FIRE-OFFICE.

Second Edition,

CORRECTED AND REVISED BY THE AUTHOR;

With upwards of Sixteen Hundred Places added thereto:
ACCOMPANIED BY A NEW MAP OF LONDON.

LONDON:

PRINTED FOR SHERWOOD, NEELY, AND JONES,
20, Paternoster Row;
AND J. M. RICHARDSON, CORNHILL.

1813.

James Compton, Printer, Middle Street, Cloth Fair, London.

TO THE

BOARD of DIRECTORS

OF THE

Phoenix Fire-Office,

THIS

WORK

IS MOST RESPECTFULLY DEDICATED,

BY THEIR

MOST OBLIGED AND OBEDIENT

HUMBLE SERVANT,

J. LOCKIE.

London, January 1813.

PREFACE.

THE flattering reception which the former Edition of this Work met with from the Public, would, perhaps, to any person except the Author, have been a sufficient inducement to reprint it, without attempting any thing like improvement.

The new Map of London, however, advertised in the former Edition, which the Author hopes shortly to publish, as well as some other pursuits in which he is engaged, rendered it necessary that he should go over the whole Metropolis again; and it was not until he had finished this arduous undertaking that he began the revisal for this new Edition.

How far his additional labours have been successfully directed towards the improvement of this Work, he leaves with the Public to decide. He begs, however, to state that, besides correcting the whole of the Descriptions, he has added upwards of sixteen hundred new ones to those contained in the former Edition.

LOCKIE'S

TOPOGRAPHY OF LONDON.

ABB

ABBEY-PL.—1st on the L. in Little Coram-st. from 54, Gt. Coram-st.

Abbey-Pl. Bethnal-Green Rd. —the continuation of Mary's-row, N.E. corner of Wilmot-sq.

Abbey-Pl. North,-N. end of the last.

Abbey-Pl. South,—S. end of the aforesaid.

Abbey-St. Bethnal-Green-Rd.- at 92, 1st on the R. below the turnpike.

Abbey-Row,—from the last to White-st.

Abchurch-Lane, Lombard-St.— at 18, 2d on the R. from the Mansion-house.

Abchurch-Yd.—S. end of the last by 67, Cannon-st.

Abel's Builds. Rosemary-Lane,- from 94, E. end, leading to Chamber-st.

Abingdon-Builds. Abingdon-St. Westr.—at 17, op. College-st.

Abingdon - Court, Abingdon-St. Bethnal-Green,—adjoins Parliament-st.

Abingdon-Place, Abingdon-St. Westr.—corner of Old Palace-yd.

Abingdon-St. Westr.—from Old Palace-yd. to Millbank-st.

ADA

Abingdon-St. (Little)—10 doors in the last from Old Palace-yd.

Abingdon St. Bethnal-Green,— 1st W. parallel to Belvedere, op. Duthie's Nursery.

Aboukir-Pl. Pleasant-Pl. Stepney-Green,—2 doors from Prospect-pl.

Academy Court, Chancery Lane, —at 93, five doors N. of Carey-st.

Acorn-Court, Rolls-Builds.— 1st on the R. from 117, Fetter-lane.

Acorn-St. Bishopsgate-without, —at 125, leading to Skinner-st.

Acorn-Yard, Trinity-St. Rotherhithe,—S. end, adjoining Russell-st.

Acton-Place, Lock's Fields, Walworth,- the continuation of York-st. to Camden-st.

Acton-St. Gray's-Inn-Lane,—¼ of a mile N. of Guildford-st.

Adam and Eve-Court, Oxford-St.—at 67, nearly op. the Pantheon.

Adam and Eve-Court, Whitecross-St. St. Luke's,—at 106, middle of the E. side.

Adam and Eve-Court, Angel-Alley,—a few yards from

A

137, Bishopsgate, towards 45, Skinner-st.

Adam and Eve-Court, Duke's-Pl.—1st on the L. from Mitre-st. Aldgate.

Adam-a-Digging-Yd. Gt. Peter-St. Westminster,—middle of the S. side.

Adam's-Court, Old Broad-St.—at 11, op. Throgmorton-st.

Adam's-Gardens, Adam-St. Rotherhithe,—1st N. parallel, from Adam's-pl. to New-court.

Adam's-Mews, Adam-St. Portman-Sq.—at 20, six doors on the L. from 26, Up. Seymour-street.

Adam's-Mews, South Audley-St.—7 doors on the L. from Grosvenor-sq.

Adam's-Pl. High-St. Boro.—at 187, about 22 doors S. of Union-st.

Adam's-Pl. Adam-St. Rotherhithe,—near the W. end, being the first on the L. from Neptune-st.

Adam's-Row, Hampstead-Road,—from the New-road to Henry-st.

Adam-St. Portman-Sq.—at 8, Baker-st. leading to 56, Manchester-st.

Adam-St. West, Upper Seymour St.—at 30, the first on the L. from Portman-sq.

Adam-St. Adelphi,—at 73, in the Strand, 73 doors on the R. from Charing-+.

Adam-St. Rotherhithe,—2d S. parallel to the Thames, from Neptune-st. (where there are 1 & 94,) to Swan-lane.

Addle-Hill, Upper Thames-St.—at 231, 1st on the L. from Earl-st. leading to 4, Gt. Carter-lane.

Addle-St. Wood-St.—at 43, 3d on the R. from 122, Cheapside.

Adelphi, Strand. See Adam-St.

Adelphi-Terrace,—2d on the R. in Adam-st. from 73, Strand.

Adelphi-Wharfs, under the Terrace,—entrance at Durham-st. 65, Strand.

Adjutant - General's Office, Whitehall,—the door on the L. under the arch in the Horse-Guards, from Whitehall towards the Park.

Admiralty, Whitehall,—a few yards on the R. from Charing-+, op. Gt. Scotland-yd.

Admiralty-Office, Doctors-Commons,—2d door on the L. from 7, Gt. Knight-Rider-st.

Affidavit-Office, Symonds-Inn,—1st on the R. from 23, Chancery-lane.

African-Company's Office,—at 3, Suffolk-lane, Cannon-st.

St. Agnes-le-Clair, Old-Street Road,—between Paul-st. and Pump-row.

St. Agnes-Crescent, Old-St.-Rd.—part of the S. side from Paul-st. to Wood-st.

St. Agnes-Pl.—the few houses which connect Old-st.-rd. with Paul-st.

St. Agnes-Street, Old-St.-Rd.—1st S. parallel to part of it, extending from Paul-st. to Wood-street.

St. Agnes-Terrace, Tabernacle-Walk,—N. continuation of it on the L. to Paul-st.

Agriculture, Board of,—at 32, Sackville-st. Piccadilly.

Air-St. Piccadilly,—27 doors on the R. from the Haymarket

Air's Alms-Houses, White's-Alley,—2d on the L. from 61, Coleman-st.

Airdrie-Pl. Alfred Mews,—1st on the R. from 199, Tottenham Court-rd.

St. Alban's-Court, Wood-St. Cheapside,—at 91, middle of the W. side.

St. Alban's-Church, Wood-St. Cheapside,—op. the last.

St. Alban's-St. Pall-Mall,—at 13, 2d on the R. from the Haymarket.

Albany, Piccadilly,—52, $\frac{1}{4}$ of a mile on the R. from the Haymarket.

Albany-New-Road, Kent-Rd.— 1st on the R. below the Green Man turnpike.

Albemarle-St. Piccadilly,-at 62, op. St. James's-st.

Albemarle-St. Clerkenwell,—at 83, St. John's-st. middle of the W. side.

Albion Brewery, Whitechapel-Rd.—at 170, a few doors W. of Mile-End turnpike.

Albion - Builds. Bartholomew-Close,—end of Westmoreland-builds. from 150, Aldersgate-st.

Albion-Builds. Shadwell,—op. Elbow-lane, from 30, High-st.

Albion-Builds. Bethnal Green,— nearly op. Patriot-sq.

Albion-Court, Albion-Pl. St. George's E.—leads to Mary-street.

Albion Fire and Life Office,—

corner of New Bridge-st. and Ludgate-hill.

Albion Information-Office,—at 21, Earl-st. Blackfriars.

Albion-Mews, Stamford-St.—3 doors on the R. from Blackfriars-road.

Albion-Pl. New Gravel-Lane,— 2d on the L. from Shadwell High-st.

Albion-Pl. Lower Chapman-St. St. George's East,—between Mary-st. and Duke-st.

Albion-Pl. Walworth,—3d on the L. from the Elephant and Castle.

Albion - Pl. East-Lane, Walworth,—part of the S. side, by the Kent-rd.

Albion-Pl. Black - friars-Road, —adjoining the bridge.

Albion-St. Commercial Road,— 4th on the R. east of Cannon-st.-road.

Albion-St. Black-friars-Rd.— continuation of Albion-pl. to Stamford-st.

Albion-St. Rotherhithe,—the E. continuation of Paradise-row, from Deptford lower rd.

Albion Terrace, Commercial-Rd.—by Mill-pl. $\frac{1}{4}$ mile W. of Limehouse church.

Aldborough - Sq.—N. end of Stratford-pl. from 160, Oxford-st.

Aldermanbury,—the continuation of Milk-st. Cheapside, to London-wall.

Aldermanbury-Postern,—the N. continuation of the last, to 32, Fore-st.

Alderman's-Walk, Bishopsgate, —at 201, N. side the church.

Aldermary Church Yard, —

at 37, Bow-lane, 18 doors on the L. from 59, Cheapside.

Aldersgate-Builds. Aldersgate-St.—at 91, 14 doors N. of Barbican.

Aldersgate Chapel,—10 doors N. of Falcon-st.

Aldersgate-School,—behind 77, Little Britain.

Aldersgate-St.—continuation of St. Martin's-Le-Grand, from 66, Newgate-st.

Aldersgate-Workhouse,—at 129, Aldersgate-st. the end of New-st. Cloth-fair.

Aldgate,—the E. continuation of Leadenhall-st. and Fenchurch-st. to Jewry-st.

Aldgate High-st.—E. continuation of the last to Somerset-street.

Aldgate-Workhouse,—the end of Cock and Hoop-yd. from 138, Houndsditch.

Aldolis-Court, John-St. Holywell Mount,—the 2d on the R. from 62, Leonard-st.

Aldridge's-Yd. Little St. Martin's-Lane,—5 doors N. of Long-acre.

Alexander-Builds. Three Oak-Lane, Horsely-down, — entrance opposite Free-school-street.

Alfred-Buildings, Castle-Lane, Westr.—2d on the R. from James-st.

Alfred - Builds. Windmill - St. Finsbury-sq.—a few yards on the R. from the N. W. corner of the sq.

Alfred-Ct. Paul's-Alley, Cripplegate,—the 2d on the L. from 17, Red-cross-st.

Alfred-Mews, Tottenham-Ct.-Rd.—at 199, op. Chapel-st.

Alfred-Pl. Goswell-St.-Road, —W. side from Rawstorne-st. to Owen's-pl.

Alfred-Pl. Kent-Road,—5th on the R. below the Bricklayers-arms.

Alfred-Pl. Bedford-Sq.—1st on the L. in Store-st. from Tottenham-court-rd.

Alfred-Pl. Gt. Surry-St. Black-Friars-Rd.—at 18, op. Christchurch.

Alfred-Pl. Newington,—nearly op. the Elephant and Castle.

Alfred-Row, Charles-St. Bethnal-Green-Rd.—2d on the L. from op. Wilmot-sq.

Alien-Office, Crown-St. Westminster,—18 doors on the R. from King-st.

Alienation-Office, King's-Bench Walk, Temple,—a few yards on the L. from Mitre-court, 44, Fleet-st.

Allen's or Allan's-Alms-Houses, Lamb-Alley,—a few doors on the R. from 144, Bishopsgate without.

Allen's-Builds. Bowling-Green-Lane, Clerkenwell,—the 1st on the L. from Coppice-row.

Allen's - Builds. Vine-Yd. St. Olave's,—2d on the L. from 110, E. end of Tooley-st.

Allen's-Court, Oxford-St. — at 388, between Wardour-st. and Chapel-st.

Allen's - Court, Harrow-Alley, Houndsditch,—2d on the R. from White-st.

Allen's-Court, Blue Gate Fields, —middle of the W. side.

Allen-St. Goswell-St.—at 113, leads to Compton-st.

Allen's Yard, Gt. Guildford-St. Russel-sq.—at 87, middle of the N. side.

Allerton-St. Hoxton Fields,—the 1st on the R. from Walbrook-pl. towards Chatham-gardens.

Alley's Alms-Houses, Gt. St. Ann's-St. Westr.—10 doors on the R. from Peter-st.

Allhallows-Church, Bread-St. Cheapside,—corner of Watling-st.

Allhallows-Church, London-Wall,—a few yards E. of Moorfields.

Allhallows-Church, 48, Lombard-st.

Allhallows-Barking-Church, —54, Gt. Tower-st. the corner of Seething-lane.

Allhallows-Church,Up.Thames-St.—at 88, corner of Allhallows-lane.

Allhallows-Staining-Church, Mark-Lane,—4 doors from 55, Fenchurch-st.

Allhallows-Lane, Up. Thames-St.—at 88, op. Bush-lane.

Allhallows-Passage, Gracechurch-St.—at 18, 6 doors N. of Lombard-st.

Allhallows-Stairs,—the bottom of Allhallows-lane, 88, Up. Thames-st.

Almack's Rooms, King-St. St. James's. See Willis's.

Almonry (Gt.) Westr.—1st in Dean-st. from Tothill-st.

Almonry(Little),—E. end of the last.

Almonry-Yd. Gt. Almonry,—middle of the S. side.

Alpha-Rd. Lisson Grove,—⅓ of a mile N. of the Yorkshire Stingo.

Alphabet-Court,Brown'sBuilds. —50, Stanhope-st. leading to Nag's head-court, and 119, Drury-lane.

St. Alphage's-Church, London-Wall,—4 doors W. of Aldermanbury.

Alport's Garden, Hackney-Rd.-⅓ of a mile on the L. from Shoreditch-church.

Alsop's-Builds. New-Rd. Marybone,—N. side op. Baker-st. Port.-sq.

Alsop's-Farm,—at the back of the last.

Alsop's-Mews,—1st on the L. in Baker-st. North from the New-rd.

Alsop's-Pl. Baker-St. North,—1st on the L. from New-rd.

Alscot-Pl. Grange Rd.—part of the R. side, ¼ of a mile from Bermondsey New-rd.

Amelia-Row, Borough-Road,—1st on the L. from the King's-Bench.

Amelia-St. Walworth,—4th on the R. from the Elephant and Castle.

Amen-Corner, Ave-Maria-Lane,—2d on the L. from 29, Ludgate-st.

America-Pl. Borough,—at 21, Queen-st. 14 doors E. of Gt. Guildford-st.

America-Mews,—behind the S. side of America-sq.

America-Sq. Minories,—at 131, middle of the W. side.

America-St. Gt.-Guilford-St. Boro.—1st on the R. from 35, Queen-st.

A 3

Amias Alms-Houses, George-yd. Old-St.—at the N. end.

Amicable Assurance - Office, Serjeant's - Inn,—6th house on the L. from 50, Fleet-street.

Amphitheatre (Astley's) Surry side of Westminster-bridge.

Amphitheatre-Row, Westminster - Bridge - Rd. — from Astley's Theatre to Stangate.

Anchor-Alley, Old-St. St. Luke's —at 99, first W. of the Church.

Anchor-Brewery, Old-St.—op. the last.

Anchor - Brewery, (Charrington's) Mile-End - Road, — about ¼ of a mile on the L. from the turnpike, and op. Stepney-green.

Anchor Brewery, Shad Thames, —on the E. side of Horsely-down Old-stairs.

Anchor and Hope Alley, St. George's East,—the continuation of Red-Lion-st. from 120, Wapping.

Anchor-St. Shoreditch or Bethnal-Green,—from the back of the Swan, 54, Shoreditch, to Club-row.

Anchor - St. (Little), Bethnal-Green,—parallel to and between Anchor-st. and Church-street.

Anchor-Lane, Mile-End,—W. side of Charrington's Brewery, ¼ of a mile on the L. from the turnpike.

Anchor-Wharf, Upper-Thames-St.—at 8, op. Addle-hill.

Anchor - Wharf, Bermondsey-Wall,—a few yards W. of Fountain-stairs.

Anderson's-Builds. City-Road, —N. side by the turnpike, about ¾ of a mile from Finsbury-sq.

Anderson's-Buildings, Grange-Road,—part of the L. side, ⅓ of a mile from Bermondsey-new-rd.

Anderson's-Court, Queen-St. Boro.—15 doors on the R. from Union-st.

Anderson's-Place, Anderson's-Walk, Lambeth,—1st on the L. from Princes-st.

Anderson's - Walk, Vauxhall-Walk,—2d on the R. from Lambeth-Butts.

Anderson's-Yard, Royal-Hospital-Row, Chelsea,—3d on the L. from the Hospital.

St. Andrew's-Church, Holborn-Hill,—a few doors on the L. from Fleet-market.

Saint Andrew's - Undershaft-Church, St. Mary-axe,—the corner of Leadenhall-st.

St. Andrew's-Court, Holborn-Hill,—20 doors on the L. from Fleet-market.

St. Andrew's-Court, White-friars,—part of Ashentree-court, Temple-st.

St. Andrew's-Hill, Black-friars, —from the E. end of Earl-st. to Gt. Carter-lane.

St. Andrew's Charity-School, Hatton-Garden,—at 43, the corner of Cross-st.

St. Andrew's-St. 7 Dials,—1st E. of Monmouth-st.

St. Andrew's-St. (Little)—the continuation of the last to St. Martin's-lane.

St. Andrew's-Warf, Earl-Street, Black-friars,—at 13, near Puddle-dock.

St. Andrew's-Workhouse,—41, Shoe-lane, a few doors from Holborn-hill.

St. Andrew's-Workhouse,—N. end of Saffron-hill, by Ray-st. Clerkenwell.

St. Andrew's Holborn and St. George the Martyr's Work-house,—on the W. side Little Gray's-inn-lane.

Angel-Alley, Long - Acre,—10 doors on the R. from St. Martin's-lane.

Angel-Alley, Aldersgate-St.— at 42, S. side of Jewin-st.

Angel-Alley, Angel-Sq.—at 138, Bishopsgate, 6 doors N. of Sun-st.

Angel-Alley, Little Moorfields, —3d on the L. from 61, Fore-street.

Angel-Alley, Ratcliffe-highway, —at 61, op. St. George's church.

Angel-Alley, Nightingale-Lane, at 22, 3d on the R. from 110, Up. E. Smithfield.

Angel-Alley, Whitechapel,—at 84, 1st W. of Osborn-st.

Angel-Alley, High-St. Boro.—at 146, near St. George's church.

Angel-Court, Prince's-St. West-minster,—2d on the L. from Story's-gate.

Angel-Court, King-Street, Saint James's-Sq.—at 20, middle of the S. side.

Angel-Court, Strand,—at 335, op. Somerset-house.

Angel-Court, Strand,—at 173, on the E. side of Surrey-st.

Angel-Court, Charing-Cross,— six doors on the L. from the Strand.

Angel-Court, Gt. Windmill-St.–

1st on the L. from Piccadilly.

Angel-Court, Angel-St.—1st on the R. from 15, St. Martin's-le-grand.

Angel-Court, Golden-Lane,—at 43, the fourth on the R. from Barbican.

Angel-Court, Grub-St. Cripple-gate,—at 68, middle of the E. side.

Angel-Court, Friday-St.-6 doors on the R. from 35, Cheapside.

Angel-Court, Skinner-St. Snow-hill,—at 24, 1st on the L. from Newgate.

Angel-Court, Throgmorton-St.–at 35, 6 doors E. of the Bank.

Angel-Court, Red-Lion-St. Spi-talfields,—on the W. side the church.

Angel-Court, Leadenhall-St.— at 64, ten doors on the L. from Aldgate.

Angel-Court, White's-Yard,— 2d on the R. from 58, Rose-mary-lane.

Angel-Court, Back-Lane, Shad-well,—4 doors E. of Blue-gate-fields.

Angel-Court, Shadwell High-St. —at 235, nine doors E. of Bluegate-fields.

Angel-Court, Nightingale-Lane, Up. E. Smithfield,—the con-tinuation of Angel-alley.

Angel - Court, Stoney-Lane,— 2d on the L. from Gravel-lane, Houndsditch.

Angel-Court, Red-Cross-St. Bo-ro.—at 82, the third on the L. from Park-st.

Angel-Court, High-St. Boro.— at 146, near St. George's church.

Angel-Court, York-St. Boro,—

2d on the R. from 276, High-st.

Angel-Court, Walworth High-St.—the corner of Amelia-st.

Angel - Gardens, Back - Lane, Shadwell,—8 doors E. of Bluegate-fields.

Angel-Inn, St. Clement's, Strand, —on the N. side the church, near Temple-bar.

Angel-Inn, St. Giles's,—adjoining E. side the church.

Angel-Inn, Angel-St.—13 doors on the R. in Butcher-hall-lane, from 82, Newgate-st.

Angel-Inn, Fleet-Market,—at 53, ten doors from Holborn.

Angel-Inn, Islington,—at the point where the City-road, Pentonville, High-st. and St. John-st.-road, all meet.

Angel-Inn, Blackman-St. Boro. —at 80, by Gt. Suffolk-st.

Angel-Livery-Stables, Earl-St. Black-friars,—3 doors on the L. from New Bridge-st.

Angel-Passage, Up. Thames-St. —at 95, op. Ducks-foot-lane.

Angel-Passage, Skinner-St.—2d on the L. from 120, Bishopsgate-without.

Angel-Pl. Broad-Wall, Lambeth, —middle of the E. side, near Hatfield-st.

Angel-Row, Islington, — from the Angel-inn towards Pentonville.

Angel-Row, Commercial-Road, —the corner of Poplar High-street.

Angel-Sq. Bishopsgate-Without, —at 138, six doors N. of Sun-street.

Angel-Street, St. Martin's-le-Grand,—1st on the L. from 66, Newgate-st.

Angel-St. Broad-Wall, S. end,— 2d on the R. in Lambeth-marsh, from Black-friars-rd.

Angel and Sun-Inn, Strand,— at 18½, about ⅛ of a mile on the R. from Temple-bar.

Angel - Yard, Piccadilly,—34 doors on the R. from the Haymarket.

St. Ann's Church, Blackfriars,— a few yards on the R. on St. Andrew's-hill, from Earl-st.

St. Ann's Church, Soho,—at the bottom of Dean-st.

St. Ann's Church, St. Ann's-Lane,—middle of the N. side, behind 41, Noble-st. Foster-lane.

St. Ann's Church, Limehouse,— on the S. side the Commercial-rd.

St. Ann's-Court, St. Ann's-St. Westr.—the first on the R. from Gt. Peter-st.

St. Ann's-Court, Wardour-St. Soho,—at 31, middle of the E. side.

Ann's-Court, Philip-Lane,—5 doors on the L. from Addle-st. Wood-st.

St. Ann's-Court, Up. Well-Alley, —2d on the L. from 110, Wapping.

St. Ann's-Court, Mary-Street, St. George's East,—between Chapel-st. and Lower Chapman-street.

St. Ann's-Lane (Little),—from 39, Old Pye-st. to Gt. Peter-street.

St. Ann's-Lane, Foster-Lane,— from 17, to 58, Saint Martin's-le-grand.

St. Ann's-Passage, Noble-St.— at 41, 3 doors N. of the last.

Ann's-Pl. Bull's-Hd.-Court, Gt. Peter-st. Westr.—1st on the R. from Strutton-ground.

Ann's-Pl. Ossulston-St. Sommers-Town,—8 doors N. of Chapel-path.

Ann's-Pl. Vincent-St. Bethnal-Green,—at the W. end facing Cock-lane.

St. Ann's-Pl. Commercial-Rd. Limehouse,—part of the N. side, op. the church.

St. Ann's-Pl. East,—op. the last on the E. side the church.

St. Ann's-Pl. North, Limehouse, —E. side of Salmon's-lane, by the Commercial-road.

Ann's-Pl. Salmon's-Lane,—the 3d on the L. from the Commercial-road.

Ann's-Pl. Jamaica-Pl. Limehouse,—1st on the L. from Gun-lane.

Ann's-Pl. St. George's-Fields, —from Webber-row to Barons-builds.

Ann's - Pl. Bethnal - Green,— nearly op. Patriot-sq.

Ann's-Row, Bethnal-Green-Rd. —on the E. side of Wilmot-sq. leading to Mary's-row.

Ann's-Pl. Stepney,—op. the S. W. corner of the church by the Ship.

Ann's-Row, Stepney-Green,— the corner of Cross-row.

St. Ann's-Row, Limehouse,— the first on the R. in St. Ann's-st. from op. the church.

St. Ann's-School, Rose-Street, Soho,—3 doors from Crown-street.

St. Ann's-School, St. Ann's-Lane,—4th house on the lt. from 17, Foster-lane.

St. Ann's-Street, Westr.—at 33, Orchard-st. six doors on the L. from Dean-st.

Ann-St. Pentonville,—2d E. of the chapel.

Ann-St. Bethnal-Green-Rd.— N. W. corner of Wilmot-sq. leading to Pollard-row.

Ann-St. op. the N. end of Black-Lion-Yard,—from 38, Whitechapel.

Ann-Street, St. George's East,— 3d on the R. in Lower Chapman-st. from Cannon - st. road.

Ann's - St. (Little), op. the last.

St. Ann's-St. Commercial-Rd. Limehouse,—op. the church.

Ann-St. Black-Wall,—1st W. of the E. India-dock-gate.

St. Ann's-Workhouse, Soho,— 1st house on the L. in Rose-st. from 6, Greek-st.

Annuity-Bank, Knightsbridge, —1st house on the R. from Hyde-park-corner.

Ansel's - Rents, Three-Colt-St. Limehouse,—at 34, nearly op. Ropemakers-fields.

Antelope - Gardens, Holywell-Mount,——the corner of Phipps-st. and Luke-st.

Anthony - St. New - Road, St. George's East, — the 2d E. of Cannon-st. turnpike.

Antigallican-Passage, Temple-Bar,—adjoining the W. side.

St. Antholin's-Church, Size-Lane,—corner of Budge-row.

Antigua-Place, Salmon's-Lane, Lime-house,—the continuation of Wilson-pl. 1st on the L. from the Commercial-rd. towards Stepney.

Antiquarian - Society. See Royal.

Apollo-Builds. St. George's Fds. —3d on the L. in Tower-st. from the Asylum.

Apollo-Builds. East-Lane, Walworth,—part of both sides, about the middle.

Apollo-Court, Fleet-St.—at 200, N. side by Temple-bar.

Apothecary's-Hall, Blackfriars, —facing Union-st. from 36, New-Bridge-st.

Appleby - Court, Bermondsey-St.—at 184, near ½ a mile on the R. from Tooley-st.

Apple-Tree-Yard, York-St.— 1st on the L. from St. James's-church, Piccadilly.

Arabella-Gardens, Chelsea,— W. side of Grosvenor-row, by the one mile stone from Buckingham-gate.

Arabella-Row, Pimlico,—1st on the R. from Buckingham-gate.

Archer-St. Gt. Windmill-St.— at 19, 1st on the R. from the Hay-market.

Archer - Yard, Christopher's-Alley, Finsbury,—1st on the L. from Wilson-st.

Archibald-Pl. Wallburge-Street, St. George's East,—1st on the R. from Back-lane.

Argyle-St. Oxford-St.—at 337, ¼ of a mile on the L. from St. Giles's.

Argyle-St. (Little),—1st on the R. in the last from Oxford-street.

Aris - Builds. Bowling - Green-Lane, Clerkenwell,—2d on the L. from Coppice-row.

Arlington - St. Piccadilly,—at 160, ½ of a mile on the L. from the Hay-market.

Armourers and Braziers Alms-Houses,—in Two Swan-yard, Bishopsgate-without.

Army-Medical-Office, Berkeley-St.—7 doors on the R. from Piccadilly.

Army - Pay - Office, Horse - Guards,—entrance, a few yards on the L. (under the arch) from White-hall.

Army-Victualling-Office. See Victualling-Office.

Arnold's - Pl. Walworth,—the continuation of Francis-st. Newington.

Arnold's-Paragon, — middle of the W. side the last.

Arthur-Pl. Bell-Alley,—the 1st on the R. from 13, Goswell-st.

Arthur-St. (Gt.) St. Luke's,— entrance by New-court, from 10, Goswell-st.

Arthur-St. (Little),—entrance the 1st on the R. in the last from Goswell-st.

Artichoke-Court, White-cross-St. Cripplegate,—at 10,7 doors S. of Beech-lane.

Artichoke-Court, Cannon-St.— at 32, op. Abchurch-lane.

Artichoke-Court, Artichoke-Yd. —1st on the L. from Lambeth-marsh.

Artichoke-Hill, Ratcliffe-High-way,—at 19, op. Princes-sq.

Artichoke-Pl. Artichoke-Row, Mile-end,—6 doors E. from the Fountain-public-house.

Artichoke-Row, Mile-End-Rd. —S. side op. the Bell and Mackarel, about 2 miles from Aldgate.

Artichoke - Yard, Newington-

Causeway, — 2d on the L. from the King's-Bench.

Artichoke-Yd. Lambeth-Marsh, —2d on the L. from Westr.-bridge-rd.

Artillery-Court, Chiswell-St.— at 53, 1st on the R. from Finsbury-sq.

Artillery-Ground, —on the W. of Finsbury-sq. entrance at 53, Chiswell-st. 29, Bunhill-row, and 13, Artillery-pl.

Artillery-Ground (Old), —part of Union-st. Bishopsgate, and Artillery-lane, the whole of Duke-st. Gun-st. Steward-st. and Fort-st.

Artillery-Lane, Bishopsgate,— at 55, near ½ a mile on the R. from Cornhill.

Artillery-Passage, Spitalfields, —the continuation of Widegate-st. Bishopsgate.

Artillery - Pl. Westminster,— from Brewers-green to Strutton-ground.

Artillery-Pl. Finsbury-Sq.—N. W. corner on the L.

Artillery-St. Bishopsgate,—the continuation of Artillery-lane.

Artillery-St. SaintJohn's,Southwark,—near the E. end of Tooley-st. the first S. parallel to St. John's-church-yd.

Artillery-Street, St. George's-Fields,—E. side Blackfriars-rd. from Bennett's-row to Higlers-lane.

Arts, Society of. See Society.

Arts, Academy of. See Royal.

Artis's - Builds. White - Hart-Row-Kennington,—2d on the R. from Clayton-pl.

Arundel-St. Strand,—at 189, 2d on the L. from Temple-bar.

Arundel - St. Coventry-St.—5 doors on the L. from the Hay-market.

Arundel-Stairs,—the bottom of Arundel-st. Strand.

Ashentree-Court, White-friars, —at the S. end of Bouverie-st. on the L. from 62, Fleet-st.

Ashby-St. Clerkenwell,—1st on the R. in Islington-rd. from St. John's-st. leading to Northampton-sq.

Ashby-St. (Upper), Goswell-St.-Rd.—2d on the L. from Goswell-st. towards Islington.

Ashfield-Pl.Stepney,—at the N. E. corner of the church-yard.

Ashton-St. Black-Wall,—N. end of Robinhood-lane, by the dock-gate.

Aske-Terrace, Hoxton,—2d on the L. north from Haberdashers-Alms-houses.

Assay-Office, Goldsmith's-Hall-the corner of Cary-lane and Gutter-lane.

Assembly-Row, Mile-End-Rd.— S. side, ⅛ of a mile on the R. below the turnpike.

Assembly-Passage,—at 13, in the last.

Astley's-Theatre,—Surrey end of Westr.-bridge.

Asylum for Female Orphans, Lambeth,—¾ of a mile towards Westr. - bridge from the Obelisk.

Asylum for Deaf and Dumb, Kent-Rd.—¼ of a mile below the Bricklayers-arms.

Asylum (Naval) Harrow-Rd. Paddington,—¾ of a mile from the W. end of Oxford-st. along the Edgware-rd.

Asylum (Royal Military) Chelsea,—between Lower Sloane-st. and the hospital.

Asylum-Builds.—from Mead-row by the Asylum to near the Obelisk.

Asylum-Pl. Mead-Row, Lambeth,—S. E. side the Asylum.

Asylum-Row, Westr.-Bridge-Road,—part of the S. side from the Asylum towards the Obelisk.

Atlas - Insurance - Company's - Office,—92, Cheapside, the corner of King-st.

Atlas-Pl. Poplar,—op. S. end of Cotton-st.

Auction-Mart, Bartholomew-Lane,—the last house on the R. from the Royal Exchange.

Auction Mart, Pancras St. Tottenham-Ct.-Rd.—the corner of Up. Thornhaugh-st.

Auditor's-Office for Public Accounts, Somerset-Pl.—on the L. side of the sq. from the Strand: there is another office at 5, Adam-st. Adelphi.

Audley-Sq. (South)—at the end of S. Audley-st. near Curzon-street.

Audley-St. (North) Oxford-St.—at 263, 2d on the R. from Hyde-park.

Audley-St. (South)—the continuation of the last from Grosvenor-sq. to Curzon-st.

St. Augustine's and St. Faith's Church, Old Change,—behind 35, St. Paul's church-yd. corner of Watling-st.

Augustus - Row, Grange - Rd. Bermondsey,—N. side, a few yards W. from the Spa.

Austin-Court, Austin-St. Beth-

nal-Green,—1st on the L from Hackney-rd.

Austin-Friars, Old Broad-St.—at 67, by Throgmorton-st.

Austin-St. Bethnal-Green,—1st on the R. in Hackney-rd. from Shoreditch-church.

Ave-Maria- Lane, Ludgate-St.—at 29, 1st on the R. from St. Paul's church-yd.

Avery-Farm - Row, Pimlico,—facing Ranelagh-walk.

Avery-Pl.—at the N. end of the last.

Avery-Row, Grosvenor-sq.—at 3, Grosvenor-st. 1st W. from New Bond-st.

Axe-Court, Hackney-Rd.—one-fifth of a mile on the L. from Shoreditch, at the back of the Axe public-house.

Axe Inn, Aldermanbury,—20 doors on the R. from Milk-st. Cheapside.

Axe-Yard, Grub-St. Cripple-gate,—2d on the L. from Fore-st.

Aylesbury-St. Clerkenwell,—at 103, St. John-st. 6th on the L. from Smithfield.

Ayliffe - St. Gt. Goodman's - Fields,—1st S. to Whitechapel from Somerset-st. to Red-Lion-st.

Ayliffe-St. (Little), E. continuation of the last to Goodman's-stile.

———

BABMAY's-MEWS, Well-St. St. James's,—at the S. end from Eagle-st. 212, Piccadilly.

Bacchus-Walk & Gardens, Hoxton,—at the back of the Bacchus-Coffee-house.

Baches-Row, Hoxton,—2d on the L. in Craven-builds. from the City-road.

Back-Alley, Great Garden,—2d on the L. from St. Catherine's-lane.

Back-Alley, Fishmonger-Alley, Borough,—2d on the R. from 255, High-st.

Back-Change, Rosemary-Lane, —at 141, N. side Swallow's Gardens.

Back-Bear-Alley. See Bear.

Back-Court, Cloth-Fair,—2d on the R. from 60, W. Smithfield.

Back-Court, Chequer-Alley,— 1st on the L. from 99, Bunhill-row.

Back-Court, Jamaica-Pl. Limehouse,— the 1st on the R. from Gun-lane.

Back-Hill, Leather-Lane,—the last on the R. from Holborn.

Back-Lane, St. Pancras,—at the back of Church-terrace, leading to Vernon's-builds.

Back-Lane, Bowling-Green-Lane, Clerkenwell,—1st W. of Rosamond-st.

Back-Lane, Bethnal-Green,— 1st E. parallel to the green, the N. continuation of Globeplace.

Back-Lane, St. George's East, —the E. continuation of the New-road and Cable-st.

Back-Lane, New-Cut, Limehouse,—the E. continuation o' Risby's-rope-walk.

Back-Lane, Poplar,—S. side the High-st. from the Commercial-rd. to op. North-street.

Back-Roll-Court, Long-Alley, —6 doors on the L. from Moorfields.

Back-St. Horsleydown,—the E. continuation of Tooley-st. on the L.

Back-St. Poplar,—from Wade's-pl. to Finch-yd.

Back-Walk, Lambeth,—1st S. parallel to Narrow-wall, near Up. Ground.

Back-Yard, White-cross St. Borough,—2d on the R. from Queen-st.

Bacon-St. (Gt.) Bethnal-Green, —at 140, Brick-lane, or the 1st on the L. in Club-row, from 170, Church-st.

Bacon-St. (Little),—at 141, Brick-lane, the 1st on the L. from Church-st.

Badger's Alms-Houses, Hoxton, a few yards on the R. from Old-st.-rd.

Badger-Court, Shoreditch,—at 43, near Webb-sq. ¼ of a mile S. from the church.

Badger-Yd. Red-Lion-St. Clerkenwell,—at 55, leading to the middle of St. John's-square.

Bagnige-Pl. Pentonville,—a few houses on the R. between Bagnige-Wells and Pentonplace.

Bagnige-Wells, Coldbath-Fields, —½ a mile from Clerkenwell-green, towards Pentonville.

Bagnio-Court, Newgate-St.—at 75, 2d on the R. from Cheapside.

Bailey's-Court, Bell-Yd. Temple-Bar,—1st on the L. from 205, Fleet-st.

Bailey's-Court, Cock-Hill, Shore

B

ditch,—1st on the L. from Webb-sq. towards Anchor-st.

Bailey's-Pl. Tower-Hill,—from the New Mint, to Upper E. Smithfield.

Bainbridge-Street, St. Giles's,—facing the E. end of Oxford-street.

Baker's-Alley, Green-Bank,—3d on the R. from 81, Tooley-street.

Baker's-Alley, Charles-St. Westminster,—middle of the S. side.

Baker's-Builds. Old Bethlem,—4 doors from Broad-st. buildings.

Baker's-Builds. Hackney-Rd.—part of the R. side from Shoreditch, adjoining Crabtree-row.

Baker's-Builds. Rotherhithe,—at 238, 5 doors on the R. below the King and Queen.

Baker's-Court, Holborn,—at 149, nearly op. Middle-row.

Baker's-Court, East-St. Manchester-Sq.—at 92, the 1st on the L. from Blandford-st.

Baker's-Court, Whetstone's-Park, Lincoln's-Inn-Fields,—middle of the N. side.

Baker's-Court, Half-moon-Alley,—the 1st on the R. from Little Moorfields.

Baker's-Court, Half-moon-St.—the 5th on the L. from 170, Bishopsgate.

Baker's-Court, Phipps-St. Holywell-Mount,—2d on the L. from Chapel-st.

Baker's-Court, Castle-St. Bethnal-Green,—at 33, six doors on the L. from the E. end of Austin-st.

Baker's-Court, Rosemary-Lane,—at 105, middle of the N. side.

Baker's-Court, Petticoat-Lane,—3d on the L. from Aldgate.

Baker's-Court, Farmer-St. Shadwell,—at 45, 2d on the L. from 38, High-st.

Baker's-Dock, Holland-Street, Blackfriars-Bridge,—E. side Northumberland wharf.

Baker's-Hall, Harp-Lane, Gt. Tower-St.—at 16, middle E. side.

Baker's-Lane, Neat Houses, Chelsea,—leading from the Monster public-house to the Thames.

Baker's-Mews, Baker-St. Portman-Sq.—5 doors on the R. from the sq.

Baker's-Pl. Duke's-Row, Tavistock-Sq.—1st on the L. from Sommers-town.

Baker's-Pl. Baker's-Row, Clerkenwell,—2d on the L. from the Workhouse.

Baker's-Row, Whitechapel-Rd.—at 94, op. Cannon-st. New-road.

Baker's-Row, Walworth High-St.— from Prospect-row to Albion-pl.

Baker's-Row, Coppice-Row, Clerkenwell,—2d coach turning on the L. from the Green.

Baker-St. Portman-Sq.—from the N. E. corner to York-pl. New-rd.

Baker-St. North,—continuation of the last from the New-road.

Balchin's-Court, Queen-St. Boro.—14 doors on the R. from Union-st.

Baldwin's-Court, Cloak-Lane,— at 18, op. College-hill.

Baldwin's - Gardens, Leather-Lane, Holborn,—at 77, leading to 32, Gray's-inn-lane.

Baldwin's-Pl. Baldwin's-Gardens,—at 48, middle of the N. side.

Baldwin's-Street, Old-Street, St. Luke's—at 104, 8 doors W. of the church.

Bales-Place, Duke-Street, St. George's-Fields,—3d on the R. from the Obelisk.

Ball-Alley, Sherbourn-Lane,— at 5, nearly op. the Post-office-yd.

Ball-Alley, Long-Alley, — the 2d on the R. from Moorfields.

Ball - Alley, or Bell - Court, Wheeler-St. Spitalfields,—at 43, op. Webb-sq.

Ball-Alley, Lombard-St.—at 50, nine doors on the R. from Gracechurch-st.

Ball-Court, Golden-Lane,—at 126, middle of the W. side.

Ball-Court, Giltspur-St.—at 15, the 3d on the R. from Newgate-st.

Ball-Court, Sampson's-Gardens, Wapping,—at the E. end of Redmaid's-lane, on the W. side of the London-docks.

Ball - Court, Cornhill,—at 38, three doors E. of Birchin-lane.

Ball-Court, Jewry-St.- at 15, 4th on the R. from Aldgate.

Ball-Court, White-Horse-Street, Ratcliffe,—1st on the L. from Butcher-row.

Ball - Court, St. Catherine's - Lane,—2d on the R. from 30, Up. E. Smithfield.

Ball's-Yard, Back Church-Lane,

Whitechapel,—1st on the R. from the Commercial-rd.

Baltic-Court, Baltic-Street, St. Luke's,—behind 20, in the said street.

Baltic-Pl. Baltic-St. St. Luke's—behind 20, in the said street.

Baltic-St. Golden-Lane,—at 99, the 1st on the R. from Old-street.

Banbury - Court, Long-Acre,—26 doors on the R. from St. Martin's-lane.

Bangor-Court, Shoe-Lane,—at 63, back of St. Andrew's-church.

Bangor-Court, High-St. Boro.—behind St. George's-church.

Bank of England, — the large stone building N. side the Royal Exchange, Cornhill.

Bank-Builds.—facing the South front of the Bank of England.

Bank's Court, Blue-Anchor-Alley,—2d on the L. from 109, Bunhill-row.

Bank-End, Southwark,—the E. end of Bankside.

Bankruptcy Information-Office, —35, Aldermanbury, 6 doors from London-wall.

Bankside, Southwark, — West continuation of the Clink, by the side of the Thames.

Bank-Street, Cornhill,—op. 14, leading to the Bank.

Banister-Court, Bluegate Fields, —1st on the L. from 95, Ratcliff-highway.

Bannister-Court, Golden-Lane, —at 67, near the middle of the E. side.

Banner - St. Bunhill-Row,—at 80, the first on the L. from Old-st.

Banner-Sq.—part of Banner-st. about the middle.

Baptist - Head - Court, White-cross-St. Cripplegate,—at 50, the 6th on the R. from Fore-street.

Barber's - Builds. Bell-Alley, — the 2d on the R. from 1, Golden-lane.

Barber's-Hall, Monkwell-St.— op. Fell-st. from 70, Wood-st. Cheapside.

Barber's- Yard, Brown's-Lane, Spitalfields,—4 doors on the R. from Brick-lane.

Barbican, — from 77, Alders-gate - st. op. Long - lane, to Redcross-st.

Barbican-Court, Barbican,—at 68, by Aldersgate-st.

Barge-House-Alley, Up Ground, —¼ of a mile on the R. above Blackfriars-bridge.

Barge (Old) Stairs. See the last.

Barge-Yard, Bucklersbury,—6 doors on the L. from the Mansion-house.

Barking -Church - Yard, Seeth-ing-Lane,—from 26, Tower-hill.

Barley-Court, Smart's-Builds.— 2d on the L. from 185, High Holborn.

Barley - Mow - Court, White-chapel,—at 39, nine doors E. of Red-Lion-st.

Barley - Mow - Passage, Cloth-Fair,—1st on the L. from 60, West-Smithfield.

Barlow-Mews, Bruton-St.— 1st on the L. from 152, New-Bond-st.

Barlow Row, Long-Lane, Ber-mondsey,—part of the S. side, op. Richardson-st.

Barlow-St. (Little) Marybone,— at 110, High-st. 2d on the L. from Charles-st.

Barlow-St. (Great)—the first on the L. in the last from High-st.

Barnard's-Inn, Holborn,—at 28, leading to 35, Fetter-lane.

Barnes-Alley, Booth-St. Spital-fields,—at 14, 2d on the L. from 50, Brick-lane.

Barnes-Builds. Castle-Alley,— 1st on the L. from 124, Whitechapel.

Barnes - Builds. Limehouse,— the E. end of Chivers's-court, entrance by Nightingale-lane.

Barnes - Builds. Wilmot - St. Bethnal-Green,—near the S. end, behind the Lamb public-house.

Barns - Builds. Gravel-Lane,— op. Fire-Ball-court, from 131, Houndsditch.

Barnes - Pl. Mile-End-Road,— adjoining the E. side the turnpike.

Barnes-Pl. Walworth-Common, op. Westmorland academy.

Barnes-Pl. Lambeth-Marsh,— middle of the N. side from Pear-tree-row to James-st.

Barnes-Terrace, James-Street, Lambeth Marsh, — by the Pen-Cutter's arms.

Barnet-Yard, Little Guildford-St. Russel-Sq.—2d on the R. from Bernard-st.

Baron-St. Pentonville,—1st on the R. from Islington.

Baron's-Builds.—3d on the L. in Webber-st. from Blackfri-ars-road.

Baron's-Pl.—2d on the L. in Webber-st. from Blackfriars-road.

Baron's - Pl. (Little), Baron's-Builds.—at 40, 1st on the R. from Webber-st.

Barracks; Knightsbridge,—⅛ of a mile on the L. from Hyde-park turnpike.

Barracks, Knightsbridge, for Cavalry,—½ a mile on the R. from Hyde-park corner.

Barracks, Pimlico,——behind Buckingham-house.

Barracks, St. James's-Park,—on the S. E. side of Buckingham-gate.

Barrack-Office, New-St. Spring-Garden,—at 20, a few yards on the L. from 52, Charing-cross.

Barrets-Court, Cavendish-Sq.—the continuation of Jees-court, from 163, Oxford-st.

Barrets-Rents, White's-Yard,—3d on the L. from 58, Rosemary-lane.

Bartholomew - Chapel, Little-Bartholomew-Close,—at 44, N. side.

St. Bartholomew the Less Church,—at the back of 44, W. Smithfield.

St. Bartholomew the Great Church, — entrance by 56, W. Smithfield.

St. Bartholomew-Church, Bartholomew-Lane,—E. side the Bank of England.

Bartholomew - Close,—at 33, Little-Britain, the 4th on the R. from 175, Aldersgate-st.; there is another entrance at 56, W. Smithfield.

Bartholomew-Close (Little), part of the N. end of the last, near King-st. Cloth-fair.

Bartholomew - Court, Ford-St.

Cripplegate,—at 88, op. Aldermanbury.

Saint Bartholomew's - Hospital, Giltspur-St.—a few yards on the R. from Newgate-st.; there is another entrance at Little Britain.

Bartholomew-Lane, — E. side the Bank, op. the Royal-Exchange.

Bartholomew-Pl. Bartholomew-Close, — at 38, near New-st.

Bartlet's Builds. Holborn-Hill, —at 50, nearly op. Hatton-garden.

Bartlet's-Builds. Richmond-St. St. Luke's,—1st on the R. from St. Luke's-hospital.

Bartlet's - Builds. Nightingale-Lane,—1st on the R. from Up. E. Smithfield.

Bartlet's-Court, Holborn-Hill, —at 53, op. Hatton-Garden.

Bartlet's-Builds. John-St. Curtain-Rd.—1st on the R. from op. William-st. Shoreditch.

Bartlet's-Passage, Fetter-Lane, —at 60, leading to 10, Bartlet's-builds.

Bartrum's-Rents, White-Lion-St. Chelsea,—1st on the L. from Lower-Sloane-st.

Barton-Court, Hoxton,—⅓ of a mile on the R. from Old-st. rd. near the Hare pub. house.

Barton - Pl. Uxbridge-Rd.—on the W. side St. George's-Burying-ground, ¼ mile on the R. from Tyburn-turnpike.

Barton-St. Westr.—2d on the L. in College-st. from 18, Abingdon-st.

Basing - House, Kingsland-Rd. —op. Union-st. ¼ of a mile on the L. from Shoreditch-church.

B 3

Basing-Lane, Bread-St.—at 40, the 2d on the L. from 47, Cheapside.

Basing-Pl. Kingsland-Road,—by the Turnpike, ⅛ of a mile on the L. from Shoreditch-church.

Basinghall-St. Cateaton-St.—at 29, 3 doors W. of the Old-Jewry.

Basinghall-St. (New), N. end of the last.

Basket-Alley, Golden-Lane,—at 89, 1st on the L. from Old-st.

Batchelor-Pl. Pentonville,—N. side the road, between the Turnpikes.

Batchelor-Pl. Borough-Road, —S. side by the King's-bench.

Bateman's-Builds. Soho-Sq. — from 127, S. side, to Queen-st.

Bateman's-Builds. Blue-Anchor-Alley,—1st on the R. from 108, Bunhill-row.

Bateman's-Row, Shoreditch,—at 159, leading to the Curtain-road.

Bate's-Row, Lisson-Green, — the N. end of Little-James-st.

Bath-Builds. Kingsland-Road, —op. the Ironmongers-Alms-Houses,⅓ of a mile on the L. from Shoreditch.

Bath-Court, Cold-Bath-Sq.—at 10, on the S. E. side.

Bath-Gardens, Kingsland-Road, —2d on the L. in Hare-walk, from op. Ironmongers Alms-houses.

Bath-Grove,Horsemonger Lane, —on the E. side the Gaol.

Bath-Pl. Brook-St. Lambeth,—part of the S. side near West-square.

Bath-Pl. Fitzroy-Sq.—N. side the New-rd. by Brook-st.

Bath-Pl. London-Road,—2d on the L. from the Obelisk.

Bath-Row, New-Road, Fitzroy-Sq.—1st W. of Hampstead-road.

Bath-Row, Cold-Bath-Sq.—at 6, leading into Baker's-row.

Bath-St.(Gt.) Cold-Bath-Fields, —N. continuation of Eyre-st. and Leather-lane.

Bath-St. (Little),—the end of Gt. Bath-st. which adjoins Eyre-st.

Bath-St. Hackney-Road,—¼ a mile on the R. from Shore-ditch-church.

Bath-St. City-Road,—N. continuation of Pesthouse-row, from the W. end of St. Luke's-hospital.

Bath-St. Bethnal-Green,—1st on the R. from the Salmon and Ball towards Dog-row.

Bath-Terrace,St. George's East, —N. side the New-road, near Cannon-st. turnpike.

Bath-Terrace, Horsemonger-Lane,—on the E. side the Gaol.

Battle-Bridge, St. Pancras,—N. end of Gray's-Inn-lane, near a mile from Holborn, and W. end of Pentonville.

Battle-BridgeMill-Lane,Tooley-St.—the end next the Thames.

Battle-Bridge-Stairs. See the last.

Batty's-Court, Batty's-St.—1st on the L. from the Commercial-road.

Batty's-Gardens, Back-Church-Lane, Whitechapel,—1st on the L. from the Commercial-road.

Batty's-Pl. Batty-St.—2d on the L. from the Commercial-rd.

Batty's-St. Commercial-Road, —2d on the right, E. from Church-lane.

Bayle's-Court, Strand,—at 411, op. Adam-st. Adelphi.

Bayles-Court, Cable-St.—at 69, nearly op. Wellclose-sq.

Bayleys-Ways, Rotherhithe, or Bermondsey-Wall,——a few yards on the left, E. of St. Saviour's-dock.

Baynes-Court, Cold-Bath-Sq. —at 4, W. side.

Baynes-Row, Cold-Bath-Fields, —on the S. side the House of Correction.

Baynes-Row (Little),—behind numbers 1 to 4, W. side of Cold-Bath-sq.

Beak-Street, Swallow-St.—at 44, middle of the E. side.

Beals-Wharf,—end of Mill-lane, from 55, Tooley-st.

Bean-St. Higlers-Lane,—5th on the R. from Blackfriars-road.

Bear-Alley, Fleet-Market,—at 27, middle of the E. side.

Bear-Alley (Back),—1st on the R. in the last from Fleet-market.

Bear-Court, Bear-Lane, Christ-Church,—middle of the E. side.

Bear-Court, Knightsbridge,—See Nag's-Head-court.

Bear-Gardens, Maid-Lane, Southwark,—the 1st E. of Thames-st.

Bear-Gardens-Stairs, Bankside, —op. the last.

Bear and Harrow-Yard, Old Boswell-Court,—1st on the R. from Clements-lane, Strand.

Bear-Lane, Christ-Church, Surrey,——continuation of Green-walk, from Holland-street.

Bear-Quay, Lower Thames-St. —at 31, E. side Billingsgate.

Bear and Ragged-Staff-Court, White-cross-st. St. Luke's,— at 176, middle of the W. side.

Bear and Ragged-Staff-Mews, Curzon-St. May-Fair,—on the W. side the Chapel.

Bear and Staff-Inn, W. Smithfield,—at 70, N. E. corner adjoining the Bell.

Bear-St. Leicester-Sq.—from 18, N. E. corner to Castle-st.

Bear-Yd. Lincoln's-Inn-Fields, —S. W. corner to 33, Vere-st.

Bear-Yard, Milford-Lane,—2d on the R. from 200, Strand.

Bear-Yard, High-St. Lambeth, —5th on the R. from the church.

Bear-Yard, Long-Walk, Bermondsey,—3 doors on the L. from Bermondsey-sq.

Bearbinder-Lane, Mansion-House,—from the E. side, to 4, St. Swithin's-lane.

Beardman's-Rooms, Hoxton-Town,—$\frac{1}{6}$ of a mile on the R. from Old-st.-road.

Beast-Lane, Stepney. See Bull-lane.

Beauchamp-St. Brook's-Market, —S. side of it, extending from 90, Leather-lane, to Brook's-street.

Beaufort-Builds. Strand,—at 95, nearly op. Southampton-st. Covent-garden.

Beaufort-Wharf, Strand,—at the bottom of Cecil-st. between Salisbury and Browning-wharfs.

Beaumonts-Builds. Blue-Anchor-Yard—3d on the L. from 48, Rosemary-lane.

Beaumonts-Builds. Cannon-St. Rd.—E. side, by Lower Chapman-st.

Beaumont-Court, Windmill-St. —8 doors on the L. from Tottenham-court.-rd.

Beaumont-Mews, Weymouth-St. Marybone, at 22, W. end.

Beaumont-Pl. Tottenham-Pl.— 1st on the L. from Tottenham-court-rd.

Beaumont-St. Marybone,—from 16, Weymouth-st. to High-st.

Beavton's-Repository, Silver-St. Golden-Sq. at 24, op. John-street.

Beckford-Pl. Beckford-Row, Walworth,—20 doors S. of East-lane.

Beckford-Row, Charles-St. Bethnal-Green-Rd—1st on the R. from op. Wilmot-sq.

Beckford-Row, Walworth High-St.—by East-lane, ¼ mile on the L. from the Elephant and Castle.

Beckford-Row, Kennington-Common,—on the W. side nearly op. the Greyhound.

Beck's-Rents, Rosemary-Lane, —at 19, the 2d on the R. from Tower-hill.

Bedford-Arms, Bedford-Sq.— by the S. E. corner: here is kept an alphabetical list of the names of all the inhabitants in the sq.

Bedford Avenue, Bow-St. Covent-Garden, — S. side the Theatre.

Bedford-Bury,—extends from 53, Chandos-st. to 10, New-st. Covent-garden.

Bedford-Court, Bedford-St. Covent-Garden,—from 16, to 63, Chandos-st.

Bedford-Court, Angel-Court,— 1st on the R. from 335, Strand.

Bedford-Court, New North-St. Red-Lion-Sq.—9 doors on the L. from 56, Theobalds-rd.

Bedford-Mews, Bedford-St.— 1st on the R. from op. Leather-lane.

Bedford-Court, Russel-St. Rotherhithe,—1st on the L. from Greenland-dock.

Bedford-Court, Bedford-St. Locksfields, Walworth,—1st on the L. from Nelson's-pl.

Bedford-Head-Yd. Up. King's-St. Bloomsbury,—2d on the R. from 120, High Holborn.

Bedford-Mews, (Up.)—behind the N. W. corner of Russel-square.

Bedford-Passage, Charlotte-St. Rathbone-Pl.—at 56, facing North-st.

Bedford-Pl. Bloomsbury-Sq.— middle of the N. side to 51, Russel-sq.

Bedford-Pl. (Up.) Russel-Sq.— at 16, op. the last.

Bedford-Pl. Thomas-St. Kent-Rd.—1st on the R. from Poplar-row.

Bedford-Pl. Deptford Lower-Rd. Rotherhithe,—on the E. side, near Paradise-row.

Bedford-Row,—N. continuation of Brownlow-st. from 50, High Holborn, bearing to the left.

Bedford-Sq. — communicates

with Tottenham-court-road by Tavistock-st. and Bedford-street.

Bedford-St. Tottenham-Court-Road,—at 268, 3d on the R. from Oxford-st.

Bedford - St. Strand,—at 423, W. side Covent Garden.

Bedford-St. Red-Lion-Street,—1st on the R. from 71, High Holborn.

Bedford - St. Leather-Lane, — the N. continuation of it, bearing to the L.

Bedford-St. Lock's-Fields, Walworth,—the continuation of York-st. to Nelson's-pl.

Bedlem. See Bethlem.

Bee - Hive - Court, Little St. Thomas Apostle,—5 doors E. of 68, Queen-st.

Beehive - Passage, Leadenhall-Market,—at 13, Lime-st. op. Cullum-st.

Beech - St. Barbican,—the E. continuation of it, to Chiswell-st.

Beech-Lane, Beech-St.—from the middle of the S. side to Whitecross-st.

Beer-Lane, Gt. Tower-St.—at 37, 1st on the L. from Tower-hill.

Belgrave-Builds. Pimlico,—at the back of 6, Lower-Belgrave-pl.

Belgrave-Pl. East-Lane, Walworth,—on the E. side Little Richmond-pl.

Belgrave-Pl. (Lower) Pimlico,—part of the R. side, ⅓ of a mile from Buckingham-gate.

Belgrave-Pl. (Upper)—the continuation of the last.

Belgrave - Terrace,—the continuation of the last towards Chelsea.

Belgrave - St. Pimlico,—5th on the R. from Buckingham-gate.

Bell-Alley, Goswell-St.—at 13, leading into Turk's - head - court, Golden-lane.

Bell - Alley, Golden-Lane,—at 1 the 5th on the L. from Barbican.

Bell-Alley (Gt.) Coleman-St.—at 56, 4th on the R. from Lothbury.

Bell - Alley (Little), London-Wall, — at Leather-sellers-builds. op. Bethlem-hospital.

Bell's - Builds. Salisbury-Sq.—2d on the L. from 32, Fleet-street.

Bell-Court, Gray's-Inh-Lane,—at 22, 3d on the R. from Holborn.

Bell-Court (Little)— the 1st on the R. in the last from Gray's Inn-Lane.

Bell-Court, Golden-Lane,—1st on the R. in Bell-alley from Golden-lane.

Bell-Court, Grub-St. Cripplegate,—at 30, 7th on the R. from 86, Fore-st.

Bell-Court, Foster Lane, Cheapside,—at 20, op. Maiden-lane, Wood-st.

Bell-Court, Bell-Yard, Doctors-Commons,—the 1st on the L. from 10, Gt. Carter-lane.

Bell-Court, Walbrook,—3 doors on the R. from the Mansion-house.

Bell-Court, Long-Alley, Moorfields,—5 doors on the R. from Crown-street towards Moorfields.

Bell-Court, Wheeler-St. Spital-fields,—at 43, op. Webb-sq.

Bell - Court, St. Catherine's-Lane,—1st on the L. from 43, Up. E. Smithfield.

Bell-Court, Fenchurch-St.—at 163, 2d on the L. from Gracechurch-st.

Bell-Court, Mincing-Lane,—at 26, seven doors from 82, Tower-st.

Bell - Court, Bermondsey-St.—at 108, 4th N. of the church.

Bell-Inn, Hay-Market,—at 70, six doors N. of the Opera-house.

Bell-Inn, (Old) Holborn,—at 123, nearly op. Fetter-lane.

Bell and Crown, Holborn,—at 133, about $\frac{1}{6}$ of a mile on the R. from Fleet-market.

Bell-Fields, Bell-St. Paddington,—S. end Stevens-builds.

Bell-Inn, West Smithfield,—at 70, between Long-lane and St. John's-st.

Bell-Inn, Warwick - Lane,—8 doors on the L. from 10, Newgate-st.

Bell-Inn, Friday-St.—3 doors on the R. from 36, Cheap-side.

Bell-Inn, Bell-Yd. Gracechurch-street.

Bell-Inn, Kent-St. Borough,—$\frac{1}{2}$ a mile on the R. from St. George's-church.

Bell-Inn, Wood-St.—at 86, $\frac{1}{5}$ of a mile on the L. from 122, Cheapside.

Bell-Lane, Spitalfields,—1st E. of Petticoat-lane, from Went-worth-st. to Raven-row.

Bell's-Messenger News-Paper-Office, Southampton-St.—1st house on the L. from 388, Strand.

Bell-Pl. Limehouse. See Five.

Bell - Pl. Prince's-St.—1st on the L. from Baker's-row, 94, Whitechapel-road.

Bell's-Rents, Tattle-Court,—2d on the L. from 247, Bermond-sey-street.

Bell-Savage-Inn, Ludgate-Hill, —at 37, first on the L. from Fleet-market.

Bell-Sq. St. Martin's-le-Grand, —at 54, 4th on the R. from Newgate-st.

Bell-Sq. Brokers-Row,—at 6, middle of the E. side of Moorfields.

Bell-St. Paddington,—1st N. of Chapel-st. Edgware-road.

Bell and Star Wharf, Upper Thames-St.—2 doors from Earl-st. Blackfriars.

Bell-Wharf, Up. Thames-St.—op. 177, 3d E. of Queen-st.

Bell-Wharf-Passage. See the last.

Bell-Wharf, Bermondsey-Wall, —a few doors below East-lane-stairs.

Bell-Wharf and Stairs, Rat-cliffe,—at 115, E. end of Shad-well-High-street.

Bell-Yard, Oxford-St.—at 108, op. Argyll-street.

Bell-Yard, York-St. Westmin-ster,—6 doors on the R. from Queen-square.

Bell-Yard, Fleet-St.—at 204, by Temple-bar.

Bell-Yard, Hay-market,—at 70, six doors from the Opera-house.

Bell-Yard, Drury - Lane.—16 doors on the L. from Holborn.

Bell-Yard, Mount-St. Grosvenor-Sq.—at 58, 6 doors on the L. from Park-st.

Bell-Yard, Strand,——E. side Drury - lane, by the New Church.

Bell-Yd. Addle-Hill,—1st on the R. from 4, Gt. Carter-lane.

Bell - Yard, Gt. Carter - Lane, Doctors-Commons,—at 10, leading to 15, Gt. Knightrider-st.

Bell-Yard, Gracechurch-St.—12 doors on the R. from Cornhill.

Bell-Yd. Fish-St. Hill,—at 13, op. the Monument.

Belmont-Pl. Vauxhall,—1-sixth of a mile on the R. south of the Turnpike.

Belmont- Row, Vauxhall,—— from the last towards Nineelms.

Belmont-Row, Bethnal-Green, —nearly op. Patriot-sq.

Belton-St. (Old),—continuation of Hanover-st. from 96, Long-Acre.

Belton-St. (New),—the N. continuation of the last.

Belvedere, Bethnal-Green,—op. Duthie's Nursery, extending towards Dog-row.

Belvedere - Brewery, Vine-St. Lambeth,—facing the end of it from Narrow-wall.

Belvedere - Builds. Belvedere-Pl.—at 45, op. the King's-bench.

Belvedere - Pl. St. George's-Fields,—W. side the King's-bench.

Belvedere-Row, Belvedere-Pl. St. George's-Fields,—N. end by Gt.-Suffolk-st.

Belvedere-Row, Narrow-Wall, Lambeth,—right side, ¼ of a mile from Westr.-bridge.

Bembers-Rents, Golden-Lane, —at 107, the fourth on the R. from Old-st.

Beuchers-Walk, Bennett's-Row, —3d on the R. from Blackfriars-rd.

Bencroft's-Alm-Houses, Mile-End-Road,—1¼ mile on the L. from Aldgate.

Bencroft's - Pl.—op. the last, leading towards Stepney.

Bengal-Pl. East Ind. Dock-Rd. —N. side, near the Dockgate.

Benjamin - St. Cow-Cross,—2d on the R. from St. John's-street.

Bennet's - Alms - Houses, St. Peter's-Hill,—2d on the L. from 216, Thames-st.

St. Bennet's, Gracechurch,— corner of Fenchurch-st. and Gracechurch-st.

St. Bennet's - Church, Upper Thames-St.—by 217, the corner of St. Bennet's-hill.

St. Benedict, or St. Bennet-Fink-Church, Threadneedle-St.—3 doors E. from the Royal-Exchange.

Bennet's Builds. Kennington-Lane,—2d on the R. from Newington.

Bennet's-Court, Drury-Lane,— at 111, op. Russel-court.

Bennet's Court, Marigold-Court, 1st on the L. from 370, Strand.

Bennet's - Court, George - St. Bethnal-Green,—2 doors S. of Spicer-st. Brick-lane.

Bennet's-Court, White-St. Borough,— at 41, first from Kent-street.

St. Bennet's-Hill, Up. Thames-St.—at 217, 2d on the L. from Earl-st. Blackfriars.

Bennett's-Pl. Bennett's-Yard, Westr.—behind 42, Tufton-street.

Bennet's - Pl. Bethnal - Green-Road,—1st E. parallel to Pollard's-row, N. end of Pollard-st.

Bennet's-Row, Paris-Pl. Chapel-St. Lisson-green,—the last on the L. from 23, Chapel-st.

Bennet's-Row, Blackfriars-Rd. —2d on the L. from Surrey-chapel, towards the Obelisk.

Bennet-St. Saint James's-St.— at 54,—1st on the R. from Piccadilly.

Bennet - St. Charlotte - Street, Rathbone-Pl.—at 87, 1st N. of Windmill-st.

Bennet-St. Princes-Street Westr. —1st on the L. from Tothill-street.

Bennet-St. Up. Ground,—1st on the L. from Blackfriars-bridge.

Bennet's-Yd. Westr.—W. end of Bennet-st.

Bennet's-Yd. Tufton-St. Westr. —at 41, leading to 13, Marsham-st.

Benson's-Wharf, Shad-Thames, —nearly op. King-st. Horsley-down.

Bentley's-Builds. Gt. Guildford-Street, Boro.—at the N. end by Maid-lane.

Bentinck - Chapel, Lisson - St. Lisson-Green,—at the corner of Chapel-st.

Bentinck - Mews, Marybone-Lane,—at 27, fourth on the R. from 157, Oxford-st.

Bentinck-St. Welbeck-Street,— from 55 to 28 Marybone-lane.

Bentinck-Street, Berwick - St. Oxford-St.—at 82, middle of the W. side.

Benton-Pl. New-St. Dock-Head, —a few doors on the L. from Russell-st. towards Tooley-street.

Berkeley-Chapel,—W. end of Charles-st. Berkeley-sq.

Berkeley - Court, Berkeley - St. Clerkenwell,—2d on the L. from 18, St. John's-lane.

Berkeley-Mews, Up. Berkeley-St. Portman-Sq.—5 doors W. from the sq.

Berkeley-Sq.—at the W. end of Bruton-st. from 146, New Bond-st.

Berkeley-St. Piccadilly,—from 76, middle of the N. side, to Berkeley-sq.

Berkeley-St. Portman-Sq.—at 7, the N. E. corner, leading to 15, Manchester-sq.

Berkeley-St. (Upper), Portman-Sq.—from the N. W. corner, to 29, Edgware-road.

Berkeley-Street, St. John's-Lane, Smithfield,—at 18, 3d on the L. from St. John's-st.

Berkeley-St. Lambeth-Walk,— 1st W. to Eleazer-pl. op. Chapman's-gardens.

Bermondsey-Builds. Bermondsey New Road,—3d on the R. from the Bricklayers-Arms.

Bermondsey-Church-Yard,—on the S. side the church.

Bermondsey New-Road,—the S. continuation of Bermondsey-street to the Bricklayers-Arms.

Bermondsey-Sq. Bermondsey,—on the S. side the church-yd.

Bermondsey-St. Boro.—op. 63, Tooley-st. where there are Nos. 1 and 284.

Bermondsey-Wall. See Rotherhithe-Wall.

Bermondsey-Workhouse, Russell-St.—a few doors on the R. from 90, Bermondsey-st.

Bernale's-Builds.Kingsland-Rd.—op. 60, 1st on the R. from Shoreditch.

Bernard-St. Brunswick-Sq.—1st N. parallel to Guilford-st.

Berners-Mews, Castle-St. Oxford-St.—4 doors E. of 11, Berner's-st.

Berners-Street, Oxford-St.—at 54, ¼ of a mile on the R. from St. Giles's.

Berner-St. Commercial-Road,—the 1st on the R. from Church-lane, Whitechapel.

Berry-Court, Love-Lane,—at 6, the back of 66, Aldermanbury.

Berry-St. Clerkenwell,—2d on the L. in Allen-st. from 113, Goswell-st.

Berwick-Street, Oxford-St.—at 373, ¼ of a mile on the L. from St. Giles's.

Berwick-Pl. Grange-Road,—the W. continuation of Fortplace.

Bethesda-Chapel, Baltic-St.—adjoins 99, Golden-lane.

Bethlem-Hospital, Moorfields,—on the S. side by Londonwall.

Bethlem (Old), Bishopsgate,—at 198, N. side the church.

Bethnal-Green,—a large green about a mile E. from the Turnpike by 65, Shoreditch, and about ½ a mile N. from Mile-End-Turnpike.

Bethnal-Green-Road,—the E. continuation of Church-st. from 65, Shoreditch, extending from the Turnpike to the Green.

Bethnal-Green-Workhouse,—at the E. end of Hare-st. from 110, Brick-lane.

Betts-Pl. Betts-St.—4 doors on the L. from 164, Ratcliffe-highway.

Betts-St.Ratcliffe-highway,—at 164,on the E. side of Princes-square.

Bevis-Marks, St. Mary-Axe,—at 30, op. Camomile-st. Bishopsgate.

Bevois-Court, Basinghall-St.—at 28, op. the church.

Bickley-Row, Trinity-Street, Rotherhithe,—E. end of it extending from Russel-st. towards the Surrey canal.

Bicknels-Rents, Kent-St. Boro.—at 76, ¼ of a mile on the L. from St. George's-church.

Bidborough-St. Judd-Street, Sommers-Town.—1st on the L. from Judd's-pl.

Billingsgate-Wharf and Market, Lower-Thames-St.—20 doors below London-Bridge.

Billingsgate-School, St. Mary's-Hill,—3 doors on the R. from Rood-lane.

Billiter-Lane, Fenchurch-St.—at 114, op. Mark-lane.

Billiter-Square,—at 12, Billiter-lane.

Bing-St. Mile-End-Road,—W.

C

side Grove-road, op. Saville-place.

Bingston's-Wharf, Wapping,—at 316, op. Globe-st. ½ a mile below Tower-hill.

B'rchin-Lane, Lombard-St.—at 61, leading to 36, Cornhill.

Bird's-Builds. Hoxton-Town,—¼ of a mile on the R. from Old-st. road, by Magna-pl.

Bird's-Builds. Green-St. Saint George's-Fields,—3d on the R. from Bennett's-row.

Bird-Cage-Alley, High-St. Boro.—at 172, nearly opposite St. George's-church.

Bird-Cage-Court, Strand,—at 393, by Southampton-street, Covent-garden.

Birdcage-Walk, Bethnal-Green,—the continuation of Crab-Tree-row, near Shoreditch-church, to the Nag's-head, Hackney-road.

Bird-Cage-Walk, St. James's-Park,—on the S. side, from Buckingham-gate to Great George-street.

Bird's-Court, Marybone-Lane, at 35, five doors from High-street.

Bird's-Court, Philip-Lane,—W. side, 10 doors from London-wall.

Bird-in-Hand-Court, Cheapside,—at 76, op. the Old-Jewry.

Bird's-Lane, Stangate, Lambeth,—2d on the L. from Westr.-bridge.

Bird's-Row, Blue-Anchor-Road, Bermondsey,—¼ of a mile on the R. from Fort-pl.

Bird-St. Grosvenor-Sq.—at 283, Oxford-st. between James-st. and Duke-st.

Bird-Street, Manchester-Sq.—at 167, Oxford-st. op. the last.

Bird-St. Saint George's East,—at the N. side of Wapping-church.

Bird-St. Lambeth,—the continuation of South-st. West-square.

Bishop's-Court, Chancery-Lane, —at 78, leading to Star-yd. and Carey-st.

Bishop's-Court, Aylesbury-St. Clerkenwell,—at 12, the 1st on the L. from St. John's-st.

B'shop's-Court, Old-St.—at 38, 3d W. of Bunhill-row.

Bishop's-Court, Coleman-St.—6 doors on the R. from London-wall.

Bishop's-Court, Old-Bailey,—3d on the R. from Snow-hill.

Bishop's-Court, King's-Head-Court,—1st on the R. from Long-alley, Moorfields.

Bishop's-Pl. Uxbridge-Road,—W. side St. George's-Burying-ground, ¼ mile on the R. from Tyburn-turnpike.

Bishopsgate - Church - Yard,—from the S. side the church to New-Broad-st.

Bishopsgate-St.-Within,— from Cornhill, (where there are Nos. 1 and 124) to the church.

Bishopsgate-St.-Without,—the N. continuation of the last, (where there are Nos. 1 and 202) to Norton-falgate.

Bishopsgate-Poorhouse, Rose-Alley,—a few yards on the L. from 34, Bishopsgate-without.

Bishopsgate-Workhouse, Dunning's-Alley,—a few yards on

the L. from 151, Bishops-
gate.
Bishop's-Head - Court, Gray's-
Inn-Lane,—6 doors on the
L. from Holborn.
Bishop's-Walk, Lambeth,—by
the side of the Thames, from
Lambeth-church to Westr.-
bridge.
Bishop's-Yd.Charles-St.—a few
yards on the L. from the S. E.
corner of Grosvenor-sq.
Bit-Alley, Turnmill-St. Clerk-
enwell,—1st on the L. from
the green.
Blacks-Court,Phœnix-St.Spital-
fields,——6 doors from 39,
Wheeler-st.
Black-Bear-Inn, Piccadilly,—
13 doors on the R. from the
Haymarket.
Black-Bear-Yd. Titchborne-St.
—1st on the L. from the Hay-
market.
Black-Bird-Alley, St. John's-
St. Bethnal-Green,—2d on
the R. from 105, Brick-lane.
Black-Boy and Camel Coach-
Office, Leadenhall-Street,—8
doors from Gracechurch-st.
Black-Boy-Alley, Chick-Lane,
—2d on the L. from Field-
lane.
Black-Boy - Court, Mile-End-
Road,—10 doors W. of Globe-
lane.
Black-Boy-Alley,Fore-St. Lam-
beth,—6th on the L. from
the church.
Black-Boy-Lane, Poplar,—½ a
mile on the L. from the
Commercial - road, op. the
Harrow.
Black-Bull (Old) Inn, Holborn,

—at 121, op. Fetter-lane, ¼
of a mile on the R. from
Fleet-market.
Black-Bull-Yard,Swallow-St.—
14 doors on the R. from Pic-
cadilly.
Blackburn's-Mews, Up. Brook-
St.—the 1st on the L. from
Grosvenor-sq.
Blackburn's-Alley,Bermondsey-
Wall,—W. side of Weslake's-
dock, and E. side Graham's
Iron-foundery.
Black - Coat - Alms - Houses,
Westr.—W. side St. Marga-
ret's-church.
Black-Dog - Alley, College-St.
Westr.—3d on the L. from
18, Abingdon-st.
Black-Eagle-St. Spitalfields,—
op. 65, Brick-lane, by Han-
bury's-Brewery.
Blackfriars,—between Ludgate-
hill and the Bridge.
Blackfriars-Alms Houses,Black-
friars,—a few doors on the L.
in Church-entry, from Shoe-
maker-row.
Blackfriars-Bridge,—S. end of
New Bridge-st. Fleet-market.
Blackfriars-Road,—from the S.
end of Blackfriars-bridge to
the Obelisk.
Black-Horse-Alley, Fleet-St.—
at 108, four doors from Fleet-
market.
Black - Horse - Court, Hay -
market. See Black-Horse-
Yard.
Black-Horse-Square, Deptford
Lower-Road,—1st on the L.
beyond the 3 mile stone.
Black-Horse-Yard,Hay-market,
—8 doors from Piccadilly.

Black-Horse-Yard, Chapel-St. Westminster,—2 doors from Tothill-st.

Black-Horse-Yard, Tottenham-Ct.-Rd.—26 doors on the L. from Oxford-st.

Black-Horse-Yd. Dean-St.—1st on the L. from 400, Oxford-street.

Black-Horse-Yard, Norfolk-St. —2d on the R. from Goodgé-st. Tottenham-Court-road.

Black-Horse-Yard, Rathbone-Pl.—6 doors on the R. from 24, Oxford-st.

Black-Horse-Yd. Newton-St.— 1st on the L. from 206, High Holborn.

Black-Horse-Yard, Grays-Inn-Lane,—at 52, fifty-two doors on the R. from Holborn.

Black-Horse-Yd. Bartholomew-Close,—2d on the L. from 56, W. Smithfield.

Black-Horse-Yd. Little Britain, —at 30, four doors N. of Cox's-court.

Black-Horse-Yd. Goswell-St.— at 115, a few doors N. of Long-lane.

Black-Horse-Yd. Fell-St. Wood-St.—middle of the N. side.

Black-Horse-Yd. Aldgate,—at 35, leading into Petticoat-lane.

Black-Horse-Yard, George-Yd. 1st on the L. from 88, White-chapel.

Black-Horse and Swan-Yard, Blackman-St. Borough,—13 doors from St. George's-church.

Black-Horse-Yd. Kent-St. Boro. —at 17½, ½ of a mile on the R. from St. George's-church.

Black-Horse-Yd. Union-Builds. Leather-Lane,—at the W. end.

Blacklands, King's-Road, Chelsea,—2d coach turning on the R. from Sloane-sq. towards Fulham.

Blacklands-Lane,—the continuation of the last to Brompton.

Blacklands-Pl. Chelsea,—facing Symonds-st. from the N. W. corner of Sloane-sq.

Black-Lion-Court, Berwick-St. —at 3, the last on the L. from 373, Oxford-st.

Black - Lion-Court, Tooley-St.—at 81, E. side of Morgan's-lane.

Black-Lion-Inn, Water-Lane,— 2d on the R. from 68, Fleet-street.

Black-Lion-Yard, Whitechapel-Road,—at 39, 2d on the L. below the church.

Blackman-St. Borough,-the continuation of High-st. from St. George's-church to Stones-end.

Blackmore-St. Drury-Lane,— at 100, 4th on the R. from 320, Strand.

Black-Prince-Row, Walworth, —a few houses on the L. from the Elephant & Castle.

Black - Raven - Alley, Upper Thames-St.-from 104, to Old-Swan-stairs.

Black-Raven-Court, Seething-Lane,—at 30, 2d on the R. from Tower-st.

Black-Raven - Court, Leadenhall-St.—3 doors on the L. from Aldgate.

Black-Swan-Alley, Market-St. St. James's,—4 doors from 127, Jermyn-st.

Black - Swan - Alley, London-Wall,—12 doors E. from Coleman-st.

Black - Swan - Court, Golden-Lane,—at 57, middle of the E. side.

Black-Swan-Alley, St. Paul's-Church-Yard,—at 21, S. side.

Black-Swan-Court, Gt. Tower-St.—at 61, six doors E. of Mark-lane.

Black-Swan-Court, High-Street, Boro.—33 doors on the L. from London-bridge.

Black-Swan-Yard, Bermondsey-St.—at 73, middle of the E. side.

Black-Swan-Yard, Cross-Street, Newington,—1st on the R. from the church.

Blacksmith's-Arms-Pl. Church-Lane, Whitechapel,—2d on the R. from Cable-st.

Blacksmith's-Arms-Court,—1st on the L. in the last from Church-lane.

Blackwall,—E. end of Poplar.

Blackwall-Bason,—E. end of the West-India-Docks.

Blackwall-Causeway,—from the E. end of Poplar to the West India-Dock.

Blackwall-Stairs,—E. end of the last.

Blackwell-Hall,—at 6, Basing-hall-st. leading to Guildhall.

Blackwell - Hall - Court,—from the last to 33, Cateaton-st.

Black and White-Court, Old-Bailey. See New-court.

Blakes-Alms-Houses, Vauxhall, —a few doors on the R. south from the Turnpike.

Blakes-Court, Catherine-St.— 6 doors on the L. from 343, Strand.

Blakes-Court, Old-Gravel-Lane, —at 150, near the middle of the W. side.

Bland's-Builds. French-Alley, —2d on the R. from 21, Goswell-st.

Bland's-Court, Great-Wild-St. Lincoln's-Inn-Fields,—2d on the R. 14 doors from Gt. Queen-st.

Blandford- Mews, Blandford-St.—5 doors from Baker-st.

Blandford-Pl.Pall-Mall,—at 83, near the Palace.

Blandford-St. Marybone,—at 47, Manchester-st. leading to 15, Baker-st. Portman-sq.

Bleeding-Heart-Yard, Charles-St. Hatton-Garden,—N. end of Union-court, from 95, Holborn-hill.

Blenheim-Mews, Blenheim-St. —1st from 351, Oxford-st.

Blenheim-St. Oxford-Street,— at 351, ¾ of a mile on the L. from St. Giles's.

Blenheim-St. New-Bond-Street, —7 doors from 307, Oxford-street.

Blewet's-Buildings, Fetter-Lane, —15 doors on the L. from 34, Holborn-hill.

Blinkford's-Builds. King-John's-Court, Shoreditch,—1st on the R. from 13, Holywell-lane.

Block's-Court, Phœnix-Street, Spitalfields,—6 doors on the R. from 33, Wheeler-st.

Bloomsbury and St. Giles's-Charity - School, — at 14, Queen-st. the corner of Hart-street.

Bloomsbury-Court, High-Holborn,—from 135, to Bloomsbury-market.

Bloomsbury Dispensary, Great-Russel-St.—at 62, nearly op. the British-Museum.

Bloomsbury-Market, Lyon-St. Holborn,—N. end, 5 doors from 143, High-Holborn.

Bloomsbury - Pl. Bloomsbury-Sq.—from the N. E. corner to King-st.

Bloomsbury-Sq.—the N. end of Southampton-st. from 126, High-Holborn.

Bloomsbury-Sq. Church-Place, Newington,—2d on the L. from op. the church.

Blossoms-Inn, Lawrence-Lane, —9 doors on the L. from 96, Cheapside.

Blossom - St. Spitalfields,—1st on the L. in White-Lion-st. from 13, Norton-falgate.

Blossom-Court,—1st on the L. in Blossom-st. from White-Lion-st.

Blue-Anchor-Alley, Brook-St. Ratcliffe,—at 106, nearly op. Stepney-causeway.

Blue-Anchor-Alley, Maid-Lane, Boro.—5th on the L. from Park-st.

Blue - Anchor - Alley, Bunhill-Row,—at 108, about the middle of the W. side.

Blue-Anchor-Court, Gt. Peter-St. Westr.—2d on the R. from Strutton-ground.

Blue-Anchor-Court, Blue-Anchor-Alley, Bunhill-Row,—

about middle of the N. side.

Blue-Anchor-Court, Brook-St. Ratcliffe,—the continuation of Blue-Anchor-alley.

Blue-Anchor-Lane, Bermondsey,—from the Blue-Anchor, to the Gregorian-arms, on the East side of the Spa.

Blue - Anchor - Lane, Bethnal Green,—near the N. E. corner of the Green, leading to Hackney-road.

Blue-Anchor-Road, Bermondsey,—the E. continuation of the Grange-road, from the turnpike, Fort-place.

Blue - Anchor - Yard, York-St. Westminster,—2d on the L. from Queen-sq.

Blue-Anchor - Yard, Coleman-St.—at No. 1, by London-wall.

Blue-Anchor-Yard, Rosemary-Lane,—at 48, 8th on the R. from Tower-hill.

Blue-Ball-Court, Lant-St. Boro.—2d on the R. from 109, Blackman-st.

Blue - Ball - Court, Tottenham-Ct.-Rd.—at 62, by Goodge-street.

Blue-Ball-Yard, St. James's-St. —at 62, 3d on the R. from Piccadilly.

Blue - Boar - Inn, Aldgate,—20 doors E. of the church.

Blue-Boar-Yard, High Holborn, —at 75, 1st W. of Red-Lion-street.

Blue-Boar-Court, Friday-St.— ten doors on the L. from 36, Cheapside.

Blue-Coat-School, Newgate-St. See Christ's-hospital.

Blue - Coat-School, Westminster,—E. end of James-st. and W. end of Little-Chapel-street.

Blue - Coat - Builds. Butcher-Hall-Lane,—the continuation of it under the arch to Little-Britain.

Blue-Court,—a few doors on the L. in Red-lion-court, from 11, Gt.-Saffron-hill.

Blue-Cross - Street, Whitcomb-St.—op. James-st. from 17, Haymarket.

Blue-Hart-Court, Little Bell-Alley,—2d on the R. from London-wall.

Blue-Gate-Court,—at the N. end of Blue-Gate-Fields.

Blue - Gate - Fields, Ratcliffe-Highway,—at 95, 1st street E. of St. George's-church.

Blue-Gate-Place,—5th on the R. in the last from Ratcliffe-Highway.

Blue-Houses, Lambeth-Marsh, —2d on the L. from Surrey-chapel.

Blue-Houses, Lambeth-Marsh, —a few houses op. the last, between the Horn-brewery and the Patent-shot-manufactory.

Blue - Last - Court, Three-Colt-St. Limehouse,—at 31, nearly op. Ropemakers-fields.

Blue-Lion - Court, Aldersgate St.—6 doors N. of Falcon-square.

Blue-Posts Coach-Office, Tottenham-Ct.-Rd.—12 doors on the L. from Oxford-st.

Blue-Posts Coach-Office, Holborn-Bars,—6 doors E. from Middle-row.

Blunden's-Court, Kent-St. Bo-

ro.—at 298, the end of Unicorn-court.

Blunderbuss-Court, Kingsland-Road,—6 doors on the L. from Shoreditch.

Blyth's - Court, Lamb - Alley, Bishopsgate,—behind 69, Sun-street.

Board of Agriculture. See Agriculture.

Boarded - Entry, New Gravel-Lane,—at 16, 2d on the L. from Wapping.

Boar and Castle Inn, Oxford-St.—6 doors on the R. from St. Giles's.

Boar's-Head-Court, Fleet-St.—at 66, middle of the S. side, by Water-lane.

Boar's-Head-Court, W. Smith-field,—at 76, N. side, by St. John's-st.

Boar's-Head -Court, Petticoat-Lane,—1st on the R. from 41, Aldgate High-st.

Boar's - Head - Court, Grace-church-St.—at 80, by Leaden-hall-market.

Boar's- Head - Court, High-St. Borough,—25 houses on the L. from London-bridge.

Boar's-Head-Yard, King-St. Westr.—3 doors N. from Gt. George-st.

Boddy's - Bridge, Up.-Ground —2d on the L. from Black-friars-bridge.

Bolingbroke-Row, Walworth,—S. side the Red Lion, by the turnpike.

Bolsover-Street, Oxford -St.—at 113, nearly op. Swallow-street.

Bolt-Court, Fleet-St.—at 151, op. Water-lane.

Bolt in Tun-Inn, Fleet-St.—at 64, middle of the South side.

Bolton-Row, Piccadilly,—at the end of Bolton-st. from Piccadilly.

Bolton-St. Piccadilly,—at 79, middle of the N. side.

Bolton-Yard, Bolton-Row,—at 10, op. Bolton-st.

Boltwright's-Court, Mount-St. Bethnal-Green,—3d on the L. from 45, Church-st. by the Charity-School.

Bombhouse-Alley, Princes-St. Lambeth, — 1st on the L. from Vauxhall.

Bond's-Buildings, Rolls Builds.—the continuation of Bond's-yard to Symonds-Inn.

Bond-Court, Walbrook, — 7 doors on the L. from the Mansion-house.

Bond-Court, Chamber-Street, Goodman's-Fields,—middle of the S. side.

Bond-Court, Horseferry-Road, Westr.—1st W. of Strutton-ground.

Bond-Place, Hackney-Road, —adjoins Durham-pl. East.

Bond-Street (New), Oxford-St.—at 307, middle of the S. side.

Bond-St. (Old), the continuation of the last to 56, Piccadilly.

Bond-St. Boro-Road,—third on the R. from the Obelisk.

Bond's-Yard, Rolls Builds.—W. end, entrance by 118, Fetter-lane.

Bone-Yard, Lemon-St. Goodman's-Fields,—a few yards behind 84, op. Prescot-st.

Bonner's-Hall, Bethnal-Green, —— a detached parcel of houses; about ¼ of a mile N. E. from the Green.

Bonner-Street, Green-St. Bethnal-Green,—⅓ of a mile on the L. East from the green.

Booker's-Gardens, Leadenhall-St.—at 93, 7 doors W. of Creechurch-lane.

Book's-Rents, Garter-Court, Barbican,—at 36, nearly op. Redcross-st.

Boot-Alley, Abchurch-Lane,—6 doors on the L. from Lombard-st.

Boot-St. Hoxton-Market,—1st on the R. in Pitfield-st. from Old-st.-road.

Booth-Court, Wells-St. Oxford-St.—at 39, 3d on the R. from Oxford-st.

Booth-Court, Twister's-Alley, —the W. end from 102, Bunhill-row.

Booth-Court, Booth-St. Spitalfields,—at 18, 3d on the R. from 50, Brick-lane.

Booth-St. Spitalfields,—at 50, Brick-lane,—¼ of a mile on the R. from Osborn-st. Whitechapel.

Boro' of Southwark,—five parishes on the S. side the Thames, St.Olave's, St.John's, St. Thomas's, St. George's, and St. Saviour's.

Borough High-Street. See High-street.

Borough-Market,—the W. end of York-st. from 275, High-street.

Boro-Road, St. George's Fields, —from the King's-bench to the Obelisk.

Boro-Skin-Market, Gt. Suffolk-St.—middle of the S. side.

Bosier-Court, Oxford-St.—the corner of Tottenham-court-road.

Boss-Alley, Lower Thames-St. —at 97, op. Billingsgate.

Boss-Alley, Gainsford-St. Horsleydown,—at 7, 1st on the L. from 34, Horsleydown-lane.

Boss-Court, Boss-Alley, Horsleydown,—1st on the L. from 7, Gainsford-st.

Boss-Court, Up. Thames-St.— at 214, W. side of Lambeth-hill.

Bostock St. Old Gravel-Lane,— at 154, 3d on the R. from Ratcliffe-highway.

Boston-Row, Brompton,—part of Queen's-buildings, at the end of Queen-st. about $\frac{1}{4}$ of a mile on the L. from Knightsbridge.

Boswell-Court New, North-St. Red-Lion-Sq.—N. end, to 20, Devonshire-st.

Boswell-Court (New), Carey-St.—at 18, 5th on the L. from 99, Chancery lane.

Boswell-Court (Old), Strand,— a few doors on the R. from Temple-bar.

Botanic-Gardens, Chelsea,— op. 31, Paradise-row, $\frac{1}{2}$ of a mile S. W. from the hospital.

St. Botolph and Aldgate-School, Tower-hill, facing the new Mint.

Botolph-Alley, Botolph-Lane, —at 40, 1st on the L. from Eastcheap.

St. Botolph-Church, Bishops-gate,—$\frac{1}{4}$ of a mile on the L. North from Cornhill.

St. Botolph-Church, Aldgate,— a few doors on the L. below Leadenhall-st.

St. Botolph and St. George's Church, Botolph-Lane,—8 doors from 16, Little East-cheap.

St. Botolph-Church, Aldersgate-St.—the corner of Little-Britain.

Botolph-Lane,—2d E. to Fish-st.-hill, from 16, Eastcheap, to 111, Lower Thames-st.

Botolph-Wharf, Lower Thames-St.—at 9, 3d below London-bridge.

Bottle-Alley, Bishopsgate-Without,—at 133, op. New-st.

Bottle of Hay-Yard, St. John-St. Clerkenwell,—at 128, $\frac{1}{4}$ of a mile on the L. from Smith-field.

Botwright's-Builds. Hackney-Road,—op. the Middlesex-chapel, $\frac{1}{3}$ of a mile on the L. from Shoreditch.

Botwright's-Builds. Bethnal-Green. See Mount Court.

Bough-Court, Shoreditch,—behind 236, leading into Plough-yard.

Bourdon-Street, Davies-St.— 4 doors on the R. from Berkeley-sq.

Bouverie-Street, Fleet-St.—at 62, middle of the S. side.

Bow-Church-Yd. Cheapside,— at 54, W. side the church.

Bow-Lane, Cheapside,—at 59, E. side the church.

Bow-Lane, Poplar,—2d on the R. also 3d on the L. from the East-India-Dock-Gate.

Bow-Lane-Court,—2d on the R. from the E.-India-Dock-Gate.

Bow-Street, Covent-Garden,—from 63, Long-Acre, to Gt. Russel-st.

Bow-St. Bloomsbury,—at 169, High-Holborn, by Broad-st. St. Giles's.

Bow-Yd.Broad-Street,St.Giles',—at 37, leading into Belton-street.

Bowling-Alley, Clerkenwell,—W. end of Bowling-st.

Bowling-Alley, Whitecross-St. Cripplegate,—at 21, 2d on the L. from Fore-st.

Bowling-Green,Edgware-Road—op. 27, ⅛ of a mile on the L. from Tyburn-turnpike.

Bowling-Green-Builds. New-Road, Marybone,—E. side the Yorkshire-Stingo.

Bowling-Green-Yard,—1st in the last from the New-road.

Bowling-Green, King-St. Boro,—at 49, 2d on the R. from 109, High-st.

Bowling-Green-House, Sommer's-Town,—in the fields, op. Judd's-place, towards the Foundling-hospital.

Bowling-Green-Lane, High-St. Marybone,—at 27, W. end of Weymouth-st.

Bowling-Green-Lane, Clerkenwell,—op. the Workhouse, Coppice-row.

Bowling-Green-Pl. Woodstock-St. Marybone,—behind 29, Weymouth-st.

Bowling-Green-Pl. Kennington-Green,—1st on the L. from the Horns.

Bowling-Green-Row, Hoxton,—the 3d on the R. from Old-st. road along Pitfield-st.

Bowling-Green-Row, Kenning-ton-Green,—1st on the L. from the Horns.

Bowl and Pin-Alley, Bream's-Builds. Chancery-Lane,—a few yards N. of the E. end.

Bowl and Pin-Alley,—1st on the R. in the last from Bream's-Buildings.

Bowling-St. Westr.—3d on the L. in College-st. from 18, Abingdon-st.

Bowling-Street, Turnmill-St. Clerkenwell,—3d on the L. from Cow-cross.

Bowls's-Wharf, Cock-Hill, Ratcliffe,—12 doors on the R. from High-st. Shadwell.

Bowman's-Builds. Aldersgate-Street,—at 140, op. Jewin-st.

Bowyer's-Buildings, James-St.—1st on the R. from Cannon-st.-road.

Boydes-Gardens, Pimlico,—1st on the L. from the S. end of Belgrave-terrace, towards the Five Fields.

Boyd's-Walk, Bermondsey-Wall,—1st on the L. west of Fountain-stairs.

Boyle-Street, New Burlington-St.—the continuation of it from 120, Swallow-st.

Brabant-Court, Philpot-Lane,—6 doors on the R. from 12, Fenchurch-st.

Braces-Builds. Blue-Anchor-Yard,—last on the L. from 48, Rosemary-lane.

Brackley-St. Golden-Lane,—at 9, 4th on the L. from Barbican.

Bradshaw's-Court, Curriers-Row, Blackfriars,—1st on the L. from Bristow-st. St. Andrew's-hill.

Bradshaw's - Rents, Portpool-Lane,—at 42, 1st on the R. from 63, Leather-lane.

Braggs - Ways, Rotherhithe,—adjoins Rotherhithe-stairs on the E. side.

Branches - Builds. Tabernacle-Walk,—at 52, nearly op. the Tabernacle.

Branches-Pl. Cable-St. Well-close-Sq.—at 72, near Rosemary-lane.

Brandon's - Fields, Bow - Lane, Black-Wall,—N. side the E. India-Dock Gate.

Brandon - Row, Newington - Causeway,—from the turnpike to Poplar-row.

Brandon-St. Bermondsey New Road,—4th on the R. from the Bricklayers-Arms.

Brandon's - Warehouses, Leadenhall-St.—at 88, W. side Creechurch-lane.

Braynes - Row, Coppice - Row, Clerkenwell, — E. side the turnpike, by the House of Correction.

Brazier's - Alms - Houses,— the end of Two Swan-yd. from 186, Bishopsgate-without.

Braziers-Builds. Fleet-Market,—at 30, 3d on the L. from Holborn-bridge.

Braziers-Hall, Coleman-St.—at 80, the corner of London-Wall.

Bread-St. Cheapside,—at 46, 3d on the R. from St. Paul's-church-yard.

Bread-Street-Hill, Up. Thames-St. — from 201 to Bread-street.

Breackneck-Steps, Bristow-St.

Blackfriars,—1st on the R. from St. Andrew's-hill.

Bream's - Buildings, Chancery-Lane, — at 27, leading to Rolls-builds. and 117, Fetter-lane.

Breezer's - Hill, Ratcliffe-Highway,— op. Ship-alley, Well-close-sq.

Brenan's-Buildings, Gibraltar-Row, Bethnal - Green,—on the S. side the Gibraltar.

Brenan's-Pl. Gibraltar-Row,—on the N. side the Gibraltar.

Brent's-Court, High-St. Boro. —at 182, the 6th S. of Union-street.

Brewer-Court, Bedfordbury,—at 34, middle of the E. side.

Brewer - Court, Gt. Wild - St. Lincoln's - Inn - Fields,—op. Wild-court.

Brewer-Court, (Two) Golden-Lane,—at 79, 4th on the L. from Old-st.

Brewer-Court, Saint Thomas's-St. Boro.—1st on the R. from 44, High-st.

Brewer-Court, Morgan's-Lane, —1st on the L. from 79, Tooley-st.

Brewer's - Green, Westr.—the continuation of James - st. from the Blue-coat-school and Bridewell.

Brewers - Hall, Addle - St.—at 19, op. 58, Aldermanbury.

Brewer-Lane, Up. Thames-St. — from 83, to Dowgate-wharf.

Brewer's-Quay, Lower-Thames-St.—⅓ of a mile below London-bridge, or the first W. from Tower-hill.

Brewer's-Row, Brewer's-Green, Westr.—1st on the R. from the E. end of James-st.

Brewer-St. Pimlico,—4th on the L. from Buckingham-gate.

Brewer-St. Bloomsbury, — 1st on the L. in Bow-st. from 169, High Holborn.

Brewer-St. Golden-Sq.—2d on the L. in Gt. Windmill-st. from the Haymarket.

Brewhouse-Alley, Cherrytree-Alley—3d on the R. from 118, Bunhill-row.

Brewhouse-Court, Long-Alley, Moorfields,—4 doors N. of 33, Sun-st.

Brewhouse-Pl. Lock's-Fields, Walworth,—1st on the R. in Queen-st. from York-st.

Brewhouse-Lane, Wapping,—at 144, op. Execution-dock.

Brewhouse-St. Shadwell,—the continuation of Pope's Hill, from 75, High-st.

Brewhouse-Turning, Vine-Yd. —2d on the R. from 110, Tooley-st.

Brewhouse-Yd. King-St.—1st on the R. from 165, Drury-lane.

Brewhouse-Yard, Cherry-Garden-St. Bermondsey,—1st on the L. from Cherry-garden-stairs, leading to West-lane.

Brewhouse-Yard, Chick-Lane, —3 doors on the L. from Saffron-hill.

Brewhouse-Yard, Shoe-Lane,—at 33, near the middle of the E. side.

Brewhouse-Yard, Angel-Alley, Bishopsgate,—2d on the L. from Long-alley.

Brewhouse-Yard, Shadwell,—at the bottom of Fox's-lane, on the R. from the church.

Brewhouse-Yard, Cartwright-St.—7 doors on the L. from 32, Rosemary-lane.

Brian's-Buildings, Green-Street, St. George's-Fields,—2d on the R. from Bennett's-row.

Brian-St. Shoreditch,—behind 47, at the entrance to Webb-square.

Brian-Court, Webb-Sq. — 1st on the L. from 48, Shoreditch.

Brick-Court, Middle Temple-Lane,—1st broad opening on the R. from Fleet-st.

Brick-Court, Gt. Shire-Lane,— 1st on the R. from Temple-bar.

Brick-Hill-Lane, Up. Thames-St.—op. 179, five doors E. of Queen-st.

Brick-Lane, Saint Luke's,—at 113, Old-st. 1st on the L. from Goswell-st.

Brick-Lane, Bethnal-Green and Spitalfields,—the North continuation of Osborn-st. op. Whitechapel-church, where there are Nos. 1 and 213, leading to 146, Church-st. Bethnal-green.

Bricklayers-Arms, Kent-Road, —at the E. end of Kent-st. ¾ of a mile from St. George's-church.

Bricklayer's-Hall, Leadenhall-Street. See Synagogue for Dutch Jews.

Brick-St. Park-Lane,—2d on the R. from Piccadilly.

Brick-Street, Borough-Road, —3d on the L. from the King's-bench.

St. Bride's-Church, Fleet-St.—6 doors on the L. from Fleet-market.

St. Bride's-Court, New Bridge-St.—4 doors on the R. from Fleet-st.

St. Bride's-Lane, Fleet-St.—at 98, 1st on the L. from Fleet-market.

St. Bride's-Passage, Fleet-St.—at 84, and at 137, Salisbury-court.

St. Bride's-Wharf,—E. side Whitefriars-dock, at the bottom of Water-lane, from 68, Fleet-st.

St. Bride's-Workhouse, Shoe-Lane,—4 doors on the R. from 128, Fleet-st.

Bridge-Court, Westr.—behind the N. side of Bridge-st.

Bridge-Dock, Limehouse,—at the E. end of Narrow-st. by the Drawbridge.

Bridge-House-Court, Grace-church-St.—at 37, op. Talbot-court.

Bridge-Pl. Deptford Lower-Rd.—N side the Surrey Canal.

Bridge-Pl. Rawston-St.—1st on the L. from Goswell-st.-road.

Bridge-Place, Bermondsey,—between the S. end of George-row, Dock-head, and the Neckinger-turnpike.

Bridge-Road, Lambeth,—from Westr.-bridge to the Marsh-gate.

Bridge-Row, Pimlico,—S. end of Belgrave-terrace, to Kemp's-row, op. Ranelagh-walk.

Bridge-St. (New), Blackfriars,—the continuation of Fleet-market to the bridge.

Bridge-St. (Little),—4 doors on the L. in the last from Ludgate-hill.

Bridge-St. Westr.—from King-st. to the bridge.

Bridge-St. (New), Vauxhall,—from the turnpike to Vaux-hall-gardens.

Bridge-Ward-School, Old Swan-Lane,—a few doors on the L. from 104, Upper Thames-st.

Bridge-Wharf, Tooley-St.—1st E. from London-bridge.

Bridge-Yard, Tooley-St.—17 doors on the L. from London-bridge.

Bridgewater-Gardens, Bridge-water-Sq.—N. side, from Brackley-st. to Fan-street, Goswell-st.

Bridgewater-Sq.—N. end of Princes-st. from 42 Barbican.

Bridle-Lane, Golden-Sq.—on the E. side, from 8, Brewer-st. to 34, Silver-st.

Bridewell, Westr.—E. end of James-st. near ½ a mile on the R. from Buckingham-gate.

Bridewell, Bridge-Street, Black-friars,—12 doors on the R. from Fleet-st.

Bridewell, Clerkenwell-Green,—on the N. side the church, facing James's-walk.

Bridewell-Precinct,—W. side of Blackfriars-bridge, to White-friars.

Bridewell-Walk, Clerkenwell-Close,—the continuation of it, entering by the church.

Brighton-Pl. Kent-Road,—S. side, by the Elephant and Castle.

Brighton-Pl. Hackney-Road,—part of the R. side, ¼ of R

D

mile from Shoreditch-church, op. Alport's nursery.

Brill-Pl. Sommers-Town, — 6 doors N. of Skinner-st. to 16, Chapel-path.

Brill-Path, Sommers-Town, — the continuation of Skinner-st.

Brill-Row—N. continuation of the last.

Brill-Terrace, —N. continuation of the last.

Brissenden-Builds. Brewer-St. Pimlico,—1st four houses adjoining Pimlico.

Bristow-St. Blackfriars,—1st on the L. on St. Andrew's-hill from Earl-st.

Britain-Court, Ratcliffe-Highway,— at 177, leading to Princes-sq.

Briton-Court, Water-Lane, — at 18, third on the R. from 67, Fleet-st.

Briton-Court, Freeman's-Lane, Horselydown,— at 22, the back of Webster's wharf.

Britain (Little), Aldersgate-St. —at 175, 1st on the L. from St. Martin's-le-Grand.

Britain (Little), Little Store-St. Bedford-Sq.—1st on the L. from Gt Store-st.

Britannia-Court, Mason-Street, Lambeth, — 4th on the L. from 30, Bridge-road.

Britannia-Court, Golden-Lane, —6 doors on the R. from Barbican.

Britannia-Gardens, Hoxton,— extends from the back of the Britannia to Haberdasher's-walk.

Britannia-Pl. Commercial-Rd. Limehouse, — W. side the Turnpike by the bridge.

Britannia-St. Gray's-Inn-Lane,

—2d on the L. from Battle-bridge.

Britannia-Row, Lambeth. See Mason-st.

British Assurance-Society,—at 129, Aldersgate-st. 10 doors S. of Long-lane.

British Brewery, Church-St. Lambeth,—between Prat-st. and Norfolk-row.

British Copper-Company, Up. Thames-St.-at 68, W. side of Queen-st.

British Fire-Office,—429, Strand, and 21, Cornhill.

British Lying-In-Hospital, — at 34, Brownlow-st. Drury-lane.

British Mercury Newspaper-Office, — at 5, Hind-court, behind 147, Fleet-st.

British Museum, Gt. Russel-St. —op. 50, near Bloomsbury-square.

British Neptune Newspaper-Office, 143, Fleet-st.

British Press Newspaper-Office, Strand,—at 127, nearly op. Exeter-change.

Britt's-Buildings, Long-Alley, Moorfields, 4th on the R. from Worship-st.

Britt's-Builds. Hoxton,—N. end of Haberdashers-walk.

Brit's-St. Sampson's-Gardens, —2d on the R. in Globe-st. from 60, Wapping-st.

Broad-Arrow-Court, Grub-St. St. Luke's,—10 doors on the L. from Chiswell-st.

Broad-Bridge, Shadwell-High-St.—at 87, fifth below the church.

Broad-Court, Drury-Lane,—at 43, leading to Bow-st. Covent-garden.

Broad-Court, Parker-St. — 1st

on the L. from 162, Drury-lane.

Broad-Pl. Shoreditch,—at the back of the church, from Austin-st. to Castle-st.

Broad-Street, St. Giles's, or Bloomsbury,—the W. continuation of Holborn, from Drury-lane to the church.

Broad-St. Carnaby-Market, — at 86, Berwick-st. fourth on the R. from 372, Oxford-st.

Broad-St. (Old), Threadneedle-St.—1st on the L. from the Royal-Exchange.

Broad-St. (New), op. Bishops-gate-church-yd. to Broker-row, also the continuation of Old Broad-st.

Broad-St. (New) Court, — 5 doors N. of Bishopsgate-ch.-yard.

Broad-St. (New) Mews, op. the last.

Broad-St.-Builds.—the N. continuation of Old and part of New Broad-st.

Broad-St.-Pl.—from 36, Broad-st.-builds. to Moorfields.

Broad-Street, Saint George's, East,—E. side the London Dock Wall, from Ratcliffe-highway, towards Wapping.

Broad-St. Ratcliffe,—the continuation of Shadwell High-st. and Cock-hill to Ratcliffe-cross.

Broad-Street, Lambeth,—from Lambeth-butts to the Thames.

Broad-St. Horselydown,—the E. continuation of Tooley-st. and Back-st.

Broad-Street Chambers, Old Broad-St.—at 37, op. Winchester-st.

Broad-Wall, Christ-Church,—W. end of Stamford-st. Black-friars-road.

Broad-Way, Westr.—at the W. end of Tothill-st. from the Abbey, and E. end of York-street.

Broad-Way, Limehouse, — the space between Narrow-st. Fore-st. and Ropemaker's-fields.

Broad-Way, Blackfriars,—1st on the L. in Cock-court from 19, Ludgate-hill.

Broad-Way, Boro.—1st on the L. in St. Thomas-st. from 43, High-st.

Broad-Way-Yard, Broad-Way, Westr.—at 9, ditto. See Broad-Way.

Broad-Way, White-Horse-Alley —1st on the L. from Cow-cross.

Broad-Yard, Lilly-St.—at the E. end from 40, Gt. Saffron-hill.

Broad-Yard, Turnmill-Street, Clerkenwell,—at 65, fourth on the L. from the Sessions-house.

Broad-Yard, Cowheel-Alley, St. Luke's,—1st on the L. from 168, Whitecross-st.

Broad-Yard, Blackman-St. Boro.—at 69, leading to Gt. Suffolk-st.

Broken-Wharf, Up. Thames-St. —at 41, op. Old Fish-street-hill.

Broker's-Alley, Drury-Lane,— at 25, op. Gt. Queen-st.

Broker-Row, Moorfields, — E. side, from London - wall to Broad-st. buildings.

Bromley-Place, Conway-St. Fitzroy-Sq.—3 doors on the L. from London-st.

Brompton,—at the W. end of Sloane-st. 3d coach turning on the L. from Hyde-park-corner.

Brompton-Chapel,—¼ of a mile on the R. from Knights-bridge.

Brompton-Crescent,—back of Michael's-pl. ½ a mile on the L. from Knightsbridge.

Brompton-Grove, Brompton,—¼ of a mile on the L. from Knightsbridge.

Brompton-Row, Brompton,—R. side the road, ⅛ of a mile from Knightsbridge.

Brompton-Terrace,—L. side the road from Knightsbridge, corner of Queen-st.

Brook's-Court, Brook's-Market, Holborn,—N. W. corner, leading to Bell-court.

Brook's-Court, Brook-St. Lambeth,—12 doors on the L. from Little Moor-pl.

Brook - Court, Brothers-Row, Lambeth,—1st on the L. from High-st.

Brook's-Court, Up. Lambeth-Marsh,—1st on the L. from the turnpike.

Brook's-Court, Vine-Yard,—3d on the R. from 110, Tooley-street.

Brook's - Gardens, Bagnige-Wells,—the back of Brook's-place.

Brook's-Market,——N. end of Brook-st. from 140, Holborn.

Brook's-Mews, Davis-St. Berkeley-Sq.—at 50, five doors S. from 40, Brook-st.

Brook's-Mews, Cleaver-St.—1st on the R. from Kennington-cross.

Brook's-Pl. Kennington-Cross,—facing Upper Kennington-lane.

Brook's-Pl. Bagnige-Wells,—on the N. side the House of Correction.

Brook's-Pl. Little Charles-St. Hampstead-Road,—middle of the S. side.

Brook-St. New-Road, Fitzroy-Sq.—1st W. of Hampstead-road.

Brook-St. (Little), 2d on the L. in the last from the New-rd.

Brook-St. Holborn,—at 140, ¼ of a mile on the R. from Fleet-market.

Brook-St. Grosvenor-Sq.—from the N. E. corner to 103, New Bond-st.

Brook-St. (Little), Hanover-Sq. —from the S. W. corner to New Bond-st.

Brook-St. (Upper), Grosvenor-Sq.—from the N. W. corner to Park-lane.

Brook - St. Ratcliffe,—the E. continuation of Back - lane and Sun-Tavern-fields.

Brook-St. Walcot-Pl. Lambeth, —from Little Moor-pl. (op. Lambeth new chapel) to South-st. West-sq.

Brook's-Wharf - Lane, Upper Thames-St.—at 51, op. Bread-st. hill.

Brook's-Wharf,—bottom of the last.

Brook's-Wharf, Willow-Street, Bankside,——between Pye-gardens and Love-lane.

Brook's-Wharf, Weaver's-Lane, Boro.—on the R. in it from 119, Tooley-st.

Brook's-Yard, Long-Alley, Moorfields,—2d on the R. north of Sun-st.

Brook's-Yard, Up. Thames-St. —at 204, E. side Lambeth-hill.

Brook's-Yd. George-St. Tower-Hill,—middle of the N. side.

Broom-Alley, Whitechapel-Rd. —at 53, two doors E. of Gt. Garden-st.

Brother's-Builds. Up. Ogle-St· —the 1st on the R. from 10, Upper Marybone-st.

Brother's-Row, High-St. Lambeth,—4th on the R. from the church.

Brown-Bear-Alley, Upper East Smithfield,—at 120, nearly op. Nightingale-lane.

Brown-Bear-Court, Queen-St. Boro.—24 doors on the R. from Union-st.

Brown-Bear-Yard, High-St. Boro.—at 247, St. Margaret's-hill.

Brown's-Builds. Stanhope-St.— at 27, 1st N. of White-Horse-yard, Drury-lane.

Brown's-Builds. St. Mary Axe, —1st on the R. from 116, Leadenhall-st.

Brown's-Builds. Princes-St.— 1st on the L. from Rosemary-lane.

Brown's-Builds. Green-Street, St. George's-Fields,—1st on the R. from Bennett's-row.

Brown's-Builds. Glean-Alley,— at the further end of it from 218, Tooley-st.

Brown-Bear-Court, Upper E.

Smithfield,—at 1, W. side Cooper's-row.

Brown's-Court, Edgware-Road, —at 81, the back of Winchester-row.

Brown's-Court, Green-St.—at 10, the 1st on the L. from N. Audley-st.

Brown's-Court, Carnaby-Market,—at 24, N. E. corner of it.

Brown's-Court, Angel-Alley, Bishopsgate,—2d on the R. from Long-alley.

Brown's-Court, James-Street, St. Luke's,—1st on the R. from 37, Featherstone-st.

Brown's-Court, Gt. Ayliff-St.— at 49, 4 doors W. of Red-lion-st. Whitechapel.

Brown's-Court, Long-Lane, Bermondsey,—4th on the R. from Kent-st.

Brown's-Lane, Spitalfields,—op. 55, Brick-lane, leading into Lamb-st. and Spital-sq.

Brown's-Passage, Green-St.— at 57, 1st on the L. from 28, North Audley-st.

Brown's-Quay, Wapping,—op. 17, Wapping-st. by Hermitage-bridge.

Brown-St. Duke-Street, Grosvenor-Sq.—at 36, the 2d on the R. from 277, Oxford-st.

Brown-St. Banhill-Row,—the E. side, at 60, near Featherstone-st.

Brown-St. Up. George-Street, —at 26, 2d on the L. from 45, Edgware-road.

Brown's-Wharf,—at the bottom of Milford-lane, from 200, Strand.

Browning's-Builds. Up. Chap-

D 3

man-St.—2d on the L. from
Cannon-st.-road.

Brownlow-Mews, Gt. Guild-
ford-St.—1st on the L. from
Gray's-Inn-lane.

Brownlow-St. Holborn,—at 50,
nearly op. Chancery-lane.

Brownlow-St. Drury-Lane,—20
doors on the R. from Hol-
born.

Brunswick-Chapel, Up. Berkeley-St. Portman-Sq.—N. side
between Quebec-st.and Cumberland-pl.

Brunswick-Court, Brunswick-
St. Christ Church,—from 84,
to Green-walk.

Brunswick-Mews, Wilmot-St.
Brunswick-Sq.—1st on the R.
from 36, Bernard-st.

Brunswick-Mews, Cumberland-
St. Portman-Sq.—4th on the
R. from 245, Oxford-st.

Brunswick-Pl. City-Road,—1st
on the R. from Old-st. by the
turnpike.

Brunswick - Pl. Brunswick-St.
Christ-Church,—at 17, middle of the N. side.

Brunswick-Pl.Kent-Road,—adjoins Nursery-pl. corner of
East-lane.

Brunswick-Row,Queen-Square,
Bloomsbury,—at the N. W.
corner.

Brunswick - Row, Horseferry-
Road, West ,—W. end, near
Bridewell.

Brunswick-Row, Brunswick-St.
Blackfriars-Road,—S. end by
Collingwood-st.

Brunswick-Sq.—on the W. side
the Foundling-hospital, Gt.
Guildford-st.

Brunswick-St.Blackwall-Cause-

way,—corner of Poplar High-
street.

Brunswick-St. Stamford-Street,
—2d on the L. from Black-
friars-road.

Brunswick-St. (Little),—continuation of the last to Cross-
street.

Brunswick-St. Hackney-Road,
—op. Brighton-pl. about ⅜
mile on the L. from Shoreditch.

Brunswick-Terrace, Hackney-
Road,—part of the L. side
from the last towards Gt.
Cambridge-st.

Brunswick-Terrace,Brunswick-
Sq. See Colonnade.

Brush-Court, Up. E. Smithfield,
—at 60, third on the R. from
Tower-hill.

Bruton-Mews, (North) Bruton-
St.—the continuation of Little Bruton-st.

Bruton-Mews, (South) Bruton-
St.—5 doors on the L. from
152, New Bond-st.

Bruton-Pl.Berkeley-Sq.—at 22,
N. W. corner leading into
Bruton-mews.

Bruton-St. Berkeley-Sq.—from
the E. side to 52, New Bond-
street.

Bruton-St. (Little),—the 1st on
the R. in the last from New
Bond-st.

Bryanstone-St. Portman-Street,
—at 19, 1st on the L. from
220, Oxford-st.

Bryanstone-St. (Up.), the continuation of the last to 9, Edgware-road.

Brydges-St. Covent-Garden,—
continuation of Catherine-st.
from 342, Strand.

Bryon's-Builds. Stangate, Lambeth,—N. end of the Bishop's-walk, near Westr.-bridge.

Buck's-Builds. Pimlico, Hoxton, —1st on the L. from the High-st.

Buck's - Head - Court, Distaff-Lane,—3 doors from 31, Old Change.

Buck's Row, Ducking - Pond-Lane, Whitechapel,—N. side by Liptrap's distillery.

Buckbridge-Court, Buckbridge-Street, St.Giles's,—middle of the N. side.

Buckbridge - Street, High - St. St.Giles's,—1st on the L.from Oxford-st.

Buckingham - Court, Charing-Cross,—at 36, N. side the Admiralty.

Buckingham-Gate, St. James's-Park, — W. end, by the Queen's-palace.

Buckingham - Gate, Buckingham-St. Strand,—S. end of it by the Thames.

Buckingham-House, St. James's Park,—W. side, ⅓ of a mile from St. James's-palace.

Buckingham-Pl. Fitzroy - Sq.— W. side, the continuation of Cleaveland-st.

Buckingham-Pl. Kent-Road,— S. side the Asylum for the Deaf and Dumb.

Buckingham - Row, James - St. Westr.—¼ of a mile on the R. from Buckingham-gate.

Buckingham-St. Strand,— 38 doors on the R. from Charing-cross.

Buckingham-St. Fitzroy - Sq.— from Buckingham-pl. to 41, Up. Norton-st.

Buckle-St. Goodman's Fields,

—at 35, Red-lion-st. 2d on the L. from Whitechapel.

Bucklersbury, Cheapside,—from 80, op. the Old Jewry, to the Mansion-house.

Buckley-Court, Church-Lane, St. Giles's,—N. end, entrance at 10, High-st. op. the church.

Budge-Row, Watling-St. — E. continuation of it to Cannon-street.

Bull-Alley, Princes - St. Lambeth,—middle of the W. side.

Bull-Alley, Up. Ground,—⅓ of a mile W. of Blackfriars-bridge.

Bullard's-Place, Bethnal-Green, —1st S. parallel to part of Green-st. from Green-pl. to West-st.

Bull-Bridge, Magdalen-St.—1st on the L. from 140, Tooley-street.

Bull - Court, Giltspur-St.—at 15, 2d on the R. from New-gate-st.

Bull - Court, Petticoat - Lane, Spitalfields,—3 doors N. of Wentworth-st.

Bull-Court, Kingsland-Road,— at 60, 3d on the L. from Shore-ditch church.

Bull-Court, Whitechapel,—at 78, 1st W. from Osborn-st. nearly op. the church.

Bull-Court, Nightingale-Lane, Limehouse,—1st on the L. from Ropemakers-fields.

Bull-Court, Kent-St. Boro.— at 290, eighteen doors on the R. from St. George's-church.

Bull - Court, Tooley - St. See Tooley's Gateway.

Bullen-Court, Strand,—at 407, nearly op. the Adelphi.

Bull and Gate-Yard, Holborn,

—at 243, E. side Little Turn-stile.

Bull's-Head-Alley, Peter-St. Clerkenwell,—at 19, 2d on the R. from Turnmill-st.

Bull's-Head-Court, Gt. Peter-St. Westr.—W. end, by the Horseferry road.

Bull's-Head-Court, Cow-Lane, W. Smithfield,—1st on the R. from Snow-hill.

Bull's-Head-Court, Newgate-St.—at 80, third on the R. from Cheapside.

Bull's-Head-Court, Lawrence-Lane,—at the back of 97, Cheapside.

Bull's-Head-Court, Newington-Causeway,—12 doors on the L. from the King's-bench.

Bull's-Head-Passage, Grace-church-St.—at 81, leading to Leadenhall-market.

Bull's-Head-Passage, Wood-St. Cheapside,—at 94, op. Love-lane.

Bull's-Head-Yard, Tottenham-Ct.-Rd.—at 101, op. Mortimer-Market.

Bull-Inn, Holborn,—at 121, ⅛ of a mile on the R. from Fleet-market.

Bull-Inn, Bishopsgate,—at 91, ¼ of a mile on the L. from Cornhill.

Bull-Inn, Leadenhall-St.—at 152, 6 doors on the L. from Cornhill.

Bull-Inn, Aldgate,—at No. 26, fifteen doors E. of Aldgate-church.

Bull-Lane, Stepney,—from the W. side the church, towards Whitechapel.

Bull Livery-Stables, Goswell-St.—at 6, ¼ of a mile N. from Barbican.

Bull and Mouth-Inn, Bull and Mouth-Street,— the 1st on the L. from St. Martin's-le-Grand.

Bull and Mouth-Street, St. Martin's-le-Grand,—2d on the L. from 66, Newgate-s.

Bull-Stake-Court, Whitechapel, —at 58, 1st W. of the church.

Bull-Stairs, Up. Ground,—N. end of Bull-alley.

Bull-Steps, Old Montague-St.— 2d on the R. from Osborn-street.

Bull-Wall, Chelsea,—at 18, Paradise-row, middle of the S. side.

Bull-Wharf-Lane, Up. Thames-St.—at 62, E. side Queen-hithe.

Bull-Wharf,— bottom of the last.

Bull-Yard, Back-Hill,—1st on the R. from Leather-lane.

Bull-Yard, White-Horse-St. Ratcliffe,— 2 doors on the L. from Butcher-row.

Bull-Yard, Gt. Windmill-St.— 14 doors on the L. from Piccadilly.

Bull-Yard, Fan-St.—the continuation of it on the L. from 1, Goswell-st.

Bull-Yard, Gray's Inn-Lane,— at 62, 6 doors S. of Liquor-pond-st.

Bullock-Court, Whitecross-St. —6th on the R. north of Chiswell-st.

Bullion-St. Stepney,—from the Green, the 2d street along Prospect-place.

Bullyrag-Row, Bethnal-Green, —at the back of the corner formed by Green-st. and Globe-st.

Bulstrode - Mews, Marybone-Lane,—at 32, 4 doors N. of Bulstrode-st.

Bulstrode-St. Marybone-Lane, —at 28, 4th on the R. from 158, Oxford-st.

Bunches-Alley, Thrawl-St. Spital-fields, — 1st on the R. from 208, Brick-lane.

Bunhill-Court, Bunhill-Row,— at 54, eight doors S. of Featherstone-st.

Bunhill-Row,—at 63, Chiswell-st. 2d on the R. from Finsbury-sq.

Burbridge-St. Lambeth-Marsh, —1st on the R. from the turnpike.

Burleigh-Court, Burleigh-St.— 2d on the L. from 365, in the Strand.

Burleigh-St. Strand,—at 365, W. side Exeter-change.

Burlington-Gardens, Old Bond-St.—1st on the L. from 56, Piccadilly.

Burlington-House,—52, Piccadilly.

Burlington-Mews (New), Swallow-St.—at 129, 5th on the L. from Piccadilly.

Burlington-Pl. Broad-St. Ratcliffe, — at 97, op. Stonestairs.

Burlington-St. (New), Swallow-St.—at 120, 4th on the L. from Piccadilly.

Burlington-St. (Old),—2d on the L. in Vigo-lane from 148, Swallow-st.

Burman's-Row, Green-St. Beth-

nal-Green,—a few yards on the R. from the Green.

Burnett's Rents, Kent-St. Boro. —behind 260, and the Green-Man.

Burr-St. Lower E.-Smithfield, —op. the Leith and Berwick Wharf, near ½ of a mile below the Tower.

Burr-St. (Little),—at 41, Burr-st. leading to King Henry-yard.

Burrows - Builds. Blackfriars-Rd.—W. side, op. Surrey-chapel, from Charlotte-st. towards the Obelisk.

Burrows-Mews,—at the back of the last.

Burton's-Builds. Back-Lane,— N. end Mercer's-row, Shadwell.

Burton - Crescent, — N. end Marchmont-st. Gt. Coram-street.

Burton-Street, Tavistock-Sq.—at the back of the E. side.

Bury-Court, St. Mary-Axe,— at 20, middle of the E. side.

Bury-Pl. Bloomsbury, — continuation of Lyon-st. from 143, High-Holborn.

Bury-St. Bloomsbury,—the continuation of Bury-pl. from 30, Hart-st. to 66, Gt. Russel-street.

Bury-St. Saint James's,—1st E. to St. James's-st. from 81, Jermyn-st. to King-st.

Bury-St. Saint Mary-Axe,—entrance by a small court at 10, leading to Bevis-Marks.

Burying - Ground - Alley, Chequer-Alley, Bunhill-Row,— middle of the N. side.

Burying-Ground-Passage, Paradise-St. Marybone,—at 11, W. end.

Busby-Court. Busby St. or New King-St. Bethnal - Green,—1st on the L. W. of James-street.

Busby-Sq. ditto,—2d on the L. W. of James-st.

Busby-Street, James-St. Bethnal-Green,—2d on the L. from 124, Church-st.

Bush-Lane, Cannon-St.—from 22, op. St. Swithin's-lane, to 158, Up. Thames-st.

Bush-Lane (Little),—from 23, Bush-lane, to 156, Thames-street.

Bush-Court, Stoney-Street, Borough,—1st on the R. from the Clink.

Bushel's-Rents, Wapping,—at 17, 3d on the L. below Hermitage-bridge.

Butcher's-Hall, Pudding-Lane, —at 34, four doors from Eastcheap.

Butcherhall-Lane, Newgate-St. —at 82, a few doors on the R. from Cheapside.

Butcher-Row, Up: East-Smithfield,—at 81, 1st coach-turning on the R. from Tower-hill.

Butcher-Row, Ratcliffe-Cross, —from the E. end of Broadst. to Brook-st.

Butcher -Row, St. George's-Market, St. George's-Fields, —N..W. side of it.

Butcer's-Alley, Moor-Lane,— N. end, on the L. from 87, Fore-st.

Butler's-Alley, Moor - Lane,— 5th on the R. from 86, Fore-street.

Butlers-Buildings, George - St. Bethnal-Green,—1st on the R. N. from Spicer-st. near 82, Brick-lane.

Butlers-Builds. Up. E.-Smithfield,—at 5, $\frac{1}{5}$ of a mile on the L. from Tower-hill.

Butlers-Builds. Artillery-Lane, Southwark,—2d on the R. down Crucifix-lane, from 50, Bermondsey-st.

Butler's-Wharf, Shad-Thames, Horselydown,—op. Thomas-street.

Button-Court, Acorn-St.—1st on the L. from 124, Bishops-gate-without.

Button's-Entry, White-Horse-St. Ratcliffe,—N.end, op. the Workhouse.

Buxton-Pl. Lambeth, — from Lambeth new chapel towards the church.

Byce-Court, Blue-Anchor-Yard, —3d on the R. from 48, Rosemary-lane.

Byde-St. Bethnal - Green,—N. side of Anchor-st. from Swan-yard to Club-row.

Byfield-Pl. Charlotte-St. Black-friars-Road,—corner of Gravel-lane.

———

CABBAGE - ALLEY, Long-Lane, Bermondsey,—middle N. side, near the King's-head.

Cable-Pl. Cable-St.—at 55, op. Short-st.

Cable - St. Wellclose - Sq.—E. continuation of Rosemary-lane.

Caddick's - Row, Whitehall,—op. the Admiralty, leading to Gt. Scotland-yd.

Cadogan Mews, Sloane - St.—1st on the L. from Knightsbridge.

Cadogan-Pl. Sloane-St. Chelsea,—op. 76, 2d on the L. from Knightsbridge.

Cadogan-Pl. (Upper), N. end of the last.

Cadogan-Pl. (Lower),—S. end of the square, op. 119, Sloane-street.

Cadogan-Pl. Little,—behind the E. side of the square.

Cain's-Pl. Church-Lane, Whitechapel,—1st on the R. from 65, Cable-st.

Calender-Yard, Long-Alley,—6th on the L. from Moorfields.

Calico-Builds. Neckinger, Bermondsey,—facing Prospect-row, ¼ of a mile on the R. from Hickman's folly.

Calthorpe - Pl. Paradise-Row, Chelsea,—op. 12, 1st on the L. a few yards from the Hospital.

Calthorpe-Pl. (Little),—1st on the L. in Paradise-walk, from op. 18, Paradise-row.

Calvert-St. Old Gravel Lane,—¼ of a mile on the R. from 65, Ratcliffe-highway.

Cambridge-Crescent, Hackney-Road,—nearly op. Matthew's-pl. extending towards Bethnal-green.

Cambridge - Heath, Hackney - Road, by the turnpike,—1¼ of a mile from Shoreditch-church.

Cambridge-Place, Buckingham-Pl. Fitzroy-Sq.—between Carburton-st. and Buckingham-street.

Cambridge-Place, Cambridge-Heath, Hackney-Road,—a few doors on the L. north from the turnpike.

Cambridge-Pl. Hackney-Road,—part of the N. side, near Gt. Cambridge-st.

Cambridge-St. (Gt.) Hackney-Road,—½ a mile on the L. from Shoreditch-church.

Cambridge-St. (Little),—8 doors on the L. in the last from Hackney-road.

Cambridge-St. Golden-Sq.—N. continuation of Windmill-st. Haymarket, to 40, Broad-st.

Camden-Court, Grub-St. Cripplegate,—3 doors on the L. from Chiswell-st.

Camden - Gardens, Camden - Row, Bethnal-Green-Road,—10 doors E. of Wilmot-st.

Camden-Row, Bethnal-Green-Road,—part of the R. side, ¾ of a mile from 65, Shoreditch.

Camden-St. East-Street, Walworth,—2d on the L. from the High-st.

Camel-Builds. Orchard-Street, Portman - Sq.—at 9, 2d on the R. from 197, Oxford-st.

Camomile-St. Bishopsgate,—1st on the R. near ¼ of a mile N. from Cornhill.

Camomile-Mews, Camomile-St.—15 doors on the R. from Bishopsgate-st.

Camperdown-Pl. Snow's-Fields,—6th on the L. from 268, Bermondsey-st.

Campeon-Lane, Up. Thames-
St.—at 89, op. Suffolk-lane.

Canal Office,—at 9, Change-
Alley, Lombard-st.

Canal-Row, Bermondsey-Wall,
—entrance by the Horse-shoe,
a few doors below East-lane-
stairs.

Candlewick - Ward -Chambers,
Crooked-Lane,—3 doors from
Cannon-st.

Cane-Pl. Gravel-Lane, Boro.
—from the S. end to Bennett's-
row.

Canon-Alley, St. Paul's Church-
Yard,—at 63, a few doors on
the R. from Cheapside.

Cannon - Brewery, Knightsbridge,—nearly op. Sloane-
street.

Cannon-Foundery, New Gravel-
Lane,—at 135, by Milk-yd.

Cannon-Pl. Mile-End,—1st W.
of the turnpike.

Cannon-Row, Westr.—from 49,
Parliament-st. to 9, Bridge-
street.

Cannon-St.—N. parallel to Up.
Thames-st. from Walbrook
to Crooked-lane.

Cannon - Street, St. George's
East,—at 143, Ratcliffe-highway, by the church.

Cannon-St.-Road,—the continuation of the last to Whitechapel.

Cannon-St. Boro.—continuation
of Lant-st. from 109, Blackman-street.

Canterbury - Builds. Lambeth,
—continuation of Hercules-
builds. from the Asylum towards the church.

Canterbury-Corner, Lambeth-

Walk,—middle of Little Canterbury-place.

Canterbury - Court, Currier's-
Row, Blackfriars,—2d on the
R. from Bristow-st.

Canterbury-Court, Phœnix-St.
Spitalfields,—at 24, five doors
W. of Grey Eagle-st.

Canterbury-Pl. Lambeth,—from
near the new Chapel (op. the
Stags), towards the church.

Canterbury-Pl. (Little), back of
the last, the 1st on the R. in
Lambeth-walk.

Canterbury - Pl. Walworth,—
from the W. end of Manor-
pl. to West-lane.

Canterbury-Row, Newington,—
L. side the road, ½ of a mile
S. from the church.

Canterbury-Sq. Dean-Street,—2
doors from 203, Tooley-st.

Canterbury-Walk,—at 15, Lambeth-terrace, op. the New-
chapel.

Canton-Pl. East - India-Dock-
Road,—L. side, ½ of a mile
from Limehouse-church.

Capel - Court, Bartholomew-
Lane,—1st on the R. from
the Royal-Exchange.

Cape of Good-Hope-Mews,—
the middle of Devonshire-
mews, East Portland-pl.

Cape Trafalgar, Deptford Lower
Road,—N. corner of China-
hall.

Captain's-Walk, Vine-St. Lambeth,—2d on the R. from
Narrow-wall.

Carburton-St. Cleveland-Street,
Fitzroy-Sq.—2d on the R.
from the New-road.

Cardigan - Place, Kennington-cross,—corner of Up. Kennington-lane.

Cardigan-St.—1st on the R. in the last from Kennington-cross.

Carey-Lane, Cheapside,—extends from 32, Gutter-lane, to 14, Foster-lane.

Carey-Pl. Oakley-St. Lambeth, —at 27, by the Oakley-arms.

Carey-St. Lambeth,—N. end of the last.

Carey-St. Chancery-Lane,—at 99, 1st on the L. from 194, Fleet-st.

Carlisle - Chapel, Kennington-Lane,—⅛ of a mile on the L. from Newington.

Carlisle-House,—W. end of Carlisle-lane, Lambeth.

Carlisle-Lane, Mount-St. Lambeth,—3 doors S. of the Marsh-gate.

Carlisle - Pl. Lambeth,—continuation of the last.

Carlisle-Sq. Carlisle-Lane,—1st on the R. from the Marsh-gate.

Carlisle-St. Soho-Sq.—at 34, W. side.

Carlton-House, Pall-Mall,—12 doors on the L. from the Haymarket.

Carlton-Pl. St. Albans-Street,— 6 doors on the L. from 13, Pall-Mall.

Carlton - Pl. White-Hart-Row, Kennington,—6 doors on the L. from Kennington-lane.

Carmarthen - St. Tottenham - Court-Road,—op. London-st. third S. from the New Road.

Carnaby - Market, Golden-Sq. —W. end of Broad-st. on the R. from 86, Berwick-st.

Carnaby-St. Carnaby-Market, —on the W. side, from 28 Gt. Marlborough-st.

Carol's-Court, Charles-Street, Horselydown,—at the back of 18, the corner of New-st.

Caroline-Court, Great Saffron-Hill,—at 18, op. Charles-st. Hatton-garden.

Caroline - Mews, Caroline - St. Bedford-Sq.—middle of the E. side.

Caroline-Pl. Gt. Saffron-Hill,— the E. end of Caroline-court.

Caroline-Pl. Gt. Guildford-St. —E. side the Foundling-hospital.

Caroline-Pl. City-Road,—part of the R. side, ¼ of a mile from Old-st. op. Fountain-pl.

Caroline-St. Bedford-Sq.—from the S. W. corner to 116, Gt. Russell-st.

Caroline-Wharf, Rotherhithe,— ⅛ of a mile below the church, nearly op. Clarence-st.

Carpenters - Builds. London-Wall,—op. the S. E. corner of Moorfields.

Carpenters-Hall, London-Wall, —at 75, by the last.

Carpenter's-Pl. High St. Shadwell,—at 128, nearly op. Gold's-hill.

Carpenter-Street, Vine-Street. Westr.—at 44, 3d on the L. from Millbank-st.

Carpenter - St. Mount-Street, Berkeley-Sq.—6 doors from Davies-st. leading into Mount-row.

Carpenter's-Yard, St. Bartholomew's-Hospital,—behind the S. side, facing the Cloisters.

E

Carpenters-Yard, Half-Moon-St.—1st on the R. from 170, Bishopsgate-without.

Carpenter's-Yard, St. Dunstan's-Alley,—6 doors from Saint Dunstan's-hill.

Carr-Sq. Cripplegate,—3d on the L. in Moor-lane, from 87, Fore-st.

Carr-Yard, Blue-Anchor-Yd.—4th on the R. from 48, Rosemary-lane.

Carrier-St. Buckbridge-Street, St. Giles's,—2d on the R. from High-st.

Carrington-Mews, Mayfair,—2d on the R. in Chapel-st. from 35, Curzon-st.

Carrington-Place, Down-St. Piccadilly,—the continuation of it to 17, Hertford-st.

Carrington-St. Shepherds-Market,—4 doors W. of White-horse-st. Piccadilly.

Carron-Wharf, Up. Thames-St.—op. 224, near Bennett's-hill.

Carron-Wharf, Lower E. Smith-field,—at 81, a few doors W. of Hermitage-bridge.

Carter-Court, Redcross-St. Boro.—at 89, 1st on the L. from Park-st.

Carter-Street, Cutler-St.—1st on the R. from 114, Hounds-ditch.

Carter-Lane (Great), Doctors-Commons,—1st on the L. in Creed-lane from 14, Ludgate-st.

Carter-Lane (Little),—the E. continuation of the last from Paul's-chain to No. 13, Old Change.

Carter-Lane, Tooley-St.——at

243, 2d on the R. from London-bridge.

Carter's-Rents, Little Minories,—at the N. end, on the L.

Carter-St. Bethnal-Green,—at 167, Brick-lane, op. Hanbury's brewery.

Carthusian-Street, Aldersgate-St.—at 107, nine doors N. of Barbican.

Cartwright's-Builds. Grange-Road,—5th on the R. from Bermondsey New Road towards Rotherhithe.

Cartwright-Sq. Rosemary-Lane,—S. end of Cartwright-st.

Cartwright-St. Rosemary-Lane,—at 32, 6th on the R. from Tower-hill.

Carteret-St. Broadway, Westr.—at the W. end of Tothill-street.

Carteret-Yard, Carteret-St.—middle of the W. side.

Cash's-Ground, Gravel-Lane, Boro.—nearly op. George-st. Blackfriars-rd.

Castle-Alley, Royal-Exchange,—W. side, from Cornhill to the Bank.

Castle-Alley, Whitechapel,—at 124, the 2d E. of Petticoat-lane.

Castle-Baynard Copper-Company, Up. Thames-St.—at 12, ⅓ of a mile E. from Black-friars-bridge.

Castle-Court, Strand,—at 430, ⅕ of a mile on the L. from Charing-cross.

Castle-Court, Poppin's-Court,—1st on the L. from 111, Fleet-st.

Castle-Court, Castle-St. Ox-

ford-St.—4 doors W. of 62,
Berners-st.

Castle-Court,Fullwood's-Rents,
—at 23, five doors on the R.
from 33, Holborn.

Castle-Court, Piccadilly,—23
doors on the R. from the
Haymarket, leading into
Castle-st.

Castle-Court, Whitecross-St.
Cripplegate,—at 55, 7th on
the R. from Fore-st.

Castle-Court, Lawrence-Lane,
—11 doors on the L. from
97, Cheapside.

Castle-Court,Budge-Row, Watling-St.—at 10, leading to 14,
Cloak-lane.

Castle - Court, Castle-St.—1st
on the L. from 40, Turnmill-
street.

Castle-Court, Kingsland-Road,
—op. Union-st. ½ of a mile on
the L. from Shoreditch.

Castle-Court, Birchin-Lane,—
at 23, 1st on the L. from
Cornhill.

Castle-Court, Castle-St. Bethnal-Green,—2d on the R.
from behind Shoreditch-chur.

Castle-Court,Old Castle-Street,
Whitechapel,—2d on the L.
from 121, Wentworth-st.

Castle-Court,Castle-Lane,Boro.
—middle of the E. side.

Castle-Court, Kent-St. Boro.—
at 248, ⅕ of a mile on the
R. from St. George's-church.

Castle and Falcon-Inn, Aldersgate-Street,—at 5, or at 6½,
St. Martin's-le-Grand.

Castle-Inn, Wood-St.—26 doors
on the R. from 122, Cheapside.

Castle-Lane, James-St. Westr.

—2d on the R. from Buck-
ingham-gate.

Castle-Lane, Upper Thames-St.
See Castle-yard.

Castle-Lane,Boro.—last on the
R. in Castle-st. from 13,
Redcross-st.

Castle-Mews, Castle-St. Oxford-St.—3 doors W. from
63, Berners-st.

Castle-Pl. Castle-Lane, Westr.
—at 22, 4th on the R. from
James-st.

Castle-Pl. New Castle-St.—1st
on the R. from 120, Whitechapel.

Castle-Pl. Old Castle-St.—1st
on the R. in Castle-alley,
from 124, Whitechapel.

Castle-Pl. Gibraltar-Row, St.
George's-Fields,—at 15, 1st
on the L. from Prospect-pl.

Castle-St. Leicester-Sq.—1st E.
parallel to it, from Gt. Newport-st. to the King's-mews.

Castle-St. Long-Acre,—1st N.
parallel to it, from Charles-
st. to Little St. Martin's-lane.

Castle-St. East,or Little Castle-
St. Oxford-Street,—from 81,
Newman-st. to Oxford-mar-
ket.

Castle-St. West, or Gt. Castle-
St.—the W. continuation of
the last.

Castle-Street, Bloomsbury,—W.
continuation of Hart-st. to
Thorney-st.

Castle-St. Gt. Saffron-Hill,—at
60, leading into Turnmill-st.

Castle-St. Air-Street,—3 doors
on the R. from 27, Picca-
dilly.

Castle-St. Holborn,—at 12, E.
side of Middle-row.

Castle-St. Falcon-Sq.—1st on the R. from Aldersgate-st.

Castle-St. Fleet-Market,——at 33, leading into Sea-coal-lane, Snow-hill.

Castle-St. Up. Thames-Street, —op. 223, ¼ of a mile on the R. from Blackfriars-bridge.

Castle-St. Finsbury-Sq.—the 2d N. from it, extending from 18, City-road to Paul-st.

Castle-St. Bethnal-Green,—from Cock-lane behind Shoreditch-church to Mount-st.

Castle-Street, (New), Bethnal-Green,—1st on the R. in the last from Shoreditch-church.

Castle-St. (New), Whitechapel, —at 120, nearly op. Red-lion-street.

Castle-St. (Old), Whitechapel, —the continuation of Castle-alley, to 121, Wentworth-street.

Castle-St. Houndsditch,—at 46, 2d on the R. from Bishops-gate.

Castle-St. Redcross-Street, Boro.—at 14, 1st on the R. from Park-st.

Castle-St. Kent-St. Boro.—at 94, ⅓ of a mile on the L. from St. George's-church.

Castle-Yard, Little Chapel-St. Westr.—op. Saint Margaret's-burying-ground.

Castle-Yard, Royal Hospital-Row, Chelsea,—2d on the L. from the Hospital.

Castle-Yard, Castle-Street, Holborn,—at 37, leading into Norwich-court.

Castle-Yard, Bolsover-St.—2d on the L. from 113, Oxford-street.

Castle-Yard, Up. Thames-St.—at 34, op. Lambeth-hill.

Castle-Yard, Gravel-Lane,—1st on the R. from Holland-st. Blackfriars-bridge.

Castle-Yard, Poplar,—1st on the L. from the Commercial-road.

Cateaton-St. Milk-Street, Cheapside,—from N. end of it, to the Old Jewry.

Catherine-Builds. William-St. Westr.—1st on the R. from James-st.

St. Catherine-Cree-Church,— between Nos. 84 and 88, Leadenhall-st.

St. Catherine Coleman's-Church, —on the E. side of Church-row, a few yards behind 67, Fenchurch-st.

St. Catherine's-Church, Tower-Hill,——behind the houses which are op. St. Catherine's-stairs.

Catherine-Court, Gt. Peter-St. Westr.—8 doors E. of Duck-lane.

Catherine-Court, Seething-Lane,—at 34, 2d on the R. from Tower-st.

St. Catherine's-Court, Saint Catherine's-Sq.—facing the W. side the church.

Catherine-Court, Catherine-St. Commercial-Road;—1st on the R. from the Commercial-road.

St. Catherine's-Cloisters, Saint Catherine's,—on the N. side the church.

St. Catherine's-Lane, Up. E. Smithfield,—6 doors on the R. from Tower-hill.

St. Catherine's-Sq.—1st on the

L. in St. Catherine's-st. from Tower-hill.

Saint Catherine's-Stairs,—at 5, St. Catherine's-street, a few doors on the R. below Tower-hill.

St. Catherine-Street, Tower-hill,—at the S. E. corner by the Thames, leading towards Wapping.

Catherine-St. William-Street, Westr.—1st on the R. from James-st.

Catherine-St. Strand,—at 342, op. Somerset-pl.

Catherine-St. (Little),—at 11, in the last.

Catherine-St. Commercial-Rd. —3d on the R. east from Cannon-st.-road.

Catherine-St. Hackney-Road,— near Brighton-pl. ¾ mile on the R. from Shoreditch.

Catherine-Wheel-Alley, Bishopsgate-Without,—at 43, 12 doors N. of New-st.

Catherine-Wheel - Sq.—1st on the L. in the last from Bishopsgate.

Catherine Wheel-Alley, Essex-St.—2d on the R. from 105, Whitechapel.

Catherine-Wheel-Court, Bridgewater-Gardens,—at 14, N. E. corner.

Catherine-Wheel-Court, Kent-St. Boro.—at 248, near ¼ mile on the R. from St. George's-church.

Catherine-Wheel-Yard, Little James-St.—W. end, by the Green-park.

Catherine-Wheel-Inn, Bishopsgate-Without,—at 40, N. side New-st.

Catherine-Wheel-Inn, High-St. Boro.—at 190, the 4th S. of Union-st.

Catherine-Wheel-Yard, Great Windmill-St.—13 doors on the R. from Piccadilly.

Cato-St. Queen-Street,—2d on the L. from 62, Edgware-road.

Catshead - Court, Orchard-St. Westr.—at 44, 3d on the L. from Dean-st.

Catshole-Court, Tower-Hill,— on the E. side, the 1st on the R. from Iron-gate.

Caulker's-St. Blackwall-Causeway,—2d on the R. from Poplar High-st.

Cavendish-Court, Houndsditch, —at 90, 12 doors on the L. from Bishopsgate.

Cavendish-Mews, South Duke-St. Portland-Pl.—at 14, 1st from 13, New Cavendish-street.

Cavendish-Mews, (North) Charlotte-St. Portland-Pl.—at 80, three doors from New Cavendish-st.

Cavendish-Sq. Marybone,—N. end of Hollis-st. from 132, Oxford-st.

Cavendish-St. (New), Portland-Pl.—from 82, Gt. Portland-st. to 24, Harley-st.

Cavendish-Street, (Old), Oxford-St.—at 140, middle of the N. side.

Causeway - Court, Stepney-Ct. —1st on the L. from Brook-street.

Cecil-Court, St. Martin's-Lane, —at 92, 4th on the L. from Charing-cross.

Cecil-St. Strand,—at 84, op. E 3

Southampton-street, Covent-garden.

Censor News-Paper-Office, Catherine-St.—1st house on the L. from 343, in the Strand.

Chad's-Row,—by Chad's-Wells.

Chad's-Wells, Gray's-Inn-Lane,—25 doors on the L. from Battle-bridge turnpike.

Chain-Gate, Boro.—at 297, 3d on the R. from London-bridge.

Chair-Court, Ship-Yard,—1st on the R. from Temple-bar.

Chalton-Gardens, Chalton-St. Sommers-Town,—at 15, middle of the E. side.

Chalton-St. Sommers-Town,—4th on the R. in the Marybone-road from the turnpike Battle-bridge.

Chamber-Sq. Upper E. Smithfield,—at 95, nearly op. the London-docks.

Chamber-St. Goodman's-Fields,—1st S. parallel to Gt. Prescot-st. from Mansel-street to Lemon-st.

Chamberlain's (Lord) Office, St. James's,—the corner of Cleveland-row and the Stable-yard.

Chamberlain's-Pl. Little Shire-Lane,—at 12, op. New-court, from 16, Carey-st. Chancery-lane.

Chamberlain's-Wharf, Tooley-St.—13 doors E. of London-bridge.

Champion-Alley, Vine-St. Westminster,—at 37, 2d on the L. from Millbank-st.

Chancellor-Court, Church-St. Bethnal-Green,—at 191, 1st

on the R. from 65, Shoreditch.

Chancery-Chambers, Quality-Court,—1st house on the L. from 48, Chancery-lane.

Chancery, Court of,—at Lincoln's-inn-hall.

Chancery-Court, Walburge-St. St. George's-East,—the corner of Up. Chapman-st.

Chancery-Lane, Fleet-St.—at 192, ten doors E. from Temple-bar, extending to 310, High-holborn.

Chancery-Masters-Office, Southampton-builds. Holborn,—facing the entrance from 318, Holborn.

Chancery Subpœna-Office,—at 6, Stone-builds. Lincoln's-inn, 1st house on the L. from op. 55, Chancery-lane.

Chandlers-Hall, Dowgate-Hill,—5 doors on the R. from Budge-row.

Chandler's-Rents, Addle-Hill,—at 7, op. Gt. Knight Rider-street.

Chandler-Street, Duke-St. Grosvenor-Sq.—at 8, 1st on the L. from 277, Oxford-st.

Chandos-St. Cavendish-Sq.—from the N. E. corner to Queen-Ann-st.

Chandos-St. Covent-Garden,—9 doors on the L. in Bedford-st. from 423, Strand.

Change-Alley,—between 24, Cornhill, and 70, Lombard-st.

Change-Court,—N. side Exeter-Change, to 21, Exeter-st.

Change (Old), Cheapside,—5 doors on the R. from St. Paul's church-yard.

Chapel-Court, Long-Acre,—14

doors on the L. from St. Martin's-lane.

Chapel-Court, Chapel-St. Bedford-row,—W. side the chapel.

Chapel-Court, Queen-Sq. — S. W. corner, by the chapel.

Chapel-Court, Oxford - St.—at 147, nearly op. New Bond-street.

Chapel-Court, Swallow-St.—at 50, near the middle of the E. side.

Chapel-Court (North), South Audley-St.—at 23, 6 doors E. of Mount-st.

Chapel-Court (South),—on the S. side the chapel, by the last.

Chapel-Court,— the continuation of Hart-st. from 63, Wood - st. facing London-wall.

Chapel-Court, Quaker-St. Spitalfields,—9 doors on the R. from 29, Wheeler-st.

Chapel-Court, Holywell-Street, Mile-End Old-Town,—at 10, 5 doors on the L. from Union-street.

Chapel-Court, Jewry-St.— 4 doors on the R. from Aldgate.

Chapel-Court, High-St. Boro. —at 124, ⅓ of a mile on the L. from London-bridge.

Chapel-Court, Norfolk-St. Boro.—1st on the L. from Little Guildford-st.

Chapel - Field, Wandsworth - Road, — ⅙ of a mile S. of Vauxhall-turnpike.

Chapel-Mews, Chapel-St. Grosvenor-Pl. Hyde-Park-Corner,

—behind 12 and 26, Grosvenor-pl.

Chapel-Mews, Duke-St. Portland-Pl.—at 20, by Portland-chapel.

Chapel-Passage, Upper Rathbone-Pl.—on the S. side the chapel.

Chapel-Path, Willsted-St. Sommers-Town,—at 35, 2d from the road to Marybone.

Chapel-Pl. Vere-St. — 1st on the R. from 154, Oxford-st.

Chapel-Pl. St. James's Park,— 4 doors N. of Gt. George-st.

Chapel-Pl. Spital-Sq.—op. the chapel, in Chapel-yd.

Chapel-Pl. Gt. Suffolk-St. Boro. —2d on the L. from 80, Blackman-st.

Chapel-Pl. Little Coram-St.— 2 doors from Tavistock-pl.

Chapel-Place, Duke-Street, St. George's-Fields,—4th on the R. from the Obelisk.

Chapel-Pl. Long - Lane, Bermondsey,—at 22, ¼ of a mile on the R. from St. George's church.

Chapel - Row, Rawstorne - St. Brompton,—by the chapel behind 28, Brompton-row.

Chapel-Row, Spa-Pl. Spa-Fields, —on the W. side the chapel.

Chapel-Row, St. George's Market, St. George's Fields,— the corner of Brick-st.

Chapel-St. Grosvenor-Pl. Hyde-Park-Corner,—at 26, middle of the W. side.

Chapel-St. (Great), Westr.— from the Broadway, and W. end of Tothill-st. to Strutton-ground.

Chapel-St. (Little),—2d on the R. in the last from Broadway.

Chapel-St. Brompton,—at 27, Brompton-row, ¼ of a mile on the R. from Knightsbridge.

Chapel-St. Lisson-Green,—at 101, Edgware-road, 9th on the R. from Tyburn-turnpike.

Chapel-Street, South Audley-St.—at 64, middle of the W. side.

Chapel-Street West, Curzon-St. May-Fair,—at 35, W. side the chapel.

Chapel-St. East,—on the E. side ditto.

Chapel-Street (Gt.), Oxford-St. —at 396, 3d on the L. from St. Giles's.

Chapel-St. (Little),—S. end of the last, leading to 19, Wardour-st.

Chapel-Street, Lamb's Conduit-St.—at 25, to Milman-st. James-st. and Bedford-row.

Chapel-St. Tottenham-Court-Rd.—at 84, 1st S. of the chapel.

Chapel-St. Great Portland-St. Marybone,—at 95, W. side the chapel.

Chapel-Street, Grub-St. Cripplegate,—by the chapel, middle of the W. side.

Chapel-St. Curtain-Road,—1st on the L. from Worship-st. op. Holywell-lane.

Chapel-Street, Wheeler-St. Spitalfields,—1st on the L. from Lamb-st.

Chapel-Street, St. George's

East,—between Upper and Lower Chapman-streets.

Chapel-Street, Mile-End New-Town,—1st on the R. in Gt. Garden-st. from 50, Whitechapel-road.

Chapel-Yd. Duke-St.—1st on the L. from Lincolns-inn-fields.

Chapel-Yd. Wilderness-Row, Clerkenwell,—2d on the L. from St. John-st.

Chapel-Yard, Spital-Sq.—2d on the L. from Bishopsgate.

Chapman's-Builds. King-St. Boro.—at the back of 49.

Chapman's-Court, Goodman's-Yd.—2d on the R. from 60, Minories.

Chapman-Pl. Up. Chapman-St. —4th on the L. from Cannon-st.-rd.

Chapman's-Pl. Lambeth-Walk, —the corner of Walnut-tree-walk.

Chapman-St. (Lower), Cannon-St.-Rd.—1st on the L. south from the Commercial-road.

Chapman-St. (Upper),—1st S. of the last.

Chapter-House-Court, St. Paul's Church-Yd.—at 67, leading to 50, Paternoster-row.

Charing-Cross,—from St. Martin's-lane to the Admiralty.

Charing-Court, Fore-St. Lambeth,—1st S. of Broad-st.

Charles-Court, Strand,—at 27, 5th on the R. from Charing-Cross.

Charles-Court-Stairs,—E. side of Hungerford-stairs. See the last.

Charles-Court, Charles-Street,

St. James's,—5 doors W. of St. Alban's-st.

Charles-Court, Charles-Street, St. George's East,—1st on the L. from 44, Old Gravel-lane.

Charles-Court, Park-St. Boro. —2 doors on the L. from the Borough-market.

Charles-Pl. Baker's-Row, Cold-Bath-Fields,—2d on the R. from Little Warner-st.

Charles-Pl. Hoxton, — 2d on the L. in Brunswick-pl. or Craven-builds. from the City-road.

Charles-Pl. Bethnal-Green-Rd. —N. W. corner of Thorold-square.

Charles-Pl. Love-Lane, Rat-cliffe,—1st on the L. from Cock-hill.

Charles-Sq. Hoxton,—N. side the Vinegar-ground, 1st on the L. in Pitfield-st. from Old-st.-rd.

Charles-St. Charles-Sq.—N.side the last.

Charles-Street, Parliament-St. Westr.—14 doors on the R. from Whitehall.

Charles-St. (Little),—E. end of the last.

Charles-Street, St. James's-Sq. —from the middle of the E. side, to St. Alban's-st.

Charles-St. (Little),—E. end of the last.

Charles-St. Long-Acre,—at 84, 1st on the R. from Drury-lane.

Charles-St.—6 doors on the R. in Russell-st. from Covent-garden.

Charles-Street, George-St. Port-

man-Sq.—at 34, 1st on the R. west from Baker-st.

Charles-St. Hampstead - Road, —3d on the L. from Totten-ham-court-road.

Charles-St. (Little),—W. end of the last, and N. end of Brook-street.

Charles-St. Lisson-Green,—1st E. of Little James-st.

Charles-St. Drury - Lane, — at 174, 2d on the L. from Hol-born.

Charles-St. Hatton-Garden,— intersects it at 24, extends from 1 r, Leather-lane, to Saf-fron-hill.

Charles-Street, Grosvenor-Sq. —from the S. E. corner, to 19, Mount-st.

Charles-St. Berkeley-Sq.—from the S. W. corner to Union-st.

Charles-St. Soho-Sq.—from the N. side, to 412, Oxford-st. 1st on the L. in it from St. Giles's.

Charles-St. Manchester - Sq.— 1st N. parallel to it, extend-ing from Manchester-st. to Thayer-st.

Charles-St. Middlesex Hospital, —S. side, from 49, Newman-st. to 13, Wells-st.

Charles-St. Bridgewater-Sq.— 1st on the R. in Princes-st. from 48, Barbican.

Charles-Street, Leonard - St.— 1st on the L. from Paul-st. towards the Curtain-road.

Charles-St. Curtain-Road,—3d on the L. from Worship-st.

Charles-Street, Bethnal-Green-Road,—¾ of a mile on the R. from 65, Shoreditch, op. Wil-mot-sq.

Charles-St. Mile - End New-

Town,—the continuation of Baker's-row, from 94, White-chapel-road.

Charles-St. Old Gravel-Lane,—at 44, middle of the E. side.

Charles-St. Westr.-Bridge-Rd. —2d on the R. from the Obe-lisk.

Charles-St. Blackfriars - Rd.— 4th on the L. from the Bridge.

Charles - St. Horselydown, — from Church-row, E. side of St. John's Church, to New-street.

Charles-St. Glean - Alley,—2d on the L. from 219, Tooley-street.

Charles-Street, (Up.), Goswell-St.—at 93, N. end, leading to Northampton-sq.

Charles-St. (Lower),—the con-tinuation of the last to St. John-st.-rd.

Charles-Street, Oakley-St. Lam-beth,—1st on the L. from Westr.-bridge-rd.

Charles-St. Goswell-Place—the E. end of it, by Northamp-ton-terrace.

Charles-Street, Phœnix-St. Som-mers-Town,—the W. conti-nuation of it, by the Polygon.

Charles-Street, Mile-End Old-Town,—from 27, Plumbers-row, to 27, Greenfield-st. Commercial-rd.

Charles-St. Globe-St. Bethnal-Green,—extends from Globe-pl. to Thurlow-pl.

Charles-St. Back-Church-Lane, Whitechapel,—1st on the L. from the Commercial-rd.

Charles-Street, Back-Lane, St.

George's East,—nearly op. the Blue-gate-fields.

Charles-St. Walworth,—op. S. end of Queen's-row, near the Red-Lion.

Charlotte-Builds. Gray's - Inn-Lane,—17 doors on the R. from Holborn.

Charlotte-Chapel, Charlotte-St. Rathbone-Place,—at 92, op. Windmill-st.

Charlotte-Court, Redcross-St. Cripplegate,—at 28, 2 doors N. of Jewin-st.

Charlotte-Court, Gt. York-St. Bethnal Green,—1st on the R. from 135, Church-st. near Shoreditch.

Charlotte-Court, Charlotte-St. Whitechapel,—1st on the L. from Fieldgate-st.

Charlotte-Court, Turville - St. Bethnal-Green,—2d on the L. from 37, Church-st.

Charlotte-Court, Black - Lion-Yd.—1st on the L. from 39, Whitechapel-road.

Charlotte-Court, Moss's-Alley, Bankside,—middle of the E. side.

Charlotte-House, Charlotte-St. —8 doors from Blackfriars-road.

Charlotte - Mews East, Char-lotte-St. Portland - Pl. — 1st on the R. from Up.-Mary-bone-st.

Charlotte-Mews West, Char-lotte-St. Portland-Pl.--at 71, 3 doors S. of Weymouth-st.

Charlotte - Mews, Tottenham-St.—2d on the R. from Tot-tenham-court-road.

Charlotte-Mews, Thorney - St.

Bloomsbury, — behind 14, Charlotte-st.

Charlotte-Pl. Up. Kennington-Lane,—adjoins the E. side of Vauxhall-Gardens.

Charlotte-Pl. New-St. Kennington-Cross,—nearly op. the W. end of Park-st.

Charlotte-Pl. Boro-Road,—N. side, near the King's Bench.

Charlotte-Pl. Grange-Road,—from the corner of Fort-pl. towards the Kent-road.

Charlotte-Pl. Lambeth-Marsh, —middle of the N. side.

Charlotte - Row, New - Road, Marybone, — adjoining the Yorkshire-Stingo.

Charlotte-Row,—W. side the Mansion-House.

Charlotte - Row, Long - Lane, Bermondsey,—part of the L. side, about ¼ of a mile from St. George's-church.

Charlotte-Row (Little),—at the back of the last.

Charlotte - Row, Walworth High-St. — adjoins the entrance to the Montpelier.

Charlotte-Row, Jamaica-Row, Bermondsey,—the W.end, by the Gregorian-arms.

Charlotte-Row, Rotherhithe-St. —at 269, E. side the Surrey-canal.

Charlotte-St. Pimlico,—1st on the L. from Buckingham-gate.

Charlotte-St. (Little), 5 doors on the R. in the last from Pimlico.

Charlotte-St. New-Road, Hans-Town,—1st N. of Exeter-st.

Charlotte-St. Portland-Pl.—1st E. to it, and 1st W. to Great Portland-st.

Charlotte-St. Rathbone - Pl.—the continuation of it, from 23, Oxford-st.

Charlotte-St.(Upper),—the continuation of the last.

Charlotte-St. (Little),—by the last, from Bennet - st. to Goodge-st.

Charlotte-St. Battle-Bridge,—op. Hamilton-pl. leading to Britannia-st. and Gray's-inn-lane.

Charlotte - St. Bloomsbury,—continuation of Plumbtree-st. from 19, Broad-st.

Charlotte - St. Bedford - Sq.—continuation of the last, from 103, Gt. Russell-st.

Charlotte-St. Old-Street-Road, —1st W. from the Curtain-road, extending to Willow-walk.

Charlotte - St. Whitechapel,—the E. continuation of Field-gate-st. from 266, Whitechapel-road.

Charlotte-St. Wapping,—on the E. side of Hermitage-dock, leading to Nightingale-lane.

Charlotte-St. (Gt.), Blackfriars-Road,—¼ of a mile on the R. from the Bridge.

Charlotte-St. (Little),—op. the last, from Surrey-chapel to Gravel-lane.

Charlotte-St. Bethnal-Green,—entrance by the second on the L. in Turville-st. from 37, Church-st.

Charlotte-Street, Union-Street, Bethnal-Green,—2d on the R. from the N. E. corner of Thorold-sq.

Charlton-Court, Charlton - St. Marybone,—3 doors N. of Clipstone-st.

Charlton-Pl. Saint Albans-St.—
at 30, 6 doors on the L. from
14, Pall-Mall.

Charlton-St. Marybone,—from
46, Up. Marybone - st. to
Clipstone-st.

Charlton-St. (Upper), the N.
continuation of the last.

Charrington-Row, George-Gardens, Bethnal-Green - Rd.—
behind the George, on the E.
side of Wilmot-sq.

Charter-House,—on the N. side
of Charter-house-sq.

Charter-House-Lane, St. John-
St.—12 doors on the R. from
Smithfield.

Charter-House-Sq.—E. end of
the last.

Charter-House-St. Long-Lane,
—at 22, middle of the N. side,
leading to the square.

Chatham-Gardens, City-Road,
—2d on the R. in Trafalgar-
st. from op. Fountain-pl.

Chatham-Pl. Bridge-St. Blackfriars,—the wide part adjoining the bridge.

Chatham-Pl. Broad-St. Bloomsbury,—3 doors W. from Holborn.

Chatham-Pl. Walworth, — op.
the Terrace, ⅓ of a mile on
the L. from the Elephant and
Castle.

Cheapside,—N. E. corner of
St. Paul's church-yd. to the
Old-Jewry.

Cheapside,(Gt. and Little)Moor-
fields. See Long-Alley.

Cheapside (Little), St. Luke's,
—1st on the R. in Cowheel-
alley, from 168, Whitecross-
street.

Cheeseman's-Court, George-St.
Bethnal-Green,—6 doors on
the R. from Carter-st.

Chelsea - Common, — between
the Queen's-Elms and the
King's-road.

Chelsea-Hospital,—1½ mile from
Hyde-park-corner, by Sloane-
st. and near 1¼ mile from
Buckingham -gate, by Pim-
lico.

Chelsea-Market,—at 27, Lower-Sloane-st. ¾ of a mile on
the L. from Knightsbridge.

Chelsea-Water - Works - Office,
—21, Abingdon-st. Westr.

Cheltenham - House, Cheltenham-Pl.

Cheltenham-Pl. Westr.-Bridge-
Rd. Lambeth,—by Oakley-
st. nearly op. the Asylum.

Chelton's-Court, Bedfordbury,
—at 44, leading to 60, Chandos-st.

Chenies-Mews,Chenies-St.Bed-
ford-Sq.—1st W. of Gower-
street.

Chenies-Mews (Up.) N. end of
the last.

Chenies-Pl. Chenies-St.—middle of the S. side.

Chenies-Street, Gower-St. Bedford-Sq.—at 61, 2d on the L.
from the sq. leading to Tottenham-court-road.

Chequer-Alley, Bunhill-Row,—
at 99, ⅖ of a mile on the L.
from 64, Chiswell-st.

Chequer-Court, Charing-Cross,
—3 doors W. of St. Martin's-
lane.

Chequer-Court, Old-Street, St.
Luke's,—at 102, W. side the
church.

Chequer-Court, Chequer-Alley,
—1st on the L. from 99, Bunhill-row.

Chequer-Court, St. Catherine's
Lane,—3d on the L. from 49,
Up. E.-Smithfield.

Chequer-Court, High-St. Boro,
—12 doors on the L. from
London-bridge.

Chequer-Pl. Chequer-Alley,—
4th on the R. from 99, Bunhill-row.

Chequer-Sq. Chequer - Alley,
—3d on the R. from 99, Bunhill-row.

Chequer-Sq. Aldgate,—8 doors
on the R. below the Minories.

Chequer-Yard, Dowgate-Hill,
—from 31 to 14, Bush-lane.

Cherry-Garden-Street,—1st W.
from Mill - pond - bridge by
the stairs.

Cherry-Garden-Stairs, Bermondsey,—1¼ mile E. from Lon-
don-bridge, op. Wapping Old-
stairs.

Cherry - Tree - Alley, Bunhill-
Row,—at 118, 1st on the L.
from Chiswell-st.

Cherry - Tree - Court, Cherry-
Tree-Alley,—the last on the
R. from 118, Bunhill-row.

Cherry - Tree - Court, Golden-
Lane,—at 103, 3d on the R.
from Old-st.

Cherry-Tree-Court, Aldersgate-
St.—at 54, between Jewin-st.
and Barbican.

Cherry-Tree-Yard, Kingsland-
Road,—by the turnpike, ⅓ of
a mile on the R. from Shoreditch-church.

Cherubim-Court, Angel-Alley,
—5th on the L. from 137,
Bishopsgate-Without.

Chester-Pl. Fleet - Market,—3
doors on the L. from Fleet-
street.

Chester-Pl. Lambeth,—E. side
the high-road, from Walcot-
pl. to Kennington-cross.

Chester-Pl. Bethnal - Green,—
a few yards on the L. from
the E. side of the Green, towards Globe-st.

Chester's-Quay, Lower Thames-
St.—2d W. from Tower-hill.

Chester-St. Lambeth,—from
the N. end of Chester-pl. to
Kennington-lane.

Chester-St. Grosvenor - Pl.—at
36, third on the R. from
Hyde-park-corner.

Chesterfield-House, South-Audley-St.—by the W. end of Curzon-st. May-fair.

Chesterfield-Street, Charles-St.
—at 29, 2d on the L. from
Berkeley-sq.

Chesterfield-Street, (Gt.) Marybone,—between the W. ends
of Weymouth-st. and Gt.
Marybone-st.

Chesterfield-St. (Little), Marybone,—4 doors S. of the last.

Cheyne - Walk, Chelsea,—N.
side the Thames, from Pa-
radise-row, towards Battersea-bridge.

Chichester-Court, Chichester-
Rents,—3 doors on the L.
from 84, Chancery-lane.

Chichester-Rents, Chancery-
Lane,—at 84, middle of the
W. side, leading into Star-yd.

Chick-Lane, Gt. Saffron-Hill,—
1st on the R. in Field-lane
from Holborn-hill, leading
into West-st. W. Smithfield.

Chicksand-Pl. Chicksand-St.—
F

2d on the L. from 10, High-street.

Chicksand-St. — the continuation of Osborn-pl. from 20, Brick-lane.

Chigwell-St. Ratcliffe-Highway, —at 51, op. Cannon-st.

Child's-Court, Tothill-St. Westr. —2d on the R. from the Abbey.

Child's-Pl. Fleet-St.—3 doors on the R. from Temple-bar.

Chimister-Alley, Bedfordbury, — at 26, middle of the W. side.

China-Court, China-Row, Lambeth,—1st on the R. from China-terrace.

China-Hall, Deptford Lower Road,—⅓ of a mile on the L. from Paradise-row.

China-Hall-Pl. S. side the last.

China-Row, Lambeth, — from the S. end of China-terrace, to Lambeth-walk.

China-Terrace, Lambeth,— by the New Chapel, ¼ a mile on the R. from Westr.-bridge.

Chirographer's-Office, Hare-Court, Temple, — at 2, the back door is op. Brick-court, Middle Temple-lane.

Chiswell-St. Finsbury-Sq.--from the S. W. corner to White-cross-st.

Chivers's - Court, Nightingale-Lane, Limehouse, — 6 doors on the R. from 60, Narrow-street.

Choppens-Court, Old Gravel-Lane,—at 25, 4th on the R. from 157, Wapping.

Christ-Church, Spitalfields,— facing Union-street, from 69, Bis .opsgate-st.

Christ-Church, Blackfriars-Rd. —⅙ of a mile on the R. from the Bridge.

Christ-Church, Newgate-Street. See the next article.

Christ-Church-Passage, Newgate-St.—at 92, middle of the N. side.

Christ's Hospital, Newgate-St. —entrance at 103, op. Warwick-lane; also op. 9, Butcherhall-lane.

Christian - Benevolence - School, —1st house in the court at the back of 26, Bedfordbury.

Christian-Street, St. George's East,— the continuation of Princes-pl. New-road.

Christopher's-Alley, Wilson-St. Finsbury-Sq.—at 39, first N. of Crown-st.

Christopher-Alley, Lambeth-St. Goodman's Fields, — 4 doors from Ayliffe-st.

Christopher-Court, Sun-Alley, —2d on the R. from . 32, Golden-lane.

Christopher - Court, Angel-Alley,—1st on the L. from Little Moorfields.

Christopher-Court, St. Martin's-le-Grand,—3d on the L. from 66, Newgate-st.

Christopher-Court, Brick-Lane, —at 20, fourth on the L. from 103, Old-st.

Christopher-Court, Tower-Hill, —on the E. side, 7 doors N. of Iron-gate.

Christopher-Court, Rosemary-Lane,—at 40, between Darby-st. and Blue Anchor-yard.

Christopher's Inn, Bermondsey-St.—35 doors on the L. from Tooley-st.

Christopher - Row, East-Lane, Walworth,-N.end of Union-st.

Christopher Square,Long-Alley, Moorfields,--2d N. of Crown-street.

Christopher-St. Hatton-Garden, —N. continuation of it, to Back-lane.

Christopher-St.Finsbury-Sq.--at 27, the N. E. corner leading into Wilson-st.

Christopher-St. (New), the continuation of the last.

Christopher-St. Bethnal-Green, —the continuation of Turville-st. bearing to the R.

Church-Alley, Basinghall-St.— at 70, middle of the W. side.

Church-Alley,Ironmonger-Lane, Cheapside,—8 doors on the R. from 90, Cheapside.

Church-Court,Church-Passage, St. James's,—1st on the L. from 200, Piccadilly.

Church-Court, Little Chapel-St. Westr.—3 doors W. of Gardener's-lane.

Church-Court, Strand,—at 466, near Charing-cross.

Church - Court, Walbrook,—6 doors on the R. from the Mansion-house.

Church - Court, Friday-St.—3 doors on the R. from 36, Cheapside.

Church-Court, Clement's-Lane, —4 doors on the R. from 53, Cannon-st.

Church-Court, Lothbury,—N. side the Bank, adjoining To-ken-house-yd.

Church - Court,——N. end of Maiden-head-court,from 101, Wapping.

Church-Entry-Shoemakers-Row,

Blackfriars,—2d on the L. west from Creed-lane.

Church-Gardens,Well-Alley,— continuation of it from 110, Wapping.

Church-Hill, St. Pancras,—E. side the church, ½ of a mile on the R. from Battle-bridge.

Church-Hill, St. Andrew's-Hill, Blackfriars,—at 29, 1st on the R. from Earl-st.

Church - Lane, George-Street. Bloomsbury,—1st on the L. from 26, Broad-st.

Church-Lane, Strand,—at 458, 30 doors on the L. from Charing-cross.

Church-Lane, Whitechapel,— the continuation of Church-st. to the Commercial-rd.

Church-Lane (Back), the continuation of the last, to 65, Cable-st.

Church-Lane,Limehouse,--from the W. side the church,to 70, Ropemakers-fields.

Church-Lane,Newington-Butts, —op. the church in the High-street.

Church-Passage,New Compton-Street. St. Giles's,—at 19, 1st from Broad-st.

Church-Passage-Yard,—N. end of the last.

Church - Passage, Covent-Garden,—W. side, by the church.

Church-Passage, Piccadilly,— at 200,by St.James's-Church.

Church-Passage, Cloth-Fair,— at 10, 1st on the R. from 60, W. Smithfield.

Church-Passage, Up. Thames-St.—at 218,W.side Bennett's-hill.

Church-Pl. Church-St. Whitechapel,—1st on the L. from the church.

Church-Pl. Newington,—op. the church.

Church-Road, Saint George's-East,—E. end of Lower Cornwall-st. Back-lane.

Church-Row, St. Pancras,—at the N. end of Pancras-place, $\frac{1}{3}$ of a mile on the R. from Battle-bridge.

Church-Row, Wenlock-St. Saint Luke's,—3 doors from Ironmonger-row.

Church-Row, Church-St. Bethnal-Green,—at 106, by the turnpike, $\frac{1}{2}$ a mile on the R. from 65, Shoreditch.

Church-Row, Aldgate,—from 8, E. side the church, to Houndsditch.

Church-Row, Fenchurch-St.—at 66, ten doors E. of Marklane.

Church-Row, Stepney-Church-Yard,—at the N. E. corner.

Church-Row, Commercial-Rd. Limehouse,—on the W. side the church.

Church-Row, Newington,—from the church to Kennington-lane.

Church-Row, Horselydown,—on the E. side of St. John's-church, from Fair-street, to Charles-st.

Church-Row, Whitechapel. See Church-st.

Church-Stairs, Rotherhithe,—nearly facing the E. end of the church.

Church-St. Bainbridge-Street, Saint Giles's,—2d on the R. from Oxford-st.

Church-Street, Dean-St. Soho,

—from the church to Moorstreet.

Church-St. Paddington,—$\frac{3}{4}$ of a mile on the L. in Edgwareroad from Tyburn turnpike.

Church-St. Boro.—from Saint George's-church to White-st. and Kent-st.

Church-St. Millbank-Street, Westr.—at 52, $\frac{1}{4}$ of a mile S. of the Abbey.

Church-St. Bethnal-Green,—at 64, Shoreditch, where there are Nos. 1 and 192: it extends to the turnpike Bethnal-green-road.

Church-Street, Mile-End New-Town,—3d on the R. along Gt. Garden-st. from 50, Whitechapel-road.

Church-St. Spitalfields,—at 187, Brick-lane, the fifth on the L. from 74, Whitechapel.

Church-St. Minories,—at 26, 1st on the L. from Aldgate.

Church-Street, Whitechapel,—at 71, 1st W. from the church.

Church-St. (New), Whitechapel. See Back-church-lane.

Church-St. Wapping,—at 98, on the W. side the church, and E. side the London-docks.

Church-St. Lambeth,—facing the Stags, from Pratt-st. to the church.

Church-St. Blackfriars-Road,—2d on the L. from the bridge.

Church-Street, Saint Saviour's, Southwark,—2d on the R. in York-st. from 276, High-st.

Church-St. Horselydown,—on the S. side St. John's-church, from Artillery-lane, to Russell-street.

Church-Street, Rotherhithe,—on the S. side the church, leading to Deptford Lower-rd.

Church-St. Newington,—1st on the R. in Manor-place, from Walworth-High-st.

Church-Terrace, St. Pancras,—at the end of Church-row, by the church.

Church-Way, Sommers-Town, —from 32, Chalton-st. to the fields.

Church-Yard, Harp-Alley,—1st on the R. from 82, Fleet-market.

Church-Yard-Court, Inner Temple-Lane,—1st on the L. from 16, Fleet-st.

Church-Yard-Passage, Upper Thames-St.—4 doors W. of London-bridge.

Church-Yard-Passage-Stairs, —end of the last.

Church-Yard-Alley, Tooley-St. —at 247, six doors on the R. from London-bridge.

Church-Yard-Row, Newington, —on the S. side the Church-yard.

Chymister-Alley. See Chimister.

Cinnamon-St.—1st on the R. in Newmarket-st. from 157, Wapping.

Circus, Royal, Blackfriars-Rd. —W. side by the Obelisk.

Circus, Minories,—at 91, three doors on the L. from Tower-hill.

Circus-St. New-Road, Marybone,—2d on the R. from the Yorkshire Stingo.

Circus-Pl.—1st in the last from the New-road.

City-Barge-Houses, Bishops-

Walk, Lambeth,—near ¼ of a mile above Westminster-bridge.

City-Chambers (New), Bishops-gate-St.—at 122, 3 doors from Cornhill.

City-Chambers (Old), Bishops-gate-St.—at 24, op. Thread-needle-st.

City-Dispensary,—at 10, Grocer's-Hall-Court.

City-Gardens, City-Road,—behind Anderson's-buildings by the turnpike, near a mile on the R. from Finsbury-sq.

City-Garden-Row,—adjoins the City-road by the last.

City-Garden-Pl.—2d on the L. in the last from the City-rd.

City-Land Coal-Meter's-Office, —at 8, Little Knight-Rider-street.

Ditto,—at 21, Garlick-hill.

City of London-Tavern, Bishopsgate-St.—14 doors N. of Leadenhall-st.

City-Lying-in-Hospital, City-Road,—at the corner of Old-st. ¼ of a mile on the L. from Finsbury-sq.

City-Repository, Barbican,—at 55, middle N. side.

City-Road, Finsbury-Sq.—extends from the N. W. corner to the Angel, Islington.

City-Terrace, City-Road,—part of the R. side, near ½ a mile from Finsbury-square, and op. Fountain-pl.

Clare-Court,—at 104, Drury-lane, to White-horse-yd.

Clare-Hall-Row, Stepney-Green, —½ of a mile on the R. from Mile-end.

Clare-Market,—near the N.end
F 3

of Newcastle-st. from 309, Strand.

Clare-St. Clare-Market,—W. side, leading to Blackmore-st. 100, Drury-lane.

Clare-St. Hackney-Road,—W. side the turnpike, Bethnal-green.

Clarendon-Court, Clarendon.Pl. —1st on the R. from Clarendon-sq.

Clarendon-Pl. Sommers-Town, —W. side of Clarendon-sq.

Clarendon-Sq. Sommers-Town, —encloses the Polygon, W. end of Phœnix-st.

Clarendon-St.—S. W. corner of the last.

Clarence - House, Wilderness-Row, Chelsea,—4th house on the R. from Royal Hospital-row.

Clarence-Passage, St. Pancras, —by the Duke of Clarence, N. side Small-pox-Hospital.

Clarence-Pl. Pentonville,—part of the S. side the road near Battle-bridge.

Clarence-Pl. Hackney-Road,— part of the R.side, from Crabtree-row to Crescent-pl.

Clarence-Pl. Boro.-Road,—10 doors on the L. from the King's Bench.

Clarence-St. Rotherhithe,—at 303, ⅛ of a mile below the church.

Clarges-St. Piccadilly,—at 84, middle of the N. side.

Clarmont — House — Academy, Brompton,—the corner of Queen's-gardens, about ½ mile on the L. from Knightsbridge.

Clarke's-Builds. Snow-Hill,—at 52,1st W. from the Saracen's-Head-inn.

Clark's Court, Bishopsgate-Within,—at 60, 6 doors S. of Camomile-st.

Clarke's - Court, Vine-St.—1st on the L. from 76, Gt. Saffron-hill.

Cock-Yard, Tothill-St. Westr. —2d on the L. from Broadway.

Clarke's-Court, Jacob-St. Dock-Head,—3d on the R. from Mill-st.

Clarke's-Mews, Beaumont-St. Marybone,—— 3 doors from Weymouth-st.

Clarke's-Orchard, Rotherhithe, —at 355, between Queen-st. and Princes-st.

Clark's-Rents, Black-Boy-Alley, Chick-Lane,—4th on the L. towards Cow-cross.

Clarke-St. Clerkenwell,—1st on the L. in Allen-st. from 113, Goswell-st.

Clarke's-Terrace, Cannon-St.-Road,—E. side, from the turnpike by Cannon-st. to the chapel.

Clay-St. Durweston-Street, Marybone,—at 16, 2d on the L. from Baker-st.

Clayton-Pl. Kennington-Road, —by the 2 mile stone, from Mansion-house-row, to White-hart-row.

Clayton-St. Kennington-Green, —2d on the L. from the Horns.

Clayton-St. (Little),—1st on the R. in the last, from Kennington-green.

Cleaver-Court, Gt. Ayliffe-St. Goodman's - Fields,—at 32, middle of the N. side.

Cleaver's-Rents,—the 1st W. of the last.

Cleaver - St. Princes-Sq. Kennington,—the continuation of the S. side to Kennington-cross.

St. Clement's-Alms-Houses,—1st on the L. from Picket-st. towards St. Clement's-Inn.

St. Clement's-Church, Strand,—a few doors W. from Temple-bar.

St. Clement's-Church, Clement's-Lane,—3 doors from Cannon-street.

Clement's-Court, Carey-Street, Chancery-Lane,—at 23, by Yeates's-court.

Clement's-Court, Milk-St.—at 22, 3d on the L. from 116, Cheapside.

Clement's - Inn, Strand,—entrance op. the N. side St. Clement's-church.

Clement's - Inn-Passage,—from the E. side the last to Clare-market.

Clement's - Lane, Strand,—op. the N. side St. Clement's-church.

Clement's-Lane, Lombard-St.—at 28, 1st on the L. from Gracechurch-st.

Clerks of Essoin's Office, Elm-Court, Temple,—at the S. W. corner.

Clerks-Hall, Wood-St. Cheapside,—at 85, the corner of Silver-st.

Clerkenwell-Church-Yard,—on the S. side the church.

Clerkenwell-Close,—on the W. side the church, leading to Spa-fields.

Clerkenwell-Green,—the open space on the S. side the church, by the Session's-house.

Clerkenwell-Workhouse, Coppice-Row,—¼ of a mile on the L. from the Session's-house.

Cleveland-Court,—8 doors on the L. from 67, St. James's-st. by the Palace.

Cleveland-Mews, Cleveland-St. Fitzroy-Sq.—at 16, 2 doors S. of London-st.

Cleveland-Row, St. James's,—W. continuation of Pall-mall, fronting the Palace.

Cleveland-Sq. St. James's,—at the W. end of the last.

Cleveland-St. Fitzroy-Sq.—W. side from Carburton-st. to Foley-st.

Cleveland-St. (Upper), the continuation of the E. side the last.

Cleveland-Yard, King-Street, St. James's,—1st on the L. from St. James's-sq.

Clifford's-Inn, Fleet-Street,—entrance by 188, W. side St. Dunstan's-church.

Clifford's-Inn-Gardens,—on the N. side the Inn.

Clifford's-Inn-Passage, Fleet-St. —at 188, by St. Dunstan's-church.

Clifford-Row, Queen-St. Chelsea,—nearly op. Ranelagh-walk.

Clifford-St. New Bond-Street,—at 14, 2d on the R. from 57, Piccadilly.

Clifton-St. Worship-Street,—1st E. parallel to Wilson-st. on the W. side of Finsbury-market.

Clink-St. Boro.—parallel to the Thames, from St. Mary-Over's dock to Bank-side.

Clipstone-St. Great Portland-

St. Marybone,—from 64, to London-st. Fitzroy-sq.

Cloak-Lane, Dowgate-Hill,—2d on the R. from the Mansion-house, down Walbrook.

Cloisters (Gt.) Westr.—on the S. side the abbey.

Cloisters (Little),—a few yards S. of the last.

Cloisters, St. Bartholomew's-Hospital,—at the S. corner, entrance by 19, Giltspur-st.

Cloisters (Little),—entrance at 44, Smithfield.

Cloisters, St. Catherine's,—on the N. side the church, entrance 1st on the L. from Tower-hill.

Cloth-Fair, W. Smithfield,—at 60, E. side by Long-lane, extending to King-st.

Clothes-Exchange (Old), Rosemary-Lane,—6 doors E. from Queen-st.

Clothes-Exchange (New),—op. the last, 3 doors E. of Princes-street.

Clothworkers - Hall, Mincing-Lane,—adjoining 43, Fen-church-st.

Clouder's-Wharf, Horselydown, —1st E. from Pickle-herring-stairs.

Club - Row, Church-St. Bethnal-Green,—at 171, 3d on the R. from 65, Shoreditch.

Coachmaker's - Hall,——at 14, Noble-st. Foster-lane.

Coach and Horses-Yard, Mount-St.—at 119, 1st on the L. from Berkeley-sq.

Coach and Horses-Yard, Old Burlington-St.—at the N. end and W. end of Boyle-st.

Coach and Horses-Yard, Castle-St. Leicester-Sq.—at 18, middle of the W. side.

Coach and Horses-Yard, Charles-St.—1st on the R. from 174, Drury-lane.

Coach and Horses-Yard, Aldersgate-St.—at 131, twelve doors S. of Long-lane.

Coach and Horses-Yard, York-St. Westr.—1st on the R. from James-st.

Coach and Horses-Yard, Wood-St. Cheapside,—at 101, middle of the W. side.

Coach and Horses Yard, Northumberland-Alley,—1st on the L. from Fenchurch-st.

Coach and Horses-Yard, Coleman-St.—at 71, 3d on the L. from London-wall.

Coad's-Row, Bridge-Road, Lambeth,—six houses on the L. from Westr.-bridge.

Coal-Exchange, Lower Thames-St.—at 93, nearly op. Billingsgate.

Coal-Harbour. See Cole-Harbour.

Coal-Meter's-Office for Westr. —at 7, Northumberland-st. Strand.

Coal-Meter's (Land) Office for the City,—at 8, Knight-rider-st. and 21, Garlick-hill.

Coal-Yard, Drury-Lane,——at 185, ten doors S. of Holborn.

Cob's-Court, Broadway, Blackfriars,—8 doors on the L. from 3, Ludgate-st. along Pilgrim-st.

Cob's-Yard, Petticoat-Lane,— 2d north of Wentworth-st.

Cobbett's Register-Office,—at 10, Bridges-st. Covent-garden.

Cobham - Row, Cold - Bath - Fields,—on the W. side the turnpike, op. the House of Correction.

Cobley's Court, Essex-St.—3d on the R. from 106, Whitechapel.

Cobley's Rents,—1st N. of the last.

Cock-Alley, Moor-Lane. See Hartshorn-Alley.

Cock - Alley, Shoreditch, — at 75, N. side the turnpike, leading to Cock-lane.

Cock-Alley, Norton-Falgate,—at 33, nearly op. White-Lion-street.

Cock-Alley, Up. E. Smithfield,—at 12, ⅛ of a mile on the L. from Tower-hill.

Cock-Alley, Tooley - St. — 22 doors on the L. from London-bridge.

Cock-Court, New-St. Carnaby-Market,—1st on the L. from 46, Broad-st.

Cock-Court, Black-Boy-Alley, Chick-Lane,—facing the N. end of it.

Cock-Court,Tottenham-Ct.-Rd. —18 doors on the L. from Oxford-st.

Cock-Court, Snow-Hill,—at 75 and 78, a few doors on the L. east from Fleet-market.

Cock-Court, Poppin's-Court,—2d on the L. from 111, Fleet-street.

Cock-Court, St. Martin's - le-Grand,—2d on the L. from 66, Newgate-st.

Cock-Court,Philip-Lane,Wood-St.—7 doors on the L. from 22, Addle-st.

Cock-Court, Ludgate-Hill,—at 19, op. the Old Bailey.

Cock-Court, Turnmill - Street, Clerkenwell,—at 71, middle of the E. side.

Cock-Court, Angel-Sq.—1st on the L. from 138, Bishopsgate-without.

Cock-Court, Norton-Falgate,—at 34, op. White-Lion-st.

Cock-Court,Jewry-St.—7 doors on the R. from Aldgate.

Cock-Court, Haymarket. See Cock-Yard.

Cock-Hill, Anchor-St. Spital-fields,—1st on the R. from 53, Shoreditch.

Cock-Hill,New-St. Bishopsgate,—from the E. end to Catherine-wheel-alley.

Cock-Hill, Ratcliffe,—the E. continuation of Shadwell High-st. to Broad-st.

Cock and Hoop-Yard, Hounds-ditch,—at 133, op. Duke-st.

Cock-Inn, Leadenhall-St. — at 51, op. Cree-church-lane.

Cock-Inn, Haymarket,—at 63, middle of the W. side.

Cock-Lane, Giltspur -St.—1st on the L. from Newgate-st. leading to 68, Snow-hill.

Cock-Lane, Shoreditch, — behind 65, leading from Church-st. to behind Shoreditch-church.

Cock and Lion-Court, Cornhill,—at 41, 6 doors E. of Birchin-lane.

Cock-Pit-Alley, Drury-Lane,—from 135, middle of the E. side, to Gt. Wild-st.

Cock-Pit-Alley, Gravel - Lane, Boro.—at 71, 1st on the L. from Bankside.

Cock - Pit - Court, Poppin's - Court,—2d on the L. from 111, Fleet-st.

Cock-Pit-Yard (Little), King's-Road, Bedford-Row,—1st on the L. from James-st.

Cock-Pit-Yard (Great), Little James-St.—4th on the L. from Gray's Inn-lane.

Cockspur-St. Charing-Cross,— the continuation of it to the Haymarket.

Cock - Yard, Haymarket, — at 63, middle of the W. side.

Coffee - House - Alley, Upper Thames - St. — from 56 to Queenhithe.

Coffee-House-Walk and Gardens, Hoxton. See Bacchus.

Cohen's Rents, Mill-Yd. Goodman's-Fields.—at 10, middle of the E. side.

Colchester-St. Savage-Gardens, —1st on the R. from Tower-hill.

Colchester-Street, Red-Lion-St. —3 doors on the L. from 32, Whitechapel.

Coldbath - Fields, Clerkenwell, —N. side towards Pentonville.

Coldbath-Sq. — facing the S. side the House of Correction.

Cole's Builds. Long-Lane,—at 30, 2d on the L. from Smithfield.

Cole's Pl. Kent-St. Boro.—S. end of White - bear - court, from 270, Kent-st.

Cole-Stairs, Shadwell.—at the bottom of Gold's hill, from 97, Shadwell-High-st.

Cole's Wharf, Horselydown, New-Stairs,—on the W. side St. Saviour's dock.

Colebrook-Pl. Hoxton,—5th on the L. ⅓ of a mile from Old-st.-road.

Colebrook-Row, Ivy-Lane, Hoxton,—a few doors on the R. from the Ivy-house.

Colebrook-Sq. Hoxton,—1st N. of Gloucester-st.

Cole-Harbour, Hackney-Road, —adjoining Alport's Nursery, ⅔ of a mile on the L. from Shoreditch.

Cole-Harbour, Blackwall,—between the Dock-bason and Marsh-wall.

Cole - Harbour - Lane, Upper Thames-St.—at 92, op. Suffolk-lane.

Cole-Harbour-Pl. White Bear-Yard,—a few yards from 270, Kent-st. Boro.

Cole - Harbour - Stairs, Upper Thames-St.—bottom of Cole-harbour-lane.

Cole-Harbour-St. Hackney-Rd. —op. Cole Harbour.

Coleman-Court, Coleman-St.— 1st on the R. from 84, Bunhill-row.

Coleman's Court, Castle-Lane, Boro.—1st on the L. from Castle-st.

Coleman-Pl. Ratcliffe-Row,— middle of the S. side, near the N. end of Ironmongers-row, from 97, Old-st.

Coleman-Pl. Coleman-St. Bunhill-Row,—1st on the R. from 45, Banner-st.

Coleman-St. Bunhill-Row,—at 83, ¼ of a mile on the L. from 63, Chiswell-st.

Coleman-St. (Lower),—the end of the last, next Bunhill-row.

Coleman-St. Lothbury, — the continuation of the Old Jewry, from Cheapside

Coleman-St.-Builds. Coleman-

St.—at 72, 6 doors from London-wall.

Coleman-St. New Gravel-Lane, —at 150, 7 doors from Wapping-wall.

Coleman's Yard, Bermondsey-St.—at 110, 12 doors N. of the church.

College-Alms-Houses, Counter-St. See College-Yard.

College-Court, Cow-Cross,—at 62, 4th on the L. from St. John's-st.

College-Mews, College-Street, Westr.—1st from Abingdon-street.

College-Hill, Up. Thames-St.—at 181, 1st E. of Queen-st. Cheapside.

College of Physicians, Warwick-Lane,—1st on the R. from 10, Newgate-st.

College - Row, Chelsea.   See Royal Hospital-row.

College - Street,   Abingdon-St. Westr.—at 18, 1st S. of the Abbey.

College-St. (Little).—from 9, in the last, to Wood-st.

College-St. Narrow-Wall, Lambeth,—1st on the L. below Westr.-bridge.

College-Street, Tooley-St.—at 140, ⅓ of a mile on the R. from London-bridge.

College-Yard,—1st on the L. in Counter-st. from St. Margaret's hill.

Collet-Pl. White-Horse-Street, Ratcliffe,—N. end by Salmon-lane.

Collier - Court, Golden - Lane, —at 12, 3d on the L. from Barbican.

Collier-Court, Fleet-St. Bethnal-Green,—2 doors on the R. from George-st. Brick-lane.

Collier's-Court, Mill-Lane,—at 89, 1st on the R. from 56, Tooley-st.

Collier's Rents, White-St. Boro. —at 23, 5th on the L. from St. George's Church.

Collier-St. Pentonville,—1st on the L. in Rodney-st. from the chapel.

Collin's-Court, Farmer - Street, Shadwell,—at 44, 1st on the L. from 58, High-st.

Collins's Pl. Poplar,—½ a mile on the L. from the Commercial-rd. E. side the Green-Dragon.

Collings's Yd. Old-St.-Road,—at the E. end of Pump-row.

Collingwood-Pl. Broad-Street, Ratcliffe, — at 102, a few doors on the L. from Cock-hill.

Collingwood-Pl. Mount-Street, Bethnal-Green,—nearly op. Collingwood-st.

Collingwood-Street, Mount-St. Bethnal-Green,—3d on the L. from 45, Church-st.

Collingwood-St. City-Road,— 1st on the L. in Trafalgar-st. from op. Fountain-pl.

Collingwood-St. Mile - End,— 1st on the R. in North-st. from 154, Whitechapel-road.

Collingwood - St. Blackfriars-Road,—3d on the R. from the Bridge.

Collitch-Pl. Cross-St. Newington,—2d on the R. from the church.

Colonnade, Grenville-St. Brunswick-Sq.—5 doors on the L. from 32, Gt. Guilford-st.

Colonnade-Mews,—W. end of the last.

Colour-Court, Worcester - St. Boro.—1st on the R. from 10, Queen-st.

Colville - Court, Charlotte - St. Rathbone-Pl.—at 17, 3 doors S. of Goodge-st.

Commander-in-Chief's Office, Horse-Guards, Whitehall,—1st door on the L. from St. James's Park.

Commerce - Row, Blackfriars-Rd.—¼ of a mile from the bridge, op. Surrey-chapel.

Commercial-Chambers, Minories,—13 doors on the L.from Aldgate.

Commercial Chronicle Newspaper-Office,—at 151, Fleet-st. by Bolt-court.

Commercial-Dock. See Greenland-Dock.

Commercial-Hall, Skinner - St. Snow-Hill,—at 9, the large house.

Commercial - Pl. Commercial-Road,—S. side, ⅛ of a mile E. of the Half-way-house.

Commercial-Road, Whitechapel,—the E. continuation of Church-lane, to the West-India-Docks.

Commercial-Road, Lambeth,—from Broad-wall and Upper Ground, towards the New Bridge.

Commercial-Sale-Rooms, Mincing-lane,—middle of the E. side.

Commercial - Terrace, Lime-house,—a few doors E. of the church.

Commissary - General's Office, Gt. George-St. Westr.—at

35, 3d door on the L. from St. James's Park.

Commons, House of,—S. side of Westminster-hall, op. the abbey.

Common - Pleas, Court of,—held at Westr.-hall, and at Guildhall, King-st. Cheapside.

Common-Pleas - Office, King's-bench-walk, Temple,—bottom of Mitre-court, on the R. from 44, Fleet-st.

Compter-Court, Poultry, — at 30, a few doors on the R. from the Mansion-house, towards Cheapside.

Compton-Mews, Compton -St. — 1st on the L. from Hunter-st. Brunswick-sq.

Compton-Passage, Compton-St. Clerkenwell,—1st on the R. from St. John's-st.

Compton-Pl. Compton-St.—1st on the R. from Hunter-st. Brunswick-sq.

Compton-Street, (New) Broad-Street, St. Giles's,—1st E. of the church, to Crown-st.

Compton-St. (Little), — continuation of the last to Greek-street.

Compton-St. (Old),—continuation of the last, to Princes-st.

Compton-St. Tavistock - Place, Tavistock-Sq.—E. end, 2d on the L. in Hunter-st. from Brunswick-sq.

Compton-St. Bloomsbury. See Bury-st.

Compton-St. Clerkenwell,—at 25, St.John's-st. extending to 107, Goswell-st.

Condemned-Hole, Trinity - St. Rotherhithe, — by Thames-

CON

st. and the S. end of Barnard's and Co.'s yard.

Conduit-Court, Long-Acre,—17 doors on the R. from St. Martin's-lane.

Conduit-St. Hanover-Sq.—from 100, Swallow-st. to 22, New Bond-st.

Coney's Court, Moss's Alley, Boro.—1st from Bankside.

Connaught-Pl. Edgeware-Road, —a few yds. on the L. from Tyburn-turnpike.

Constable-Row. See Five Ditto.

Constable's-Wharf, Horsely-down,—2d E. from George's stairs, nearly facing Thomas-street.

Constitution-Brewery, Bell-Lane, Spitalfields, — middle of the W. side.

Constitution-Hill, Green-Park, —the road rising between St. James's park and Hyde-park-corner.

Constitution-Row, Gray's Inn-Lane,—from op. Sidmouth-pl. to Chad's Row.

Contentment-Row, Hoxton,—on the N. side of Bacchus-walk, op. Brit's buildings.

Conway-Court, Paradise-Street, Marybone,—at 10, 1st on the L. in Grafton-court, leading to Burying-ground-passage.

Conway-Mews, Conway-Street, Fitzroy-Sq.—S. end by London-st.

Conway-St. Fitzroy-Sq.—from the S. W. corner, to 26, London-st.

Conway-St. (Upper),—from op. the last, to the New-road.

Cook's Alms-Houses, Spring-St.

COO

Shadwell,—on the S. side the church-yd.

Cook's (Captain) Alms-Houses, Mile-End,—2⅛ miles on the L. from Aldgate-pump, op. York-pl.

Cook's Builds. Stoney-Lane,—3d on the L. from Gravel-lane, Houndsditch.

Cook's Court, Primrose-St.—at 15, a few doors on the R. from 110, Bishopsgate.

Cook's Court, Carey-St.—at 36, 2d on the R. from 99, Chancery-lane.

Cook's Court, Booth-St. Spital-fields,—at 16, 2d on the R. from 50, Brick-lane.

Cook's Passage, North-Row,—a few yards on the L. from Park-st. Oxford-st.

Cook's Place, Long-Alley, Moor-fields,—at 11, 4th on the L. from Worship-st.

Cook's Row, St. Pancras,—14 doors from the church, towards Camden-town.

Cook's Wharf, Shadwell,—at the bottom of Gold's hill, from 97, Shadwell High-st.

Cooper's Alms-Houses. See Coopers-Sq.

Coopers-Court, Gt. Windmill-St.—10 doors on the R. from Piccadilly.

Coopers-Court, Portpool-Lane, —at 27, 3 doors from 64, Leather-lane.

Cooper's Court, Seward-St.—3 doors on the R. from 30, Brick-lane, Old-st.

Coopers-Court, White-Cross-St, —at 83, 13 doors N. of Chis-well-st.

G

Coopers-Court, Blue - Anchor-Yard,—last on the L. from 48, Rosemary-lane.

Coopers - Gardens, Hackney-Road,—2d on the R. from Shoreditch.

Cooper's Hall, Basinghall-St.—at 71, middle of the W. side.

Coopers-Pl. Salisbury - Mews, New-Road, Marybone, — 4 doors from Gt. Quebec-st.

Coopers-Rents, St. Catherine's Sq. Tower-Hill,—N. E. corner.

Coopers-Row, Crutched-Friars, —3d on the R. from 64, Mark-lane.

Coopers-Row, Up. East-Smithfield,—at 110, op. Nightingale-lane.

Coopers - Sq. School - House - Lane, Ratcliffe,—a few doors on the R. from Cock-hill.

Coopers-Street, Orchard-Street, Westr.— from 29 to 3, Dacre-street.

Coopers-Yard, Carnaby-St.—at 38, middle of the W. side.

Coopers-Yard, John-St. Holywell-Mount,—1st on the R. from 62, Leonard-st.

Copenhagen-Pl. Limehouse,—1st on the R. in Salmon-lane, from the Commercial-road.

Copenhagen - Wharf,—by the last.

Cope's-Rents, Limehouse,—1st on the R. in Chivers's court, from Nightingale-lane.

Copper's Wharf,—bottom of Salisbury-st. or Cecil-street, Strand.

Copper - Wharf, Up. Thames-St.—at 12, between Anderson's and Carron-wharf.

Coppice - Row, Clerkenwell,—the continuation of Ray-st. from the N. W. corner of the Green.

Copping-Court, St. Dunstan's Hill,—3 doors from 11, Gt. Tower-st.

Copthall-Builds. — from Copthall-chambers to Bell-alley.

Copthall-Chambers,— he continuation of Copthall-court.

Copthall-Court, Throgmorton-St.—at 30, 10 doors from the Bank.

Coram-Pl. Little Coram-St.— 1st on the R. from 54, Gt. Coram-st.

Coram-St. (Gt.), Brunswick-Sq.—from the N. W. corner to Russel-sq.

Coram-St. (Little),—from 54, Gt. Coram-st. to 10, Tavistock-pl.

Corbets - Court, Gracechurch-St.—7 doors on the R. from Cornhill.

Corbets-Court, Brown's Lane, Spitalfields,—at 36, 3d on the R. from op.55, Brick-lane.

Corder's Wharf, Horselydown, —2d E. from Pickle-herring-stairs.

Cordwainers - Charity - School, Old Change,—corner of Watling-st. by St. Paul's Church-yard.

Cordwainers-Hall, Gt. Distaff-Lane,—4 doors W. of 21, Friday-st.

Cordwells-Yard, Queen-Street, Golden-Sq.—at 7, middle of the W. side.

Corkcutters-Alley, Princes-St. Westr.—1st on the L. from Tothill-st.

Cork-Mews, Cork-St.—at 12, 5 doors from Burlington-Gardens.

Cork-St. Burlington - Gardens, —1st E. of 1, New Bond-st.

Corn-Exchange (New), Mark-Lane,—at 26, middle of the W. side.

Corn-Exchange (Old), Mark-Lane,—at 53, nearly op. the last.

Cornbury - Pl. Kent - Road,— part of the R. side, $\frac{1}{8}$ of a mile below the Bricklayers-arms.

Cornhill,—from the Mansion-house to 124, Bishopsgate-st.

Corney's Yd. Tufton-St. Westr. —at 47, near Wood-st.

Cornycap-Alley, Bankside, Boro.—at 50, 2d W. of Thames-street.

Cornwall-Street, St. George's East,—1st N. parallel to Back-lane, near Cannon-st.-turnpike.

Cornwall-St. (Lower),—E. end of the last.

Corporation for working Mines in Scotland,—Office at the Sun Fire-Office, Cornhill.

Corporation - Court, Corporation-Row,—5 doors from the N. end of St. John's st.

Corporation-Lane, Corporation-Row,—the W. end of it.

Corporation-Row, St. John's-St.—last on the L. from Smithfield.

Cotchett's Builds. French-Alley,—1st on the R. from 21, Goswell-st.

Cottage-Court, Horseferry-Rd. Westr.—W. end, behind the Ship.

Cottage - Gardens, Stepney-Green,—1st on the R. from Mile-End-road.

Cottage - Lane, Dorans - Row, Commercial - Road,—1st on the L. near $\frac{1}{3}$ of a mile E. from Cannon-st. road.

Cottage-Pl. Chapel-Path, Sommers-Town,—at 16, 10 doors from Brill-Path.

Cottage-Pl. Poplar,—about $\frac{1}{4}$ a mile on the R. in the East-India Dock-road, from Lime-house.

Cottage-Pl. Bird-St. Lambeth, —3d on the L. from Brook-street.

Cottage-Pl. Lion-St.—2d on the L. from the Kent-road.

Cottage-Row, Bermondsey New-Road,—part of the E. side, by the Bricklayers-arms.

Cottage-Row, Poplar,—W. side of Cottage-st.

Cottage-Street, Poplar High-St. —1st E. of the East-India-Alms-Houses.

Cottons-Gardens, Old Palace-Yard, Westr.—E. side by the Thames.

Cottons-Gardens, Hackney-Rd. —3d on the L. from Shoreditch-church.

Cotton-St. Poplar,—2d on the L. from the East-India-Dock.

Cotton's Wharf, Tooley-St.— entrance 17 doors E. of London-bridge.

Cotton-Yard, Poplar High-St. —about $\frac{1}{4}$ a mile on the L. from the Commercial-road, nearly op. the Town-hall.

Counter-Alley, High-St. Boro. —at 254, by St. Margarets' hill.

Counter-St. Boro.—from Saint Margaret's-hill to the Boro.-market.

Counting-House-Yard, Christ's Hospital,—1st on the L. in Butcherhall-lane, from 82, Newgate-st.

County-Chronicle Newspaper-Office,—18, Warwick-sq. 5 doors on the L. from Warwick-lane.

County Fire-Office,—25, Southampton-st. Strand, 3 doors on the R. from Covent-garden.

County-Gaol (for Surrey),—a few yards on the L. in Newington-causeway, from Stones-end.

County Herald Newspaper-Office,—18, Warwick-sq.

County Newspaper-Office,—at 5, Warwick-sq.; here advertisements are taken in for every newspaper in the United Kingdom.

County-Row, Mill-Lane,— 1st on the L. from 55, Tooley-st.

County-Terrace (Webb's), Kent-Road,—¼ of a mile on the L. from the Elephant and Castle.

County-Terrace-St.—E. end of the last.

Courier D'Angleterre Newspaper-Office,—4 doors on the R. in Crane-court, from 174, Fleet-st.

Courier Newspaper -Office, Strand,—at 348, 6 doors E. of Exeter-change.

Courier De Londres, Newspaper-Office,—behind 73, Gt. Queen-st. Lincoln's Inn-Fields.

Court of Delegates, Doctors-Commons,— 5th door on the L. from op. 14, Great-Knight-rider-st.

Court of Requests, Osborn-St.—5 doors on the R. from 74, Whitechapel.

Court of Requests, Castle-St. Leicester-Sq.—12 doors on the R. from Hemmings-row.

Court of Requests, Vine-Street, Piccadilly,—10 doors from the W. end of Brewer-st.

Court of Requests, Fullwood's Rents,— at 13, the last house on the L. from 34, High-Holborn.

Court of Requests, Guildhall,—3d door on the R. from 23, King-st. Cheapside.

Court of Request-Office, Weston-St. Maze, Boro.—at 17, 6 doors on the L. from 35, Snow's fields.

Court-St. Whitechapel-Road,—at 110, op. the London-hospital.

Cousin-Lane, Up. Thames-St.—at 84, op. Dowgate-hill.

Covent-Garden, — the end of Southampton-st. from 387, Strand, or of James-st. from 43, Long-acre.

Covent-Garden-Theatre, — at the N. E. corner of Covent-garden, extending to Bow-st. and Hart-st.

Covent-Garden-Workhouse,—N. end of Norfolk-st. Middlesex-Hospital.

Coventry-Court, Haymarket,—at 29, leading to 6, Coventry-street.

Coventry-Place, Willow-Walk, Bermondsey,—a few houses on the L. east from Page's-walk.

Coventry-St. Haymarket,—E. continuation of Piccadilly.

Coventry-St. Bethnal-Green,—2d W. parallel to Belvedere, op. Duthie's Nursery.

Cow-Alley, Free-School-Street, Horselydown,—at 26: it leads to Goat-st. and John-st.

Cow-Court, Old-St.—at 122, 3d on the L. from Goswell-street.

Cow-Court, Hare-St. Bethnal-Green,—at 30, 1st on the R. a few doors from 103, Brick-lane.

Cow-Court,—near 333, Rother-hithe-st. S. E. corner of the church-yd.

Cow-Cross, St. John's Street,—at 87, 2d on the L. from Smithfield.

Cow-Lane, W. Smithfield,—at 93, 3d on the L. from Newgate-st. leading to Snow-hill.

Cow-Lane, New Gravel-Lane,—at 97, 2d on the L. from 23, High-st. Shadwell.

Cow-Lane, Stepney,—1st N. parallel to the church-yd.

Cow-Lane, Rotherhithe, — between Lower Queen-st. and Trinity-st. near $\frac{1}{2}$ a mile from Greenland-dock.

Cow-Yard, Liquorpond - St. — 1st on the R. from 68, Gray's-inn-lane.

Cow-Yard, Hackney - Road,— 1st on the L. from Shore-ditch-church.

Cowheel-Alley, White - Cross-Street, St. Luke's,—at 168, nearly op. Banner-st.

Cowley-Street, Wood-St. Westminster,—2d on the R. from 64, Millbank-st.

Cowper's Court, Cornhill, — from 32 to 6, Birchin-lane.

Cox's Court, Aldersgate-St.—at 160, 2 doors S. of West-moreland-builds.

Cox's Court, Little Britain,—at 27, 2d on the L. from St. Bartholomew's hospital.

Cox's Court, Green-Walk,—1st on the L. from Holland-st. Blackfriars-bridge.

Cox's Court, Petticoat-Lane,—at 102, 8 doors S. of Wentworth-st.

Cox and Curling's Dock,—between Limehouse-hole-stairs and the entrance to the West-India-docks.

Cox's Dock, Fore-St. Limehouse,—at 23, on the E. side of Duke's Shore.

Coxhead's Gateway, Bermondsey-St.—at 221, middle of the W. side.

Cox's Rents, City-Road,—a few doors on the L. from the Angel, Islington.

Cox's Sq. Spitalfields,—behind the N. corner of Wentworth-st. and Petticoat-lane, entrance by Short's-st.

Cox-St. Tavistock-Pl. Tavistock-Sq.—the E. continuation of it from Marchmont-st.

Cox's Quay, Lower Thames-St. —6 doors from London-bridge.

Cox's Wharf, Fountain-Court, Cecil-St. Strand, — between Browning's and Winckworth's Wharfs.

Coy's Yard, Henrietta-St. Cavendish-Sq. — W. end, op. Marybone-lane.

Crabtree-Row, Hackney-Road,

G 3

—3d on the R. from Shore-
ditch-church.

Cradle-Court, St. Mary-Axe,—
at 21, middle of the E. side.

Cradle-Court, Aldersgate-St.—
at 50, 3 doors N. of Jewin-
street.

Cradle-Court, Red-Cross-St.—
at 51, 10 doors on the L. from
Barbican.

Cradle-Court, Love-Lane, Shadwell,—the W. corner of High-
street.

Craigs-Court, Charing-Cross,—
20 doors on the L. from the
Strand.

Cranbourne-Alley, Cranbourne-
St.—at 10, middle of the S.
side.

Cranbourne - Passage, Cran -
bourne-St.—corner of Castle-
street.

Cranbourne-St. Leicester-Sq.—
N. E. corner to Castle-st.

Crane-Court, Fleet-St.—at 174,
5 doors E. from Fetter-lane.

Crane-Court, Lambeth-Hill,—3
doors from Old-Change.

Crane-Court, Old Gravel-Lane,
—at 92, 1st on the L. from
66, Ratcliffe-highway.

Cranes (Three). See Three
Cranes.

Crane (New) Dock, Wapping,
—1st E. from New Crane-
stairs.

Crane-Stairs (New), Wapping,
—at 198, op. New Gravel-
lane.

Crane-Yard (Old), Leicester-St.
—3 doors W. of 31, Swallow-
street.

Craven-Builds. Drury-Lane,—
at 94, 2 doors from Wych-st.

Craven-Builds. City-Road,—1st
on the R. north from Old-st.

Craven - Court, Craven-Street,
Strand,—at 34, middle of
the E. side.

Craven-St. Strand,—10 doors on
the R. from Charing-cross.

Craven-St. City-Road,—1st on
the L. in Craven-builds. from
the turnpike.

Craven-Yard, Drury-Lane,—at
97, 4 doors from Wych-st.

Crawford's-Court, Rotherhithe.
See Cow-Court.

Crawford's Court, Rosemary-
Lane. See Windmill-court.

Crawfords-Passage, Ray-Street,
Clerkenwell,—3d on the R.
from the Green.

Crawford-St. Baker - St.—4th
on the L. from Portman-sq.

Creak and Co.'s Mast Yard and
Block-Manufactory, Trinity-
Street, Rotherhithe. See Du-
rand's Wharf.

Creechurch-Lane, Leadenhall-
St.—at 87, 1st on the R.
from Aldgate.

Creed - Lane, Ludgate-St.—at
15, 5 doors on the L. from
St. Paul's church-yd.

Crescent (North), Chenies-St.
Bedford-Sq.—2 doors from
209, Tottenham-court-road.

Crescent (South), Gt. Store-St.
Bedford - Sq. —2 doors from
Tottenham-court-road.

Crescent, Sommers-Town,—E.
end of Phœnix-st. Clarendon-
square.

Crescent, Jewin-St. Cripplegate,
—2 doors on the R. from 29,
Redcross-st.

Crescent, New Bridge-Street,

Blackfriars,—part of the E. side, 6 doors on the L. from Ludgate-hill.

Crescent, Minories, — at 102, 2d on the L. from Tower-hill.

Crescent-Mews,—S. end of the last.

Crescent - Pl. New Bridge-St. Blackfriars,—8 doors on the L. from Ludgate-hill.

Crescent-Pl.Tavistock-Sq.–from the N. E. corner to Burton-crescent.

Crescent-Pl. Hackney-Road,— at 12, Clarence-pl. 3d on the R. from Shoreditch-church.

Crescent - Pl. Lambeth-Road, —S. side, from the Obelisk towards Lambeth.

Cressey-Pl. Harpur's Fields,— about ⅓ of a mile W. from 37, Edgeware-road.

Cressey-Sq.—on the W. side the last.

Crimscott-St. Grange-Road,— 2d on the R. from Bermond-sey New-road towards Ro-therhithe.

Cripplegate - Builds. Wood-St. — continuation of it from London-wall to Fore-st.

Cripplegate-Church, Fore-St.— nearly op. Red-cross-st.

Crispin-St. Spitalfields,—at 25, Union-st.4th from69,Bishops-gate.

Crocker's-Builds. Hoxton-Sq.— 1st on the L. from Pitfield-street.

Crombie's or Doran's - Row, Commercial-Road,—W. side the George, or Half - way-house.

Cromers-Pl.—N. end Marson-st. Sommers-Town.

Crooked-Lane, Cannon-St.—at 49, leading into Miles's lane and to Fish-st.-hill.

Crooket's Alley, High-St. Lam-beth,—2d on the L. from Broad-st.

Crooked - Billet - Court, Long-Alley,—7 doors on the L. from Moorfields.

Crooked-Billet-Court, Mint-St. Boro.—1st on the L. from 156, High-st.

Crooked - Billet - Wharf, Mill-bank-St. Westr.—nearly op. 53, by Wallinger's wharf.

Crooked - Billet - Yard, Kings-land-Road,—at 53, 6th on the L. from Shoreditch.

Crosby's-Builds. French-Alley, —1st on the L. from 150, Shoreditch.

Crosby-Row, Snow's Fields,— 3d on the R. along King-st. from 108, Borough High-st.

Crosby-Row, Walworth High-St.—part of the L. side, ¼ a mile from the Elephant and Castle.

Crosby-Sq. Bishopsgate-Within, —23 doors N. of Leadenhall-street.

Crosby-Street, St. Mary Axe,— 7 doors on the L. from Lead-enhall-st.

Cross-Alley, Shoe - Lane,—at 32, near the middle of the E. side.

Cross-Alley, Gun - Alley, — 2 doors on the R. from 105, Wapping-st.

Cross-Alley, Butcher-Row,--1st on the L.from Ratcliffe-cross.

Cross-Alley, King-St. Rother-hithe,—1st on the L. from 375, Rotherhithe-st.

Cross-Alley, Cherry-Garden-St. Bermondsey,—2d on the R. from Rotherhithe-wall.

Cross-Court, Broad-Court,—1st on the L. from 44, Drury-lane.

Cross-Court, Carnaby-Market, —at the S. W. corner.

Cross-Gun - Court, Rosemary-Lane,—at 111, middle of the N. side.

Cross-Keys-Alley, Bermondsey-St.—at 268, 13 doors on the R. from Tooley-st.

Cross-Key-Buildings, London-Wall,—at 42, 3d E. of Cole-man-st.

Cross-Keys-Inn, Wood-St.—3 doors on the L. from 122, Cheapside.

Cross-Keys-Inn, Gracechurch-St.—16 doors on the R. from Cornhill.

Cross-Keys-Inn, Saint John's St.—at 108, 17 doors on the R. from Smithfield.

Cross-Key - Mews, Marybone-Lane,—at 31, six doors on the L. from High-st.

Cross-Key-Sq. Little Britain,—8 doors on the R. from 75, Aldersgate-st.

Cross-Keys-Yd. Whitecross-St. Cripplegate,—4 doors on the R. from Fore-st.

Cross-Key-Yard, Bermondsey-St.—at 266, 20 doors on the R. from Tooley-st.

Cross-Lane, Neat-Houses, Chelsea,—2d on the L. from the bridge, Pimlico.

Cross-Lane, Long - Acre, —at 106, middle of the N. side.

Cross-Lane, Newton-St.—continuation of it from 206, High Holborn.

Cross - Lane, Bush - Lane,—8 doors on the L. from 23, Can-non-st.

Cross-Lane, St. Mary's Hill,—at 28, 11 doors from East-cheap.

Cross-Lane, St. Dunstan's Hill, —2d on the L. from 11, Tower-st.

Cross-Row, Ratcliffe-Sq.—last on the L. in Periwinkle-st. from Brook-st.

Cross-Row, Stepney-Green,—4th on the R. from Mile-end-road.

Cross-Street, New-Road, Hans-Town,—1st on the R. from North-st.

Cross-St. Hatton-Garden,—at 43, 2d from Holborn.

Cross-St. King-Street, Golden-Sq.—at 17, 4th on the L. from 323, Oxford-st.

Cross-St. Queen's-Sq. Blooms-bury,—S. side, from 32, Devonshire-st. to 23, Glouces-ter-st.

Cross-St. Wilderness - Row,—1st on the R. from 135, Goswell-st.

Cross-St. Finsbury-Pl.—at 22, 1st on the R. from Moor-fields.

Cross-St. Westmoreland-Row, City-Road,—1st on the R. from Providence-st.

Cross-Street, Church-St. Beth-nal-Green,—at 17, 2d on the L. from 65, Shoreditch.

Cross-Street, Myrtle-St. Hoxton,—1st on the R. from Hoxton-town.

Cross-Street, Leonard-St. Shoreditch,—2d on the R. east from Paul-st.

Cross-Street, Morgan-St.—1st on the L. from the Commercial-road.

Cross-Street, Thomas-St. Whitechapel,—1st on the R. from Greyhound-lane.

Cross-St. Blackfriars-Rd.—4th on the R. from the bridge.

Cross-St. Newington,—op. the church, 1st S. of the Elephant and Castle.

Cross-St. Lock's Fields, Walworth,—2d in Queen-st. from York-st.

Cross-Street, Brandon-St.—1st on the L. from Bermondsey New-road.

Cross-Street, Cherry-Garden-St. Bermondsey,—1st on the R. from Rotherhithe-wall.

Cross-St. Fair-Street, Horselydown,—at 25, 1st on the L. from the E. end of Tooley-street.

Cross-St. King-Street, Rotherhithe,—at ·10, 2d on the L. from 274, Rotherhithe-st.

Cross-Street, Green-St. Bethnal-Green,—near ⅓ of a mile on the L. from the Green.

Cross-St. Bethnal-Green,—on the N. side of Three-colts-lane, op. Duthie's nursery.

Cross-St. Limehouse,—between the church and the West-India-docks, extending from Rich-st. to Jamaica-pl.

Cross-Street, Lower Cornwall-Street, St. George's East,—

nearly op. the Jolly Sailor, Back-lane.

Cross-St. Mews, Finsbury,—1st on the R. in Cross-st. from Wilson-st.

Crow-Court, Whitecross-Street, St. Luke's,—at 128, S. side Banner-st.

Crown and Anchor, Strand,—at 139, ⅛ of a mile on the L. from Temple-bar.

Crown-Brewery, Stanhope-St. Drury-Lane,—at 45, 3 doors N. of Denzell-st.

Crown-Brewery, Golden-Lane, —middle of the W. side.

Crown-Court, Crown-St. Westr. —middle of the S. side.

Crown-Court, Fleet-St.—at 72, between Salisbury-sq. and Water-lane.

Crown-Court, Tudor-St.—W. continuation of it from 15, New Bridge-st.

Crown-Court, Russel-St.—10 doors on the R. from Drury-lane.

Crown-Court, Strand,—op. 218, 3d on the R. from Temple-bar.

Crown-Court, Chancery-Lane, —at 221, ten doors on the L. from 193, Fleet-st.

Crown-Court, Pall-Mall,—at 66, op. the Palace.

Crown-Court, Liquorpond-St.— at 5, 2d on the R. from 67, Gray's-inn-lane.

Crown-Court, Sherrard-St. Golden-Sq.—at 10, three doors from 35, Brewer-st.

Crown-Court, Little Pulteney-St. Soho,—at 38, leading to 23, Gt. Windmill-st.

Crown-Court (Little), Princes-St. Soho,—at 22, op. Compton-st.

CRO

Crown-Court, Dean-St. Soho,—at 68, 2d on the R. from 399, Oxford-st.

Crown-Court, Portpool-Lane,—at 24, six doors from 64, Leather-lane.

Crown-Court, West-St. West-Smithfield,—2d on the L. from 87, Smithfield.

Crown-Ct. Butcherhall-Lane,—at 5, four doors from 82, Newgate-st.

Crown-Court, Golden-Lane,—at 16, 2d on the L. from Barbican.

Crown-Court, Bell-Alley,—1st on the L. from 12, Goswell-street.

Crown-Court, Grub-St. Cripplegate,—at 8, 4th on the L. from Chiswell-st.

Crown-Court, Warwick-Lane,—at 37, 1st on the L. from 10, Newgate-st.

Crown-Court, Old Change,—at 10, behind the S. E. corner of St. Paul's Church-yard.

Crown-Court, Whitecross-Str. St. Luke's,—at 153, 1st on the R. from Old-st.

Crown-Court, Charter-House-Lane,—at 26, 1st on the L. from 100, St. John's-st.

Crown-Court, Aldersgate-St.—at 52, six doors N. of Jewin-street.

Crown-Court, Cheapside,—at 64, between Bow-church and Queen-st.

Crown-Court, Trinity-Lane,—3 doors W. of Bow-lane.

Crown-Court, Holywell-Lane,—at 26, the last on the R. from 194, Shoreditch.

Crown-Court, White's-Alley,—1st on the L. from 60, Coleman-st.

Crown-Court, Old Broad-St.—at 62, E. side the church.

Crown-Court, Little Pearl-St. Spitalfields,—six doors S. from 10, Great Pearl-st.

Crown-Court, Quaker-St. Spitalfields,—1st on the L. from 29, Wheeler-st.

Crown-Court, Threadneedle-St.—at 45, op. Merchant-Taylors-hall.

Crown-Court, White's-Yard,—4th on the R. from 57, Rosemary-lane.

Crown-Court, Jewry-St.—at 12, 2d on the R. from Aldgate.

Crown-Court, Sun-Tavern-Fields,—by the Ship public-house, near ¼ mile E. of Cannon-st. turnpike.

Crown-Court, Cartwright-St.—4th on the L. from 32, Rosemary-lane.

Crown-Court, Queen's-Row, Prussian-Island,—3d on the R. from 188, Wapping.

Crown-Court, Wapping,—at 30, ⅛ of a mile on the L. below Hermitage-bridge.

Crown-Court, Wentworth-St.—at 99, the 1st W. of George-yard.

Crown-Court, Seething-Lane,—1st on the L. from 55, Great Tower-st.

Crown-Court, Narrow-Wall, Lambeth,—⅓ of a mile on the L. from Westr.-bridge.

Crown-Ct. Horselydown-Lane,—at 26, 2d on the R. from Broad-st.

Crown-Court, Bankside, Boro.—at 53, E. side Moss's-alley.

Crown-Court, Glean-Alley,— 2d on the R. from 218, Tooley-street.

Crown-Court, Garlick-Hill,—2 doors from 191, Up. Thames-street.

Crown - Court, Mile-End-Terrace, Mile End-Road,—1st on the L. from Savile-row.

Crown-Ct. Foster-Lane, Cheapside,—at 19, nearly op. Maiden-lane.

Crown-Court, High-St. Boro.—at 269, 6th on the R. from London-bridge.

Crown-Court (or Alley), Crown-St.—3d on the L. from Finsbury-sq.

Crown - Court, Curtain-Road, —10 doors N. from Holywell-lane, Shoreditch.

Crown-Court (Little),—1st on the R. in the last from the Curtain-road.

Crown and Cushion-Court, W. Smithfield,—at 1, the corner of Cow-lane.

Crown-Mews, Crown-St. Westr. —N. side of it.

Crown - Office, King's Bench-Walk, Temple,—at the bottom of Mitre-court, on the L. from 44, Fleet-st.

Crown-Office, Rolls-Yard,—at the back of 14, Chancery-lane.

Crown-Office-Row, MiddleTemple-Lane,—the last on the L. from 4, Fleet-st.

Crown-Pl. Crown-Court, Strand, —1st on the R. from op. 218, Strand.

Crown-Pl. Walworth,—8 doors S. from Cross-st. Newington.

Crown - Row, Mile-End-Road,

—op. the King Harry, 1½ mile on the R. from Aldgate.

Crown-Row, Walworth,—a few doors on the L. from the Elephant and Castle.

Crown and Sceptre-Court, St. James's-St.—at 36, 3d on the L. from 164, Piccadilly.

Crown and Shears-Pl. Rosemary-Lane,—1st on the L. from the Minories.

Crown-Sq. High-St. Boro.—at 269, 6th on the R. from London-bridge.

Crown-St. Westr.—3d on the R. from Charing-cross towards the Abbey.

Crown-St. (Up.)- W. end the last.

Crown-St. Soho,—from 440, Oxford-street, by St. Giles's, to Moor-st. Seven Dials.

Crown-St. Hoxton-Sq.—at the S. W. corner, leading into Old-st. road.

Crown-St. Finsbury-Sq.—at the S. E. corner, continued by Sun-st.

Crown-St. Walworth,--by Cross-st. and op. Crown-row.

Crown and Thistle-Court, Swallow-St.—at 46, two doors W. of Beak-st.

Crown-Wharf, Bankside,—⅓ of a mile E. from Blackfriars-bridge, by Thames-st.

Crown-Yard, Swallow-St.—at 112, nine doors N. of New Burlington-st.

Crown-Yard, Kent-St. Boro.—at 53, 3d on the L. from St. George's-church.

Crucifix-Lane, Bermondsey-St. —at 50, ⅙ of a mile on the L. from Tooley-st.

Crutched-Friars, Mark-Lane,—

at 64, 2d on the L. from Fen-church-st.

Cuckolds-Court, Maid-Lane, Bo-ro.—3d on the L. from Park-street.

Cuckold's-Point, Rotherhithe, —at 126, about a mile below the church.

Cullum-St. Fenchurch-Street,— at 135, 2d on the L. from Gracechurch-st.

Culver-Court, Fenchurch-St.— at 130, middle of the N. side.

Cumbers-Court (Gt.) Blackman-St. Boro.—at 52, op. Suffolk-street.

Cumbers - Court (Little), two doors S. of the last.

Cumberland-Court, Black-Bird-Alley, Bethnal-Green,—1st on the right, S. from Fleet-street.

Cumberland-Court, Tottenham-St. Tottenham-Court-Road, —at 20, two doors from Nor-folk-st.

Cumberland-Gardens, Vauxhall, —at the back of the Royal-oak by the turnpike.

Cumberland - Mews, Edgware-Road,—5 doors on the R. from Tyburn-turnpike.

Cumberland-Pl. Gt. Cumber-land-St.—12 doors from 246, Oxford-st.

Cumberland - Pl. New-Road, Marybone,—S. side, near the Yorkshire Stingo.

Cumberland-Pl. Kent-Road,— part of the L. side, ¼ of a mile below the Bricklayers arms.

Cumberland-Row, Kennington-Green,—nearly op. Upper Kennington-lane.

Cumberland-Row, Pentonville,

—S. side from the turnpike, by the Bell, to Battle-bridge.

Cumberland-St. (Gt.) Oxford-St.—at 246, the 1st on the L. from Tyburn-turnpike.

Cumberland-Street, New-Road, Marybone,—3d on the R. from the Yorkshire Stingo.

Cumberland-St. Goodge-Street, —at 23, 3d on the R. from 64, Tottenham-court-rd.

Cumberland-St. Curtain-Road, —1st on the R. from Wor-ship-st. Finsbury.

Cumberland - St. John - Street, Blackfriars-Road,—1st on the L. from Holland-st.

Cumberland - Wharf, Rother-hithe,—⅛ of a mile below the church, nearly op. Clarence-street.

Cummings - Sq. Fitzroy - Row, New Road,—N. end on the R.

Cumming-Pl. Pentonville,—N. side the road, from the chapel to Southampton-st.

Cumming-St.—West side the chapel, by the last.

Cumming-St. (Upper),—the con-tinuation of the last.

Cupers - Bridge, Narrow-Wall, Lambeth,—¼ a mile on the L. from Westr.-bridge.

Cupers-Gardens, Narrow-Wall, —op. Cupers-bridge.

Cupid's-Court, Golden-Lane,— at 131, 6th on the L. from Barbican.

Curling's-Dock, Limehouse,— between Limehouse-hole and the entrance to the West-India-docks.

Curriers - Hall-Court, London-Wall,—4 doors E. of Wood-st.

Currier's-Row, Bristow-Street,

Blackfriars,—1st on the R. from St. Andrew's-hill.

Cursitor-St. Chancery-Lane,— at 39, middle of the E. side.

Curtain-Road,—1st on the R. in Worship-st. from 250, Shoreditch.

Curtis's-Row, Broadwall,—op. Cross-st. from Blackfriars-road.

Curzon-St. Mayfair,—1st on the L. in Clarges-st. from Piccadilly.

Cushion-Court, Old Broad-St. —10 doors on the R. from Threadneedle-st.

Custom-House, Lower Thames-St.—op. 60, ¼ of a mile below London-bridge.

Custom-House-Court, Beer-Lane,—1st on the R.from 37, Gt. Tower-st.

Custom-House-Quay, Lower-Thames-St.—S. side the Custom-house.

Custom-House-Stairs,—opposite Water-lane.

Custos-Brevium-Office, Elm-Ct. Temple,—3 doors on the L. from Middle Temple-lane.

Cutlers-Hall, Cloak-Lane,—at 5, corner of College-hill.

Cutlers-St. Houndsditch,—at 114, middle of the N. side.

———

Dacre's ALMS-HOUSES, Westr. See Emanuel's Hospital.

Dacre-St. New Tothill-Street, Westr.—at 25, leading to Gt. Chapel-st.

Daffey's-Rents, Glean-Alley,—

the continuation of it from 218, Tooley-st.

Dagger-Court, Fore-St. Cripplegate,—at 110, nearly op. Wood-st.

Dagger-Court, Quaker-St. Spitalfields,—at 16, 15 doors on the R. from 29, Wheeler-st.

Dagget's-Court, N. E. corner of Moorfields.

Dagget's-Passage, Long-Alley, —1st on the R. from Moorfields.

Daker's-Rents, Whitecross-St. Cripplegate,—at 14, 3d on the L. from Fore-st.

Dalby-Terrace, City-Road,— part of the S. side by the New river.

Danish-Church, Wellclose-Sq. —in the centre of the sq.

Darby-St. Rosemary-Lane,—at 38,6th on the R. from Tower-hill.

Darkhouse-Lane,LowerThames St.—at 16, W. side Billings-gate.

Dark-Entry, Duke-St.—2d on the L. from Aldgate.

Dark-Entry, Lower E. Smithfield,—at 59, facing Butcher-row.

Darling-Place, Dog-Row, Mile-End,—3d on the L. from the turnpike.

Darling-Row,—the continuation of the last.

Darnal's-Row, Willow-Walk, Bermondsey,—1st on the L. from Page's-walk.

Dartmouth-Row, Westr. See Lewsham-St.

Dartmouth-St. Westr.—the 1st on the R. in Tothill-st. from the Abbey.

H

Darts-Alley, Whitechapel,—25 doors W. of the church.

David-St.York-Pl.Baker-Street, —six doors on the L. from the New-road.

Davis's-Builds.Hoxton,—by the corner of Workhouse-lane, ¼ mile on the L. from Old-st.-road.

Davis's-Builds. Vine-St. Spital- fields,—at 11, 3 doors N. of Phœnix-st.

Davies's - Builds. Penny-Fields, Poplar,—1st on the R. from the Commercial-road.

Davies-Court, Chequer-Sq. Che- quer-Alley,—N. W. corner, a few doors on the R. from 99, Bunhill-row.

Davies-Mews,Davies-St.Berke- ley-Sq.— at 53, 2d on the L. from Oxford-st.

Davies-Street, Berkeley-Sq.— N. W. corner, extending to 292, Oxford-st.

Davis's-Rents,Austin-St.Shore- ditch,—a few yards on the L. from Hackney-road.

Davis's-Wharf, Horselydown, —entrance by Potters-fields, E. end of Tooley-st.

Daws-Court,Gunpowder-Alley, —7 doors on the L. from 95, Shoe-lane.

Day's-Court, Gutter-Lane,—5 doors from Cheapside.

Day Newspaper-Office, Pickett- St. Strand,—11 doors on the R. from Temple-bar.

Deacon-Court, Quaker-St. Spi- talfields,—2d on the L. from 29, Wheeler-st.

Deadman's-Pl. Park St. Boro. —4th on the L. from the Borough-market.

Deal's-Court, Flower and Dean- St. Spitalfields,—1st on the L. from 200, Brick-lane.

Deal-St. Mile-End New-Town, —last on the R. in Pelham- st. from 63, Brick-lane.

Dean's-Builds.Commercial-Rd. —N. corner of Poplar High- street.

Dean's - Builds. Lock's-Fields, Walworth,—1st on the L. in Flint-st. from Apollo-builds.

Dean's-Court, New Round-Ct. —1st on the R. from 447, Strand.

Dean's-Court, Hatfield-St.—1st on the R. from 25, Goswell- street.

Dean's-Court, St. Martin's-le- Grand,—at 50, 3d on the R. from 66, Newgate-st.

Dean's-Court (Little), N. side the last.

Dean's-Court, Old-Bailey,—at 24, op. Newgate.

Deans-Court, St.Paul's Church- Yard,—at 5, 2d on the R. from Ludgate-st.

Dean's-Court, Kingsland-Road, —at 48, ⅛ of a mile on the L. from Shoreditch.

Dean's-Court, Church-St. Beth- nal-Green,—at 143, on the E. side of Brick-lane.

Dean's-Mews, Holywell-Lane, —at 22, the 5th on the R. from 193, Shoreditch.

Dean's-Pl.Westr.-Bridge-Rd.— part of the R. side, from the Asylum towards the Obelisk.

Dean's-Pl. Walworth,—S. end of Dean's-row.

Dean's-Row, Walworth High- St.—from Amelia-st. to Ma- nor-row.

Dean-St. Westr.—1st on the L. west from the abbey.

Dean-St. Soho,—at 400, Oxford-st. 2d on the L. from St. Giles's.

Dean-St. (Little),—at 44, in the last, 4 doors N. of Compton-street.

Dean-St. South Audley-Street, —op. 9, from Hill-st. Berkeley-sq. to Park-lane.

Dean-St. Fetter-Lane,—at 43, middle of the E. side.

Dean-St. High-Holborn,—at 92, leading into Red-lion-sq.

Dean-St. Finsbury - Sq.—from the S. E. corner to Wilson-street.

Dean-St. Mile-End New-Town. See Deal-st.

Dean-St. Up. East Smithfield,— at 95, $\frac{1}{6}$ of a mile on the R. from Tower-hill.

Dean-St. Shadwell,—the 1st in Gould's-hill, from 98, High-street.

Dean - St. Tooley - Street,—at 200, the fifth on the R. from London-bridge.

Dean's-Yd. Dean-St.—1st on the R. from Park-lane.

Dean's-Yd. Dean-St. Soho,—at 10, middle E. side.

Dean's - Yard, Westr.—S. W. corner of the abbey.

Dean's-Yard (Little),—1st on the R. in the last from College-st.

Dean's-Yard, Dean-St. Park-Lane,—7 doors on the L. from op. 9, South Audley-st.

Dear's Pl. Sommers-Town,— from the Crescent to the fields.

Deaton's-Court, Phœnix-Street,

Spitalfields,—entrance by the 2d on the R. from 38, Wheeler-st.

Debtors Charity-School, Newington-Road, Surrey,—third house on the R. from the King's-bench.

Delahay-St. Gt. George-Street, Westr.—at 34, 3 doors E. of the Park.

Delap-Court, Broadway, Westr. —2 doors E. of Queen-sq.

Denham-Court, Drury-Lane,— 7 doors from the New Church, Strand.

Denmark - Court, Strand,—at 382, W. side of Exeter - Change.

Denmark- Court, Denmark-St. St. Giles's,—3 doors from High-st.

Denmark-Court, Golden-Lane, —at 20, 1st on the L. from Barbican.

Denmark-Street, High St. Saint Giles's,—1st on the R. from Oxford-street.

Denmark-St. (Little),—1st on the L. in the last from High-street.

Denmark - St. Ratcliffe - Highway,—at 153, 1st W. parallel to Cannon-st.

Dennis or Dennets-Court, King-St. Boro. See Tennis-Court.

Dennis-Builds. Garden-Walk, —2d on the R. from Willow-walk, Tabernacle-sq.

Dennis-Row,—op. the last.

Dennis-Row, Willsted-St. Sommers-Town,—1st on the L. from the road to Marybone.

Denton's-Builds. Chapel-Path, Sommers-Town,—op. 22, between Brill-row and Middle-sex-st.

Denzell-St. Stanhope-Street,—at 48, the continuation of White-horse-yard from 110, Drury-lane.

Deptford Lower-Road,—from Paradise-row, near Rother-hithe-church, Deptford.

Derby - Court, Piccadilly,—at 208, 8 doors E. of St. James's church.

Derby-Street, Curzon-St. May-fair,—at 22, three doors E. of South Audley-st.

Derby - Street, Parliament-St. Westr.—at 46, 2d on the L. from the Horse-guards.

Derby-St. Rosemary-Lane. See Darby.

Dermer's-Passage, Fetter-Lane. See Bartlet's-Passage.

Devereux - Court, Strand,—at 218, 3d on the L. from Tem-ple-bar.

Devonshire-Builds. Worship-St.—4th on the L. from 249, Shoreditch.

Devonshire - Court, Sutton-St. Maze,—op. the S. side of Guy's-hospital.

Devonshire - Court, Hounds-ditch. See Cavendish-court.

Devonshire-House, Piccadilly,—near the middle of the N. side.

Devonshire-Mews East, Devon-shire-St.—6 doors W. of Port-land-pl.

Devonshire-Mews North, Devon-shire - St.—3 doors W. of Portland-pl.

Devonshire-Mews South, Devon-shire-St.—between Up. Wim-pole-st. and Up. Harley-st.

Devonshire-Mews West, Devon-shire - St.—between Devon-shire-pl. and Up. Harley-st.

Devonshire-Mews, Devonshire-Sq. Bishopsgate,—at the S. E. corner.

Devonshire - Pl. Marybone,—the continuation of Up. Wim-pole-st.

Devonshire-Pl. Old Nicol-St. Bethnal-Green,—a few yards on the R. from Cock-lane.

Devonshire - Pl. Stepney,—by the World's-end, N. E. cor-ner of the Church-yard.

Devonshire - Pl. Commercial-Road,—S. side, the corner of Albion-st.

Devonshire-Pl. Up. Kennington-Lane,—1st on the R. from Vauxhall-gardens.

Devonshire-Pl. Mews, Mary-bone,—1st W. of Devonshire-place.

Devonshire-Row, Devonshire-St.—6 doors E. of Portland-place.

Devonshire-Sq. Bishopsgate,—at the E. end of Devonshire-street.

Devonshire-St. Bishopsgate,—at 18, 1st on the R. north of the church.

Devonshire - St. Marybone,—last on the L. in Portland-road, entering by John-st. 101, Oxford-st.

Devonshire - St. Queen-Sq.—S. E. corner, to 59, Theobalds-road.

Devonshire-St. Up. Kenning-ton - Lane,—1st on the R. from Kennington-cross.

Devonshire-Yard, Devonshire-Sq.—at S. E. corner.

Diamond-Builds. White-Hart-Row, Kennington,—1st on the R. from Clayton-pl.

Diamond-Court, Hosier-Lane, —at 6, 1st on the L. from 24, W. Smithfield.

Diamond-Court, Gt. Pearl-St. Spitalfields,—at 21, 3 doors from Grey-eagle-st.

Diamond - Point, East - India Dock-Road,—N. side, by the Dock-gate.

Diamond-Row, Stepney,—part of the R.side from Redman's-row towards the church.

Diana-Pl. New-Road,—op. Conway-st. Fitzroy-sq.

Dibbles-Builds. Up. E. Smithfield,—at 20, op. Butcher-row.

Dice-Quay, Lower Thames-St. —at 23, E. side of Billings-gate.

Digby-Row, Bethnal-Green,— the E. continuation of Digby-street.

Digby-Street, Globe-St. Bethnal-Green,—1st on the L. from Green-st. towards Mile-end.

Digby's-Walk,—1st on the L. in the last from Globe-st.

Dingle-Lane, Poplar,—1st on the R. from the Commercial-road.

St. Dionis Back-Church, Lime-St.—behind 160, Fenchurch-street.

Diot-Street, St. Giles's. See George-st.

Dirty-Lane, Strand,—at 88, op. Southampton-st.

Dirty-Lane, Shoreditch,—at 73, by the turnpike, leading to Cock-lane.

Dirty Lane,Blackman-St.Boro. See Great Suffolk-st.

Dispatch Newspaper-Office,— behind 15, Fleet-st.

Dispensary for Relieving the Sick Poor at their own Habitations,—at 29, Alderman-bury.

DissentersLibrary,—at 49,Red-cross-st. Cripplegate.

Distaff-Lane (Gt.) Friday-St.— at 31, 2d on the R. from 36, Cheapside.

Distaff-Lane (Little),—middle of the S. side the last.

Ditchman's - Builds. Hackney-Road,—op. the Nag's-head, towards Goldsmith's-pl.

Ditchman's - Gardens, Old-St.-Road,—behind Fuller'sAlms-houses, near Shoreditch - church.

Dobney's-Pl. Penton-St. Pentonville,—6 doors on the R. behind 1, Winchester-pl.

Doby - Court, Monkwell-St.— 2d on the L. from Falcon-square.

Doby-Court, Maiden-Lane,Up. Thames-St.—1st on the R. a few yards from 37, Queen-street.

Doctors-Commons,—on the S. side St. Paul's church-yard, entrance op. 14, Gt. Knight-rider-st.

Dock - Head, Horselydown,— from the E. end of New-st. and Russell-st. to Hickman's Folly.

Dock-Head-Court,—at the E. end of the last, op. Mill-st.

Dock - Side, Hermitage-Dock, Wapping,—on both sides of it, by Hermitage-bridge.

H 3

Dock-St. Up. E. Smithfield,—from 37, to 68, Rosemary-lane.

Dock-St. Commercial-Road,—4th on the R. from Cannon-st.-road towards Limehouse.

Dock-Yard, Hermitage-Dock, Wapping,—on the E. side, from the bridge towards Charlotte-st.

Dod's-Pl. Hanover-St. Rother-hithe,—last on the R. from Hanover-stairs.

Dodd's-Pl. Three Colts-Lane, Bethnal-Green,—a few yards on the L. from Dog-row.

Dog and Bear-Inn, High-St. Boro.—at 196. See the next article.

Dog and Bear-Yard, High-St. Boro.—at 196, sixteen doors S. of Union-st.

Dog and Bear-Yard, Tooley-St.—at 127, ⅓ of a mile on the R. from London-bridge.

Dog and Duck-Yard, Princes-St. Red-Lion-Sq.—7 doors W. of Bedford-row.

Dog and Duck-Stairs,—1st below Greenland-dock.

Dog's-Head-Court, Old-Street, St. Luke's,—at 106, ten doors W. of the church.

Dog-Row, Bethnal-Green,—from the W. side the green to Mile-end turnpike.

Dogwell-Court, Lombard-St.—2d on the L. from 56, Fleet-street.

Dolley's-Court, Ropemakers-St.—3d on the L. from Moor-fields.

Dolphin-Court, High-Holborn,—at 289, between Chancery-lane and Gt. Turnstile.

Dolphin-Court, Ludgate-Hill,—12 doors on the R. from Fleet-market.

Dolphin-Court, Noble-St. Foster-Lane,—at 40, ⅛ of a mile on the L. from Cheapside.

Dolphin-Court, Old-St.—at 135, 2d on the L. from Goswell-street.

Dolphin-Court, Rose and Crown Court,—2d on the L. from the N. E. corner of Moor-fields.

Dolphin-Court, Raven-Row, Artillery-Pl. Spitalfields,—between the S. end of Gun-st. and Crispin-st.

Dolphin-Court, Whitechapel-Road,—at 53, two doors E. of Gt. Garden-st.

Dolphin-Lane, Poplar High-St.—3d on the R. from the Commercial-road.

Domingo-St. Old-Street,—at 14, 2d on the R. from Goswell-st.

Denaldson's-Builds. Tottenham-Court-Road,—8 doors on the L. from Oxford-st.

Doran's or Crombie's-Row, Commercial-Road,—on the W. side the George, or Halfway-house.

Dorrington-St. Leather-Lane,—at 87, 3d on the L. from 129, Holborn-hill.

Dorrington-St. Coldbath-Fields,—the W. continuation of Bayne's-row by the House of Correction.

Dorset-Court, Dorset-St.—six doors on the L. from Salisbury-sq.

Dorset-Mews West, Dorset-St. Portman-Sq.—1st on the R. west from Baker-st.

Dorset-Mews East, Dorset-St. Portman-Sq.—1st on the L. east from Baker-st.

Dorset-Pl. St. Pancras,—from Church-row, near the church, to Back-lane and Vernon's-buildings.

Dorset-Sq. Canon-Row, Westr. —1st on the L. from 46, Parliament-st.

Dorset-St. Salisbury-Sq.—the continuation of the E. side, entering at 82, Fleet-st.

Dorset-Street, Manchester-St. Manchester-Sq.—at 28, the last on the L. from the sq.

Dorset-St. Spitalfields,—from the S. end of Crispin-st. to Red-lion-st.

Dorset-Wharf, Whitefriars,—E. side Whitefriars-dock, and W. side the New-river-office.

Doublet's-Wharf, Up. Thames-St.—entrance by 89, W. side Cole-harbour-stairs.

Doughty-St. Guilford-Street,—ten doors from Gray's-inn-lane.

Doughty-Mews, Guilford-St.—from 12, to Henry-st. Gray's-inn-lane.

Dove-Court, Leather-Lane, Holborn,—at 59, op. Cross-street.

Dove-Court, New Street-Hill,—1st on the L. from King's-head-court.

Dove-Court, St. Martin's-le-Grand,—4th on the L. from 66, Newgate-st.

Dove-Court, Old Jewry,—3 doors on the R. from 42, Poultry.

Dove-Court, Old Fish-St.-Hill, —1st on the R. from 204, Up. Thames-st.

Dove-Court, St. Swithin's-Lane, —1st on the R. from 10, Lombard-st.

Dove-Court, Pavement, Moor-fields,—4 doors S. of Rope-makers-st.

Dove-Court, Dog-Row,—1st on the R. from Mile-end-turn-pike.

Dove-St. Wade's-Pl. Poplar,-1st on the R. from the High-st.

Dover-Pl. Kent-Road,—part of the R. side, ½ of a mile from the Elephant and Castle.

Dover-St. Piccadilly,—at 68, op. Arlington-st. St. James's.

Dover-St. Blackfriars-Road,—2d on the R. from the Obelisk.

Dover-Yard, Dover-St.—at 41, six doors from Piccadilly.

Dowgate-Hill, Up. Thames-St. —from 168, to Cannon-st. op. Walbrook.

Dowgate-Wharf, and Dock,—bottom of the last.

Dowgate-Stairs, Cousin-Lane, —1st E. of the last.

Down-St. Piccadilly,—1st E. from Park-lane.

Downd's Yard, Rupert-St.—2d on the L. from Coventry-st.

Downe's Wharf, Lower East-Smithfield,—at 94, W. side Hermitage-bridge.

Downing-St. Westminster,—S. side of the Treasury, White-hall.

Downing and Mills's Wharf, Horselydown,—nearly op. Thomas-street, 1st E. from George-stairs.

Dowsing-Pl. Whitechapel,—1st on the R. in Osborn-pl. from 20, Brick-lane.

Drake-Pl. St. Pancras,—N. end of Clarence-passage.

Drake-St. Red-Lion-Sq.—N.W. corner, to Theobald's road.

Drapers-Alms-Houses, Kingsland-Road,—¼ of a mile on the R. from Shoreditch.

Drapers-Alms-Houses, Old-St.-Road,—a few doors on the R. from Shoreditch-church.

Drapers-Alms-Houses, Coopers-Row,—3 doors on the R. from Crutched-friars.

Drapers-Alms-Houses, N. side Cross-St. Newington, — op. the church.

Drapers-Alms-Houses, Beech-Lane, Barbican,—the N. side of it.

Drapers-Alms-Houses, Whitechapel-Road, — at 160, W. side the turnpke.

Drapers-Builds. Old-St.—at 32, 1st E. from Whitecross-st.

Drapers-Builds. London-Wall, —at 62, op. Bethlem-hospital, from Winchester-st.

Drapers - Gardens, — between Drapers-builds. and Drapers-hall.

Drapers - Hall, Throgmorton-St.—at 27, 3 doors W. of Broad-st.

Drapers-Pl. Old-St.—at 33, 8 doors E. of Whitecross-st.

Drill-Pl. Poplar,—E. side the Commercial-road, by the turnpike.

Drum-Yard, Whitechapel,—at 50, 3d W. from the church.

Drury-Lane,—W. end of Hol-

born, where there are Nos. 1 and 194, to the New-church, Strand.

Duchess-St. See Dutchess-st.

Duck-Lane, Gt. Peter-Street, Westr.—5 doors from Strutton-ground.

Duck-Lane, Edward-St. Soho, —4 doors W. from 95, Wardour-st.

Duck-Yd. Duck-Lane, Westr. —1st on the R. from Peter-street.

Ducksfoot-Lane, Up. Thames-St.—at 145, 4th on the R. from London-bridge.

Ducking-Pond-Lane,—N. end of Greyhound-lane, from 105, Whitechapel-road.

Ducking-Pond-Mews, Mayfair, —on the S. side Shepherd's market.

Dudley-Court, High-Street, St. Giles's,—at 52, by the church.

Dudley-Grove, Paddington,— on the Harrow-road, near the Green.

Dudman's Court, George-St. Deptford,—6 doors W. of Grove-st.

Dudman's Ship-Yard, Deptford, —S. side George-stairs and Greenland-dock.

Duff's-Court, Queen-St. Boro. —at 99, 2d on the L. from Union-st.

Dufours-Pl. Broad-St. Carnaby-Market,—at 21, 8 doors W. of Poland-st.

Duke's Court, Little Almonry, Westr.—4 doors from Dean-street.

Duke's Court, James-St. Westr. —at the E. end, op. York-st.

Duke's Court, Saint Martin's Lane, Charing-Cross,— at 134, op. the church.

Duke's Court, Duke-Street, St. James's,—at 33, middle of the W. side.

Duke's Court, Drury-Lane,— at 50, 10 doors S. of Long-acre.

Duke's Court, Gt. Earl-St.— 1st on the R. from the Seven Dials.

Duke's Court, Black Boy-Alley, —1st on the L. from Chick-lane.

Duke's Court, Kingsland-Road, —4 doors on the R. north from Union-st.

Duke's Court, Crown-St. Finsbury,—1st on the R. from the square.

Duke's Court, Fore-St. Lime-house,—1st on the L. from the E. end of Narrow-st. op. Duke's shore.

Duke's Court, Totterburn-Alley, Boro.—1st on the R. from Duke-st.

Duke's Ct. New-Lane, Horse-lydown,—1st on the L. from 32, Gainsford-st.

Duke's Head-Passage, Ivy-Lane,—at 22, 2d on the R. from 50, Newgate-st.

Duke's Head-Yard, Rose-Court, —1st on the L. from 42, Tower-st.

Duke's Head-Court, White-Cross-St. Cripplegate,— at 42, 3d on the R. from 115, Fore-st.

Duke's Head-Court, Red-Lion-St. Spitalfields,—2d S. of the church.

Duke's Head-Court, New-St.

Boro.—on the E. side Guy's hospital.

Duke-Mews, Duke-St.—at 20, 5 doors from Manchester-square.

Duke's Place, Aldgate,— the end of Duke-st. from 28, Houndsditch.

Duke's Pl. (Little),—the end of Mitre-st. from 29, Aldgate.

Duke's Pl. Duke's Row, Pimlico,—nearly op. Arabella-row.

Duke's Row, Pimlico,—L. side, $\frac{1}{4}$ of a mile from Buckingham-gate.

Duke's Row, Sommers-Town, —op. Sommers-pl. West, towards Tavistock-sq.

Duke's Shore, Fore-St. Lime-house,—3 doors on the R. from Narrow-st.

Duke's Shore-Alley,—op. the last, leading to Ropemakers-fields.

Duke-Street, Manchester-Sq.— middle of the S. side, to 171, Oxford-st.

Duke-St. Grosvenor-Sq.—from the N. E. corner to 277, Oxford-st. op. the last.

Duke-St. Portland-Chapel,— on the W. side, from 33, Queen Ann-st. East, to New Cavendish-st.

Duke-St. Westr.—W. end of Charles-st. Parliament-st.

Duke-Street, St. James's,—at 182, Piccadilly, op. Burlington-house.

Duke-St. Adelphi,—2d on the L. in Villiers-st. from 32, Strand.

Duke-St. Lincoln's-Inn-Fields,

—at 52, W. side under the arch.

Duke-Street, Gt. Russell - St. Bloomsbury,—at 42, middle of the S. side.

Duke-St. W.-Smithfield, — at 52, S. E. corner, leading into Little-Britain.

Duke-Street, Worship-St. Finsbury,—1st on the R. from Paul-st. towards the Curtain-road.

Duke-St. Long - Alley, Moorfields,—nearly op. Primrose-st. from 110, Bishopsgate-without.

Duke-St. Houndsditch,—at 27, —1st on the L. from Aldgate.

Duke-St. Aldgate,—at 19, 4 doors W. of Houndsditch.

Duke-St. Old Artillery-Ground, —9 doors in Union-st. from 69, Bishopsgate.

Duke-Street, Turk-St. Bethnal-Green,—middle of the E. side.

Duke-Street, St. George's East,— the continuation of Union-st. from op. Blue - gate - fields, Back-lane.

Duke-Street, Princes-St. Lambeth,—2d on the R. from Vauxhall.

Duke - Street, Saint George's Fields,—1st on the R. from the Obelisk towards Westr.-bridge.

Duke-St. Commercial - Road, Lambeth,— 1st on the L. from Up. Ground.

Duke-St. Boro. — from Charlotte-st. Blackfriars-road, to Queen-st.

Duke-Street, Mint-St. Boro.—

3d on the R. from 156, High-street.

Dulwich-Alms-Houses,—N.W. corner of St. Luke's hospital.

Dulwich-Alms-Houses, Lamb-Alley, Bishopsgate - St. See Allen's.

Dumb-Alley, High-Holborn,— at 153, 1st on the L. from St. Giles's.

Dun-Horse-Yard, High-St. Boro.—at 162, op. St. George's church.

Duncan - Court, Poplar, — N. end of Hale-st.

Duncan-Place, Leicester-Pl.— at 14, by the N. E. corner of Leicester-sq.[1]

Duncan-Pl. City-Road,—part of the N. side, by High-st. Islington.

Duncan-Street, Red - Lion-St. —2d on the R. from 30, Whitechapel.

Duncan-Terrace, City-Road,— by Duncan-place, on the W. bank of the New-river.

Duncomb - Court, Cock-Lane, Shoreditch,—behind Shore-ditch-church, 4th on the L. from Church-st.

Dundee - Arms Wharf, Wapping,—at 253, ⅛ of a mile below the church.

Dundee - Wharf, Wapping,— op. 27, a few doors below Hermitage-bridge.

Dunk-Street, Princes-St. Mile-End New-Town,—1st.on the L. from Great Garden - st. Whitechapel.

Dunkin's Gateway, Gt. Tower-Hill,—at 38, 4 doors S. of Coopers-row.

Dunning's Alley, Bishopsgate-

Without,—at 151, 3 doors S. of Sun-st.

St. Dunstan's Alley, St. Dunstan's Hill,—3 doors from 10, Gt. Tower-st.

St. Dunstan's Church, St. Dunstan's Hill,—on the S. side the last.

St. Dunstan's Church, Fleet-St.—at 185, 17 doors E. of Temple-bar.

St. Dunstan's Church, Stepney, —near ½ a mile from Mile-end, by Stepney-green.

St. Dunstan's Court, Fleet-St. —at 160, middle of the N. side.

Dunstan's Court, Old-Bailey, —at 20, op. Newgate.

St. Dunstan's Hill, Gt. Tower-St.—at 10, op. Mincing-lane.

St. Dunstan's Pl. Stepney,—by the Ship, W. side the Church-yard.

St. Dunstan's Pl. Brook-Street, Ratcliffe,— op. 41, near Stepney-causeway.

St. Dunstan's Workhouse, St. Dunstan's Hill,—4 doors on the L. from Thames-st.

Dunster's Court, Old-Bailey,— 3d on the R. from Snow-hill.

Dunster-Court, Mincing-Lane, —2 doors on the L. from Fenchurch-st.

Durand's Wharf, Rotherhithe, —1st in Trinity-st. below Cuckold's Point.

Durham-House, Chelsea,—last house in Durham-pl. from Gt. Smith-st.

Durham-House, Durham-Pl. Hackney-Road.

Durham-Pl. Chelsea,—W. side

the hospital, extending from Ormond-row to Smith-st.

Durham-Pl.-Mews, Chelsea,— between Durham-place and Ormond-row.

Durham-Place, East, Hackney-Road,—part of the R. side, ¾ of a mile from Shoreditch.

Durham-Place, West,—the W. continuation of the last.

Durham-Place, Wolsingham-Place, Lambeth,—from the Three Stags to Wallers-pl.

Durham-Row, Stepney, — adjoins the N. side the church-yard.

Durham-St. Strand,—at 64, ⅓ of a mile on the R. from Charing-cross.

Durham-Yard, West-St.—1st on the R. from 86, N. W. corner of Smithfield.

Durweston-Mews, Crawford-St. Portman-Sq.—1st on the L. from York-pl.

Durweston-St. Baker-Street,— at 45, 4th on the L. from Portman-sq.

Durweston-St. (Little),—at 19, in the last, 6 doors W. of Gloucester-pl.

Durweston-St. (Upper), — the E. continuation of John-st. from the Edgware-road.

Dutch-Alms-Houses, Crown-St. Finsbury,—at the S. end of Duke's-court.

Dutchess-Mews, Dutchess-St. —1st W. of Portland-pl.

Dutchess-St. Marybone,—from 17, Duke st. by Portland-chapel, to 2, Mansfield-st.

Dutch-Church, Austin-Friars, —5 doors on the R. from 67, Old Broad-st.

Dutch-Pin-Row, Tabernacle-
Sq.—1st on the L. from Old-
st.-road.

Dutch-Prize-Office, Old Broad-
St.—at 55, nearly op. the
Excise-office.

Dutsom's Ways, Wapping,—
between King Edward's stairs
and New Crane.

Dyers-Alms-Houses, City-Road,
—by the turnpike, near 1
mile on the L. from Fins-
bury-sq.

Dyers-Alms-Houses, St. John-
St. Bethnal-Green,—last on
the R. from 105, Brick-lane.

Dyer's Builds. Holborn-Hill,—
at 18, 11 doors W. from
Fetter-lane.

Dyer's Builds.-Passage,—leads
from the last to 40, Castle-
street.

Dyer's Court, Noble-Street,
Foster-Lane,—at 34, middle
of the W. side.

Dyer's Court, Aldermanbury,
—10 doors on the R. from
Lad-lane.

Dyer's Court, James-Street, St.
Luke's,—1st on the R. from
37, Featherstone-st. City-
road.

Dyer's Court, Whitechapel,—
at 52, 2d W. of the church.

Dyers-Hall, Elbow-Lane,—2
doors from 14, Dowgate-hill.

Dyers-Hall-Wharf, Up. Thames-
St.—at 95, op. Lawrence-
Pountney-lane.

Dyer's Pl. Sommers-Town,—a
few yards on the R. from the
turnpike, Battle-bridge, towards Marybone.

Dyer's Pl. Long-Alley, Moor-

fields,—1st on the L. from
Worship-st.

Dyer's Place, Parsonage-Walk,
Newington,—1st on the R.
from the High-road.

Dyer-Street, William-St. Blackfriars-Rd.—nearly op. York-
street.

Dyers-Wharf, Stangate, Lambeth,—3d wharf above Westminster-bridge, by Searls's,
the boat-builder.

Dyson's Yard, Park-Lane,—1st
on the R. from Piccadilly.

———————

EAGLE-COURT, St. John's
Lane, Clerkenwell,—at 5;
1st on the L. from St. John-
street.

Eagle-Court, Dean-St. Red-
Lion-Sq.—6 doors from 92,
High-Holborn.

Eagle-Court, White-Hart-Yd.
—2d on the L. from 83,
Drury-lane.

Eagle and Child-Alley, Fleet-
Market,—at 61, 1st on the
R. from Holborn.

Eagle and Child-Court, Princes-
St. Lambeth,—6 doors on
the R. from Broad-st.

Eagle Insurance-Office,—at 83,
Cornhill, 6 doors E. of the
Royal-Exchange.

Eagle-Place, Mile-End,—¼ of a
mile on the L. below the
turnpike.

Eagle-Pl. Princes-St.—3d on
the L. from Bakers-row, 94,
Whitechapel-road.

Eagle-Pl. Back-Lane, Poplar,—

2d on the L. from the Commercial-road.

Eagle-St. Piccadilly,—at 212, 1st on the L. from the Haymarket.

Eagle-Street, Red-Lion-St.—at 65, 1st on the L. from 72, High-holborn.

Eagle-Wharf,—at the bottom of Milford-lane, from 200, Strand.

Eam's Yard, Piccadilly, — at 21, op. the Green-Park.

Earl's Court, Cranbourne-St.— 5 doors on the R. from Castle-st.

Earl's Court, Gt. Earl-St.—1st on the R. from the Seven-dials.

Earl-St. (Gt.) Seven-Dials,— op. Cross-lane from 106, Long-acre.

Earl-St. (Little), Seven-Dials,— from op. the last to the W. end of Monmouth-st.

Earl-St. Blackfriars,—1st on the R. north from the Bridge.

Earl-St. London-Road,—1st on the L. from the Obelisk.

Earl's Yard, Castle-St. Long-Acre,—6 doors from St.Martin's-lane.

Easley's Mews, Wigmore-St. —at 24, op. Marybone-lane, from 158, Oxford-st.

East-Country-Dock, — on the S. side of Greenland, or the Commercial-Dock.

East-Court, East-St. Walworth, —4 doors on the R. from the High-st.

Eastcheap (Gt.)—the continuation of Cannon-st. to Grace-church-st.

Eastcheap (Little), — op. the last, 2d on the R. from London-bridge.

Eastern Dispensary, Gt. Ayliffe-St.—at 46, 6 doors W. of Red-lion-st. Whitechapel.

East-India Alms-Houses, Poplar,—⅓ of a mile on the L. from the Commercial-road, nearly opposite the Spotted-dog.

East-India-Chambers, Leadenhall-St.—at 23, 3 doors E. of Lime-st.

East-India-Dock, Blackwall.

East-India-Dock-Road, Limehouse,—on the L. east from the church.

East-India-Dock-Company's-House,—at 3, Lime-st. sq.

East-India-House, Leadenhall-St.—13 doors from Gracechurch-st.

East India Military-Fund-Office,—at 4, Lime-st.-sq.

East-India-Row, Poplar,—between Cotton-st. and Garden-st.

East-India-Tavern, Blackwall, —N. side the Dock-gate.

East-Lane, Poplar,—1st E. of the King's-road.

East-Lane, Kent-Road,—6th on the R. below the Bricklayers-arms: it leads to Walworth.

East-Lane, Bermondsey, — op. East-lane-stairs, ¼ of a mile below St. Saviour's dock.

East-Lane-Stairs, Bermondsey, —⅔ of a mile W. from Rotherhithe-church, nearly op. Union-stairs, Wapping.

East-London Water-Works-Office,—at 16, St. Helen's-pl. Bishopsgate.

I

Eastman's Court, Wentworth-St. Spitalfields,—at 16, 4th on the L. from Petticoat-lane.

East-Mews, East-St. Lambeth, —1st on the R. from East-place, Walcot-pl.

East-Passage, Cloth-Fair,—between Middle-st. and Long-lane.

East-Pl. Lambeth,—the W. side the Surrey-road, from Walnut-tree-walk to East-st.

East-Pl. (Little)—1st on the R. in East-street from the last.

East-Pl. East-St. West-Sq.—4 doors on the L. from the square.

East-Row, City-Rd.—op. Winkworth's-builds. 2d on the R. north of Old-st.

East-Row, Commercial-Road, Limehouse,—at the E. end of St. Ann's-row.

East-Smithfield. See Smithfield.

East-St. Manchester-Sq.—1st E. parallel to part of Baker-st. from 4, Blandford-st. to David-st.

East-St. Red-Lion-Sq.—6th on the L. from 71, High-Holborn, along Red-lion-st.

East-St. Spitalfields-Market,—middle of the E. side of it, to 35, Red-lion-st.

East-Street, Smart-St. Bethnal-Green,—1st on the L. from Green-st.

East-St. West-Sq. St. George's Fields,—at the S. E. corner.

East-St. Walworth,—that part of East-lane which is next to Walworth High-st.

East-St. Lambeth,—3d on the R. from the Stags, towards Kennington.

Estate and Mortgage-Office, —at 56, Pall Mall, near the Palace.

Eaton-Lane, Pimlico,—4th on the R. from Buckingham-gate.

Eaton-Pl. Little Eaton-St. Pimlico,—middle of the N. side.

Eaton-St. Pimlico,—3d on the R. from Buckingham-gate.

Eaton-St. (Upper)—the continuation of the last to Grosvenor-pl.

Eaton-St. (Little), Pimlico,— 2d on the R. from Buckingham-gate.

Ebden-Court, Pearl-Row,— 1st on the R. from Blackfriars-rd.

Ebenezer-Chapel,—N. side of Brill-pl. Sommers-town.

Ebenezer-Chapel, Shadwell High-St.—at 240, ten doors W. of Union-st.

Ebenezer-Chapel, Albion-St. Rotherhithe,—a few doors on the R. from Neptune-st.

Ebenezer-Pl. Commercial-Rd. Limehouse,—R. side, ⅓ of a mile below the church.

Ebenezer-Pl. Lambeth-Road,— 1st on the L. from the Obelisk.

Ebenezer-Pl. Cherry-Tree-Alley,—2d on the R. from 118, Bunhill-row.

Ebenezer-Pl. Kennington-Lane, —N. side, ⅓ of a mile from the Plough and Harrow, Newington.

Ebenezer - Row, Kennington - Lane,—1st on the R. from Newington.

Ebenezer - Sq. Stoney-Lane,—1st on the L. from Gravel-lane.

Ebenezer-St. London-Road, St. George's-Fields,—at 19, 1st on the R. from the Obelisk.

Ebenezer-St. Plumbers-Street, City-Road,—1st on the L. from Caroline-pl.

Ebury-House, Chelsea,—at the S. end of Ebury st.

Ebury-Pl. See Avery-farm-row.

Ebury-St. Five-Fields, Chelsea, —from Ecclestone - st. to Grosvenor-row.

Ecclestone-St.—5th on the R. ½ a mile from Buckingham-gate.

Eden - House, Paradise - Row, Chelsea,—11 doors on the L. from the Hospital.

Eden-St. Hampstead-Road,—1st on the L. from Tottenham-court.

Ede's-Yard, Brompton-Road,—2d on the R. from Knightsbridge.

Edington's-Wharf, Earl-Street, Blackfriars,—adjoining the bridge.

Edgware-Road, Tyburn-Turnpike,—W. end of Oxford-st. where the Nos. begin.

Edinburgh-Castle Coach-Office, Strand,—at 322, nearly op. Somerset-pl.

Edith-Place, Bird-Cage-Walk, Hackney-Road,—1st on the L. a few doors from the Nag's head.

Edmonds-Court, Princes-Street,

Soho,—at 27, 3d on the L. from Coventry-st.

Edmonds-Pl. Union-Street, St. George's Fields,—1st on the R. from the London-rd.

Edmond-St. Battle-Bridge, Saint Pancras,—N. side the Small-pox - hospital, W. side the Maiden-head.

Edmond-St. (Up.)—N. end of the last.

St. Edmond the King's Church, Lombard-St.—2 doors E. of Birchin-lane.

Edna-Pl. E. India-Dock-Road, —1st W. of the Dock-gate.

Edward's Alms-Houses, Church-St.—1st on the L. from Black-friars-road.

Edward-Court, Edward-St. Cavendish-Sq.—at 14, 4 doors S. of Foley-pl.

Edward's-Court, Oxendon-St.—5 doors from Coventry-st.

Edward's-Court, New Round-Court,—1st on the L. from 447, Strand.

Edward's-Mews, Duke-St.—at 37, 3d on the L. from 175, Oxford-st.

Edward-Pl. Old-St.-Road,—a few yards on the R. from the Curtain-road towards Shoreditch-church.

Edward's-Pl. Kingsland-Road, —by the turnpike, 3 doors N. of the Basing-house.

Edward-Pl. Hackney-Road,—R. side, adjoining Brighton-pl. ¼ of a mile from Shoreditch.

Edward-Pl. Westr.-Bridge-Rd. See Asylum-builds.

Edward-St. Hampstead-Road, —1st N. of the chapel.

Edward-St. Cavendish-Sq.—N. continuation of Bolsover-st. from 113, Oxford-st.

Edward-St. Manchester-Sq.— 3d in Duke-st. from 174, Oxford-st.

Edward-Street, Wardour-St.— at 95, 3d on the R. from 381, Oxford-st.

Edward-Street, Church-Street, Bethnal-Green,—at 116, ⅓ of a mile on the R. from 65, Shoreditch.

Edward-Street, Hare-St. Bethnal-Green,—at 28, 2d on the L. from 110, Brick-lane.

Edward-St. Stepney,—N. end Nelson-st. near the church.

Edward-St. Mile-End New-Town. See King Edward-st.

Edward-St. Blackfriars-Rd.— 3d on the L. from the bridge.

Edward-Street, Market-St. Kennington-Lane,—1st on the L. from White-hart-pl.

Edward-Yard, Edward-St. Cavendish-Sq.—at 14, 4 doors S. of Foley-pl.

Egleston's Builds. Paradise-Pl. Marybone,—1st on the R. from 6, Paradise-st.

Egleton's Pl. Twisters-Alley, —1st on the R. from 102, Bunhill-row.

Egypt (Little), Jamaica-Row, Bermondsey,—at 13, op. the Rev. Townsend's chapel.

Eight-Houses, Deptford Lower-Road,—op. the three milestone.

Elbow-Lane, Dowgate-Hill,— 3d on the R. from the Mansion-house, continuing down Walbrook.

Elbow-Lane (Little), Upper

Thames-St. — from 175, to the last.

Elbow-Lane, Shadwell High-St. —at 30, 7 doors E. of New Gravel-lane.

Elbow-Pl. City-Gardens,—1st on the L. from the City-rd.

Elder-Street, White-Lion-St. Spitalfields,—2d on the L. from 13, Norton-Falgate.

Elder-Court, Fleur-de-Lis-St.— 3 doors E. from 13, Elder-street.

Eldon-Builds. Bagnige-Wells,— first row on the L. from the Wells towards Pentonville.

Eleazer-Pl. Lambeth-Walk,— W. side, op. Chapman's gardens.

Elephant and Castle-Court, Whitechapel,—at 22, 8 doors W. of Red-lion-st.

Elephant and Castle-Court, Kent-St. Boro.—at 248, near ¼ of a mile on the R. from St. George's church.

Elephant and Castle, Newington,—a mile nearly S. from London-bridge.

Elephant-Lane, Rotherhithe,— at 344, Rotherhithe-st. 1st W. from the church.

Elephant-Stairs, Rotherhithe,— op. Elephant-lane, and op. Execution-dock, Wapping.

Elger's-Court, Three Tuns Alley,—2d on the L. from 99, Petticoat-lane.

Elgers-Pl. Essex-St.—the last on the L. from 105, Whitechapel.

Elgers-Sq. Essex-St. Whitechapel,—4th on the L. from 105, Whitechapel High-st.

Elizabeth-Court, Whitecross-

St.—at 146, 2d on the L. from Old-st.

Elizabeth - Court, Phœnix - St. Spitalfields,—2d on the L. from 38, Wheeler-st. leading into King-st.

Elizabeth - Court, Hickman's Folly, Dock-Head,—last on the R. towards Rotherhithe.

Elizabeth-Pl. Gt. Peter-Street, Westr.—6 doors E. of New Peter-st.

Elizabeth-Pl. Dog-Row, Mile-End,—10 doors on the L. from the turnpike.

Elizabeth-Pl. Queen Ann-St. Whitechapel,—2d on the L. from op. Court-st.

Elizabeth-Pl. Bethnal - Green, —1st on the L. from Patriot-sq. towards Hackney-road.

Elizabeth-Pl. Hoxton,—by the corner of Workhouse-lane, ½ a mile on the L. from Old-st.-road.

Elizabeth - Pl. Brook-St. Ratcliffe,—at 70,nearly op.Love-lane.

Elizabeth-Place, Prince-Road, Lambeth,—a few doors on the R.from Kennington-cross.

Elizabeth-Pl. Maid-Lane, Boro. —N. side, at the corner of Gravel-lane.

Elizabeth-Pl. Westr. - Bridge - Road, St. George's Fields,— from the Free-masons-school to Melina-pl.

Elizabeth-Place, Webber-Row, St.George's Fields,—between Ann's-pl. and Duke-st.

Elizabeth - Pl. Prospect - Row, Bermondsey,—on the E. side the Marine-crescent, nearly up Printers-pl.

Elizabeth-Row, George-Street, Bethnal-Green,—part of the W. side, near the N. W. corner of the Green.

Elizabeth-St. Hans-Pl. Sloane-St.—at 46, the N. W. corner, leading to Queen-st. and the High-road, Brompton.

Elizabeth-St. Hackney - Rd.— between Durham-pl. West and James's-pl.

Elliott's Court, Old-Bailey,—at 20, op. Newgate.

Elliott's Court, Elliott's Row, St. George's Fields,—1st on the R. from Prospect-pl.

Elliott's Row, Saint George's Fields,—3d on the L. from the Elephant and Castle towards West-sq.

Elliott's Row, Bethnal-Green-Road,—1st on the L. in White-st. from 72 in the said road.

Ellis-Sq. Penton-St. Walworth, —middle of the E. side.

Ellison-St. Petticoat-Lane,—20 doors on the L. from 41, Aldgate.

Elm - Court, Middle Temple-Lane,—2d on the L. from 6, Fleet-st.

Elm-Court, Elm-St. Gray's-Inn-Lane,—1st on the L. from 86, Gray's-inn-lane.

Elm-Court, Fetter-Lane,—at 108, middle of the W. side.

Elm-Pl. Fetter-Lane, Fleet-St. —at 105, middle of the W. side.

Elm-Pl. Walworth High-St. or Road,—⅓ of a mile on the L. from the Elephant and Castle.

Elm-Row, Love - Lane, Shadwell,—middle of the W. side.

Elm-St. Gray's-Inn-Lane,—at 85, near ⅓ of a mile on the R. from Holborn.

Elsworth-Pl. Golden-Lane, Barbican. See Colliers-Court.

Ely-Chapel, Ely-Pl. Holborn-Hill,—14 doors on the L. from 102, Holborn-hill.

Ely-Court, Holborn-Hill,—at 117, 7 doors W. of Hatton-garden.

Ely-Pl. Holborn-Hill,—at 101, 25 doors on the R. from Fleet-market.

Ely-Pl.-Mews,—at 20, the last on the L. from Holborn.

Ely-Pl. Whitechapel,—3d on the R. in Osborn-pl. from 20, Brick-lane.

Ely-Pl. King Edward-St. Mile-End New-Town,—at 11, middle of the E. side.

Ely-Pl. Bethnal-Green,—1st on the R. in Digby-street from Globe-st.

Ely-Pl. West-Sq. St. George's Fields,—from the N. W. corner to Prospect-pl.

Emanuel's Hospital, James-St. Westr.—⅓ of a mile on the R. from Buckingham-gate.

Embroiderers - Hall, Gutter - Lane,—at 36, 12 doors on the L. from 132, Cheapside.

Emery - Hill's Alms - Houses, Westr.—middle of Rochester-row.

Emigrant-Office,—at 10, Queen-st. Bloomsbury.

Endenbury Court, Gravel-Lane, Boro.—12 doors S. of Duke-street.

Engine-St. Piccadilly,—4th on the L. ¼ of a mile from Hyde-park.

England-Row, Poplar,—E. side Black-Boy-lane.

English - Copper - Company's - Wharf, — op. 215, Upper Thames-st. near St. Peter's-hill.

English's Wharf,—entrance by Water-st. behind the Crown and Anchor, 190, Strand.

Englishman Newspaper-Office, —at 5, Hind-court, 147, Fleet-street.

Enoch-Court, Goodman's Yard, —1st on the L. from 60, Minories.

Epping-Pl. Mile-End-Road,— on the S. side, by the turn-pike.

Equitable - Assurance - Office, Bridge-St. Blackfriars, — E. side, 8 doors from the bridge.

St. Ermin's Hill, Chapel-Street, Westr.—1st on the R. from the Broadway.

Essex-Alley, Essex-St. Whitechapel,—the continuation of it to Wentworth-st.

Essex-Court, Essex-St.—4th on the L. from 105, Whitechapel.

Essex-Court, Middle Temple-Lane,—at the back of Brick-court, 1st on the R. from 5, Fleet-st.

Essex-Pl. Rotherhithe-St.— at 170, 27 doors below Globe-stairs.

Essex-Pl. Well-St. Poplar,—2d on the L. from Robinhood-lane.

Essex-Pl. Lambeth, — adjoining the Workhouse, near Lambeth-butts.

Essex-St. Strand,—at 210, 1st on the L. from Temple-bar.

Essex-St. (Little),—1st on the R. in the last, from 210, Strand.

Essex-Street, Bouverie-St.—2d on the R. from 62, Fleet-st.

Essex-St. Kingsland-Road,—⅓ of a mile on the L. from Shoreditch-church, op. Gloucester-st. Hoxton.

Essex-St. (Little),—6 doors on the R. in the last from Kingsland-road.

Essex-Street, Whitechapel,—at 105, nearly op. Red-lion-st.

Essex-St. Mile-End Old-Town, —1st W. of Cannon-st.-road, from 38, Charlotte-st. to the Commercial-road.

Essex-Wharf,—at the bottom of Essex-street, from 210, Strand.

Etham-Pl. Kent-St.-Road,—N. side, near the turnpike, by the Bull.

St. Ethelburga's Church, Bishopsgate-Without, — behind 54, E. side of St. Helen's-pl.

Euston-Pl. New-Road, Tottenham-Court,—op. Southampton-pl.

Euston-Sq.—E. end of the last.

Europe-Pl. St. John's-Row, Ratcliffe-Row, St. Luke's,—middle of the S. side, 15 doors on the R. from 41, Brick-lane.

Evangelist-Court, Little Bridge-St. Blackfriars,—1st on the L. from Cock-court, Ludgate-hill.

Evans-Court, Basinghall-St.— at 45, 6 doors from London-wall.

Evan's-Place, Star-Corner, Bermondsey,—3d S. of Long-lane, op. the Grange-road.

Evan's Rents, Turners-Sq. Hoxton,—at the N. W. corner.

Evan's Row, Middlesex-Street, Sommers-Town,—part of the E. side.

Evan's Yd. Poplar,—1st E. of Wade's-pl.

Eve's-Place, Adam-St. Rotherhithe,—at 95, 2d on the L. from Neptune-st.

Evelyn's-Place, Oxford-St.—27 doors on the R. from St. Giles's.

Evelyn-Place, Deptford.—near the S. end of Victualling-Office-row.

Evening-Mail Newspaper-Office, Printing-House-Square, Blackfriars.

Evening-Post Newspaper-Office,—at 5, Hind-court, 147, Fleet-st.

Everard's Builds. Church-Lane, Whitechapel,—W. side, adjoining 66, Cable-st.

Everards-Pl.—1st on the L. in the last from Cable-st.

Everett-Street, Bernard-St.—at 48, 2d on the R. from Brunswick-sq.

Evesham-Buildings, Sommers-Town,—the continuation of Chalton-st. to Clarendon-sq.

Ewer's Buildings, White-Hart-Row, Kennington, — middle of the S. side.

Ewer-Street, Duke-St. Boro.— 1st on the R. from Queen-st. leading to Gravel-lane.

Ewing's Builds. Mile-End-Rd. —S. side, op. the New Globe, two miles from Aldgate.

Examiner Newspaper-Office,—

at 15, Beaufort - buildings, Strand.

Exchange-Alley. See Change.

Exchange (for Clothes), Rosemary-Lane. See Clothes.

Exchange (Coal), Thames - St. See Coal.

Exchange (Corn), Mark-Lane. See Corn.

Exchange (Royal). See Royal.

Exchange (Stock). See Stock.

Exchequer, New Palace-Yard, Westr.—S. E. corner, between Westr. - hall and the Thames.

Exchequer-Office, Lincoln's Inn, —at 9, 1st door on the L. from op. 56, Chancery-lane.

Exchequer-Office, Somerset-Pl. —1st door on the L. in the sq. from under the archway.

Exchequer-Office, King's Bench-Walk, Temple,—at the bottom of Mitre-court, on the R. from 44, Fleet-st.

Excise-Office, Old Broad-St.— between 22 and 33, and at 103, Bishopsgate-within.

Excise-Office, Tower-Hill,—W. side, the corner of Tower-st.

Execution-Dock,—at 243, Wapping, op. Princes-stairs, Rotherhithe.

Exeter - Change, Strand, — at 355, middle N. side.

Exeter-Court, Strand,—adjoining the E. side of the last.

Exeter-Place, Exeter-St. Hans-Town,—4th on the L. from 32, Sloane-st.

Exeter-Street, Catherine-St.— ten doors on the L. from 343, Strand.

Exeter-St. Hans-Town,—from

32, Sloane-st. to New-street, Brompton.

Exeter-St. (Little),—3d in the last from Sloane-st.

Eye and Ear Infirmary. See London Infirmary.

Eyre-Court, Eyre-St. — at 22, 1st on the L. from Leather-lane.

Eyre-Pl. Eyre-St.—at 10, 2d on the R. from Leather-lane.

Eyre-St. Leather - Lane, Holborn,—the continuation of it towards Coldbath-fields.

———

FACTORY-COURT, Rose - Lane, Spitalfields, — 1st on the R. from Wentworth-st.

Fair-St. Horselydown,—the E. continuation of Tooley-st. on the R.

Faircloth-Court, High-St. Lambeth,—1st on the L. from Broad-st.

Falcon - Brewery, Portpool - Lane,—10 doors on the R. from 52, Gray's-inn-lane.

Falcon-Wharf, Bankside,—$\frac{1}{4}$ of a mile below Blackfriars-bridge.

Falcon-Court, Fleet-St.—at 32, op. St. Dunstan's church, near Temple-bar.

Falcon-Court, Shoe-Lane,—at 84, $\frac{1}{8}$ of a mile on the L. from 129, Fleet-st.

Falcon-Court, Benjamin-Street, Clerkenwell,—1st on the R. from Turnmill-st.

Falcon-Court, High-St. Boro.— at 178, 3d N. of Mint-st.

Falcon-Court (Little), High-St. Boro.—W. continuation of the last.

Falcon-Court, White-St. Boro. —at 40, 2d E. of Kent-st.

Falcon-Court, Fishmongers-Alley, High-St. Boro.—1st on the R. from 234, by St. Margaret's hill.

Falcon-Place, Coppice-Row, Clerkenwell,—1st on the L. from Ray-st.

Falcon-Foundery, Bankside,— op. Falcon-wharf, by Gravellane.

Falcon-Sq.—E. end of Falcon-street.

Falcon-Street, Aldersgate-St.— at 16, 1st on the R. from St. Martin's-le-Grand.

Falcon-Yard, Portpool-Lane,— at 15, 2d on the R. from 53, Gray's-inn-lane.

Falconbridge-Court, Crown-St. Soho,—3 doors on the R. from the E. end of Oxford-street.

Falstaff-Yard, Kent-St. Boro. —at 141, ¼ mile on the L. from St. George's church.

Fan-Alley, Fan-St. Goswell-Street, St. Luke's,—at the E. end from 11, Goswell-st.

Fan-Alley, Webb-Sq.—at the N. side : it leads to Cock-hill and to 47, Wheeler-st.

Fan-Court, Fan-St.—1st on the L. from Goswell-st.

Fan-Court, Miles's Lane,—2 doors from 131, Up. Thames-street.

Fan-Court, Bakers-Row,—2d on the L. from 93, Whitechapel-road.

Fan-St.—between 106, E. side

of Aldersgate-st. and 1, Goswell-st.

Farm-Mews, Hill-St.—1st on the R. from Berkeley-sq.

Farm-St. Berkeley-Square,—the continuation of the last to Union-st.

Farmer's Journal Newspaper-Office,—at 49, Watling-st.

Farmer's-Rents, Crown-St. Soho, —1st on the L. from Oxford-street.

Farmer's-Row, Salmon-Lane, Limehouse,—R. side, ⅛ of a mile from the Commercial-rd.

Farmer-Street, High-St. Shadwell,—at 38, 18 doors W. of the church.

Farrer's-Rents, Bishopsgate-Without,—at 163, op. Wide-gate-st.

Farrer-Builds. Inner-Temple-Lane,—10 doors on the R. from 15, Fleet-st.

Farringdon-Within Charity-School, Bull and Mouth-St.— nearly facing Butcher-hall-lane.

Farthing-Alley, Up. East-Smithfield,—at 8, 14 doors on the L. east from Butcher-row.

Farthing-Alley, Jacob-St. Dock-Head, — middle of the S. side.

Farthing-Fields, New Gravel-Lane,—at 40, middle of the W. side.

Farthing-Hill, Farthing-St. Spitalfields,—the N. continuation of it, to Sclater-st.

Farthing-Street, Phœnix-St. Spitalfields,—1st on the L. from 39, Wheeler-st. leading to Club-row.

Fashion-St. Brick-Lane,—at

194,4th on the L. from White-chapel.

Faulkner's-Court, Cow-Cross, West-Smithfield,—4th on the R. from St. John-st.

Faulkner's-Pl. George-Passage, —1st on the R. from St. George's Market.

Feathers-Court, Drury-Lane,— at 86, 2d on the L. from the New-church, Strand.

Feathers-Court, High-Holborn, —at 264, nearly op. Red-lion-street.

Feathers-Court, Fox-Court,—5 doors on the L. from 10, Gray's-inn-lane.

Feathers-Court, Castle-St.Beth-nal-Green,—1st on the R. from the back of Shoreditch-church.

Feathers-Mews, Old Millman-St. Bedford-Row,—N. conti-nuation of it, to Long's-yard.

Feathers-Yard, Oxford-St.—at 336, ½ mile on the L. from St. Giles's.

Featherbed-Lane, Fetter-Lane, —18 doors on the R. from 180, Fleet-st.

Featherstone-Builds. High-Hol-born,—at 62, 8 doors E. of Red-lion-st.

Featherstone - Builds. Salmon-Lane, Limehouse,—1st on the R. from the Commercial-road.

Featherstone - Court, Feather-stone-St.—at 46, 2d on the R. from the City-road.

Featherstone-St. City-Road,— 1st on the L. from Finsbury-square.

Felix-St. Hackney - Road,—2d

on the L. from Cambridge-heath turnpike towards Shore-ditch.

Felix-St. Bridge-Road, Lambeth, —2d on the R. from Westr.-bridge.

Fellowship-Hall, St. Mary's-Hill, Lower Thames-St.—at 17, 3 doors on the L. from op. Billingsgate.

Fell-Street, Wood-St.—at 71, 6th on the L. from 122, Cheap-side.

Fen-Court, Fenchurch-St.—at 125, op. Mincing-lane.

Fen - Office, Tanfield- Court, Temple,—at 3, on the S. side.

Fenchurch-Builds. Fenchurch-St.—at 108, 2d on the R. from Aldgate.

Fenchurch - Chambers, Fen-church-St.—at 63, four doors east of London-st.

Fenchurch-Street, Gracechurch-St.—3d on the R. from Lon-don-bridge.

Fendal - St. Grange-Road,—2d on the L. from Bermondsey New-road.

Fenwick-Court, High-Holborn, —at 291, 17 doors W. of Chancery-lane.

Ferguson's-Rents, Snow's-Fields, —the 3d on the L. from 238, Bermondsey-st.

Ferry-St. Lambeth,—1st S. to the church, extending from High-st. to Fore-st.

Fetter-Lane, Fleet-St.—at 180, 6 doors E. of St. Dunstan's-church.

Field-Builds. Battle-Bridge,— E. end of Fifteenfoot-lane, Gray's-inn-lane.

Field-Court, Gray's-Inn-Sq.—at the S. W. corner, also the N. end of Fullwood's rents.

Field-Court, Field-Lane, Holborn,—the 1st on the R. from 83, Holborn-hill.

Field - Court, Ducking - Pond-Lane, Whitechapel,—5th on the R. from Court-st.

Field-Lane, Holborn-Hill,—at 83, 6 doors on the R. from Fleet-market.

Field-Pl. Battle-Bridge,—S. end of Field-terrace.

Field-St. Battle-Bridge,—1st on the R. from the Turnpike, by the Bell, towards Clerkenwell.

Field-Street, Poplar High-St.—½ a mile on the L. from the Commercial-road, 2d below the East-India alms-houses.

Field-Terrace, Battle-Bridge,—from the Bell by the Turnpike, towards Clerkenwell.

Fieldgate-Street, Whitechapel-Road,—at 266, 2d on the R. below the church.

Fife's-Court, Fleet-St. Bethnal-Green,—3d on the R. from George-st.

Fife's - Gardens, Granby - Pl. Lambeth Lower Marsh,—from Granby-pl. to Vine-st. Narrow-wall.

Fifteen-Foot-Lane, Gray's-Inn-Lane,—1st on the L. from the Turnpike, Battle-bridge.

Fig-Tree-Court, Temple,—entrance by 3d on the L. in Temple-lane from 6, Fleet-street.

Fig-Tree-Court, Barbican,—at 15, 2d on the R. from 77, Aldersgate-st.

Filacer, Court of,—at 4, Elm-Court, Temple, 2d door on the R. from op. Fountain-court, Middle Temple-lane, Fleet-st.

Finch-Builds. Ewer-St. Boro.—at the E. end of it, 4 doors on the L. from Duke-st. or from the W. end of Queen-street.

Finch-Court, Poplar High-St.—1st east of the E. India alms-houses.

Finch-Lane, Cornhill,—at 80, ten doors E. of the Royal-Exchange.

Finch-St. Whitechapel,—at the S. end of Dowsing-pl. Osborn-pl. Brick-lane.

Finch-Yard, Poplar,—2d on the L. below North-st.

Finchet's-Builds. Ewer-St. Boro.—1st on the L. from Duke-street.

Findall-St. See Fendal.

Finmore - Court, Blue-Anchor-Yard,—3d on the R. from 48, Rosemary-lane.

Finnemore-Court, Artillery-St. Boro.—op. the S. side of St. John's church.

Finnemore's-Rents, Russell-St.—1st on the L. from 90, Bermondsey-st.

Finsbury-Court. See Finsbury-Passage.

Finsbury-Dispensary,—at 123, St. John's-st. 12 doors S. of Corporation-row.

Finsbury - Dispensary (New),—35, West Smithfield.

Finsbury - Market,—at the E. end of Christopher-st. from the N. E. corner of Finsbury-square.

Finsbury - Passage, Wilson-St.
Moorfields,—op. Princes-st.
N. E. corner of Finsbury-
square.

Finsbury-Pl. Moorfields,—from
the N. W. corner to Finsbury-
square.

Finsbury-Sq.—on the N. side of
Moorfields, ¼ of a mile W.
from 148, Bishopsgate, along
Sun-st.

Finsbury-Street, Chiswell-St.—at
36, 1st on the L. from the sq.

Finsbury-Terrace, City-Road,
—R. side, ⅕ of a mile from
the sq. op. Featherstone-st.

Fire-Ball-Court, Houndsditch,
—at 131, middle of the N.
side.

First-Fruits-Office, Inner-Temple-Lane,—at 10, on the R.
from 15, Fleet-st.

Fish-St. (Old).—from Bread-st.-
Hill to Lambeth-Hill, S. end
of the Old-change.

Fish-St.-Hill (Old), late Labour-
in-vain-Hill,—at 6, Old Fish-
st. by the church.

Fish - St. - Hill,—from Gracechurch-st. to London-bridge.

Fisher's Alms-Houses, Dog-Row,
Mile-End,—3 doors on the L.
from the Turnpike.

Fisher's-Alley, Dorset-St. Fleet-
St.—at 62, 2d on the R. from
Salisbury-sq.

Fisher's-Alley, Petticoat-Lane,
—3d on the R. north of Wentworth-st.

Fisher's-Court, Broad-Street, St.
Giles's,——12 doors from
Drury-lane.

Fisher's-Court, Eagle-St. Red-
Lion-Sq.—7 doors on the L.
from Red-lion-st.

Fisher-St. Red-Lion-Sq.—S. W.
corner to Kingsgate-st.

Fishmonger's - Alley, High-St.
Boro.—at 235, nine doors S.
of St. Margaret's-hill.

Fishmongers Alms-Houses, Newington,—op. the Elephant
and Castle.

Fishmongers-Hall, Up. Thames-
St.—10 doors W. of London-
bridge.

Fishmongers - Passage, Fenchurch - St.—from 118, to
Billiter-sq.

Fitchet's-Court, Noble-St. Foster-Lane,—3 doors on the
L. from Falcon-sq.

Fitzroy - Chapel, London-St.—
9 doors on the R. from Tottenham-court-road.

Fitzroy-Market,—1st on the R.
in Grafton-st. from Tottenham-court-road.

Fitzroy - Mews, Hertford - St.
Fitzroy-Sq.—3 doors on the
L. from London-st.

Fitzroy - Pl. New - Road,—op.
Fitzroy-st. from the sq.

Fitzroy-Pl. (Upper),—N. continuation of the last.

Fitzroy - Row, Fitzroy-Pl.—1st
on the L. from the New-rd.

Fitzroy-Sq.—W. end of Grafton-st. from 119, Totten-
ham-court-road.

Fitzroy-St. Fitzroy-Sq.—S. E.
corner.

Fitzroy-St. (Upper),—N. E. corner, op. the last.

Fives-Court, Saint Martin's-St.
Leicester - Sq.—4 doors on
the R. from Whitcomb-st.

Fives-Court, St. Dunstan's-Alley,—at 7, three doors on the
R. from St. Dunstan's-hill.

Fives-Court, Mansel-St. Goodman's-Fields,—at 13, 5 doors
N. of Swan-st.

Five-Bell - Court, Wheeler-St.
Spitalfields,—at 43, nearly
facing Webb-sq.

Five-Bell - Pl. Three Colt - St.
Limehouse,—op. the E. side
of the church.

Five-Bell-Court, Bermondsey-
Sq.—on the W. side, leading
to Star-corner.

Five-Constable-Row, Mile-End,
—a few yards on the L. east
from the Turnpike.

Five-Fields, Chelsea,—between
Grosvenor-pl. at the back of
the Queen's Gardens, and
Sloane-st.

Five-Field-Row. See Ebury-
Street.

Five-Foot-Lane, Up. Thames-
St.—at 203, leading to 7,
Old Fish-st.

Five-Foot-Lane, Bermondsey.
See Russell-St.

Five-Garden-Row, Artillery-St.
St. John's, Boro. See Finnemore-Court.

Five-Houses-Corner, Tyson-St.
Bethnal - Green,—ten doors
from 52, Church-st; op. Brick-
lane.

Five-Inkhorn - Court, White -
chapel,—at 91, 3d W. of
Osborn-st.

Flask-Row, Five-Fields, Chelsea,—from the Old Red-lion
to Avery-row.

Fleet - Gardens, Horseferry -
Road, Westminster,—W. side
of Marsham-st.

Fleet-Lane, Fleet-Market,—at
16, 1st on the R. from Ludgate-hill.

Fleet-Market,—between Ludgate-hill and Fleet-st. extending to Holborn-bridge.

Fleet-Prison, Fleet-Market,—4
doors on the R. from Ludgate-
hill.

Fleet - Row, Eyre-St.—at 15,
4th on the R. from Leather-
lane.

Fleet-St. Temple-Bar,—E. side,
where there are Nos. 1 and
206, to Fleet-market.

Fleet-St. Spitalfields,—1st S.
parallel to St. John-st. Brick-
lane, from George-st. to Fleet-
st.-hill.

Fleet-St.-Hill, St. John-Street,
Bethnal-Green,—3d on the
R. from 105, Brick-lane.

Flemish - St. Tower - Hill,—E.
side, 2d on the R. from Iron-
gate.

Fletcher's - Court, Church-St.
St. Giles's,—1st E. of Buck-
bridge-st.

Fletcher-Row, Vineyard-Gar-
dens, Clerkenwell,—2d on
the R. from Bowling-green-
lane.

Fletcher's-Ways, Shadwell,—1st
E. of Shadwell - dock, op.
the Surrey - canal, Rotherhithe.

Flint - Street, Higlers-St.—4th
on the R. from Blackfriars-
road.

Flint-St. East-Lane, Walworth,
—the 5th on the R. from the
Kent-road.

Floating-Dock, Rotherhithe,—
⅛ of a mile E. of Rotherhithe-
church, op. King Edward-
stairs, Wapping.

Flower and Dean-St. Spitalfields,—at 200, Brick-lane,
K

3d on the L. from 74, White-chapel.

Flower-de-Luce-Court, Gray's-Inn-Lane,—at 85, ⅓ of a mile on the R. from Holborn.

Flower-de-Luce-Court, Fleet-St.—at 179, on the E. side Fetter-lane.

Flower-de-Lis-Court, Shoemakers-Row,—at 2, the 3d on the L. from Creed-lane, Ludgate-street.

Flower-de-Lis-Court,St.Peter's-Lane, West-Smithfield,—the continuation of New-court.

Flower-de-Lis-Court, Turnmill-St. Clerkenwell,—2d on the L. from Cow-cross.

Flower-de-Luce-Court,Houndsditch,—at 111, nearly op. St. Mary-Axe.

Flower-de-Lis-Court, Shoreditch,—at 10, 13 doors on the R. north of White-lion-st.

Flower-de-Lis-St. Spitalfields,—E. continuation of the last, to 72, Wheeler-st. op. Great Pearl-st.

Flower-Pot, Coach-Office,—at 115, Bishopsgate-within, corner of Threadneedle-st.

Floyd's-Court, Black-Swan-Alley,—1st on the L. from London-wall.

Fludyer-St. Westr.—2d S. of the Horse-guards.

Flushing-Court, Lower East-Smithfield,—a few doors W. of Hermitage-bridge.

Flying-Horse-Court, Maiden-Lane,—4 doors on the R. from 110, Wood-st.

Flying-Horse-Yard, Grub-St. Cripplegate,—at 58, 13 doors on the R. from 97, Fore-st.

Flying-Horse-Yard, Rose and Crown-Court,—2d on the L. from the N. E. corner of Moorfields.

Flying-Horse-Yard, Crown-St. Finsbury,—1st on the L. from Wilson-st.

Flying-Horse-Yard,Half-Moon-St.—1st on the L. from 170, Bishopsgate-st.

Flying-Horse-Yard, Worship-St.—2d on the R. from the Curtain-road, towards Paul-street.

Flying-Horse-Yard, Camomile-St. Bishopsgate,—at 25, 1st on the L. from 1, Bishopsgate-st.

Flying-Horse-Yard, Brick-Lane, Spitalfields,—at 31, opposite Fashion-st.

Flying-Horse-Yard, Blackman-St. Boro.—at 31,the 5th from St. George's-church.

Flying-Horse-Yard, Stamford-St.—1st on the L. from Black-friars-road.

Foley-House, Chandos-St. Cavendish-Sq.—middle of the E. side.

Foley-Pl. Gt. Portland-St.—at 33, 6th on the L. from 102, Oxford-st.

Foley-St.—the W. end of the last from 27, Gt. Titchfield-st. (late Queen Ann-st. E.)

Foley-Yard, Foley-Pl.—at 23, W. side Gt. Portland-st.

Fore-St. Cripplegate,—from the S. W. corner of Moorfields to Red-cross-st.

Fore-St. Limehouse,—continuation of Narrow-st. from the 2d Drawbridge to Three-colts-st.

Fore-St. Lambeth,—from the church to New-st. near Vauxhall.

Fore and Aft-Dock, Bermondsey-Wall,—E. side of East-lane-stairs.

Fort-Pl. Lambeth,—corner of Bird-st. and South-st. West-square.

Fort-Pl. Grange-Road, Bermondsey,—part of the S. side, near the Turnpike and Blue-anchor-road.

Fort-St. Old Artillery-Ground, —the N. end of Duke-st. from 38, Union-st.

Foss-Side Warehouses, Tower-Hill,—on the E. side, extending to Iron-gate.

Foster's Builds. Whitecross-St. St. Luke's,—at 123, 6 doors south of Banner-st.

Foster's Builds. Shoreditch,— entrance by 133, op. Church-st. : it leads into King John's court.

Forsters Court, Lombard-St. Boro.—3 doors W. of Mint-street.

Foster-Lane, Cheapside,—at 148, 8 doors from Newgate-street.

Foster-St. op. Rose and Crown-Alley,—from the N. E. corner of Moorfields.

Foster's Yard, High-St. Marybone,—1st on the L. from the New-road.

Foulk's Builds. Bethnal-Green-Road,—behind the George on the N. side of Wilmot-square.

Founders-Court, Lothbury,—10 doors east from Coleman-street.

Founders-Hall-Chapel,—N. end the last.

Foundery-Place, Bowling-green-Row, Hoxton,—1st on the L. from op. Haberdashers-alms-houses.

Foundery-Row,—on the E. side the last.

Foundling-Hospital, Guilford-St.—20 doors on the R. from Gray's-inn-lane.

Fountain-Alley, Maid-Lane, Boro.—the N. end of Castle-lane.

Fountain-Court, Strand,—at 104, $\frac{3}{8}$ of a mile on the R. from Charing-cross.

Fountain-Court, Middle-Temple-Lane,—2d on the R. from 5, Fleet-st.

Fountain-Court, Cheapside,— 24 doors on the R. from St. Paul's-church-yard.

Fountain-Court, Aldermanbury, —2 doors on the R. from Milk-st.

Fountain-Court, Old Bethlem, —1st on the L. from 199, Bishopsgate.

Fountain-Court, Virginia-St. Bethnal-Green,—middle of the N. side, at the back of the Fountain Public-house.

Fountain-Court, Minories,—at 20, 3d on the L. from Aidgate.

Fountain-Court, New-St. Dock-Head,—14 doors on the L. from the E. end of Fair-st.

Fountain-Court, Lambeth-Walk,—2d N. of King-st.

Fountain-Gardens, Lambeth,— entrance by the last.

Fountain-Gardens, Crab-Tree-Row, Bethnal-Green, — the

3d on the R. from Hackney-road.

Fountain-Pl. City-Road,—part of the L. side, $\frac{3}{8}$ of a mile from Finsbury-sq.

Fountain-Pl. (Upper),—the W. continuation of the last.

Fountain-Stairs, Bermondsey-Wall,—N. end of Salisbury-st. from Jamaica-row.

Four Swans-Inn, Bishopsgate,—at 83, S. side the church.

Fowk's Builds. Gt. Tower-St.—at 25, nearly op. Mark-lane.

Fowlers-Rents, Poplar,—N.end of Cottage-st.

Fox-Alley,Princes-St. Lambeth,—middle of the W. side.

Fox-Builds. Kent-St. Boro.—at 37, 2d on the L. from St. George's church.

Fox-Court, Gray's-Inn-Lane,—10 doors on the R. from Holborn.

Fox-Court,Ray-St.Clerkenwell,—10 doors on the L. from the green.

Fox-Court, Long-Lane. See Three Fox.

Fox-Court, Petticoat-Lane,—E. side, 9 doors S. from Went-worth-street, opposite Stoney lane.

Fox-Court, Gun-Alley,—at the E. end of Wapping-church.

Fox's Lane, Shadwell High-St.—at 55, E. side the church.

Fox and Goose-Yard, London-Wall,—3 doors E. of Basing-hall-st.

Fox and Goose-Yard, Coleman-St. Shadwell,—3 doors W. of Star-st.

Fox and Hounds-Yard,Swallow-

St.—3 doors from 323, Ox-ford-st.

Fox and Hounds-Yard, Totten-ham-Court-Road,—at 197, op. the chapel.

Fox and Hounds-Yard, Curtain-Road,—2d on the R. from Old-st.-road.

Fox and Hounds-Yard, Bish-opsgate-Without,—at 62, by Union-st.

Fox and Knot-Court,Cow-Lane,—at 42, 10 doors on the L. from Snow-hill.

Fox and Knot-Yard,—bottom of the last.

Fox-Pl. Fox-Court,—3 doors on the L. from 10,Gray's-inn-lane.

Fox-Ordinary-Court, Nicholas-Lane,—12 doors on the R. from 24, Lombard-st.

Fozard's Yard, Park-Lane,—5th on the R. from Picca-dilly.

Frame-Work-Knitters Alms-Houses, Kingsland-Road,—E. side, $\frac{3}{4}$ of a mile on the R. from Shoreditch-church.

Frances-Court, Maiden-Lane, Covent-Garden,—at 33, mid-dle N. side.

Francis-Court, Berkeley-Street, Clerkenwell,—4 doors on the L. from St. John's lane.

Frances-Court, Lambeth-Walk,—between King-street and Union-st.

Francis-Pl. Francis-St.—9 doors on the R. from Tottenham-court-road.

Francis-Pl. Hare-Walk, Kings-land-Road,—1st on the R. from op. the Ironmongers-alms-houses.

Francis-Pl. Princes-St.—2d on the L. from Baker's row, 9½, Whitechapel-road.

Frances - Pl. Westr. - Bridge-Road, Lambeth,—N. side the Asylum.

Francis - Pl. Palmers - Village, Westr.—E. end of Goodman's gardens.

Francis-St. Tottenham-Court-Road,—at 192, 6th on the R. from Oxford-st.

Francis-St. Golden-Sq.—the N. continuation of Air-st. from 27, Piccadilly.

Frances-St. Westr.-Bridge-Rd. Lambeth,—op. the N. side the Asylum.

Francis St. High-Street, Newington,-nearly op. the church.

Franklin's Court, Robinson's Lane, Chelsea,—at 23, the 1st on the R. from Paradise-row.

Franklin's Row, Chelsea,—E. side the Hospital, from Royal Hospital-row to Turk's row.

Frazer's Court, Green-Walk, Blackfriars - Road,—S. side of Christ-church.

Frederick-Pl. Hampstead-Road, —W. side, by Frederick-st.

Frederick Pl. Goswell-St.-Road, —E. side, from the New River to Sidney-st.

Frederick-Pl. Old-Jewry,—1st on the L. from 81, Cheapside.

Frederick-Pl. Newington,—2d S. from the church.

Frederick-Pl. Walworth-Common,—op. the chapel, Villa-place.

Frederick - Row, Goswell-St.-Road,—1st from Sidney-st. towards Islington.

Frederick-St. Hampstead-Road, —4th on the L. from Tottenham-court.

Free-Chapel, West-St. 7 Dials, —middle of the N. side.

Free-Court, Princes-St. Lambeth,—3d on the R. from Broad-st.

Free-Passage-Alley, Cock-Hill, Ratcliffe,—1st on the R. from High-st. Shadwell.

Freebrothers-Wharf, Millbank-St. Westr.—op. Vine-st.

Freeman's Builds. Walworth-Common,—nearly op. the Paul's head.

Freeman's Court, Cheapside,—at 102, nearly op. Bow-church.

Freeman's Court, Cornhill,—at 83, 6 doors E. of the Royal-Exchange.

Freeman's Court, Old Montague-St.—2d on the L. from Osborn-st.

Freeman's Court, Freeman's Lane, Horselydown,—at 19, 1st on the L. from Back-st.

Freeman's Lane, Horselydown, —2d on the L. from the E. end of Tooley-st.

Freeman's Wharf, Horselydown, —entrance by Potter's fields, E. end of Tooley-st.

Freeman's Wharf, Millbank-St. Westr. — between Fairbrother's and Hadley's wharfs, op. Vine-st.

Freemasons Charity-School,—a few doors on the R. from the Obelisk towards Westminster-bridge.

K 3

Freemasons Tavern and Hall, —at 62, Gt. Queen-st. Lincoln's-inn-fields.

Free-School -St., Horselydown, —E. continuation of Tooley-st. betweenBack-st. and Fair-street.

French-Alley, Goswell-St.—at 21, 15 doors S. from Old-st.

French-Alley, St. Luke's,—on the S. side the French-hospital.

French-Alley, Shoreditch,—at 150, nearly op. the Jane Shore.

French-Chapel, Threadneedle-St.—facing Finch-lane.

French-Chapel, St. John-St. Spitalfields,—14 doors on the L. from 105, Brick-lane.

French-Court,Threadneedle-St. —8 doors on the L. from the Royal-Exchange.

French-Court, Gt. Hermitage-St. Wapping,—at 47, middle of the N. side.

French-Court, Old-St.-Sq. Saint Luke's,—at the N. E. corner.

French - Hospital, Pesthouse - Row, Old-St.—a few doors on the L. from the W. end of St. Luke's hospital.

French-Row, City-Road. See Bath-St. and Ratcliffe-Row.

French - Yard, Bowling-Green-Lane, Clerkenwell,—2d on the R. from Coppice-row.

French-Horn-Yard, High-Holborn,—at 88, W. side Red-lion-st.

French-Horn-Yard, Crutched-Friars,—at 26, 2d on the R. from Mark-lane.

Fresh-Wharf, Lower Thames-St.—2 doors from London-bridge.

Friar's Alley, Wood - St.—12 doors on the R. from Cheap-side.

Friar's Alley, Up. Thames-St. —at 82, nearly op. Dowgate-hill.

Friar's Pl. Higglers-Lane,—1st on the R. from Blackfriars-road.

Friars-St. and Courts. See Fryer.

Friars - St. Blackfriars - Road. See Higglers-Lane.

Friary, St. James's Palace,—the E. end, from Pall-mall to St. James's Park.

Friday-St. Cheapside,—at 37, 2d on the R. from St. Paul's church-yard.

Friday-St. (Little),—at 42, in the last, 2d on the L. from Cheapside.

Friendly - Institution, for the Cure of Cancers, &c. Kent-Road,—¼ of a mile on the L. from the Elephant and Castle, nearly opposite Rodney's buildings.

Friendly-Pl.Sun-Tavern-Fields, Shadwell,—S. side the Rope-ground, entrance by the 1st on the R. in King David-lane from No. 193, Shadwell High-street.

Friendly - Pl. Benchers-Walk, Blackfriars-Road,—W. side, adjoining Bennett's row.

Friendly-Pl. Coleman-St.—1st on the L. from 84, Bunhill-row.

Friendly-Pl.Castle-St.Finsbury-

Sq.—2 doors on the R. from 18, Paul-st.

Friendly-Pl. Mile-End-Road,—E. side the Bell and Mackarel, op. Savile-row.

Friendly-Pl. Vine-St. Narrow-Wall,Lambeth,—between the Belvedere-brewery and Neptune-pl.

Friendly-Pl. Kent-Road,—part of the R. side, ⅛ of a mile below the Bricklayers-arms.

Friendly-Pl. Chapel-Street, St. George's East,——between Mary-st. and Duke-st.

Friendly-Row,Old Gravel-Lane, —at 114, 2d on the R. from Ratcliffe-highway.

Frith - Street, Soho - Square,—S. W. corner, and 48, Old Compton-st.

Frog-Island, Nightingale-Lane, Limehouse,—at the N. end, near the New-cut.

Frog - Island, Narrow - Wall, Lambeth,—near the New-bridge.

Frogwell-Court, Charterhouse-Lane,—1st on the R. from 100, St. John-street.

Frost's Alley, Old Montague-St.—1st on the L. from Osborn-st.

Fryer's Alley, Up. Thames-St. See Friar.

Fry's Alley, Middle Turning, Shadwell,—1st on the R. from 67, Shakespear's walk.

Fryers-Court, Gt. Tower-Hill, —at 48,3 doors S. of Coopers-row.

Fryers-Hill, Gt. Hermitage-St. Wapping,—at 41, middle of the N. side.

Fryer's St. Shoemakers-Row,—

1st on the L. west from Creed-lane.

Frying-Pan-Alley, Turnmill-St. Clerkenwell,—at 60, 2d on the L. from the Sessions-House.

Frying-Pan - Alley, Petticoat-Lane,—1st on the L. from Widegate-st. Bishopsgate.

Frying-Pan-Alley, Princes-St. Lambeth,—2d on the R. from Broad-street.

Frying Pan-Alley, Maze, Boro. —10 doors on the L. from 195, Tooley-st.

Frying-Pan-Alley, High-St. Boro.—at 287, 4th on the R. from London-bridge.

Fugen's Row, Palmer's Village, Westr.—N. end of Paradise-row.

Fullbrook's Buildings,North-St. Pentonville, — 10 doors on the R. from the Turnpike.

Fuller's Alms - Houses, Mile-End-Road,—entrance by Eagle-pl.

Fuller's Alms-Houses, Hoxton-Town,—L. side, ⅛ of a mile from Old-st.-road.

Fuller's Alms - Houses, Gloucester-St. Hoxton,— middle of the S. side.

Fuller's Alms-Houses, Old-St.-Road,—6 doors on the L. from op. Shoreditch-church.

Fuller's Court, Up. E.-Smith-field,—at 35, 1st on the L. from Tower-hill.

Fuller's Rents, Princes-Street, Westr.—1st on the L. from Tothill-st.

Fuller's Rents, Ducking-Pond-Lane, Whitechapel,—6 doors W. of North-st.

Fuller's Rents, Poplar. See Fowler.

Fuller-Street, Church-St. Bethnal-Green,—at 115, $\frac{3}{8}$ of a mile on the R. from 65, Shoreditch.

Fuller-Street, Hare-St. Bethnal-Green,—at 37, 3d on the L. from 110, Brick-lane.

Fullwood's Rents, High-Holborn, — at 33, nearly op. Chancery-lane.

Fulmer's Row, Palmer's Village, Westr.—1st on the R. in Providence-row from Paradise-row.

Furnival's Inn, Holborn, — at 135, 6 doors W. of Leather-lane.

Furnival's-Inn-Court, Holborn, —at 137, on the W. side of Furnival's-inn.

Furnival's-Inn - Gardens, — on the N. side of Furnival's-inn.

Fye-Foot-Lane, Up. Thames-St. See Five-Foot.

———

GAGEN's COURT, Poplar, —behind the White-Horse, by North-st.

Gainsford-St. Horselydown,— at 34, Horselydown-lane, 10 doors on the R. from Backst. E. end of Tooley-st.

Galley-Quay, Lower-Thames-St.—1st E. of the Custom-house.

Gardens (Great), St. Catherine's Lane,—5th on the L. from 50, Upper East-Smithfield.

Garden-Court, Middle Temple-Lane,—3d on the R. from 6, Fleet-st.

Garden-Court, Baldwin's Gardens,—at 15, 1st on the R. from 31, Gray's-inn-lane.

Garden - Court, Gt. Turnstile, —at 10, 9 doors on the L. from 283, High-Holborn.

Garden-Court, Hull-St. Ratcliffe-Row, St. Luke's,— behind Garden-terrace.

Garden-Court, Petticoat-Lane, —at 14, 2d on the L. from Aldgate.

Garden-Court, Risby's Rope-Walk, Limehouse,—middle of the N. side.

Garden-Court, George-Yard,— 1st on the R. from 88, Whitechapel.

Garden-Court, Red-Lion-Alley, Cow-Cross,—1st on the L. from 70, Cow-cross.

Garden-Court, Lee's-Court, St. Catherine's Lane,—N. side, leading to Gt.-Gardens.

Garden-Court, Mason-St. Lambeth,—1st on the L. from 30, Bridge-road.

Garden-Court, Garden - Row, London - Road, — middle of the E. side.

Garden-Passage, Willow-Walk, —2d on the L. from Tabernacle-sq.

Garden-Pl. Union-St. Bethnal-Green,—3d on the L. from the N. E. corner of Thorold-square.

Garden-Place, Chicksand - St. Mile-End New-Town,—1st on the L. from 16, High-st.

Garden-Pl.—1st on the L. in Garden-court, from 14, Petticoat-lane.

Garden-Pl. Well-St. Poplar,—
1st on the L. from Robin-
hood-lane.

Garden-Pl. Vine - St. Narrow-
Wall, Lambeth,—by the Belvedere-brewery.

Garden-Pl. Blackman-St. Boro.
—at 59, nearly op. the King's
Bench.

Garden-Pl. St. George's Fields,
—S. end of Temple-st. near
the Elephant and Castle.

Garden-Place, Walworth,—by
Hampton-st. ¼ of a mile on
the R. from the Elephant
and Castle.

Garden-Row, Chelsea,—at the
W. end of Turk's-row, by the
Hospital-wall.

Garden-Row, Hoopers - Court,
Brompton,——W. side of
North-st.

Garden-Row, Brick-Lane, St.
Luke's,—at 43, near the N.
end.

Garden-Row, Old-St.-Road,—
part of the S. side, between
St. Agnes - le-Clair and the
Curtain-road.

Garden-Row, Gibraltar-Walk,
Bethnal-Green,—part of the
E. side of King-st.

Garden-Row, North-St. Whitechapel,—1st on the R. north
of Ducking-Pond - lane, op.
the Jews' burying-ground.

Garden-Row, Stangate-St. Lambeth,—at 12, middle of the
S. side.

Garden-Row, Duke-Street, St.
George's Fields,—2d on the
R. from the Obelisk.

Garden-Row, London-Road,—
1st on the R. from the Obelisk.

Garden-Row, Walworth, — at
the back of Garden-place.

Garden-Row, Snow's Fields,—
5th on the L. from 138, Bermondsey-st.

Garden-St. (Gt.) Whitechapel-
Road,—at 50, 4th on the L.
below the church.

Garden-St. Well-St. Poplar,—
3d on the L. from Robinhood-
lane.

Garden-Terrace, Hull Street,
Ratcliffe-Row, St. Luke's,—
at the N. end, on the R.

Garden-Walk, Vineyard - Gardens, Clerkenwell, — 2d on
the R. from Bowling-green-
lane.

Garden-Walk, Willow-Walk,—
1st on the L. from Tabernacle-sq.

Gardner's Lane, York - Street,
Westr.—3d on the L. from
Queen-sq.

Gardner's Lane, King - Street,
Westr.—5th on the R. from
the Horse-Guards.

Gardner's Lane, High - Timber-
Street, Upper Thames-St.—
middle of the S. side.

Garlick-Hill, Up. Thames - St.
—from 190, to Bow-lane,
Cheapside.

Garmouth-Row, Kent-Road,—
S. end of Rodney-row.

Garrett's Alms-Houses, Elder-
St. See Weavers.

Garter-Court, Barbican, — at
36, 5 doors on the R. from
Red-cross-st.

Gascoigne-Pl. Crabtree - Row,
Bethnal-Green,—1st on the
R. from Hackney-road.

Gate-St. Lincoln's-Inn -Fields,
—N. W. corner by Queen-st.

Gate-Yard, America-Sq. — op. Hanover-court, from 109, Minories.

Gatward's Builds. Hill-St. Finsbury,—1st on the R. 6 doors from 9, Windmill-st.

Gaywood-St. London-Road,— 2d on the L. from the Elephant and Castle.

Gaywood-Court, Gaywood-St. —2d on the L. from the London-road.

Gazette-Office,—at 46, Parliament-st. Westr.

Gees-Court. See Jees.

Gee-St. Sommers-Town, — at the N. W. corner of Clarendon-sq.

Gee-St. Goswell-Street,—at 52, 17 doors N. of Old-st.

General-Agency-Office,—at 34, Gt. George-st. Westr.

General - Dispensary, Aldersgate-St.—at 38, 10 doors S. of Jewin-st.

General-Evening - Post, Newspaper-Office,—at 28, Paternoster-Row.

George-Alley, Field-Lane,—1st on the L. from 84, Holbornhill, op. Chick-lane.

George-Alley, Fleet-Market,— at 70, middle of the W. side.

George-Alley, Up. Thames-St. — at 98, op. Lawrence - Pountney-lane.

George-Alley, Pelham-St. Spitalfields,— at 31, 10 doors from Brick-lane.

George-Alley, Lower Shadwell, —at 64, E. side Shadwell-Dock.

George-Alley, Lombard-St.—at 52, 10 doors on the R. from Gracechurch-st.

St. George's Builds. Hoxton-Sq.—at the N. W. corner.

George's Chapel, George - St. Chelsea,—a few yards on the L. from Royal Hospital-row.

St. George's Church, Hanover-Sq.—the corner of Maddox-st. George-st.

St. George's Church, Hart-St. Bloomsbury,—$\frac{1}{8}$ of a mile on the R. from the S. side of Bloomsbury-sq.

St. George the Martyr's Church, Queen-Sq.—S. W. corner.

St. George's Church, Botolph-Lane,—7 doors from Eastcheap.

St. George's Church in the East, —8 doors on the R. in Cannon-st. from 143, Ratcliffe-highway.

St. George's Church, High-St. Boro.—$\frac{1}{2}$ a mile on the L. from London-bridge.

George-Cottage (Lower), George St. Chelsea,—a few yards on the R. from Sloane-sq.

George-Court, Perkin's Rents, Westr.—middle of the E. side.

George-Court, Gt. Saint-Ann's-St. Westr.—middle of E. side.

George-Court, David-St. Marybone,—op. East-st.

George-Court, Strand,—at 50, on the R. 50 doors from Charing-cross.

George-Court, Piccadilly,—at 40, op. St. James's church.

George-Court, Dorset-St. White Friars,—at 66, last on the R. from 82, Fleet-st.

George-Court, Water-Lane,— 4th on the R. from 67, Fleet-street.

George - Court, George - Yard,

Hatton-Wall,—at the N. E. corner.

George-Court, Rupert-St. Haymarket,—1st on the R. from Coventry-st.

George-Court, Cross - St. Carnaby - Market,—at 4, middle of the N. side.

George-Court, George - Alley, Field-Lane,—the middle of the S. side.

George-Court, Bennett's Hill, —at 5, 1st on the L. from 217, Upper Thames-st.

George-Court, Old Fish-St.-Hill, —behind 204, Up. Thamesstreet.

George-Court, St. John's Lane, W. Smithfield,—2d on the L. from St. John's-st.

George-Court, Stoney-Lane,— 3 doors on the R. from 38, Petticoat-lane.

St. George's Court, John-St.— 2d on the R. from Cannonst.-road.

George-Court, George-St. Spitalfields,—1st on the R. from Wentworth-st.

George-Court, George-St. Mile-End New-Town,—2 doors on the L. south from Chicksandstreet.

George-Court, White-Horse-St. Ratcliffe,—7 doors on the L. from Butcher-row.

George-Court, White-St. Boro. —at 35, 3d E. of Kent-st.

George-Court, Horselydown,— 3 doors W. from Georgestairs and Thomas-st.

St. George's Fields, Southwark, — the district around the Obelisk, Blackfriars-road.

George - Gardens, Bethnal -

Green-Road,—by the N. E. corner of Wilmot-sq.

St. George's Gardens, Webber-Row,—corner of Duke-st.

St. George's Hospital,—W. side the turnpike, Hyde park-corner.

George-Inn, Haymarket,— at 67, 10 doors N. of the Operahouse.

George and Blue-Boar-Inn,—at 270, High-Holborn, op. Redlion-st.

George-Inn, West - Smithfield, —at 16, 8 doors N. from Husier-lane.

George-Inn, Aldermanbury,— behind 22, op. Addle-st.

George-Inn, Boro High-St.—at 70, near St. Margaret's-hill.

George-Inn, Snow-Hill,—at 82, 6 doors from Fleet-market.

George Coach-Office, Old-Bailey,—W. side, 12 doors on the R. from Skinner-st.

George and Gate Coach-Office, —at 15, Gracechurch-st. 8 doors N. from Lombard-st.

George-Lane, Pudding-Lane,— 5 doors from Eastcheap.

St. George's Mall,—2d on the L. from the Obelisk towards the Asylum.

George's Market, Oxford-St.— at 289, between Davis-st. and James-st.

St. George's Market, London-Rd.—3d on the L. from the Obelisk.

St. George's New-Town, St. George's Fields, — op. the Elephant and Castle.

St. George's Parade, North Audley-St.—7 doors on the L. from 263, Oxford-st.

St. George's Passage, Saint George's Market, St. George's Fields,—N. E. corner.

George-Passage, Pelham-Street, Spitalfields,—at 30, 9 doors on the L. from 62, Brick-lane.

George-Pl. George-Row, Neat Houses, Chelsea,—12 doors from the bridge at Pimlico.

St. George's Pl. New-Road, St. George's East,—the corner of Cannon-st. by the turn-pike.

St. George's Place, Blackfriars-Road,—E. side, from Surrey-chapel towards the Obelisk.

St. George's Pl. Duke-Street, St. George's Fields,—N. end, by Barons-builds.

George-Pl. White-St. Boro.—at 37, by Long-lane.

St. George's Pl. Walworth High-St.—the corner of Amelia-street.

George-Pl. Wood-St. Westr.—3d on the R. from Millbank-street.

George-Pl. Paradise-Row, Chelsea,—nearly op. the Physic-gardens.

St. George's Road,—from the Elephant and Castle to Waller-pl. Lambeth-chapel.

St. George's Row, Neat-Houses, Chelsea,—1st row over the bridge, at Pimlico.

St. George's Row, Uxbridge-Road,—N. side, $\frac{1}{6}$ of a mile on the R. from Tyburn-turn-pike.

St. George's Row, Blackfriars-Rd.—7th on the R. from the bridge.

St. George's Row, Westminster-Bridge - Road, St. George's Fields. See Tower-St.

George-Row, Bermondsey,—1st on the R. below Mill-stairs, leading to the Neck-inger-turnpike.

George's Row, Locks - Fields, Walworth,—the continuation of Townsend-st.

George-Row, City-Road,—$\frac{5}{8}$ of a mile on the L. from Finsbury-sq. entering by Nelson-st.

George's-Row-Buildings,—W. side the last, and E. side of Pitman's-builds.

George's Sq. Hoxton,—by the Coffee-house, N. E. corner of Hoxton-sq.

St. George's Sq. Saint George's Mall, St. George's Fields,—middle of the E. side.

George-Stairs, Horselydown,—N. end of Thomas-st. near $\frac{1}{4}$ of a mile below London-bridge.

George-Stairs, Greenland-Lock,—$\frac{1}{6}$ of a mile below the said dock.

George-St. (Upper), Sloane-Sq. Chelsea,—N. E. corner.

George-St. (Lower), Sloane-Sq.—S. E. corner, leading to Royal Hospital-row.

George-Street, James-St West.—between the E. end of it and York-st.

George-St. (Gt.) Westr.—the continuation of Bridge-st. to St. James's Park.

George-St. (Little), Westr.—12 doors in the last from St. James's Park.

George-St. Adelphi,—continuation of George-court from 50, Strand.

George-Street, St. James's Sq.
—from the S. W. corner to
44, Pall-mall.

George-Street, James-St. Lisson-
Green,—3d E. of Bell-st.

George-St. (Upper), Edgware-
Road,—at 44, 4th on the R.
from Tyburn-turnpike.

George-St. Portman-Sq.—2d in
Baker-st. from the N. E. corner, leading to the last.

George-St. (Little),—at 39 in
the last, 2d W. of Baker-st.

George-St. Gt. Portland-Street,
Marybone,—1st E. to it from
12, Foley-pl. to 23, Upper
Marybone-st.

George-Street, Oxford-St.—at
267, 3d on the R. from Park-
lane.

George-St. Hanover-Sq.—middle of the S. side, to 25, Conduit-street.

George-St. Tottenham-Court,
—1st E. of Hampstead-road.

George-Street, Broad-St. Bloomsbury,—at 25, middle of the
N. side.

George-St. Battle-Bridge,—1st
S. of Britannia-st. and op.
Weston-st. Pentonville.

George-St. Foster-Lane,—at
28, 1st on the L. from Cheapside.

George-St. Mansion-House,—
E. side, from Lombard-st. to
Bearbinder-lane.

George-St. Shoreditch,—at 208,
15 doors S. of Holywell-
lane.

George-Street, Union-St. Bethnal-Green,—3d on the R.
from the N. E. corner of
Thorold-sq.

George-St. (Little), Bethnal-

Green,—N. W. corner of
the Green, near Patriot-sq.

George-St. (Great), extends from
the last towards Hackney-
road.

George-St. Bethnal-Green, or
Spitalfields,—1st on the L.
in Carter-st. op. Hanbury's
brewery, from 68, Brick-
lane.

George-St. Spitalfields,—1st on
the R. in Wentworth-st. from
Osborn-st. Whitechapel.

George-St. Gt. Tower-Hill,—N.
side, behind Postern-row.

George-St. Minories,—at 142,
1st on the R. from Ald-
gate.

George-St. (Little),—1st on the
R. in the last from the Minories.

George-St. Mile-End New
Town,—op. Black-lion-yard
from 38, Whitechapel-road.

George-St. Commercial-Road,
Ratcliffe,—6 doors W. of
White Horse-st.

St. George's Street, St. George's
Fields. See Tower-St.

George-St. Blackfriars-Road,—
5th on the L. from the
bridge.

George-St. (New),—E. end of
the last.

George-St. (Old) Gt. Suffolk-
St. Boro.—4th on the R.
from 80, Blackman-st.

George-St. Trafalgar-Street,
Walworth,—1st on the L.
from Beckford-row.

St. George's Terrace, Commercial-Road,—4th on the L.
from Cannon-st.-road towards
Whitechapel.

St. George's (Hanover-Square)
L

Workhouse,—at 102, Mount-st. Berkeley-sq.

St. George's East Workhouse, —back of the Iron-foundry, near 27, Old Gravel-lane.

George-Yard, Duke-St. Grosvenor-Sq.—at 39, 3d on the R. from 276, Oxford-st.

George-Yard, Haymarket,—at 68, 9 doors from the Opera-house.

George-Yard, Titchborne-St.— 4 doors from Coventry-st.

George-Yard, Piccadilly,—at 32, ⅝ of a mile on the R. from the Haymarket.

George-Yard, Crown-St. Soho, —3d on the R. from Oxford-street.

George-Yard, Princes-St. Soho. —at 14, between King-st. and Gerrard-st.

George-Yard, Whitcomb-St.— at the corner of Panton-st. Haymarket.

George-Yard, Long-Acre,—14 doors from Drury-lane.

George-Yard, Drury-Lane,—12 doors on the L. from the Strand.

George - Yard, Coal-Yard,—4 doors on the L. from 185, Drury-lane.

George-Yard, Little Queen-St. —12 doors from 223, High-Holborn.

George - Yard, Holborn,— 17 doors W. of Gray's-inn-lane.

George - Yard, Leather-Lane, Holborn,—at 80, 4 doors S. from Baldwin's Gardens.

George-Yard, Hatton-Wall,—at 22, nearly op. Hatton-garden.

George - Yard, Islington,—17

doors on the R. from the City-road.

George - Yard, Dorset-St.—at 18, the 3d on the L. from Salisbury-sq. Fleet-st.

George-Yard, Water-Lane,—at 18, the 4th on the R. from 67, Fleet-st.

George-Yard, Up. Thames-St. —at 37, nearly op. Lambeth-hill.

George-Yard, Coleman-St.—4 doors from London-wall.

George-Yard, Seacoal-Lane,— 1st on the L. from 40, Fleet-lane.

George-Yard, Grub-St. Cripplegate,—the 3d on the L. from 93, Fore-st.

George - Yard, Old-Street, St. Luke's,—at 108, 12 doors W. of the church.

George-Yard, Golden-Lane,— at 45, 5th on the R. from Barbican.

George - Yard, Bow-Lane,—8 doors on the L. from 59, Cheapside.

George-Yard, Lombard-St.—at 56, 1st E. of Birchin-lane.

George-Yard, Coleman-St. Lothbury,—at 56, E. side Bell-alley.

George-Yard, Crown-St. Hoxton,—2d on the L. from Old-st.-road.

George-Yard, Whitechapel,— at 88, 2d W. of Osborn-st.

George-Yard, Aldgate,—at 1, the corner of Fenchurch-st.

George-Yard, New-Road, St. George's East,—op. Bett's st.

George-Yard, Brook-St. Ratcliffe,—at 115, E. side of Blue Anchor-alley.

George - Yard, Fore-St. Lambeth,—12 doors on the L. from the church.

George-Yard, Red-cross-Street, Boro.—at 47, the 4th S. of Union-st.

George - Yard (Old), Kent-St. Boro.—at 241, ¼ of a mile on the R. from St. George's church.

George - Yard (New),—at the back of the last.

George and Catherine-Wheel-Yard, Bishopsgate-Without, —at 80, ten doors N. of Union-st.

George and Catherine-Wheel-Inn, Bishopsgate. See the last article.

German-Chapel (Lutheran), Savoy,—entrance by 125,Strand.

German - Chapel (Calvinistic), Savoy, — entrance by 137, Strand, 1st W. of Somerset-place.

German-Chapel, Trinity-Lane, —6 doors on the L. west from Bow-lane, Cheapside.

German-Chapel, Little Ayliffe-St. Goodman's Fields,—2d door on the L. from Red-lion-street.

German-Chapel, Brown's Lane, Spitalfields,—3 doors E. from Wood-st.

German-School,Savoy,—behind 124, Strand.

German and English - School, Little Ayliffe-St. Goodman's-Fields,—at 26,a few doors on the L. east from Red-lion-st.

Gerrard's Hall - Inn, Basing-Lane,—3 doors from 40, Bread-st. Cheapside.

Gerrard - Street, Princes - St. Soho,—2d on the R. north from Coventry-st.

Gibb's Yard, Mount - St.—at 115, 2d on the L. from the N. W. corner of Berkeley-square.

Gibbon's Court, New-Lane, Horselydown,—7 doors on the L. from 32, E. end of Gainsford-st.

Gibbon's Rents, Bermondsey-St.—26 doors on the L. from Tooley-st.

Gibbon'sWharf,—25,Millbank-st. Westr.

Gibraltar - Chapel, Samuel-St. Bethnal - Green, — 3 doors from 73, Church-st.

Gibraltar-Court,Elliott's Court, —the last on the L. from 20, Old Bailey.

Gibraltar Fields,Bethnal Green, —a district now chiefly built upon, situate between the middle of Church - st. and Birdcage-walk.

Gibraltar - Gardens, Bethnal-Green,—on the N. side the Gibraltar, Gibraltar-walk.

Gibraltar-Pl. Gibraltar-Row,St. George's Fields,—at 20, middle of the E. side.

Gibraltar - Row, St. George's Fields,—4th on the L. from the Elephant and Castle, towards West-sq.

Gibraltar - Walk, Church - St. Bethnal-Green,—entrance at 73, ⅓ of a mile on the L. from 65, Shoreditch.

Gibson's Court, Marybone-St. Piccadilly,—at 39, 2d on the L. from the Haymarket.

Gibson's Court, Horselydown.
See Gibbon's.

Gilbert's Builds. Vauxhall,—W.
side of the gardens.

Gilbert's Builds. Westr.-Bridge-
Road,—N. side, by Tower-st.
op. the Asylum.

Gilbert's Builds. St. George's
Fields,—the continuation of
Tower-st. on the N. side.

Gilbert's Court, Tower-Street,
St. George's Fields,—at 29,
op. Duke-st.

Gilbert's Passage, Clare-Market,—from the middle of the
E. side, to Portugal-st.

Gilbert-St.—the E. side of
Clare-Market.

Gilbert - St. Bloomsbury,—1st
S. to Gt. Russell-st. from
Queen-st. to Bury-st.

St. Giles's Alms-Houses,—S.
end of Smart's builds. 185,
High-Holborn.

St. Giles's Church,—S. side,
High-st. St. Giles's.

St. Giles's Church, Cripplegate,
—near the N. end of Wood-st.

Giles - Pl. Battle - Bridge, St.
Pancras,—N. W. corner of
the Small-Pox-hospital.

St. Giles's Workhouse,—at 55,
Broad-st. St. Giles's, also in
the Vinegar-yard, behind.

Gilham's Court, Hickman's
Folly,—1st on the L. from
Dock-head.

Gilham's Court, Rotherhithe,—
2d on the R. a few doors below Cherry-garden-stairs.

Gilham's Fields, Worship-St.
Finsbury,—5 doors from the
Curtain-road towards Paul-
street.

Gill - St. Commercial - Road,
Limehouse,—2d on the R.
below the church.

Giltspur-Street, Newgate-St.—
last on the R. from Cheapside.

Giltspur - St. Compter, — the
large building adjoining Newgate-st.

Gimber's Rents, Snow's Fields,
—the 1st on the L. from
239, Bermondsey-st.

Gin-Alley, Queen-St. Ratcliffe,—
1st on the R. below London-st.

Gingerbread-Court, Lamb's Alley,—1st on the R. from 144,
Bishopsgate.

Girdler's Alms-Houses,—by the
N. W. corner of St. Luke's-
hospital.

Girdler's Hall, Basinghall-St.—
at 40, near London-wall.

Glasgow-Wharf, Lower E. Smithfield,—near ¼ mile below the
Tower, op. Burr-st.

Glasshouse-Alley, Whitefriars,
—on the W. side of Water-
lane, Fleet-st.

Glasshouse Court, Mutton-Lane,
Clerkenwell,—3 doors from
the Green.

Glasshouse-Court, Glasshouse-
Yard, Minories,—entrance of
the said yard.

Glasshouse-Court, Glasshouse-
St.—1st on the R. from
Vauxhall-walk.

Glasshouse-St. Swallow-Street,
Piccadilly,—at 20, 2d on the
R. from 43, Piccadilly.

Glasshouse-St. Goswell-Street,
—at 108, 2d N. of Long-
lane.

Glasshouse-St. Vauxhall-Walk,

—N. side the Gardens, Vauxhall-walk.

Glasshouse-Wharf, Cock-H'll, Ratcliffe,—6 doors on the R. from High-st. Shadwell.

Glasshouse-Yard, Blackfriars, —on the E. side of Apothecaries-hall, entrance by Playhouse-yard.

Glasshouse-Yard, Goswell-St.— entrance by 108, nearly op. Fan-st.

Glasshouse - Yard, Goodman's Yard,—1st on the R. from 60, Minories.

Glasshouse - Yard, Sampson's Gardens, Wapping,—2d on the R. in Redmaid's lane from Hermitage-yard.

Glasshouse-Yard, Gravel-Lane, Boro.—12 doors N. from Dake-st.

Glasshouse - Yard, Boro.-Market,—1st on the L. from York-st. towards the church.

Glasshouse - Yard, Cock-Hill, Ratcliffe,—at 120, 10 doors on the L. from High-st. Shadwell.

Glean - Alley, Tooley-St.—at 218, 5th on the R. from London-bridge.

Globe-Alley, Narrow-St. Limehouse,—at 54, 2d on the L. below the Drawbridge.

Globe-Court, Fish-St.-Hill,—at 22, nearly op. the Monument.

Globe-Court, Wapping-St.—at 58, 2 doors W. from Globe-street.

Globe-Court, Lambeth-Walk, —bottom of King-st. on the R. from the said walk.

Globe - Court, Ratcliffe-High-

way,—at 78, E. side Old Gravel-lane.

Globe-Court, Maid-Lane, Boro.—4th on the L. from Park-street.

Globe-House, Globe-Pl. Bethnal-Green,—a few doors on the L. from Green-st.

Globe-Insurance-Office, Cornhill,—5 doors on the R. from the Mansion-house, also near the Palace, Pall-mall.

Globe-Lane, Mile-End-Road,— near ½ a mile on the L. below the turnpike.

Globe Newspaper Office, Strand, —at 127, op. Exeter-change.

Globe-Pl. Bethnal-Green,—N. continuation of Globe-st. on the L. towards Hackney-road.

Globe-Pl. Westr.-Bridge-Road, Lambeth,—E. side, near the Marsh-gate.

Globe-Stairs,—at 104, Rotherhithe-st. ¾ of a mile below the church, op. Ratcliffe-cross.

Globe - Stairs-Alley,—op. the last.

Globe-St. Bethnal-Green,—1st on the R. from the Green, towards Green-st.

Globe-St. Wapping,—at 60, the 1st street west from the London-docks.

Globe - Terrace, Globe-Lane, Bethnal-Green,—part of the L. side, ⅕ mile from the Old Globe, Mile-end.

Globe-Yard, South-Molton-St. —at 55, middle of the N. side.

Globe-Yard,—N. end of Baker's-builds. Old Bethlem.

L 3

Globe-Yard, Lower Thames-St.
--at 58, op. the Custom-house.

Gloucester-Builds. Brompton,
--from Sloane-st. to Hooper's
court.

Gloucester-Builds. Albion-Pl.
Walworth,—from the E. end
to Weymouth-st. Kent-road.

Gloucester-Court, St. James's
St.—9 doors on the R. from
the Palace.

Gloucester-Court, Whitecross-
Street, St. Luke's,—at 114,
middle of the E. side.

Gloucester-Court (Little),—at
the E. end of the last.

Gloucester-Court, Curriers-
Row, Blackfriars,—1st on the
L. from Ireland-yard, St. An-
drew's-hill.

Gloucester-House, Up. Grosvenor-St.—17 doors on the L.
from Grosvenor-sq.

Gloucester-Mews West, George-
St. Portman-Sq.—3 doors W.
of 71, Gloucester-pl.

Gloucester-Mews North, New-
Road, Marybone,—at 24,
Gloucester-pl.

Gloucester-Mews East, King-St.
Portman-Sq.—at 13, 3d on
the R. from 69, Baker-st.

Gloucester-Pl. New-Road,
Marybone,—N. side, op.
Salisbury-pl. and Cumber-
land-pl.

Gloucester-Pl. Portman-Sq.—
from the N. W. corner to the
New-road.

Gloucester-Pl. Holborn,—at
147, 6 doors E. from Gray's-
inn-lane.

Gloucester-Pl. Vauxhall-Walk,
—adjoining Glasshouse-st.
near the gardens.

Gloucester-Pl. (New), Vauxhall-
Walk,—N. end of the last.

Gloucester-Pl. Kent-Road,—
N. side the Asylum for the
Deaf and Dumb.

Gloucester-Row, Walworth,—
from the E. end of Prospect-
row, to Union-row, Kent-
road.

Gloucester-Pl. Walworth-Common,—W. end of Westmore-
land-row.

Gloucester-Row,—at the W.
end of the last.

Gloucester-Row, Gloucester-
St. Hoxton,—parallel to the
N. side of it.

Gloucester-St. Curtain-Road,
Shoreditch,—2d on the R.
from Worship-st.

Gloucester-St. Portman-Sq.—
from the N. W. corner to
George-st.

Gloucester-St. (Little), George-
St. Portman-Sq.—15 doors
on the R. from Baker-st.

Gloucester-Street, Queen-Sq.—
S. W. corner to Kingsgate-st.
Holborn.

Gloucester-St. Hoxton,—⅓ of a
mile on the L. from Old-st.-
road.

Gloucester-St. Mile-End Old-
Town,—from 59, Charlotte-
st. to the Commercial-road.

Gloucester-St. (New), Vauxhall-
Walk,—¼ of a mile on the R.
from Lambeth-butts.

Gloucester-St. Oakley-Street,
Lambeth,—1st on the R. from
Westr.-bridge-road.

Gloucester-Terrace, Hoxton,—
the N. continuation of Haberdashers walk, on the R.

Gloucester-Terrace, Cannon-

St.-Road,—W. side, from the Commercial-road to Charlotte-st.

Gloucestershire - Pl. Salmon's Lane, Limehouse, — 4th on the L. from the Commercial-road.

Glovers - Hall - Court, Beech-Lane, Barbican,—7 doors on the L. from 3, Whitecross-street.

Goat - Street, Free - School-St. Horselydown,—2d on the L. from the E. end of Tooley-st.

Goat-Yard, Whitecross Street, St. Luke's,—at 163, 3d on the R. from Old-st.

Goat-Yard, Blackman-St. Boro. —at 25, 4th on the L. from St. George's church.

Goat-Yd. Queen-St. Horsely-down,—2d on the L. from Freeschool-st.

Goater's Farm, New-St. Newington,—2d on the R. from op. the chapel.

Goby's Court, Denmark-St.— 10 doors on the R. from 153, Ratcliffe-highway.

Goddards-Rents, Webb-Sq.— continuation of the N. side, entering by 47, Shoreditch.

Godfrey's Court, Milk-St.—at 24, 2d on the L. from Cheapside.

Godfrey's-Row, Mason-Street, Lambeth, — 3d on the L. from 30, Bridge-road.

Godliman-St. — the continuation of St. Paul's chain from 14, St. Paul's-church-yard.

Goff's Coal-Wharf, Whitehall, —entrance by Gt. Scotland-yard.

Gold or Gould-Sq. Coopers-

Row, Tower-Hill, — 1st on the L. from Crutched-friars.

Gold-St. King - Street, Saint George's East,—1st on both the R. and L. from 30, New-Gravel-lane.

Gold-St. Stepney-Green,—the continuation of Prospect-pl.

Golden-Builds.Strand,—at 169, nearly op the New-church.

Golden-Court, Golden-Lane,— at 117, 5th on the R. from Old-st.

Golden - Cross - Inn, Charing-Cross,—10 doors W. of St. Martin's-lane.

Golden - Lane, St. Luke's or Cripplegate,—2d on the L. in Barbican from 77, Aldersgate-st.

Golden-Pl. Drury - Lane, — at 138, middle of the E. side.

Golden-Place, Market-St. Kennington-Lane,—2d on the L. from White Hart-pl.

Golden-Sq.— $\frac{1}{3}$ of a mile N. from 28, Piccadilly, along Air-st. Francis-st. and John-street.

Golden - Fleece - Court, Minories,—2 doors on the L. from Aldgate.

Golden - Fleece - Yard, Tothill-St. Westr.—4th on the R. from the Abbey.

Golden - Griffin - Yard, Long-Lane,—at 19, 3d on the R. from Aldersgate-st.

Golden-Hart-Wharf, — bottom of Joiners-hall-lane, from 79, Up. Thames-st.

Golden-Horse-Yard, Oxford-St. —at 156, middle of the N. side.

Golden-Leg-Court, Cheapside,

—at 66, 3 doors W. of Queen-street.

Golden-Lion-Inn, Saint John-St.—at 111, 2d inn on the R. from Smithfield.

Golden-Lion-Yd. Gravel-Lane, Boro.—op. Price's-pl. Edward-st. Blackfriars-rd.

Golden-Lion-Court, Aldersgate-St.—4 doors N. from Falcon-square.

Goldsmiths-Alley, Charles-St.—2d on the L. from 174, Drury-lane.

Goldsmiths-Alms-Houses, Hackney-Road, — left side the foot-way, from the Nag's head to London-field.

Goldsmith-Court, Gt. New-St. Fetter-lane, — at 20, 2d on the L. from West-Harding-street.

Goldsmiths-Hall, Foster-Lane, —at 16, that number on the R. from Cheapside.

Goldsmiths-Pl. Hackney-Road, —op. the Nag's head, ¾ of a mile on the L. from Shore-ditch-church.

Goldsmiths-Row or Walk, — the continuation of the last.

Goldsmith-Row, East Harding-St. Fetter-Lane,—part of the S. side of it.

Goldsmith-Street, Gough-Sq.—N. W. corner, entrance by 145, Fleet-st.

Goldsmith-Street, Wood-St.—at 124, 10 doors on the L. from Cheapside.

Goldsworthy-Row, Deptford Lower-Road, —¼ of a mile on the R. from Paradise-row.

Goodge-St. Tottenham-Court-Road,—at 64, 3d on the L. from Oxford-st.

Goodman's Fields, Whitechapel,—a large district E. of the Minories.

Goodman's Green, Palmer's Village, — S. end of Goodman's-row.

Goodman's Gardens, Middlesex-Pl. Hackney-Road,—¼ of a mile on the L. from Shoreditch.

Goodman's Row, Palmer's Village, — 2d on the L. from Brewers-green.

Goodman's-Sq.—op. the E. end of Church-st. Blackfriars-Rd.

Goodman's Stile, Church-St.—2d on the R. from 72, Whitechapel.

Goodman's Yard, Minories,—at 60, 22 doors on the R. from Sparrow-corner, Tower-hill.

Goodwin's Court, St. Martin's Lane, Charing-Cross,—at 55, S. side New-st.

Goodwin and Powell's Wharf, Rotherhithe-wall,—E. side of Fountain-stairs.

Goose and Gridiron Coach-Office, St. Paul's Church-Yard, —behind 74, corner of London-House-yard.

Gossip-Builds. Ducking-Pond-Lane, Whitechapel,—4th on the R. from Court-st.

Goswell-Place, Goswell-St.-Rd.—E. side the turnpike, 1st on the R. from Goswell-st.

Goswell-St.—the continuation of Aldersgate-st. and St. Martin's le-grand, entering by 66, Newgate-st.

Goswell-St.-Rd.— continuation of Goswell-st. to Islington.

Goswell-Street-Repository,—2 doors N. of Fan-st.

Gough-House, Paradise - Row, Chelsea,—a few yards on the L. from the Hospital.

Gough-Sq. Fleet - St. — behind the middle of the N. side, entrance by 145 and 151.

Gould's Court, Lambeth Upper-Marsh,—nearly op. Staugate-street.

Gould's Hill, Shadwell High-St. —at 97, 6th E. of the church.

Gouldstone-Court, Three-Tun-Alley,—2d E. of New Goulstone-st.

Goulston-Sq.—N. end of Goulston-st.

Goulston-St. Whitechapel,—at 140, 1st 'E. of Petticoat-lane.

Goulston-St.(New),—the continuation of the last to Wentworth-st.

Gower- Mews, Gower - St.--5 doors on the L. from Bedford-sq.

Gower-Mews (Up.)—1st on the L. in Francis-st. from Gower-st. towards Tavistock-sq.

Gower's-Pl.Mill-Yard,—1st on the R. from 80, Cable-st.

Gower's-Row,— from the last to Gower's-walk.

Gower-St. Bedford-Sq.—from the N.E. corner to Francis-st.

Gower-St. (Upper),—continuation of the last.

Gower-St. North,—the continuation of the last to the New-road.

Gower's Walk, Church-Lane,

Whitechapel,—3 doors E. of Goodman's stile.

Govey's-Pl. Mile-End-Road,— by the Three Mackarel, nearly two miles on the L. from Aldgate.

Graces-Alley, Wellclose-Sq.— from the N. W. corner to Well-st.

Graces-Yd. Minories,—at 46, middle of the E. side.

Gracechurch-St.—N. continuation of Fish-st.-hill, London-bridge.

Grafton-Court,Paradise-Street, Marylebone,— 10 doors on the R. from 82, High-st.

Grafton-Mews, Grafton - St.— by the S. E. corner of Fitzroy-square.

Grafton-St. Tottenham-Court-Road, — at 120, 2d S. of the New-road.

Grafton-St. East,—op. the last.

Grafton-St. (Up.) Fitzroy-Sq.— S. W. corner.

Grafton-St. Soho, — N. continuation of Gerrard-street, to Monmouth-st.

Grafton-Street, Dover-St.—the continuation of it from 68, Piccadilly.

Grafton-Yard, Tottenham - Ct. —1st E. of the Hampstead-road.

Graham's Builds. Blue-Anchor-Alley,—1st and 2d on the L. from 108, Bunhill-row.

Granby's Builds. Drury-Lane, —at 111, N. side Whitehorse-yard.

Granby's Buildings, Vauxhall-Walk,—N. end, the corner of Lambeth-butts.

Granby-Gardens,—a few doors
on the R. in Artichoke-yard,
from 18, Lambeth-marsh.

Granby-Pl. Lambeth-Marsh,—
N. end of Artichoke-yard.

Granby-Row, Bethnal-Green-
Road,—1st on the L. in Abbey-st. from 92, said road.

Granby-Row, Granby-St. Bethnal-Green,—1st on the L.
from James-st.

Granby-St. James-Street, Bethnal-Green, — 1st on the R.
from 124, Church-st.

Grand-Junction-St.Whitefriars,
—the continuation of Bou-
verie-st. bearing to the L.
from 62, Fleet-st.

Grand-Junction-Wharf, White-
friars,—(Messrs. Harvey and
Napier's) at the S. end of the
last.

Grange-Court, Carey-St.—at
27, 1st on the R. from Portugal-st.

Grange-House-Lodge, Mi-
chael's-Grove, Brompton.

Grange-Road, Bermondsey,—
at Star-corner: it branches
off on the R. by Fort-pl. to
the Green-man, Kent road,
and on the L.to Jamaica-row.

Grange-Terrace, Grange-Road.
See Anderson's-Builds.

Grange-Walk, Bermondsey-Sq.
—from the S. E. corner, to
what was lately called the
Grange.

Grange-Yard, Carey-St.—at 31,
near Portugal-st.

Grantham-Pl. Park-Lane,—10
doors on the R. from Piccadilly.

Grasshopper-Court, White-

cross-Street, St. Luke's,—at
217, 3 doors N. of Beech-st.

Gravel-Lane, Houndsditch,—at
148, 10 doors from Aldgate-
church.

Gravel-Lane (Old), Ratcliffe-
Highway,—at 65, nearly op.
St. George's-church.

Gravel-Lane (New), Shadwell
High-St.—at 23, 1st E. of
Old Gravel-lane.

Gravel-Lane, Southwark,—1st
E. on both the R. and L.
from Surrey-chapel, Blackfriars-road.

Gravel-Walk, Blue-Anchor-Alley,—3d on the L. from 109,
Bunhill-row.

Grave's Alley, Poplar,—op. the
Town-hall.

Gray's Builds. Duke-St. Manchester-Sq.—at 28, 2d on the
L. from 174, Oxford-st.

Gray's Inn,—N. side of Holborn, op. Middle-row, and
W. side of Gray's-inn-lane.

Gray's-Inn-Gardens,—princi-
pal entrance at the N. end of
Fullwood's rents, from 24,
Holborn.

Gray's-Inn-Lane, Holborn,—
5th coach-turning on the R.
about ¼ of a mile W. from
Fleet-market.

Gray's-Inn-Lane (Little),—at
73, in the last, ½ of a mile on
the R. from Holborn.

Gray's-Inn-Passage, Red-Lion-
St.—18 doors on the R. from
71, High-Holborn.

Gray's-Inn-Place,—N. end of
Warwick-court, from 40,
High-Holborn.

Gray's-Inn-Square,—W. side of

Gray's-inn-lane, entrance op. 30.

Gray-Street, Duke-St.Manchester-Sq.—2d on the R. from 174, Oxford-st.

Gray-St. Blackfriars-Rd.—continuation of George's - row, from the John o'Groats to Baron's-builds.

Gray's Walk, Lambeth, — the W. continuation of East-st.

Gray's Yard, James-St. Manchester-Sq.—at 44, 2 doors N. of Gray-st.

Graystock-Pl. Fetter-Lane. See Greystock-Pl.

Great-Yard, Gun-Alley,—2d on the R. from 104, Wapping-street.

Great-Yd. Parish-St.—2d on the R. from the bottom of Tooley-st.

Greek's Court, Bermondsey-St. —39 doors on the L. from Tooley-st.

Greek-St. Soho-Sq. — from the S. E. corner to King-st.

Green-Bank, Wapping,—from the N. side the church to 160, Old Gravel-lane.

Green-Bank, Tooley-St.—at 31, —3 doors below Morgan's-lane.

Green's Builds.Lambeth-Marsh, —3d on the L. from Blackfriars-rd.

Green-Church-Yard, St. Catherine's,—on the S. side St. Catherine's-church.

Green-Court, Tothill-Fields, Westr.—behind the Horseguards-hospital, Rochester-row.

Green-Court, Coleman-St. — 9

doors on the R. from London-wall.

Green-Court, Green-Walk,— op. the E. end of Church-st. Blackfriars-rd.

Green-Park, St. James's Park, —from St. James's Park to Piccadilly.

Green-Pl. Green-St. Bethnal-Green, — by the Weavers-arms, ⅓ of a mile on the R. from the Green.

Green's Row, Chelsea,—op. the Hospital-wall, 2d on the L. in Smith-st. from the King's road.

Green's Row, Bermondsey New-Rd.—4th on the L. from the Bricklayers-arms.

Green's Row,Kennington-Road, Newington,—behind the Mansion-house Public-house.

Green-St. Leicester-Sq.—from the S.E. corner, to 6, Castle-st.

Green-Street, Theobald's Road, Red-Lion-Sq.—6 doors E. of Lamb's-conduit-st.

Green-Street, North Audley-St.—at 27, 2d on the R. from 262, Oxford-st.

Green's Court, Little Pulteney-St.—10 doors on the R. from Wardour-st.

Green-St. Bethnal-Green,—entrance by the S. E. corner of the Green, towards Bow-common.

Green-St. Church-St.—3 doors from Blackfriars-road.

Green-St. Bennet's Row,—3d on the R. from Blackfriars-road.

Green-St. (Up.) Higlers-Lane, —op. the last.

Green's Walk, James-St. Westminster, — E. side of Lady
Dacre's alms-houses.

Green-Walk, Christ - Church,
Surrey,—2d on the R. in
Holland-st. from Blackfriars-
bridge.

Green-Walk, Blackfriars-Road,
—3d on the R. from the
bridge.

Green-Walk, St. George's Fields.
See Green-St.

Green-Walk, Hickman's Folly,
Bermondsey,— the last on
the R. from Dock-head.

Green - Yard (for the City),
White-Cross-St. Cripplegate,
—at 34, 2d on the R. from
115, Fore-st.

Green-Yd. Pepper-Alley, Boro.
—1st on the L. from 314,
High-st.

Green-Yard, Up. East-Smithfield,—at the back of 110,
op. Nightingale-lane.

Green-Coat-School, Westr.—
S. side of Bridewell, by
Palmer's village.

Green-Dragon-Yard, King-St.
—at 37, 1st on the L. from
322, Oxford-st.

Green-Dragon-Court, Fore-St.
Cripplegate,—at 102, W. side
of Grub-st.

Green - Dragon - Court, Cow-
Lane, W. Smithfield,—at 43,
21 doors on the L. from
Fleet-market.

Green-Dragon-Court, St. Andrew's Hill, Blackfriars,—at
10, op. the church.

Green-Dragon-Yd. High-Holborn,—at 199, op. Blooms-
bury-court.

Green-Dragon-Yard, Worship-
St.—1st on the L. from 21,
Norton-falgate.

Green-Dragon-Yd. Whitechapel,—at 10, op. the church.

Green-Dragon-Alley, Wapping,
—at 194, 2 doors W. of New
Gravel-lane.

Green-Dragon-Alley, Narrow-
St. Limehouse,— 2d on the
L. below Turner's wharf.

Green-Dragon-Court, York-St.
Boro.—1st on the R. from
276, High-st.

Green-Dragon-Gardens, Spring-
Garden-Pl. Stepney,—2d on
the L. from the church.

Green - Dragon - Inn, Bishopsgate,—at 85, 20 doors S. of
the church.

Green-Dragon-Inn, Giltspur-St.
—1st gateway on the R.
from Newgate-st.

Green-Dragon-Coach-Office,—
at 56, Fleet-st. middle of the
S. side.

Greenfield-Street, Commercial-
Road,—4th on the L. from
Whitechapel.

Green-Gate-Court, Hampstead-
Road,—by the turnpike, N.
side the chapel.

Green-Gate-Gardens, Hackney-
Road,—⅕ of a mile on the
R. from Shoreditch, behind
the Green-gate.

Green-Gate-Yard, Curtain-Rd,
—1st on the L. from Wor-
ship-st.

Green-Arbour-Court, Lambeth-
Hill,—5 doors on the R. from
the Old-change.

Green - Harbour - Court, Old-
Bailey,—at 16, 5 doors from
Snow-hill.

Green-Harbour-Court (Little),

—a door or two S. of the last.

Green-Harbour - Court, Little Moorfields, — 5 doors from 62, Fore-st.

Green-Harbour-Court, French-Alley,—4th on the R. from 21, Goswell-st.

Greenhill's Rents, Saint John-St.—14 doors on the L. from 75, N. side of West-Smith-field.

Green-House - Row, Westmin-ster-Bridge-Rd.—N. side, by the Obelisk.

Greenland or Commercial-Dock, —at the lower part of Ro-therhithe, 3 miles from Lon-don-bridge.

Greenland-Pl. Lucas-St. Gray's Inn-Lane,—W. end, between Joseph-st. and Judd-st.

Green-Lettuce-Court, Fore-St. Cripplegate,—at 106, 6 doors W. of Grub-st.

Green-Lettuce - Lane, Cannon-St.—at 30, nearly op. Ab-church-lane.

Green-Man and Still Waggon-Office, Oxford-St. — at 324, corner of Swallow-st.--Coach-office is nearly opposite.

Green-Man-Yard, Coleman-St. —3 doors on the L. from London-wall.

Greenwich (Little), 43, Alders-gate-St. See Horn-Alley.

Greenwich-St. Dowgate,—bot-tom of Brewer-lane, from 83, Up. Thames-st.

Greenwood's Court, Nightin-gale-Lane,—at 25, 5th on the R. from 110, Up. E.-Smith-field.

Greenwood's Court, Harrow-

Alley, Houndsditch,—3d on the R. from White-st.

Greenwood's Rents, Angel-Sq. Bishopsgate, — west end of Slade's builds.

Gregg's Alley, Essex-St.—6th on the R. from 105, White-chapel.

Greigg's Court, Goodman's Yd. —2d on the L. from the Mi-nories.

Grieg's Gardens, Commercial-Rd.—N. side, by Doran's row.

Gregory's Builds. New-Road, St. George's East,—nearly op. Betts-street.

Gregory's Court, Corporation-Row, Clerkenwell, — 2d on the L. from St. John-st.

Gregory's Court, High-Holborn, —at 244, E. side Little Turn-stile.

Gregory's Pl. Half-Moon-Al-ley,—1st on the R. from 138, Aldersgate-st.

Gregory's Pl. Maze, Boro.—op. Dean-st. from 201, Tooley-st.

Gregory's Terrace, Hull-Street, St. Luke's,—N. end, op. the Market-garden.

Grenville-St. Brunswick-Sq.— from the S. W. corner, to 83, Gt. Guilford-st.

Grenville-St. Sommers - Town, —1st parallel to the N. side of Clarendon-sq.

Grenville-Mews,—at the back of the last.

Gresham - Alms - Houses,—be-hind 34, Whitecross-st. Crip-plegate.

Gresham-Pl. Moor-Lane, Crip-plegate,—at the N. end, on the L. from 37, Fore-st.

Gresham-Lecture-Room, Royal-
M

Exchange,—1st door on the R. in the Staircase from Cornhill.

Gresse-Mews, Gresse-St. Rathbone-Pl.—at 21, S. end.

Gresse-St. Rathbone-Pl. — 22 doors on the R. from 24, Oxford-st.

Greville-Street, Brook - Street, Brook's-Market,—1st on the R. from 140, Holborn-hill.

Greville-Court, Greville-St.—at 9, leading into Beauchampst. and Brook's-market.

Grey-Coat-Place, Westr.—op. the Grey - coat - school, by Strutton-ground.

Grey-Coat-School, Westr.—W. end of Gt. Peter-st. and S. end of Strutton-ground.

Grey-Eagle - St. Spitalfields,— 1st on the R. in Phœnix-st. from 38, Wheeler-st.

Grey-Friars, Newgate - St.—at 108, op. Warwick-lane.

Greyhound - Alley, St. Mary-Axe,—6 doors on the R. from Leadenhall-st.

Greyhound - Court, Water - St. Strand,—1st on the L. from 37, Arundel-st.

Greyhound-Court, Chick-Lane, —6 doors on the R. from Field-lane or from Saffronhill.

Greyhound - Court, St. Catherine's Lane,—2d on the L. from 49, Up. E.-Smithfield.

Greyhound-Inn, W.-Smithfield, —12 doors N. from Hosier-lane.

Greyhound-Lane, Whitechapel-Road,—at 106, op. the London-hospital.

Greyhound-Yard, Brick-Street,

Mayfair,—op. Engine-st. Piccadilly.

Greyhound-Yd. High-Holborn, —at 82, 10 doors W. of Redlion-st.

Greyhound-Yard, Grub-Street, Cripplegate, — 12 doors on the L. from 100, Fore-st.

Greystock-Pl. Fetter-Lane,—at 101, 3d on the R. from 33, Holborn-hill.

Greystock-Pl. Bethnal- Green, —between North - st. and Dog-row.

Grice's-Wharf, Rotherhithe,— by Church-stairs, on the E. side of the church.

Grievson's Rents, Melior-Street, Snow's Fields, Boro.—middle of the N. side.

Griffin-Inn, Boro.—S. side St. George's church, 6 doors from Kent-st.

Griffin-Passage, Half-Moon-St. —at 28, 1st on the L. from Piccadilly.

Griffin-Pl. Dog-Row, Bethnal-Green,—1st on the R. a few doors from Mile-end-turnpike.

Griffin-St. Shadwell,—continuation of Peal-alley, from 61, High st.

Griffin's Wharf,—at the bottom of Morgan's lane, from 80, Tooley-st.

Griffith's Rents, Bermondsey-St.—34 doors on the L. from Tooley-st.

Grindon's Builds. Tabernacle-Walk,—at 54, nearly op. the Tabernacle.

Grivson's Rents - Melior-St.— 1st on the L. from Snow's Fields.

Grocer-Court, Shoreditch,—at 33, 13 doors N. of the turnpike.

Grocer-Court, Kingsland-Road, —at 55, a few doors on the L. from Shoreditch.

Grocer-Court, Well-Alley,— 2d on the R. from 110, Wapping.

Grocers-Hall-Court, Poultry,— at 35, 10 doors W. of the Mansion-house.

Grocers-Hall,—N. end of the last.

Grog-Court,—N. end of Nightingale-lane, Limehouse.

Grass's Builds. Cannon - St.-Road, — N. end of Beaumont's-builds.

Grose's-Rents, Long-Lane, Bermondsey, — 4th on the L. from the church.

Grosvenor-Chapel, South Audley-St.—22 doors on the L. from Grosvenor-sq.

Grosvenor-Gate, Park-Lane,— ½ a mile from Piccadilly.

Grosvenor-Market, Davies-St. —1st on the L. from 292, Oxford-st.

Grosvenor-Mews, Grosvenor-St. —4 doors on the L. from 130, New Bond-st.

Grosvenor-Pl. Hyde-Park-Corner,—S. side the turnpike.

Grosvenor-Place (Lower),—the continuation of the last to Arabella-row.

Grosvenor-Row, Chelsea,—the E. continuation of Royal Hospital-row, to Ebury-st.

Grosvenor-Pl. Boro.-Road,— 15 doors on the R. from the Obelisk.

Grosvenor-Sq.—S. end of Duke-st. from 277, Oxford-st.

Grosvenor-Street, New Bond-St. —at 130, 4th on the L. from 58, Piccadilly, extending to Grosvenor-sq.

Grosvenor-St. (Upper),—continuation of the last from the square to Park-lane.

Grosvenor-St. (Little),—at 63, Grosvenor-st. 9 doors E. of Davies-st.

Grosvenor-St. West, Pimlico, —the E. side of the King's road, by Up. Eaton-st.

Grosvenor - St. Millbank-Row, Westr.—at 6, under the archway.

Grotto - Pl. Paddington-Street, Marybone,—8 doors on the L. from High-st.

Ground's Brewers - Alley,—1st on the R. from 5, Morgan's-lane, Tooley-st.

Grove, Gt. Guildford-St. Boro. —1st on the L. from 35, Queen-st.

Grove, Chapel-Path, Sommers-Town,—between Chalton-st. and Willsted-st.

Grove (New), Mile-End-Road, —part of the S. side, 2¼ miles from Aldgate.

Grove-Cottage, Rowland's Row, Stepney-Green,—1st on the R. from Mile-end.

Grove (New) Cottage, Mile End-Road,—about ½ mile on the L. below the Plough.

Grove, Grange-Road,—1st on the R. from Star-corner.

Grove's Court, White-Horse-St. Ratcliffe,--nearly op. Butcher-row.

GRO   GUN

Grove - Pl. Lisson - Grove,—⅓ mile on the R. north from the Yorkshire Stingo.

Grove-Pl. James-St.—1st on the L. from Lisson-grove.

Grove-Lane, Lambeth-Marsh, —E. side the Pear-tree Public-house.

Grove - Pl. Northampton-Terrace,—2d on the R. from the City-road.

Grove-Pl. Mile-End,—by the turnpike, to S. end of Epping-place.

Grove-Pl. Grove-St.—1st on the R. from the Commercial-road.

Grove - Pl. Deptford,—the S. end of Victualling - office-row.

Grove-Row, Cambridge-Heath, Hackney-Road,— behind the Hare Public-house, by the turnpike.

Grove - Road, Mile-End-Road, —op. Savile-place, about 2¼ miles on the L. from Aldgate.

Grove-St. Lisson-Grove,--⅓ mile on the R. north from the Yorkshire Stingo.

Grove-St. Greenland-Dock,— on the W. side Dudman's yard, to Victualling - office-row.

Grove-St. Commercial-Road,— 5th on the L. west of Cannon-st.-road.

Grotto - Gardens, Cannon - St. Mint-St. Boro.—a few doors W. from the S. end of Lombard-st.

Grub-St. Westr.—at 33, Vine-st. 8 doors from Millbank-st.

Grub-St. Cripplegate,—at 97, Fore-st. 3d on the R. from Moorfields.

Grub's-Yard, Castle-Lane, Boro. —3 doors N. of Morris's walk.

Guildford - Mews, Gt. Guildford-St.—5 doors W. of the Foundling-hospital.

Guildford-Pl. Gt. Guildford-St. —middle of the S. side, op. the Foundling-hospital.

Guildford-St. (Gt.) Russell-Sq. —from the E. side, to Gray's-inn-lane.

Guildford-St. (Up.)—W. end of the last.

Guildford-St. (Little),—at 49, Bernard-st. 1st on the L. from Russell-sq.

Guildford-St.(Gt.)Queen-Street, Boro.—at 35, 3d on the R. from 219, High-st.

Guildford-St. (Little),—op. the last.

Guildhall,—N. end of King-st. from 92, Cheapside.

Guinea-Mews, Bruton-Pl. See North Bruton-Mews.

Gullan's Yard, Princes-Street, Westr.—behind 1, Gt.George-street.

Gullan's Yard, New Bond-St.— at 52, between Maddox-st. and Brook-st.

Gullman's Mews, Bruton-St.— 2d on the L. from 152, New Bond-st.

Gun-Alley (Little), Moorfields, —at 27, middle of the W. side.

Gun-Alley (Up.) Wapping,—at 104, 7 doors on the L. below the London-docks.

Gun - Alley. (Lower), Green-Bank,—the continuation of the last.

Gun-Alley, Bermondsey-St.—at 84, 6 doors N. of Russell-street.

Gun-Court, White-Horse-Alley, —1st on the R. from Cow-cross.

Gun - Court, St. John - Street, Clerkenwell,—at 155, 2 doors S. from Wilderness-row.

Gun and Holybush-Court, Cable-St.—at 58, 7 doors E. of Church-lane.

Gun-Dock, Wapping,—op. 104, 3 doors E. of the London-docks.

Gun - Lane, Limehouse,—from 23, Three-colt-st. to the Commercial-road.

Gun-Sq. Houndsditch,—at 150, —2d on the R. from Aldgate-church.

Gun-St. Old Artillery-Ground, —3d in Union-st. from 69, Bishopsgate.

Gun-St. Higlers-Lane,—3d on the R. from Blackfriars - road.

Gun-Yard, Pepper-Alley, Boro. —1st on the L. from 314, High-st.

Gunhill-Court, Cherry-Garden-St. Bermondsey,—2d on the L. from Cherry-garden-stairs.

Gun-House-Alley and Stairs, Lambeth. See Bomb-house-Alley.

Gunpowder-Alley, Shoe-Lane, —at 95, 18 doors on the L. from 130, Fleet-st.

Gunpowder - Court, Crutched-Friars,—3 doors N. of John-st. America-sq.

Gun and Shot Wharf, Morgan's Lane,—N. end on the R. from 80, Tooley-st.

Gunt's Yard, Wigmore-St.—at 23, by Marybone-lane.

Gut-Lane, Poplar. See Dolphin-Lane.

Gutter - Lane, Cheapside,—at 132, 2d on the L. from St. Paul's-church-yard.

Guy's Hospital, St. Thomas's St. Boro.—a few doors on the R. from 43, High-st.

Gwyn's Builds. Goswell - St.-Road,—W. side, adjoining the City-road.

Gynn's Pl. Lisson-Grove,—¼ of a mile on the R. north from the Yorkshire-stingo.

HABERDASHERS - ALMS - Houses, Hoxton,—at the N. end of Pitfield-st.

Haberdashers - Alms - Houses, Snow-Hill,—at 62, on the N. side of Skinner-st.

Haberdashers - Hall, Maiden-Lane,—8 doors on the R. from 110, Wood-st.

Haberdashers-Pl. Hoxton,—adjoins the N. side Haberdashers-alms-houses.

Haberdashers-School, Bunhill-Row,—at 103, about the middle of the W. side.

Haberdashers-Sq. Grub-Street, Cripplegate,—1st on the R. from Chiswell-st.

Haberdashers-St. Hoxton,—N. side of Haberdashers-alms-houses.

Haberdashers-Walk, Hoxton,—

the N. continuation of Pit-field-st. from Old-st.-road.

Hacker's-Court, Nicholas-Lane, —at 27, middle of the E. side.

Hackney-Coach - Office, Essex-St. Strand,—S. end by the Thames.

Hackney-Road,—at Shoreditch-church on the R.: its extent from thence to Hackney-church is about 2 miles.

Hackney-New-Road, Mile-End, —from op. the Plough, 2¼ miles on the L. below Ald-gate-pump to Hackney.

Hackney-Road-Crescent,—¼ of a mile on the R. from Shore-ditch-church, op. Middlesex-place.

Haddon's Gardens, Old - St.-Road,—1st on the R. from the N. end of Paul-st.

Hadley's Wharf, Millbank-St. Westr.——nearly op. Vine-street.

Hadlow-St. Leigh-Street, Bur-ton-Crescent,—2d on the R. from Hunter-st. Brunswick-square.

Hagley-Pl. Kent-Road,—part of the R. side, ⅛ of a mile from the Elephant and Castle.

Hagen's-Wharf, Mill-St.—2d on the L. from Dock-head.

Haglin's-Gateway, Tooley - St. —at 44, op. Dean-st.

Hairbrain-Court, Blue-Anchor-Yard,—2d on the R. from 43, Rosemary-lane.

Hale-St. Poplar,—the 3d E. of North-st.

Hale's-Pl. South-Lambeth,—2d on the L. from Vauxhall-turnpike.

Half-Farthing-Alley, Jacob-St.

Dock-Head,—4th on the R. from Mill-st.

Half-Moon - Alley, Aldersgate-St.—at 138, middle of the W. side.

Half-Moon-Alley, Whitecross-St. Cripplegate,—at 46, 5th on the R. from 115, Fore-street.

Half-Moon-Alley, Little Moor-fields,—2d on the L. from 61, Fore-st.

Half-Moon-Alley, Whitechapel, —18 doors E. from Somerset-st. Aldgate.

Half-Moon-Court, Stanhope-St. —at 32, 4 doors from Prin-ces-st. Drury-lane.

Half - Moon - Court, Portpool-Lane,—at 20, 12 doors on the L. from 64, Leather-lane.

Half-Moon-Court, Wapping,— at 8, 1st below Hermitage-bridge.

Half-Moon-Inn, High-St. Boro. —at 130, 22 doors N. of St. George's church.

Half - Moon - Passage, Grace-church - St.—8 doors S. of Leadenhall-st.

Half-Moon-St. Piccadilly,—at 86, middle of the N. side.

Half-Moon-St. Bishopsgate,—at 170, ⅛ of a mile N. of the church.

Half-Moon-Yard, Clipstone-St. Marybone,—6 doors on the L. from Gt. Portland-st.

Half-Nicol-St. Bethnal-Green. See Nicol.

Half-Paved - Court, Dorset-St. —3d on the L. from 82, Fleet-st. along Salisbury-court.

Halfpenny-Hatch (Old), Broad-Wall,—1st on the L from

HAL

Charlotte - st. Blackfriars - road.

Halfpenny - Hatch (Curtis's), Broad - Wall,—op. Cross-st. Blackfriars-road.

Halifax - St. Mile - End New-Town,—2d on the R. from 50, Whitechapel-road, along Gt. Garden-st.

Halifax-St. (Little),—4th on the L. in Chicksand-st. from the last.

Halkin-St. Grosvenor-Pl. Hyde-Park-Corner,—10 doors from the turnpike towards Buckingham-gate.

Halkin-Mews,—1st on the L. in the last from Grosvenor-place.

Hall's Court, Great Gardens, St. Catherine's,—1st on the L. in Helmet-court, from 30, Butcher-row.

Hall's Passage, Cursitor - St. Chancery-Lane,—at 25, nearly op. Castle-st.

Hall's Pl.—N. end of Cottage-lane, from Doran's - row, Commercial-road.

Hall's Pl. Kennington-Lane,—6 doors on the R. from Newington.

Hall's Yard, Down-St.—1st on the L. from Piccadilly.

Hall's Yard, Swallow-St.—at 96, 3 doors S. of Maddox-st.

Ham - Yard, Gt. Windmill-St. Haymarket,—at 37, op. Archer-st.

Ham-Yard, North-Row, Park-Lane;—10 doors W. from 56, Park-st.

Hambro' Wharf, Up. Thames-St.—bottom of Queen - st. Cheapside.

HAM

Hamilton-Gardens,—S. end of York-st. Pentonville.

Hamilton-Pl. Pentonville-Road, Clerkenwell,—from Weston-st. to the turnpike, Battle-bridge.

Hamilton-Pl. Piccadilly,—1st on the L. from Hyde-park-corner.

Hamilton-Row, Pentonville,—N. end of Hamilton-pl.

Hammer-Alley (Three), Glean-Alley,—the continuation of it, bearing to the L. from 218, Tooley-st.

Hammer and Crown - Court, Broad-St. Ratcliffe,—at 80, middle of the N. side.

Hammet-St. Minories,—at 102, 2d on the L. from Tower-hill.

Hammond-Court, Haymarket,—8 doors from Piccadilly.

Hammond - Court, Mincing - Lane,—at 23, 4 doors from Tower-st.

Hammonds Quay, Lower Thames St.—at 9, W. side Botolph-Wharf.

Hamden-Pl. Bethnal-Green,—op. the S. end of Smart-st. from Green-st.

Hampden-St. Sommers Town, —at the N. E. corner of Clarendon-sq.

Hampshire-Court, Berner-St.—1st on the L. from the Commercial-road.

Hampshire-Court, Whitechapel-Road,—at 237, 4th on the R. below the church.

Hampshire-Hog-Yard, High-St. St. Giles's,—at 10, nearly op. the church.

Hampstead-Road,—the N. continuation of Tottenham-court-road.

Hampstead-Yard, Leather-Lane, —4 doors on the R. from 128, Holborn-hill.

Hampton-St. Walworth,—2d on the R. from the Elephant and Castle.

Hanbury-Pl. Poplar,—1st on the R. from the Commercial-road.

Hand-Alley, Long - Alley,—at 42, 7th on the L. from Moor-fields.

Hand - Court, Maiden - Lane, Covent-Garden,—at 26, by Bedford-st.

Hand-Court, High-Holborn,—at 57, nearly op. Gt. Turn-stile.

Hand-Court, Golden-Lane,—at 71, near the middle of the E. side.

Hand-Court, Up. Thames-St.—at 160, 2 doors W. of Bush-lane.

Hand-Court, New-St. Bishops-gate,—E. end, by the India-warehouses.

Hand - Court (Three), Cree-church-Lane,—3 doors from the church by 87, Leadenhall-street.

Hand-Yard, Bermondsey-St.—at 154, op. the church.

Hand in Hand Fire-Office, New Bridge - St.—1st on the R. from Fleet-st.

Hand and Pen-Court, Leaden-hall-St.—at 60, op. Cree-church.

Hand and Pen-Court, Tower-Hill,—at 36, between Steel-yard and Coopers-row.

Handcock's Rents, Hackney-

Road,—the 3d on the L. from Shoreditch-church.

Hancock's Yard, White-Friars, —at the bottom of Water-lane, on the L. from 68, Fleet-st.

Hansard's Pl. Blackfriars-Road, —1st on the R. from Surrey-chapel, towards the Obe-lisk.

Hanging-Sword - Alley, Water-Lane,—3 doors on the L. from 68, Fleet-st.

Hanks-Court, Robin-Hood-Lane, Blackwall,—1st on the R. from the East-India Dock-gate.

Hanley's Builds. Chequer-Alley, —a few doors on the L. from 99, Bunhill-row.

Hanover-Court, Grub-St. Crip-plegate,—at 74, op. the cha-pel.

Hanover-Court, Houndsditch,—4 doors on the L. from Ald-gate.

Hanover - Court, Minories,—at 108, 3d on the L. from Tower-hill.

Hanover - Court, Brick-Lane, Spitalfields,—at 10, 3d on the R. from 74, Whitechapel.

Hanover-Court, Hanover-St. Ro-therhithe,—at 23, the S. end of it.

Hanover-Sq.—op. 132, Oxford-st. E. side of New Bond-st.

Hanover-St. Hanover-Sq.—from the S. E. corner, to 92, Swallow-st.

Hanover-St. Long-Acre,—at 96, 2d on the R. from Drury-lane.

Hanover-Stairs, Rotherhithe,— ¼ of a mile below the

church, and op. New Crane, Wapping.

Hanover-St. Rotherhithe,—2d st. on the R. below the church.

Hanover-St. Walworth,—3d on the R. from the Elephant and Castle.

Hans-Place, Hans-Town,—the square at the W. end of Hans-st.

Hans-Street, Sloane-St.—at 63, 3d on the R. from Knights-bridge.

Hans-Town,—W. side of Sloane-street.

Hanson's Gains, St. Catherine's Lane,—the last on the R. from 48, Up. E. Smithfield.

Hanway-Street, Oxford-St.—22 doors from and leading to Tottenham-court-road.

Harbour-Masters-Office,—at 2, Little Thames-st. between St. Catherine's dock and Lower E. Smithfield.

Harden's Rents,—behind the 4th house on the R. in Snow's fields from the E. end of King-st.

Harding-St. (East), Gt. New-St. Fetter-Lane,—1st on the R. from West Harding-st.

Harding-St. (West), Fetter-Lane, —20 doors on the R. from 179, Fleet-st.

Hare-Alley, Shoreditch,—at 80, 12 doors on the R. north from the turnpike.

Hare-Alley, Hare-St. Bethnal-Green,—at 58, a few doors W. from the Workhouse.

Hare - Court, Inner Temple - Lane,—1st on the R. from 15, Fleet-st.

Hare - Court Builds. Middle Temple-Lane,—3d on the L. from 5, Fleet-st.

Hare-Court, Aldersgate-St.—at 62, 10 doors S. of Barbican.

Hare-Court, Hare-St. Bethnal-Green,—4 doors on the L. from 110, Brick-lane.

Hare-Gardens, Hoxton,—at the E. end of Hare-st.

Hare-Marsh, Hare-St. Bethnal-Green,—at 61, 2d on the R. from 109, Brick-lane.

Hare-Row, Cambridge - Heath, Hackney - Road, — between the Hare Public-house and Cambridge-house.

Hare-Sq. Hoxton,—1st on the R. in Hare-st. from Hoxton.

Hare-St. Hoxton,—by the Hare Public-house, ⅓ of a mile on the R. from Old-st.-road.

Hare-St. Brick-Lane, Bethnal-Green,—at 110, 2d on the L. from 144, Church-st.

Hare-Street, Poplar High-St.—1st W. from the East-India alms-houses.

Hare-Walk, Hoxton-Town,—by the Hare Public-house, ⅓ of a mile on the R. from Old-st.-road.

Harewood-Pl. Oxford-St.—from op. 132, middle of the S. side, to Hanover-sq.

Harford - Pl. Walworth,—the continuation of West-lane.

Harford -Pl. Drury-Lane,—at 116, op. the theatre.

Harley - Mews, Wigmore-St.—1st on the R. from the N. W. corner of Cavendish-sq.

Harley - Mews North,—at 58, Harley-st. 2d on the L. from Cavendish-square.

Harley-Pl. New-Road, Marybone, —E. side of Devon-
shire-pl.

Harley-Street, Cavendish-Sq.—
from the N. W. corner to
Weymouth-st.

Harley-St. (Upper), — the N.
continuation of the last.

Harleyford-Place, Kennington-
Common,—W. side the Clap-
ham-road.

Harleyford-St. Harleyford - Pl.
—3d on the R. from the
Horns towards Clapham.

Harlow-Place, Mile-End,—15
doors on the R. below the
turnpike.

Harrard's-Alley, Wellclose - Sq.
—from the S. W. corner to
Well-st.

Harp-Alley, Fleet-Market,—at
82, 16 doors on the L. from
Fleet-st.

Harp-Alley, Grub-St. Cripplegate,—5 doors on the R.
from 96, Fore-st.

Harp-Court, Black-Horse - Alley,—N. end from 98, Fleet-
street.

Harp-Lane, Lower Thames-St.
—from 77 to 19, Gt. Tower-
street.

Harpur's Fields, Edgware-Rd.
—op. King-st. ½ of a mi'e on
the L. from Tyburn turnpike.

Harpur's Mews, Theobald's Rd.
—3 doors W. of Lamb's Conduit-st.

Harpur-St. Theobald's Road,—
at 47, 9 doors from Red-
Lion-st.

Harpur's Walk, High-St. Lambeth,—2d on the R. from
the church.

Harrel's Row, Green-Bank, St.

George's in the East,—2d on
the L. from Wapping-church.

Harriot's Pl. Fashion-St. Spitalfields,—at 56, 1st E. of
Red-lion-st.

Harris's Builds. Whitechapel-
Road,—at 130, op. the London-hospital.

Harris's Court, Ratcliffe-Highway,—at 122, op. Old Gra-
vel-lane.

Harris's Court, Brook-St. Ratcliffe,—at 115, E. side Blue-
anchor-alley.

Harris's Pl. Oxford-St.—at 364,
between Poland-st. and the
Pantheon.

Harris's Pl. White-Bear-Gardens, Hackney-Road,—a few
yards N. from Harris's-row.

Harris's Row, White-Bear-Gardens, Hackney - Road,—1st
on the R. from the N. end of
Union-walk.

Harrison's Builds. Back-Lane,
St. George's. East,—9 doors
W. of King Dav d-lane.

Harrison-St. Gray's Inn-Lane,
—1st N. of Sidmouth-street,
near Acton-st.

Harrison's Wharf, St. Catherine's-St.—a few doors E.
from St Catherine's-stairs.

Harrow-Alley, White-St. — 2d
on the L from Cutler-st. 114,
Houndsditch.

Harrow-Alley, Aldgate - High-
St.—at 68, 2d E. of the Minories.

Harrow-Court, St. Peter's-Hill,
—6 doors on the L. from
216, Up. Thames-st.

Harrow-Court, Harrow-Street,
Mint-St. Boro. — middle of
the S. side.

Harrow - Lane, Poplar. See King's Road.

Harrow-Road, Paddington,—⅘ of a mile on the L. from Ty-burn-turnpike along the Edg-ware-road.

Harrow-Street, Mint-St. Boro. —2d on the L. from 156, High-st.

Harrow-St. (Little), — op. the last.

Hart-Court, Bridgewater-Sq.— at the N. W. corner.

Harts-Lane, Bethnal-Green-Rd. —1st on the L. below the turnpike, near ½ a mile from 65, Shoreditch.

Harts-Row, Marsh-Wall, Pop-lar, or Isle of Dogs,—near a mile below the entrance to the West-India-ducks.

Hart-Street, Duke-St. Grosve-nor-Sq.—1st on the R. 12 doors from 276, Oxford-st.

Hart-St. Bloomsbury,—1st on the L. in King-st. from 120, High-Holborn.

Hart-St. Covent-Garden, — 1st on the L. in Bow-st. from Gt. Russell-st.

Hart-Street, Wood-St. Cripple-gate, — at 63, op. London-wall.

Hart-St. Crutched-Friars,—at 64, Mark-lane, 1st on the L. from Fenchurch-st.

Hart-Street, Weymouth-St.— 2d on the R. from Brighton-pl. Kent-road.

Hartley-Pl. Kent-Road, — op. the Asylum for the Deaf and Dumb.

Hartley's Wharf, Horselydown, —W. side of Horselydown

Old-Stairs, entrance by Free-man's-lane.

Hartshorn-Court, Moor - Lane, Moorfields,—4th on the R. from 86, Fore-st.

Hartshorn-Court, Leadenhall-St.—at 66, 8 doors on the L. from Aldgate.

Hartshorn-Court,Golden-Lane, —at 82, 3d on the L. from Old-st.

Hartshorn-Wharf, Lower East-Smithfield,—between the Ar-my Victualling - Office and Glasgow-wharf.

Harvey's Buildings, Strand,—at 426, 3 doors W. of Bedford-street.

Harvey's Court, Mason-Street, Lambeth,—2d on the L. from 30, Bridge-road.

Hasley-Court,Blackman-Street. See Nelson's Pl.

Hat and Mitre-Court, St. John-St.—at 150, ⅕ of a mile on the R. from Smithfield.

Hatchet-Court, Little Trinity-Lane,—3 doors on the R. from 199, Up. Thames-st.

Hatfield-Pl. St. George's-Fields, —on the W. side the Obe-lisk.

Hatfield-Pl. Cross-St. — 3d on the R. from Blackfriars-rd.

Hatfield-Street, Stamford-St.— 3d street from Blackfriars-road.

Hatfield-St. Goswell-Street,— at 25, a few doors S. from Old-st.

Hatfield - Yard, Gray's Walk, Lambeth,—E. end from Lam-beth-walk.

Hatton - Court, Threadneedle-

St.—at 49, 3 doors E. of the church.

Hatton-Court, Saffron - Hill,—12 doors on the L. from Field-lane, Holborn-bridge.

Hatton-Garden, Holborn-Hill, —at 106, 2d coach - turning on the R. from Fleet-market.

Hatton's Rents, Lombard - St. Boro.—1st on the R. south of Mint-st.

Hatton-Wall, Hatton - Garden, —at the N. end, 3d from Holborn.

Hatton-Yard, Cross-Street,—8 doors E. of 44, Hatton-garden.

Haughton-St. Clare-Market,—2d on the R. in Newcastle-st. from 308, Strand.

Haunch of Venison-Yd. Brook-St. Grosvenor-Sq.—3 doors from 103, New Bond-st.

Hawkers-Office, Somerset - Pl. —1st door on the R. in the square, from 159, Strand.

Hawkins's Court, Pedlars-Acre, —1st on the L. from Westr.-bridge.

Hawkins's Court, Miles's Lane, —11 doors on the R. from 49, Cannon-st.

Hawkins's Court, Charles-St.—3d on the L. from 174, Drury-lane.

Hawkins's Court, Rosemary-Lane,—at 82, op. Dock-st.

Hawkins's Court, Risby's Rope-Walk, Limehouse,—1st on the L. from the W. end.

Hawksbury-Pl. Lock's Fields, Walworth,—the E. end of Salisbury-pl.

Hawley-Wharf. See Downe's.

Hawley's Pl. North-St. White-chapel,—2d on the R. from Ducking-Pond-row, op. the Jews-Burying-ground.

Haw's-Alms-Houses, Bow-Lane, Poplar,—1st on the R. from the High-st.

Hay's Court, Gerrard-St. Soho, —E. end, from Newport-market to Greek-st.

Hay's Court, White's Yard,—1st on the L. from 58, Rose-mary-lane.

Hay-Hill, Berkeley-St.—4 doors from the S. E. corner of Berkeley-sq.

Hayse's Court, White's Yard,—1st on the L. from 58, Rose-mary-lane.

Hay's Lane, Tooley-St.—at 44, nearly op. Dean-st. leading to Hay's wharf.

Hay's Mews, Charles - St. — 5 doors on the R. from Berke-ley-sq.

Hay's Row, Paris - Pl. Lisson-Green,—a few yards on the L. from 23, Chapel-st.

Hay's Wharf. See Hay's Lane.

Haydon-Passage, Mansel-St.—from 21, to the N. E. corner of Haydon-sq.

Haydon-Sq. Minories,—at the E. end of Haydon-yard.

Haydon-Sq. (Little), N. side the last.

Haydon-Yd. Minories,—at 40, middle of the E. side.

Hayfield-Yard, Mile-End,—25 doors below Stepney-green.

Haymarket,—from the E. end of Piccadilly to Pall-Mall.

Haymer-Court, Maid-Lane, Boro.—middle of the S. side, op. Rose-alley.

Hazlewood-Court, Twisters-Alley,—1st on the L. from 103, Bunhill-row.

Heath-Court, Strand,—at 412, nearly op. Adam-st. Adelphi.

Heath-Pl. Hackney-Road,—a mile on the L. from Shoreditch, between the turnpike and the Hare public-house.

Heath-St. Commercial-Road, Stepney,—nearly op. Stepney-causeway.

Heddon-Court, Swallow-St.—at 131, 4th on the L. from 44, Piccadilly.

Heddon-Street, Leicester-St. —4 doors on the R. from 139, Swallow-st.

Hedger's Court, Webber-Row, St. George's Fields, — near the Jolly Miller.

St. Helena, Deptford Lower-Road, — W. side the Halfway-house, 2¼ miles from London-bridge.

St. Helena-Place,—W. side the last.

St. Helen's (Great),—from 35, Bishopsgate-within, to 61, St. Mary-Axe.

St. Helen's Place,—the bottom of Gt. St. Helen's from Bishopsgate.

St. Helen's Pl.—1st N. of the last.

St. Helen's Passage,—N. side Gt. St. Helen's.

St. Helen's-Chambers, Gt. St. Helen's—E. side, entrance by 33.

St. Helen's Church, Great St. Helen's.

Helen's Place, Pitt-St. Bethnal-Green,—1st on the L. from Chester-pl.

Helmet-Court, Strand,—at 337, op. Somerset-house.

Helmet-Court, Helmet-Row, St. Luke's,—at 15, N. side the church.

Helmet-Court, London-Wall, —at 25, 6 doors E. of Basinghall-st.

Helmet-Court, Upper Thames-St.—at 230, 3 doors E. of Addle-hill.

Helmet-Court, Wormwood-St. —7 doors on the L. from 65, Bishopsgate.

Helmet-Court, Butcher-Row, —at 31, a few doors on the R. from Up. E.-Smithfield.

Helmet-Row, Old-Street, St. Luke's,—at 97, W. side the church.

Helvetic-Chapel, Moore-St. Seven-Dials,—by the W. end of Monmouth-st.

Hemlock-Court, Carey-St.— 3d on the L. from 99, Chancery-lane.

Hemming's Row, St. Martin's Lane,—at 119, 1st on the L. from Charing-cross.

Hemus-Terrace, Chelsea,—between the Hospital and the King's road, E. side Smith-street.

Hen and Chickens-Court, Fleet-St.—at 184, between St. Dunstan's church and Fetter-lane.

Heneage-Lane, Duke's Pl.—3d on the R. in Creechurch-lane from 87, Leadenhall-st.

Heneage-St. Mile-End New-Town,—the continuation of N.

Flying-horse-yard, from 31, Brick-lane.

Henrietta-Mews, Henrietta-St. Brunswick-Sq.—E. end, by the Foundling-hospital.

Henrietta - Passage, Henrietta-St.—5 doors on the L. from the S. W. corner of Cavendish-sq.

Henrietta-St. Cavendish-Sq.— from the S.W. corner to Marybone-lane.

Henrietta-St. Manchester-Sq.— 1st on the R. in Duke-st. from 173, Oxford-st.

Henrietta-St. Covent - Garden, —from the S. W. corner to 34, Bedford-st.

Henrietta-Street, Hunter-St.— 1st from the N. W. corner of Brunswick-sq.

Henrietta-St. Hackney-Road,— nearly op. Gt. Cambridge-st. ½ a mile on the R. from Shoreditch.

Henry-Passage, Henry-St.—2d on the R. from the Hampstead-road.

Henry-Pl. Castle-Lane, Westr. —last on the L. from James-street.

Henry-Pl. Walworth-Common, —at the W. side of Surrey-square.

Henry-St. Hampstead-Road,— 2d on the L. from Tottenham-court.

Henry-St. Gray's-Inn - Lane,— op. 91. ¾ of a mile on the L. from Holborn.

Henry-Street, Pentonville,—the continuation of White-lion-st. from Islington.

Henry-Street, Old-St.—at 30,

2d W. of St. Luke's hospital.

Henry-St.Blackwall-Causeway, —1st on the R. from Poplar High-st.

Heralds-College, Doctors-Commons,—at 15, Bennet's hill, S. side St. Paul's-church-yd.

Herbert's Passage, Beaufort's Builds.—3 doors from 95, Strand.

Hercules-Builds. Lambeth,—S. side the road from the Asylum to the church.

Hercules Coach-Office, Leadenhall-St.—at 119, nearly op. Lime-st. and the East-India-house.

Hercules - Tavern,—at 79, Old Broad-st. by Threadneedle-street.

Hereford-Pl. Commercial - Rd. —N. side, the corner of Cannon-st.-road.

Hereford-Street, Park-St.—1st on the R. from 257, Oxford-st.

Hermes - St. Pentonville, — 3d on the R. from Islington.

Hermes-Hill,—op. the N. end of Hermes-st.

Hermitage, Brompton,—N.side of Yeoman's-row.

Hermitage-Bridge, Hermitage-Dock,—⅓ of a mile below the Tower.

Hermitage - Dock,——divides Lower E. Smithfield from Wapping.

Hermitage-Stairs, Wapping-St. —op. 14, and op. Mill-stairs.

Hermitage-St. (Great),—1st N, parallel to Wapping-st. from Hermitage - bridge, to the London-docks.

Hermitage-St. (Little),—at 14, Wapping-st. 1st on the L. below Hermitage-bridge.

Hermitage-Yd. — continuation of Little Hermitage-st. from 14, Wapping-st.

Hern's Builds. Up. East-Smithfield,—at 7, ⅙ of a mile on the L. from Tower-hill.

Hern's Court, Dock - St.—1st on the L. from 88, Up. East-Smithfield.

Hertford-Row, Battle - Bridge, —op. Weston-street, Pentonville, and Hamilton-pl.

Hertford-St. Fitzroy-Sq. — 1st on the R. in London-st. from 108, Tottenham-court-road.

Hertford-St. Mayfair,—3d on the R. in Park-lane from Piccadilly.

Hertford - Street, Skinner - St. Sommers-Town,—2d on the R. from 15, Judd's-pl.

Hert's Row, Marsh-Wall, Poplar,—⅛ of a mile below the King's-arms.

Hewet's Court, Strand, — at 461, near Charing-cross.

Hewit's Court, Mutton-Lane,— 1st on the R. from Mile-End-road.

Hickman's Folly, Dock-Head, —E. continuation of Dock-head to George's-row.

Hickman's Rents, Russell-St. Bermondsey. See Hillman's Rents.

High-Row, Knightsbridge,—N. side the High-road, opposite Sloane-st.

High-St. Marybone,—continuation of Thayer-st. E. side of Manchester-sq. to the New-road.

High-Street, St. Giles's,—W. continuation of Broad-st. by the church.

High-St. Islington,—from the Angel-inn towards the church.

High-St. Mile-End New-Town, —the continuation of Great Garden-st. from 50, Whitechapel-road.

High-St. Stepney,—W. side the church-yard.

High-St. Lambeth,—from op. the church, to Broad-st.

High-St. Boro.—from London-bridge (where there are 1 and 325) to St. George's church.

High-St. Newington,—on the E. side the High-road, op. the church.

High-Timber-St. Up. Thames-St.—from Broken-wharf to Brook's-wharf, op. Bread-st.-hill.

Higlers-Lane, Lambeth-Marsh or New-Cut,—2d on the L. from Surrey-chapel : it leads to Webber-st.

Higlers-Lane, Blackfriars-Rd. —3d on the R. from the Obelisk.

Hill's Alms - Houses, Westr. See Emery-Hill's.

Hill's Builds. Avery-Row, Pimlico, —a few doors on the R. from op. Ranelagh-walk.

Hill-Court, Hill-St. Finsbury-Sq.—1st on the L. 3 doors from Paul-st.

Hill-Court, Shoreditch,—at 51, 3 doors N. of Webb-sq.

Hill-Mews, Hill-St.—at 35, 1st on the L. from Berkeley-sq.

Hill's Pl.—the continuation of Pancras-st. Tottenham-court-road.

Hill-St. Berkeley-Sq.—at 41, middle of the W. side.

Hill-St. Finsbury-Sq.—2d parallel to the N. side, from Paul-st. to 10, Windmill-st.

Hill-St. Little Tower-Hill,—the E. side, from the Minories to the New-Mint.

Hilliard's Court, Old Gravel-Lane,—at 15, 2d on the R. from 157, Wapping.

Hillman's Rents, Russell-Street, Bermondsey,—1st on the R. from Dock-head.

Hind-Court, Fleet-St.—at 147, op. Water-lane.

Hind-Court, Noble-St. Foster-Lane,—at 19, the corner of Falcon-sq.

Hind-Mews, Marybone-Lane, —at 61, 3d on the L. from Oxford-st.

Hind-Street, Manchester-Sq.— from the E. side to 58, Marybone-lane.

Hind-St.-Chapel,—the corner of Thayre-st.

Hinton's Alms-Houses, Plough-Alley, Barbican,—a few yards on the R. from nearly op. Redcross-st.

Hob's Court, Old Castle-Street, Whitechapel,—1st on the L. from 121, Wentworth-st.

Hobson's Buildings, Russell-St. Bermondsey,—1st on the L. in Church-st. towards Dockhead.

Hobson's Pl. Pelham-St. Mile-End New-Town,—4th on the R. from 63, Brick-lane.

Hobson's Rents,—E. side of the last.

Hodge's Builds. Ratcliffe-Row,

St. Luke's,—op. Nelson-st. City-road.

Hodge's Court,—a few yards W. of the last.

Hodge's-Court, Denmark-St. St. George's East,—1st on the R. from 153, Ratcliffe-highway.

Hodge's Pl. Gill-St. Limehouse, —E. side of it.

Hodgson's Builds. Arnold-Pl. Walworth,—op. Hanover-st.

Hodgson's Place, Lock's Fields, Walworth, — between Salisbury-pl. and Paragon-pl.

Hodgson-Street, Francis-St. Walworth, — 1st on the R. from op. Newington-church.

Hog-Lane, Shoreditch. See Worship-St.

Hog-Yard, White's Yard,—3d on the L. from 58, Rosemary-lane.

Hog-Yd. Castle-Lane, Boro.— 1st on the R. from Castle-street.

Holborn-Bars, Holborn,— the boundary of the city, by Middle-row, op. Gray's-inn-lane.

Holborn-Bridge, Fleet-Market, —N. end, between Snow-hill and Holborn-hill.

Holborn-Court, Gray's Inn,— entrance by 20, High-holborn.

Holborn-Hill,—from the N. end of Fleet-market to Middle-row.

Holborn (High),—the W. continuation of the last from Middle-row, (where the numbers begin and end, viz. 1 and 320), to Drury-lane.

Holbrook-Builds. Tottenham-

Court-Road,—from 127, to
Fitzroy-market.

Holbrook-Court,—W. side the
last.

Holden's Yard, Crown-St. Soho,
—2d on the L. from Oxford-st.

Holding's Rents, Rotherhithe-
St.—W. side the Surrey-
canal-dock.

Holdsworth's Yard, Tottenham-
Court-Road,—9 doors on the
R. from Oxford-st.

Hole in the Wall-Court, 160,
Fleet-St. See St. Dunstan's
Court.

Hole in the Wall-Passage, Baldwin's Gardens,—at 24,12 doors
on the L. from 77, Leather-
lane.

Holland-St. Blackfriars-Road,—
1st on the L. from the bridge.

Hollen-Street, Wardour-St. Soho,—9 doors on the L. from
332, Oxford-st.

Holles - St. Cavendish - Sq.—at
123, Oxford-st. middle of the
N. side.

Holles-St. Clare - Market,—3d
on the R. from 306, Strand,
along Newcastle-st.

Holliday - Yard, Creed-Lane,—
1st on the R. from 14, Ludgate-st.

Hollow-Mitchell - Street, Saint
Luke's,—the 1st on the R.
from 11, Helmet-row.

Holloway-St. (Gt.)—2d on the
L. in Union-st. from 281,
Whitechapel-road.

Holloway-St. (Little),—E. continuation of the last.

Holyfield - Row, Elizabeth-Pl.
Lambeth, — 2d on the L.
from Kennington-cross.

Holywell-Lane, Shoreditch,—at
194, near the turnpike.

Holywell-Mount, Shoreditch,—
the neighbourhood around
Chapel-st. and Holywell-row
is called so.

Holywell-Row,Worship-St.—2d
coach-turning on the R. from
Shoreditch, leading to Chapel-street.

Holywell-St. Shoreditch,—part
of the High-st. particularly on
the W. side, say from 194 to
249.

Holywell-St. Strand,—from the
W. side St. Clement's church
to the New-church.

Homer-Court,Blue-Gate-Fields,
—3d on the R. from 95,
Ratcliffe-highway.

Homer-Pl. Winchester-Row,—
continuation of it from 82,
Edgware-road.

Homer-Row, Winchester-Row,
—1st on the R. from 82,
Edgware-road.

Homer-St. Marybone,—1st N.
parallel to the last.

Honduras-Street, Old-Street,—
at 23, 4th on the R. from Goswell-st.

Honduras-Wharf, Bankside,—
E. side Falcon-wharf.

Honey - Lane, Cheapside,—at
110, op. Bow-church.

Honey-Lane-Market,—N. end
the last.

Honeysuckle-Court,Moor-Lane,
—1st on the L. from 87,
Fore-st.

Hood's Builds. Gt. Saint Ann's
St. Westr.—middle of Johnson's builds.

Hood's Pl.Bethnal-Green-Rd.—

N 3

the N. end of George-Gardens, E. side of Wilmot-sq.

Hood's Wharf, Earl-St. Blackfriars,—op. 10, the 4th E. of the bridge.

Hook's Gardens, Silver-St.—1st on the L. from Canterbury-square.

Hooper's Builds. Brompton. See the next.

Hooper's Court, Brompton,—1st on the L. from Knightsbridge.

Hooper's Court, Up. E. Smithfield,—at 28, 2d on the L. from Tower-hill.

Hooper's Sq. Goodman's Fields, —at 82, Lemon-st. op. Prescott-st.

Hooper's Street, Gt. Sutton-St. Clerkenwell,—1st on the R. from 128, Goswell-st.

Hooper-St. Westr.-Bridge-Road, — from op. the Asylum to Gloucester-st.

Hop - Gardens, St. Martin's Lane, Charing-Cross,—at 50, S. side New-st.

Hope - Alley, Broad-Wall.—2d on the L. from Charlotte-st. Blackfriars-road.

Hope Coach-Office, Charing-Cross,—nearly op. the gate of the King's Mews.

Hope - Court, Wentworth - St. Spitalfields,—at 54, 2 doors W. of George-st.

Hope-Court, Angel-St. Broad-Wall, Lambeth,—1st on the L. from Charlotte-st.

Hope Insurance - Office, Ludgate - Hill,—10 doors from New-Bridge-st.

Hope-Pl. Bishop's Walk, Lam-

beth, — middle of the N. side.

Hope-Pl. Whitechapel-Road,— at 134, op. the London-hospital.

Hope-Street, Quaker-St. Spitalfields,—2d on the R. from 173, Brick-lane.

Hope-Town, Church-St. Bethnal-Green, — by the turnpike, ½ a mile on the L. from 65, Shoreditch.

Hopkins-Street, Broad-St. Carnaby-Market,—4 doors W. of 87, Berwick-st.

Hopton's Alms-Houses, Green-Walk,—a few doors on the L. from Holland-st.

Horatio-Pl. Portland-St. Walworth-Common,—part of the S. end, by the Paul's head.

Hore's Wharf, Wapping,—by Hermitage-stairs, near a mile below London-bridge.

Horham's Court,—S. E. corner of Ratcliffe-sq.

Horn-Alley, Liquor-Pond-St.— at 30, 1st on the R. from Leather-lane.

Horn-Alley, Aldersgate-St.—at 43, 4 doors S. of Jewin-st.

Horn-Brewery, Lambeth-Marsh, —3d on the R. ¼ of a mile from Surrey-chapel.

Horn-Court, Golden-Lane,—at 123, near the middle of the W. side.

Horn - Court, Vine-Yard,—the 4th on the L. from 109, Tooley-st.

Horse-Row, King-St. Boro.— behind 59, 1st on the R. from 109, High-st.

Horse and Dolphin-Yard, &c.

Martin's St.—1st on the R. from Whitcomb-st.

Horse and Dolphin-Yard, Macclesfield - St. Soho,—middle of the E. side.

Horse-Ferry, Rotherhithe-St.—at 118, $\frac{3}{4}$ of a mile below the church.

Horse-Ferry, Limehouse,—from the E. end of Queen-st. to Turner's wharf, op. the last.

Horse-Ferry - Road, Millbank-St. Westr.—5th on the R. from the Abbey.

Horse and Groom-Yard, Oxford-St.—at 129, middle of the N. side.

Horse and Groom-Yard, Green-St.—at 41, 2d on the R. from Park-lane.

Horse and Groom-Yard, Dean-St. Soho,—behind 400, Oxford-st.

Horse and Groom-Yard, Holborn,—at 129, nearly op. Fetter-lane.

Horse and Groom-Yard, Wood-St. Westr.—3 doors from 63, Millbank-st.

Horse and Groom-Yard, Bedfordbury,—at 32, middle of the E. side.

Horse and Groom-Yard, Theobald's Road,—at 66, by North-street.

Horse and Groom-Yard, Gt. St. Thomas-Apostle,—3 doors W. of Queen-st.

Horse and Groom-Yard, Chiswell-St.—20 doors on the L. from Finsbury-sq.

Horse and Groom-Yard, Curtain-Road, Shoreditch, — a few doors on the R. from Worship-st.

Horse and Groom-Yard, Blackfriars-Road,—12 doors S. of Holland-st.

Horse and Groom-Yard, Newington,—$\frac{1}{4}$ of a mile on the L. south from the church.

Horse - Guards, Whitehall,—$\frac{1}{6}$ of a mile on the R. from Charing-cross.

Horse-Shoe-Alley, York-St.—2d on the R. from James-st.

Horse-Shoe - Alley, Old-Street, St. Luke's,—at 99, 3 doors W. of the church.

Horse-Shoe - Alley, Petticoat-Lane,—at 110, 7th on the R. from 41, Aldgate High-st.

Horse - Shoe - Alley, Bankside, Southwark,—14 doors from Clink-st.

Horse-Shoe- Alley - Stairs,—N. end of the last, op. Threecranes, Bankside, Southwark.

Horse-Shoe-Alley, Wilson-St.—at 14, 2d on the R. from Moorfields.

Horse-Shoe-Court, St. Clement's Inn,—middle of the E. side, leading to Clement's lane.

Horse - Shoe - Court, Ludgate-Hill,—at 32, 5 doors W. of the Old-Bailey.

Horse-Shoe-Court, Long-Lane, W. Smithfield,—at 24, middle of the N. side.

Horse-Shoe-Inn, Stones - End, Boro.—op. the King's Bench.

Horse-Shoe-Inn, Goswell-St.—37 doors on the R. from Barbican.

Horse-Shoe-Passage, Newgate-St.—at 60, 3 doors from Cheapside.

Horse-Shoe - Wharf,—W. side Horse-Shoe-alley.

Horse-Shoe-Wharf, Up. Thames-St.—at 10, op. Addle-hill.

Horse-Shoe-Yard, Brook-St. Grosvenor-Sq.—2 doors from 104, New Bond-st.

Horse-Shoe-Yard, James-St.—at 42, 2d on the L. from 287, Oxford-st.

Horse and Trumpet-Yard, Jewry-St.—at 18, 2d on the L from Aldgate.

Horsley-Street, Mount-Street, Walworth,—2d on the R. from op. the Montpelier.

Horselydown, Southwark,—from the E. end of Tooley-st. to Dock-head.

Horselydown-Lane,—3d coach-turning from the E. end of Tooley-st. bearing to the L.

Horselydown Old-Stairs,—½ a mile below London-bridge, and op. Iron-gate, entrance by Horselydown-lane.

Horselydown New-Stairs,—W. side St. Saviour's dock.

Horselydown-Wharf, Shad-Thames,—W. side of George-stairs.

Horsemonger-Lane, Stones-End, Borough,——op. the King's Bench.

Hosier-Lane, West Smithfield,—at 25, 2d on the L. from Newgate-st.

Houndsditch,—from op. Bishopsgate-church, to Aldgate-church.

House of Correction for Middlesex, Coldbath-Fields,—¼ of a mile on the L. from Clerkenwell-green.

Howard's Court, Risby's Rope-Walk. See Garden-Court.

Howard's Green, City-Gardens,

—behind Anderson's builds. City-road.

Howard's Pl. Hackney-Road,—N. side, by the turnpike, Cambridge-heath.

Howard's Row, Bowling-Green-Lane, Clerkenwell,—3d on the L. from Coppice-row.

Howard-Street, Arundel-St.—1st on the R. from 189, Strand.

Howard's or Howe's Rents, Chigwell-St.—3 doors on the R. from 51, Ratcliffe-highway.

Howford-Builds. Fenchurch-St.—at 148, nearly op. Rood-lane.

Howland-Mews, West Howland-St.—4th on the L. from Tottenham-court-road.

Howland-Mews, East Howland-St.—3 doors on the L. from Tottenham-court-road.

Howland-St. Tottenham-Court-Road,—at 94, the 1st N. of Whitfield's chapel.

Howland-St. (Little),—3 doors in the last from Tottenham-court-road.

Hoxton-Academy, Hoxton,—2d on the L. from Old-st.-road.

Hoxton-Market-Place,—the 1st on the L. in Crown-st. from Old-st.-road.

Hoxton-Sq.—2 doors from that part of Old-st.-road which is op. the Curtain-road.

Hoxton-Sq.-Court,—by the S.W. corner of the last.

Hoxton-Town or High-St.—1st on the R. in Old-st.-road, from Shoreditch-church.

Hudson's Bay-House, Fenchurch-St.—3 doors on the R. from Gracechurch-st.

Hudson's Court, Wheeler-St. Spitalfields,—at 52, nearly op. Quaker-st.

Hudson's Court, Strand,—at 482, 6 doors E. of St. Martin's lane.

Hudson's Wharf, Up. Thames-St.—5 doors on the R. from Earl-st. Blackfriars.

Huggin - Lane, Wood - St.—at 115, 2d on the L. from 122, Cheapside.

Hugging-Lane, Up. Thames-St. —from 200, to Trinity-lane, 3 doors E. of Bread-st.

Hugging-Court,—middle of the E. side the last.

Hugh'sCourt,Newington-Causeway,—3d on the L. from Stones-end.

Huish-Court,Water-Lane,Blackfriars,—1st on the R. from Earl-st.

Hull's Pl. John's Row, St. Luke's, —2d on the L. from Brick-lane.

Hull-Street, John's Row, St. Luke's,—3d on the L. from Brick-lane.

Hull's Terrace,—at the N. end of the last.

Humberston - St. Commercial-Road,—2d on the L. from Cannon-st.-road.

Humphrey's Court, Castle-St. —2d on the R. from 60, Gt. Saffron-hill.

Humphrey's Wharf, Limehouse, —1st below Limehouse-hole-stairs.

Hungerford-Market. See Hungerford-St.

Hungerford-Stairs, Strand,—at the bottom of Hungerford-street.

Hungerford-St. Strand,—at 20, the third on the R. from Charing-cross.

Hunt's Court, St. Martin's Lane, —1st on the R. from the Strand.

Hunt's Court, Castle-St. Leicester-Sq.—at 20, op. Cecil-court.

Hunt's Court, Hunt-St. Spitalfields,—10 doors on the L. from Spicer-st.

Hunt's Court, Gale's Rope - Walk, Shadwell,—1st on the R. from King-David-lane.

Hunt's Court, Queen-St. Horselydown,—a few doors on the R. from the E. end of Free-school-st.

Hunt-St. Spitalfields,—3d on the R. in Spicer-st. from 32, Brick-lane.

Hunter - Mews, Henrietta - St. Brunswick-Sq.—6 doors W. of Hunter-st.

Hunter's Museum, Portugal-St. Lincoln's Inn - Fields, — the stone - fronted building op. Carey-st.

Hunter - St. Brunswick - Sq.— N. W. corner towards Sommers-town.

Hunter-St. (North),—N. end of the last.

Huntingdon-Passage, Huntington-St.—6 doors on the R. from Kingsland-road.

Huntingdon-Pl.—1st on the L. in the last from 6, Huntington-st.

Huntingdon-St. Kingsland-Rd. —1st on the L. ¼ of a mile from Shoreditch-church.

Hurle's Builds. Garlick-Hill,—6 doors on the L. from Bow-lane, Cheapside.

Hurst's Pl. New-St. Kent-Road, —part of the E. side.

Husband-Street, New-St. Carnaby-Market,—E. end from 46, Broad-st.

Hyde-Park,—W. end of Piccadilly and of Oxford-st.

Hyde-Park-Corner,—the corner by Piccadilly and Knightsbridge.

Hyde-Park, Walworth,—S. end of Thurlow-pl. East-lane.

Hyde-St. Bloomsbury,—1st on the L. in Lyon-st. from 143, High-holborn.

Hylord'sCourt, Crutched-Friars, —at 46, op. Savage-gardens.

———

JACK'S BUILDS. Vine-Yard, —2d on the R. from 110, Tooley-st.

Jackson's Builds. Paul's Alley, Cripplegate,—1st on the L. from 13, Redcross-st.

Jackson's Builds. Long-Alley, Moorfields, — the 1st S. of Crown-st.

Jackson's Court, Curriers-Row, Blackfriars,—3 doors on the R. from Bristow-st. St. Andrew's hill.

Jackson's Pl. Long-Alley, Moorfields,—11 doors S. of 29, Sun-st.

Jackson's Wharf, Horselydown, —on the E. side of Horselydown New-stairs, near St. Saviour's-dock.

Jackson's Yard, Bermondsey-

St.—at 105, 5th N. of the church.

Jacob's Court, Turnmill-Street, Clerkenwell,—1st on the L. from Cow-cross.

Jacob's Mews, Charles-St. Manchester-Sq.—on the E. side of the chapel.

Jacob-Street, Mill-St. Bermondsey,—3d on the R. from Dock-head:

Jacob's Well's Court, Barbican, —at 20, middle of the S. side.

Jamaica - Court, Commercial-Road, Limehouse,—1st on the L. below the church.

Jamaica-Level, Bermondsey,— E. side the Blue-anchor, and ½ a mile from Fort-pl.

Jamaica-Pl. Commercial-Road, Limehouse,—3d on the R. below the church.

Jamaica - Pl. Boro-Road,—2d on the L. from the Obelisk.

Jamaica-Row, Bermondsey,— the E. continuation of Parker's row, Prospect-row, and Printers-pl. to Mill-pond-st.

Jamaica New-Wharf, Upper-Ground,—a few doors above Blackfriars-bridge.

Jameno-Gallery,—the corner of Welbeck-st. and Henrietta-st. Cavendish-sq.

St. James's Builds. Rosamond-St. Clerkenwell,—at 51, 5 doors from Corporation-row.

St. James's Chapel, Hampstead-Road,—¼ of a mile on the R. from Tottenham-court-road.

St. James's Chapel, Pentonville, —⅜ of a mile on the R. from Islington.

St. James's Chronicle Newspaper-Office,—1st door on the R. in Union-st. from 36, New Bridge-st. Blackfriars.

St. James's Church, Piccadilly, —$\frac{1}{6}$ of a mile on the L. from the Haymarket.

St. James's Church, Clerkenwell,—on the N. side the green.

St. James's Church, Garlick-Hill, — behind 190, Upper Thames-st.

St. James's Church, Little Duke's Pl.—5 doors on the R. from 32, Aldgate.

James-Court, James-Street, St. Luke's,—the 1st on the L. from 33, Featherstone-st.

St. James's Court, Duke's Pl.—on the W. side of Heneage-lane.

James-Court, James-Street, St. George's East,—2d on the L. from Cannon-st.-road.

James's Court, Farmer-St. Shadwell,—behind 65, towards Shakespear's-walk.

James's Court, Lambeth-Butts, —by the E. corner of Vauxhall-walk.

James-Court, Union-Street, St. George's Fields,—5th on the R. from the London-road.

James-Court, Golden-Lane,—at 100, 2d on the R. from Old-street.

St. James's Infirmary, Poland-St.—at 48, 2d on the R. from 365, Oxford-st.

St. James's Market,—W. end of Norris-st. from 56, Haymarket.

St. James's Palace,—W. end of Pall-mall, and S. end of St. James's st.

St. James's Park, — between Charing-cross and Buckingham-gate.

James's Pl. Hampstead-Road,—$\frac{1}{8}$ mile on the R. from Tottenham-court.

St. James's Pl. Saint James's St.—at 66, 3d on the R. from 162, Piccadilly.

St. James's Pl. Clerkenwell-Green,—E. side the church.

James's Pl. Hackney-Road,—part of the R. side, $\frac{3}{4}$ of a mile from Shoreditch.

St. James's Pl.—N. E. corner of Bethnal-green.

James-Pl. Silver-St. Old Gravel-Lane,—2d on the R. from King-st.

James - Pl. Salisbury-St. Bermondsey,—5 doors on the L. from the Admiral Hawk, Jamaica-row.

James's Place, Salisbury - Pl. Bermondsey,—the W. end on the R. from Salisbury-st.

St. James's Pl. Walworth-Common,—nearly op. the Paul's head.

St. James's Row, Gt. Suffolk-St. Boro.—continuation of it to Gravel-lane.

St. James's Sq. Saint James's, —entrance by 29, Pall-mall.

James-St. Westr.—from Buckingham-gate to York-st.

Saint James's Street, St. James's, —at 163, Piccadilly, 3d st. on the L. from the Haymarket.

Saint James's St. (Little),—11 doors on the L. in the last from the Palace.

James-St. Haymarket,—at 17, middle of the E. side.

James-St. Grosvenor-Sq.—from 29, Brook-st. to 287, Oxford-street.

James-St. Manchester-Sq.—at 163, Oxford-st. op. the last.

James-St. (Upper), Golden-Sq. —from the N. E. corner, to 33, Silver-st.

James-St. (Lower), Golden-Sq. —from the S. E. corner, to 12, Brewer-st.

James-St. Lisson-Grove,—1st N. from the Yorkshire - stingo.

James-St. (Little),—continuation of Lisson-st. from Bell-street.

James-St. Adelphi,—W. end of William st. 65, Strand.

James-St. Covent-Garden,—middle of the N. side, to 43, Long-acre.

James-St. (Gt.) Bedford-Row, —N. continuation of it, to Chapel-st.

James-St. (Little),—at 16, in the last, 1st on the R. from the King's road.

James-Street, Skinner-St. Sommers-Town,—1st on the L. from Judd's-pl. E.

Saint James's Street, St. James-Pl. Clerkenwell,—N. side the church.

James-Street, Featherstone-St. —at 37, 9 doors on the R. from the City-road.

James-Street, Church-St. Bethnal-Green,—at 124, 1st E. of Brick-lane, extends to 18, Hare-st.

James-Street, Leonard-St. Shoreditch,—at 51, 1st on the right E. from Paul-st.

James-Street, Cannon-St.-Road,

—1st on the R. south from the Commercial-road.

James - St. Stepney,—back of the N. E. corner Trafalgar-square.

James-St. Boro.-Road,—S. end of Dover-st. Blackfriars-rd.

James-St. Lambeth-Marsh,—3d on the L. from the Marsh turnpike, towards Blackfriars-road.

Saint James's Walk, St. James-Pl. Clerkenwell,—1st on the R. north of the church.

Jane-Court, Little York-Mews, Marybone,—1st on the L. from Gloucester-pl.

Jane-Court, Jane - St.—1st on the R. from the Commercial-road.

Jane-Pl. Kent-Road,—3d on the L. below the Bricklayers-arms.

Jane-St. Commercial - Road,—2d on the R. east from Cannon-st.-road.

Jane-St. Hackney-Road,—a few doors W. of the Nag's head, $\frac{1}{2}$ mile on the R. from Shoreditch.

Jane-Shore-Alley, 101, Shoreditch. See Wilkie's-Court.

Jay's Yard, Brick-St.—2d on the L. from Park-lane.

Idol-Lane, Tower-St.—5th on the R. from Fish-st. hill.

Jealous - Row, New-Road, St. George's East,—N. side, op. Betts-st.

Jees-Court, Oxford-St.—at 163, near a mile on the R. from St. Giles's.

Jeffries-Builds. New Tothill-St. Westr.—middle of the E. side.

Jeffery's Court, Grey-Eagle-St. Spitalfields,—3 doors N. of Quaker-st.

Jeffry's Gardens, Horseferry-Road, Westr.—op. the Ship, near New Peter-st.

Jeffries-Sq. St. Mary-Axe,—12 doors on the R. from Leadenhall-st.

Jeffrie's Yard, Chamber-St. Goodman's Fields, — 1st on the R. from Mansel-st.

Jenkin's Court, Ropemakers-Fields, Limehouse,—at 49, 1st on the L. from the E. end of Narrow-st.

Jennerian-Society's Central-House, — at 14, Salisbury-square.

Jennings's Yard, Bermondsey-St.—at 102, 12 doors S. of Russell-st.

Jericho-Court, Jerusalem-Court, —behind 58, Gracechurch-street.

Jermyn-St.—1st S. parallel to Piccadilly, from the Haymarket to St. James's st.

Jermyn-St. (Little),—W. end of the last.

Jersey-Court, White's Yard,—1st on the L. from 58, Rosemary-lane.

Jerusalem-Court, Gracechurch-St.--at 58, 6 doors S. of Fenchurch-st.

Jerusalem-Court, Saint John-St. —at 89, 5th on the L. from Smithfield.

Jerusalem-Passage, St. John-Sq. —N. side, leading to 16, Aylesbury-st.

Jetsom-St. Bennet's Row,—2d on the R. from Blackfriars-road.

Jewin-Court, Jewin-St.—1st on the R. from 46, Aldersgate-st.

Jewin-St. Cripplegate,—at 46, Aldersgate-st. middle of the E. side.

Jewin-St. Crescent. See Crescent.

Jewry (Old), Cheapside,—at 81, 1st on the R. from the Mansion-house.

Jewry (Old) Chapel, Jewin-St. Cripplegate,—12 doors on the R. from 29, Redcross-street.

Jewry-St. Aldgate,—1st on the R. from Fenchurch-st.

Jews-Chapel, Church-St. Spitalfields,—the corner of Brick-lane.

Jews-Harp-Court, Angel-Alley, —2d on the R. from Long-alley, Moorfields.

Jews-Harp-Passage, Marybone-Park,—in the field op. Devonshire-pl.

Jews-Hospital (Dutch), Mile End-Road,—op. the Three Crowns, about 1½ mile on the R. from Aldgate.

Jews-Hospital (Portuguese), Mile End-Road,—between the Three Crowns and the King-Harry, about 1½ mile on the L. from Aldgate.

Jews-Row, Chelsea. See Royal Hospital-Row.

Jews-Walk, Bethnal-Green,—N. side the Green.

Imperial Gazette-Office,—at 45, Old Bailey, corner of Fleet-lane.

Imperial Insurance-Office,—at 6, St. James's-st. and Sun-court, Cornhill.

O

India-House, Dock, &c. See
East-India.

Industry-Row, Vine-St. Lambeth,—near the Belvedere-
brewery.

Ingram-Court, Fenchurch-St.—
8 doors from 69, Grace-
church-st.

Inner-Court, Johnson's Builds.
Rosemary - Lane, — 1st on
the R. from Swallows-gar-
dens.

Innholders-Hall, Little Elbow-
Lane,—behind 175, Upper
Thames-st.

Inkhorn-Court (Five), Whitechapel High-St.—at 91, ½ of
a mile on the L. below Ald-
gate-pump.

Inman's Buildings, Thomas-St.
Kent-Road,—2d on the L.
from Poplar-row.

Innage-Lane,Creechurch-Lane.
See Heneage-Lane.

Inrolment - Office, Chancery -
Lane,—4th house on the R.
from 310, High-Holborn.

Jobbins-Court, Knightsbridge,
—½ a mile on the R. from
Hyde-park - corner, 6 doors
from the Barracks.

Jockey-Fields, Bedford - Row,
—between the E. side and
Gray's-inn-gardens.

John's Builds. Gt. Peter-Street,
Westr.—between Great St.
Ann's-st. and Little Saint
Ann's-lane.

St. John's Chapel, Gt. James-
St. Bedford-Row,—N. end,
being the corner of Chapel-
st. from 25, Lamb's-conduit-
street.

St. John's Chapel, St. John
Street, Spitalfields,—18 doors

on the L. from 105, Brick-
lane.

St. John's Chapel, West-Lane,
Walworth, — middle of the
N. side.

St.John the Evangelist's Church,
Westr. — op. 18, Millbank-
street.

St. John the Baptist's Church,
Savoy,—behind 125, in the
Strand.

St. John's Church, St. John's
Square,—E. side, near the
Gate.

St. John's Church, Wapping,—
a few yards N.from 98, Wapping-st.

St. John's Church, Fair-Street,
Horselydown,—middle of the
S. side.

John's Court, Edward-St. Manchester-Sq.—from the E. end
to 65, Marybone-lane.

John's Court, Hanway-St.—4
doors from 6, Tottenham-
court-road.

John's Court, Farm-St. Berkeley-Sq.—op. John-st.

John's Court, John-St. Golden-
Sq.—2 doors from the S. W.
corner of the square.

St. John's Court, Cow-Lane,—
at 36, 1st on the R. from 87,
W.-Smithfield.

St. John's Court, Corporation-
Row, Clerkenwell,—1st on
the L. from St. John-st.

St. John's Court, St. Martin's-
le-Grand,—5 doors from 66,
Newgate-st.

John's Court, Chalton-St. Sommers-Town,—12 doors on the
R. from the road to Mary-
bone.

John's Court, John-St. Holywell-Mount,—2 doors on the L. from Phips-st. Chapel-st.

John's Court, George-St. Mile-End New-Town,—at 21, 4 doors N. of Chicksand-st.

John's Court, Somerset-Street, Aldgate,—16 doors on the L. from Whitechapel.

John's Court, Up. East-Smith-field,—at 54, 2d on the R. from Tower-hill.

John's Court, Church-Lane,—1st on the R. from Cable-st.

John's Court, John-St.—5 doors on the L. from 35, Ratcliffe-highway.

John's Court, White-Horse-St. Ratcliffe. See Pipemakers-Alley.

John's Court, New-Walk, Horse-lydown,—1st on the L. from Shad-Thames.

St. John's Gate, St. John's-Sq. —the S. entrance from St. John's lane.

St. John's Lane, St. John-Street, —3d on the L. from Smith-field.

John's Hill, Ratcliffe-Highway. See John-St.

John's Mews, John-St. Edgware-Road,—at 6, under the archway, 1st N. from Cato-st.

John's Mews, Little James-St. —3d on the L. from Gray's-inn-lane.

St. John's Passage, Smith-Sq. Westr.—from the S. W. corner to Vine-st.

St. John's Passage, Cloak-Lane, —1st on the R. from Dowgate-hill.

John's Pl. Robert-St. Bedford-Row,—3d on the L. in Henry-st. from Gray's-inn-lane.

St. John's Pl. St. John's Row, St. Luke's,—1st on the L. 7 doors from Pittman's buildings.

John's Place, Old-St.-Road,—6 doors on the L. from op. Shoreditch-church.

John's Place, Back-Lane, St. George's East,—1st W. of King-David-lane.

St. John's Place, Lock's Fields, Walworth,—on the N. side of Salisbury-pl.

John's Rents, Silver-Street, Old Gravel-Lane,—N. end of it, behind Raine's hospital.

John's Row, Tottenham-Court, —E. end of Phillips's gardens.

St. John's Row, St. Luke's,—at 42, the N. end of Brick-lane, Old-st.

St. John's Sq. Clerkenwell,—N. end of St. John's lane from 68, St. John's-st.

John's Sq. Church-Lane, White-chapel,—4th on the R. from Cable-st.

St. John-Street, Wood-St. Westminster,—2d on the L. from 63, Millbank-st.

John-Street, Adam-St. Adelphi, —3 doors from 72, Strand.

John-Street, St. James's Sq.—from the S. E. corner to 29, Pall-mall.

John-St. New-Road, Marybone, —4th on the R. from the Yorkshire-st'ngo.

John-Street, Oxford-St.—at 101, near half a mile on the R. from St. Giles's.

John-St. Tottenham-Ct.-Rd.—1st W. from 31, Windmill-st. to 7, Howland-st.

John-St. (Up.) Tottenham-Ct.-Road,—continuation of the last.

John-St. King's Road, — at 6, 2d on the R. from Gray's-inn-lane.

John-St. Edgware - Road,—at 78, 7th on the R. from Tyburn-turnpike.

John-St. Berkeley-Sq.—at 20, N. E. corner.

John-Street, Hill-St. — at 15, 2d from the W. side of Berkeley-sq.

John-St. (Lower), Golden-Sq.—from the S. W. corner to 20, Brewer-st.

John-St. (Upper), Golden-Sq.—from the N. W. corner to 30, Silver-st.

John-St. Maiden-Lane, Battle-Bridge, St. Pancras,—W.side, from Edmond-st. to Union-place.

St. John-Street, W.-Smithfield, —at 74, N. side: it extends to Corporation-row.

St. John-Street-Road, Clerkenwell, — continuation of the last to Islington.

John-St. Pentonville, — 2d on the R. in Rodney-st. from the Chapel.

St. John-Street, Brick - Lane, Bethnal-Green,—at 106, 3d on the L. from 145, Church-street.

John-Street, St. Luke's. See John's Row.

John-St. Curtain-Road,—1st on the R. from Old-st.-road.

John-St. Holywell - Mount,— the last on the R. in Leonard-st. from Paul-st.

John-St. Brown's-Lane, Spital-fields,—at 30, the continuation of Wood-st. from the church.

John-St. America - Sq. — from 122, in the Minories, to Crutched-friars.

John-Street, Cannon-St.-Road, —1st on the L. from the turnpike, Cannon-st.

John's Street, or Hill, Ratcliffe-Highway,—at 34, 3d on the R. from Wellclose-sq.

John-St. Whitechapel,—1st on the L. in Osborn-pl. from 20, Brick-lane.

John-St. Ducking-Pond-Lane, —nearly op. Court-st. from 110, Whitechapel-road.

John-Street, St. George's East, —nearly op. the E. end of Lower Chapman-st.

John-Street, Lucas-Pl. Commercial-Rd.—a few doors below the Halfway-house.

John-Street, Bonner-St. Bethnal-Green, — 2d on the R. from Green-st.

John-Street, Union - St. Lambeth,—2d on the L. from Walcot-pl.

John-St. Blackfriars - Rd.—1st on the R. from Surrey-chapel towards the Obelisk.

John-St. Holland-St. — 1st on the R. from Blackfriars-bridge.

John-St. East-Lane, Walworth, — 3d on the R. from the Kent-road.

John-Street, Webb-St. Boro.— 1st on the L. from 248, Bermondsey-st.

John-St. Kent-Road, — 2d on the L. below the Bricklayers-arms.

John-St. Hickman's Folly,—4th on the R. from Dock-head, E. side Parker's-row.

John-St. Horseydown,—at the E. end of Broad-st. on the L. extending to Gainsford-st.

John-St. (Little),—S. end of the last, leading to Free-School-street.

John-St. Mint, Boro.—1st on the L. in Lant-st. from 108, Blackman-st.

Saint John's Wharf, Millbank-St. Westr.—10 doors from Abingdon-st.

St. John's Workhouse, Horse-lydown,—a few doors on the L. in Parish-st. from Tooley-street.

Johnson's Builds. Gt. St. Ann's-st. Westr.—1st on the L. from Gt. Peter-st.

Johnson's Builds. Rosemary-Lane,—behind 141, 6th on the L. from the Minories.

Johnson's Builds. Church-St. Lambeth,—W. end by the church.

Johnson's Builds. St. George's Fields,—behind the Circus, by the Obelisk.

Johnson's Change, Rosemary-Lane. See Johnson's Builds.

Johnson's Court, Charing-Cross. See Angel-Court.

Johnson's Court, Gt. Peter-St. Westr.—2 doors W. of Gt. St. Ann's st.

Johnson's Court, Fleet-St.—at 166, 12 doors E. of Fetter-lane.

Johnson's Court, Rupert-Street, Goodman's Fields,—middle of the E. side.

Johnson's Court, Shakespear's

Walk, Shadwell,—at 62, 3d on the L. from 48, High-st.

Johnson's Court, Duke-Street, St. George's Fields,—1st on the R. from the Obelisk.

Johnson's Place, Marsham-St. Westr.—at 48, 7 doors from the Horseferry-road.

Johnson's Pl. Globe-St. Bethnal-Green,—1st on the L.from Green-st. towards North-row.

Johnson-St. King Edward - St. Mile-End New-Town,—at 5, 1st on the L. from Church-street.

Johnson-St. Old Gravel-Lane,—at 156, 4th on the R. from Ratcliffe-highway.

Johnson's Wharf, Millbank-St. Westr.—op. Church-st.

Joiner's Court, Jacob-St. Dock-Head, — middle of the N. side.

Joiners-Hall-Buildings, Upper Thames-St.—at 79, 3d W. of Dowgate-hill.

Joiners-Pl. Curtain-Rd. Shore-ditch,—1st on the L. from Old-st.-road, 3 doors N. of William-st.

Joiners-Pl. St. George's Fields,—1st on the L. from the Obelisk, towards the Asylum.

Joiner-Street, Tooley-St.—at 240, 14 doors on the R. from London-bridge.

Jolly - Gardener - Court, Lambeth-Butts,—at the corner of Vauxhall-walk.

Jones's Court, Bainbridge-St. St. Giles's,—3d on the R. from Oxford-st.

Jones's Court, Jacob-St. Dock-Head, Bermondsey,—1st on the left E. from Mill-st.

O 3

Jones's Rents, Silver-St. Old Gravel-Lane,—3d on the R. from King-st.

Jones's Row, Tottenham-Court, —E.end, by Phillips's gardens.

Jones's Pl. Fore-St. Lambeth, —4th S. of Broad-st.

Joseph's Alley, Gravel-Lane, Boro.—W. side, nearly op. Maid-lane.

Joseph-Street, Lucas-St. Gray's Inn-Lane,—at 112, W. end.

Ipswich-Arms-Inn, Cullum-St. —4 doors from 135, Fenchurch-st.

Ipswich-Arms, Lower Thames-St.—at 22, ⅛ of a mile on the R. from London-bridge.

Ireland-Row, Mile-End-Road, —N. side, ¼ of a mile below the turnpike.

Ireland-Yard, Blackfriars,—S. end of New-st. and Creed-lane, from 14, Ludgate-st.

Irish-Court, Glasshouse-Yard, Goodman's Yd. Minories,— middle of the S. side.

Irish-Court, Whitechapel, — 3 doors E. of Somerset-st. Aldgate.

Irongate Stairs and Wharf, Tower-Hill,—at the S. E. corner, by St. Catherine's-st.

Ironmongers-Alms-Houses, Kingsland-Road,—⅓ of a mile on the R. from Shoreditch.

Ironmongers-Hall, Fenchurch-St.—at 118, nearly op. Mark-lane.

Ironmonger-Lane, Cheapside, —at 90, 2 doors E. of King-street.

Ironmonger-Row, Old-Street, St. Luke's,—at 97, on the E. side the church.

Isaac's Place, Willsted-St. Sommers-Town,—13 doors on the R. from Judd's pl. New-road.

Isabella-Row, William-Street, Westr.—at 22, 1st on the L. from James-st.

Island-Row, Commercial-Road, Limehouse,—⅛ of a mile on the L. west of the church.

Isle of Dogs, or Poplar-Marshes, —the ground on the S. side the West-India-docks.

Islington-Road. See St. John-Street-Road.

Islington-Spa,—S. side of Sadler's Wells.

Jubilee-Court, Royal Hospital-Row, Chelsea,—5th on the L. from the Hospital.

Jubilee-Pl. Commercial-Road, Stepney,—W. side the Half-way-house.

Jubilee-Pl. King's Road-Terrace, Chelsea,—about ¾ of a mile on the R. from Sloane-sq. towards Battersea-bridge.

Jubilee-Pl. Parliament-St. Bethnal-Green,—2d on the L. from op. Duthie's nursery.

Judd's Alms-Houses, Great St. Helen's,—adjoining 36, Bishopsgate.

Judd's Pl. E., Sommers-Town, —N. side the road to Marybone, a few doors from the turnpike, Battle-bridge.

Judd's Pl. W.—the continuation of the last.

Judd-St.—op. Judd's Pl. E. 2d from the turnpike.

Judge-Advocate's Office, —. Fludyer-st. Westr.

Judson's Row, St. George's Fields. See Jetsom-St.

Juniper's Court, Park-St. Boro. —1st on the R. from the Boro.-market.

Juniper-Court, Chigwell-St.— 3 doors on the R. from 51, Ratcliffe-highway.

Juniper - Row, Sun - Tavern - Fields, Shadwell,—S. side the Rope - ground, entrance by the first on the R. in King David-lane from 193, Shadwell High-st.

Jurstone-St. Lambeth,—1st on the R. in Hooper-st. from the Asylum.

Justice-Court, Harrow-St. Boro. —1st on the R. from Mint-st.

Ivy-Court, Ivy-Street, St. Giles's, —corner of George-st.

Ivy-Lane, Newgate-St.—at 30, —middle of the S. side.

Ivy-Lane, Hoxton,—by the Ivy-house, near ½ a mile on the R. from Old-st. along Pit-field-st.

Ivy-Pl. Hoxton,—on the N. side the Ivy-house, by the last.

Ivy-Street, St. Giles's,—2d on the L. in George-st. from 25, Broad-st.

Ivy-Terrace, Hoxton,—op. Ivy-place.

KEATE-STREET, Spitalfields, —the continuation of Thrawl-st. from 208, Brick-lane.

Keate-St. (Up.)—the W. end of the last.

Keate-Court,—at the W. end of the last.

Keen's Row, Walworth High-St.—part of the R. side, ½ a

mile from the Elephant and Castle.

Kemp's Court, Berwick-St. Oxford-St.—at 89, 3 doors E. of Broad-st.

Kemp's Row, Chelsea,—facing Ranelagh-walk.

Kendal's Court, Stangate-St. Lambeth,—op. Felix-st.

Kendal's Farm, Marybone,—N. side the New-road, nearly op. Fitzroy-sq.

Kendal's Mews, George-Street, Portman-Sq.—at 18, 5 doors E. of Baker-st.

Kendrick-Pl. Chenies-St. Tottenham-Ct.-Rd.—op. Thornhaugh-st.

Kenedy's Court, Cross-Lane,— op. the E. end of King-st. Drury-lane.

Kennet's Wharf-Lane, Upper Thames-St.—at 66, op. Garlick-hill.

Kennet's Wharf,—bottom of the last.

Kennington-Chapel, — by the 2 mile-stone, op. New-st.

Kennington - Common,——the open space fronting the Horns tavern.

Kennington-Cross, Kennington, —between Upper and Lower Kennington - lane, by the White-hart.

Kennington-Gardens, Kennington-Pl.—1st on the L. from the Green.

Kennington-Green,—from Kennington-cross to the Horns tavern.

Kennington-Lane,—1st on the R. south from Newington-church.

Kennington - Lane (Upper),—

the continuation of the last to Vauxhall.

Kennington-Passage, Kennington-Common,—10 doors N. of the Horns tavern.

Kennington-Pl. Up. Kennington-Lane,—S. side, by the Windmill tavern.

Kennington-Place, Kennington-Green,—behind the Horns tavern.

Kennington-Row, Kennington, —op. the Common, by the Horns tavern.

Kent and Essex-Inn, Whitechapel,—at 114, op. Red-Lion-street.

Kent-Pl. Kent-Road,—op. the Asylum for the Deaf and Dumb.

Kent-Road, — from the Elephant and Castle to Blackheath, Greenwich, &c.

Kent-St. Boro.—a few doors on the R. east from St.George's church.

Kent-St.-Road, the continuation of Kent-st. to the Bricklayers-arms.

Kentish-Builds. High-St. Boro. —at 94, ¼ of a mile on the L. from London-bridge.

Kenton-Street,Brunswick-Sq.— continuation of Wilmot-st. from 26, Bernard-st.

Keppel-Mews North, Keppel-St. Bedford-Sq.—1st on the L. from 11, Gower-st.

Keppel-Mews South,—op. the last.

Keppel's Row, New-Road,—S. side, near the N. W. corner of Fitzroy-sq.

Keppel-St. Russell-Sq. — from

30, on the W. side, to 10, Gower-st.

Keppel-St. Old Gravel-Lane,— at 71, 2d on the L. from 66, Ratcliffe-highway.

Keppel-Street, Gt. Guildford-St. Boro.—10 doors on the R. from 35, Queen-st.

Key-Court, Little St. Thomas Apostle,—4 doors on the R. from 34, Bow-lane.

Kidney-Stairs, Narrow-Street, Limehouse,—a few doors W. of the Draw-bridge.

Kilvinton's Coal-Wharf, Bankside,—on the E. side of Honduras-wharf.

King's Builds. Marybone-Lane, —at 67, 1st on the L. from 158, Oxford-st.

King's Court, Pimlico,—10 doors S. of Arabella-row.

King's Court, Blue-Anchor-Alley,—at 22, 4th on the R. from 99, Bunhill-row.

King's Court, King-St. Bethnal-Green,—2d on the R. from 158, Brick-lane.

King's Court, Gt. Suffolk-Street, Boro.—last on the R. from 80, Blackman-st.

King-Court (Three), Whitecross-St. Cripplegate,—at 9, 6 doors on the R. south from Beech-lane.

King-Court (Three), Lombard-St.—at 33, 4 doors E. from Clement's lane.

King-Court (Three), Minories, —10 doors on the L. from op. the Church, Aldgate.

King's Arch-Court, East-Street, Walworth, — 3d on the L. from the High-st.

King's Court, Half-Moon-St.—
2d on the R. from 170, Bishopsgate-without.

King's Mews, Charing-Cross,—
a few yards on the R. from
the Strand.

King's Mews (Up.)—on the N.
side of the last.

King's Mews (Back),—W. side
the King's mews, and at the
corner of Whitcomb-st.

King's St.-Mews, Park-Lane,—
5th on the L. from Oxford-
street.

King-St.-Mews, King-St. Portman-Sq.—3 doors on the L.
from 70, Baker-st.

King's Mews, King's Road,—
1st on the R. from Gray's-
inn-lane.

King's Mill, Rotherhithe,—¼ of
a mile below the church, op.
King James's stairs, Wap-
ping-wall.

King's Mill - Wharf,—on the
W. side the last.

King's Place, Pall-Mall,—at 58,
13 doors on the L. from St.
James's-street.

King's Place, Church-Row, St.
Pancras,—¼ of a mile on the
R. from Battle-bridge to-
wards Camden-town.

King's Pl. Commercial-Road,—
S. side, between Batty-st.
and King-st.

King's Pl. Blackman-St. Boro.
—at 63, op. the King's Bench.

King's Place, Boro.-Road,—W.
side the King's Bench.

King's Place,—N. side Queen's
gardens, Crosby-row, Snow's
fields.

King's Road, Grosvenor-Pl.—
4th on the R. from Hyde-
park-corner.

King's-Road-Terrace, Chelsea,
—a part of the King's road
by Manor-place, nearly op.
Smith-st.

King's Road, Gray's-Inn-Lane,
—1st on the L. ¼ of a mile
from Holborn.

King's Road, Poplar,—by the
Harrow public-house, ½ a
mile on the R. from the Commercial-road.

King's Row, Brompton, — R.
side the High - road from
Knightsbridge.

King's Row, Pimlico,—the R.
side, from Arabella-row to
Eaton-st.

King's Row, Pentonville,——
nearly op. the New-river re-
servoir, from Penton-st. to
the chapel.

King's Row, Dog-Row, Bethnal-
Green,—part of the L. side,
¼ of a mile from Mile-end-
turnpike.

King's Row, Smart's Gardens,
Bethnal-Green,—behind the
Lamb public-house, by the
S. end of Wilmot-st.

King's Row, Walworth High-
St.—nearly op. the Montpellier.

King's Row, Newington,—E.
side, between the Elephant
and Castle and the church.

King's Row, Horselydown. See
King-St.

King's Sq. Brick-Lane, Spitalfields,—at 165, 2 doors N.
from Phœnix-st.

King's Square, Horseshoe-Alley,
Moorfields,—1st on the L.
from Wilson-st.

King's Sq.-Court, Chapel-St.—
the S. end from 396, Oxford-
street.

King's Stairs, Rotherhithe-St.—
at 18, op. King-st. ⅕ of a
mile W. of the church.

King-Street, Ebury-St. Chelsea,
—1st on the R. from the
Watch-house towards Five-
fields.

King-St. West, Edgware-Road,
—at 53, 5th on the R. from
Tyburn-turnpike.

King-Street, Baker-St.—at 70,
3d on the L. from Portman-
square.

King-Street, Park-St.—at 23,
5th on the L. from Oxford-
street.

King-St. Golden-Sq.—at 323,
Oxford-st. E. side of Swallow-st.

King-Street, St. James's Sq.—
from the W. side, to Little
King-st.

King-St. (Little),—W. end of
the last to 12, St. James's
street.

King-St. Westr.—from Whitehall to the Abbey.

King-Street, Covent-Garden,—
N. W. corner, to New-st.
and St. Martin's lane.

King-Street, Drury-Lane,—at 165,
10 doors N. of Gt. Queen-
street.

King-Street, Princes-St. Soho,
—at 18, E. side the church.

King-Street, Broad-Street, St.
Giles's,—1st on the L. from
Holborn.

King-St. High-Holborn,—from
120, to Hart-st. Bloomsbury-sq.

King-St. (Up.)—continuation of
the last.

King-Street, Snow-Hill,—from
Fleet-market towards Smithfield.

King-Street, Goswell-St.—at

96, about ½ a mile on the L.
from Barbican.

King-Street, Long-Lane, West-
Smithfield,—at 70, middle of
the S. side.

King-St. Blackfriars,—last on
the L. in Church-entry from
Shoemakers-row.

King-Street, Cheapside,—from
92, N. side, to Guildhall.

King-Street, Wilson-St.—at 45,
nearly op. the N. E. corner
of Finsbury-sq.

King-Street, Old-St.—at the
N. W. corner of St. Luke's
hospital.

King-Street, Old-St.-Rd.—2d
on the R. from Shoreditch-
church.

King-Street, Turk-St. Bethnal-
Green,—1st on the L. from
Virginia-st. behind Shore-
ditch-church.

King-Street, (New), James-St.
Bethnal-Green,—2d on the
R. from 124, Church-st.

King-St. Brick-Lane, Spitalfields,—at 158, 4th on the
R. from 145, Church-st.

King-St. Creechurch-Lane,—the
continuation of it on the R.
from 87, Leadenhall-st.

King-St. Tower-Hill,—1st on
the R. in Rosemary-lane.

King-St. Mile-End New-Town,
—3d on the L. in Princes-st.
from Gt. Garden-st. Whitechapel-road.

King-St. Commercial-Road,—
3d on the R. from Church-
lane, Whitechapel.

King-St. Sampson's Gardens,
Wapping,—the continuation
of Globe-st. from 60, Wapping-st.

King-St. Old Gravel-Lane,—at

17, 2d on the R. from **157,** Wapping.

King-Street, Lambeth-Walk,—middle of the E. side.

King-St. Boro.-Road,—W. side the King's Bench.

King-Street, Mint-St. Boro.—4th on the R. from op. St. George's church.

King-Street, High-St. Boro.—at 109, ¼ of a mile on the L. from London-bridge.

King-St. Horselydown, — the continuation of Queen-street from the E. end of Free-School-st. to Shad-Thames.

King-St. Bermondsey New-Rd. —4th on the R. from the Bricklayers-arms.

King-Street, East St. Walworth, —1st on the L. from the High-st.

King-Street, Rotherhithe-St.—at 375, op. King's stairs, ⅖ of a mile W. of the church.

King's Yard, South-St. Grosvenor-Sq.—at 17, 2d on the L. from Park-lane.

King's-Arms-Builds. Wood-St. —10 doors on the R. from 122, Cheapside.

King's-Arms - Builds. Change-Alley,—at 24 and 23, Cornhill.

King's-Arms - Court, Princes-Row, Chelsea,—1st on the L. from King's-st.

King's-Arms-Court, Windmill-St.—at 17, 17 doors on the R. from the N. W. corner of Finsbury-sq.

King's-Arms-Court, Whitechapel-Road, — at 29, nearly op. the church.

King's-Arms-Gardens, Sun-Ta-

vern-Fields,—a few doors E. of King David-lane, Shadwell.

King's-Arms-Inn, Oxford-St.—at 264, 4 doors E. of N. Audley-st.

King's - Arms - Inn, Holborn-Bridge,—op. the N. end of Fleet-market.

King's-Arms- Inn, Leadenhall-St.—at 121, op. the India-House.

King's-Arms-Coach-Office, Bishopsgate - Within, — at 106, 10 doors N. of Threadneedle-street.

King's-Arms-Place, Tottenham-Ct.-Rd.—5 doors N. of Whitfield's chapel.

King's - Arms - Row, Bethnal - Green,—¼ of a mile E. of Bonner's Hall.

King's-Arms-Stairs, College-St. Lambeth,—¼ of a mile below Westr.-bridge.

King's-Arms-Stairs, Mill-Wall, Poplar,—¾ of a mile below the entrance to the West-India-docks.

King's-Arms - Yard, Silver - St. Bloomsbury,—1st on the L. from Southampton-st.

King's-Arms-Yd. Drury - Lane, —at 130, 2d on the L. from Holborn.

King's-Arms-Yd. Marybone-St. Piccadilly,—at 12, op. Air-street.

King's-Arms-Yard, Whitecross-St. Cripplegate,—at 40, 3d on the R. from 115, Fore-street.

King's-Arms-Yd. Chick - Lane, —at 57, 2d on the R. from Field-lane.

King's-Arms-Yard, Coleman-St.
—at 51, 10 doors on the R.
from Old-Jewry.

King's-Arms-Yard, Shoreditch,
—at 120, op. the church.

King's-Arms-Yard, Princes-St.
Lambeth,—1st on the R.
from Vauxhall.

King's-Arms-Yard, Blackfriars-
Road,—24 doors on the R.
from the Bridge.

King's-Arms-Yard, Hickman's
Folly,—4th on the R. from
Dock-head.

King's Bench (Courts of). See
Westr.-Hall and Guildhall.

King's-Bench-Office, Temple,
—on the S. side of King's-
Bench-walk.

King's-Bench-Prison, Boro.—
by Stones-End, ⅔ of a mile
on the R. from London-
bridge.

King's-Bench-Row,— S. side
the King's Bench.

King's-Bench-Terrace,— the
entrance to the King's-Bench-
prison.

King's-Bench-Walk, Temple,—
the open space on the N.
side the Temple gardens, at
the bottom of Mitre-court
from 44, Fleet-st.

King's-Bench-Walk, Bennet's
Row,—4th on the R. from
Blackfriars-road.

King David-Fort, Back-Lane, St.
George's East,— op. King
David-lane.

King David-Lane, Shadwell
High-St.—at 198, 1st on the
R. west of the church.

King David-Street, King David-
Lane,—middle of the W.
side.

King-Edward's-Stairs, Wapping,
—at 221, nearly op. Rotherhithe church.

King Edward-St. Wapping,—
op. the last.

King Edward-Street, Tudor-St.
—1st on the L. from 15, New
Bridge-st.

King Edward-Street, Mile-End
New-Town,—2d on the L.
in Princes-st. from Gt. Garden-st. Whitechapel-road.

King's Gardens, Gravel-Lane,
—14 doors on the R. from
Holland-street, Blackfriars-
bridge.

King's-Head-Alley, Rose-Lane,
Spitalfields,—at the back of
King's-head-court.

King's-Head-Alley, Virginia-St.
Parson's St. Up. East-Smithfield,—op. Pennington-st.

King's-Head-Court, Wood-St.
Westr.—3d on the L. from
63, Millbank-st.

King's-Head-Court, James-St.
Westr.—1st on the L. from
Buckingham-Gate.

King's-Head-Court, Broadway,
Westr.—middle of the N. side.

King's-Head-Court, Shoe-Lane
—at 98, 1st on the L. from
130, Fleet-st.

King's-Head-Court, 326, High-
Holborn. See Middle-Row-
Place.

King's-Head-Court, Holborn-
Hill,—at 40; leads to 63, Fetter-lane.

King's-Head-Court, Gray's-Inn-
Lane,—24 doors on the R.
from Holborn.

King's-Head-Court, St. Martin's-
le-Grand,—at 17, 5th on the
L. from 66, Newgate-st.

King's Head-Court, Beech-St. Barbican,—at 42, 8 doors E. of Golden-lane.

King's Head-Court, St. Paul's Church - Yard, — at 27, S. side.

King's Head-Court, Shoreditch, —at 214, 6 doors N. from Worship-st.

King's Head-Court, Long-Alley, Moorfields,—3 doors N. of Crown-st.

King's Head-Court, Whitecross-St. Cripplegate,—at 42, the 4th on the R. from 115, Fore-street.

King's Head-Court, Gutter-Lane, —at 14, 2d on the R. from Cheapside.

King's Head - Court, Fish-St.-Hill,—4 doors on the R. from London-bridge.

King's Head-Court, Kingsland-Road,—2d on the R. from Shoreditch.

King's Head-Court, Petticoat-Lane,—2d on the L. from Widegate-st. Bishopsgate.

King's Head - Court, Gravel - Lane, Boro. — 1st N. from Price's-st.

King's Head-Gardens, Holywell-Row, Holywell-Mount,—1st on the L. from Worship-sq.

King's Head-Inn, Old-Change, —10 doors from the S. E. corner of St. Paul's church-yard.

King's Head-Inn, High-St. Boro.—at 53, 8 doors S. of St. Thomas-st.

King's Head-Yard, Duke-St.— 1st on the R. from 52, W. side of Lincoln's-inn-fields.

King's Head-Yard, Russell-St.—

12 doors on the R. from Drury-lane.

King's Head-Yard, Charles-St. Hatton-Garden,—at 14, seven doors E. of 24, Hatton-garden.

King's Head - Yard, Broad-St. Bloomsbury,—17 doors on the R. from Holborn.

King's Head-Yard, Duke-Street, Bloomsbury,—3 doors from 43, Gt. Russell-st.

King's Head-Yard, High-Street, Lambeth, — 3d on the R. from the church.

King's Head-Yard, Tooley-St.— at 178, by the corner of Bermondsey-st.

King Henry-Court, King-Street, St. George's East,—1st on the R. from 29, New Gravel-lane.

King Henry-Yard, Nightingale-Lane, East-Smithfield,—at 38, two doors N. of Burr-st.

King James's Stairs, Wapping-Wall,—at 70, op. Star-st.

King John's Pl. Holywell-Lane, —13 doors on the R. from 193, Shoreditch.

King John's Court (Little),—1st W. of the last.

King John's Court, Limehouse-Causeway,—op. the Lime - kilns-dock.

King John's Palace, Tottenham-Court,—6 doors E. of the Hampstead-road.

King and Key Coach - Office, Fleet-St.—at 142, 11 doors W. of Shoe-lane.

King's Printing-Office,—at 12, East Harding-street, Shoe-lane.

King and Queen - Court, Old

P

Gravel-Lane,—at 114, 2d on the R. from Ratcliffe-high-way.

King and Queen-Stairs, Rother-hithe,—E. side the Surrey-Canal, ¼ a mile below the church.

Kingsbury-Pl. Bowl and Pin-Alley, Chancery-Lane,—at the E. end, entrance op. Bream's-builds.

Kingsgate-St. High-Holborn,—at 118, W. side of Red-lion-square.

Kingsland-Road,—at Shoreditch-church, on the L. to Kings-land.

Kingsland-Row, Old Gravel-Lane,—at 114, 10 doors on the R. from 65, Ratcliffe-highway.

Kinning's Builds. Swan-Lane, Rotherhithe,—a few doors on the R. from Rotherhithe-street.

Kirby-Court, West-St. W. Smith-field,—a few doors on the R. from the N. W. corner of Smithfield.

Kirby-Street, Charles-St. Hatton-Garden,—at 33, 4 doors E. from 25, Hatton-garden.

Kirk's Place, Pitt-Street, St. George's Fields,—part of the E. side.

Kirkman's Pl. Tottenham-Court-Road,—at 54, between Wind-mill-st. and Goodge-st.

Kitten-Court, Orchard-St. West-minster,—back of Cat's head-court.

Kittisford-Pl. Hackney-Road,—R. side, adjoining the chapel, ¼ of a mile from Shoreditch.

Kittleby-Court, Blue-Anchor-

Yard,—5th on the R. from 48, Rosemary-lane.

Knightsbridge,—from the turn-pike, Hyde-park-corner, to-wards Kensington.

Knightsbridge-Green,—from op. the Barracks, to Brompton high-road.

Knight's Court, Tench-Street, St. George's East,—2d on the R. from the London-docks.

Knight's Court, Green-Walk,—2d on the L. from Holland-st. Blackfriars-bridge.

Knight-Rider-Court, Little Knight-Rider-St.—15 doors on the R. from the Old-change.

Knight-Rider-St. (Gt.) Doctors-Commons,—2d on the R. south from 14, St. Paul's-church-yard.

Knight-Rider-St. (Little),—op. the last.

Knowle's Court, Little Carter-Lane,—at 10, 2d on the L. from 14, Old-change.

——————

LABOUR-IN-VAIN-COURT, Old Fish-St. Hill, Up. Thames-St.—middle of the W. side.

Labour-in-Vain-Court, Upper Thames-St. See Brook's Wharf-Lane.

Labour-in-Vain-Hill, Upper Thames-St. See Old Fish-St.-Hill.

Labour-in-Vain-St. Shadwell-Market,—S. E. corner.

Labour-in-Vain-St. (Little),—on the S. side Shadwell-water-works.

Lad-Court, White-Hind-Alley, Bankside, Boro. — 1st from Maid-lane.

Lad-Lane, Wood-St.—at 19, 1st on the R. from 122, Cheapside.

Lady's Yard, Harrow-Alley,— 1st on the L. from Aldgate.

Lamb-Alley, Bishopsgate-Without,—at 144, N. side of Sun-street.

Lamb-Alley, Blackman-St. Boro.—at 34, 6th on the L. from St. George's church.

Lamb-Alley (Little), Blackman-St.—7 doors from St. George's church.

Lamb-Alley, Bermondsey-St.— at 185, 5th on the L. from the church towards Tooley-street.

Lamb's Builds. Inner Temple-Lane,—2d on the L. from 16, Fleet-st.

Lamb's Builds. Cherry-Tree-Alley,—1st on the R. from 118, Bunhill-row.

Lamb's Court, Clerkenwell-Green,—at 23, S. side the Sessions-house.

Lamb's Chapel-Court, Monkwell-St. — continuation of Hart-st. Wood-st.

Lamb's Court, Red-Lion-Court, Spitalfields,—middle of the N. side.

Lamb's Court, Whitechapel-Road,—at 65, ⅙ of a mile on the L. below the church.

Lamb-Green, Lamb-Alley,—1st on the L. from 185, Bermondsey-st.

Lamb's Passage, Chiswell-St.—

at 75, 3d on the R. from Finsbury-sq.

Lamb's Pl. Swan-St.—the 1st on the R. from the Kent-road.

Lamb-Row, Wilmot-St. Bethnal-Green,—S. end on the L. by the Lamb public-house.

Lamb-Square, Clerkenwell-Green,—the S. end of Lamb-court.

Lamb-St. Spitalfields,—E. continuation of Spital-sq. from 103, Bishopsgate-without.

Lamb-Yard, Lamb's Conduit-St.—3 doors on the L. from op. the Foundling-hospital.

Lamb's Conduit-Passage, Red-Lion-Sq.—at 25, N. E. corner.

Lamb's Conduit-St. Red-Lion-St. Holborn,—N. continuation of it, to the Foundling-hospital.

Lambeth-Butts, Lambeth,— between Vauxhall-walk and Lambeth-walk, by Broad-st.

Lambeth-Chapel,—op. the Three Stags, S. side the Asylum.

Lambeth's Court, Webber-Row, —1st on the L. from Blackfriars-road.

Lambeth-Hill, Up. Thames-St. —from 212, to the Old-Change.

Lambeth-Marsh, Westr.-Bridge-Road,—2d on the L. ¼ of a mile from the bridge.

Lambeth-Upper-Marsh,— from the turnpike to Stangate-street.

Lambeth-Mews,—N. end Clarges-st. Piccadilly.

Lambeth - Palace, Lambeth,—N. side of Lambeth-church.

Lambeth - Pl. West - Sq.—the continuation of Brook - st. Lambeth.

Lambeth - Road, St. George's Fields,—from the Obelisk towards Lambeth.

Lambeth-Stairs, Lambeth,—W. side Lambeth-church.

Lambeth-St. Goodman's Fields, —2d on the L. from behind 32, Lemon-st.

Lambeth-Terrace, Lambeth,—op. the New-chapel, towards Lambeth-church.

Lambeth-Walk, Lambeth,—1st on the L. from the New-chapel towards the church.

Lambeth-Water - Works, Narrow-Wall, Lambeth,—$\frac{1}{2}$ of a mile from Westr.-bridge.

Lambeth-Workhouse,—near the S. end of Lambeth-walk.

Lamp - Office - Court, Lamb's Conduit-St.—at 54, nearly op. Chapel-st.

Lancashire-Court, New Bond-St.—at 121, 3d on the R. from 307, Oxford-st.

Lancaster - Court, Strand,—at 474, a few doors on the L. from Charing-cross.

Lancaster - Court, Bankside, Southwark,—between Smith's Rents and Rose-alley.

Land-Revenue - Office, Whitehall,—2d door on the L. from nearly op. the Admiralty towards Middle Scotland-yard.

Land of Promise, Hoxton - Town,—nearly op. Workhouse lane, $\frac{1}{2}$ a mile on the R. from Old-st.-road.

Lane's-Court, Cold-Bath-Sq.— behind No. 4, W. side.

Langadale -Street, Cannon-St.-Road,—1st W. to it, from William-st. to James-st.

Langbourn - Chambers, Fen-church-St.—14 doors on the L. from Gracechurch-st.

Langbourn-Ward-School, Lime-St.—by the church, two doors from 160, Fenchurch-st.

Langley-Buildings, Walworth-Common,—W. side of Surrey - sq. by the Hen and Chickens.

Langley-Pl. Commercial-Road, —N. side, between Greenfield-st. and Gloucester-st.

Langley-St.Long-Acre,—at 115, 4th on the R. from Drury-lane.

Langthorn-Court, Little Bell-Alley, London-Wall,—S. side Leathersellers-builds.

Lanham's Builds. Mount - St. Bethnal-Green,—1st on the R. from Rose-st.

Lansdown - House,——S. side Berkeley-sq.

Lansdown-Mews, Great Guildford-St. Russell-Sq.—at 33, op. Lansdown-pl.

Lansdown-Mews, Clarges-St.— 2d on the R. from Piccadilly.

Lansdown-Passage, Berkeley-St. —a few yards on the R. from Berkeley-sq.

Lansdown-Pl. Gt. Guildford-St. —3d on the R. from Gray's-inn-lane.

Lant-St. (Old), Blackman - St. Boro.—at 109, 1st on the R. from St. George's church.

Lant-St. (New),—W. end of the last.

Lant-St. (Little),—2d on the R. in Lant-st. from 109, Blackman-st.

Larger's Yard, Angel - Alley, Bishopsgate,—middle of the N. side.

Lark-Row, Bethnal - Green,— 2d on the L. east from Cambridge-heath turnpike.

Lascell's Court, Broad-Street, St. Giles's,—at 42, op. Plumtree-street.

Lascell's Pl.—5 doors E. of the last.

Latham's Builds. South - Row, Sommers - Town,—op. Chalton-st.

Latham's Pl. Sommers Town,— behind 1, Sommers-pl. West, New-road.

Laudable-Society for the Benefit of Widows,—held at 4, Crane-court, Fleet-st.

Laundry -Yard, Gt. Peter - St. Westr.—7 doors W. of Marsham-st.

Lavender-Lane, Rotherhithe-St. — op. 118, by the Horse-ferry.

Lavender-Pl. Rotherhithe,—at 142, op. Lavender-wharf.

Lavender-Wharf, Rotherhithe-St.—nearly op. 140, by the Pageants.

Lawn, South Lambeth,—⅛ of a mile on the L. from Vauxhall-turnpike.

Lawn-Lane,—3d on the L. from Vauxhall-turnpike.

St. Lawrence Jewry - Church, Cateaton - St. — N. end of King-st. Cheapside.

Lawrence-Lane, Cheapside,—at

96, 4th on the R. from the Mansion-house.

Lawrence-Pountney-Hill,—bottom of Green - lettuce-lane, from 30, Cannon-st.

Lawrence-Street, High-St. Saint Giles's,—1st on the L. from Oxford-st.

Lawrence-Pountney-Lane, Cannon-St.—from 38, to 141, Up. Thames-st.

Laxton-Court, Long-Lane, Bermondsey,— 7th on the L. from St. George's church.

Laystall-St. Leather-Lane,—N. continuation of it, bearing to the L.

Layton's Grove, High-St. Boro. —at 138, 16 doors N. of St. George's church.

Layton's Builds.—4 doors S. of the last.

Lazenby-Court, Conduit-Court, —behind 17, W. end of Long-acre.

Lead-Company's Office,—at 9, St. Martin's Lane, Cannon-st.

Lead-Yard, Kingsland-Road,— 3d on the R. from Shoreditch, 8 doors S. of Union-st.

Lead-Yard, Plough-St.—2d on the L. from 45, Whitechapel.

Leadenhall - Buildings, Gracechurch-St.—at 80, 10 doors N. of Fenchurch-st.

Leadenhall-Market,——by the last.

Leadenhall-Street, Gracechurch-St.—at 98, op. Cornhill.

Leading-St. Fox's Lane, Shadwell,—1st on the L. from 56, High-st.

Leaping-Bar-Yard, Old-St.—at 117, 1st on the L. from Goswell-st.

P 3

Leaping-Bar-Yard, Blackfriars-Road,—op. Stamford-st.

Leather-Lane, Holborn, — at 129, 3d coach-turning on the R. from Fleet-market.

Leather-Lane - Chapel,—at 26, Leather-lane, op. Baldwin's gardens.

Leathersellers-Alms-Houses,—N. side of Hart-st. facing London-wall, or behind 63, Wood-st.

Leathersellers-Alms-Houses,—bottom of Clark's court, on the R. from 60, Bishopsgate-st.

Leathersellers-Builds. London-Wall, — op. the centre of Bethlem-hospital.

Leathersellers-Hall,—E. end St. Helen's pl. Bishopsgate.

Leaves-Court, Fore-St. Lambeth,—¼ of a mile on the L. from the church.

Leblond's Builds. William-St. Curtain-Road, — last on the R. from 137, Shoreditch.

Lee's Court, St. Catherine's Lane,—2d on the R. from St. Catherine's church.

Lee's Mews, North Audley-St. —a few yards on the L. from the N. W. corner of Grosvenor-square.

Lee's Row, St. George's Fields, —behind Hatfield-pl. by the Obelisk.

Leech's Court, Collingwood-St. Blackfriars-Road,—corner of Charlotte-st.

Leg-Alley, Long-Acre,—at 34, 10 doors W. of James-st.

Leg-Alley, Shoreditch,—at 240, 10 doors N. of Worship-st.

Leg-Court, Oxford-St.—at 417, 1st on the L. from St. Giles's.

Leg-Court, Gt. Peter-St. Westr. —middle of the N. side.

Leg-Court (Three), Whitecross-Street, St. Luke's,—at 207, 13 doors on the L. from Beech-st.

Leg of Mutton-Gardens, Kingsland-Road,—back of Taylor's builds. ⅖ of a mile on the L. from Shoreditch.

Leghorn-Alley, Rotherhithe-St. —at 215, near Globe-stairs.

Leicester-Court, Castle-St. Leicester-Sq.—5 doors N. of Green-st.

Leicester - Pl. Leicester - Sq.—N. E. corner to Lisle-st.

Leicester-Sq.—op. the E. end of Panton-st. from '25, in the Haymarket.

Leicester - St. Leicester - Sq.—N. W. corner to Lisle-st.

Leicester-Street, Swallow-St.—31 doors from 43, Piccadilly.

Leigh - Street, Red-Lion-Sq.—middle of the S. side to Dean-st. and 93, High-holborn.

Leigh-St. Burnton-Crescent,—3d on the L. in Hunter-st. from Brunswick-sq.

Leith and Berwick-Wharf, Lower East-Smithfield,—op. Burr-st. near ¼ of a mile below the Tower.

Lemon-Court, Old Nicol-Street, Bethnal-Green,—2d on the L. east from Cross-st.

Lemon-Row, Lemon-St. Goodman's Fields,—S. end, near Rosemary-lane.

Lemon-Court (Gt.) Princes-St. Lambeth,—1st on the L. from Broad-st.

Lemon-Court (Little),—S. side the last.

Lemon-St. Goodman's Fields, —the continuation of Red-Lion-st. from 30, Whitechapel.

Lemon-St. Loman's Pond, Boro. —3d from Gravel-lane.

Lemon-Tree-Yard,—corner of the Haymarket and Piccadilly.

Lemon-Tree-Yd. Bedfordbury, —3 doors from 53, Chandos-street.

Lenham's Buildings, Mount-St. Bethnal-Green,—a few doors on the R. from 44, Church-street.

St. Leonard's Charity-School, —1st house on the R. in Kingsland-road from Shoreditch.

St. Leonard's Church, Shoreditch,—a mile on the R. north from Cornhill along Bishopsgate and Shoreditch.

Leonard-Court, Paul-St. Finsbury,—N. side of Leonard-square.

Leonard-Sq. Paul-St. Finsbury, —the space where Paul-st. and Leonard-st. intersect each other.

Leonard-St. Shoreditch, — the continuation of Tabernacle-row, from 35, City-road.

Leonard-St. (Little), Paul-St. —1st on the R. north of Leonard-sq.

Leopard-Court, Baldwin's Gardens, Leather-Lane,—at 37, 6 doors on the R. from 76, Leather-lane.

Leopard - Court, Rotherhithe-St.—at 173, 24 doors below Globe-stairs-alley.

Lestock-Pl. East-St. Walworth,

—4th on the L. from the High-st.

Levant-Company's- House, St. Helen's Pl.—a few doors on the L. from Bishopsgate.

Lewer-Row, Lambeth-Butts,— N. side, by Lambeth-walk.

Lewington's Builds. City-Road, —W. side the turnpike by St. Luke's hospital.

Lewsham - Street, Princes - St. Westr.—3d on the R. from Storey's gate.

Life-Guards - Stables, King-St. Portman - Sq.—5 doors on the R. from Baker-st.

Life-Guards-Stables, Portman-St.—4 doors on the R. from 220, Oxford-st.

Lilly-St. Gt. Saffron-Hill,—at 40, 5th on the R. from Field-lane.

Lillyput-Lane, Noble-St. Foster-Lane,—at 6, 3d on the R. from Cheapside.

Lime-Street, Fenchurch-St.—at 160, 1st on the L. from Gracechurch-st.

Lime-Street-Passage, Lime-St. —at 18, leading to Leadenhall-market.

Lime-Street-Sq. Lime - St.—3 doors on the L. from 21, Leadenhall-st.

Limehouse-Causeway,—at 41, Three-Colts-st. extending to the Commercial-road by the W. India-docks.

Limehouse - Hole, — continuation of Three Colt-st. from the Lime-kilns towards Mill-wall.

Limehouse-Hole-Stairs,—a few yards on the R. below the Lime-kilns-dock.

Lime-Kilns-Dock, Limehouse,
—E. end of Fore-st. and S.
end of Three Colt-st.

Lime-Kilns-Hill, Limehouse,—
a few yards on the R. from
the E. end of Fore-st.

Lime Tree-Court, Narrow-Wall,
Lambeth,—between Peach's
yard and Cupers-bridge.

Lincoln's-Inn, Chancery-Lane,
—op. 40, ½ of a mile on the
L. from 193, Fleet-st.

Lincoln's-Inn-Fields,—by Great
Turnstile, 282, Holborn, and
by Serle-street, Carey-street,
Chancery-lane.

Lincoln's - Inn - Gardens, —W.
side of Lincoln's inn.

Lincoln's - Inn - Hall,— facing
the entrance from op. 40,
Chancery-lane.

Lincoln's-Inn New Sq.—2d on
the R. in Carey-st. from 99,
Chancery-lane.

Lincoln's-Inn Old Sq. or Builds.
See Lincoln's-Inn.

Linnean - Society,—at 9¾, Gerrard-st. Soho.

Linny-Court, Queen-St. Bloomsbury,—at 21, near the W. end
of Hart-st.

Linton-Pl. Bell-St. Paddington,
—a few doors on the L. from
Edgware-road.

Lion-Pl. Battle-Bridge,—op. S.
end of York-st. Pentonville.

Lion-St. Holborn. See Lyon-St.

Lion-St. Kent - Road,—2d on
the R. from the Elephant and
Castle.

Lion and Lamb-Alley, Princes-
St. Lambeth,—3d on the L.
from Vauxhall.

Lion and Lamb-Court, Play-

house-Yd.—1st on the R.
from 50, Golden-lane.

Lion in the Wood-Yard, Wilderness-Lane,—5 doors on
the R. from Dorset-st. Salisbury-sq.

Liquor-Pond - St. Gray's - Inn-
Lane,—at 68, ¼ of a mile on
the R. from Holborn.

Lisbon-S. Dog-Row, Mile-End,
—12 doors on the L. from
the turnpike.

Lisle-St. Leicester-Sq.—1st parallel to the N. side.

Lisle-St. (New),—E. end of the
last.

Lisson-Green, Marybone,—op.
the Yorkshire-stingo.

Lisson-Grove, Marybone,—N.
side the New-road, op. the
Yorkshire-stingo.

Lisson - Mews, Southampton -
Row,—1st on the L. from 82,
Edgware-road.

Lisson-Pl. Lisson-Green, Paddington,—2d N. from Bell-
street.

Lisson-Row, Lisson - Grove,—
2d on the L. north from the
Yorkshire-stingo.

Lisson-St. Lisson-Green,— 1st
on the L. in Southampton-
row, from 82, Edgware-road.

Lisson-St. (Up.)—continuation
of the last.

Litchfield-Street, King-St. Soho,
—3d on the R. from Princes-
street.

Literary-Fund, — 36, Gerrard-
st. Soho, middle of the S.
side, 12 doors on the L. from
Little Newport-st.

Literary-Panorama-Office,—at
108, Hatton-garden, 5 doors

on the L. from 111, Holborn-hill.

Little-Court, Castle-St. Leicester-Sq.—4 doors from Great Newport-st.

Little-Court, Gt. Arthur-St.—the last on the L. from 10, Goswell-st.

Lloyd's Court, St. Giles's,—W. side the church.

Lloyd's Evening-Post Newspaper-Office,—at 12, Warwick-square.

Lloyd's Yard, Black-Swan-Alley,—1st on the L. from London-wall.

Loader's-Pl. James-St. Westr.—E. end, op. the Blue-coat-school.

Lock's Fields, Walworth,—the space between Walworth High-st. and the Kent-road, on the N. side of East-lane.

Lock's Gardens, Bowling-Green-Lane, Clerkenwell,—3d on the L. from Coppice-row.

Lock-Hospital, Grosvenor-Pl.—30 doors on the R. from Hyde-park-corner.

Lock-Hospital (Old),—at the E. end of Kent-st. Boro.

Lock's Pl. Lock's Fields,—1st on the R. in York-st from Walworth High-st.

Lock's Row,—the S. side Lock's place.

Lock's Yard, Blackman-St. Boro.—at 62, op. the King's Bench.

Lockwood-Court, Gt. Saffron-Hill,—at 47, middle of the E. side.

Loggerhead-Court, Gascoigne-Pl. Bethnal-Green,—1st on the L. from 40, Castle-st.

Loman's Pond, Gravel-Lane, Boro.—2d on the L. south of Charlotte-st.

Loman's St. — E. end of the last.

Lombard-Court, Tower-St. 7 Dials,—at 21, 5 doors on the R. from Little St. Martin's-lane.

Lombard-St. 7 Dials,—op. the last.

Lombard-Street, Gracechurch-St.--from 24, to the Mansion-house.

Lombard-Street, Fleet-St.—at 56, middle of the S. side, 12 doors W. of Water-lane.

Lombard-St. Mile-End New-Town,—3d on the R. from 55, Brick-lane, along Pelham-street.

Lombard-St. (Great), Boro.—at the W. end of Mint-st.

Lombard-St. (Little),—N. end of the last.

London-Annuity-Office for Widows,—at 25, Old Fish-st. 4 doors E. of the Old-Change.

London-Assurance-Office, Birchin-Lane,—2 doors on the R. from 62, Lombard-st.

London-Bridge,——the lowest bridge over the Thames.

London-Chronicle Newspaper Office,—at 151, Fleet-st. by Bolt-court.

London-Court, White's Yard,—1st on the R. from 57, Rosemary-lane.

London-Docks, Wapping,—between 72, Wapping-st. and the church.

London Dock-Office,—N. end of Princes-st. Bank.

London-Dock-Office, — 110,

Fenchurch-street, nearly op. Mark-lane.

London-Electric-Institution, — at 16, Bunhill-row, also at 26, Tabernacle-row, City-road.

London-Evening-Post Newspaper-Office,—Union-st. Black-friars.

London-Female-Penitentiary, Pentonville,—W. side the chapel, op. Weston-st.

London-House, Aldersgate-St.—at 155, near the middle of the W. side.

London-Hospital, Whitechapel, —⅓ of a mile on the R. below the church.

London-House-Yd. St. Paul's-Church-Yd.—at 74 and 79, 1st on the L. from Ludgate-street.

London-Infirmary, Charter-house-Sq.—at 40, 2d house on the L. from Carthusian-street.

London-Institution, Old-Jewry,—under the gateway, 8 doors on the R. from 81, Cheapside.

London-Journal Newspaper-Office,—Union-street, Black-friars.

London-Life-Association,—at 48, St. Paul's church-yard, near Cheapside.

London-Mews, London-St.—14 doors on the L. from Tottenham-court-road.

London-Packet Newspaper-Office,—at 12, Warwick-sq. Warwick-lane.

London-Registry-Office, — at 16, Gt. Knight-Rider-street, Doctors-commons.

London-Rd. St. George's Fields,—from the Obelisk to the Elephant and Castle.

London-Society-Protestant-School,—a few doors on the L. in Ropemakers-st. from Moorfields.

London-Stone, Cannon-St.—between 81 and 82, by the church.

London-St. Tottenham-Court-Road,—at 108, ½ a mile on the L. from Oxford-st.

London-St. (Old), Fenchurch-St.—at 59, 5th on the R. from Gracechurch-st.

London-St. (New),—the continuation of the last.

London-St. Hackney-Road,—from the Nag's head towards the Bird-cage.

London-Street, Queen-St. Ratcliffe,—1st on the L. from Ratcliffe-cross.

London-Street, London-Road, St. George's Fields,—2d on the R. from the Elephant and Castle towards the Obelisk.

London-St. Bermondsey,—entrance by the first bridge on the R. in Mill-st. from Dock-head.

London-Tavern, Bishopsgate-St.—2 doors from Cornhill.

London-Tavern (New), Cheapside,—at 140, 10 doors on the L. from St. Paul's-church-yd.

London Terrace, Hackney-Rd.—R. side, op. Gt. Cambridge-st. ½ a mile from Shoreditch.

London-Terrace, Commercial-Road,—1st on the L. west of Cannon-st.-road.

London-Wall, Moorfields,—S.

side of Bethlem-hospital, 4th street on the R. in Wood-st. from 122, Cheapside.

London - Workhouse, Bishopsgate,—at 173; ⅛ of a mile N. of the church.

Long-Acre, Drury - Lane,—40 doors on the R. from St. Giles's.

Long-Alley, Moorfields,—2d on the R. from the N. E. corner.

Long-Alley, Worship -St.—the N. continuation of the last from Crown-st.

Long's Builds. Whitecross-St. —at 104, 7th on the R. north from Chiswell-st.

Long's Court, Saint Martin's St.—4 doors on the L. from 38, Leicester-sq.

Long's Court, Rotherhithe-St. —6 doors E. of the church.

Long-Lane, West-Smithfield,— at 66, E. side, extending to op. 77, Aldersgate-st.

Long-Lane, Bermondsey, — at 149, Bermondsey-st. 6 doors S. of the church.

Long-Walk, Half-Moon-Alley, —2d on the L. from 48, Whitecross-st. Cripplegate.

Long-Walk, Bermondsey-Sq.— —at the N. E. corner, leading eastward.

Long's Yard, Lamb's-Conduit-St.—10 doors on the L. from the Foundling-hospital.

Looker's Court, King - St.—at 84, 4th on the R. from 323, Oxford-st.

Lords, House of,—E. side New Palace - yard, adjoining the House of Commons.

Lothbury,—N. side the Bank,

1st on the R. in Old-Jewry, from Cheapside.

Lottery-Office, Somerset-Pl.— 2d door on the L. in the sq. from the Strand.

Love-Court, George - Alley,— 1st on the L. from 70, Fleet-market.

Love-Court, Mutton - Lane,— 2d on the L. from Clerkenwell-green.

Love-Court, Petticoat-Lane,— at 120, 5th on the R. from 41, Aldgate High-st.

Love-Court, Little Middlesex-St.—1st on the L. from 120, Petticoat-lane.

Love-Court, Love-Lane, Shadwell,—4 doors on the R. from 117, High-st.

Love-Court, Tooley-Street,—at 157, nearly op. Green-bank.

Love-Lane, Wood-St.—at 36, 2d on the R. from 122, Cheapside.

Love-Lane (Little),—N. side the last.

Love-Lane, Little Eastcheap,— from 19 to 102, Lower Thames-st.

Love-Lane, Shadwell High-St. —at 117½ by Cock-hill.

Love-Lane, Old Gravel-Lane, —at 160, 4th on the L. from 157, Wapping.

Love-Lane, Willow-St. Bankside,—1st on the R. from Holland-street, Blackfriarsbridge.

Love-Lane, Rotherhithe-St.— at 384, op. Rotherhithe-stairs, near Millpond-bridge.

Love-Place, Hackney-Road,— W. side, part of Middlesexplace.

Lovel's Court, Paternoster-Row, —at 20, 3d on the R. from Cheapside.

Lovers-Court, White-Horse-St. Ratcliffe,—9 doors on the L. from Butcher-row.

Loveland's-Yard, Royal - Hospital-Row, Chelsea,—1st on the L. from the Hospital.

Lowdell's Court, Gt. Guildford-St. Boro.—1st on the right N. from 35, Queen-st.

Lowdell-Passage, Broad-Wall, —1st on the L. from Great Charlotte-st. Blackfriars-road.

Lower-Mews, Crescent, Minories,—behind the S. side.

Lower - Turning, Shakespear's Walk, Shadwell,—last on the L. from 49, High-st.

Lownds-Court, Carnaby-St.— at 24, 2d on the L. from Gt. Marlborough-st.

Loxwood-Place, Fitzroy-Place, Marybone,— 1st on the R. from the New-road.

Lucas-Pl. Commercial-Road,— E. side the Halfway-house.

Lucas-St. Commercial-Road,— 1st E. of the Halfway-house.

Lucas-St. Gray's Inn-Lane,— N. side Sidmouth-pl. and op. Acton-st.

Lucas-Street, Paradise-St. Rotherhithe,—at 80, 1st on the R. below Millpond-bridge.

Ludgate (Old), Half-Moon-St. —2d on the L. from 170, Bishopsgate.

Ludgate-Court,—the entrance to the last.

Ludgate-Hill,—at the S. end of Fleet-market, extending to St. Martin's church.

Ludgate-Pl. Ludgate - Hill,—3

doors on the R. from Bridge-street.

Ludgate-Street, St. Paul's-ch.-yd.—W. end, extending to St. Martin's-church.

Saint Luke's Charity - School, Golden - Lane,—5 doors on the L. from Old-st.

St. Luke's Church, Old-Street, —middle of the N. side.

St. Luke's Hospital, Old-St.— N. side, near the City-road.

St. Luke's Pl. Stepney,—op. the W. side of the church-yard.

Luke-Street, Paul-St. Finsbury, —at 49, 1st on the R. from Worship-st.

St. Luke's Workhouse, City-Rd. —W. side of the Shepherd and Shepherdess.

Lumley's Alms-Houses, City-Road,—N. side the Shepherd and Shepherdess Tea-gardens.

Lumley-Court, Strand,—at 398, 12 doors W. from Southampton-st.

Lumley-Court, Bowl and Pin-Alley, Chancery-Lane,—1st on the L. from Bream's buildings.

Luntley-Pl. Whitechapel,—2d on the R. in Osborn-pl. from 20, Brick-lane.

Luxford-Row, North-Green,— 1st on the R. from 12, Worship-st.

Lyceum, Strand,—at 352, about ¼ of a mile on the R. from Temple-bar.

Lying-in-Hospital, St. Luke's, —the corner of Old-st. and the City-road.

Lynn-Street, Gaywood-Street, St. George's Fields,—1st on

the L. from the London-road.

Lynn-Court, Lynn-St.—middle of the N. side.

Lyon's Inn, Holywell - Street, Strand,—16 doors on the R. from St. Clement's church.

Lyon's Inn - Passage,—op. the last to the Strand.

Lyon's Quay, Lower Thames-St.—12 houses on the R. below London-bridge.

Lyon-St. High - Holborn, — at 143, 1st on the L. from Broad-st. St. Giles's.

———

MABLEDON-PLACE, Sommers-Town, — op. Willsted-st. to Burton-crescent.

Macclesfield - Street, Gerrard-St. Soho,—from 15, to Dean-s'reet.

Macord's Rents, Choppens-Ct. —1st on the R. from 25, Old Gravel-lane.

Maddox-St. Hanover - Sq.—3d on the R. in Swallow-st. from 322, Oxford-st.

Maddox-St. (Little), —op. the last, extending to 43, New Bond-st.

Magdalen - Circus, Magdalen-St.—behind 154, Tooley-st.

Magdalen-Hospital,Blackfriars-Rd.—½ a mile on the R. from the bridge.

Magdalen-Passage, Gt.Prescot-St. Goodman's Fields,—middle of the S. side.

Magdalen-Place,Tooley-St.—at 143, nearly op. Stoney-lane.

Magdalen-Row, Gt. Prescot-St.

Goodman's Fields,—middle of the S. side.

Magdalen-Street, Tooley-St.— at 143, extending to 23, Bermondsey-st.

Magna-Place, Hoxton-Town,— a few doors fromOld-st.-road.

St. Magnus-Church,—N, end of London-bridge.

Magpye-Alley, Wentworth-St. Spitalfields,—at 41, 3 doors E. of Rose-lane.

Magpye-Alley, Shoreditch,—at 10, nearly op. Worship-st.

Magpye-Court, Glass - House-Alley, Whitefriars,—at the N. end of it.

Magpye-Court, Aldersgate-St. —at 180, op. the Castle and Falcon-Inn.

Magpye and Stump Coach-Office,—at 117, Newgate-st.

Mahogany-Court, Whitecross-St.—at 81, 11 doors N. of Chiswell-st.

Maid-Lane,Southwark,—parallel to the Thames, from Park-st. to Gravel-lane.

Maida-Place, Printers-Pl. Bermondsey,—nearly op. the Gregorian-Arms, W. end of Jamaica-row.

Maiden-Lane, Southampton-St. —10 doors on the L. from 388, Strand.

Maiden-Lane, Battle - Bridge, St. Pancras, — E. side the Small-pox-hospital.

Maiden-Lane, Wood - St.—at 110, 3d on the L. from 122, Cheapside.

Maiden-Lane, Queen-St.Cheapside,—at 37, extending from Garlick-hill to College-hill.

Q

Maiden-Row, Boro.-Road,—1st on the L. from the King's Bench.

Maidenhead - Court, Berwick-Street, Oxford-St.—at 99, 4 doors N. of Peter-st.

Maidenhead-Ct. Snow's Rents, Westr.—1st on the R. from York-st.

Maidenhead-Court, Aldersgate-St.—at 28, 10 doors N. of Falcon-st.

Maidenhead - Court, Little St. Thomas Apostle,—3 doors E. of 69, Queen-st.

Maidenhead-Court, Moor-Lane, Cripplegate,—3 doors from 86, Fore-st.

Maidenhead - Court, Wheeler-St. Spitalfields,—at 67, 2d on the L. north of White-lion-street.

Maidenhead-Court, Broad-Wall, —a few doors S. of Stamford-st. Blackfriars-road.

Maidenhead Court, Gt. Gardens, —3d on the L. from St. Catherine's-lane.

Maidenhead-Court, Wapping, —at 102, 4 doors on the L. below the London-docks.

Maidenhead-Court, Farmer-St. Shadwell,—at 61, 5th on the L. from 38, High-st.

Maidenhead-Yard, George-St. Bloomsbury,—1st from 25, Broad-st.

Maidenhead-Yard, Addle-Hill, —at 24, 1st on the L. from Gt. Carter-lane.

Maidman's Court, Blue-Gate-Fields,—2d on the L. from 95, Ratcliffe-highway.

Maidman's Row, Mile-End-Rd. —⅙ of a mile on the R. be-

low Bencroft's alms-houses, near two miles from Aldgate.

Maidstone-Buildings, High-St. Boro.—at 228, 10 doors N. of Union-st.

Maidstone-Court, Old Nicol-St. Bethnal - Green,—2d on the R. from Cock-lane.

Maidstone-New-Wharf, Queen-hithe,—W. side the dock.

Major Foubert's Passage, Swallow-St.—at 61, op. Conduit-street.

Malaga-Ct. Nightingale - Lane, —at 36, a few doors on the L. below the entrance to the London-docks.

Malaga-Court (Little),—on the N. side the last.

Manchester - Builds. Cannon-Row, Westminster,—2d N. to Bridge-st.

Manchester-House, Manchester-Sq.—at 20, N. side.

Manchester-Mews, Manchester-St.—4 doors on the R. from the square.

Manchester-Mews North, Manchester-St.—14 doors on the R. from the square.

Manchester-Square,—N. end of Duke-st. from 173, Oxford-street.

Manchester - St. Manchester-Sq.—N. W. corner.

Mandana's Lane, Bethnal - Green-Road, — the last on the L. from 65, Shoreditch, towards the Green.

Manley-Pl.—S. W. corner of Kennington-common.

Manuer's Court, Gt. Winchester-St. Boro.—1st on the R. from St. Saviour's church.

Manor-Buildings, King's Road, Chelsea,—behind Manor-Pl.

Manor-Court, Perriwinkle-St. Ratcliffe,— 1st on the R. from Brook-st.

Manor-Pl. King's Road, Chelsea,—¼ of a mile on the R. from Smith-st. towards Battersea-bridge.

Manor-Pl. Walworth,—5th on the R. from the Elephant and Castle.

Manor-House-Academy, Kennington-Lane,— nearly op. Carlisle-chapel.

Manor-Row, Robinson's Lane, Chelsea,—part of the L. side, ⅛ of a mile from Paradise-row.

Manor-Row, Manor-Pl. Walworth,—the S. side of it.

Manor-Row, Deptford Lower Road, — S. side the seven houses.

Manor-Row, Little Tower-Hill, —from the E. side to Upper East-Smithfield.

Manor-Row (Little),—on the S. side the last.

Manor - Row (Old), Salmon's Lane, Limehouse,—the N. end of Featherstone-builds.

Manor-St. Chelsea,—between 13 and 14, Cheyne-walk, by the side of the Thames.

Manor-Terrace, King's Road, Chelsea,—near Manor-place, extending towards Battersea-bridge.

Mansel-St.—the S. continuation of Somerset-st. from Aldgate High-st.

Mansfield-Mews, Mansfield-St. Marybone,—at 11 and at 10, Harley-st.

Mansfield-Pl. Boro.-Road,—S. side, by the Obelisk.

Mansfield-St. Marybone,—1st E. to Harley-st. from Queen-Ann-st. West to New Cavendish-st.

Mansfield-St. Boro.-Road,—1st on the R. from the Obelisk.

Mansion - House, — the large building at the W. end of Lombard-st.

Mansion-House Coach-Office, —nearly op. the Mansion-house.

Mansion -House - Alley, Newington,— by the Mansion-house public-house.

Mansion-House-How, Kennington High - Road,—near the two mile stone, extending to Kennington-lane.

Mansion-House-Street, — from Cornhill to the Poultry.

Manson's Ways, Bermondsey-Wall,—on the E. side of Mill-stairs and St. Saviour's dock.

Map's Row, Stepney-Green,—¼ of a mile on the L. from Mile-End.

Marble-Court, Webb-St. Boro. —1st on the R. from Weston-street.

Marble-Hall-Lane, Vauxhall,— op. the W. end of the Gardens.

Marchmont-Pl. Little Coram-St.—2d on the L. from 10, Tavistock-pl.

Marchant's Row, Limehouse, —a few yards E. of St. Ann-st. by the Barge-river.

Marchmont-Street, Gt. Coram-St. Brunswick - Sq.—at 44, middle of the N. side.

Marden - Court, Broad - Wall, Christ-Church. See Maidenhead-Court.

St. Margaret's Chapel, Westr. —on the S. side of Little Chapel-st.

St. Margaret's Chapel, Margaret-Street, Cavendish-Sq.—9 doors from 63, Wells-st.

St. Margaret's Church, Westr. —N. side the Abbey.

St. Margaret's Church, Lothbury,—N. side the Bank of England.

St. Margaret-Patten's Church, Rood-Lane, Fenchurch-St.— corner of Tower-st.

Margaret-Court, Margaret-St. Cavendish-Sq.—at 59, middle of the S. side.

St. Margaret's Hill, High-Street, Boro.—the open space, ½ of a mile on the R. from London-bridge.

Margaret's Rents, Snow's Fields, Boro.— behind 35, by Weston-st.

Margaret-Row, Marchmont-St. —N. end, by Burton-crescent, Tavistock-sq.

Margaret-St. Cavendish-Sq.— from the S. E. corner to 63, Wells-st.

Margaret-St. Westr.—S. continuation of Parliament-st. E. side the Abbey.

Saint Margaret's Workhouse, Westr.—W. end of Orchard-st. by Gt. Chapel-st.

Maria-Pl. Baker's Row, — 1st on the L. from 94, Whitechapel-road.

Maria-Pl. Blue-Anchor-Road, Bermondsey, —¼ of a mile on the R. from the turnpike, Fort-pl.

Marigold - Stairs, Up.-Ground, —W. side of Blackfriars-bridge.

Marigold-Court, Strand, — at 370, W. side Exeter-Change.

Marigold-Court, Star - Corner, Bermondsey,—2d S. of Long-lane.

Marigold-St. Bermondsey,—1st W. parallel to Cherry-garden-st. extending to Millpond-st.

Marine-Brewery, Broad-Street, Ratcliffe,—op. 81, by Stone-stairs.

Marine - Crescent, Prospect-Row, Bermondsey,—1st on the L. from the Neckinger-turnpike towards Jamaica-row.

Marine-Society,—at 54; Bishopsgate-within.

Mariners (Three) Court, Fore-St. Cripplegate,—at 102, 4 doors W. of Grub-st.

Mark-Lane, Fenchurch-St.—at 55, 4th on the R. from Gracechurch-st.

Mark-Street, Paul-St. Finsbury, —at 54, 2d on the R. from Worship-st.

Mark's Yard. See Stacey's Repository.

Market-Court, Oxford-St.—at 92, ¾ of a mile on the R. from St. Giles's.

Market-Court, Market - St.— 1st on the L. from Shadwell-market.

Market-Hill, Shadwell High - St. — at 65, 2d E. of the church.

Market-Lane, Pall-Mall,—behind the Opera-House, Haymarket.

Market-Lane, White-Hart-Pl. Kennington-Lane,—13 doors on the L. from Kennington-cross.

Market-Row North, South, East, and West, St. James's,—are merely the different sides of St. James's market.

Market-Row, Oxford-Market, —the S. and W. sides of the said market.

Market-Row, Saint George's Fields,—S. end of Mansfield-street.

Market-Row, East and West, Carnaby-Market,—the sides of the said market.

Market-Street, Hart-St. Bloomsbury,——S. W. corner of Bloomsbury-sq.

Market-St.—the builds. around Fitzroy market.

Market-Street, Oxford-St.—at 87, ¾ of a mile on the L. from St. Giles's.

Market-Street, St. James's Market,—from the N. W. corner to 127, Jermyn-st.

Market-St. Horseferry-Road, Westr.—part of the E. end, by Millbank-st.

Market-St. May-Fair,—on the W. side of Shepherd's market.

Market-St. Soho,—W. side of Newport-market to Little Newport-st.

Market-St. Shadwell,—at the S. E. corner of Shadwell-market.

Market-St. Boro.-Road,—2d on the R. from the Obelisk.

Market-St. Lambeth, — from Walcot-pl. to Kennington-lane.

Marlborough-Court, Pall-Mall, —at 82, 9 doors E. of the Palace.

Marlborough-Court, Carnaby-St.—at 24, 3d on the L. from Gt. Marlborough-st.

Marlborough-Court, Green-Walk, Blackfriars-Rd.—10 doors on the R. from Holland-st.

Marlborough-Mews, Queen-St. —at the S. end, from 340, Oxford-st.

Marlborough-Pl. Pall-Mall,— at 81, near the Palace.

Marlborough-Pl. Walworth,— R. side, ¼ of a mile from the Elephant and Castle, from Hampton-st. to the Terrace.

Marlborough-Pl. Kennington-Cross,—E. side, op. Up. Kennington-lane.

Marlborough-Row, Carnaby-Market,—S. W. corner.

Marlborough-Square, Whisters-Ground, Westr.—the corner of Gt. Peter-st.

Marlborough-St. (Gt.)—1st on the R. in Poland-st. from 365, Oxford-st.

Marlborough-St. (Little), — at 34, King-st. 2d on the L. from 323, Oxford-st.

Marlborough-Street, Charlotte-St. — 1st on the L. from Blackfriars-road, towards Lambeth.

Marlow's Rents, St. Catherine's Sq. Tower-Hill,—N. side, by Catshole-court.

Marmaduke-Court, Marmaduke-St.—1st on the R. from John-st.

Q 3

Marmaduke-Street, John - St. St. George's East,—1st on the R. from Cannon-st.-road.

Marman - Street, St. George's East,—continuation of Humberstone-st. from the Commercial-road.

Marquis-Court, Drury-Lane,— at 70, S. side the Theatre.

Marsh-Pl. Lambeth - Marsh,— 1st on the L. from the turnpike towards Blackfriars-rd.

Marsh's Pl. Princes-St. London-Road,—the E. end of Princes-court.

Marsh-Wall, Poplar. See Mill-Wall.

Marshall-Street, Silver-Street, Golden-Sq.—1st on the R. from Little Windmill-st.

Marshall-St. London - Road,— 3d on the R. from the Obelisk.

Marshalsea - Prison, High - St. Boro.—behind 118, ¼ of a mile on the L. from London-bridge.

Marsham-St. Westr.—continuation of Great Smith-st. and Dean-st.

Marson-Pl. Sommers-Town,— N. end of Marson-st.

Marson-St. Sommers-Town,— 1st on the L. in Phillips's-builds. from 20, Willsted-st.

Martha - Street, St. George's East, — 2d on the R. in Charles-st. from op. Bluegate-fields.

Martha-St. Hackney - Road,— 1st on the R. north from Cambridge-heath-turnpike.

Saint Martin's Alms - Houses, Crown-St. Soho,—6 doors N. of Compton-st.

Martin's Builds. Old-St.—at 69, op. the Hospital.

Martin's Builds. Milk - Yard, Shadwell,—op. the S. end of Farmer-st.

St. Martin's Church (in the Fields), St. Martin's Lane, Charing-Cross.

St. Martin's Church, Ludgate-St.—a few doors on the R. from St. Paul's-church-yard.

Saint Martin's Church, St. Martin's Lane,—3 doors from 42, Cannon-st.

St. Martin's (Outwitch) Church, Threadneedle - St.—the corner of Bishopsgate-st.

Saint Martin's Court, St. Martin's Lane, Charing-Cross,— at 89, op. New-st.

St. Martin's Lane, Charing-Cross,—from 487, Strand, to Long-acre.

St. Martin's Lane, (Little),— continuation of the last.

Saint Martin's Lane, Cannon-St. — from 42 to 138, Upper Thames-st.

St. Martin's-le-Grand,—at 65, Newgate-st. 8 doors on the R. from Cheapside.

St. Martin's St. Leicester-Sq.— at 38, middle of the S. side.

Martin - St. Westmoreland-Pl. City-Road,—1st on the L. from Providence-st.

St. Martin's St. Higlers-Lane,— 2d on the R. from Blackfriars-road.

Martin-St. (New), White's Yd. —1st on the L. from 97, Up. E. Smithfield.

Martin - Street, Essex-St.—2d on the L. from 105, Whitechapel.

Saint Martin's Workhouse, St. Martin's Lane, Charing-Cross, —behind 128, to Hemming's row.

Martlet'sCourt, Bow-St. Covent-Garden,—at 30, middle of the E. side.

St. Mary Abchurch, Abchurch-Lane, by Cannon-st.

St. Mary-Axe, Leadenhall-St. —at 117, 1st on the L. from Cornhill.

St. Mary's Church, Aldermanbury,—at 66, the corner of Love-lane.

Saint Mary's Church, St. Mary's Hill, Lower Thames-St.—op. Billingsgate.

St. Mary Aldermary - Church, Bow-Lane,—behind 38, Watling-st.

St. Mary-le-Bow-Church, Cheapside,——middle of the S. side.

St. Mary - Magdalen - Church, Old Fish-St.—corner of the Old-Change.

St. Mary-Magdalen-Church,— S. end of Bermond-ey-st.

St. Mary's Church, Whitechapel, —¼ a mile E. of Aldgate.

St. Mary-le-Strand-Church,— 2d church, ¼ of a mile from Temple-bar.

St. Mary's Church, Newington, —⁵⁄₆ of a mile S. of the Elephant and Castle.

St. Mary's Church, Rotherhithe, —1½ mile below London - bridge, op. Wapping -dock-stairs.

St. Mary's Church, Lambeth,— ¾ of a mile above Westr.-bridge.

St. Mary-Somerset-Church, Up. Thames-St.—at 203, corner of Old Fish-st.-hill.

St. Mary - Woolnoth's-Church, Lombard - St.—W. side the General-post-office.

St. Mary's Hill, Lower Thames-St.—from 93 (op. Billingsgate), to Rood-lane.

St. Mary-Overy's-Dock, Boro. —W. side of St. Saviour's church, ⅛ of a mile above London-bridge.

Mary's Pl. Mary - St. Hampstead-Road,—N. end, on the R. from Brook-st.

Mary's Pl. Bethnal-Green-Road, —1st on the R. in Mary's row, from the N. E. corner of Wilmot-sq.

Mary's Row, Bethnal - Green-Road, — on the E. side of Wilmot-sq.

Mary-St. Hampstead - Road,— W. end of Charles-st. on the R.

Mary-St. Whitechapel-Road,— at 76, ¼ of a mile on the L. below the church.

Mary-Street, St. George's East, —4th E. of Cannon-st.-road, from Up. Chapman - st. to Lower Chapman-st.

Mary-St. Stepney,—1st on the R. in Ocean-st. from op. the Walnut-tree.

St. Marybone-Church,—N. end of High-st. op. Beaumont-street.

Marybone - Court, Weymouth-St. Marybone,—at 26, three doors E. of Little Marybone-street.

Marybone - Court - House,—at

159, Oxford-st. middle of the N. side.

Marybone-Dispensary,—at 77, Welbeck-st. 2 doors from Henrietta-st.

Marybone-Infirmary, New-Rd. —12 doors E. of York-pl. Baker-st.

Marybone-Lane, Oxford-St.— at 158, nearly op. New Bond-street.

Marybone - Mews, Gt. Marybone - St.—at 49, between Welbeck-st. and Wimpole-street.

Marybone-Passage, Wells-St.— at 68, 2d on the L. from Oxford-st.

Marybone - School,——at 110, High-st. Marybone.

Marybone-St. (Great),—at 51, Harley-st. 2d on the L. from Cavendish-sq.

Marybone-St. (Little),—at 23, in the last, 5 doors E. of High-st.

Marybone - St. (Upper),—from 53, Gt. Portland-st. to Howland-st. Tottenham - court - road.

Marybone-St. Piccadilly,—the continuation of Titchborn-street.

Marybone - Workhouse, Northumberland- St.—middle of the W. side.

Marygold. See Marigold.

Mason's Alley, Basinghall-St.— 1st on the R. from Cateaton-street.

Mason's Arms-Yard, Maddox-St.—at 15, 2d on the R. from 92, Swallow-st.

Mason's Builds. City-Road,—⅕

of a mile on the L. north from Winkworth's builds.

Mason's Builds. Bencher's Row, St. George's Fields,—1st on the R. from Bennett's row.

Mason's Court, George and Catherine-Wheel-Yard,—1st on the R. behind 80, Bishopsgate-without.

Mason's Court, Shoreditch,—at 109, 10 doors on the L. from the church.

Mason's Court, Brick-Lane,— 2d on the R. from 74, Whitechapel.

Mason's Court, High - St.—1st on the L. from Gt. Garden-st. Whitechapel.

Masons-Hall,—S. side of Mason's alley, Basinghall-st.

Mason's Pl. Little Prescot-St. —6 doors S. of Chamber-st.

Masons - Stairs, Bankside, — near Corny-cap-alley, ⅓ of a mile below Blackfriars-bridge.

Mason -St. Sommers-Town, — 1st on the R. in Northam's builds. from Weston-st.

Mason-St. Bridge-Road, Lambeth,—at 30, 3d on the R. from Westr.-bridge.

Mason-St. Kent-Road,—2d on the R. below the Bricklayers-arms.

Mason's Yard, Duke - St.—2d on the L. from 132, Piccadilly.

Mason's Yard, Queen-Ann-St. East, or Foley-Pl.—at 54, behind 83, Great Portland-street.

Mason's Yard, Broad-Street, St. Giles's,—2 doors from Drury-lane.

Masters in Chancery's Office,—at 24, Southampton - builds. Holborn, 4 doors on the R. from 53, Chancery-lane.

Match-Walk, Back-Lane,—N. end of Mercers-row, Shadwell.

Mathematical-Society, Crispin-St. Spitalfields,—behind 35, 8 doors on the L. from Union-street.

Matilda-Pl. North East Passage, Wellclose-Sq.—1st on the L. from 35, Cable-st.

Matthew's Builds. King - St. Spitalfields,—3 doors on the R. from 153, Brick-lane.

St. Matthew's Church, Friday-St.—2 doors from 36, Cheapside.

St. Matthew's Church, Bethnal-Green,—½ a mile on the R. along Church-st. from 65, Shoreditch.

Matthew's Pl. Hackney-Road, —part of the N. side, near Cambridge-heath-turnpike.

Matthew-Street, Paul-St. Finsbury,—1st on the L. in Market-st. from 54, Paul-st.

Maudlin's Rents, Lower East Smithfield,—at 41, extending to 53, Nightingale-lane.

Maxwell's Court, Long- Alley, —2 doors on the L. from Moorfields.

May's Builds. Brick-St. Piccadilly,—N. side, nearly op. Down-st.

May's Builds. (Gt.) St. Martin's Lane, Charing-Cross,—at 40, middle of the E. side.

May's Builds.(Little), Bedford-bury,—at 39, op. the last.

May's Builds. Kennington-Oval,

—from Bowling - green - pl. to Clayton-st.

May-Bush-Alley, Shoreditch,—at 216, about 25 doors S. of Holywell-lane.

May-Fair,—the neighbourhood on the N. side of Piccadilly near Park-lane is so called.

May-Fair-Chapel, Curzon-St.—middle of the S. side, near Shepherds-market.

May's Row, New-Cut, Limehouse,—at the N. end of Nightingale-lane.

Mayfield's Builds. Princes-Sq. St. George's East, — at the N. E. corner.

Maynard-Street, St. Giles's,—1st on the R. in Bainbridge-st. from Oxford-st.

Maypole-Alley, High-St. Boro. —at 203, 5 doors S. of Union-street.

Maypole-Alley, Up. E. Smithfield,—at 22, op. Butcher-row.

Maze, Tooley-St.—at 194, 7th on the R. from London - bridge.

Maze-Court (Little),—the 1st on the L. in Maze-pond, from the last.

Maze - Court (Great),—at the back of the last.

Maze-Pond (Great), Boro.—the continuation of New-st. from Guy's hospital to Snow's fields.

Maze-Pond (Little),—the last on the R. in the Maze from 194, Tooley-st.

Mead's Court, Old Bond-St.—19 doors on the R. from 57, Piccadilly.

Mead-Pl. Westr.-Bridge-Road,

Lambeth,—E. side the Asylum.

Mead-Row,—from the last to Woolsingham-pl.

Mead-St. Bethnal-Green,—the 5th on the L. in Turville-st. from 37, Church-st.

Meadow - Row, Kent-Road,— 2d on the L. from the Elephant and Castle.

Meard's Court, Wardour - St. Soho,—at 57, 10 doors N. of Compton-st.

Medical-Society, Bolt-Court,— 3 doors on the R. from 151, Fleet-st.

Medway-St. Horseferry-Road, Westr.—op. the Ship, 2d on the L. from Gt. Peter-st.

Meeting-House-Alley, Johnson-St.— the 1st on the L. from 156, Old Gravel-lane

Meeting-House-Court, Drury-Lane,—at 29, N. side Long-acre.

Meeting-House-Court, Water-Lane, Blackfriars,—5 doors N. of Union-st.

Meeting - House - Court, Old-Jewry,—at 17, 2d on the R. from Cheapside.

Meeting - House -Court, Long-Alley, Moorfields, — 2d on the R. from Worship-st.

Meeting-House-Court, Miles's Lane,—16 doors on the R. from 49, Cannon-st.

Meeting-House-Court, Tooley-Street,—at 108, op. College-street.

Meeting-House-Court, Gains-ford - St. Horselydown,—at 18, 2 or 3 doors W. of Thomas-st.

Meeting-House - Walk, Snow's Fields,—4th on the R. from 109, High-st. Boro.

Meeting-House-Yard, Redcross-St. Cripplegate,—at 15, middle of the W. side.

Meeting-House-Yard, St. Martin's Lane,—8 doors on the L. from 41, Cannon-st.

Meeting-House - Yard, Stoney-Lane,—1st on the R. from Gravel-lane, Houndsditch.

Meeting - House - Yard, Dock-Head,—1st on the R. from New-st.

Megg's - Alms-Houses, White-chapel-Road,—at 223, op. the Workhouse.

Melish's Yard, Kent-St. Boro. —at 117, ⅓ of a mile on the L. from St. George's church.

Melina-Pl. St. George's Fields, —on the R. from the Obelisk towards the Asylum.

Melina-Builds.—E. end the last by Charles-st.

Melior-St. Boro.—2d st. on the L. from 194, Tooley-st. along the Maze and Weston-st.

Memel -Street, Domingo-St.— 1st on the R. from 14, Old-street.

Mercers-Alms-Houses, White-Horse-St. Ratcliffe,—at the N. end of it, op. Stepney-church-yard.

Mercers-Court, St. Mary's Hill, Tower - St.—at 30, op. the church.

Mercers-Court, Mercers-Row, —4 doors from 210, High-st. Shadwell.

Mercers-Hall, Ironmonger-Lane,

—4 doors on the R. from 90, Cheapside.

Mercers-Row, High-St. Shadwell,—at 209, 2d on the R. west from the church.

Mercers-School, College - Hill, —at 20, 3 doors on the L. from Cloak-lane.

Mercers-St. Long-Acre,—at 123, 1st on the L. from St. Martin's lane.

Merchants-Builds. Poplar,—W. side the East-India Almshouses.

Merchants (Company of) trading to Africa, Bush - Lane,—2 doors on the R. from 22, Cannon-st.

Merchant - Seamen's - Office,— over the S. side of the Royal-Exchange.

Merchant-Taylors Alms-Houses, Princes - St.—5 doors from Rosemary-lane.

Merchant-Taylors-Hall,—at 32, Threadneedle-st.

Merchant-Taylors-School, Suffolk-Lane,—by 151, Upper Thames-st.

Meriton's Wharf, Mill-St. Dock-Head,—a few yards on the R. from Mill-stairs.

Merlin's Mechanical-Museum, Hanover-Sq.—from the N. E. corner to 315, Oxford-st.

Merlin's Pl. Spa-Fields,—W. side the New River-head.

Merlin's Rents, Shoe-Lane,—at 50, by St. Andrew's church, Holborn.

Mermaid-Court, Royal-Hospital - Row, Chelsea,—4th on the L. from the Hospital.

Mermaid-Court, High-St. Boro.

—at 120, ⅓ of a mile on the L. from London-bridge.

Mermaid-Row, Snow's Fields. See Ship and Mermaid - Row.

Merret's Builds. Peter-St. —1st on the R. from 25, Sun-st. Bishopsgate.

Merton's Court, Ratcliffe-Highway,—at 198, W. end, by Wellclose-sq.

Mesnard's Dock, Horselydown, —W. side St. Saviour's dock, ¾ of a mile below London-bridge.

Mestaer's Rents, Rotherhithe, —at 235, about ½ mile below the church.

Mestaer's-Ship - Yard, Rotherhithe,—E. side of King and Queen - stairs, and op. the last.

Metcalf's Buildings, Phillips's Builds. Walworth-Common,-- 1st on the R. from Westmoreland-row.

Metcalf-Court, Essex-St.—5th on the R. from 106, Whitechapel.

Metcalf-Court, Jacob-St. Dock-Head,—1st on the R. from Mill-st.

Metilda-Pl. North-East-Passage, Wellclose-Sq.—2 doors from 35, Cable-st.

St. Michael's Alley, Cornhill,— at 44, 7 doors E. of Birchinlane.

St. Michael's Church. See the last.

St. Michael Bassishaw's Church, Basinghall-St.—middle of the W. side.

St. Michael's Church, Wood-St.

Cheapside,—20 doors on the L. from 122, Cheapside.

St. Michael's Church, Crooked-Lane,—4 doors from 49, Cannon-st.

St. Michael's Church, Upper Thames-St.—at 200, middle of N. side.

St. Michael's Church, College-Hill,——middle of the E. side.

Michael's Grove, Brompton-Road,—5th coach-turning on the L. from Knightsbridge.

Michael's Pl. Brompton High-Road,—by the last.

Middle-Row, Knightsbridge,—at the commencement of the Brompton-road.

Middle-Row, Holborn,—a pile of houses which stand out in the street op. Gray's-inn-lane.

Middle-Row, St. Giles's,—from 37, Broad-st. to King-st.

Middle-Row, Goswell-St.—the corner of Old-st.

Middle-Row-Pl. Holborn,—at 326, High-Holborn, on the W. side of Middle-row.

Middle-St. Cloth-Fair,—the continuation of it, entering by 60, West-Smithfield.

Middle-Shadwell, — 1st S. parallel to part of High-st. from Pope's hill to Broad-bridge.

Middle-Turning, Shakespear's Walk, Shadwell,—4th on the L. from 49, High-st.

Middle-Yard, Gt. Queen-St. Lincolns-Inn-Fields,—at 65, middle of the S. side.

Middlesex-Builds. Hackney-Road, — behind Middlesex-

pl. ¼ of a mile on the L. from Shoreditch.

Middlesex-Chapel, Hackney-Road,—¼ of a mile on the R. from Shoreditch-church.

Middlesex-Court, Drury-Lane,—at 35, 6 doors N. of Long-acre.

Middlesex-Court, Bartholomew-Close,—at 61, a narrow dark passage leading to Little Bartholomew-close.

Middlesex-Hospital, Marybone,—op. Berners-st. from 54, Oxford-st.

Middlesex-Mad-House, Hackney-Road,—¼ of a mile on the L. from Shoreditch-chur.

Middlesex-Pl. New-Road, Lisson-Green,—nearly op. the Yorkshire-stingo.

Middlesex-Pl. Middlesex-St. Sommers-Town,—middle of the E. side.

Middlesex-Pl. Hackney-Road,—part of the L. side, ½ of a mile from Shoreditch-church.

Middlesex-Society's Charity-School,—at 18, Cannon-st.-road, op. Lower Chapman-street.

Middlesex-St. Sommers-Town,—1st E. to Ossulston-st. from Chapel-path to Hampden-st.

Middlesex-Street, Aldgate-High. St.—at 41, ⅛ of a mile E. of the church.

Middlesex-St. (Little),—20 doors on the R. in the last from Aldgate.

Middlesex-Terrace, Hackney-Road,—by Middlesex-chapel, ¼ of a mile on the R. from Shoreditch.

Middleton's Builds. Foley - Pl. Marybone,—4 doors from 87, Gt. Titchfield-st.

Middleton's Alley, Crucifix-Lane,—1st on the R. from 50, Bermondsey-st.

Middleton's Rents, Bermondsey-St.—at 56, 5 doors S. of Crucifix-lane.

Midford-Pl. Tottenham-Court-Road,—at 113, between London-st. and Grafton-st.

Midway-Pl. Deptford Lower-Road,—S. side the Halfway-house.

St. Mildred's Church, Bread-St.—12 doors from 47, Cheapside.

St. Mildred's Church, Poultry, —nearly op. the Mansion-house.

St. Mildred's Court, Bread-St. —at 36, S. side the church.

St. Mildred's Court, Poultry,— on the E. side St. Mildred's church.

Mile-End-Charity-School, Stepney-Green,—⅓ of a mile on the R. from Mile-end-road.

Mile - End - Corner, Dog-Row, Mile-End,—14 doors on the L. from the turnpike.

Mile-End-Green,—near the S. E. corner of the London-hospital.

Mile-End New-Town,—a large district on the N. side of Whitechapel-road.

Mile-End Old-Town,—a large district on the N. side the Commercial-road, extending W. to Whitechapel-church-yard.

Mile-End Poor-House,—6 doors

L. of the Old-globe, Mile-end.

Mile-End-Road,—the continuation of Whitechapel - road, from the turnpike, to Bow.

Mile-End-Terrace,—10 doors on the L. in Maidman's row, from op. the New Globe, Mile-end-road.

Miles's Lane, Upper Thames-St. —at 130, 10 doors W. of London-bridge.

Miles's or Meymott's Rents, Church-St. Horselydown,— a few yards on the L. from St. John's church-yard.

Miles's Rents, Long - Lane, Bermondsey,——1st coach-turning on the L. from the church.

Milford - House - School, — at 30, Canterbury-Row, Newington-butts.

Milford-Lane, Strand,—at 200, op. St. Clement's church.

Milford-Lane-Wharf,—at the bottom of the last, on the L. from 200, Strand.

Milk-Alley, Wardour-St. Soho, —at 62, 3 doors N. of Compton-st.

Milk-Court, Gravel-Lane, Boro. —7 doors S. of Duke-st.

Milk-St. Walworth,—between the Red-lion and Queen's Row.

Milk-St. Cheapside,—at 116, 4th on the L. from St. Paul's church-yard.

Milk-Yard, Poppin's Court,— at 19, the last on the L. from 102, Fleet-st.

Milk-Yard, New Gravel-Lane, —at 133, 3d on the R. from Wapping.

R

Millbank-Row, Westminster,—the continuation of Millbank-st. by the Thames.

Millbank-Stairs, Westr.—S. end of Millbank-st. op. the Horse-ferry-road.

Millbank-St. Westr.—the continuation of Abingdon-st. from the Abbey.

Millbank-Walk,—the continuation of Millbank-row, to the Neat-houses.

Mill's Builds. Knightsbridge,—½ a mile on the R. from Hyde-park-corner.

Mill's Court, Type-St.—2 doors from 24, Chiswell-st.

Mill's Court, Curtain-Road,—2d on the R. from Old-st.-rd.

Mill's Court, Petticoat - Lane,—3d on the L. from Wide-gate-st. Bishopsgate.

Mill-Lane, Tooley-St.—at 55, 1st open lane on the L. from London-bridge.

Mill-Place, Commercial-Road, Limehouse,—⅓ of a mile on the L. west of the church.

Mill's Rents, East-St. Walworth,—4 doors on the R. from the High-st.

Mill - Stairs, Bermondsey,—on the E. side St. Saviour's dock, op. Hermitage-stairs.

Mill-St. Bermondsey,—the continuation of Dock-head, bearing to the L. on the E. side of St. Saviour's dock.

Mill-St. Lambeth - Walk,—N. side the Windmill, leading to Pratt-st.

Mill-Street, Maddox-St. Hanover-Sq.—at 19, behind Saint George's church.

Mill-wall, Poplar,—the bank of the Thames, below Lime-

house - hole towards Blackwall.

Mill-Wharf, Bermondsey,—E. side of Mill-stairs and St. Saviour's dock.

Mill's Yard, Gt. Peter-Street, Westr.—W. end of it, nearly op. the Gray-coat-school.

Mill-Yard, Lemon-Street, Goodman's Fields,—from behind 82, on the R. to 80, Cable-st.

Mill-Hill-Mews, Wimpole-St. Marybone,—at 91, 6 doors from Henrietta-st.

Mill-Pond-Bridge, Rotherhithe,—1st on the L. in West-lane from the Thames near Cherry-garden-stairs.

Mill-Pond - Row, Rotherhithe,—from Mill-pond-bridge towards the Blue-anchor-road.

Mill-Pond - St. Bermondsey,—E. continuation of Jamaica-row, leading to Mill - pond-row and bridge.

Millard's Court, Duke's Court, Chick-Lane, — entrance the 1st on the L. in Black-Boy-alley from Chick-lane.

Miller's Court, Aldermanbury,—at 36, 6 doors from London-wall.

Miller's Rents, East-St. Walworth,—1st on the R. from Walworth High-st.

Miller's Wharf, Lower East-Smithfield,—on the E. side the Leith and Berwick-wharf, ¼ of a mile below the Tower.

Millman-Mews, New Millman-St.—6 doors from Gt. Guilford-st.

Millman-Pl. Gt. James - St.—2d on the R. from Bedford-row.

Millman-Street, Gt. James-St.

Bedford-Row,—continuation of it by the chapel.

Millman-St. (New), Gt. Guilford-St.—16 doors on the L. from Gray's-inn-lane.

Mincing-Lane, Fenchurch - St. —at 43, 3d on the R. from Gracechurch-st.

Minor-Pl. Boro. - Road,—middle of the N. side, and op. Flint-st.

Miner-Court, Anchor & Hope-Alley, Wapping,—at 13, 6 doors on the R. from the London-docks.

Minories,—from op. Aldgate-church to Tower-hill.

Minories (Little), Church-St.— 1st on the L. from the Minories.

Mint (New), Tower-Hill,—the large new building on the E. side.

Mint, Borough,—(a mart for household-goods)—at the S. end of Redcross-st. and W. end of Mint-st.

Mint-Sq.--the centre of the last.

Mint-Street, Hi.h-St. Boro.— at 156, op. Saint George's church.

Mirror of the Times Newspaper-Office,—in Hind - court, 147, Fleet-st.

Mitcham-St. Lisson - Green,— 1st N. of Chapel-st.

Mitchell - Court, Mitchell - St. St. Luke's,—at 18, by Brick-lane.

Mitchell-Street, Brick-Lane, St. Luke's,—at 64, 1st on the R. from 113, Old-st.

Mitchell-St. (Little), — the E. end of the last.

Mitchell's Wharf,—at 28, Millbank-st. Westr.

Mitre-Builds. Temple,—the S. -end of Mitre-court from 44, Fleet-st.

Mitre - Builds. Three Colt-St. Limehouse,—middle of the W. side.

Mitre-Court, Fleet-St.—at 44, op. Fetter-lane.

Mitre-Court, St. Paul's-Church-Yard, — at 71, leading into London-house-yard.

Mitre-Court, Hatton - Garden, —3 doors on the R. from Holborn-hill.

Mitre-Court, St. John-Street, —at 143, near ½ of a mile on the R. from W.-Smithfield.

Mitre-Court, Cheapside, — 14 doors on the R. from St. Paul's-church-yard.

Mitre-Court, Milk-St.—5 doors on the L. from 116, Cheap-side.

Mitre-Court (Little), Duke-St. —1st on the L. from Aldgate.

Mitre-Court, Fenchurch-St.— 20 doors on the R. from Gracechurch-st.

Mitre-Court, Mint-St. Boro.— 3d on the L. from op. St. George's church.

Mitre-St. Aldgate,—-at 29, 1st on the L. from Leadenhall-st.

Modiford's Court, Fenchurch-St.—at 40, 3 doors W. of Mincing-lane.

Moffat's Court, Gascoigne-Pl. Crabtree-Row, Hackney-Rd. —middle of the W. side.

Moffat-Street, City-Road,—the continuation of Trafalgar-st. entering op. Fountain-place.

Moffling's Court, New Gravel-Lane,—at 25, 3d on the L. from Wapping.

Molton-St. See South-Molton.

Moley's Court, Fleet-St. Bethnal-Green,—middle of the N. side, op. Ram-alley.

Molyneux-Street, Queen-St.— 3d on the L. from 61, Edgware-road.

Monastery-Court, — N. end of Wade's-pl. Poplar.

Monday-Court, Carnaby-Market,—at 23, N. E. corner.

Money - Bag - Alley, Blue-Anchor-Yd.—2d on the L. from 48, Rosemary-lane.

Monk's Builds. Hoxton,—on the N. side of Bacchus-walk, op. Britt's-builds.

Monkwell-Builds. Coffee-House-Walk, Hoxton,—a few doors on the L. from op. Renton's gardens.

Monkwell-St. Falcon-Sq. — 13 doors on the R. in Silver-st. from 81, Wood-st.

Monmouth-Court, Whitcomb-St.—2d on the R. from Charing-cross.

Monmouth-Court, Monmouth-Street, St. Giles's,—4 doors from White-Lion-st.

Monmouth-Pl. Walworth-Common, — on the W. side of Surrey-square.

Monmouth-Street, St. Giles's, —2d E. of the church.

Monmouth-Street, Market-Hill, Shadwell, — 1st on the L. from 67, High-st.

Monster - Row, Neat - Houses, Chelsea, — the continuation of George's row.

Montague - Close, Boro. — between St. Saviour's church and the Thames, entrance by Pepper-alley.

Montague-Court, Little-Britain, —at 32, op. St. Bartholomew's hospital.

Montague-Court (Little),—12 doors from the last towards Aldersgate-st.

Montague-Court, Bishopsgate-Without,—at 94, op. Skinner-street.

Montague - Court (Old), Old Montague - St.—adjoins the R. corner of Black-lion-yard, from 38, Whitechapel-road.

Montague-House, Portman-Sq. —at the N. W. corner.

Montague-Mews West, Montague-Sq.— behind the W. side.

Montague-Mews South, — op. the last.

Montague-Mews North, Montague-Pl. Portman-Sq. — 1st on the R. from the W. end of Dorset-st.

Montague-Mews, Montague-St. Russell-Sq.—middle E. side.

Montague - Pl. Portman-Sq.— the W. continuation of Dorset-st.

Montague-Place, Bedford-Sq.— from the N. E. corner to 37, Russell-sq.

Montague-Sq. Marybone,—op. the N. end of Montague-st.

Montague-St. Marybone,—the continuation of Quebec-st. from 236, Oxford-st.

Montague-St. (Up.)—the continuation of the last.

Montague-Street, Russell-Sq.— from the S. W. corner to 85, Gt. Russell-st.

Montague-St. Brick-Lane, Spitalfields,—at 55, op. Brown's lane.

Montague-St. (Old), Osborn-St.

—1st on the R. from 74, Whitechapel.

Montague-St. Bell-Lane, Spitalfields,—1st on the L. from Wentworth-st.

Montfort - Place, Kennington-Green,—3d on the L. from the Horns tavern.

Montpelier Tea-Gardens, Walworth,—$\frac{3}{4}$ of a mile on the R. from the Elephant and Castle.

Monument-Yard, Fish-St.-Hill, —the open space by the Monument.

Moody's Gardens, Gt. Peter-St. Westr. — middle of the S. side.

Moon-Alley or Street, Bishopsgate - Without, — at 103, 10 doors N. of Primrose-st.

Moon-Rakers-Alley, Gt. Suffolk-St. Boro.—last on the R. from 80, Blackman-st.

Moorfields,—on the N. side of London-wall, towards Finsbury-sq.

Moorfields (Little), Fore-Street, Cripplegate,—at 61, 1st W. of the last.

Moorfields(Little),Broker-Row, —the S. end of it, by London-wall.

Moorfields (Upper),—a part of the N. end of Wilson-st.

Moor-Lane, Fore-St. Cripplegate,—at 87, nearly op. Basinghall-st.

Moor-Place, Lambeth, — from Woolsingham-pl. by the Asylum to Walcot-pl.

Moor-Place (Little),— S. end of the last,and corner of Brook-st.

Moor-Sq. Moor-Lane, Cripple-

gate,—2d on the L. from 87, Fore-st.

Moor-Street, Seven - Dials,—at Compton-st. and 22, Greek-street.

Moore's Alley, Norton-Falgate, —at 38, nearly op. Spital-sq. leading to Long-alley.

Moore's Court, Batchelor-Pl. Pentonville,—3 doors from the Maidenhead.

Moore's Court, Old Fish-St.— at 3, op. the Old-change.

Moore's Court, Essex-St.—3d on the L. from 105, Whitechapel.

Moore's Gardens, Long-Alley, Moorfields,—3d on the L. from Worship-st.

Moore's Pl. Long-Alley,— 1st on the L. in the last from Long-alley.

Moore-Street, Queen-St. Edgware-Road,—1st S. parallel to it.

Moore's Yard,St.Martin's Lane, Charing - Cross,—at 23, N. side the church.

Moore's Yard (Little),—E. end of the last.

Moore's Yard, Clarges-St.— 2d on the R. from Piccadilly.

Moore's Yard, King-Street, St. James's,—2d on the L. from St. James's-sq.

Mop-Spinners - Court,—1st on the L. in Duke's court from Chick-lane.

Morden's Court, Up.-Turning, Shadwell,—middle of the E. side.

Morgan-Court, Mile-End,—36 doors E. of Stepney-Green.

Morgan's Lane, Tooley-St.—at

R 3

79, 2d open turning on the L. from London-bridge.

Morgan-St. Commercial-Road, —2d on the L. west of Cannon-st.-road.

Morning-Advertiser Newspaper-Office,—at 12, Catherine-st. Strand.

Morning-Chronicle Newspaper-Office,—at 143, Strand, op. Catherine-st.

Morning - Herald Newspaper-Office,—at 18, Catherine-st. 3 doors from 342, Strand.

Morning-Post. Newspaper-Office,—at 335, Strand, nearly op. Somerset-house.

Morris's Causeway, Narrow - Wall, Lambeth,—E. side the Patent - shot - manufactory, near $\frac{1}{8}$ of a mile above Blackfriars-bridge.

Morris's Court, New-Sq. Horse-lydown,—1st on the R. from 102, Shad-Thames.

Morris's Walk, Castle - Lane, Boro.—4th on the L. from Castle-st.

Mortimer-Market, Tottenham-Court-Road,—op. 103, near Howland-st.

Mortimer-St. Cavendish-Sq.—from the N. E. corner to 49, Wells-st.

Morton-St. Newington - Causeway,—1st on the L. from the Elephant and Castle.

Morton-Court,—1st in the last from the Causeway.

Mosley-Pl. Brick-Lane,—at 204, 3d on the L. from op. the church, Whitechapel.

Mosman's Pl. Hackney-Road, —about $\frac{1}{8}$ of a mile on the R. north of Cambridge-Heath turnpike.

Moss's Alley, Bankside, Boro. —20 doors W. of Thames-st.

Moss's Court, Queen-St. Boro. —4 doors from Union-st.

Motley-Court, Motley-St. Curtain-Road,—at 10, leading to 24, Chapel-st.

Motley-St. Curtain-Road,—2d on the L. from Worship-street.

Mouldmakers - Row, Foster-Lane,—1st on the L. from 148, Cheapside.

Mount, Kent - St. Boro.—entrance by 298, 10 doors on the R. from St. George's church.

Mount's Court, Harrow-Alley, Houndsditch,—1st on the R. from White-st.

Mount-Court, Mount-St. Bethnal-Green,—2d on the R. from Rose-st.

Mount-Court, Mount-St. Walworth,—1st on the R. from the road.

Mount - Gardens, Mount - St. Lambeth,—12 doors S. of the Marsh-gate.

Mount's Gateway, Up. E. Smithfield,—at 85, by Butcher-row.

Mount-Pl. Whitechapel-Road, —from Cannon-st.-road, to the London-hospital.

Mount-Pl. Gibraltar-Row, St. George's Fields,—3d on the L. from Prospect-pl

Mount-Pl. Walworth High-St. —op. the Montpelier.

Mount-Pleasant,—the end of Elm-st. from 86, Gray's-inn-lane.

Mount-Pleasant, City-Road,— at 12, in East-row, nearly op. Winckworth's builds.

Mount-Pleasant, Stepney,—N. end of York-pl. by the World's End public-house.

Mount-Row, Davies-St.—at 22, 7 doors on the L. from Berkeley-sq.

Mount-Row, City.Road,—behind the houses which form Eastrow, op. Winckworth's builds.

Mount-Row, Kent - Road,—N. side, between the Bricklayersarms and the Paragon.

Mount - Row, Bridge - Road, Lambeth,—from the Marshgate to Oakley-st.

Mount-Sq. Mount-St. Bethnal-Green,—at 67, 1st on the L. from Rose-st.

Mount St. Berkeley-Sq.—N. W. corner where there are 1 and 131, extending to Park-lane.

Mount-St. Bethnal-Green,—the continuation of Rose-st. from 45, Church-st. nearly op. Brick-lane.

Mount-St. Whitechapel-Road, —behind Mount-pl.

Mount -St. Old, Whitechapel-Road,—at 206, on the E. side the London-hospital.

Mount-St. Bridge-Road, Lambeth,—from the Marsh-gate to op. the Asylum.

Mount-Street, Walworth High-St.—op. the Montpelier-gardens.

Mount - Terrace, Cannon - St.-Road, — E. side, adjoining Whitechapel-road.

Moxley's Court, White's-Row, —2 doors on the L. from Baker's row, Whitechapel-rd.

Mud's Court, Lamb's Conduit-St.—at 54, leading into Ormond-pl.

Muggeridge's Builds. Castle-St. Boro.—at 46, 1st on the R. from 13, Redcross-st.

Mulberry-Court, Bell-Alley,— 1st on the L. from 57, Coleman-st.

Mulberry - Court, Horse-Shoe-Alley, Moorfields,—the E. end, from 14, Wilson-st.

Mulberry - Court, Petticoat -Lane,—at 99, 1st S. of Wentworth-st.

Mulberry-Court, Three Colt-St. Limehouse,—between the S. side of the church and Mitrecourt.

Mulberry - Court, Castle - St. Boro.—at 23, 3d on the L. from 14, Red-cross-st.

Mulberry-Tree-Court, Stepney-Green,—$\frac{1}{4}$ of a mile on the L. from Mile-end.

Mulberry - Court, Long - Lane, Bermondsey,—2d on the L. from the church.

Mulberry-Gardens, Nightingale-Lane, East-Smithfield,—nearly op. Burr-st.

Mulberry-St. Commercial-Road, —2d on the L. from Whitechapel.

Mullings's Builds. Blue-Anchor-Road, Bermondsey,—a few doors on the R. east of Fort-pl.

Mumford-Court, Milk-St.—10 doors on the R. from 116, Cheapside.

Munday's Court. See Monday's.

Murden's Pl. Batty-St.—1st on the L. from the Commercial-road.

Muscovy-Court, Great Tower-Hill,—at 17, W. side of Savage-gardens.

Music - House- Court, High-St.

Shadwell,—at 54, 2 doors W. of the Church-yard.

Mutton-Court, Maiden-Lane,—8 doors on the L. from Wood-st. Cheapside.

Mutton-Lane, Clerkenwell,—at the N. W. corner of the green.

Mutton-Lane, Mile - End,—3d on the R. below the turnpike.

Myers's Builds. Salmon's Lane, —the 1st on the R. from the Commercial-road.

Myrtle-Row, Hoxton,—part of the L. side, ¼ of a mile from Old-st.-road.

Myrtle-St. Hoxton-Town,—3d coach-turning on the L. ¼ of a mile from Old-st.-road.

———

NAG'S - HEAD - COURT, Knightsbridge,—½ a mile on the R. from Hyde-park-corner, 3 doors E. of the Barracks.

Nag's Head-Court, Drury-Lane, —at 119, S. side Princes-st.

Nag's Head - Court, Golden-Lane,—at 86, 2d on the L. from Old-st.

Nag's Head - Court, Golden-Lane,—at 25, 3 doors on the R. from Barbican.

Nag's Head - Court, Grace-church-St.—at 34, leading to 28, Clement's lane.

Nag'sHead-Court,Cooper'sRow, —at 40, corner of Tower-hill.

Nag's Head-Inn, Boro. High-St.—at 100, op. Union-st.

Nag's Head - Yard, Oxford-St. —at 344, ⅓ of a mile on the L. from St. Giles's.

Nag's Head-Yard, Gray's-Inn-Lane,—at 80, opposite Little James-st.

Nag's Head - Yard, Leather-Lane,—at 40, 3 doors S. of Hatton-wall.

Nag's Head-Yard, Whitcomb-St.—3d on the R. from Charing-cross.

Nag's Head - Yard, Hackney-Road,—⅔ of a mile on the R. from Shoreditch-church.

Nag's Head-Yard, Whitechapel, —at 7, op. the church.

Nailsey-Pl. Salmon-Lane,Lime-house,—5th on the L. from the Commercial-road.

Naked-Boy-Alley, Up. Thames-St.—at 53, op. Bread - st.-hill.

Naked-Boy - Alley, Princes-St. Lambeth,—1st on the R. from Broad-st.

Naked - Boy - Court, Ludgate-Hill,—at 34, 7 doors W. of the Old-Bailey.

Naper's Court, Little Mitchell-Street, St. Luke's, — behind 21, Ironmonger-row.

Narrow-St. Limehouse,—from Ratcliffe-cross-stairs to Fore-st. by the Thames.

Narrow-Wall, Lambeth,—continuation of Pedlar's Acre, to Upper-ground.

Nassau-Street, King-St. Soho,—from 12, to Newport-market.

National-Register Newspaper-Office,—corner of Pickett-st. Temple-bar.

Naval-Row, Blackwall,—continuation of Poplar High-st.

Navy-Office, Somerset-Pl.—S. side, facing the entrance from the Strand.

Navy - Pay - Office, Somerset-Pl. — on the R. from the Strand.

Naylor's Yard, Silver-St. Golden-Sq.—at 24, op. John-street.

Neal's Passage, Gt. Earl - St. Seven-Dials,—3 doors from King-st.

Neal's Yard,—continuation of the last.

Neat-Boys-Court, Fashion-St. Spitalfields,—at 54, middle of the N. side.

Neat-Houses,—a district on the N. bank of the Thames, from Tothill-fields to Chelsea.

Neat - Houses - Row,—by the Monster Public-house, near the bridge at Pimlico.

Neckinger-Road or Lane, Parker's Row, Bermondsey,—extends from the turnpike to the Grange-road.

Nell-Gwine - Passage, Grosvenor-Row, Chelsea,—E. side of Wilderness-row.

Nelson's Court, Ratcliffe-Highway, — at 123, nearly op. Old Gravel-lane.

Nelson's Court, Salmon's Lane, Limehouse,—6th on the L. from the Commercial-road.

Nelson's Passage, Gt. Arthur-St.—the 1st on the R. from 10, Goswell-st.

Nelson-Passage,Bowling-Green-Builds. Marybone, — 2d on the L. from the New-road.

Nelson's Pl. Circus-St. Marybone,—1st on the R. from the New-road.

Nelson-Court,—N. end of the last.

Nelson's Pl. City - Road,—1st on the L. in New-st. from Up. Fountain-pl.

Nelson-Pl. City-Road,—S. end of Nelson-terrace.

Nelson's Pl. Fashion-St. Spitalfields,—2d on the L. from 194, Brick-lane.

Nelson's Pl. Poplar,—6 doors W. of Bow-lane.

Nelson's Pl. Blackman-St. Boro. —at 102, 6 doors S. of Lant-st.

Nelson's Pl. Lock's Fields, Walworth,—from the Obelisk to Sun-st.

Nelson's Pl. Kent - Road,—L. side, ⅛ of a mile below the Bricklayers-arms.

Nelson's Pl. London-Road,—10 doors on the L. from the Elephant and Castle.

Nelson's Row, Deptford Lower-Road,—¼ of a mile on the L. below the Halfway-house.

Nelson-Sq. Blackfriars-Road,—1st on the L. from Surrey-chapel towards the Obelisk.

Nelson-St. City - Road,—⅔ of a mile on the L. from Finsbury-sq. nearly op. the Shepherd and Shepherdess.

Nelson-St.Bethnal-Green,—behind Shoreditch-church, 1st on the L. in Mount-st. from 45, Church-st.

Nelson-St. Hackney-Road,—op. Gt. Cambridge-st. ½ a mile on the R. from Shoreditch.

Nelson-Street, Red-Lion-St.—6 doors on the R. from 30, Whitechapel.

Nelson-Street, Cannon-St.-Rd. —1st N. of the Commercial-road.

Nelson-St. Stepney,—2d E. of Ocean-st. N. side the Church-yard.

Nelson's Terrace, City-Road,— op. Sidney-st. a mile on the R. from Finsbury-sq.

Neptune - Court, Neptune - St. Lock's Fields, — middle of the N. side.

Neptune - Court, Neptune - St. Rotherhithe,—E. end of New-st. near Albion-st.

Neptune-Court, Lambeth Marsh, —S. end of Neptune-pl.

Neptune-Pl. Lambeth-Marsh,— ⅓ of a mile N. of the Horn-brewery towards Narrow-wall.

Neptune-Pl. Lock's Fields,—on the E. side of Neptune-st.

Neptune-Street, Lock's Fields, Walworth, — 3d on the L. from Rodney - row, Kent-road.

Neptune - St. Wellclose - Sq.— from the middle of the S. side, to 71, Parsons-st.

Neptune-St. Rotherhithe,—S. continuation of Elephant lane, entering by 344, Rotherhithe-st. near the church.

Nesbitt's Rents, Three Colt-St. Limehouse,—at 26, 8 doors N. from op. Ropemakers-fields.

Nevil's Court, Fetter-Lane,—at 37, middle of the E. side.

New-Alley, Three Colt-Street, Limehouse,—at 63, 1st N. of Ropemakers-fields.

New-Alley, High-St. Boro.—at 155, N. side of St. George's church.

New-Builds. Rotten-Row,—2d

on the R. from 30, Goswell-street.

New-Builds. Dark-Entry,—1st on the L. from 59, Lower E. Smithfield.

New-Builds. King Henry-Yard, —1st on the L. from Night-ingale-lane.

New - Builds. Fox and Knot-Court,—1st on the R. a few yards from 41, Cow-lane, W. Smithfield.

New-Builds. Half-Moon-Alley, —1st on the L. from 48, Whitecross-st. Cripplegate.

New-Builds. Little Bell-Alley. See New-Court, Swan-Alley.

New-Church, Strand. See St. Mary-le-Strand.

New-Court, New - St. Bromp-ton,—8 doors from the High-road.

New-Court, Little Chapel-St. Westr.—a few doors on the L. from the E. end of James-street.

New-Court, Duck-Lane, Westr. —8 doors from 58, Orchard-street.

New - Court, Strand,—at 205, op. St. Clement's church.

New-Court, Carey-St. Chancery-Lane, — at 16, nearly op. Serle-st.

New-Court, Temple,— 1st on the L. in Devereux - court, from 218, Strand.

New-Court, Gt. New-St. Fet-ter-Lane,—at 24, 3 doors on the L. from West Harding-street.

New-Court, Fleet-Market,—at 19, 2d on the R. from Lud-gate-hill.

New-Court, Old-Bailey,—at 50, middle of the W. side.

New-Court, Portpool-Lane,—at 50, 1st on the L. from Gray's-inn-lane.

New-Court, Goswell-St.—at 10, $\frac{1}{6}$ of a mile on the R. from Barbican.

New-Court, Allen-St.—1st on the R. from 113, Goswell-street.

New-Court, St. Peter's Lane, Smithfield,—2d on the R. from 68, St. John-st.

New-Court, Saint John's St. Clerkenwell,—at 123, $\frac{1}{3}$ of a mile on the L. from W. Smithfield.

New-Court, Cloth-Fair,—2d on the L. from 60, W. Smithfield.

New-Court, Brick-Lane, Saint Luke's,—at 80, 1st on the R. from 113, Old-st.

New-Court, Fore-St. Cripplegate,—at 122, op. the church.

New-Court, Moor-Lane, Cripplegate,—4th on the L. from 87, Fore-st.

New-Court, Gravel-Walk,—1st on the R. from Blue-Anchor-alley, Bunhill-row.

New-Court, Swan-Alley,—E. end, on the R. from 67, Coleman-st.

New-Court, Bow-Lane,—6th on the R. from 58, Cheapside.

New-Court, St. Swithin's Lane, —at 10, middle of the W. side.

New-Court, Throgmorton-St. —6 doors on the R. from the Bank.

New-Court, Old Broad-St.—7

doors from Threadneedle-street.

New-Court, Long-Alley,—4 doors on the L. from Moorfields.

New-Court, Long-Alley, Moorfields,—2d on the L. from Worship-st.

New-Court, Crown-St. Finsbury,—W. side of Maxwell-court, 2d on the L. from Wilson-st.

New-Court, Holywell-Lane, Shoreditch,—at 13, 3d on the R. from 193, Shoreditch.

New-Court, Holywell-Lane,—at 20, 2 doors W. of the last.

New-Court, Holywell-Lane,—at 48, nearly op. the last.

New-Court, Bough-Court,—1st on the L. entering by 236, Shoreditch.

New-Court, Angel-Alley,—1st on the R. from 124, Bishopsgate-without.

New-Court, Hackney-Road,—3d on the R. a few doors from Shoreditch-church.

New-Court, Hackney-Road,—2d on the L. from Shoreditch-church.

New-Court, Church-St. Bethnal-Green,—at 49, nearly op. Brick-lane.

New-Court, New Nicol-Street, Bethnal-Green,—the last on the L. from Cock-lane.

New-Court, Dorset-St. Spitalfields,—at 34, middle of the N. side.

New-Court, Brown's Lane, Spitalfields,—at 34, 2d on the L. from Red-lion-st.

New-Court, Vine-St. Spitalfields,—1st on the R. from 23, Lamb-st.

New-Court, Gt. Pearl-St. Spitalfields,—at 34, 5 doors on the L. from 20, Wheeler-st.

New-Court, Quaker-St. Spitalfields,—15 doors on the R. from 29, Wheeler-st.

New-Court, Carter-Street, Bethnal-Green,—1st on the R. from 67, Brick-lane.

New-Court, Fashion-St. Spitalfields,—3d on the L. from 194, Brick-lane.

New-Court, Wentworth-St. Spitalfields,—7 doors on the L. from Petticoat-lane.

New-Court, Wentworth-St.—at 26, the 4th E. of the last.

New-Court, Creechurch-Lane, —2d on the R. from 87, Leadenhall-st.

New-Court, Crutched-Friars,— at 45, nearly op. Savage-gardens.

New-Court, Goodman's Fields, —the continuation of Wellyard, from 82, Lemon-st.

New-Court, Blue Anchor-Yard, —3d on the R. from 48, Rosemary-lane.

New-Court, St. Catherine's Sq. —N. W. corner, and E. end of Catshole-court.

New-Court, Nightingale-Lane, —at 43, 1st on the L. from the entrance to the London-docks.

New-Court, Upper Chapman-St. St. George's East,—2d on the L. from Cannon-st.-road.

New-Court, Frying-Pan-Alley, —1st on the R. from Petticoat-lane, near Widegate-st.

New-Court, George-Yard,—2d

on the L. from 88, White-chapel.

New-Court, New-St.—1st on the R. from Fieldgate-st. Whitechapel.

New-Court, Bethnal-Green,—a few doors on the L. from the N. W. corner of the Green.

New-Court, Thomas-St. Whitechapel,—1st on the L. from Ducking Pond-lane.

New-Court, Blue-Gate-Fields, —4th on the L. from 95, Ratcliffe-highway.

New-Court, High-St. Newington,—a few doors on the L. from the church towards Kennington.

New-Court, White-St. Boro.— at 17, 3d on the L. from St. George's church.

New-Court, Castle-Lane, Boro. —8 doors on the L. from Castle-st.

New-Court, Queen-St. Horselydown,—2d on the L. from Free School-st.

New-Crane-Stairs and Dock, Wapping,—at 198, the bottom of New Gravel-lane, op. Hanover-stairs, Rotherhithe.

New-Cut, Narrow-St. Limehouse,—from the E. side the Drawbridge to the Commercial-road.

New-Cut, Lambeth-Marsh,— continuation of Charlotte-st. op. Surrey-chapel.

New-Grove, Mile-End-Road, —between the Plough and Thompson's nursery, 2¼ miles from Aldgate.

New-Inn, Tottenham-Court-Road,—at 187, 5 doors N. of Francis-st.

New-Inn, Wych-St.—a few doors on the R. from St. Clement's church.

New-Inn, Old-Bailey,—behind 51, op. the Sessions-house.

New-Inn-Builds. Wych-St.—at 30, a few doors on the R. from St. Clement's church.

New-Inn-Passage, Haughton-St. —7 doors on the R. from Newcastle-st. Strand.

New-Inn-Yard, Shoreditch,—at 176, by the turnpike.

New-Inn-Sq. Bateman's Row, —2d on the L. from 159, Shoreditch.

New-St. New-Inn-Yard,— 2d st. on the R. from 176, Shoreditch.

New-Lane, Shad-Thames,—at 102, op. Horselydown Newstairs.

New-Place, Poplar High-St.—R. side, ½ a mile from the Commercial-road.

New-Prison, Clerkenwell, — facing St. James's pl. from the Green.

New-Rents, St. Martin's-le-Grand,—5 doors on the R. from Newgate-st.

New-River-Head, Spa-Fields, —on the W. side of Sadler's Wells.

New-River-Office, Whitefriars, —facing the S. end of Dorset-st. Salisbury-sq.

New-Road, Marybone,— at 82, Edgware-road, ½ a mile on the R. from Tyburn-turnpike, leading to Sommers-town, Pentonville, and Islington.

New-Road, Hans-Town,—1st W. parallel to Sloane-st. near Knightsbridge.

New-Road, St. George's East, —the E. continuation of Cable-st.

New-Road, Cannon-Street, St. George's East,—the N. continuation of Cannon-st. to 210, Whitechapel-road.

New-Road, Dock-Head or Bermondsey. See Parker's Row.

New-Road, Bermondsey. See Bermondsey New-Road.

New-Row, Kennington-Common,—by the foot-path, middle of the E. side.

New-Sq. Orchard-St. Westr.— at 38, 2d on the L. from Dean-st.

New-Sq. Lincoln's-Inn. See Lincoln's-Inn New-Sq.

New-Sq. Minories,—at 130, middle of the W. side.

New-Sq. Stepney. See Trafalgar-Sq.

New-Sq. New-Lane,—the broadest part of it, adjoining 102, Shad-Thames.

New-St. Brompton,—1st street on the L. from Knightsbridge.

New-St. Hanover-Sq.. See Swallow-St.

New-Street, Broad-St. Carnaby-Market,—at 46, op. Poland-street.

New-St. Spring-Gardens,— 1st E. from 52, Charing-cross.

New-St. Covent-Garden,—continuation of King-st. to 57, St. Martin's lane.

New-Street, Baker-St. North, Marybone,—10 doors on the L. from the New-road.

New-Street, George St. Saint Giles's,—4 doors from 23. Gt. Russell-st.

New-St. (Gt.) Fetter-Lane,—1st
S

on the L. in West-Harding-st. from 20, Fetter-lane.

New-St. (Little),Shoe-Lane,—at 39, 1st street on the L. from 130, Fleet-st.

New-St. (Middle),—op. the W. end of the last.

New-St.-Hill,—1st on the L. in Little New-st. from 39, Shoe-lane.

New-St.-Sq.—op. Dean-st. from 43, Fetter-lane.

New-St. Blackfriars,—the continuation of Creed-lane,entering by 14, Ludgate-st.

New-Street,Old-St. Saint Luke's, —at 91, 2d E. of the church.

New-Street, Aldersgate-St.—at 126, leading to Cloth-fair.

New-Street, Peter-St. Clerken-well,—1st on the R. from Turnmill-st.

New-St. City-Road,—2d on the L. north from Old-st. by Up. Fountain-pl.

New-St.—the continuation of St. Mary-Axe, from Camo-mile-st. to 55, Houndsditch.

New-Street, Bishopsgate-St.— at 30, 2d on the R. north from the church.

New-St. Gibraltar-Fields, Beth-nal-Green,—1st on the R. in Duke-st. from Turk-st.

New-Street, Fieldgate-St.—ten doors on the R. from 266, Whitechapel-road.

New-Street, Cannon-St.-Road, —3d on the L. from White-chapel.

New-Street, St. Catherine's Lane,—the continuation of it, entering by 48, Upper East-Smithfield.

New-St. Lower E. Smithfield,—

at 66, a few doors on the R. from Butcher-row.

New-St. Shadwell-Market,—at the L. corner, from 67, High-street.

New-St. Holyfield-Row, Lam-beth,—op. W. end of Park-st. Kennington-cross.

New-Street,Union-St. Lambeth, —3d on the L. from Walcot-place.

New-Street, Princes-St. Lam-beth,—1st on the L. from Vauxhall.

New-Street, Gt. Guildford-St. Boro.—3d on the R. from 35, Queen-st.

New-St. Maze, Boro,—the con-tinuation of Joiner-st. from 241, Tooley-st.

New-St. Blackfriars-Road,—op. the E. side of the Obelisk.

New-St. (Little), Boro.-Road,— 2d on the R. from Stones-end.

New-St. Newington,—op. the 2 mile-stone, $\frac{3}{8}$ of a mile on the L. south from the church.

New-Street, Lion-St. Walworth, —1st on the L. from the Kent-road.

New-St. East-Lane, Walworth, —1st on the R. in Camden-st. from the chapel.

New-St. Horselydown,—the E. continuation of Fair-st. and of Free-School-st. to Russell-st. and Dock-Head.

New-Street, Adam-St. Rother-hithe,—at 76, middle of the N. side.

New-Street, Neptune - St. Ro-therhithe,—3d on the L. from Elephant-lane.

New - Terrace, Tabernacle -

Walk, Moorfields, -1st on the L. from 36, City-road.

New-Walk, Shad-Thames,—1st on the L. from Dockhead, extending to Thomas-st.

New-Way, Orchard-St. Westr. —12 doors on the R. from Dean-st.

New-Way -Court,—7 doors in the last from Orchard-st.

New - Way, Maze, Boro.—1st on the R. from 196, Tooley-street.

New - Wharf, Limehouse-Hole, —between Limehouse-hole-stairs and the entrance to the West-India-docks.

New-Yard, Lisle - St.—4 doors from Newport-market.

New-Yard, Gt. Queen-St. Lincoln's-Inn-Fields,—at 55, ten doors from Drury-lane.

New-Yard, Camomile-St.—4th on the R. from Bishopsgate.

Newby's Pl. Poplar,—¼ a mile on the L. from the Commercial-road, near the Green-dragon.

Newcastle-Court, Strand,—entrance op. 218, a few doors on the R. from Temple-bar.

Newcastle-Court, College-Hill, —3 doors on the R. from Cloak-lane.

Newcastle-Place, Clerkenwell-Close,—part of the E. side, adjoining the church.

Newcastle - Pl. Mile-End,—10 doors E. of the turnpike.

Newcastle - Row, Clerkenwell-Close,—on the E. side of Newcastle-pl.

Newcastle-St. Strand,—at 309, by the New-church.

Newcastle-St. Fleet-Market,—at 33, 2d on the L. from Holborn-bridge.

Newcastle-St.Whitechapel. See Castle.

Newcastle-Street, Clerkenwell-Close,—the 2d on the R. north of the church.

Newgate-Market,—entrance by 20, Newgate-st. or by 30, Paternoster-row.

Newgate - Prison, Old -Bailey, —at the N. end of it, adjoining Newgate-st.

Newgate-St.—the W. continuation of Cheapside on the R. extending to the Old-Bailey.

Newington - Butts,—the neighbourhood about the Elephant and Castle.

Newington-Causeway,—L. side, from Stones-end to the Elephant and Castle.

Newington-Road,—R.side,from the King's Bench to the Elephant and Castle.

Newington-Pl. Newington,—E. side the High-road, by Kennington-Common.

Newington-Terrace,—the N. E. corner of Kennington-common.

Newman's Court, Cornhill,—at 73, 4th E. of the Royal-Exchange.

Newman's Mews, Castle - St. Oxford-St.—at 74, three doors W. of Newman-st.

Newman's Passage, Newman-St.—26 doors on the R. from Oxford-st.

Newman's Row, Lincoln's-Inn-Fields,—6 houses at the N. E. corner, by Gt. Turnstile.

Newman's Row, Bermondsey-
St.—at 117, 6 doors N. of
the church.

Newman-Street, Oxford-St.—
39 doors on the R. from St.
Giles's.

Newman's Yard, Newman-St.
—10 doors on the R. from
Oxford-st.

Newmarket-St. Wapping,—at
157, the continuation of Old
Gravel-lane.

Newmarket-Terrace, Cam-
bridge-Heath, Hackney-Rd.
—part of the E. side, adjoining the turnpike.

Newnham-Place, Bishopsgate-
Without,—at 134, 10 doors
N. of Sun-st.

Newnham-Street, Queen-St.—
1st on the L. from 61, Edgware-road.

Newport-Court, — S. end of
Newport-market, op. Great
Newport-st.

Newport-Market,—W. end of
Gt. Newport-st.

Newport-St. (Gt.) St. Martin's
Lane,—op. Long-acre.

Newport-St. (Little),—continuation of the last from Castle-
st. to Grafton-st.

News Newspaper-Office,—at
28, Brydges-st.

Newton-Court, Strand,—from
Old Round-court to Vine-st.

Newton-St. High-Holborn,—
from 207, to Charles-street,
Drury-lane.

St. Nicholas-Church, Old Fish
St.—4 doors E. of the Old-
Change.

St. Nicholas-Church-Yd. Bread-
St. Hill,—5 doors on the R.
from Bread-st.

Nicholas-Lane, Lombard-St.—
at 24, 3d on the R. from the
Mansion-house.

Nicol's Court, Rosemary-Lane,
—at 88, nearly op. Dock-st.

Nicol's Row, Church-St. Bethnal-Green, — at 30, ⅛ of a
mile on the L. from 65, Shoreditch.

Nicol's Sq. Cripplegate; — N.
end of Castle-st. Falcon-sq.

Nicol-St (Old), Bethnal-Green,
—1st on the R. in Cock-lane,
from 65, Shoreditch.

Nicol-St.(New),Bethnal-Green,
—1st N. parallel to the last,
2d on the R. in Cock-lane.

Nicol-St.(Half),Bethnal Green,
—3d on the R. in Cock-lane,
from behind 65, Shoreditch.

Night-Lane,St. Luke's,—N.end
of Brick-lane.

Nightingale-Court,Nightingale-
Lane,—1st on the R. from
Up. E.-Smithfield.

Nightingale-Lane,Up.E.-Smith-
field,—at 110, op. the entrance to the London-docks.

Nightingale-Lane, Fore-Street,
Limehouse,—at 60, by the W.
end of Ropemakers-fields.

Nile-Pl. Weymouth-St.—1st on
the R. from the Kent-road.

Nile-St. Hoxton-Fields,—2d on
the L. north of Winkworth's
builds. City-road.

Nine-Elms,—1st on the R. ¼ of
a mile from Vauxhall-turnpike towards Wandsworth.

Nixon-Square,—W. end of the
Crescent, Jewin-st. Criople-
gate.

Nixon's Yard, Princes . Pimlico. See Princes-Court.

No Name-Court, Bedfordbury,

—3 doors on the L. from New-st. St. Martin's lane.

Noah's-Ark-Alley, Queen - St. Ratcliffe,—2d on the R. east of London-st.

Noah's - Ark - Court, Stangate, Lambeth, — 1st on the R. from Westr.-bridge.

Noble-Street, Falcon-Sq.—the continuation of Foster-lane, Cheapside.

Noble-Street, Goswell - St.—at 57, 2d N. of Old-st.

Noble-St. Poplar,—1st W. of the East-India Alms-houses.

Noel-Street, Berwick-St. — at 45, 10 doors from 373, Oxford-st.

Noel-St. Bermondsey New-Rd. —2d on the L. from the Bricklayers-arms.

Norfolk-Pl. Curtain-Road,—3d on the L. from Old-st.-road.

Norfolk-Place (Little),—1st on the R. in the last from the Curtain-road.

Norfolk-Place, Church-St. Lambeth,—1st E. of High-st.

Norfolk-Pl. St. George's Road, —the N. side, op. the Elephant and Castle.

Norfolk-Pl. East - Lane, Walworth,— ⅙ of a mile on the R. from High-st. op. Richmond-pl.

Norfolk-Pl. Salisbury-St. Bermondsey,—2d on the L. from Rotherhithe-wall.

Norfolk-Row, Church-St. Lambeth,—2d E. from High-st.

Norfolk-St. Park-Lane, Oxford-Street,—from North-row to Wood's mews.

Norfolk-St. Middlesex - Hospital, — continuation of Newman-st. from 39, Oxford-st.

Norfolk-St. Strand,—at 180, 3d on the L. from Temple-bar.

Norfolk-St. Kingsland-Road,— part of the said road, ⅛ of a mile from Shoreditch.

Norfolk-Street, Cannon-St.-Rd. —2d N. of the Commercial-road.

Norfolk - St. Little Guildford-St. Boro.—1st on the R. from 75, Queen-st.

Norfolk - Waggon - Office, —at 32, Sun-st. Bishopsgate-without.

Norman-Builds. Wenlock - St. St. Luke's, — 3d on the R. from op. 36, Ironmonger-row.

Norman-Court, Cable-St. Well-close-Sq.—at 41, op. N. E. passage.

Norman - Street, St. Luke's,— continuation of Helmet-row, W. side the church.

Norris-Court, Nightingale-Lane, —at 26, 3d on the L. from the entrance to the London-docks.

Norris-Court, Snow's Fields,— 1st on the R. from 238, Bermondsey-st.

Norris-St. Haymarket,—at 56, 1st on the R. from Piccadilly.

North-Court, South-St. Berkeley-Sq.—3 doors E. from 17, South Audley-st.

North-East-Passage, Wellclose-Sq.—from the N. E. corner to 35, Cable-st.

North-Green, Worship-St.—12 doors on the L. from Paul-st.

North-Mews, Little James-St.
—1st on the R. from Gray's-
inn-lane.

North-Mews, North-St. Tottenham-Ct.-Rd.—middle of the
N. side.

North-Pl. Gray's-Inn-Lane,—
op. 80, part of the W. side,
from Little James-st. to Henry-st.

North-Place, (Upper),—the N.
continuation of the last.

North-Place, Phillips's Builds.
Sommers-Town,—1st on the
L. from 20, Willsted-st.

North-Pl. Banner-St.—8 doors
on the R. from 80, Bunhill-
row.

North-Place, Globe-St. Bethnal-
Green,—1st on the R. north
from Green-st.

North-Pl. Ducking-Pond-Lane,
Whitechapel, — 3d west of
North-st.

North's Pl. Lambeth,—op. W.
side the Asylum.

North-Place, West-Square, St.
George's Fields,——at the
N. E. corner.

North-Row, Grosvenor-Sq.—
1st on the R. in George's-st.
from 267, Oxford-st.

North-Row-Mews, — at 14, in
the last.

North-Row, East-St. Walworth,
—2d on the L. from the High-
street.

North-St. (Up.) Hans-Town,—
6 doors on the R. in Sloane-
st. from Knightsbridge.

North-St. (Lower),—the continuation of the last.

North-Street, Wood-St. Westr.
—1st on the L. from 63, Millbank-st.

North-St. Manchester-Sq.—

from 12, South-st. to 12, Paradise-st.

North-St. Tottenham-Court-
Road, — behind Whitfield's
chapel, from 70, John-st. to
35, Charlotte-st.

North-St. Pentonville,—4th on
the R. from the Chapel towards Sommers-Town.

North-St. (Old), Red-Lion-Sq.
—at 32, middle of the N.
side.

North-St.(New),—continuation
of the last.

North-Street, Ropemakers-St.
—2d on the L. from Moor-
fields.

North-St. City-Road,—4th on
the R. ¼ of a mile from Finsbury-sq.

North-Street, Lamb-St. Spitalfields,—at 11, 3d on the R.
from Spital-sq.

North-St. Whitechapel-Road,
—at 154, a few doors W. of
Mile-end-turnpike.

North-St. Wilmot-St. Bethnal-
Green, — near the S. end,
leading to the last.

North-St. Bethnal-Green,—1st
on the L. in West-st. entering by Green-st.

North-St. Poplar,—1st on the
L. from the Commercial-rd.

North-St. Lambeth,— op. the
W. side of the Asylum.

North-Street, East-Lane, Walworth,—middle of the N. side.

Northam's Buildings, Sommers-
Town,—the continuation of
Phillips's builds. to 20, Will-
sted-st.

Northampton-Buildings, Rosamond-St. Clerkenwell, — at
45, 2d on the R. from Corporation-lane.

Northampton - Court, North-ampton-St. Clerkenwell,—2 doors N. of Perceval-st.

Northampton-House, Ashby-St. Clerkenwell,—1st on the R. from St. John-st.

Northampton-Pl.St.John Street, —N. end, on the R. ½ a mile from Smithfield.

Northampton-Place, Hackney-Road,—part of the R. side, adjoining James's pl. ¾ of a mile from Shoreditch.

Northampton-Place, North-St. Walworth,—2d on the R. from East-lane.

Northampton-Row, Rosamond-St. Clerkenwell,—at 24, leading to Spa-fields.

Northampton-Sq.—between St. John-st.-road and Goswell-st.-road, entrance by Ashby-street.

Northampton-St. Battle-Bridge, St. Pancras,—between Up. Edmond-street and Vernon's buildings.

Northampton-St. Clerkenwell, — E. side of St. John-st. and the corner of Compton-st.

Northampton - St. (Lower),—a few yards from the last.

Northampton - Terrace, City-Road,—by the turnpike, ¾ of a mile on the L. from Finsbury-sq.

Northcote's Wharf, Rotherhithe, —op. 179, a few doors below Globe-stairs.

Northern - Dispensary, South-Row, Sommers-Town,—corner of Duke's row, Tavistock-square.

Northumberland - Alley, Fen-church-St.—at 78, 10 doors on the L. from Aldgate.

Northumberland Coal-Company's-Office, — at 12, New Bridge-st. Blackfriars, middle of the W. side.

Northumberland-Court, Strand, —1st on the R. from Charing-cross.

Northumberland-Court, South-ampton-Builds.—at 40, 10 doors on the L. from 320, High-Holborn.

Northumberland-Court, Compton-Street, Clerkenwell,—14 doors on the L. from Goswell-street.

Northumberland - Court, Northumberland Alley,—1st on the R. from 78, Fenchurch-street.

Northumberland-House, Strand, —op. St. Martin's lane, Charing-cross.

Northumberland - Mews, Northumberland-St. Marybone, —behind the E. side.

Northumberland-Passage, Northumberland-St.—12 doors on the L. from the Strand.

Northumberland-Place, Lamb-Alley, Bishopsgate,—1st on the L. from 58, Sun-st.

Northumberland-St. Strand,— 1st on the R. from Charing-×.

Northumberland-St. New-Road, Marybone,—from the turnpike, to 18, Paddington-st.

Northumberland-Wharf, — 3d E. of Blackfriars-bridge, Surrey side.

Norton-Falgate,—the N. continuation of Bishopsgate-st. to Shoreditch.

Norton-Falgate Alms-Houses, —op. the N. end of Blossom-st. entering by 27, White-Lion-st.

Norton-Street, Up. Marybone-St.—at 32, 3d on the R. from Howland-st.

Norton-St. (Up.)—the continuation of the last.

Norway-Pl. Hackney-Road,—part of the R. side, adjoining Brighton-pl. ⅓ of a mile from Shoreditch.

Norway-Pl. Commercial-Road, Limehouse,—⅛ of a mile on the L. west of the church.

Norway-Street, Old-St.—at 19, 3d on the R. from Goswell-street.

Norway-Wharf, Millbank-St.—S. end of Abingdon-st. on the L. ¼ of a mile above West-minster-bridge.

Norwell-Place, Bethnal-Green-Road, — by the turnpike, about ½ a mile on the L. from 65, Shoreditch.

Norwich-Court, Fetter-Lane,—at 92, 16 doors on the R. from 33, Holborn-hill.

Norwich-Court, Upper East-Smithfield,—at 24, op. Butcher-row.

Nottingham-Court, Short's Gardens,—2d on the L. from 15, Drury-lane.

Nottingham-Mews, High-Street, Marybone,—at 58, 2d on the R. from the New-road.

Nottingham-Place, New-Road, Marybone,—between High-st. and Northumberland-st.

Nottingham-Pl.—at 51, Charlotte-st. Whitechapel, 3d W. of Cannon-st.-road.

Nottingham-Place, East-Lane, Walworth,—1st on the R. in South-st. from Apollo-builds.

Nottingham-Street, High-St. Marybone,—at 61, 1st on the R. from the New-road.

Nottingham Waggon-Office,—at 90, London-wall, 3 doors from Wood-st.

Nova-Scotia-Gardens, Crabtree-Row, Bethnal-Green,—at the E. end, op. the Bird-cage.

Nun's Court, Coleman-St.—at 74, 6 doors on the L. from London-wall.

Nursery-Pl. St. George's Fields,—op. the S. side the Philanthropic-Reform.

Nursery-Row,—from the last towards Lambeth.

Nursery-Pl. Kent-Road, —at the corner of East-lane.

Nursery-Row, Lock's Fields, Walworth,—S. parallel to Bedford-st.

Nutkin's Corner, Bermondsey-Wall.—1st on the R. below Mill-st.

OAKEY-STREET, Thomas-St. Bethnal-Green,—5 doors on the L. from 119, Brick-lane.

Oakley's Court, Hare-St. Bethnal-Green,—at 35, between Edward-st. and Fuller-st.

Oakley-St. Bridge-Road, Lambeth,—3d on the L. from Westr.-bridge.

Oat-Lane, Noble-St. Foster-

Lane,—at 11, 4th on the R. from Cheapside.

Oatmeal-Yard, Dog and Bear-Yard,—last on the R. from 128, Tooley-st.

Obelisk, Fleet-Market,—S. end of it, between Ludgate-hill and Fleet-st.

Obelisk, Blackfriars-Road, St. George's Fields,—S. end of it, $\frac{2}{3}$ of a mile from the bridge.

Obelisk, Lock's Fields, Walworth,—W. end of Salisbury-pl. near Neptune-pl.

Observer Newspaper-Office,—at 169, Strand, nearly op. the New-church.

Ocean-Row, Stepney,—1st N. parallel to the church-yd.

Ocean-St. Cow-Lane, Stepney, —1st on the L. from Stepney Old-sq.

Octagon-Pl. Kennington-Common,—W. side, op. the Horns Tavern.

Off-Alley, Villiers-St.—4 doors on the L. from 32, Strand.

Offertory or Offerty-School, Little Vine - St. Piccadilly,—3 doors on the L. from 5, Swallow-st.

Ogle-Mews, Upper Ogle-St.—4 doors on the R. from Foley-place.

Ogle-Sq. Upper Ogle-St.—behind 10, 3 doors from 9, Up. Marybone-st.

Ogle-St. Foley-Pl. Marybone, —6 doors E. from 28, Great Titchfield-st.

Ogle-St. (Up.)—6 doors E. from the last.

Ohren's Court, Ratcliffe-Sq.—

at the S. E. corner, by Perriwinkle-st.

St. Olave's Church, Tooley-St. — 8 doors E. of London-bridge.

St. Olave's Church, Old-Jewry, —middle of the N. side.

St. Olave's Stairs, Tooley-St.— 7 doors E. of London-bridge.

St. Olave Workhouse, Parish-St.—a few doors on the L. from Tooley-st.

Old-Bailey, Ludgate - Hill,—at 28, 1st on the L. from Fleet-market.

Old-Bethlem. See Bethlem.

Old-Buildings or Square, Lincoln's Inn. See Lincoln's Inn.

Old - Change, Cheapside, — 6 doors on the R. from St. Paul's-church-yard.

Old-Jewry. See Jewry.

Old-Court, Hackney - Road,— 3d on the L. from Shoreditch-church.

Old Pay-Office, Old Broad-St. —at 54, nearly op. the Excise-Office.

Old-Street, St. Luke's,—2d on the L. $\frac{1}{4}$ of a mile from the N. W. corner of Finsbury-sq.

Old-St.-Rd.—the E. continuation of Old-st. from the City-road to opposite Shoreditch-church.

Old-St.-Sq.—at the N. end of Henry-st. a few doors W. of St. Luke's hospital.

Old Swan-Lane and Stairs. See Swan.

Oliver-Court, Bowling-St. Westminster, —at 23, 5 doors from Wood-st.

One-House-Court, Miles's Lane, —14 doors on the R. from Cannon-st.

One-Swan - Yard, Bishopsgate, —at 180, N. side the church.

One-Tun-Yard, Davies-St. — 6 doors on the L. from 292, Oxford-st.

One-Tun-Ct. Strand,—24 doors on the R. from Charing-cross.

Onslow-Street, Vine - St.—1st on the L. from Mutton-lane, Clerkenwell-green.

Opera-House, Haymarket,—on the W. side near Pall-mall.

Orange-Court, Swallow-St. See Orange-St.

Orange-Court, Castle-St. Leicester-Square,—1st from the King's mews.

Orange-Court, Drury-Lane,— from 130, middle of the E. side, to op. Wild-st.

Orange-Court, Rose-St. Soho, —at 10, middle of the N. side.

Orange-Court, Wapping-St.— at 23, near Hermitage-bridge.

Orange - Place, Old Nicol-St. Bethnal-Green,—on the E. side of Cross-st.

Orange-Place, Deptford Lower-Rd.—nearly op. China-hall.

Orange-Row, Fieldgate - St.— 1st on the L. from 266, Whitechapel-road.

Orange - Row, Newington, — from the Plough and Harrow towards Kennington.

Orange-Street, Swallow-St.—at 55, near the middle of the N. side.

Orange-St. Leicester - Sq.—S. side, from St. Martin's-st. to Castle-st.

Orange-Street, Red-Lion-Sq.— N. W. corner, to 20, King-st.

Orange-St. Loman's Pond, Boro.—1st on the L. in Gravel-lane, from Duke-st. towards the King's Bench.

Orchard, New-St.—1st on the L. from Shadwell market.

Orchard, Broad-St. Ratcliffe,— at 80, middle of the N. side.

Orchard, Nightingale - Lane, Limehouse,—the E. end of Chiver's court.

Orchard-Place, White - Bear - Gardens, Hackney-Road,— entrance by Union-walk, Union-st.

Orchard, Blackwall, — by the river entrance to the East-India-Dock.

Orchard-St. Portman-Sq.—S.E. corner, to 197, Oxford-st.

Orchard-St. Westminster,—1st on the R. in Dean-st. from Tothill-st.

Orchard-Street, St. Luke's,— the N. continuation of Ironmonger-row, from 97, Old-st.

Ordnance-Office, Pall-Mall,— at 91, op. George-st. late Cumberland-house.

Ordnance-Office, Tower,— op. the bridge or first turning or entrance on the R. from Iron-gate.

Orford-Row, Kent - Road, — part of the R. side, ½ of a mile below the Bricklayers-arms.

Ormond-House, Paradise-Row, Chelsea,—3d house on the R. from the hospital.

Ormond-Pl. Gt. Ormond-St.— bottom of Little Ormond-yd.

Ormond-Row, Chelsea,— W.

side the hospital, from Paradise-row to Durham-pl.

Ormond-St. (Gt.) Lamb's-Conduit-St.—at 50, 5th on the L. from 71, High-holborn.

Ormond-St. (Little), Queen-Sq.—op. the last, leading to Southampton-row.

Ormond-St. (New), Lamb's-Conduit-St.—at 31, op. Gt. Ormond-st.

Ormond-Yard (Great), Gt. Ormond-St. Queen-Sq. — middle of the S. side.

Ormond-Yard (Little), Gt. Ormond-St.—8 doors from 50, Lamb's-conduit-st.

Ormond-Yard, York-Street,—4 doors on the L. from St. James's-sq.

Orphans-School, City-Road,—on the S. side the turnpike, ⅞ of a mile from Finsbury-square.

Orton's Builds. Castle-St. Boro.—last on the L. from 13, Redcross-st.

Osband-Buildings, Bermondsey New-Road,—2d on the R. from the Bricklayers-arms.

Osborn-Pl.—2d on the R. from op. Whitechapel-church, along Osborn-st.

Osborn-Pl. Poplar,—W. end of Ashton-st. Robinhood-lane.

Osborn-St. Whitechapel, — at 74, nearly op. the church.

Osman's Pl. Swan-Yard, Boro.—1st on the L. from St. George's church.

Osnaburgh-Row, King's Road, Pimlico,—1st on the R. from Up. Eaton-st.

Ossulstone-St. Sommers Town,

—continuation of Willsted-street.

Oval, Kennington,—S. end of Bowling-green-row, op. the Horns Tavern.

Overman's Alms-Houses, Montague-Close,—on the N. side St. Saviour's church.

Owen's Alms-Houses,—6 doors on the L. from Islington towards Sadler's Wells.

Owen's Court, Owen's Place,—1st N. of Rawstorne-st.

Owen's Place, Goswell-St.-Rd.—W. side, adjoining Owen's-row.

Owen's Row, Goswell-St.-Rd.—2d on the R. from Islington.

Oxendon-Chapel, Oxendon-St.—4 doors from Coventry-st.

Oxendon-Street, Coventry-St.—8 doors on the R. from the Haymarket.

Oxford-Arms-Inn, Warwick-Lane,—3d on the R. from 10, Newgate-st.

Oxford-Arms-Passage,—between the Inn-yard and Warwick-lane.

Oxford-Buildings, Oxford-St.—at 299, 10 doors W. of New Bond-st.

Oxford-Chapel, Vere-St.—8 doors on the R. from 151, Oxford-st.

Oxford-Court, Oxford-St. — at 319, 4 doors W. from Swallow-st.

Oxford-Court, Salters-Hall-Ct.—1st on the L. from 82, Cannon-st.

Oxford-Dairy, Oxford-St.—at 71, nearly op the Pantheon.

Oxford-House, Hackney-Road, —near the Nag's-head, ¾ of a mile on the R. from Shoreditch.

Oxford-Market, Oxford-St.—at 87, ¾ of a mile from Saint Giles's.

Oxford-Pl. Westr.-Bridge-Rd. —R. side, a few doors from the Obelisk.

Oxford-Rhedarium, Oxford-St. —27 doors on the R. from St. Giles's.

Oxford-St.—from Saint Giles's, where the numbers begin and end, viz. 1 and 440, to Tyburn-turnpike, where there is 245, about 1½ mile in length.

Oxley-Court, Parker's-Row, Dock-Head,—a few doors on the L. from Hickman's Folly.

Oxley-Pl. Hickman's Folly,— 2d on the R. from Dockhead.

——

Packer-Court, Still-Alley,—1st on the R. from 104, Houndsditch.

Packer-Court, Coleman-St.—4 doors from the Old-Jewry, Cheapside.

Packston's-Alley, Rotherhithe-St.—at 312, 3d on the R. below the church.

Paddington-Builds. Paddington, —between the Edgware-rd. and the Harrow-road.

Paddington-Green, Paddington, —the open space by Paddington-church.

Paddington-St. Marybone,—

5th on the R. in Baker-st. from Portman-sq.

Pageants, Rotherhithe,—at 125, near a mile below the church, op. Duke's-shore, Limehouse.

Page's Walk, Grange-Road,— 1st coach-turning on the R. from Bermondsey New-road.

Pagets-Place, Blue-Gate-Fields, —4 doors on the R. from 95, Ratcliffe-highway.

Painter's Builds. Norfolk-Pl.— N. side, a few yards on the L. from the Curtain-road.

Painter's Court, Bury-Street, St. James's,—5 doors on the R. from Jermyn-st.

Painters-Hall, Little Trinity-Lane,—middle of the W. side.

Painter's Rents, Broad-St. Ratcliffe,—at 66, 3 doors W. of Butcher-row.

Palace-Court-Office, Clifford's Inn,—1st door on the R. from 138, Fetter-lane.

Palace-Row, Tottenham-Court, —from the Hampstead-road to the turnpike.

Palace-St. Westr.—the continuation of Charlotte-st. Pimlico.

Palace-Wharf, Lambeth,—op. Ferry-st. on the S. side of the church.

Palace-Yard (New),—between Bridge-st. and Wesminster-hall.

Palace-Yard (Old),—S. side of Westminster-hall by the Abbey.

Palatine-Pl. Commercial-Road, —part of the N. side, between Plumbers-row and Greenfield-st.

Pall-Mall, St. James's,—from the S. end of the Haymarket to the Palace.

Pall-Mall-Court, Pall-Mall,—at 102, middle of the S. side.

Palmer's Rents, Snow's Fields, —4th on the L. from 238, Bermondsey-st.

Palmer's Village, Westminster,— N. side of Bridewell, Brewers-green.

Palmer's Yard, Bermondsey - Wall,—2d on the R. a few doors below East - lane, by Palmer's rope-walk.

Palsgrave - Court, Strand,—at 222, twelve doors on the L. from Temple-bar.

Pancras Female-Charity-School, Hampstead - Road,—S. side the chapel.

Pancras - Lane, Queen - St.—3 doors on the L. from 70, Cheapside.

Saint Pancras-Pl. St. Pancras, —from the Small-pox-hospital towards the church.

Pancras-St. Tottenham - Court-Road,—at 175, op. Howland-street.

Pancras-St. (Little),—1st on the L. in the last from Tottenham-court-road.

Pancras- Walk, St. Pancras,— N. end of Vernon's builds. near the church.

Pannier - Alley, Newgate-St.— at 50, 3 doors on the L. from Cheapside.

Panorama, Leicester-Sq.—N. E. corner, by Cranbourn-st.

Panorama, Strand, — at 169, nearly op. the New-church.

Panorama (Marshall's), Old

Bond-St.—13 doors on the R. from 57, Piccadilly.

Pan's Head-Yard, Leicester-St. —3 doors on the L. from 32, Swallow-st.

Pantheon, Oxford-St.—at 360, $\frac{1}{3}$ of a mile on the L. from St. Giles's.

Panton-Sq. Haymarket,—end of Arundel - st. from Coventry-street.

Panton-St. Haymarket,—at 24, 1st on the L. from Piccadilly.

Paper-Builds. Temple,—W. side King's - bench - walk, by the Temple-gardens.

Parade, St. James's Park,—the E. end of it, by the Horse-guards.

Parade (Old), North Audley-St.—7 doors on the L. from 263, Oxford-st.

Parade, Du Four's Place,—1st on the L. from 21, Broad-street.

Paradise-Builds. Lambeth Up. Marsh,—nearly facing Stangate-st.

Paradise-Chapel, Paradise-Walk, Chelsea,—a few doors on the L. from op. 18, Paradise-row.

Paradise - Court, Paradise - St. Battle-Bridge,—4 doors from Britannia-st.

Paradise-Court, Castle - Yard, Gravel - Lane, Boro. — the S. end of it.

Paradise-Pl. Paradise-St. Mary-bone,—6 doors on the R. from 82, High-st.

Paradise-Pl. Tabernacle-Walk, —at 44, the corner of Leonard-st.

T

Paradise-Pl. or Row, Lambeth Up.Marsh,—the continuation of it on the L. to Royal-row.

Paradise-Pl. Paradise-Row, Rotherhithe,—at 10, a few doors on the L. from Deptford Lower-road.

Paradise-Pl. Poplar,—op. the Black-horse.

Paradise-Row, Paradise-Place, Marybone,—at the N. end, from 6, Paradise-st.

Paradise-Row, Chelsea,—on the W. side the hospital, extending towards Battersea-bridge.

Paradise-Row, Palmer's Village, Westr.—N. side of Bridewell, Brewers-green.

Paradise-Row, St. Pancras,—1st W. of the Small-pox-hospital.

Paradise-Row, Bethnal-Green, —W. side of the Green, from Bethnal-green-road to Peacock-court.

Paradise-Row, Charles-Street, Saint George's East,—the continuation of it bearing to the L. from 44, Old Gravel-lane.

Paradise-Row, Ratcliffe-Sq.—at the S. E. corner, by Perriwinkle-st.

Paradise-Row, High-St. Lambeth,—1st on the L. from the church.

Paradise-Row, Gravel-Lane, Boro.—10 doors S. of Charlotte-st.

Paradise-Row, Rotherhithe,—1st S. parallel to Paradise-st. from Lucas-st. to Deptford Lower-road.

Paradise-Street, High-St. Marybone,—at 82,3d on the L. from Charles-st. Manchester-sq.

Paradise-Street, Britannia-St. Battle-Bridge,—6 doors from Gray's-inn-lane.

Paradise-Street, Paul-St.—at 30, 4th on the L. from the N. E. corner of Finsbury-sq.

Paradise-St. Rotherhithe,—1st S. parallel to part of Rotherhithe-st. from Mill-Pondbridge, towards Deptford Lower-road.

Paradise-Walk, Paradise-Row, Chelsea,—op. 18, leading towards the Thames.

Paragon, Kent-Road,—W. side the turnpike, by the Bricklayers-arms.

Paragon-Chapel,—S. end of Webb-st. Bermondsey New-road.

Paragon-Mews, Kent-Road,— at the back of the W. side of the Paragon.

Paragon-Pl. Kent-Road,—S.side, adjoining the Paragon.

Paragon-Pl. Lock's Fields, Walworth,—the continuation of Trafalgar-pl. from Rodney-row, Kent-road.

Paragon-Row, Lock's Fields, Walworth,—2d on the L. from Garmouth-row, Kent-road.

Paragon-Walk, Webb-St.—1st on the L. from Bermondsey New-road.

Pardon-Passage, Saint John-St. Clerkenwell,—at 54, leading into Wilderness-row.

Pardon-Court,—1st on the L. in the last from St. John-st.

Parietalia-Pl. Snow's Fields,— 6th on the R. from 109, High-st. Borough.

Paris-Place, Chapel-St. Lisson-

Green,—1st on the L. from
Edgware-road.

Paris-Garden-Lane, Holland-St.
Blackfriars - Road,—op. the
Falcon Glass-house.

Paris-Garden-Stairs,—N. end of
the last.

Parish-Street, Tooley-St.—last
on the R. from London-
bridge.

Parker's-Court, Whitechapel,—
16 doors E. of Red-lion-st.

Park-Lane, Piccadilly,—2d on
the L. from Hyde-park-corner,
extending to Oxford-st.

Park-Lane, Baker-St. North,
Marybone,—1st on the L.
from the New-road.

Park-Place, Baker-St. North,
Marybone,—continuation of
it on the L. from the New-
road.

Park-Place, Knightsbridge,—E.
side the barracks, ½ a mile
on the R. from Hyde-park-
corner.

Park-Pl. Saint James's St.—at
60, 2d on the R. from 163,
Piccadilly.

Park-Pl. Carlisle - Lane, Lambeth,—last on the R. from
the Marsh-gate.

Park-Pl. (Little),—E. end of
the last.

Park-Pl. Kennington - Cross,—
W. side, op. the White-hart.

Park-Pl. East-Lane, Walworth,
—4th on the R. from the
Kent-road.

Park - Prospect, Knightsbridge,
—W. end of the Cannon-
brewery.

Park-Row,—E. end of the barracks, Knightsbridge.

Park-Row, Limehouse - Cause-

way,—a few doors on the L.
from Three-Colt-st.

Park-Street, Oxford-St.—at 257,
2d on the R. from Hyde-park.

Park-St. Westr.—N. end of
Carteret-st. Broadway.

Park-Street, New-St. Marybone,
—2d on the R. from Baker-
st. North.

Park-St. Little,—S. end of the
last.

Park - St. Limehouse-Hole,—a
few doors on the L. from the
Lime-kilns.

Park-St. Kennington - Cross,—
nearly op. the White-hart.

Park-St. (Little),—the W. continuation of the last.

Park-St. Boro.-Market,—from
the middle of the W. side, to
Bankside.

Parker's Builds. Grange-Road,
—by the Queen's head, 3d on
the R. from Bermondsey New-
road.

Parker's Pl. Middlesex-St. Sommers - Town,—3 doors from
Phœnix-st.

Parker's Rents, Shoe-Lane,—
at 43, 3d on the L. from Holborn.

Parker's Row, Bermondsey,—
1st coach-turning on the R.
in Hickman's Folly from
Dock-head.

Parker's St. Drury - Lane,—at
161, 1st N. of Great Queen-
street.

Parker's Yard. See Bartholomew-Pl.

Parliament - Court, Artillery -
Lane,—2d on the R. from 55,
Bishopsgate.

Parliament-Court (Little),—on
the E. side the last.

Parliament-Pl. Old Palace-Yard, Westr.—from the corner of Abingdon-st. to the Thames.

Parliament - Pl. Parliament-St. Bethnal-Green,—1st on the R. from op. Duthie's nursery.

Parliament - St. Westr.—from Bridge-st. to Whitehall..

Parliament-St. Bethnal-Green, —op. Duthie's nursery, 2d on the R. from the Salmon and Ball towards Dog-row.

Parliament-Street, St. George's Fields,—E. side St. George's Market.

Parrot-Alley, Playhouse-Yard, St. Luke's,—the 1st on the R. from 188, Whitecross-st.

Parr's Builds. North-Row, Grosvenor-Sq.—at 20, 6 doors E. of Park-st.

Parr's Head-Yard, Leicester-St. —3 doors from 31, Swallow-street.

Parsey's-Gardens, North-St.—6 doors from 152, Whitechapel-road.

Parson's Court, Bride-Lane,—a few yards on the L. from 10, New Bridge-st. Blackfriars.

Parson's-Stairs, Lower E. Smithfield,—by 82, ¼ of a mile below the Tower.

Parson's-St. Upper E.Smithfield, —the continuation of it to Ratcliffe-highway.

Parson's and Syme's Waggon-Office,—at 69, Old-Bailey, 3 doors on the L. from Ludgate-hill.

Parsonage-Row, Newington,— from the church towards the Elephant and Castle.

Parsonage - Walk, Newington,

—from the last to the Churchyard.

Parsonage-Yard, Shoreditch,— 3 doors from the church.

Partridge - Court, Houndsditch, —at 130, middle of the N. side.

Partridge-Court, Gravel-Lane, —2d on the L. from 148, Houndsditch.

Pasfield's Rents, Paradise - St. Rotherhithe,—2d and 3d on the L. from Mill - pond - bridge.

Passing - Alley, Saint John-St. Clerkenwell,—at 66, the 4th on the L. from Smithfield.

Patent-Office,—at 4, Lincoln's-Inn Old - Square, entrance op. 40, Chancery-lane.

Paternoster - Row, St. Paul's Church-Yard,—1st on the R. in Ave-maria-lane from 29, Ludgate - st. extending to Cheapside.

Paternoster-Row, Spitalfields,— continuation of Union-st. from 69, Bishopsgate-without.

Paternoster - Row (Little),—4 doors on the R. in the last, from Union-st.

Patience - Street, Wheeler - St. Spitalfields,—at the N. end, near Webb-sq. entering by 47, Shoreditch.

Patriot-Row, Bethnal-Green,— adjoining Patriot-sq. and extending towards the Green.

Patriot-Sq. Bethnal-Green,—1st on the R. a few doors from the Green towards Hackney-road.

Patriot-St. Commercial - Road, —the continuation of Morgan-st. by Cannon - st.-road.

Patton's Pl. Lock's Fields, Walworth,—op. Paragon-row.

Paty's Court, Holywell-Lane,—
2d on the L. 15 doors from
194, Shoreditch.

Paul's Alley, Redcross-St. Cripplegate,—at 13, 10 doors S.
of Barbican.

St. Paul's Alley, St. Paul's
Church - Yard,—at 69, middle of the N. side.

Paul's Bakehouse-Court, God-
liman - St.—6 doors on the
R. from 15, St. Paul's church-
yard.

St. Paul's Chain, St. Paul's
Church-Yard,—15 doors on
the L. from Ludgate-st.

St. Paul's Church - Yard,—the
houses which surround and
front St. Paul's Cathedral: the
numbers begin and end at
Ludgate-st.

St. Paul's Church, Covent-Garden,—on the W. side of
Covent-garden-market.

St. Paul's Church, Shadwell,—
on the S. side Shadwell High-
street.

St. Paul's College, St. Paul's
Church - Yard,—3 doors on
the R. from Ludgate-st.

Paul's Court, Huggin-Lane,—3
doors on the L. from 115,
Wood-st. Cheapside.

St. Paul's Pl. Walworth-Common,—by the Paul's head.

St. Paul's School, St. Paul's
Church - Yard,—6 doors on
the L. from Cheapside.

Paul-Sq. Paul-St. Finsbury,—at
44, 1st on the R. from Worship-st.

Paul-St. Finsbury-Sq.—the continuation of Wilson-st. com-

mencing at Worship-st. and
leading to Old-st.-road.

Paul's Wharf, Up. Thames-St.—
at 22, op. Bennet's hill.

Paul's Head-Court, Cateaton-St.
—5 doors from Milk-street,
Cheapside.

Paul's Head-Court, Fenchurch-
St.—at 154, nearly op. Rood-
lane.

Paved-Alley, Pall-Mall,—at 66,
6 doors on the L. from St.
James's-st.

Paved-Alley, Paternoster-Row,
—at 30, leading to Newgate-
market.

Paved-Alley, Leadenhall-Market,—N. side, by the Red-
lion.

Pavement, Moorfields,—the W.
side, from Moorgate to Finsbury-pl.

Paviours-Arms-Court, Wardour-
St.—at 50, 14 doors N. of
Compton-st.

Payn's-Place, Aldersgate-St.—at
142, op. Jewin-st.

Peacock-Alley, Morgan's Lane,
—2d on the L. from 80,
Tooley-st.

Peacock -Brewery, Whitecross-
St. Cripplegate,—a few doors
on the L. from 116, Fore-
street.

Peacock-Court, Bethnal-Green,
—N. W. corner of the Green.

Peacock-Place, Minories,—at 12,
middle of the E. side.

Peacock-St. Newington,—3d on
the L. south from the church.

Peacock-Sq.—1st on the L. in
the last from the road.

Peal-Alley, Shadwell High-St.—
at 61, 6 doors below the
church.

T 3

Pea-Hen-Court, Bishopsgate-St.
—at 75, 12 doors S. of the
church.

Pearl-Pl. Stepney,—1st on the
R. from Redman's row, Mile-
end.

Pearl-Row, City-Gardens,—behind Anderson's-builds. City-
road..

Pearl-Row, Blackfriars - Road,
—last on the L. from the
bridge.

Pearl-St. (Gt.) Spitalfields,—the
continuation of Flower - de -
Lis-st. entering by 10, Shoreditch.

Pearl-St. (Little),—continuation
of Vine-court, from 24, Lamb-
st. leading into the last.

Pearl-Street, St. George's East,
—entrance the 1st on the R.
in King-st. from 30, New
Gravel-lane.

Pearson's Alley, High-St. Lambeth,—1st on the L. from the
church.

Pearson's Wharf, Up. Thames-
St.—E. side of Puddle-dock, ⅛
of a mile below Blackfriars-
bridge.

Pearson's Wharf, Shad-Thames,
—op. King-st. Horselydown.

Pear-St. Strutton-Ground, Westminster,—middle of the E.
side.

Peartree-Alley, Shadwell High-
St.—at 46, 10 doors W. of
the church.

Peartree - Alley, — nearly op.
King Edward-st. from 272,
Wapping.

Peartree - Court, Clerkenwell -
Close,—at 20, a few doors on
the L. north from the church.

Peartree-Court, Coppice-Row,

Clerkenwell,—at 51, 1st on
the R. from the Green.

Peartree-Court, Aldersgate-St.
—at 42, E. end of Angel-
alley.

Peartree-Court, Shoreditch High-
St.—at 132, nearly op. the
church.

Peartree-Court, Lambeth-Marsh,
—behind the Peartree public-
house.

Peartree-Pl. Peartree - St.—behind the last.

Peartree-Row, Lambeth-Marsh,
—middle of the N. side the
road.

Peartree-St. Lambeth-Marsh,—
behind the last.

Peartree-Street, Goswell-St.—at
72, 3d N. of Old-st.

Peck's Builds. King's Bench-
Walk, Temple,—on the W.
side, a few yards on the R.
from the S. end of Mitre-
court, entering by 44, Fleet-
street.

Peck's Rents, Cherrytree-Court,
—1st on the L. from Golden-
lane.

Pedlars - Acre, Lambeth,—1st
on the L. from Westminster-
bridge.

Peerless-Place, City-Road,—W.
side, between the turnpike
and Peerless-row.

Peerless-Pool, City-Road,—W.
side of Peerless-pl.

Peerless-Row, City-Road,—1st
on the L. north of Old-st.

Pekin-Pl. East - India Dock -
Road, Poplar,—S. side, from
Bow-lane to Cotton-st.

Pelham-Pl. Grange-Road,—W.
end of Fort-pl.

Pelham-St. Brick-Lane, Spitalfields,—at 63, middle of the E. side, opposite Hanbury's brewery.

Pelican-Court, Little-Britain,— at 59, two doors from Bluecoat-buildings.

Pelican Life-Insurance-Office,— at 70, Lombard-st. and at Spring - gardens, Charing - cross.

Pelican-Stairs, Wapping - Wall, —at 57, near Foxes - lane, Shadwell-church.

Pell-Pl. Pell-St.—1st on the R. from 6, New-road.

Pell-St. Ratcliffe-Highway,—at 194, five doors from Wellclose-sq.

Pellet's Row, Garden-Walk,— 1st on the R. from Willowwalk, Tabernacle-sq.

Pemberton - Row, Fetter-Lane, —the continuation of Featherbed-court, from 18, in the said lane.

Pendrey's Yard, Marybone - Lane,—at 23, 5th on the R. from Oxford-st.

Pennington - St. Ratcliffe-Highway,—between it and the London-docks-wall, extending to Old Gravel-lane.

Penny - Court, Hatton-Wall,— behind 59, Hatton-garden.

Penny-Fields, Poplar,—1st N. of the High-st. from the Commercial-road.

Penson-Pl. Commercial - Road, Limehouse,—part of the R. side, ¼ of a mile below the church.

Penton-Grove, White - Lion-St. Pentonville,—at 44, ⅙ of a

mile on the L. from Islington.

Penton-Pl. Pentonville,—nearly op. the chapel, towards Clerkenwell.

Penton-Pl. Walworth,—at the W. end of Manor-pl.

Penton-Row, Walworth High-St. —part of the W. side, from Manor-row to Westlane.

Penton-St. Walworth,—the W. continuation of Amelia-st.

Penton-St. Pentonville,—2d on the R. from the Angel-inn, Islington.

Pentonville, — between Islington and Battle-bridge.

Pepper-Alley, Boro.—4 doors on the R. from London-bridge.

Pepper - Alley - Stairs,—by the last.

Pepper-Street, Duke-St. Boro. —1st on the L. from Queenstreet.

Perceval-St. Clerkenwell,—N. end of St. John-st. the last on the R. from Smithfield.

Percy-Chapel,—W. end of Windmill-st. Tottenham-court-road.

Percy-Mews, Rathbone-Pl.—at 26, 3 doors S. of Percy-st.

Percy - St. Tottenham - Court-Road,—op. Bedford - st. 40 doors on the L. from Oxfordstreet.

Periwinkle-Court, Turk's Row, Chelsea,—nearly op. Lower Sloane-st.

Periwinkle - Court, Periwinkle-St. Ratcliffe,—1st on the R. from Brook-st.

Periwinkle-Street, Brook-St.

Ratcliffe,—nearly op. But-cher-row, Ratcliffe-cross.

Perkins's Rents, Gt. Peter-St. Westr.—middle of the N. side, to 48, Old Pye-st.

Perry's Court, Hackney-Road, —at N. end of Union-builds. Union-st.

Perry's Dock,—from the E. side of Blackwall-causeway to the East-India-dock.

Perry's Place, Oxford-St.—30 doors on the R. from St. Giles's.

Perry's Rents, Providence-Row, Palmers-Village,—1st on the L. from Paradise-row.

Perry's Rents, Hackney-Road, —$\frac{4}{5}$ of a mile on the L. from Shoreditch-church.

Perry's Rents, New Gravel-Lane, St. George's East,— entrance by 40, middle of the W. side.

Pesthouse-Row, Old-St.—at the W. end of St. Luke's Hos-pital.

St. Peter's Alley, Cornhill,— from 55, to 2, Gracechurch-street.

St. Peter's Church. See the last.

St. Peter-Cheap-Church, Wood-St.—20 doors on the L. from 123, Cheapside.

St. Peter-le-Poor's Church, Old Broad-St.—at 63, nearly op. the Excise-office.

Peter's-Court, Saint Martin's-Lane,—at 111, 3d on the L. from Charing-cross.

Peter's Court, Rosemary-Lane, —at 28, 4th on the R. from Tower-hill.

St. Peter's Hill, Up. Thames-St.—at 216, $\frac{1}{4}$ of a mile on the L. from Blackfriars-bridge.

Peter and Key-Court, St. Peter's Lane,—1st on the L. from Cow-cross.

St. Peter's Lane, Saint John-St. —3d on the L. from 75, Smithfield, or 1st on the R. in Cow-cross.

St. Peter's Place, Walworth-Common,—op. the Paul's-head.

St. Peter-Street,—by the last.

Peter-Street, Redcross-St. Bo-ro.—at 45, 1st S. of Queen-st.

Peter-St. (Little), Westr.—the continuation of Wood-street, from 63, Millbank-st.

Peter-St. (Gt.)—continuation of the last to the Grey-coat-school.

Peter-Street, (New), Gt. Peter-St. Westr.—1st on the R. from Strutton-ground.

Peter-Street, Wardour-St.—4th on the R. from 381, Oxford-street.

Peter-St. Bloomsbury,—the continuation of Bow-st. from op. Drury-lane.

Peter-St. Gt. Saffron-Hill,—at 29, $\frac{4}{5}$ of a mile on the R. from Holborn-bridge along Field-lane.

Peter-Street, Sun-St.—at 25, 1st on the L. from 149, Bish-opsgate.

Peter-Street, Mount-St. Beth-nal-Green,—1st on the R. from 45, Church-st. along Rose-st.

Peterborough-Court, Fleet-St. —at 135, 5th on the R. from Fleet-market.

Petersburg - Wharf, Narrow - Wall, Lambeth, — by the Lambeth-water-works, $\frac{1}{3}$ of a mile below Westminster-bridge.

Petticoat - Lane,—at 41, Aldgate High-st. $\frac{1}{4}$ of a mile below the church.

Petticoat-Sq. Petticoat-Lane,— nearly op. Wentworth-st.

Petty's Court, Hanway-St.—6 doors on the L. from 22, Oxford-st.

Petty-Bag-Office,—behind 14, Chancery-lane, 2d gateway on the R. from 192, Fleet-street.

Petty's Walk, Lock's Fields, Walworth,—1st on the R. in York-st. from Pitt-st.

Pettyfield-Court, Drury-Lane, —4 doors on the R. from the Strand.

Pewter-Platter Coach-Office,— at 86, Gracechurch-st. by the Spread-eagle.

Pewter-Platter-Yard, St. John-St.—at 79, $\frac{1}{4}$ of a mile on the L. from Smithfield.

Pewterers - Hall,—behind 15, Lime-st. on the E. side of Leadenhall-market.

Pewtner's Court, Charterhouse-Lane,—at 20, 1st on the R. from the square.

Pheasant and Cock-Court, Angel-Sq.—4th on the L. from 137, Bishopsgate-without.

Phil's Builds. Houndsditch,—at 106, nearly op. St. Mary-Axe.

Philadelphian - Church, Windmill-St. Finsbury,—entrance by the 1st on the R. from Providence-row.

Philanthropic-Annuity - Office, —at 89, Pall-mall, 16 doors on the R. from the Palace.

Philanthropic-Charity, Grange-Road,—the W. end of Fort-place.

Philanthropic-Reform, London-Road,—entrance by the 1st on the R. from the Obelisk.

Phillips's Builds. Willsted-St. Sommers - Town,—20 doors on the R. from Judd's pl. New-road.

Phillips's Builds. Walworth,— continuation of Thurlow-pl. from 20, Apollo-builds. East-lane.

Phillip's Court, Brackley - St. Golden-Lane, Cripplegate,— 3 doors on the R. from Golden-lane, near Barbican.

Phillip's Court, Grub-St. Cripplegate,—4th on the R. from 96, Fore-st.

Phillips's Gardens, Tottenham-Pl.—2d on the L. from Tottenham-court-road.

Philip-Lane, London - Wall,— between Wood-st. and Aldermanbury.

Phillips's Row, Tottenham - Court,—E. end, by Phillips's gardens.

Philips-Street, Charles-St. Saint George's East,—1st on the R. from Lower Cornwell-st.

Philological-Society, King - St. Edgware-Road,—1st door E. of Brown-st.

Philpot's-Gardens, Up. Ground, —the corner of Broad-wall.

Philpot-Lane, Fenchurch-St.— 12 doors on the R. from Gracechurch-st.

Philpot's-Row, Broad-Wall,—

E. side, from Stamford-st. to Up. Ground.

Philpot-Terrace, Edgware-Rd. —¾ of a mile on the L. from Tyburn-turnpike.

Phipps-Court, Phipps-St.—1st on the L. from Chapel-st.

Phipps-Street, Chapel-St. Holywell-Mount,—1st on the R. from the Curtain-road.

Phœnix-Alley, Long-Acre,—at 56, op. Hanover-st.

Phœnix - Court, West-St.—1st on the L. from 86, Smithfield.

Phœnix-Court, Newgate-St.—3 doors on the R. from the Old-Bailey.

Phœnix-Court, Old-Change,— at 27, op. Little Carter-lane.

Phœnix-Court, Butcher - Row, —at 38, the 2d on the R. from Up. East-Smithfield.

Phœnix Fire-Office, Lombard-St.—op. Change-alley. Also, at Charing - cross, op. the King's Mews.

Phœnix Newspaper - Office, Strand,—at 163, S. W. corner of Exeter-change.

Phœnix - Place, Ratcliffe,—by the Phœnix-Tavern, Ratcliffe-cross.

Phœnix-Pl. Phœnix - St. Sommers-Town,—between Ossulston-st and Middlesex-st.

Phœnix-Row, Blackfriars-Road, —by Webber-st. near ½ a mile on the R. from the bridge.

Phœnix-Street, Crown-St. Saint Giles's,—5 doors N. of Compton-st.

Phœnix - St. Bloomsbury,—1st on the L. in Plumbtree-st. from 19, Broad-st.

Phœnix-St. Sommers-Town,—

from the S. E. corner of Clarendon-sq. to the Crescent.

Phœnix - Street, Wheeler - St. Spitalfields,—at 40, 3d on the R. from Lamb-st. extending to 159, Brick-lane.

Phœnix-Street, South-St. East-Lane, Walworth,—2d on the R. from Apollo-builds.

Phœnix-Coal-Wharf, Clink-St. Boro.—on the W. side St. Mary-Overy's-Dock, ⅛ of a mile above London-bridge.

Phœnix-Wharf, Wapping,—by 248, on the W. side of Execution-dock.

Phœnix Stone-Wharf, Fore-St. Lambeth,—a few doors from Broad-st. towards Vauxhall.

Phœnix-Yard, Oxford -St.—at 126, ¼ a mile on the R. from St. Giles's.

Physic-Gardens, Chelsea,—entrance opposite 30, Paradise-row.

Piccadilly, — N. end of the Haymarket, where the numbers begin and end, viz. 1 and 142, extending to Hyde-park-corner.

Pichegrue-Pl. London-Road,— middle of the R. side, from the Obelisk.

Pike's Gardens, Maid - Lane, Boro.—1st W. of Thames-street.

Pike's Pl. Union-St.—4th on the R. from the London-road.

Pickering's Pl. Saint James's St. —4 doors on the R. from the Palace.

Pickering's Pl. or Court, Union-Street, St. George's Fields,

—3d on the L. from op. West-sq.

Pickering-Pl. East India-Dock-Road, Poplar, — 2d on the L. west of the Dock-gate.

Pickett - St. Strand,—part of the R. side, commencing near Temple-bar.

Pickett-Pl. Strand,—at 243, six doors W. of Temple-bar.

Pickle-Herring-Stairs,—the end of Vine - yard, from 110, Tooley-st.

Pickle-Herring-Wharf,—the E. side of the Stairs.

Pidcock's Builds. Boro.-Road, —op. the King's Bench.

Pig-Alley, Wheeler-St. Spital-fields,—1st on the R. 15 doors from 32, Lamb-st.

Pig's Head-Court, Shoreditch, —at 140, 3 doors S. of William-st.

Pig's Quay, W. side of Black-friars-Bridge,—last on the L. in William-st. from 20, New Bridge-st.

Pigeon-Court. See Three.

Pilgrim - Street, Ludgate-St.— at 3, 2d on the L. from St. Paul's Church-yard.

Pilgrim - St. Up. Kennington-Lane,—1st on the L. from Kennington-cross.

Pillory-Lane, Lower East-Smith-field,—2d on the L. in St. Catherine's st. from Tower-hill.

Pilot Newspaper - Office, 104, Strand.

Pimlico, — from Buckingham-gate to Chelsea, ¾ of a mile.

Pimlico, Hoxton,—¼ of a mile on the L. from Old-st.-road,

and nearly op. the White-hart.

Pimlico-Alley, Gravel-Lane,—1st on the R. from 148, Houndsditch.

Pimlico-Wharf, Pimlico,—⅓ of a mile on the L. from Buckingham-gate.

Pin-Court, Blue-Anchor-Yard, —1st on the R. from 48, Rosemary-lane.

Pindar - Passage, Gray's - Inn-Lane,—8 doors S. of Britannia-st.

Pine-Apple-Court, Castle-Lane, Westminster,—middle of the N. side.

Pink's Row, Ratcliffe - Row, City-Road,—1st on the right W. from Bath-st.

Pinner's Court, Gray's Inn-Lane, —at 35, that number on the R. from Holborn.

Pinner-Court, Old Broad-St.—at 55, op. the Excise - office.

Pipemakers-Alley, Cow-Cross, —at 75, 1st on the L. from St. John-st.

Pipemakers-Alley, Bedfordbury —at 35, middle of the E. side.

Pipemakers-Alley, Old Montague-St.— 1st on the L. from Osborn-st.

Pipemakers-Alley, White-Horse-St. Ratcliffe,—at 35, 1st on the L. north of the Commercial-road.

Pipemakers-Alley, Narrow-St. Limehouse,—at 32, 3d on the L. below Mr. Turner's wharf.

Pipemakers-Alley, Maze, Boro.

—2d on the R. from 195, Tooley-st.

Pitchers-Court, White's Alley, —the continuation of it, from 60, Coleman-st.

Pitfield-St. Hoxton,—1st on the L. in Old-st. road, from the City-road.

Pitt's Court, Crispin-St. Spitalfields,—3 doors S. from 25, Union-st. Bishopsgate.

Pitt's Pl. Bankside, Southwark, —N. end of Williams's court, Maid-lane.

Pitt's Place, Kent-Road,—nearly op. the Bricklayers-arms.

Pitt-St. Bethnal-Green,—2d on the L. from the Green towards Globe-st.

Pitt-St. Kent-Road,—1st on the R. below the Bricklayers-arms.

Pitt-Street, St. George's Fields, —2d on the L. from the Elephant and Castle, towards West-sq.

Pitt-St. Blackfriars-Road,—6 doors N. of Surrey-chapel.

Pitt-Street, Charlotte-St. Rathbone-Pl.—at 25, 5 doors N. of Goodge-st.

Pitt's Head-Mews, Park-Lane, —7th on the R. from Piccadilly.

Pitt's Yard, Downing-St.—1st on the R. from Whitehall.

Pitt's Head-Grove, Grange-Road,—1st on the R. from Star-corner.

Pittman's Builds. Ratcliffe-Row, St. Luke's,—op. the N. end of Ironmonger-row.

Pittman's Builds. Spa-Road-Passage, Bermondsey,—1st

on the R. from 13, Printers-place.

Pittman's Pl. Bermondsey,—at the back of Printers-pl. near the W. end of Jamaica-row.

Pittman's Yard, Dean-St.—2d on the L. from 400, Oxford-street.

Plantation-Place, Commercial-Road,—W. side White-horse-st. Ratcliffe.

Plasterers-Hall, Addle-St.—6 doors on the L. from Wood-st. Cheapside.

Platform, Rotherhithe-St.—W. side of Rotherhithe-stairs, $\frac{1}{4}$ of a mile W. from the church.

Platina-St. Tabernacle-Walk, Finsbury-Sq.—at 30, between Castle-st. and Paradise-st.

Playhouse-Yard, Whitecross-Street, St. Luke's,—at 189, middle of the W. side.

Playhouse-Yard, Water-Lane, Blackfriars,—3d on the R. from Earl-st.

Pleasant-Court, Broadwall,—middle of the W. side.

Pleasant-Passage, Mile-End-Road,—1st on the left E. of the Old Globe, $1\frac{1}{2}$ mile on the L. from Aldgate.

Pleasant-Pl. Pentonville,—N. side the High-road, op. the Bell, Battle-bridge.

Pleasant-Pl. Stepney-Green,—at the E. end of Redman's-row, Mile-end.

Pleasant-Pl. Kingsland-Road,—part of the R. side, adjoining the Alms-houses, $\frac{1}{2}$ a mile from Shoreditch-church.

Pleasant-Pl. Bonner-St. Bethual-Green,—1st on the R. from Green-st.

Pleasant-Pl. William-St. Shoreditch,—at the N. end of Pleasant-row.

Pleasant-Pl. Pleasant-Retreat, —the corner of George's row from Blackfriars-road.

Pleasant - Pl. Lambeth, or St. George's Fields,—at the S. end of Gibraltar-row, West-square.

Pleasant-Pl. Pleasant-Row,— 1st on the L. from Kennington-lane.

Pleasant-Pl. Walworth - Common,—E. end of Portland-pl. near the Paul's head.

Pleasant-Retreat, Palmers-Village, Westr.—the end of Paradise-row.

Pleasant-Retreat,—continuation of George's row from Blackfriars-road.

Pleasant - Row, New - Road, Marybone,—1st E. of Baker-st. North.

Pleasant-Row, Latham's Place, Sommers-Town,—2d from 1, Sommers-pl. West.

Pleasant-Row, Pentonville,—N. side the High-road, from the turnpike to Southampton-street.

Pleasant-Row, Britannia-Gardens, Hoxton,—a few houses on the L. entering by Haberdashers-walk.

Pleasant-Row, Kingsland-Road, —part of the L. side, about ½ a mile from Shoreditch-church, op. Pleasant-pl.

Pleasant-Row, William - St.— 1st on the R. from 137, Shoreditch.

Pleasant-Row, Bethnal-Green-Road,—part of the N. side, adjoining Wilmot-sq.

Pleasant-Row, North-St. Whitechapel,—3d on the R. north of Ducking Pond-lane.

Pleasant-Row, Mile-End New-Town,—the continuation of Pelham-st. from 63, Brick-lane.

Pleasant-Row, Church - Lane, Whitechapel,—on the E. side of John's sq.

Pleasant - Row, Globe - Alley, Limehouse,—2d on the R. from 54, Fore-st.

Pleasant-Row, Stepney-Green, —W. end of Prospect-pl.

Pleasant-Row, Mile-End-Road, —the N. end of Pleasant-passage, on the E. side the Old Globe.

Pleasant-Row, Stepney-Causeway,—at 5, middle of the E. side.

Pleasant - Row, Kennington - Lane,—1st on the L. from the Plough and Harrow.

Pleasant-Row, Wagstaff's Builds. Boro.—3 doors on the R. from Maid-lane.

Pleasant-Row, East - St. Walworth,—W. side of Camden-st. by the chapel.

Pleasant-Row, South-St. East-Lane, Walworth,—1st on the R. from Apollo-builds.

Pleasant-Row, Deptford Lower-Road. See Black Horse-Sq.

Plough-Alley, Barbican,—at 51, near the middle of the N. side.

Plough - Alley, Wapping,—43 doors on the L. below Hermitage-bridge.

U

Plough-Court, Carey-St. Lincoln's-Inn-Fields,—at 21, that number on the L. from 99, Chancery-lane.

Plough-Court, Gray's-Inn-Lane, —24 doors on the R. from Middle-row, Holborn.

Plough-Court, Fetter - Lane,— at 48, the 4th on the L. from Holborn.

Plough-Court, Holborn-Hill,— at 86, 2d on the R. 10 doors from Fleet-market.

Plough-Court, Lombard - St.— 6 doors on the L. from 24, Gracechurch-st.

Plough-Court, Seething - Lane, —2d on the L. from 56, Tower-st.

Plough-Pl. Plough-Court,—1st on the L. from 48, Fetter-lane.

Plough-Street, Whitechapel,— at 44, 14 doors E. of Red-lion-st.

Plough-Yard, Crown-St. Soho, —middle of the W. side.

Plough-Yard, Shoreditch,—entrance by Rose-court, 223, Shoreditch.

Plough-Yard, Bermondsey - St. —at 79, 12 doors N. of Russell-st.

Plough and Harrow-Yard, Tooley-St—at 99, E. s.de of Stoney-lane.

Plough and Harrow - Yard, Kent-St. Boro.—at 84, ⅓ of a mile on the L. from Saint George's church.

Plumber's Builds. Wilmot-St. Bethnal-Green-Road,—at the S. end, behind the Lamb public-house.

Plumber's Court, High - Hol-

born,—at 111, 5 doors E. of Kingsgate-st.

Plumbers - Row, — from 266, Whitechapel - road, to the Commercial-road.

Plumbers-Row, City-Road,—E. side, by the turnpike, op. Peerless-place.

Plumbers-St. City-Road,—op. Fountain-pl. the 3d on the right N. from Old-st.

Plumb-Tree - Court, Holborn-Hill,—3 doors on the L. from Fleet-market.

Plumb-Tree-Street, Broad-St. Bloomsbury,—20 doors on the R. from Holborn.

Poets-Corner, Westminster,— adjoining the S. side of the Abbey.

Pointers-Pl. Old-St.-Road,—1st on the L. 6 doors from Shoreditch-church.

Pointers-Builds.—the continuation of French-alley, on the L. entering by 150, Shoreditch.

Poland-Street, Oxford - St.—at 365, 6th on the L. ⅓ of a mile from St. Giles's.

Polen-Street, Hanover-St. Hanover-Sq.—at 13, middle of the S. side.

Police-Office, Queen-Sq. Westminster,—3 doors on the L. from the Broad-way.

Police-Office, Gt. Marlborough-St.—at 20, W. end.

Police-Office, Bow-St. Covent-Garden,—4 doors on the L. from Gt. Russell-st.

Police-Office, 54, Hatton-garden.

Police-Office, Worship-St.—at 23, near the Curtain-road.

Police-Office, Lambeth-Street, Goodman's Fields,—1st door on the R. from Little Ayliffe-street.

Police - Office, High-St. Shad-well,—at 157, 20 doors on the L. below the church.

Police - Office for the River Thames,—by 260, Wapping, op. King's. stairs, Rother-hithe.

Police-Office, Union-Hall, Bo-ro.—a few doors on the L. in Union-st. from 218, High-street.

Pollard's Row, Bethnal-Green-Road,—a few doors W. of Wilmot-sq. ¾ of a mile from 65, Shoreditch.

Pollard-St. Bethnal-Green-Rd. —1st E. parallel to Pollard-row, from 1 to 16.

Polygon, Sommers-Town. See Clarendon-Sq.

Pomona-Pl. Little James - St. Lisson-Green,—1st N. of Bell-street.

Pond-Yard, Mosses-Alley, Bank-side,—2d on the R. from Maid-lane.

Ponder's-Court, Butler's Alley, Grub - St. Cripplegate,—2d on the R. from Grub-st.

Ponder's-Pl. Ropemaker-St.— 5th on the L. from Moor-fields.

Pontipool-Pl. Webber-St —2d on the R. from Blackfriars-road.

Pool's Builds. Mount-Pleasant, —3d on the R. from 72, Gray's-inn-lane.

Pool's Pl.—1st on the L. in the last.

Pope's Head-Alley, Cornhill,—at 19, op. the Royal - Ex-change.

Pope's Head-Court, Bell-Yard, Temple-Bar,—at 20, 2d on the R. from 204, Fleet-st.

Pope's Head-Court, Quaker-St. Spitalfields,—4 doors on the R. from 29, Wheeler-st.

Pope's Hill, Shadwell High-St. —at 75, 4th E. of the church.

Popham-Pl. City-Gardens,—be-hind Anderson's builds. City-road.

Poplar High-St.—from the Com-mercial-road, by the W. India-docks, to Blackwall.

Poplar-Grove, Oval, Kenning-ton,—W. side of Clayton-street.

Poplar - Marsh. See Marsh-Wall.

Poplar-Pl. Compton-St. Bruns-wick-Sq.—N. side of Comp-ton-pl.

Poplar-Row, Kent-Road,—1st on the L. from the Elephant and Castle.

Poplar - Row, Lock's Fields, Walworth,—3d on the L. in Pitt-st. from the Kent-road.

Poppin's-Court, Fleet-St.—at 111, 7 doors on the R. from Fleet-market.

Porridge - Pot - Alley, Old-St. See Dog's Head-Court.

Portobello - Passage, Lisle-St. Leicester-Sq.—3 doors on the L. from Little Newport-st.

Porter's Court, Old Montague-St. Whitechapel,—2d on the L. a few doors from Osborn-street.

Porter-St. Leicester-Sq.—from

14, Gt. Newport-st. to Litch-field-st.

Porter's Quay, Lower Thames-St.— at 32, W. side the Custom-house.

Portland-Chapel, Gt. Portland-St.— at 95, by Foley-pl.

Portland-Mews, Portland-St.— at 20, 8 doors W. of 72, Berwick-st.

Portland-Pl. Marybone,—parallel to and between Charlotte-st. and Harley-st.

Portland-Pl. Walworth - Common,—near Queen's row.

Portland-Road, Marybone,— the continuation of Gt. Portland-st. to the New-road.

Portland - Row, New-Road,— N. side, op. the last.

Portland-Row, Walworth-Common,—W. end of Portland-pl. near Queen's row.

Portland-St. (Gt.) Marybone,— the continuation of John-st. entering by 102, Oxford-st.

Portland-St. (Little), Marybone, —at 7 in the last, the 4th from Oxford-street.

Portland-Street, Wardour - St. Soho,—at 112, 2d on the R. from 382, Oxford-st.

Portland-St. Walworth - Common,—nearly op. the Paul's head.

Portland - Terrace, Walworth-Common,—op. Portland-pl. near Queen's row.

Portland - Yard, Buckingham-Pl. Fitzroy-Sq.—op. Warren-st. 5 doors from the New-rd.

Portman-Grove, Lisson-Grove, —⅓ of a mile north of the Yorkshire-stingo.

Portman-Mews (North), Port-

man-Sq.—1st parallel to the N. side, from Baker-st. to Gloucester-st.

Portman-Mews (South), Portman-Sq.—from 10, Portman-st. to 24, Orchard-st.

Portman-Pl. Edgware-Road,— E. side, ⅞ of a mile on the R. from Tyburn-turnpike.

Portman-Sq.—at the N. end of Orchard - st. from 197, Oxford-st.

Portman - Street, Oxford-St.— at 220, 3d on the L. from Tyburn-turnpike.

Portpool - Lane, Gray's - Inn-Lane,—at 52, ½ of a mile on the R. from Holborn.

Portsmouth-Place, Kennington-Lane,—a few doors from the Plough and Harrow, Newington.

Portsmouth-St. Lincoln's - Inn-Fields,—from the S.W. corner, to Clare-market.

Portugal-Pl. Dog-Row, Mile-End,—12 doors on the L. from the turnpike.

Portugal-Row, Lincoln's - Inn-Fields,—S. side the square.

Portugal-Street, Lincoln's-Inn-Fields,—8 doors from the S. E. corner.

Portugal-St. Grosvenor-Sq.— from 80, Mount - st. near Park-st. to 3, Chapel-st.

Post-Office (General), Lombard-St.—by 11, E. side the church.

Post-Office (General Two-penny Post),—38, Gerrard - st. Soho.

Postern - Row, Tower-Hill,— facing the N. side the Tower, about the middle of it.

Potier's Pl. Bermondsey New-Road,—3d on the L. from the Bricklayers-arms.

Potter's Fields, Pratt-St. Lambeth,—S. end, by Paradise-row.

Potter's Fields, Horselydown,—at the E. end of Tooley-st. ½ a mile on the L. from London-bridge.

Potter's Row, Cambridge-Heath, Hackney-Road,—1st on the L. from the turnpike, towards Bonner's-hall.

Poultry,—continuation of Cheapside, from the Old-Jewry to the Mansion-house.

Poultry - Compter,—at 30, N. side.

Powell's Alley, Kent-St. Boro.—at 296, 12 doors on the R. from St. George's church.

Powell's Pl. City-Road,—op. the Shepherd and Shepherdess-walk, ¼ a mile on the L. from Finsbury-sq.

Powis-Pl. Great Ormond-St.—at 50, 8 doors on the L. from Queen-sq.

Pownal - Terrace, Lambeth,—op. Chester - pl. near Kennington-cross.

Poynder's Wharf, Earl-Street, Blackfriars,—the 3d E. of the bridge.

Pratt's Builds. New Gravel-Lane,—at 76, 12 doors on the R. from 22, High-st. Shadwell.

Pratt's Row, Ducking Pond-Lane, Whitechapel,—6 doors W. of North-st.

Pratt-St. Lambeth,—3d on the L. from the Three Stags, towards the church.

Prerogative-Office,—at 6, Gt. Knight - Rider - st. Doctors-commons.

Prescot - St. (Gt.) Goodman's Fields,—op. Goodman's yard, from 60, Minories.

Prescot-St. (Little),—the continuation of Mansel-st. from the last.

Preston's Dock, Shad-Thames,—W. side of Horselydown New-stairs.

Price's Builds. Bowling-Green, King-St. Boro.—nearly op. Mermaid-court.

Price's Court, Old-St.—at 48, 1st W. of Bunhill-row.

Price's Court, Redcross - St. Boro.—the 1st on the R. from the Mint.

Price's Court, Queen-St. Boro.—at 90, 4th on the L. from Union-st.

Price's Court, Gravel - Lane, Boro.—2d on the R. south from Maid-lane.

Price's Pl. Gravel -Lane,—1st N. of George-st. Blackfriars-road.

Price's Row, Back-Lane, Saint George's East,—3 doors W. of King David-lane.

Price's St. Gravel-Lane,—last on the L. in Green-walk from Holland-street, Blackfriars-bridge.

Priest-Alley, Tower-St.—at 48, 4 doors on the L. from Tower-hill.

Priest-Court, Foster-Lane,—4 doors on the R. from 147, Cheapside.

Primrose - Alley, Church - St. Boro.-Market,--nearly op. the W. side St. Saviour's church.

U 3

Primrose - Court, Primrose-St. —the last on the R. from 110, Bishopsgate.

Primrose-Hill, Salisbury-Sq.— at the S. W. corner, entering by 82, Fleet-st.

Primrose-St. Bishopsgate-With-out,—at 110, op. Spital-sq.

Primrose-St. Three Colts-Lane, Bethnal-Green,—op. Dodd's pl. between Dog-row and Wilmot-st.

Princes-Alley, Princes-St. Rotherhithe,—at 15, middle of the E. side, leading into Elephant-lane.

Princes-Builds. White - Hart-Row,—1st on the R. from Kennington-lane.

Princes-Court, Princes-Street, Westminster,——corner of George-st.

Princes-Court, James-St. Westminster,—1st on the R. from Buckingham-gate.

Princes-Court, Princes-St. Pimlico,—1st on the R. from Queen's row.

Princes - Court, Whitcomb-St. Charing - Cross,—middle of the W. side.

Princes-Court, Duke-Street, St. James's,—4th on the R. entering by 182, Piccadilly.

Princes-Court, Drury-Lane,— at 144, 1st S. of Gt. Queen-street.

Princes-Court, Newport-Market,—middle of the E. side.

Princes - Court, Coleman-St.— 15 doors on the R. from London-wall.

Princes-Court, Banner - St.—5 doors on the R. from 80, Bunhill-row.

Princes - Court, Old Gravel-Lane,—at 27, 5th on the R. from 157, Wapping.

Princes-Court, Tyssen-St. Bethnal - Green,—2d on the R. from op. Brick-lane.

Princes-Court, Princes-St. London-Road,—middle of the E. side.

Princes-Court, Fore-St. Lambeth,—3d N. of New-st.

Princes-Court, Green Bank,— 1st on the R. from 81, Tooley-st.

Princes - Court, Commercial-Road, Lambeth,—the corner of Broad-wall.

Princes-Court, Surrey-Sq.—on the W. side, at the back of Monmouth-pl.

Princes-Court, Princes-Street, Lambeth,—3d on the R. from Vauxhall.

Princes Gate-Way, Hampstead-Road,—nearly op. the chapel.

Princes-Mews, Princes-Street, Westminster,—1st on the L. from George-st.

Princes-Place, Hart-St. Covent-Garden,—1st on the L. from Bow-st.

Princes-Place, Duke-Street, St. James's,—at 40, 4th on the R. from Piccadilly.

Princes-Place, New-Road, St. George's East,—1st on the L. from Cable-st.

Princes-Place, Princes-St. Mile-End New-Town,—2d on the R. from Great Garden-st.

Princes-Pl. Mile-End-Terrace, Mile-End-Road,—2d on the L. from Savile-row.

Princes-Pl. Commercial-Road, —part of the S. side, from

near Cannon-st.-road towards Whitechapel.

Princes-Pl. Pimlico,—E. end of Princes-st. or row.

Princes-Pl. Princes-St. Bethnal-Green,—1st on the R. from Virginia-st.

Princes-Place, Lambeth,—op. Chester-pl. near Kennington-cross.

Princes-Place, Great Suffolk-St. Boro.—the corner of King's court.

Princes-Place, Newington High-Road,—op. Newington-pl. near Kennington-common.

Princes-Pl. Surrey-Sq.—at the W. side, near Monmouth-place.

Princes-Road, Princes-Pl. Kennington-Cross,—at 10, op. Chester-pl.

Princes-Row, Loman's Pond, Boro.—2d in Totterbourne-alley from Duke-st.

Princes-Row, King-St. Chelsea, —at 5, 1st on the R. from Queen-st.

Princes-Row, Pimlico,—3d on the L. from Buckingham-gate.

Princes-Row, Newport-Market, —E. side of it.

Princes-Row, Walworth High-St.——the entrance to the Montpelier-gardens.

Princes-Sq. Princes-St. Lincoln's-Inn-Fields,—nearly op. New-turnstile.

Princes-Sq. St. George's East,—6 doors on the L. in Princes-st. from 173, Ratcliffe-highway.

Princes-Sq. Kennington,—the termination of Cleaver-st.

from the White-hart, Kennington-cross.

Princes-Stairs, Rotherhithe-St. —at 40, near 1½ mile below London-bridge, and op. Execution-dock.

Princes-St. Pimlico,—3d on the L. from Buckingham-gate.

Princes-St. Westr.—1st on the R. from the W. end of the Abbey.

Princes-Street, Oxford-St.—at 119, ½ a mile on the R. from St. Giles's.

Princes-Street, Drury-Lane,—at 123, op. Russell-st.

Princes-St. Little Queen-St.—8 doors on the L. from 222, High-holborn.

Princes-St. Hanover-Sq.—from the N. W. corner to Swallow-street.

Princes-St. Soho,—continuation of Wardour-st. to Whitcomb-st. Charing-cross.

Princes-St. Red-Lion-Sq.—middle of the E. side, to 31, Bedford-row.

Princes-Street, Queen-St. Clerkenwell,—the 1st on the R. from Perceval-st.

Princes-St. Barbican,—at 42, 10 doors on the R. from Redcross-st.

Princes-St. Mansion-House-St.—W. side the Bank of England.

Princes-Street, Wilson-St.—1st on the R. from the N. E. corner of Finsbury-sq.

Princes-Street, Virginia-Street, Bethnal-Green,—1st on the L. a few doors from the Birdcage.

Princes-Street, Mile-End New-

Town,—1st on the R. in Gt. Garden-st. from 50, White-chapel-road.

Princes-St. Brick-Lane, Spital-fields,—at 186, the 1st N. from the church.

Princes-St. Rosemary-Lane,—2d on the L. from the Mino-ries.

Princes-St. Ratcliffe-Highway,—at 173, 2d on the L. from Wellclose-sq.

Princes-Street, Charles-St.—1st on the R. from 46, Old Gravel-lane.

Princes-Street, Gt. Hermitage-St. Wapping,—at the E. end, by the London-docks-wall.

Princes-St. Lambeth,—2d E. parallel to the Thames, from Broad-st. to Vauxhall.

Princes-St. London-Road,—1st on the L. from the Elephant and Castle.

Princes-Street, Duke-St. Boro.—from the middle of the S. side, to Loman's pond.

Princes-St Lock's Fields, Wal-worth,—1st on the L. in Queen-st. from York-st.

Princes-Street, Rotherhithe-St.—at 350, 2d W. from the church.

Princes-Wharf, Lambeth,—S. corner of Broad-st.

Printers-Court, Bury-Street, St. James's,—5 doors on the R. from Jermyn-st.

Printers-Pl. Bermondsey,—S. side the road which leads from the Neckinger-turnpike to Jamaica-row.

Printers-Row, Printers-Pl. Ber-mondsey,—at the W. end of the last.

Printers-St. Shoe-Lane,—at the W. end of Little New-st. on the L. from 88, Shoe-lane.

Printers-Street, Earl-St. Black-friars,—at 10, 2d on the L. from Bridge-st.

Printing-House-Lane, Water-Lane, Blackfriars,—2d on the R. from Earl-st.

Printing House-Sq.—E. end of the last.

Printing-House-Yard, Gt. Swan-Alley,—1st on the R. from 66, Coleman-st.

Prior-Court, Chamber-St. Good-man's Fields,—middle of the S. side.

Prior-Pl. East-Lane, Walworth,—part of the R. side, ⅕ of a mile from the Kent-road.

Prisoners of War Office,—at the Transport-office, Dorset-sq. Cannon-row, Westminster.

Privy-Gardens, Whitehall,—nearly op. the Horse-guards.

Privy-Seal-Office, Somerset-Pl.—3d door on the L. in the sq. entering from the Strand.

Produce-Court, Lower-Turning, Shadwell,—at 11, 4 doors from Star-st.

Property-Tax-Office,—at 107, Fenchurch-st.

Prospect-Pl. Stepney-Green,—3d on the R. from Mile-end.

Prospect-Place, Church-Lane, Whitechapel,—1st on the R. from Cable-st.

Prospect-Place, New-Road, St. George's East,—1st on the R. below Cannon-st.

Prospect-Pl. Back-Lane, Pop-lar,—3d on the L. from the Commercial-road.

Prospect-Pl. St. George's Fields,

—from the Elephant and Castle to the Philanthropic-reform.

Prospect-Pl. Bermondsey,—the continuation of Parker's row, Dockhead, from the Neckinger-turnpike towards Jamaica-row.

Prospect-Pl. Paradise-St. Rotherhithe,—1st on the R. a few yards from Mill-pond-bridge.

Prospect-Row, Henry-St. Pentonville,——2 doors E. of Hermes-st.

Prospect - Row, Cambridge-Heath, Hackney-Road,—N. side the road which leads from the turnpike towards Bonner's hall.

Prospect-Row, Mile-End-Road, —part of the N. side, op. Ewing's-buildings, two miles from Aldgate.

Prospect-Row, Walworth,—2d on the L. from the Elephant and Castle.

Prospect-Row, Blue - Anchor-Road, Bermondsey,—part of the R. side, by the turnpike from Fort-pl.

Prospect-Terrace, Gray's-Inn-Lane,—1st S. of Sidney-st. towards Guildford-st.

Protestant-Dissenter's Charity-School, Ball-Court, Giltspur-St.—a few doors on the R. from Newgate-st.

ProtestantCharity-School,Moorfields. See London-Society-School.

Protestant Dissenters- School, LittleBartholomew-Close,W. Smithfield,—at 44, W. side.

Protestant -Dissenters - School, Maze-Pond,—6 doors from the Maze, Tooley-st.

Providence-Builds. Mill-Street, Dock-Head,—1st on the R. from Jacob-st. towards the Thames.

Providence-Builds. Kent-Road, —L. side, ⅜ of a mile from the Elephant and Castle.

Providence-Chapel,Gray's-Inn-Lane,-nearly op.Guildford-st.

Providence-Chapel, Holborn,—at 143, 4 doors E. of Gray's-inn-lane.

Providence-Court, Gt.Peter-St. Westr.—op. Gt. St. Ann's st.

Providence-Court, North Audley-St.—12 doors on the L. from 263, Oxford-st.

Providence - Court, White's Ground, Bermondsey,—1st on the R. from Crucifix-lane.

Providence-Court,White'sYard, Rosemary-Lane,—middle of the E. side.

Providence-Gardens, Hackney-Road,—3d on the L. from Shoreditch-church.

Providence-Pl. Baker's Row, Clerkenwell,—4th on the L. from the Workhouse, Coppice-row.

Prov dence-Pl.Ball-Court,—the 2d on the R. from 136, Golden-lane.

Providence-Pl. Petticoat-Lane, —on the L. 28 doors from Aldgate.

Providence-Place, Commercial-Road, Limehouse,—part of the R. side, 5 doors E. of the church.

Providence-Pl. Up. Kenning-ton-Lane, — part of the N. side, near Vauxhall-gardens.

Providence-Pl.Lambeth-Marsh, —¼ of a mile on the R. from the Marsh - gate towards Blackfriars-road.

Providence - Pl. Webber-Row, St. George's Fields,—op. 10, middle of the S. side.

Providence-Place, St. George's Fields,—S. end of Bond-st. Borough-road.

Providence-Pl. Crosby-Row,— the last on the R. from Snow's fields.

Providence-Pl. Kent-St. Boro. —the E. side of Fox's buildings.

Providence-Pl. Walworth-Common,—op. Portland-pl. near Queen's row.

Providence-Pl. Providence-St. Walworth-Common,—1st on the R. from Westmoreland-academy.

Providence - Row, Walworth-Common,—6 doors W. of Westmoreland-academy.

Providence-Row, Palmer's Village, Westminster,—1st on the L. from the N. side of Bridewell.

Providence-Row,Battle-Bridge, —op. the Bell, by the turn-pike.

Providence-Row, Finsbury-Sq. —1st N. from it, extending from the City-road to Paul-street.

Providence-Row, Duke-Street, Bethnal-Green,—2d on the R. from the middle of Gibral-tar-row.

Providence-Row, Mile - End-Road,—S. end of Mile-end-terrace, Maidman's row.

Providence - Row, York-St.— 1st on the L. from the Lon-don-road.

Providence - Row, Lambeth-Marsh, — adjoining Green's-row, ⅛ of a mile on the R. from the Marsh-gate towards Blackfriars-road.

Providence-St.City-Road,—5th on the R. north from Old-st.

Providence-St. Walworth-Common,—W. side of Westmore-land-academy.

Providence-St. Walworth-Common,—op. Portland-pl. near Queen's row.

Provident - Institution for Insurance on Lives. See County-Fire-Office.

Prujean-Sq. Old-Bailey,—at 61, 7 doors on the L. from Lud-gate-hill.

Prussian-Island, Wapping,—at 188, 5 doors W. of New Gravel-lane.

Prussian-Court,—2d on the R. in the last from Wapping.

Public - Dispensary, Bishop's Court, Chancery - Lane,—4 doors on the R. from 78, Chancery-lane.

Public-Ledger Newspaper-Office,—at 12, S. W. corner of Warwick-sq.

Pudding-Lane, Lower-Thames-St.—at 120, 6 doors from Fish-st.-hill.

Puddle-Dock, Earl-St. Black-friars,—op. Saint Andrew's hill, at the W. end of Up. Thames-st.

Pugh's Court, Rotherhithe. See Cow-Court.

Pulteney - Court, Little Wind-mill-St. Haymarket,—at 20, op. Silver-st.

Pulteney-Street, (Gt.) Brewer-St. Golden-Sq.—5 doors on the R. from Windmill-st.

Pulteney-St. (Little), Gt. Wind-mill-St.—2d on the R. from Coventry-st.

Pump - Alley, St. Luke's,—at the end of Foster's builds. from 123, Whitecross-st.

Pump-Alley, Ewer-St. Boro.—-1st on the R. from Duke-street.

Pump-Court, Perkins's Rents, Westr.—3 doors from 49, Old Pye-st.

Pump-Court, George-St. West-minster,—1st on the L. from James-st.

Pump-Court, Middle Temple-Lane,—1st on the L. from 6, Fleet-st.

Pump-Court, White's Yard,—1st on the L. from 24, Gt. Saffron-hill.

Pump-Court, White-Horse-Al-ley,—2d on the R. from Cow-cross.

Pump - Court, Snow - Hill,—at 62, on the N. side of Skinner-street.

Pump-Court, Moor-Lane, Crip-plegate,—3d on the R. from 86, Fore-st.

Pump-Court, Bridgewater-Gar-dens,—behind the Catherine-wheel, N. E. corner.

Pump-Court, Frying-Pan-Alley,—2d on the R. from Petti-coat-lane towards Bell-lane.

Pump-Court, Dean-St.—at 32,

1st on the L. from 94, Up. E. Smithfield.

Pump - Court, Shadwell High-St.—at 4, op. the corner of West's gardens.

Pump-Court, Boddy's Bridge, Blackfriars-Road, — 6 doors from Up. Ground.

Pump-Court, Duke - St. Boro.—1st on the R. from Queen-street.

Pump-Court, Tooley's Gate-way,—the further end, from 63, Tooley-st.

Pump-Court, Long-Lane, Ber-mondsey,—middle of the N. side.

Pump-Row, Old - St. - Road,—part of the S. side, from the City-road towards St. Agnes-le-Clair.

Pump - Yard, Queen - St. Rat-cliffe,—the W. end of the said street still retains that name.

Punderson's Gardens, Bethnal-Green-Road,—2d on the R. from the Green towards Shoreditch.

Punderson's P. Bethnal-Green-Road, — N. side, near the Green.

Punnet's Ways, Rotherhithe,—by Globe-Stairs, ⅔ of a mile below the church.

Purim-Pl. Dog-Row,—E. side, by Mile-end-turnpike.

Purse-Court, Old-Change,—at 40, 10 doors on the L. from Cheapside.

Pye-Corner, W. Smithfield. See Giltspur-st.

Pye-Gardens, Bankside, Boro.—W. side of White-Hind-al-ley.

Pye - Street, (New), Orchard-St. Westminster,—2d on the R. from Strutton-ground.

Pye-St. (Old),—1st in the last from Orchard-st.

Pyed-Bull-Yard, Little Russell-St. Bloomsbury,—E. end, 5 doors from Bury-st.

Pyed-Horse-Yard, Chiswell-St. —3 doors from Finsbury-square.

QUAKER - STREET, Brick-Lane, Spitalfields,—at 173, N. side Hanbury's brewery.

Quakers-School, Islington-Road, —nearly op. Sadlers-wells.

Quality-Court, Chancery-Lane, —at 47, ¼ of a mile on the R. from 192, Fleet-st.

Quarter-Master-General's Office, Horse-Guards,—N. of the Commander in Chief's-Office.

Quebec-Chapel, Quebec-Street, 10 doors on the L. from 237, Oxford-st

Quebec-Mews, New Quebec-St. Portman-Sq.—at 20, middle of the W. side.

Quebec-Street, Oxford-St.—at 236, 2d on the L. from Tyburn-turnpike.

Quebec-St. (New), Portman-Sq. —W. side, from Up. Seymour-st. to Up. Berkeley-st.

Quebec-St. (Gt.) New-Road, Marybone,—5th on the R. from the Yorkshire-stingo.

Quebec-St. (North),—op. the last.

Quebec-Wharf (Old), Rotherhithe-St.—op. 179, between

Globe-stairs and the Horse-ferry.

Queen Ann's Bounty - Office, Dean's Yard, Westminster,— 2d door on the R. from under the archway, entering by the W. end of the Abbey.

Queen Ann's Mews, Chandos-St.—4 doors from the N. E. corner of Cavendish-sq.

Queen Ann-St. East. See Foley-St.

Queen Ann-St. West, Cavendish-Sq.—at the N. end of Chandos-st.

Queen Ann-St. Ducking-Pond-Row, —op. Court-st. entering by 110, Whitechapel-road.

Queen's Arms - Court, Upper Ground-St.—3 doors on the L. from Blackfriars-road.

Queen's Builds. Brompton-Road, —the L. side, by Knights-bridge.

Queen's Builds. (Up.)—the continuation of the last.

Queen Catherine-Court, Brook-St. Ratcliffe,—at 23, a few doors on the R. from Butcher-row.

Queen Catherine-Court (Little), —west side the last.

Queen Charlotte-Court, Moses-Alley, Bankside, Boro.— 3d on the R. from Maid-lane.

Queen Charlotte - Row, New-Road, Marybone,—S. side, commencing on the E. side the Yorkshire-stingo.

Queen's Court, Pimlico,—1st on the R. from Buckingham-gate.

Queen's Court, King-St. Covent-Garden,—at 30, 1st on the

R. 13 doors from the N. W. corner of Covent-garden.

Queen's Court, Gt. Queen-St. Lincoln's-Inn-Fields,—at 58, middle of the S. side.

Queen's Court, High-Holborn, —at 246, nearly op. Dean-st. Red-lion-sq.

Queen's Court, Circus, Minories,—at the N. side.

Queen's Court, King-St. Bethnal-Green,—at 20, 3d on the R. from 157, Brick-lane.

Queen's Court, King-St. Commercial-Road, Whitechapel, —from 12 to 13, Batty-st.

Queen's Court, Dog-Row, Bethnal-Green,—at the S. end of Queen's row, adjoining Redcow-lane.

Queen's Court, Queen's Row, St. George's East,—a few doors from Prussian-island, Wapping-st.

Queen's Court, Queen-St. Ratcliffe,—1st on the R. east of London-st.

Queen's Head-Court, Lambeth Upper Marsh,—nearly op. Stangate-st.

Queen's Head-Court, Lambeth-Butts,—the corner of Vauxhall-walk.

Queen's Court, Gt. Suffolk-St. Boro.—W. side of George-st. 5th on the R. from 80, Blackman-st.

Queen's Court, Queen-St. Mint, Boro.—6 doors on the R. from Lombard-st.

Queen's Court, Little Queen-St. Boro.—1st on the L. from 20, King-st.

Queen's Court, (Little),—a few doors N. of the last.

Queen's Court, Queen-St. Boro. —at 40, 4 doors W. of Guildford-st.

Queen's Gardens, Brompton,— 3d on the L. from Knightsbridge.

Queen's Gardens, Crosby-Row, —last on the L. from Snow's Fields.

Queen's Head-Alley, Wapping, —at 122, 5th below the church.

Queen's Head - Alley, White-Horse-St. Ratcliffe,—at 83, a door or two on the R. from the Commercial-road.

Queen's Head - Builds. Marybone-Park,—in the field op. Portland-road.

Queen's Head-Court, Strand, —at 405, nearly op. Adam-st. Adelphi.

Queen's Head-Court, Gt. Windmill-St.—at 24, 5th on the R. from the Haymarket.

Queen's Head - Court, Gray's Inn-Lane,—at 38, that number on the R. from Holborn.

Queen's Head-Court, Giltspur-St.—2d on the R. from Newgate-st.

Queen's Head-Court, Charlotte-St—at 23, 3d on the L. from Whitechapel-road.

Queen's Head-Gardens, Hoxton, —near ½ a mile from Old-st.-road, leading to Kingsland-road.

Queen's Head-inn, Boro.—at 83, near St. Margaret's hill.

Queen's Head-Passage, Newgate-St.—at 41, 2d on the L. from Cheapside.

Queen's Head - Sq. Lambeth Up. Marsh,—by Stangate-st.
X

Queen's Head-Yard, Gt. Queen-St.—4 doors from Lincoln's-inn-fields.

Queen-Hithe Charity-School,—at 5, Old Fish-st. by the church.

Queen-Hithe Dock and Stairs, Up. Thames-St.—at 60, E. side of Bread-st.-hill.

Queen's Pl. Gt Peter-St. Westminster,—2d on the L. from Strutton-ground.

Queen's Pl. Chelsea,—S. side of Queen-st

Queen's Pl. New-St. Kennington-Cross,—op. the W. end of Park-st.

Queen's Pl. Kennington,—W. side the common.

Queen's Pl. Little Queen-St. Boro.—at the N. end of it.

Queen's Row, Brompton. See Queen's Builds.

Queen's Row, Pimlico,—op. the Barracks, from Ward's row to Duke's row.

Queen's Row, Palmer's Village, —N. end, on the R. from Brewer's green.

Queen's Row, Pentonville,—part of the L. side the road, ¼ of a mile from Islington.

Queen's Row, Hoxton,—part of the W. side, between Turner-sq. and Workhouse-lane, ¾ of a mile on the L. from Old-st.-road.

Queen's Row, Dog-Row, Bethnal-Green,—part of the R. side, ¼ of a mile from Mile-end-turnpike.

Queen's Row, King-Street, St. George's East,—2d on the R. from 17, Old Gravel-lane.

Queen's Row Kennington High-

Road,—nearly op. the Common.

Queen's Head-Row, Newington,—R. side, from the Elephant and Castle towards the church.

Queen's Row, Walworth,—E. end of King's row, on the R. from nearly op. the Montpellier.

Queen's-Sq. Westminster,—middle S. side of St. James's park, by Broadway.

Queen-Sq.-Pl.—1st on the L. in the last from York-st.

Queen-Sq. near Bloomsbury,—end of Gt. Ormond-st. from 50, Lamb's Condu t-st.

Queen-Sq. Aldersgate - St.—at 140, op. Jewin-st.

Queen-Sq. Moorfields,—at 12, near the middle of the N. side.

Queen-Sq. Hoxton,—between Turner-sq. and Workhouse-lane, near ½ a mile on the L. from Old-st.-road.

Queen-St. Brompton,—4th on the L. from Knightsbridge.

Queen-St. Chelsea or Pimlico,—from near Ranelagh-walk towards the hospital.

Queen-St. (Great), Westminster,—the continuation of Little Queen-st.

Queen-Street (Little), Princes-St. Westminster,—3 doors on the R. from Gt. George-street.

Queen-St. Edgware-Road,—at 61, 6th on the R. from Tyburn-turnpike.

Queen-St. (Little),—1st on the R. in the last from Edgware-road.

Queen-Street, Oxford - St.—at 272, 4th on the R. from Hyde-park.

Queen-Street, Oxford - St.—at 340, ⅓ of a mile on the L. from St. Giles's.

Queen-Street, Curzon-St. Mayfair,—at 10, 1st W. of Half-moon-st.

Queen-Street, Gt. Windmill-St. Haymarket,—at 47, 10 doors from Piccadilly.

Queen-Street, Dean-St. Soho,— at 18, 2d on the L. from 400, Oxford-st.

Queen-Street, Gt. Russell- St. Bloomsbury,—at 49, op. the British-museum.

Queen-St. 7 Dials,—the continuation of Short's-gardens, from 15, Drury-lane.

Queen-St. (Gt.) Lincoln's-Inn-Fields,—N. W. corner, to 155, Drury-lane.

Queen-St. (Little),—from the last to 222, High-holborn.

Queen-Street, Perceval-Street, Clerkenwell,—2d on the L. from 96, Goswell-st.

Queen-St. Cheapside,—at 70, 6th on the R. from St. Paul's church-yard.

Queen-Street, Worship-St.—2d on the R. from Paul-st.

Queen-St. Hoxton,—2d on the R. in Pitfield-st. from Old-st.-road.

Queen-Street, Quaker-St. Spitalfields,—1st on the R. a few yards from 173, Brick-lane.

Queen-Street, Church-St. Mile-End New-Town,—at 26, 2d on the R. from Baker's row.

Queen-St. Tower-Hill,—2d on the R. in Rosemary-lane.

Queen - Street, St. George's East,—entrance by the 1st on the R. in King-st. from 17, Old Gravel-lane.

Queen-St. Ratcliffe,—the continuation of Broad-st. from Ratcliffe-cross.

Queen-Street, Poplar High-St. —by the Queen's Head, ⅓ of a mile on the R. from the Commercial-road.

Queen-St. Boro.—the continuation of Union-st. from 218, High-st.

Queen-St. Mint, Boro.— the 2d on the R. in Redcross-st. from Union-st.

Queen-Street (Little), King-St. Boro.—at 20, 1st on the L. from 109, High-st.

Queen-St. Lock's Fields, Walworth,—1st on the R. in York-st. from the High-st.

Queen-St. Horselydown,—4th on the L. in Free-School-st. from the E. end of Tooley-st.

Queen-St. Rotherhithe,—at 368, few doors below King's stairs, ⅘ of a mile W. of the church.

Queen-St. (Lower), Rotherhithe-St.—the continuation of it, 1¼ mile below the church, leading to Trinity-st.

Quickset - Row, New-Road,— N. side, nearly op. Fitzroy-square.

————

RADCLIFFE-PLACE, &c.— See Ratcliffe.

Raquet - Court, Fleet - Street, —at 114, 10 doors on the R. from Fleet-market.

Ragged'-Staff-Court, Drury-Lane,—10 doors on the R. from Holborn.

Rahn's-Pl.Church-Lane,White-chapel,—3d on the R. from 65, Cable-st.

Raine's Hospital, St. George's East,—facing the E. end of Charles-st. from 46, Old Gravel-lane.

Rainy's Yard, Little Guildford-St. Russell-Sq.—1st on the R. from Bernard-st.

Ralph's Quay, Lower Thames-St.-at 23, E. side Billingsgate.

Ram-Alley, Spicer-St. Spital-fields,—3d on the L. from 83, Brick-lane.

Ram-Alley, Rotherhithe-St.—at 217, near Globe-stairs, ⅔ of a mile below the church.

Ram-Court, Fleet-St.—at 47, nearly op. Fetter-lane.

Ram-Inn, W. Smithfield,—at 79, 4 doors W. from the entrance to St. John-st.

Ram-Mews, King-St. Westr.—8 doors N. of George-st.

Ramsden's Yd. Beckford-Row, Walworth,—at 20, ⅔ of a mile on the L. from the Elephant and Castle.

Ramsgate-Harbour-Office,—at 22, Austin-friars.

Rance's Court, Lower-Turning, Shadwell,—behind 75,Shakes-pear's-walk.

Randall's Causeway, Rother-hithe,--at the entrance to the Surrey-canal.

Randall's Rents, Rotherhithe,—on the N. side of Green-land-dock.

Randall and Brent's Lower-Yard,—on the N. side Green-land-dock.

Randall and Brent's Up. Yard, Rotherhithe,——1st below Cuckold's Point.

Randall's Wharf,—E. side of Broken-wharf, entrance 42, Up. Thames-st.

Ranelagh-Green, Chelsea,—at the W. end of Ranelagh-walk.

Ranelagh-Pl. Pimlico,—2d on the R. from Arabella-row.

Ranelagh-St.—1st on the L. in Arabella-row from Pimli-co.

Ranelagh-St. (Upper),—the con-tinuation of, the last.

Ranelagh-Walk, Chelsea,—1st on the L. west from the bridge at the Neat Houses.

Ranelagh (New) Gardens, Mill-bank,—S. side the Spread-Eagle, near the New-bridge.

Ratcliffe,—a large district in the parish of Stepney, from the E. end of Shadwell High-st. to Limehouse.

Ratcliffe or Radcliffe-Court, John's Row, St. Luke's,—1st on the L. from the N. end of Brick-lane.

Ratcliffe-Court, Ratcliffe-High-way,—at 115, 30 doors E. of Cannon-st.

Ratcliffe-Cross,—from the E. end of Broad-st. to the Thames.

Ratcliffe-Cross-Stairs,—W. end of Narrow-st. 2½ miles below London-bridge.

Ratcliffe-Dock,—W. side the last, and E. side of Mr. Whi-ting's Wharf.

RatcliffeGardens,Ratcliffe-Row, St. Luke's,—3d on the L. west from Bath-st.

Ratcliffe-Highway,—the E.continuation of Parsons-st. and Up. East-Smithfield, where the numbers begin and end, viz. 1 and 198 : it extends to Shadwell High-st.

Ratcliffe - Layer, Brick - Lane, St. Luke's,—last on the L. from 113, Old-st.

Ratcliffe-Pl. Ratcliffe-Row, St. Luke's,—a few yards on the L. from Bath-st.

Ratcliffe-Row, St. Luke's,—a few doors on the R. in Bath-st. from the City-road.

Ratcliffe-Sq. Commercial-Road, —between White - horse-st. and Stepney-causeway.

Ratcliffe - Workhouse,—at the N. end of White-horse-st. by Salmon's-lane.

Rathbone-Pl. Oxford - St.—23 doors on the R. from Tottenham-court-road.

Rathbone-Pl. (Up.)—continuation of the last.

Raven-Court, Fetter-Lane,—at 101, nearly op. Dean-st.

Raven-Row, Spitalfields,—the continuation of Widegate-st. Bishopsgate.

Raven-Row, Whitechapel-Rd. —E. side the London-hospital.

Raven and Sun-Yard, Russell-St. Bermondsey,—middle of the S. side, nearly op. Church-street.

Ravenshear's Rents, Vine-St. Leather-Lane,—1st on the L. from Bedford-st.

Rawstorne-St. Brompton,—3d on the R. from Knightsbridge.

Rawstorne-St. Islington-Road,

—5th on the R. from St. John-st.

Ray's Builds. Ebury-St. Chelsea,—at the W. end, by the Watch-house.

Ray-Street,—N. W. corner of Clerkenwell-green, bearing to the L.

Ray-St.-Pl.—3 doors on the R. in the last from the Green.

Rayner-Pl. Chelsea,—N. side the Hospital, by Great Smith-street.

Rayner's Wharf, Broad-St. Ratcliffe,—at 28, W. side of Stone-stairs.

Read's Alley, Rotherhithe,—at 235, 10 doors on the R. below King and Queen-stairs.

Rebecca-Court, Wells - St.—at 48, the last on the R. from 63, Oxford-st.

Recorder Newspaper-Office,— at 45, Old-Bailey, op. Newgate-prison.

Red-Bull-Court, Harp-Alley,— 1st on the R. from 46, Grubstreet.

Red-Bull-Wharf, Up. Thames-St.—at 93, op. Duck's-foot-lane.

Red-Bull-Yard,—the entrance to the last.

Red-Cow-Alley, Kent-St. Boro. —at 105, ⅓ of a mile on the L. from Saint George's church.

Red-Cow-Lane, Mile-End, -1st on the L. below the turnpike.

Red-CrossCoal-Wharf, Thames-Street,—W. side of Londonbridge.

Red-Cross-Court, High-St. Bo-

X 3

RED

Red-Cross-Court, Cow-Lane,—at 20, 2d on the L. from 93, W. Smithfield.

Red-Cross-Court, Barbican,—at 32, behind the Red-cross public-house.

Red-Cross-Sq. Cripplegate,—2d on the R. in Jewin-st. from 46, Aldersgate-st.

Red-Cross-Sq. Tower-St.—at 60, 9 doors E. of Mark-lane.

Red-Cross-St. Cripplegate,—W. end of Fore-st. by the church, extending to Barbican.

Red-Cross-Street, Nightingale-Lane,—at 7, 2d on the R. from Up. E. Smithfield.

Red-Cross-St. Boro.—1st in Union-st. from 218, High-street.

Red-Gate-Alley, Minories,—at 71, nearly opposite the Crescent.

Red-Gate-Court, Minories,—at 79, 6 doors on the R. from Tower-hill.

Red-Lion-Alley, Cow-Cross, W. Smithfield,—at the W. end of Greenhill's Rents, entrance by 93, St. John-st.

Red-Lion Alms-Houses, York-St. Westr.—W. end, by James-street.

Red-Lion Coach-Office, Strand,—at 339, E. side of Catherine-st.

Red-Lion-Court, White-Hart-Yard,—1st on the R. from 82, Drury-lane.

Red-Lion-Court, Fleet-St.—at 169, 10 doors E. of Fetter-lane.

Red-Lion-Court, Shoe-Lane,—at 42, the 4th on the L. from Holborn.

Red-Lion-Court, Great Saffron-Hill,—at 11, 3d on the R. from Holborn-hill along Field-lane.

Red-Lion-Court, Silver-St.—6 doors on the R. from 81, Wood-st. Cheapside.

Red-Lion-Court, Watling-St.—at 19, E. side of Bread-st.

Red-Lion-Court, Saint John-St.—at 153, ¼ of a mile on the R. from Smithfield.

Red-Lion-Court, Charterhouse-Lane,—1st on the L. from the sq. towards 100, St. John-street.

Red-Lion-Court (Little),—entrance by the last.

Red-Lion-Court, London-Wall,—at 38, 1st E. of Coleman-street.

Red-Lion-Court, Holywell-Lane,—at 58, 1st on the L. from 194, Shoreditch.

Red-Lion-Court, Hoxton,—nearly op. the Britannia, ¼ of a mile on the R. from Old-st.-road.

Red-Lion-Court, Kingsland-Road,—at 62, 2d on the L. from Shoreditch.

Red-Lion-Court, Red-Lion-St. Spitalfields,—at 19, 8 doors N. of the church.

Red-Lion-Court, George-St. Bethnal-Green,—10 doors on the L. north from Spicer-st. Brick-lane.

Red-Lion-Court, Minories,—at

70, 2d on the R. from Tower-hill.

Red-Lion-Court, St. Catherine's Lane,—3d on the R. from 48, Up. E. Smithfield.

Red-Lion-Court, Pennington-St. Ratcliffe-Highway,—at 81, 3 doors E. of Breezers-hill.

Red-Lion-Court, Red-Lion-St. —1st on the L. from 120, Wapping.

Red-Lion-Court, Bermondsey-St.—at 44, ⅛ of a mile on the L. from Tooley-st.

Red-Lion-Inn, Whitechapel,— at 30, the corner of Red-lion-street.

Red-Lion and Spread-Eagle-Inn, Whitechapel,—at 94, op. Plough-st.

Red-Lion-Inn, Aldersgate-St.— at 110, and at 12, Long-lane, W. Smithfield.

Red-Lion-Market, Whitecross-Street, St. Luke's,—at 213, 2d on the L. from Chiswell-street.

Red-Lion-Passage, St. Pancras-Pl. St. Pancras,—at 26, W. side the Small-pox-hospital.

Red-Lion-Passage, Red-Lion-Sq.—from the S. E. corner, to 62, Red-lion-st.

Red-Lion-Passage, Fleet-St.— the continuation of Red-lion-court.

Red-Lion-Passage, Whitecross-Street, St. Luke's,—at 213, leading from Red-lion-market to King's-Head-court, Beech-street.

Red-Lion-Passage, Hoxton,— nearly op. the Britannia, leading to Kingsland-road.

Red-Lion-Passage, Red-Cross-St. Boro.—at 37, 10 doors S. of Queen-st.

Red-Lion-Passage, Cloth-Fair, —3d on the R. from 60, W. Smithfield.

Red-Lion-Pl. Cock-Lane, West-Smithfield,—1st on the L. from Giltspur-st.

Red-Lion-Row, Walworth,—be-hind Bolingbrook-row and the Red-lion.

Red-Lion-Sq.—end of Dean-st. and Leigh-st. from 92, High-holborn.

Red-Lion-St. Holborn,—at 71, ½ a mile on the R. from Fleet-market.

Red-Lion-Street, Clerkenwell-Green,—middle of the S. side.

Red-Lion-St. Spitalfields,—W. side the church, 5th from 69, Bishopsgate, along Union-street.

Red-Lion-St. Whitechapel,—at 30, 4th on the R. from Ald-gate.

Red-Lion-Street, Wapping,—at 120, 4th on the L. near ⅛ of a mile below the church.

Red-Lion-Street, High-St. Boro. —at 263, by St. Margaret's hill.

Red-Lion-Wharf, Up. Thames-St.—E. side Three Cranes, Queen-st.

Red-Lion-Wharf, Wapping,— at 264, op. Red-lion-st.

Red-Lion-Yard, Princes-St. Westr.—2d on the L. from Tothill-st.

Red-Lion-Yard,—W. end of Charles-st. Berkeley-sq.

Red-Lion-Yard, Tottenham-

Court . Road,—60 doors on the L. from Oxford-st.

Red-Lion-Yard, Swallow St.—at 62, near the middle of the E. side.

Red-Lion-Yard, Old Cavendish-St.—1st on the R. from 140, Oxford-st.

Red-Lion-Yard, High-Holborn, —at 255, op. Dean-st. Red-lion-sq.

Red-Lion-Yard, Up. King-St. Bloomsbury,—at 52, N. side Hart-st.

Red-Lion-Yard, Eagle-St. Red-Lion-Sq.—2 doors from Red-lion-st.

Red-Lion-Yard, Castle-Street, Leicester-Sq.—the corner of Hemming's-row.

Red-Lion-Yard, Gt. Warner-St. —at 12, a few yards on the R. from Bayne's row.

Red-Lion-Yard, Coppice-Row, Clerkenwell,—at 46, 3d on the R. from the Green.

Red-Lion-Yard, Red - Lion-St. Clerkenwell,—at 70, 3 doors on the L. from the Green.

Red-Lion-Yard, Long-Lane, W. Smithfield,—10 doors on the R. from 115, Aldersgate-st.

Red-Lion-Yard, Stangate,—1st on the R. from Westminster-bridge.

Red-Rose - Alley, Whitecross-St. Cripplegate,—at 56, 2d S. of Chiswell-st.

Redmaid's Lane, Wapping,—on the N. side of Gt. Her-mitage - st. by the London-docks-wall.

Redman's Row, Mile - End,—the continuation of Grove-pl. by the turnpike.

Reed's Wharf, St. Saviour's Dock,—on the W. side of Mill-stairs.

Reeve's Arch, Princes-St. Lam-beth,—4th on the R. from Broad-st.

Reeve's Court, Angel-Sq. Bish-opsgate,—at the W. end of Slade's-builds.

Reeve's Court, White's Yard,—2d on the L. from 58, Rose-mary-lane.

Reeve's Mews, South-Audley-St.—7 doors on the R. from Grosvenor-sq.

Refuge for the Destitute, Nar-row - Wall, Lambeth,—W. side the Patent Shot manu-factory.

Regent's Park, Marybone-Park, —N. side the New-road, to-wards Hampstead.

Regent-St. Blackwall Causeway, —W. end of Caulker-st.

Regency-Pl. Blackfriars-Road, —24 doors on the L. from Surrey-chapel, towards the Obelisk.

Reliance-Sq. New - Inn-Yard, —at 29, 2d on the R. from 175, Shoreditch.

Renney's Court, Webb-St. —a few doors on the R. from 240, Bermondsey-st.

Renney's Rents, Maze, Boro.—at 29, the 6th on the L. from 196, Tooley-st.

Renou's Court, Whitecross-Pl. Moorfields,—1st on the L. from 22, Wilson-st.

Reputation - Row, Kingsland-Road,—L. side, ⅓ of a mile from Shoreditch, and op. the Alms-houses.

Retreat, South-Lambeth,—1st

on the L. from Vauxhall-turnpike.

Revel-Row, Blackman-St. Borough,—at 64, by the King's Bench.

Reynolds-Court, Ropemakers-St. Moorfields,—op. Type-st. Chiswell-st.

Rhodes-Wells, Stepney,—⅓ of a mile E. of the church.

Rice's Rents,Shakespear's Walk, Shadwell,—at 41, 2d on the L. from High-st.

Rich-Street, Commercial-Road, Limehouse,—4th on the R. below the church.

Richards-Buildings, Shoe-Lane, Fleet-St.—at 72, 3d on the R. from Holborn-hill.

Richards-Builds. Cherry-Tree-Court,—2d on the R. from Golden-lane.

Richards-Court, Bainbridge-St. St. Giles's,—4th on the R. from Oxford-st.

Richard-St. Commercial-Road, —1st on the R. east of Cannon-st.-road.

Richardson's Builds. Spa-Road-Passage, Bermondsey,—1st on the L. from 13, Printers-pl.

Richardson's Mews, Warren-St. Fitzroy-Sq.—at 23,middle of the S. side.

Richardson-St. Long-Lane, Bermondsey,—middle of the N. side.

Richbell - Court, Lamb's Conduit-St.—10 doors on the R. from Red-lion-st.

Riches-Court, Lime-St.—at 50, 5 doors from Leadenhall-st.

Richmond-Builds. Dean-Street, Soho,—at 58, 5th on the R. from 400, Oxford-st.

Richmond-Mews,—W. end of the last.

Richmond-Hall, Prospect-Row, Bermondsey, — E. side the Marine Crescent, nearly op. Printers-pl.

Richmond - Gardens, New-St. Brompton,—6 doors from the High-road.

Richmond-Pl. Walworth,—part of East-lane, by the chapel.

Richmond-Pl. (Little),—op. the chapel and Camden-st.

Richmond - Street, Princes-St. Soho,—2d on the L. from Coventry-st.

Richmond-Street, St. Luke's,— 2d N. from 66, Old-st. by the hospital.

Rickets-Court, Morgan's Lane, —1st on the L. from 79, Tooley-st.

Rider-Court. See Ryder.

Riding-House-Lane, Gt. Tichfield-St. Marybone,—at 96, 5th on the L. from Oxford-market.

Risby's Rope-Walk, Narrow-St. Limehouse,—entrance on the L. below Mr. Turner's wharf.

Ritchie's Pl. Deptford Lower-Road,—op. China-hall.

Ritchie's Wharf, Lower Queen-St. Rotherhithe,—½ of a mile below Cuckold's point.

River-Terrace, City-Road,—on the E. side the New-river.

Rivet-Place,London-Road,—1st on the L. from the Elephant and Castle.

Roberts-Builds. Pimlico,—1st on the R. from Belgrave-terrace, towards Five-fields.

Roberts-Court, Charles-Street,

Hampstead - Road,—at 14, 6 doors from Brook-st.

Roberts-Pl. Commercial-Road, —3d on the R. west of Cannon-st.-road.

Roberts-Place, Wade's-Pl. Poplar,—1st on the R. from op. the Green-man.

Robert-St. Hampstead-Road,— op. the chapel.

Robert-Street John-St. Adelphi, —1st on the L. from Adam-st. 73, Strand.

Robert-Street, Little James-St. Bedford-Row,—1st on the L. from 17, Great James-street.

Robert-St. Blackfriars-Road,— 1st E. parallel to part of the said road, from Edward-st. to George-st.

Robinhood-Court, Church-Lane, —4 doors from George-st. Bloomsbury.

Robinhood - Court, Newcastle-Court, Strand,—on the W. side, a few yards on the L. from Pickett-st.

Robinhood Court, Shoe - Lane, —at 67, 2d on the R. from St. Andrew's church, Holborn-hill.

Robinhood - Court, Bow-Lane, Cheapside,—19 doors on the R. from Cheapside.

Robinhood-Court, Milk-Street, Cheapside,—2 doors N. of Honey-lane-market.

Robinhood - Court, Bell-Alley, —3d on the R. from 1, Golden-lane.

Robinhood-Court, Mill-Lane,— at 23, 2d on the R. from 55, Tooley-st.

Robinhood-Lane,—E. end Poplar-High-st. to the E. India dock-gate.

Robinhood-Yard, Leather-Lane, Holborn,—8 doors on the R. from 128, Holborn-hill.

Robinson's Lane, Paradise-Row, Chelsea,—by Cheyne-walk, ¼ of a mile on the R. from the Hospital.

Robinson's Place, Farmer-St. Shadwell,—at 64, last on the L. from 39, High-st.

Robinson's Place, Shakespear's Walk, Shadwell,—last on the R. from 49, High-st.

Rochester-Row, Westr.—by the Grey-coat-school, near the W. end of Gt. Peter-st.

Rochester-St. Boro.-Market,— the continuation of York-st. from 276, High-st.

Rock Life-Insurance-Office,— at 14, New-Bridge-st. Blackfriars, a few doors on the R. from Fleet-st.

Rockingham-Court, Newington-Causeway,—3 doors N. of the Kent-road.

Rockingham-Pl. Kent-Road,— N. side, by the Elephant and Castle.

Rockingham-Row West,—the E. continuation of the last.

Rockingham - Row Middle,— the continuation of the last.

Rockingham - Row East,—the continuation of the last.

Rodney's Builds. Kent-Road,— part of the R. side, ¼ of a mile from the Elephant and Castle.

Rodney's Court, Chapel-Street, Holywell-Mount,—at 10, 1st on the L. from the Curtain-road.

Rodney's Row, Kent-Road,—4th on the R. from the Elephant and Castle.

Rodney - Row, Shadwell,—op. Elbow-lane, from 30, High-street.

Rodney-Street, Pentonville,—E. side the chapel, ¼ of a mile on the R. from Islington.

Rodney-St. Mint, Boro.—between Lant-st. and Great Suffolk-st.

Roebuck - Court, Turnmill-St. Clerkenwell,—at 20, middle of the W. side.

Roebuck-Yard, Kent-St. Boro. —at 225, ¼ of a mile on the R. from St. George's church.

Rogers' Court, Lower E. Smithfield,—3 doors W. of Hermitage-bridge.

Rogers' Court, Denmark-St.— 6 doors on the R. from 153, Ratcliffe-highway.

Rogers' Rents, Webb-St. Boro. —a few doors on the R. from 248, Bermondsey-st.

Rogues - Lane, Rotherhithe,— from Jamaica-Level to the St. Helena.

Rollinson's Court, Jacob - St. Dock-Head,—2d on the R. from Mill-st.

Rolls-Builds. Fetter-Lane,—at 117, 2d on the L. from 180, Fleet-st.

Rolls - Chapel, Rolls - Yard,— facing the entrance from 14, Chancery-lane.

Rolls-Workhouse,—at the N. end of Acorn-court, Rolls-builds.

Rolls-Yard, Chancery-Lane,— 15 doors on the R. from 192, Fleet-st.

Romney-Row, Westminster,— the continuation of Vine-st. from Millbank-st.

Rood-Lane, Fenchurch-St.—23 doors on the R. from Gracechurch-st.

Roope's Tenements, Rotherhithe-St.—at 391, leading to Pasfield's rents and Mill-pond-bridge.

Roper's Builds. White-St.—1st on the L. from Cutler-st. 114, Houndsditch.

Roper's Place, Borough-Road,— middle of the S. side.

Ropemakers - Alley, Row, or Walk, Moorfields,—S. side of Ropemakers-st.

Ropemakers-Fields, Limehouse, —E. continuation of Narrow-st. bearing to the L.

Ropemakers-St. Moorfields,— from the N. W. corner to Type-st.

Rosamond-St. Clerkenwell,— 2d on the R. in Corporation-row from St. John-st.

Rose-Alley, High-Holborn,—at 88, from French-horn-yard to Eagle-st.

Rose-Alley, Turnmill-St. Clerkenwell,—at 64, op. Castle-street.

Rose-Alley, Golden-Lane,—at 62, middle of the E. side.

Rose-Alley, Bishopsgate-Without,—at 34, 4 doors N. of New-st.

Rose-Alley, Flower and Dean-St. Spitalfields,—1st on the R. from 200, Brick-lane.

Rose-Alley, Bankside, Southwark,—at 21, 4th from Clink-street.

Rose-Court, Long - Acre,—12

doors on the R. from Saint Martin's lane.

Rose-Court, Cursitor-St. Chancery-Lane,—at 25, nearly op. Castle-st.

Rose-Court Turnmill-St. Clerkenwell,—1st on the L. from Clerkenwell-green.

Rose-Court, Fore-St. Cripplegate,—at 100, 3 doors W. of Grub-st.

Rose-Court, Bow-Lane,—4 doors on the L. from 59, Cheapside.

Rose-Court, New-St. Bishopsgate-Without,—1st on the L. from 30, Bishopsgate-st.

Rose-Court, William-St. Shoreditch,—at 13, 2d on the R. from 136, Shoreditch.

Rose-Court, Wheeler-St. Spitalfields,—at 62, nearly opposite Quaker-st.

Rose-Court, Gt. Tower-St.—at 42, 8 doors on the L. from Tower-hill.

Rose-Court, Up. E. Smithfield,—at 16, 5 doors on the L. east of Butcher-row.

Rose-Court, Blue-Anchor-Yard,—6th on the L. from 48, Rosemary-lane.

Rose-Court, Hickman's Folly,—1st on the R. from Dock-head.

Rose-Court, Newington,—nearly op. the church.

Rose's Gateway, Russell-Street, Bermondsey,—by the Ship and Ball, 3d on the R. east of Church-st.

Rose-Inn, West-Smithfield,—at 80, 6 doors W. from the entrance to St. John-st.

Rose-Lane, Wentworth-Street,

Spitalfields,—at 38, middle of the N. side.

Rose-Lane, Whitehorse-Street, Ratcliffe,—at 91, by the Commercial-road.

Rose-Place, Turk-St. Bethna. Green,—1st on the L. from Tyson-st.

Rose-Street, Greek-St.—6 doors on the L. from Soho-sq.

Rose-St. Newport-Market,—N. side, to Litchfield-st.

Rose-Street, King-St. Covent-Garden,—at 23, adjoining New-st.

Rose-Street, Newgate-St.—at 20, 2d on the L. from Cheapside.

Rose-Street, Brick-Lane, St. Luke's,—at 50, 2d on the R. from 113, Old-st.

Rose-Street, Church-St. Bethnal-Green,—at 44, 5th on the L. from 65, Shoreditch.

Rose-Yard, Shoreditch,—at 223, leading into Plough-yard.

Rose-Yard, Redcross-St. Boro.—at 85, 2d on the L. from Park-st.

Rose and Crown Alley, Whitefriars,—nearly op. Bouverie-st. from 62, Fleet-st.

Rose and Crown-Alley, Rose and Crown-Court,—the 1st on the R. from Moorfields.

Rose and Crown-Court, Turk's Row, Chelsea,—nearly op. Lower Sloane-st.

Rose and Crown-Court, Moorfields,—at the N. E. corner.

Rose and Crown-Court, Islington,—9 doors from the City-road.

Rose and Crown-Court, Shoe-

Lane,—at 26, four doors N of Stonecutter-st.

Rose and Crown-Court, Foster-Lane,—7 doors on the R. from Cheapside.

Rose and Crown-Court, Essex-St. Whitechapel,—1st on the L. from 105, Whitechapel.

Rose and Crown-Court, Saint Catherine's Lane,—4th on the L. from 49, Up. E. Smithfield.

Rose and Crown-Court, Booth-St. Spitalfields,—2 doors on the R. from 49, Brick-lane.

Rose and Crown-Yard, Saint John-St.—at 126, $\frac{1}{8}$ of a mile on the R. from Smithfield.

Rose and Rainbow-Court, Aldersgate-St.—8 doors from Falcon-st. towards Barbican.

Rosemary-Lane, Tower-Hill,—near the N. E. corner, extending to Cable-st.

Rosemary-Branch-Alley, Rosemary-Lane,—4th on the L. from the Minories.

Rosher's Wharf, Trinity-Street, Rotherhithe, — entrance by 11, S. side Durand's wharf.

Rotherhithe -Charity-School,—on the S. side Rotherhithe-church.

Rotherhithe-Stairs,—at 74, Rotherhithe-st. $\frac{1}{4}$ of a mile W. of the church.

Rotherhithe-St.—parallel to the Thames from West-lane, where the numbers begin and end, viz. 1 and 397, to Lower Queen-st. $1\frac{1}{2}$ mile in length.

Rotherhithe-Wall, Bermondsey,—parallel to the Thames, from the E. side of Saint

Saviour's dock to West-lane, $\frac{1}{3}$ of a mile in length.

Rotherhithe-Workhouse, Deptford Lower-Road,—$\frac{1}{6}$ of a mile on the R. from Paradise-row.

Rotten-Row, Goswell-St.—at 30, leading into Old-st.

Round-Court (New), Strand,—at 447, op. Buckingham-st.

Round-Court (Old), Strand,—at 436, E. side the last.

Round-Court, Sharp's Alley, Cow-Cross,—1st on the L. from Cow-cross or from Turnmill-st.

Round-Court, Onslow-St.—1st on the L. from Mutton-lane.

Round-Court, St. Martin's Le-Grand,—1st on the R. from 66, Newgate-st.

Round-Court, Butlers-Alley,—1st on the R. from Moor-lane.

Round-Court, Shacklewell-St. Bethnal-Green,—3 doors on the R. from 18, Tyssen-st.

Rouse's Buildings, Robinson's-Lane, Chelsea,—op. 25, 1st on the L. from Paradise-row.

Rowcroft's Wharf, Bermondsey,—W. side of Cherry-garden-stairs, $1\frac{1}{4}$ mile below London-bridge.

Rowland's Row, Stepney-Green,—a few doors on the R. from Mile-end-road.

Rowlandson's Court, Russell-St.—1st on the L. from 90, Bermondsey-st.

Rowlandson-Place, St. Luke's. See Bath-St.

Rowlandson's Row, City-Road. See Peerless-Row.

Royal-Adelphi-Terrace. See Adelphi.

Y

Royal-Academy of Arts, Somerset-Pl.—the door on the R. under the archway, from the Strand.

Royal-Antiquarian-Society, Somerset-Pl.—the door on the L. under the archway, from the Strand.

Royal - Court, Horselydown - Lane,—3 doors on the L. from Shad-Thames.

Royal-Exchange, Cornhill,—N. side, entrance op. 23.

Royal-Exchange Assurance-Office, —over the W. side of the Royal-Exchange, and at 37, Pall-mall.

Royal-Hospital-Row, Chelsea, —from the Hospital-gate to Grosvenor-row and Pimlico.

Royal-Infirmary for Diseases in the Eye,—at 4, Nassau-st. Soho.

Royal - Institution, Albemarle-St.—21 doors on the R. from 62, Piccadilly.

Royal - Row, Lambeth Upper Marsh,—last on the L. from the turnpike.

Royal-Oak-Court, Beak-St.—3 doors from 45, Swallow-st.

Royal-Oak-Court, Broad-Street, Ratcliffe,—at 119, near Cockhill.

Royal-Oak-Court, Park-St. Boro.—2d on the R. from the Boro.-market.

Royal-Oak-Court, Kent-Street, Boro.—at 279, 30 doors on the R. from St. George's church.

Royal-Oak-Lane, Maid - Lane, Boro.—1st on the L. from Park-st.

Royal-Oak-Tents, Kent-Street, Boro.—at 293, 14 doors on the R. from St. George's church.

Royal-Oak - Walk, Haberdashers - Walk, Hoxton,—at 10, 4th on the R. from Old-st.-rd.

Royal-Oak-Yard, Christopher-St.—1st on the R. from Hatton-garden.

Royal-Oak-Yard, Kent-Street, Borough,—at 284, about 24 doors on the R. from St. George's church.

Royal-Oak-Yard, Bermondsey-St.—at 173. 10 doors on the L. north of the church.

Royalty-Theatre, Well-St. Wellclose-Sq.—5 doors on the R. from Cable-st.

Ruddicks - Builds. Long-Alley, Moorfields,—op. Skinner-st. Bishopsgate.

Rufard's Builds. Islington,—op. White-lion-st. by the City-rd.

Ruins, Lower Shadwell,—at 15, the 2d W. of Gould's hill.

Rumbal's Court, Long-Alley, Moorfields,—2d S. of Crown-street.

Running-Horse - Yard, Davis's St.—at 54, 1st on the L. from 292, Oxford-st.

Running-Horse-Yard, Piccadilly,—5 doors E. of Park-lane.

Running-Horse-Yard, Lambeth-Street, Goodman's Fields,—3 doors on the R. from Ayliffe-st.

Rupert-Pl. Rupert - St. Goodman's Fields,—6 doors from Ayliffe-st.

Rupert-Passage, Rupert-Street, —1st on the L. from Coventry-st.

Rupert-Street, Coventry - St.— 2d on the L. from the Haymarket

Rupert-St. Goodman's Fields, —1st E. parallel to Lemon-street.

Rural-Place, Mile-End-Road,— 6 doors E. of the Old Globe.

Russell-Builds.Wapping-Street, —at 72, W. side the London-docks.

Russell-Court, Cleveland-Row, —3 doors on the R. from St. James's st.

Russell-Court, Drury-Lane,— at 75, 4th on the L. from the New-Church, Strand.

Russell-Court, Rosemary-Lane, —at 50, by Blue Anchor-yard.

Russell-Court, Ratcliffe - High-way,—at 119, nearly opposite Old Gravel-lane.

Russell-Institution, Gt. Coram-St.—a few yards on the L. from Wooburn-pl. Tavistock-square.

Russell-Mews, Howland-St.— at 37, 4th on the R. from Tottenham-court-road.

Russell-Mews, Keppel-St.—1st on the L. from 30, Russell-square.

Russell-Mews, Cleveland-Row, —N. end of Russell-court.

Russell-Pl. New-Road, Hans-Town,—W. end, by Sloane-street.

Russell-Pl. Lisson-Grove,—op. the White-lead Manufactory.

Russell-Pl. Little Coram-St.— middle of the E. side.

Russell-Pl. Fitzroy-Sq.—4th on the L. in London - st. from Tottenham-court-road.

Russell-Place, Bow-St. Covent-Garden,—from 38, to Russell-st.

Russell-Pl. Kent - St.-Road,— 2d on the R. from the Brick-layers-arms.

Russell-Sq.—$\frac{1}{6}$ of a mile N. of Bloomsbury-sq.

Russell-St. (Gt.) Bloomsbury-Sq.—from the N. W. corner to Tottenham-court-road.

Russell-St.(Little),Bloomsbury, —1st S. to the last, from Bury-st. to Duke-st.

Russell-St.(Little), Drury-Lane, —at 61, on the N. side the Theatre.

Russell-St. (Gt.) Covent-Garden,—the continuation of the last.

Russell-Street, Bermondsey-St. —at 90, near $\frac{1}{3}$ of a mile on the L. from Tooley-st.

Russell-St. (Upper),—op. the last.

Russell-St. Rotherhithe,—the continuation of Trinity-st. to Greenland-dock.

Russia-Court, Honey-Lane-Market,—on the N. side of it.

Russia-Row, Milk-St. Cheap-side,—N. side of Honey-lane-market.

Rust's Builds.—bottom of Palmers-rents from Snow's fields, Borough.

Rutland-Court, Glasshouse-St. —1st on the R. from 108, Goswell-st.

Rutland-Pl. Charterhouse - Sq. —at 12, 1st on the R. from Carthusian-st.

Rutland-Pl. Up. Thames-St.— at 4, on the E. side of Puddle-dock.

Rutland - Street, Cannon - St.-Road,—4th ou the right, N. of the Commercial-road.

Rutland-Yard, Up. Thames-St. —op. Rutland-pl.

Rycroft's Court, Old Gravel-Lane,—at 152, middle of the W. side.

Ryder's Court, Leicester-Sq.—from the N. E. corner to Little Newport-st.

Ryder's Court, Little Ryder-St. —5 doors on the R. from St. James's st.

Ryder's Mews, Gt. Ryder-St.— 2d on the L. from St. James's street.

Ryder-Street (Little), St. James's St.—at 26, middle of the E. side.

Ryder-St. (Gt.)—E. end of the last, to Duke-st.

Rye-Loaf - Court, Cock - Hill, Ratcliffe,—at 119, W. side of Glasshouse-yard.

———

Sabb's Quay, Lower Thames-St.—op. 75, W. side of Bear-quay.

Sackville-St. Piccadilly,—at 48, nearly op. St. James's church.

Saddlers Arms-Yard, Swallow-St.— at 147, 2d on the L. from Piccadilly.

Saddlers-Hall, Cheapside,—at 143, near Newgate-st.

Sadler's Wells,—⅓ of a mile on the L. from the N. end of St. John-street towards Islington.

Saffron-Court, Gt. Saffron-Hill,

—at 67, 8 doors from Vine-street.

Saffron-Hill (Great), Holborn-Bridge,—the continuation of Field-lane, where there are Nos. 1 and 150, extending to Vine-st.

Saffron - Hill (Little),—the N. continuation of the last.

Saffron-Pl. Gt. Saffron-Hill,—at 57, 4 doors S. of Castle-street.

Saffron - Street, Peter-St.—1st on the L. from 30, Great Saffron-hill.

Saffron-Terrace,—part of the W. side Gt. Saffron-hill, say at No. 100.

Salem-Chapel, Leading-Street, Shadwell,—between Foxes-lane and Griffin-st.

Salisbury-Arms Canal - Ware-house,—behind 36, Cow-lane, 12 doors on the L. from Snow-hill.

Salisbury-Court, Fleet-St.—at 81, 2d coach-turning on the L. from Fleet-market.

Salisbury - Crescent, Lock's Fields, Walworth,—the continuation of Pitt-st. Kent-road.

Salisbury-Lane, Bermondsey,— 2d on the R. below Mill-stairs.

Salisbury-Mews, Gt. Quebec-St. Marybone,—1st on the L. from the New-road.

Salisbury-Pl. New-Road, Mary-bone,—S. side, from John-st. to Gloucester-pl.

Salisbury-Pl. Lock's Fields, Wal-worth,—part of the L. side the road from Rodney-row

Kent-road, to Park-pl. East-lane.

Salisbury-Pl. Salisbury-St. Bermondsey,—2d on the R. from Rotherhithe-wall.

Salisbury-Sq.—a few doors on the R. in Salisbury - court from 81, Fleet-st.

Salisbury-St. Strand,—at 77, 5 doors E. of Adam-st. Adelphi.

Salisbury-St. Bermondsey,—op. Fountain-stairs, ⅓ of a mile below St. Saviour's dock.

Sally's Alley, London-St. Ratcliffe,—at 44, 1st on the R. from Queen-st.

Salmon's Lane, Ratcliffe,—from the N. end of White-horse-st. to Limehouse.

Salmon's Place, Salmon's Lane, —7th on the L. from the Commercial-road.

Salmon's Row, Salmon's Lane, —at the back of the last.

Salmon and Ball-Court, Bunhill-Row,—at 94, S. side of Banner-st.

Salmon and Ball-Passage,—the E. end of Salmon and Ball-court.

Salter's Alley, Green-Bank,— 2d on the L. from Wapping-church.

Salters-Alms - Houses, Monkwell - St. — 12 houses on the E. side, adjoining Hart-street.

Salter's Court, Bow-Lane,—14 doors on the R. from Bow-church, Cheapside.

Salter's Court, Russell-St. Bermondsey,—2d on the L. from Church - st. towards Dock-head.

Salters-Hall-Court, Cannon-St. —at 82, by the church.

Salters-Hall. Entrance by the last.

Saltpetre-Bank, Rosemary-Lane. See Dock-St.

Salutation-Court, Broad-Street. St. Giles's,—5 doors E. of Monmouth-st.

Salutation Court, Lower Thames-St.—at 101, op. Billingsgate.

Salvadore-House, Bishopsgate, —behind 200, 2 doors N. of the church.

Samaritan-Society,—held at the London-hospital, Whitechapel-road.

Sambrook-Court, Basinghall-St. —at 25, nearly opposite the church.

Sampson's Gardens, Wapping, —the N. end of Globe-st.

Sampson's Pl. Mile-End,—W. side the Jews-hospital, 1¼ mile on the R. from Aldgate.

Samuel-Pl. George-St. Portland-Pl.—2 doors from 23, Upper Marybone-st.

Samuel - Street, Church-Street, Bethnal-Green,—at 74, ⅓ of a mile on the L. from 65, Shoreditch.

Samuel-Street, Booth-St. Spitalfields,—the E. end, from 50, Brick-lane.

Samuel - Street, St. George's East,—2d W. of Cannon-st.-road, extending from John-st. to James-st.

Sand-Yard, Clerkenwell-Green, —at the S. W. corner.

Sandall-Street, Grange-Walk,— 1st on the L. from Bermondsey-sq.

Sanders's Builds. Horse-Shoe-

Alley, Moorfields,—3d on the L. from 14, Wilson-st.

Sanders's Court,—on the S. side the last.

Sanders's Court, Gt. Peter-St. Westr.—3 doors W. of Perkins's rents.

Sanders's Court, Saint John-St. Clerkenwell,—nearly opposite Corporation-row.

Sanders's Court, Peter-St. Mint, —3d on the L. from Redcross-street.

Sanders's Gardens, Kingsland-Rd.--at 60, a few doors on the L. from Shoreditch-church.

Sandford-Row, South-St. East-Lane, Walworth,—3d on the R. from Apollo-builds.

Sandy's Row, Artillery-Lane,— the 1st on the R. from 54, Bishopsgate.

Sandy's Street, Widegate-St.— 1st on the R. from 50, Bishopsgate.

Sans-Pareil-Theatre,410,Strand, —op. Adam-street, Adelphi.

Saracen's Head-Inn, Snow-Hill, —W. side St. Sepulchre's chur.

Saracen's Head-Inn, Friday-St. —6 doors on the R. from 36, Cheapside.

Saracen's Head-Inn, Aldgate,— 3 doors on the R. from Fenchurch-st.

Saracen's Head - Yard, Camomile-St.—7 doors from Bishopsgate.

Sarah-St. New Gravel-Lane,— at 145, 12 doors from Wapping-wall.

Sarah-St. Bethnal-Green,—continuation of Nicols-row, entering by 30, Church-st.

Sardinian-Chapel, Duke-Street, — a few yards on the L. from 52, Lincoln's-inn-fields.

Sarn's Alley, Rotherhithe-St.— at 376, near Rotherhithe-stairs.

Sarnell-Court, Dock - Head,— 1st E. from Charles-st. Horse-lydown.

Sash-Court, Wilson-St.—1st on the R. from Moorfields.

Satchwell's Rents, Church-St. Bethnal-Green,—at 82, W. side of Thorold-sq.

Satchwell-St.—1st on the R. in the last from 82, Church-street.

Sauer's Court, Phœnix-Street, Spitalfields,—3d on the L. from 168, Brick-lane.

Savage-Court, Widegate-St.— at 30, 7 doors on the L. from 52, Bishopsgate.

Savage - Gardens, Crutched - Friars,—at 21, 3d on the R. from 64, Mark-lane.

Savannah-Pl. Essex-St. Kingsland-Road,—6 doors on the R. from the said road.

Saville-Builds. Aldgate,—at 17, 10 doors E. of the church.

Saville-Builds. Stepney-Green, —the corner of Cross-row.

Savil-Builds. Lambeth-Walk,— op. Winter's-pl. and Walnut-tree-walk.

Saville-Passage, Saville-Street, Burlington-Gardens,—the N. end, under the archway.

Saville-Pl. Lambeth,—the W. continuation of Canterbury-place.

Savil-Pl. Lambeth - Walk,—2d on the R. from the New chapel.

Saville-Pl. Mile-End-Road,—S.
side, near the Plough, 2¼
miles on the R. from Aldgate.
Saville - Row, Mile-End-Road,
—S. side, op. the Bell and
Mackarel, near the last.
Saville-Row, Walworth High-
St.—L. side, ¼ of a mile from
the Elephant and Castle.
Saville-St. or Row, Burlington-
Gardens,—1st on the R. in
Vigo-lane,from 148,Swallow-
street.
Saint Saviour's Church-Yard,
High-St. Boro.—at 296, 3d
on the R.from London-bridge.
Saint Saviour's Dock, Horsely-
down,—¾ of a mile below
London-bridge, op. Hermi-
tage-dock.
St. Saviour's Workhouse, Pep-
per-St. Boro.—S. end of it,
entering by the W. end of
Queen-st.
Savory's Wharf, Millbank-St.
Westr.—op. Wood-st. ¼ of a
mile above the bridge.
Savoy, Strand, — entrance by
124, middle S. side, and op.
Exeter-change.
Savoy-Steps,—at 107, Strand,
W. side the last.
Sawyers-Court,Clement's Lane,
—1st on the R. from Clare-
market.
Sawyer's Yard (Old),—3 doors
S. of the last.
Sawyer's Yard(New), Clements-
Lane,—at 60, 7 doors S. of
the last.
Sawyer's or Sayer's Buildings,
Phœnix-St. Spitalfields,—be-
tween Hope-st. and Grey
Eagle-st.

Sawyer - St. Blackwall Cause-
way,—4th on the R. from
Poplar.
Sayer's Builds,—on the S. side
of Park-st. a few doors on
the L. from Lime Kilns-dock,
Limehouse-hole.
Say's Craftsman Newspaper-
Office,—at 10, Ave - maria-
lane.
Scale's Builds. Spa Road-Pas-
sage, Bermondsey,—2d on
the L. from 13, Printers-pl.
Scalesbury-Row, Battle-Bridge,
St. Pancras, — N. end of
Clarence-passage.
Scallop-Court,Gt. Carter-Lane,
—2 doors on the L. from
Creed-lane, entering by 14,
Ludgate-st.
School for Female Orphans of
the Clergy,—next door to the
chapel in Chapel-st. Lisson-
green.
School for the Indigent Blind,
St. George's Fields,—on the
S. side the Obelisk, Black-
friars-road.
School for Licensed Victuallers
Friendly-Society, Up. Ken-
nington-Lane,—a few doors
W. of the Windmill-tavern.
School for Debtors - Children,
Newington - Road,—3 doors
on the R. from the King's
Bench.
School-House-Court, Nightin-
gale-Lane, E. Smithfield,—at
2½, 1st on the R. from Burr-
street.
School-House-Lane, Cock-Hill,
Ratcliffe,—at 104, 2d on the
left from Shadwell High-st.
School - House - Passage, Up.

Thames-St.—at 184, W. side
Queen-st.

School-House-Yard, Aylesbury-
St. Clerkenwell,—14 doors
on the R. from 103, St. John-
street.

School-House-Yard, Ironmonger-Row, St. Luke's,—7 doors
on the R. from 97, Old-st.

School-House-Yard, Felix-St.
Lambeth,—1st on the L. from
Bridge-road.

Sclater-St. Brick-Lane, Bethnal-
Green,—at 154, the 3d on
the R. from Church-st.

Sclater-Court, Sclater-St.—3
doors on the L. from Brick-
lane.

Scooner's Alley, Wapping-Wall,
—at 28, three doors E. of
Star-st.

Scotch-Church, Swallow-St.—
3 doors from Piccadilly.

Scotch-Church, London-Wall,—
N. end of Coleman-st.

Scotch-Court, Cross-Lane,—op.
the E. end of King-st. Drury-
lane.

Scotland-Yard (Gt.), Whitehall,
—35 doors on the L. from
the Strand.

Scotland-Yard (Middle), Whitehall,—2 doors S. from the last.

Scotland-Yard (Little or Inner).
See the last.

Scottish-Hospital, Crane-Court,
—the centre house facing the
entrance from 174, Fleet-st.

Scott's Wharf, Mill-St.—a few
doors on the L. from Dock-
head.

Scott's Yard, Dowgate-Hill,—
W. corner, by Up. Thames-st.

Scott's Yard, Bush-Lane,—7

doors on the R. from 22,
Cannon-st.

Scott's Yard, Whitecross-St.
St. Luke's,—at 176, middle
of the W. side.

Scotten's Gardens, Duke-Street,
St. George's Fields,—middle
of the E. side.

Seabrook-Pl. White-Lion-St.
Pentonville,—2d on the L.
from Islington.

Sea-Coal-Company's Office,—at
29, New Bridge-st. Black-
friars, 3 doors from Earl-
street.

Sea-Coal-Lane, Skinner-Street,
Snow-Hill,—at 14, 2d on the
R. from Fleet-market.

Seager-Pl. George-St. Battle-
Bridge,—middle of the N.
side.

Seal-Office, Somerset-Pl.—3d
door on the L. from the archway, 152, Strand.

Seal-Office, Inner Temple-Lane,
—a few yards on the R. from
15, Fleet-st.

Secondaries-Office, King's-Bench-
Walk, Temple,—at the bot-
tom of Mitre-court, on the L.
from 44, Fleet-st.

Secondaries-Office,—at 28, Coleman-st. 16 doors on the L.
from Lothbury.

Secretary of Bankrupts-Office,
—bottom of Quality-court,
from 47, Chancery-lane.

Secretary of State's Office,
Home Department,—1st door
on the L. in the small square
at the W. end of Downing-
st. from Whitehall.

Secretary of State's Office,
Foreign Department, White-

hall,—3d house on the R. from the Horse Guards, towards Westminster.

Secretary of State's Office, War-Department,--the door facing the W. end of Downing-st.

Seething-Lane, Gt. Tower-St.—at 56, 1st E. of Mark-lane.

Selby's Mews, Berkeley-St.—1st on the R. from Portman-square.

Selector Newspaper-Office,—at 10, Ave-maria-lane, opposite Paternoster-row.

St. Sepulchre's Charity-School, Ball-Court,—entrance by 14, Giltspur-st.

St. Sepulchre's Church, Snow-Hill,—at the corner of Gilt-spur-st.

Saint Sepulchre's Workhouse, West-St.—4 doors on the R. from 88, W. Smithfield.

Seran's Place, Bethnal-Green,—W. side of Abingdon-st. by Duthie's nursery.

Serjeants-Inn, Fleet-St.-50 doors on the R. from Temple-bar.

Serjeants-Inn, Chancery-Lane,—4 doors on the R. from 192, Fleet-st.

Serle-St. Lincoln's - Inn-Fields,—at the S. E. corner, extending to 50, Carey-st. Chancery-lane.

Sermon - Lane, Little Carter-Lane,—at 7, op. Black Swan-alley, from 20, St. Paul's church-yard.

Sessions-House, Old - Bailey,—op. 52, middle of the E. side.

Sessions - House, Clerkenwell-Green,—the large building on the W. side.

Sessions - House, Borough,—at the Town-hall, St. Marga-ret's hill.

Sessions-House, Horsemonger-Lane,—W. side the County-Gaol.

Seven Dials, St. Giles's,—S. end of Gt. St. Andrew-st. from Broad-st. and N. end of Little-st. Saint Andrew's st. from St. Martin's lane.

Seven Houses, Deptford Lower-Road,—part of the R. side, $\frac{1}{4}$ of a mile S. of China-hall.

Seven-Houses, Trinity - Street, Rotherhithe,—op. 29, by the 3 mile stone.

Seven-Islands, Mill-Pond, Bermondsey,—S. side Mill-pond-street.

Seven - Star - Alley, Ratcliffe-Highway,—at 81, E. side Old Gravel-lane.

Seven-Star-Court, Nightingale-Lane, East - Smithfield,—at 30, middle of the W. side.

Seven-Star - Court, Rosemary-Lane,—at 22, 3d on the R. from Tower-hill.

Seven-Star - Yard, Brick-Lane, Spitalfields,—at 188, 6th on the L. from Whitechapel.

Seven - Steps - Alley, Rother-hithe - St.—at 360, $\frac{1}{4}$ of a mile W. of the church.

Seven-Steps-Alley, Gt. Gardens,—1st on the L. from Saint Catherine's lane.

Seward-Street, Goswell-St. —at 80, the 4th N. of Old-st.

Seymour-Court, Latham's Place, Sommers-Town,—1st on the R. from 1, Sommers-place West.

Seymour - Court, Chandos-St.

—9 doors on the R. from 27,
St. Martin's lane.

Seymour-Mews, Lower Sey-
mour-St.—3 doors on the L.
from Portman-sq.

Seymour-Mews, Lower,—the E.
end of the last.

Seymour-Pl. Portman-Sq.—the
continuation of Adam-street
West.

Seymour-Pl. Sommers-Town,—
⅓ of a mile on the R. from
the turnpike, Battle-bridge,
towards Marybone.

Seymour-Pl. Curzon-St. May-
fair,—W. end, near South
Audley-st.

Seymour-Pl. York-St. Walworth,
—⅛ of a mile on the L. from
Walworth High-st. and op.
the chapel.

Seymour-St. (Lower), Portman-
Square,—S. E. corner, leading
into Edward-st.

Seymour-St. (Upper),—the continuation of the last, to 12,
Edgware-road.

Shacklewell-Street, Tyssen-St.
Bethnal-Green,—10 doors
on the R. from 54, Church-st.

Shad-Thames, Horselydown,—
the last on the R. from Broad-
st. Horselydown-lane, extending to Dock-head.

Shadwell-Dock,—at the end of
Fox's lane from Shadwell-
church.

Shadwell-Dock-Stairs,—on the
E. side the last.

Shadwell High-St.—the E. continuation of Ratcliffe-highway to Cock-hill.

Shadwell-Gap,—at 161, High-
st. op. Market-hill.

Shadwell-Market,—S. side Shad-

well High-st. 10 doors below
the church.

Shadwell-Mews, Coleman-St.—
1st on the L. from 150, New
Gravel-lane.

Shadwell (Middle),—the 1st S.
to part of the High-st. from
Pope's hill to Broad-bridge.

Shadwell (Little),—the E. continuation of Lower Shadwell
to Bell-wharf.

Shadwell (Lower),—the E. continuation of Wapping-wall by
the Thames.

Shadwell (Upper). See Shadwell High-St.

Shadwell Water-Works,—at the
end of Pope's hill on the L.
from 75, Shadwell High-st.

Shadwell-Workhouse,—middle
of the W. side of Union-st.

Shaft's Court, Leadenhall-St.—
at 133, op. the East India-
house.

Shafts or Shaftsbury-Sq. York-
St. Westr.—between Horse-
shoe-alley and Smith's Rents.

Shaftsbury- Aldersgate-St.—
at 34, 15 doors N. of Falcon-
street.

Shaftsbury-Chapel. See the last.

Shakespear's Row, Pimlico,—3d
on the R. in Ranelagh-st.
from Arabella-row.

Shakespear's Walk,—at 48,
Shadwell High-st. leading to
24, Wapping-wall.

Shard's Row, New-Road, St.
George's East. See Saint
George's Place.

Sharp's Alley, West-St. West-
Smithfield,—2d on the R.
from 87, N. W. corner of
Smithfield.

Sharp's Buildings, Rosemary-

Lane,—part of the S. side, by Tower-hill.

Sharp's Court, Little Trinity-Lane,—3 doors from 199, Up. Thames-st.

Shaw's Court, Charles-St.—10 doors from 174, Drury-lane.

Shaw's Court, New-Alley, Boro.—at the S. end, behind St. George's church.

Shears-Alley, Twisters-Alley,—2d on the R. from 102, Bunhill-row.

Shearwood-Place, Turville-St. Bethnal-Green,—2d on the R. from 38, Church-st.

Sheen's Court, Holborn-Hill,—12 doors on the R. from Fleet-market.

Sheffield-St. Clare-Market,—the N. side, from Vere-st. to Portsmouth-st.

Shepherd's Alley, Up. Thames-St.—at 64, op. Garlick-hill.

Shepherd's Court, Up. Brook-St.—8 doors on the R. from the N. W. corner of Grosvenor-sq.

Shepherd's Court, Old Nicol-St. Bethnal-Green,—1st on the L. from Cock-lane.

Shepherd's Market, Mayfair,—N. end of White-horse-st. from Piccadilly.

Shepherd's Pl.—1st on the R. from the City-road towards the Shepherd and Shepherdess.

Shepherd's Place, White's Row, Spitalfields,—3 doors from Bell-lane.

Shepherd's Row, Bethnal-Green-Road,—part of the R. side, op. Wilmot-sq.

Shepherd's Square, Curzon-St. Mayfair,—at 38, 7 doors W. of Halfmoon-st.

Shepherd-St. Shepherd's Market,—from the S. side of it to Hertford-st.

Shepherd-Street, Oxford-St.—at 310, 3 doors E. of New Bond-st.

Shepherd and Flock-Court, White's Alley,—4th on the L. from 61, Coleman-st.

Shepherd and Shepherdess-Walk, City-Road,—E. side St. Luke's workhouse, $\frac{1}{2}$ a mile on the R. from Finsbury-square.

Sherborne-Lane, Lombard-St. —by 10, behind the church.

Sheriffs-Court, Guildhall,—entrance by the 1st door on the R. in the hall from King-st.

Sheriff of Middlesex-Commissioners-Office, Bedford-St.—at 15, op. Bedford-row.

Sheriffs-Office, Giltspur-Street Compter,—a few yards on the R. from Newgate-st.

Sherrard-Court, Tooley-St.—at 223, between Glean-alley and Joiner-st.

Sherrard-St. Golden-Sq.—1st on the R. in Titchborn-st. from the Haymarket.

Ship-Alley, Wellclose-Sq.—from the S. E. corner to Ratcliffe-highway.

Ship-Gardens, Horseferry-Road, Westr.—W. end, by the Ship.

Ship-Court, York-St. Westr.—1st on the L. from James-st.

Ship-Court, Old-Bailey,—at 66, 5 doors on the L. from Ludgate-hill.

SHI   SHO

Ship-Court, Poplar,—1st on the L. from Blackwall.

Ship-Court, Green-Bank,—1st on the R. from 81, Tooley-street.

Ship - Coach - Office,—at 46, Charing-cross.

Ship-Inn, High - St. Boro.—30 doors on the L. from London-bridge.

Ship - Place, Strand,—at 266, leading to Ship-yard.

Ship-St. Prussian - Island,—2d on the R. from 188, Wapping.

Ship-Yard, Strand,—at 266, about 12 doors on the R. west of Temple-bar.

Ship-Yard, Wardour-St. Soho, —ht 37, middle of the E. side.

Ship-Yard, Redcross-St. Cripplegate,—at 38, nearly op. Jewin-st.

Ship-Yard, Bishopsgate-Street Without,—at 118, N. side of Skinner-st.

Ship-Yard, Minories,—32 doors on the L. from Aldgate.

Ship-Yard, Green - Bank,—2d on the R. from 81, Tooley-street.

Ship-Yard, High-St. Boro.—33 doors on the L. from London-bridge.

Ship and Mermaid-Row, Snow's Fields,—7th on the L. from 237; Bermondsey-st.

Ship and Mermaid-Court,—1st on the R. in the last from Snow's fields.

Ship and Sun-Yard, East-St. Walworth,—1st on the L. from the High-st.

Ship-Tavern - Passage, Grace-church-St.—from 76, leading to Leadenhall-market.

Ship-Tavern-Wharf,—W. side of Ratcliffe-cross-stairs.

Shipwright-St. Blackwall-Cause-way,—3d on the R. from Poplar.

Shire-Lane (Gt.), Fleet-St.—adjoining the E. side of Temple-bar.

Shire-Lane (Little),—1st on the L. in the last, from Fleet-street.

Shire - Lane, Chelsea, — from behind the Bun-house towards Sloane-st.

Shirley's Court, Old Montague-St.—2d on the R. from Os-born-st.

Shoe-Lane, Fleet-St.—at 130, 24 doors on the R. from Fleet-market.

Shoemakers-Row, Blackfriars, —the last on the R. in Creed-lane, from 15, Ludgate-st.

Shoreditch High-St.—the N. continuation of Bishopsgate-street from Norton-falgate (where there are 1 and 249) to the church.

Short's Builds. St. James's Pl. Clerkenwell,—2d N. of the church.

Short-Cut, Hickman's Folly,—2d on the R. from Dock-head.

Short's Gardens, Drury-Lane,—15 doors on the R. from Broad-st. St. Giles's.

Short-Street, Cumberland - St. Shoreditch,—1st on the L. a few yards from the Curtain-road.

Short-St. Pavement, Moorfields,

—at 15, middle of the W. side.

Short-Street, Wentworth-St.—2d on the L. from Petticoat-lane.

Short - Street, Huntington - St. Kingsland-Road,--at 17, leading to Essex-st.

Short-St. Bethnal-Green,—1st on the L. in New Nicol-st. from Cock-lane.

Short-Street, Goulstone-St.—1st on the L. from 140, Whitechapel.

Short-Street, Tower-Street,—5 doors on the L. from the Asylum.

Short's Yard, Broad-St. Lambeth,—op. High-st.

Shorter's Court, Throgmorton-St.—1st on the R. from the Bank.

Shorter's Rents, White's Yard, —3d on the L. from 58, Rosemary-lane.

Shorter-St. Wellclose-Sq.—middle of the N. side, to 26, Cable-st.

Shoulder of Mutton-Alley, Fore-St. Limehouse,—at 52, a few yards on the L. below the Drawbridge.

Shouldham-Street, Queen-St.—4th on the L. from 61, Edgware-road.

Shovel-Alley, Great Gardens, St. Catherine's,—4th on the L. from Catherine's lane.

Shovel-Alley, Princes - Square, St. George's East,—at the N. E. corner.

Shovel-Court, Wood - St.—12 doors on the L. from 123, Cheapside.

Shrewsbury-Court, Whitecross-Street, St. Luke's,—at 192, 4th on the L. north of Chiswell-st.

Shropshire-Court, Pancras - St. Tottenham-Court-Road,—the corner of Up. Thornhaugh-street.

Shuter-Court, Basinghall-St.—at 42, 10 doors from London-wall.

Sick and Wounded-Office,—at the Transport-office, Dorset-sq. Cannon-row, Westr.

Sidmouth-Mews, Gray's - Inn-Lane,—1st N. of Sidmouth-street.

Sidmouth-Pl. Gray's-Inn-Lane, —W. side, nearly op. Acton-street.

Sidmouth-St. Gray's-Inn-Lane, —at the S. end of the last.

Sidney's Alley, Leicester-Sq.—N. W. corner, to Coventry-street.

Sidney-Grove, Sidney - St.—1st on the R. from the City-road.

Sidney's Pl. Sidney-St.—a few doors on the L. from the City-road.

Sidney-Pl. Upper Kennington-Lane,—a few doors E. of Vauxhall-gardens.

Sidney-St. City-Road,—the 1st on the R. from Islington, extending to Goswell-st.-road.

Sidney-Street,- Green-St. Bethnal-Green,—2d on the L. east from Bonner-st.

Signet-Office, Somerset-Pl.—the 3d door on the L. from the archway, entering between 151 and 152, Strand.

Silk-Street, Grub-St. Cripplegate,—by the chapel, middle of the W. side.

Z

Silver-Court, Silver-St. Mile-End New-Town,—middle of the W. side.

Silver-Court, Silver-St. Golden-Sq.—at 3, op. Gt. Pulteney-street.

Silver-Lion-Court, Poplar,—1st W. of North-st.

Silver-Pl. Stepney-Green,—2d along Prospect-pl.

Silver-St. Golden-Sq.—the continuation of Beak-st. from 45, Swallow-st.

Silver-Street, Southampton-St. Bloomsbury,—6 doors on the L. from 127, High-Holborn.

Silver-Street, Fleet-St.—behind 62, bearing to the R. in Bouverie-st.

Silver-Street, Wood-St. Cheapside,—from 32, to Falcon-square.

Silver-St. Bridgewater-Sq.—1st on the R. in Charles-st. from the S. E. corner.

Silver-St. Mile-End New-Town,—2d on the R. from 62, Brick-lane, along Pelham-st.

Silver-St. Stepney,—2d on the R. from Redman's row, Mile-end.

Silver-Street, King-St.—1st on the L. from 18, Old Gravel-lane.

Silver-St. Loman's Pond, Borough,—2d on the L. from Gravel-lane.

Silver St. Canterbury-Sq. Tooley-St.—at the back of the W. side.

Silver-St. Rotherhithe,—1st on the R. below Cuckold's Point.

Silver-St. Clerkenwell,—N. end of Turnmill-st. by the Sessions-house.

Silver-Lion-Gardens, Poplar,—3d on the L. from the Commercial-road.

Simpson's Pl. Birdcage-Walk, Bethnal-Green,—1st on the L. from the Nag's head, Hackney-road.

Simon's Buildings, Old Pye-St. Westr.—at 55, by Duck-lane.

Simonds-St. See Symonds-St.

Sion-Chapel. See Sion-Sq.

Sion's Court, Bermondsey-St.—at 122, three doors N. of the church.

Sion-Court, Philip-Lane,—10 doors on the L. from London-wall.

Sion-College, London-Wall,—7 doors W. of Aldermanbury.

Sion-Gardens, Aldermanbury,—at 44, 4 doors S. of London-wall.

Sion-Pl. East-Lane, Walworth,—part of the R. side, ⅛ of a mile from the Kent-road.

Sion-Sq. Mile-End Old-Town,—1st on the L. in Union-st. from 281, Whitechapel-road.

Sister's Close, Green-Church-Yard,—the houses immediately behind St. Catherine's st. S. side the Church-yard.

Six Clerks-Office, Chancery-Lane,—op. 62, six doors on the R. from 310, High-holborn.

Six Garden-Court, Paul's Alley,—a few doors on the L. from 62, Aldersgate-st. entering by Hare-court.

Size-Lane, Pancras-Lane, Cheapside,—8 doors on the R. from 83, Queen-st.

Size-Yard, Whitechapel-Road,

—at 22, nearly opposite the church.

Skin-Market, Blackman-Street, Boro.—at 63, op. the King's Bench.

Skinners Alms-Houses, Mile-End,—10 doors on the L. below the turnpike.

Skinners-Hall, Dowgate-Hill,—middle of the W. side.

Skinner's Place, Weston-Place, Sommers-Town,—1st on the L. from the turnpike.

Skinner's Pl. Sommers-Town,—op. Judd's pl. E. 1st on the L. from Battle-bridge.

Skinner's Pl. Leadenhall-Market,—E. end of Bull's head-passage.

Skinner-St. Sommers-Town,—1st on the R. from the turnpike, Battle-bridge, towards Marybone.

Skinner-Street, Snow-Hill,—the continuation of Holborn from Fleet-market to the Old Bailey.

Skinner-Street, Bishopsgate-Without,—at 120, about 24 doors N. of Sun-st.

Skinner's Yard, Old Bethlem,—N. end of Baker's builds.

Slade's Builds. Angel-Alley,—2d on the L. from 138, Bishopsgate.

Slade's Court, Red-Cross-Street, Boro.—at 54, twelve doors S. of Union-st.

Slade's Pl. Little Sutton-St.—3d on the R. from Goswell-street.

Slater-Court, Blue-Anchor-Yard,—4th on the L. from 43, Rosemary-lane.

Slater or Slaughter-St. Bethnal-Green. See Sclater-St.

Sleep's Alley, Saint John-St. Clerkenwell,—at 129, near ½ a mile on the L. from Smithfield.

Sloane-Pl. North-St. Brompton,—2d on the R. from Sloane-street.

Sloane-Sq. Chelsea,—between Sloane-st. and Lower Sloane-st. through which passes the King's road.

Sloane-St. Knightsbridge,—1st on the L. ⅜ of a mile from Hyde-park-corner.

Sloane-St. (Lower),—op. the last, from Sloane-square to Turks-row.

Sloane-Terrace,—opposite 134, Sloane-st.

Sly-Corner, Charlotte-Mews West, Portland-Pl.—L. corner, from 71, Charlotte-street.

Small-Pox-Hospital, Battle-Bridge,—facing the N. end of Gray's-inn-lane.

Smart's Builds. High Holborn,—at 184, 1st E. of Drury-lane.

Smart's Court, Cartwright-St.—2 doors on the L. from 32, Rosemary-lane.

Smart's Gardens, Bethnal-Green,—a group of small houses at the S. end of Wilmot-st.

Smart's Quay, Lower Thames-St.—at 21, E. side of Billingsgate.

Smart-Street, Green-St. Bethnal-Green,—2d on the R. east from Bonner-st.

Smith's Alley, Ropemakers-

Fields, Limehouse,—at 60, middle of the N. side.

Smith's Arms-Pl. See Black-smiths.

Smith's Buildings, Gray's-Inn-Lane,—end of White-hart-row, Battle-bridge.

Smith's Builds. Chequer-Alley,—the 3d on the R. from 99, Bunhill-row.

Smith's Builds. Angel-Sq.—the 2d on the L. from 137, Bish-opsgate-without.

Smith's Buildings, Long-Alley, Moorfields,—3d on the R. from Worship-st.

Smith's Builds. Leadenhall-St.—at 74, by Aldgate-pump.

Smith's Builds. Long-Lane, Ber-mondsey,—1st on the L. from the church.

Smith's Court, Gt. Windmill-St.—at 31, 5th on the L. from the Haymarket.

Smith's Court, Holborn-Hill,—at 93, opposite St. Andrew's church.

Smith's Court, Brackley-St.—2d on the R. from 9, Golden-lane.

Smith's Court, Whitechapel-Road,—at 65, ⅙ of a mile E. of the church.

Smith's Court, Lower Chapman-St.—5th on the L. from Can-non-st.-road.

Smith's Place, Skinner-St. Som-mers-Town,—1st on the R. from Judd's pl.

Smith's Pl. Gray's-Inn-Lane,—1st on the L. from Battle-bridge.

Smith's Pl. Cooper's Gardens, Hackney-Road,—the last on the R. towards Gascoigne-pl.

Smith's Pl. Wapping-St.—at 65, between Globe-st. and the London-docks.

Smith's Pl. Salmon-Lane, Lime-house,—6th on the L. from the Commercial-road.

Smith's Pl. Gibraltar-Row, St. George's Fields,—2d on the R. from Prospect-pl.

Smith's Rents, York-St. Westr.—4th on the L. from Queen-sq.

Smith's Rents, Saint John-St.—at 140, ⅙ of a mile on the R. from Smithfield.

Smith's Rents, Bankside, South-wark,—at 16, the 2d from Bank-end.

Smith's Rents, Union-Street, St. George's Fields,—last on the R. from the London-rd.

Smith's Rents, Birdcage-Alley, Boro.—the continuation of it, from 172, High-st.

Smith's Rents, Bermondsey-St.—at 165, nearly opposite the church.

Smith's Row, Bluegate-Fields, Shadwell,—middle of the E. side.

Smith-Square, Westr. (St. John's Church-Yard),—at 52, Mill-bank-st.

Smith-St. (Great), King's Road, Chelsea,—⅓ of a mile on the L. from Sloane-sq. leading to the W. side the Hospital.

Smith-St. (Little),—at 22, the 1st on the L. in the last from the King's road.

Smith-St. (Gt.) Westminster,—S. continuation of Dean-st. near the Abbey.

Smith-St. (Little),—1st in the last from Dean-st.

Smith-St.(Lower) Northampton-Sq.—1st on the R. in King-st. from 96, Goswell-st.

Smith-St. (Upper),—the continuation of the last.

Smith's Ways, Bermondsey-Wall,—E. side of Mill-stairs and St. Saviour's dock.

Smith's Ways, Wapping,—E. side the Dundee-wharf, ⅛ of a mile below Hermitage-bridge.

Smith's Wharf, Rotherhithe-Wall,—between East-lane-stairs and Fountain-stairs.

Smith's Yard, Up. Marybone-St.—at 44, 2d on the R. from Howland-st.

Smith's Yard, Curzon-St. Mayfair,—op. Half-moon-st.

Smith's Yard, Shepherd's Market,—1st W. of White-horse-street.

Smith's Yard,—op. Engine-st. Piccadilly.

Smith's Yard, Bermondsey-St.—at 101, 12 doors S. of Russell-st.

Smithfield-Bars, West-Smithfield,—at 74, N. side, being the entrance to St. John-st.

Smithfield-Market, West-Smithfield,—at the N. end of Giltspur-st. from Newgate-st.

Smithfield (Up. East),—extends from the E. side of Tower-hill to Parsons-st. Ratcliffe-highway.

Smithfield (Lower East),—the continuation of Butcher-row from the last to the Hermitage-bridge.

Smock-Alley, Spitalfields. See Artillery-Passage.

Snead's Court, Engine-St. Pic-

cadilly,—the N. end, opposite Brick-st.

Snipe-Alley, Arundel-St.—at 24, the 2d on the L. from 180, Strand.

Snow's Fields, Bermondsey,—the continuation of King-st. entering by 109, High-street, Borough.

Snow-Hill, Holborn-Bridge,—N. side Skinner-street, from Fleet-market to St. Sepulchre's church.

Snow's Rents, York-St. Westminster,—nearly op. Queen-square.

Snug's Builds. Little Warner-St. Clerkenwell,—at 14, 1st on the L. from Ray-st.

Society for the Encouragement of Arts,—12, John-st. Adelphi.

Society for the Suppression of Vice,—at 31, Essex-street, Strand.

Society for the Relief of Persons imprisoned for Small Debts,—7 doors on the R. in Craven-st. from 10, in the Strand.

Society for the Encouragement of Servants,—at 10, Pall-Mall.

Socrates-Pl. New-Inn-St. Shoreditch,—8 doors on the R. from New-inn-yard.

Soho-Sq.—end of Charles-st. from 412, Oxford-st.

Soll's Row, Hampstead-Road,—W. side, from Charles-st. to Frederick's pl.

Somerset-Buildings, Hackney-Road,—1st on the L. in Crabtree-row, from the said road.

Somerset-Court, Little Somer-

Z 3

set-St. Aldgate,—a few yards on the R. from 22, Somerset-street.

Somerset-House or Pl. Strand, —at 151, ¼ of a mile on the L. from Temple-bar.

Somerset-Pl. Castle-St. Finsbury-Sq.—2d on the L. from 18, Paul-st.

Somerset-Pl. Kennington-Common,—a few yards S. of the Horns-tavern.

Somerset-Pl. Deptford Lower-Road,—S. side Rotherhithe-Workhouse.

Somerset-Row, Palmer's Village,—a few doors on the R. from Brewers-green.

Somerset-Street, Duke-St. Manchester-Sq.—at 45, 5 doors on the L. from 174, Oxford-street.

Somerset-St. Aldgate,—1st E. of the Minories.

Somerset-St. (Little),—at 22, in the last, W. side.

Somerset-St.—bottom of Beaufort-builds. from 95, Strand.

Sommer's Pl. East, Sommers-Town,—the R. side the road to Marybone, ¼ of a mile from Battle-bridge.

Sommer's Pl. West,—continuation of the last.

Sommers-Quay, Lower Thames-St.—1st W. of Billingsgate.

Sommers-Stairs,—E. side the last.

Sommers-Town, St. Pancras,—on the R. from Battle-bridge turnpike towards Marybone.

Sommers-Town Terrace,—continuation of Ossulston-street from Phœnix-st.

Sope-Yard, Park-St. Boro.—4

doors on the L. from the Boro.-market.

Sophia-Place, Duke-Street, St. George's Fields,—1st S. of Webber-row.

Sots-Hole, Archer-Street, Gt. Windmill-St. Haymarket,—at the E. end, leading to Rupert-st.

South-Crescent, Tottenham-Court-Road. See Crescent.

South-Lambeth,—S. side of Vauxhall-turnpike, on the L.

South-London Water-Works, UpperKennington-Lane,—2d on the L. from Kennington-cross.

South-Mews, South-St. Manchester-Sq.—at 17, 3 doors from Manchester-st.

South-Molton-Street, Oxford-St.—at 294, 2d W. of New Bond-st.

South-Molton-Lane, Oxford-St. —on the W. side the last.

South-Pl. Moorfields,—part of the N. side, adjoining South-street.

South-Pl. Kennington-Cross,— N. side, the corner of Devonshire-st. Upper Kennington-lane.

South-Pl. Kennington,—N. side of the Common.

South-Row, New-Road, Sommers-Town,—op. Sommers-pl. West.

South-Sea-Chambers, Threadneedle-St.—at 41, W. side the South-Sea-House.

South-Sea-Court, Mint, Boro.— 2d on the L. in Little Guildford-st. from 75, Queen-street.

South-Sea-Court, Maze, Boro.

—20 doors on the L. from 195, Tooley-st.

South - Sea - House, Thread-needle-St.—adjoins 115,Bishopsgate-st.

South-Sea-House (Old),—at 19, Old Broad-st. op. the church.

South-St. King's Road, Chelsea, —1st on the R. from Sloane-sq. towards Fulham.

South-St. Manchester-Sq.—2d on the R. in Manchester-st. from the sq.

South-Street, South Audley-St. —at 17, 4th from Grosvenor-sq.

South-St. Moorfields,—N. side, between Finsbury-place and Wilson-st.

South-St.Spitalfields-Market,— 5th on the L. from 69, Bishopsgate, along Union-st.

South - St. Lambeth,—N. side the Terrace, op. the Three Stags.

South-St. Whitechapel-Road,— 2d E. of the London Hospital.

South-Street, West - Sq. Saint George's Fields,—middle of the S. side.

South-St. East-Lane, Walworth, —middle of the S. side, by Apollo-builds.

Southampton-Builds. Holborn, —at 318, W. side of Middle-row.

Southampton-Court, Southampton-Builds.—3 doors on the R. in the last from Holborn.

Southampton-Court, Southampton-Row,Bloomsbury,—from the middle of the E. side to Queen-sq.

Southampton - Court, Totten-

ham - Court-Road,—at 140, nearly op. Warren-st.

Southampton-Mews,New-Road, Tottenham - Court,—on the N. side of Southampton-pl.

Southampton-Mews, Southampton-Row, Bloomsbury,—middle of the W. side.

Southampton-Pl. New - Road, Tottenham-Court,—N. side, by the turnpike.

Southampton - Row, Edgware-Road,—at 83, op. Winchester-row, $\frac{1}{2}$ a mile on the R. from Tyburn-turnpike.

Southampton-Row,Bloomsbury, —continuation of King - st. from 120, High-Holborn.

Southampton-Street, Strand,--at 337, middle of the N. side.

Southampton-St. High-Holborn, —from 126, to Bloomsbury-square.

Southampton-St. Pentonville,— 2d on the R. from the chapel towards Battle-bridge.

Spa-Fields,—N. side of Clerkenwell, towards Islington.

Spa - Fields - Chapel, Clerkenwell,— 12 doors E. of the turnpike by the House of Correction.

Spa-Place, Spa-Fields,—E. side the turnpike by the House of Correction.

Spa-Road,—op. Rawstorne-st. to Sadlers-wells.

Spa-Row,—op. Owen's pl. to Sadlers-wells.

Spa - Road, Bermondsey,—the continuation of the Grange-road to Printers-pl.

Spa-Road - Passage, Bermondsey,—1st on the left E. from the Spa.

Span's Builds. St. Pancras,—the continuation of Vernon's builds. towards the church.

Span's Place, Brill-Pl. Sommers-Town,—N. end of Marson-street.

Spanish-Place, Manchester-Sq.—N. E. corner, extending to Charles-st.

Spark's Place, (Gt.) Duke's Pl. Aldgate,—at the S. E. corner.

Sparrick's or Spurrick's Row, Boro.—1st on the L. in Weston-st. from 35, Snow's fields.

Sparrow's Builds. Potters-Fields, Horselydown,—1st on the L. from the E. end of Tooley-street.

Sparrow - Corner, Rosemary - Lane,—N. side, adjoining the Minories.

Sparrow's Rents, Portpool-Lane,—at 47, 2d on the R. from 64, Leather-lane.

Speck's Builds. Booth-St. Spitalfields,—last on the R. from Brick-lane.

Speding's Gardens, North - St. Poplar,——1st from High-street.

Speldhurst-Street, Judd-St. Sommers-Town,—2d on the L. from Judd's pl.

Spencer-Place, Battle-Bridge,—N. W. corner of the Small-Pox-Hospital.

Spencer-Pl. Kennington-Common,—by the White Swan, Croydon-road.

Spencer-Row, Goswell-St.-Rd.—part of the W. side, by the turnpike.

Spencer-St. Northampton - Sq.—from the turnpike, Goswell-st. - road, to St. John-st.-road.

Spencer-Street, New-Inn-Yard, Shoreditch,—1st on the R. from 176, Shoreditch.

Spencer-Street, Saint George's East,—3d on the R. in Charles-st. from op. Bluegate-fields.

Spicer-Court, Spicer-St. Bethnal-Green,—1st on the R. from 82, Brick-lane.

Spicer-St. Brick - Lane, Spitalfields,—at 82, op. Hanbury's brewery.

Spikeman's Court, Little Portland-St. Marybone,—3 doors E. of Gt. Portland-st.

Spiller's Court, Webber-Row,—3d on the L. from Black-friars-road.

Spital-Court, Spital-St.—1st on the right N. of Pelham-st.

Spitalfields-School,—on the W. side the church.

Spital-Sq. Bishopsgate-Without,—at 10½, ⅓ of a mile on the right N. from the church.

Spital-St. Spitalfields,—2d on the R. in Spicer-st. from 82, Brick-lane.

Spital-St. Little,—the S. end of the last.

Spitalfields-Market, Spitalfields,—at 23, Paternoster-row, W. side the church.

Spitalfields -Work - House,—E. side of Charles-st. Mile-end New-Town.

Spital-Yard, Spital-Sq.—1st on the R. from Bishopsgate.

Splidt's Terrace, Church-Lane, Whitechapel,—1st on the R. from Cable-st.

Spotted-Dog Coach-Office,—at 298, Strand.

Spotted - Horse - Court, Shore-ditch,—at 197, 5 doors S. of Holywell-lane.

Spread - Eagle - Court, Gray's-Inn-Lane,—27 doors on the R. from Holborn.

Spread - Eagle - Court, Finch-Lane,—3 doors on the L. from Cornhill.

Spread-Eagle-Court, Kingsland-Road,—6 doors on the L. from Shoreditch.

Spread-Eagle-Court,Limehouse-Causeway, — 1st on the L. from Three-Colt-st.

Spread-Eagle - Court, Rother-hithe,—on the S. side the church, near Cow-court.

Spread-Eagle-Inn,Gracechurch-St.—at 84, twelve doors S. of Leadenhall-st.

Spring-Garden, Charing-Cross, —behind the W. side, entrance by 66, or at 51.

Spring-Garden-Pl.Pimlico,—N. side of Flask-row.

Spring-Garden, Mile-End New-Town. See Spring-St.

Spring-Garden-Court,Mile-End-Road,—⅓ of a mile on the L. below the turnpike, and the 1st E. from op. Stepney-green.

Spring-Garden-Mews, Charing-Cross, — on the S. side of New-street.

Spring-Garden - Pl. Stepney,—from the W. side the church towards the fields.

Spring-Garden (Old), Stepney, —1st on the L. in the last from the church.

Spring-Street, Dorset-St. Port-man-Sq.—5 doors W. from Baker-st.

Spring-Street, King Edward-St. Mile-End New-Town,—1st on the R. from Princes-st.

Spring-St. (Upper),—N. continuation of the last to York-street.

Spring-St. (Great), Shadwell,—adjoins the S. side the church-yard.

Spring-St. (Little), Shadwell,—4 doors from the E. end of the church-yard.

Spurling's Yard, Brick-St.—1st on the L. from Park-lane.

Spur-Inn, High - St. Boro.—at 98, ¼ of a mile on the L. from London-bridge.

Spyer's-Court, Back-St. Horse-lydown,—at 8, 1st on the L. from the E. end of Tooley-street.

Stable-Yard, St. James's,—from the W. end of the Palace, to St. James's Park.

Stable-Yard, St. John's Sq.—at 40, middle of the W. side.

Stacy's Repository, Gt. Port-land-St.—at 108, op. Little Titchfield-st.

Stacey - Street, Monmouth-St. St. Giles's,—2d on the R. from Broad-st.

Stafford's Alms-Houses, Gray's Inn-Lane,—at 78, op. Little James-st.

Stafford-Pl. Pimlico,—10 doors from Buckingham-gate.

Stafford-Pl. Hill-St. Finsbury-Sq.—1st on the R. from Paul-st.

Stafford-Row, Pimlico,—from Buckingham-gate to Ward's row.

Stafford-Street, Lisson - Green, —op. the Yorkshire-stingo.

Stafford-Street, Old Bond-St.— 1st on the L. from 58, Piccadilly.

Stag-Brewhouse, Westr. — W. end of Castle-lane, James-st.

Stag and Hounds-Yard, Blackman-St. Boro.—at 50, op. the Angel-inn.

Staining-Lane, Wood-St. Cheapside,—op. the N. end of Gutter-lane.

Stamford-St. Blackfriars-Road, —2d on the R. from the bridge.

Stamford-St. (Up.)—continuation of the last.

Stamp-Office, Somerset - Pl.— S. E. corner of the sq.

Stanbrook-Court, Piccadilly,— at 53, 3 doors E. of Bond-st.

Standige's Builds. Stoney-Lane, —2d on the L. from 95, Tooley-st.

Standcliffe's Lecture Room,— at 11, Took's court, Chancery-lane.

Stanford-Pl. East-Lane, Walworth,—1st on the R. from the Kent-road.

Stangage's Builds. Bermondsey New-Road,—1st on the R. from the Bricklayers-arms.

Stangate, Lambeth, —7 doors on the R. from Westminster-bridge.

Stangate-Street,—the continuation of the last, bearing to the L.

Stongate Pl. Stangate,—at 36, N. side Felix-st.

Stangate-Wharf, Lambeth,—1st above Westminster-bridge.

Stanhope - Row, Long - Lane, Bermondsey,—part of the L. side, near the church.

Stanhope-St. May - Fair,—1st on the L. in South Audley-street, from Curzon-st.

Stanhope-St. (Little), Hertford-St. May-Fair,—1st on the L. from Park-lane.

Stanhope-St. Clare - Market,— continuation of Newcastle-st. Strand.

Stanton's Wharf,—N. end of Stoney-lane, from 95, Tooley-st.

Staple-Court, Bermondsey-St.— at 166, nearly op. the church.

Staple's-Inn, Holborn,—8 doors on the R. from Middle-row.

Staple's-Inn-Buildings, Middle-Row, Holborn,—at 10, W. side the last.

Staple's Rents, Paradise-St. Rotherhithe,—at 85, a few doors on the R. from Mill-pond-bridge.

Stapleton's Coal-Wharf, Whitefriars,—W. side Whitefriars-dock.

Stapleton's Court, Ropemakers-St.—2d on the R. from Moorfields.

Star-Alley, Upper East-Smithfield,—10 doors on the L. east of Butcher-row.

Star-Alley, Fenchurch-Street,— from 52, to Mark-lane.

Star-Corner, Bermondsey-St.— the continuation of it, from Long-lane to the Grange-rd.

Star-Court, Strand,—entrance op. 218, a few doors on the R. from Temple-bar.

Star-Court, Chancery-Lane,—at 114, 18 doors on the L. from 193, Fleet-st.

Star-Court, Cross-Lane, — 3 doors on the L. from S. end of Newton-st. High-Holborn.

Star-Court, Little Compton-St. Soho, — between Greek - st. and Crown-st.

Star-Court, Grub-St. Cripplegate,—op. 68, middle of the W. side.

Star-Court, Bread-St.—9 doors on the L. from 46, Cheapside.

Star-Court, Bread-St. Hill,—5 doors from Bread-st.

Star-Court, Mint-St. — at 30, 4th on the L. from 156, Boro.-High-st.

Star-Court (Little), — 2 doors W. of the last.

Star-Court, Bermondsey-St.—at 250, 35 doors on the R. from Tooley-st.

Star-Court, Gt. Eastcheap,—7 doors on the L. from Fish-st. hill.

Star-Court, Nightingale-Lane, E.-Smithfield,—at 30, middle of the W. side.

Star Newspaper - Office, — on the N. side of Fleet-st. by Temple-bar.

Star-Passage, Piccadilly, — 20 doors on the R. from the Haymarket.

Star-Pl. Lower Chapman-St.—last on the L. from Cannon-st.-road.

Star-St. Shadwell,—the continuation of Shakespear's walk from 48, High-st. to 24, Wapping-wall.

Star-Yard, Carey-St. Lincoln's-

Inn-Fields,—1st on the R. from 99, Chancery-lane.

Star-Yard, Blackman-St. Boro. —at 96, middle of the W. side.

Star-Yard, Old Gravel-Lane,—at 103, by 65, Ratcliffe-highway.

Star and Garden - Yard, Ratcliffe Highway,—at 90, op. Bluegate-fields.

Starch-Alley, Goswell - St.—at 30, on the S. side of Old-st.

Starch-Yard. Old Gravel-Lane. See Star-Yard.

State-Paper-Office, Inner Scotland-Yd.—1st house on the L. from Gt. Scotland-yard.

Statesman Newspaper-Office,—at 87, Fleet-st.

Stationers-Alley, Ludgate-St.—at 35, 2d on the R. from St. Paul's-church-yard.

Stationers-Court, — N. end of the last.

Stationers - Hall, — on the N. side of Stationers-court.

Stave Yard, Wapping-St. — at 332, ⅛ of a mile below Hermitage-bridge.

Staverton - Row, Newington - Butts,—E. side, by the Elephant and Castle.

Steamfield-St. Ocean, Stepney, —1st on the L. from the N. side the church-yard.

Stebonheath-Terrace, Salmon-Lane, Ratcliffe,—part of the N. side, ⅛ of a mile from White-horse-st.

Steel's Court, Lee's Mews, Grosvenor-Square,—1st on the L. from 41, Park-st.

Steel's Yard, Gray's-Inn-Lane, —1st N. of Portpool-lane.

Steel-Yard, Up. Thames-St.—at 87, op. Bush-lane.

Steel's Yard, Gt. Tower-Hill,—at 33, 8 doors from Coopers-row.

Steel's Yard, Maze-Pond, Boro.—1st on the L. from Guy's Hospital.

Steelhouse-Lane, Stepney,—'from op. the Causeway towards the church.

Steers's Buildings, Robinson's Lane, Chelsea,—op. 28, 2d on the L. from Paradise-row.

Steers-Pl. Barbican,—10 doors on the R. from Aldersgate-street.

St. Stephen's Chapel,—E. side Westminster-hall.

St. Stephen's Church, Coleman-St.—7 doors on the L. from Lothbury.

St. Stephen's Church, Walbrook,—by the Mansion-house.

St. Stephen's Court, New Palace-Yard, Westminster,—E. side, by the Thames.

Stephen-Mews, Gresse-St.—5 doors on the L. from 23, Rathbone-pl.

Stephen-St. Tottenham-Court-Road,—at 29, 2d on the L. from Oxford-st.

Stepney-Causeway, Brook-St. Ratcliffe,—from the middle of the N. side, to the Commercial-road.

Stepney-Gap, Stepney-Causeway,—1st on the L. from the Commercial-road.

Stepney-Green,—¼ of a mile on -the R. in Mile-end-road, E. of the turnpike.

Stepney-Green-Passage, — 3 doors E. of the last.

Stepney-Green-Terrace,—from Prospect-pl. to Cross-row.

Stepney-Meeting-House-Charity-School,—at the N. end of White-horse-st.

Stepney-New-Sq. See Trafalgar-Sq.

Stepney-Old-Square, Stepney-Green,—near the N. side the Church-yard.

Stepney's Rents, Hackney-Rd.—8 houses on the R. side, between Shoreditch-church and Crabtree-row.

Steven's Builds. Bell-St. Paddington,—12 doors on the L. from Lisson-green.

Stew-Alley, Up. Thames-St.—at 54, op. Bread-st.-hill.

Stew-Alley-Stairs,—bottom of the last.

Steward's Court, Clerkenwell-Green,—at 33, N. side the Sessions-house.

Stewards-Office, Gray's-Inn,—by the Chapel, at the N. E. corner of Holborn-court.

Steward's Rents, Drury-Lane,—from 128, middle of the E. side, to Wild-st.

Steward-St. Spitalfields,—2d in Union-st. from 69, Bishopsgate.

Still-Alley, Bishopsgate-Without,—at 196, six doors N. of the church.

Still-Alley, Houndsditch.—at 104, nearly opposite St. Mary Axe.

Still-Alley, Blue-Gate-Fields,—6 doors from 245, High-st. Shadwell.

Still-Stairs, Horselydown,—N. end of Potter's fields from the bottom of Tooley-st.

Stillwell-Court, Maze, Boro.— at 25, 5th on the L. from 195, Tooley-st.

Stock-Exchange, — E. end of Capel-court, Bartholomew-lane.

Stock's Terrace, Poplar High-St.—middle of the S. side, op. the E.-India-Alms-Houses.

Stock-Weavers Alms - Houses, Kingsland -Road, — near ½ a mile on the R. from Shoreditch.

Stone-Builds. Lincoln's-Inn,— 1st on the R. from op. 55, Chancery - lane, near Holborn.

Stone - Court, Laundry - Yard, Westminster,—5 doors from Gt. Peter-st.

Stones-End, Borough,—at the S. end of Blackman-st. by the King's Bench.

Stone's Row, New-Road, Sommers - Town,.— nearly op. Chalton-st.

Sone-Stairs, Broad-St. Ratcliffe, —at 30, W. side the India-warehouse.

Stone-Stairs-Court, Broad-St. Ratcliffe, — at 94, op. the stairs.

Stone-Yard, Queen-St. Boro.— 20 houses on the R. from Union-st.

Stonecutters-Alley, Blackfriars, —the end of Cock-court, on the L. from 18, Ludgate-hill.

Stonecutters - Buildings, Little Queen-St.—17 doors on the L. from 223, High-Holborn.

Stonecutters-Court, Little St.

Martin's Lane,—13 doors on the R. from Long-acre.

Stonecutters-Court, Old-Street, St. Luke's,—at 89, E. side the church.

Stonecutters-St. Fleet-Market, —at 75, middle of the W. side.

Stonecutters-Yard, Kent-Street, Boro.—22 doors on the L. from St. George's church.

Stonemason's Yd. Stoney-Lane, —1st on the R. from 96, Tooley-st.

Stoney-Lane, Gravel - Lane,— 2d on the R. from 148, Houndsditch.

Stoney-Lane, Tooley -St.,— at 95, 3d open turning on the L. from London-bridge.

Stoney-St. Boro.-Market,—the W. side, extending to Clink-street.

Store- St. (Great) Tottenham-Court-Road,—4th on the R. from Oxford-st.

Store-St. (Little),—4 doors in the last from 78, Gower-st.

Story's Gate, St. James's Park, —at Gt. George-st. Westminster.

Strand,—extends from Charing-cross, where there are 1 and 487, to Temple-bar, where there is 236, about ¾ of a mile in length.

Strand-Lane, Strand,—at 168, nearly op. the New Church.

Strand - Lane - Stairs,—at the bottom of the last.

Stratford - Mews, Marybone - Lane,—at 67, 1st on the L. from Oxford-st.

Stratford-Mews, Oxford - St.— at 160, W. side the next.

A a

Stratford-Pl. Oxford - St.— at 159, op. South - Mo.ton-st. ¼ a mile on the L. from Tyburn-turnpike.

Streatham-Street, Charlotte-St. Bloomsbury,—6 doors south from 34, Gt. Russell-st.

Streatham-Mews, Streatham-St. Bloomsbury,——1st W. of Charlotte-st.

Street's Buildings, Mount - St. Grosvenor-Square,—at 75, 6 doors E. of Park-st.

Stretton-St. Piccadilly,—at 78, middle of the N. side.

Stretton-Yard,—2 doors in the last from Piccadilly.

Stringer's Row, Deptford Lower-Road, Rotherhithe,— 1st on the L. from the E. end of Paradise-row.

Strong's Buildings, East-India-Dock-Road, Poplar,—S. side, near the Dock-gate.

Stroud Waggon-Office, Grub-St. —6 doors on the R. from 97, Fore-st.

Strumbolo - House, Grosvenor-Row, Chelsea,—op. the Bun-House.

Strutton-Ground, Westminster, —the continuation of Great Chapel-st. from Broadway.

Strutton-Pl. Strutton - Ground, —8 doors on the L. from Gt. Peter-st.

Suffolk-Court, Harrow-St. Boro. —7 doors on the R. from Mint-st.

Suffolk-Lane, Up. Thames-St. —from 152, to Green-Lettuce-lane, and 30, Cannonstreet.

Suffolk-Mews, Middlesex-Hospital, Marybone,—W. side of it.

Suffolk-Pl. Bateman's Row,— 1st on the R. from 158, Shoreditch.

Suffolk-Pl. Hackney - Road,— adjoins Cambridge - heath - turnpike, near a mile on the R. from Shoreditch.

Suffolk-St. Marybone,—3 doors W. of Middlesex - Hospital, near Berner's-st.

Suffolk-St. (Little), Haymarket, —7 doors on the R. from Cockspur-st.

Suffolk-St. (Gt.)—1st in the last from the Haymarket to Cockspur-st.

Suffolk-St. Battle-Bridge, Saint Pancras,—1st on the L. in Edmond-st. from the Small-Pox-hospital.

Suffolk-St. Pentonville,—1st on the R. in White-lion-st. from Islington.

Suffolk-Street, Cannon-St.-Rd. —op. William-st. a few doors N. of the Commercial-road.

Suffolk-St. (Gt.) Blackman-St. Boro,—at 80. 1st on the L. from the King's Bench.

Suffolk-St. (Little),—3d on the R. in the last from 80, Blackman-st.

Sugar Bakers-Yard, Duke's Pl. —3d on the R. along Creechurch-lane, from 87, Leadenhall-st.

Sugar - Loaf - Alley, Bethnal - Green,—middle of the E. side the Green.

Sugar-Loaf - Court, Dorset-St. Salisbury-Sq.—at 100, 5th on the L. from 82, Fleet-st.

Sugar-Loaf-Court, Garlick-Hill, —10 doors on the R. from Bow-lane, Cheapside.

Sugar - Loaf - Court, Little-Elbow - Lane, — 3 doors from 176, Up. Thames-st.

Sugar-Loaf-Court, Long-Alley, —5th on the L. from Moorfields.

Sugar-Loaf-Cour', Bishopsgate-Without,—at 130, 12 doors N. of Sun-st.

Sugar-Loaf-Court, Angel-Alley. —3d on the L. from 138, Bishopsgate-without.

Sugar - Loaf - Court, Holywell-Lane,—at 52, 3d on the L. from 194, Shoreditch.

Sugar-Loaf-Court, Leadenhall-St.—at 50, op. Creechurch-lane.

Sugar-Loaf-Court, Bermondsey-St.—46 doors on the L. from Tooley-st.

Sugar-Loaf-Court, Essex-St.— 1st on the R. from 105, Whitechapel.

Sugar-Loaf-Court, Swan-St.— 2d on the R. from the Minories.

Summer-Pl. Stepney,—1st E. of Ocean-st. N. side the Churchyard.

Summer-Street, Eyre-St. — 12 doors on the R. from the N. end of Leather-lane.

Sumner's Builds. Bishopsgate, —at 22, a few doors on the R. north from the church.

Sun-Alley, Up.-E.-Smithfield,— at 20, nearly op. Butcher-row.

Sun-Alley, Golden - Lane,—at 32, 3d on the R. from Barbican.

Sun-Court,—1st in the last from Golden-lane.

Sun-Court, Grub-St. Cripple-

gate,—5th on the L. from Cmswell-st.

Sun-Court, Cloth-Fair,—3d on the L. from 60, West-Smithfield.

Sun-Court, Cornhill,—at 68, 7 doors W. of Bishopsgate - street.

Sun-Court, Little Swan-Alley, —last on the L. from 67, Coleman-st.

Sun-Court, Aldgate High-St.— at 20, 12 doors E. of the church.

Sun - Court, Curzon - St. May-Fair,—at 43, W. side of Half-moon-st.

Sun-Court, King-David-Fort,— 1st on the L. from King-David-lane, Shadwell.

Sun-Court, Mile-End,—$\frac{1}{8}$ of a mile on the L. below the turnpike.

Sun Fire-Office, Cornhill,—2d door W. of the Royal-Exchange ; also in Craig's-court, Charing-cross.

Sun Newspaper Office, Strand, —at 112, op. Exeter-Change.

Sun - Passage, Paddington - St. Marybone,—6 doors on the R. from High-st.

Sun-Place, Princes-Road, Lambeth,—1st on the L. from Kennington-cross.

Sun-Sq. Sun-St.—at 13, 1st on the L. from 149, Bishopsgate-without.

Sun-St. Bishopsgate - Without, —at 149, $\frac{4}{6}$ of a mile on the L. north of the church.

Sun-St. East-Lane, Walworth, —4th on the L. from the High-st.

Sun-Yard, Gray's-Inn-Lane,— 2d N. of Liquorpond-st.

Sun - Yard, Nightingale - Lane, East-Smithfield,—at 28, middle of the W. side.

Sun-Tavern-Fields, Shadwell,— on the N. side High-st. from King David-lane to Love-lane.

Sun-Tavern-Row, Gale's Rope-Walk,—2d on the R from King David-lane.

Sunday-Advertiser Newspaper-Office,—Catherine-st.Strand.

Sunday-Observer Newspaper-Office, — at 272, Strand, 5 doors W. of St. Clement's church.

Surat-Place; Smart-St. Bethnal-Green,—2d on the L. from Green-st.

Surgeons-College or Hall, Portugal-St. Lincoln's-Inn.Fields,—middle of the N. side, op. Carey-st.

Surrey-Builds. East-Lane, Walworth,—1st on the L. from Surrey-pl. Kent-road.

Surrey - Canal - Dock, Rotherhithe,—⅓ of a mile below the church.

Surrey-Chapel, Blackfriars-Rd. —¼ of a mile on the L. from the bridge.

Surrey - Dispensary, Union-St. Boro.—a few yards on the L. from 218, High-st.

Surrey-Gazette-Office,—at 154, High-st. Boro. by St. George's church.

Surrey-Institution, Blackfriars-Rd.—6 doors on the R. from the bridge.

Surrey - Mills, Rotherhithe,— near the Platform, ¼ of a mile W. of the church.

Surrey-Pl. Surrey-St.—at 30, 8 doors on the R. from 170, Strand.

Surrey-Place, Lower Queen-St. Rotherhithe,——behind 50, from Cow-lane to Silver-st.

Surrey - Pl. Kent-Road,—part of the R. side, ½ of a mile below the Bricklayers-arms.

Surrey-Road. See Blackfriars-Road.

Surrey-Row, Blackfriars-Road, —2d from Surrey-chapel towards the Obelisk.

Surrey - Square, Kent-Road,— 1st on the R. below East-lane.

Surrey-Stairs,—at the bottom of Surrey-st. Strand.

Surrey-St. Strand,—at 172, the 4th on the L. from Temple-bar.

Surrey-St. (Gt.) Blackfriars-Rd. —part of the E. side, say from Holland-st. to Surrey-chapel ; also part of the op. side, say from Cross-st. to Christ-church.

Surrey-St. (New), Blackfriars-Road,—part of the W. side, say from Stamford-st. to Christ-church.

Susannah-Place, Curtain-Road, —part of the W. side, near Old-st.-road.

Susannah-Row, Curtain-Road, —5th on the L. from Worship-st.

Sussex-Pl. Kent-Road,—part of the R. side, ¾ of a mile below the Bricklayers-arms.

Suter's-Buildings, Chapel-Path, Sommers-Town,—at 29, between Ossulston-st. and Middlesex-st.

Sutton's Court, Bishopsgate,—at 77, twelve doors S. of the church.

Sutton-Place, Lisson-Green,—nearly op. 18, Lisson-st.

Sutton-St. Soho-Sq.—at 21, E. side, leading to Crown-st.

Sutton-St. (Little),—1st on the L. in the last, from 21, in the square.

Sutton-St.(Great),—at 128,Goswell-st. extending to 45, St. John-st.

Sutton-St. (Little),—6 doors N. of the last.

Sutton-St. Maze-Pond, Boro.—op. S. end of Guy's hospital.

Swain's Alley. Castle-Lane, Boro.—2d on the L. from Castle-st.

Swain's Yard, Park-Lane,—6th on the R. from Piccadilly.

Swallow - Gardens, Rosemary-Lane,—at 128, 6th on the L. from the Minories.

Swallow-St. Piccadilly,—at 45, op. St. James's church, where there are Nos. 1 and 160.

Swan-Alley, St. Ann's Court,—a few yards on the R. from 31, Wardour-st.

Swan-Alley (Little), Saint John-St. Clerkenwell,—at 72, third on the L. from West-Smithfield.

Swan-Alley (Great), Coleman-St.—at 66, 6th on the R. from Lothbury.

Swan-Alley (Little),—E. end of the last.

Swan-Alley, Up. E. Smithfield,—at 102, 8 doors W. of Nightingale-lane.

Swan-Alley, Rotherhithe-St.—

at 311, ⅛ of a mile on the R· below the church.

Swan-Brewery,Chelsea,—at the S. end of Swan-walk.

Swan-Court,· Mount-St. Grosvenor-Sq.—at 48, 3d on the L. from Park-lane.

Swan-Court, Bream's Buildings,—E. end, entrance by 37, Chancery-lane.

Swan - Court, Golden-Lane,—behind 75, 1st on the R. in Cowheel-alley.

Swan-Court, Swan-St. Bethnal-Green,—4 doors on the R. from 155, Church-st.

Swan-Court, Petticoat-Lane,—at 114, 6th on the R. from Aldgate.

Swan-Court, Mansel-St. Goodman's Fields,—2 doors N. of Swan-st.

Swan-Court, Rosemary-Lane,—at 57, W. side of White's yd.

Swan-Court, Narrow-Wall, Lambeth,—a few doors W. of Cuper's Bridge.

Swan-Court, William-St. Blackfriars-Road,—nearly opposite York-st.

Swan-Gardens, Haberdashers-Walk, Hoxton,—on the S. side Pimlico, by Gloucester-terrace.

Swan-Inn, Holborn - Bridge,—op. the N. end of Fleet-market.

Swan with Two Necks-Inn,Lad-Lane,—at 10, op. Milk - st. Cheapside.

Swan with Two Necks-Inn, Gt. Carter - Lane, — op. Dean's court, from 4, Saint Paul's-church-yard.

A a 3

SWA

Swan-Inn (One), Bishopsgate, —at 180, twenty doors N. of the church.

Swans-Inn (Two), Bishopsgate, —at 186, 15 doors N. of the church.

Swans-Inn (Four), Bishopsgate, —at 82, 18 doors S. of the church.

Swan Coach - Office, Charing-Cross,—3 doors on the R. towards the Horse-guards.

Swan-Inn, Whitechapel,—at 20, 10 doors W. of Red-lion-st.

Swan-Inn, Blackman-St. Boro. —S. side of Saint George's church.

Swan-Lane, Swan-Yard, Blackman-St.—1st on the L. from St. George's church.

Swan-Lane, Up. Thames-St.—at 102, 1st W. of London-bridge.

Swan-Lane (Old),—1st W. of the last.

Swan - Lane, Rotherhithe,—at 310, ⅛ of a mile below the church.

Swan-Mead, Bermondsey-New-Road,—E. end of Brandon-street.

Swan-Passage, Gt. Portland-St. —at 100, 4 doors S. of Foley-place.

Swan-Pl. Kent-Road,—4th on the R. below the Bricklayers-arms.

Swan-Pl. Mile-End,—S. end of Epping-place, by the turn-pike.

Swan-Stairs (Old), Up. Thames-St.—1st stairs above London-bridge.

Swan-Street, Church-St. Beth-

SWE

nal-Green,—at 154, 10 doors W. of Brick-lane.

Swan-St. Minories,—at 47, middle of the E. side.

Swan-St. Nightingale-Lane,—at 5, 1st on the R. from Up. E. Smithfield.

Swan-St. Kent-Road,—4th on the L. below the Bricklayers-arms.

Swan-Walk, Paradise-Row, Chelsea,—op. 30, by the Botanic-garden.

Swan-Yard, Oxford-St.—at 270, 8 doors E. of N. Audley-st.

Swan - Yard, Knightsbridge,—W. side of Sloane-st.

Swan - Yard, Strand,—at 331, op. Somerset-house.

Swan-Yard, Tothill-St. Westr. —1st on the R. from the Abbey.

Swan-Yard, Shoreditch High-St. —at 54, nearly op. Holy-well-lane.

Swan - Yard, Whitechapel,—at 20, 10 doors W. of Red-lion-street.

Swan-Yard, Mile-End-Road,—3d on the left E. from the Old Globe, ½ a mile below the turnpike.

Swan-Yard, Blackman-St. Boro. —at 1, by Saint George's church.

Swan-Yard, Lambeth,—op. the church.

Swan-Yard, Bermondsey-Street. See Black Swan.

Swan and Hoop Passage, Cornhill,—11 doors on the R. from the Mansion-house, leading to 78, Lombard-st.

Swedish Church, Princes - Sq.

St. George's East,—in the centre of the square.

Sweeds-Court, Trinity-Lane,— 6 doors W. of Bow-lane, Cheapside.

Sweedland-Passage, Moor-Lane, Cripplegate,—N. end, on the left.

Sweedland-Court, Bishopsgate-Without,—at 48, 4 doors S. of Widegate-st.

Sweetapple-Court, Bishopsgate-Without,—at 157, 8 doors S. of Sun-st.

Sweetapple - Court, Austin-St. Bethnal-Green,—at 29, the last on the L. from Shoreditch-church.

Sweeting's Alley, Cornhill,—at 87, E. side the Royal-Exchange.

Sweeting's Rents,—E. side the last.

Swinton-St. Gray's-Inn-Lane,— ¾ of a mile on the R. from Holborn.

Swiss-Chapel, Moor-St. Seven-Dials,—3 doors on the R. from Monmouth-st. towards Crown-st.

Saint Swithin's Church, Saint Swithin's Lane,—corner of Cannon-st.

St. Swithin's Lane, Lombard-St.—1st on the R. from the Mansion-house.

Sycamore-Row, Old-St.—1st on the R. from Goswell-st.

Symond's Inn, Chancery-Lane, —23 doors on the R. from 193, Fleet-st.

Symond's St. Sloane-Sq. Chelsea, —N. W. corner.

Symond's Wharf, Tooley-St.—

on the W. side of Stanton's wharf, Stoney-lane.

Synagogue (Gt.) Duke's Pl.—a few doors on the L. in Duke-st. from Aldgate.

Synagogue (for Dutch Jews), —behind 53, Leadenhall-st.

Synagogue (for Dutch Jews), Church-Court,—a few yards on the L. from 66, Fenchurch-street.

Synagogue (for Portuguese Jews), Bevis-Marks,—at 10, by Heneage-lane.

Synagogue (for German Jews), Denmark - Court,—1st door on the R. from 382, Strand.

TABERNACLE, Moorfields, —a few doors on the L. in Tabernacle - row, from 36, City-road.

Tabernacle-Alms - Houses,—on the W. side the Tabernacle.

Tabernacle - Alley, Fenchurch-St.—at 128, op. Mincing-lane.

Tabernacle-Place, Tabernacle-Walk,—at 56, nearly facing the Tabernacle.

Tabernacle-Row, City-Road,— at 36, 3d on the R. ⅕ of a mile from Finsbury-sq.

Tabernacle-Sq. Old-St.-Road,— N. end of Paul-st.

Tabernacle-Walk, Finsbury-Sq. —the continuation of Windmill-st. to the Tabernacle.

Talbot-Court, Gracechurch-St. —from 55 to 46, Little East-cheap.

Talbot-Inn, High-St.—at 74, by St. Margaret's-hill.

Talbot-Inn, Whitechapel,—at 25, five doors W. of Red-Lion-street.

Talbot-Yard, Gray's Inn-Lane, —op. the King's road.

Tallow-Chandlers Hall, Dowgate-Hill,—5 doors on the R. from Cannon-st.

Tanfield-Court, Temple,—E. side of Lamb's builds. being the 2d on the L. in Inner Temple-lane from 15, Fleet-street.

Tapping's-Rents, Ewer-St. Boro. —10 doors from Duke-st.

Tash-Court, Tash-St.—1st on the L. from 43, Gray's Inn-lane.

Tash-St. Gray's Inn-Lane,—at 43, 1st street on the R. from Holborn.

Tattersall's Repository, Grosvenor-Pl.—1st on the R. from Hyde Park corner.

Tattle-Court, Bermondsey-St. —at 246, six doors N. of Snow's fields.

Tatum's Place, Lock's Fields, Walworth,—1st from East-lane, extending from John-st. to Park-pl.

Tavern-Terrace, Blackwall,— by E. India-dock-gate.

Tavistock-Court, Covent-Garden,—S. E. corner.

Tavistock-Mews, Tavistock-St. —3 doors from Tottenham-court-road.

Tavistock-Mews, Little Coram-St. Russell-Sq.—middle of the W. side.

Tavistock-Pl. Tavistock-Sq.—

2d on the right N. from Russell-sq.

Tavistock-Row, Covent-Garden, —S. side, E. from Southampton-st.

Tavistock-Sq.—N. side Russell-sq. towards Sommers-town.

Tavistock-Street, Bedford-Sq.— S. W. corner, to Tottenham-court-road, near Oxford-st.

Tavistock-St. Covent-Garden,— 1st on the R. in Southampton-st. from 387, Strand.

Tax-Office, Somerset-Pl.—2d door at the back of the building which forms the E. side of the sq.

Tax-Office, Bermondsey-St.—at 280, middle of the W. side.

Taylor's Builds. Kingsland-Rd. —part of the L. side, ⅓ of a mile from Shoreditch.

Taylor's Court, Bow-Lane,—at 30, 28 doors from Cheapside.

Taylor's Court, Lambeth-Hill, —2 doors from the Old Change.

Taylor's Court, Saint John-St.-Road,—at 13, a few doors N. of Ashby-st.

Taylor's Court, Hare-Walk, Hoxton,—1st on the L. from op. the Ironmongers-alms-houses, Kingsland-road.

Taylor's Court, Farmer-St. Shadwell,—at 58, middle of the W. side.

Taylor's Passage, St. Martin's Lane, Charing-Cross,—at 31, N. side Chandos-st.

Taylor's Row, Islington-Road, —2d on the R. from St. John-st.

Taylor's Yard, Whitehind-Alley,

Bankside, Boro.—2d on the R. from Maid-lane.

Teanby's Buildings, Old-St.—at 135, 2d on the L. from Goswell-st.

Tear's Alley, High-St. Lambeth, —3d on the L. from the church.

Temple, —a number of builds. law-offices, &c. between the W. end of Fleet-st. and the Thames.

Temple-Bar,—the gate which divides Fleet-st. from the Strand.

Temple-Court, Inner Temple-Lane,—a few yards on the L. from 16, Fleet-st.

Temple-Gardens, Temple,—— upon the bank of the Thames, on the S. side the Temple.

Temple-Hall,—on the L side of Fountain-court, from Middle Temple-lane.

Temple-Lane,—the continuation of Lombard-st. bearing to the R. from 56, Fleet-st.

Temple-Lane (Inner), Fleet-St. —at 16, op. Chancery-lane.

Temple-Lane (Middle), Fleet-St.—4 doors on the R. from Temple-bar.

Temple-Pl. Blackfriars-Road, —E. side; by the Obelisk.

Temple-St. Whitefriars,—last on the R. in Water-lane, from 67, Fleet-st.

Temple-Street, St. George's Fields,—1st on the L. from the Elephant and Castle, towards West-sq.

Temple-Stairs, Middle Temple-Lane,—S. end, entrance by 5, Fleet-st.

Temple-Stairs (New), Lower

Thames-St.—by 22, on the E. side of Billingsgate.

Tenbury-Pl. Commercial-Road, Limehouse,—2d on the R. in Jamaica-place, towards Gunlane.

Tench-Street, St. George's East, —2d N. of Wapping-church, by the London-docks.

Tenfoot-Way, Nightingale-Lane, Up. East Smithfield,— nearly op. Burr-st.

Tennis-Court, Middle-Row, Holborn,—at 8, W. side of Staple's inn.

Tennis-Court, Church-Entry, Blackfriars,—1st on the L. from Shoemakers-row.

Tennis-Court, King-St. Boro.— at 60, 1st on the R. from 109, High-st.

Tennis-Pl.—near the last.

Tent's Court, Silver-St. Golden-Sq.—at 5, nearly op. Great Pulteney-st.

Tenter-Alley, Little Moorfields, —the 5th on the L. from 61, Fore-st.

Tenter-Ground, Goodman's Fields,—at 39, Prescot-st. six doors from Mansel-st.

Tenter-Row, Shepherd and Shepherdess-Walk,—2d on the R. from the City-road.

Tenterden-St. Hanover-Sq.—at 16, the N. W. corner.

Tenths-Office, Garden-Court, Temple,—4th door on the R. from Middle Temple-lane.

Terling-Street, St. George's East,—near the E. end of Lower Chapman-st.

Terrace-Walk,——bottom of Buckingham-st. from 38, Strand.

Terrace, Temple,—2d on the R. in King's-bench-walk, from Mitre-court, Fleet-st.

Terrace, High-St. Marybone,—W. side of the New-road.

Terrace, Brompton High-Road,—by the corner of Queen-st. about ¼ of a mile from Knightsbridge.

Terrace, Tottenham-Court-Rd.—E. side, op. Whitfield's chapel.

Terrace, Gray's-Inn-Lane,—part of the W. side, op. 69 to 80.

Terrace, Walworth,—R. side, ¼ of a mile from the Elephant and Castle, between Hanover-st. and Amelia-st.

Terrace, Cannon-Street-Road. See Clark's Terrace.

Terrace, Kent-Road,—part of the L. side, ¼ of a mile below the Bricklayer's-arms.

Terrace, Grange-Walk, Bermondsey. See Anderson's Buildings.

Terrace, Broad-Wall, Christ-Church, or Lambeth,—E. side, near Stamford-st.

Terrace, Vauxhall. See Vauxhall.

Terrace, Poplar,—op. the India-alms-houses, ⅓ of a mile on the R. from the Commercial-road.

Terrace-Place, Stepney-Green,—4th on the R. from Mile-end.

Tewkesbury-Court, Whitechapel,—at 100, nearly op. Red-Lion-st.

Thackham's-Court, Vine-Street,—N. end of Church-lane, 456, Strand.

Thames-Street (Lower),—from London-bridge to Tower-hill.

Thames-Street (Upper),—from London-bridge to Earl-st. Blackfriars, where there are 1 and 240.

Thames-Street (Little),—the continuation of St. Catherine's-st. to 80, Lower East-Smithfield.

Thames-St. Bankside, Southwark,—at 31, first street from Clink-st. towards Blackfriars-bridge.

Thames-Street, Rotherhithe,—between Russell-st. and the Thames, on the N. side of Greenland-dock.

Thanet-Place, Strand,—at 231, six doors on the L. from Temple-bar.

Thatched-House-Court, Little St. James's-Street,—3 doors from 75, St. James's-st.

Thatched-House-Court, Strand,—at 418, nearly op. Adam-street, Adelphi.

Thavies-Inn, Holborn-Hill,—at 56, six doors W. of St. Andrew's-church.

Thayer-Street,—first on the L. in Hinde-st. from the W. side Manchester-sq.

Theobald's-Road, Red-Lion-Sq.—3d coach-turning in Red-lion-st. from 71, High Holborn.

Thirteen Houses, Stepney-Green,—W. side, between Union-pl. and Prospect-pl.

St. Thomas-Apostle's(Gt.), Bow-Lane,—at 27, third st. on the L. from Cheapside.

St. Thomas-Apostle's (Little),—Bow-Lane,—at 35, second st. on the L. from Cheapside.

St. Thomas - Apostle's - Court, Gt. St. Thomas-Apostle's,—at 22, first E. of Queen-st.

St. Thomas's-Church-Yard, St. Thomas's - St.—2d on the R. from 43, Boro. High-st.

Thomas-Court, Bar-Court, —3d on the L. from 126, Golden-lane.

Thomas-Court, Crabtree-Row, Bethnal-Green,—4th on the R. from Hackney-road.

St. Thomas's Hospital, High-St. Boro.—36 doors on the L. from London-bridge.

Thomas - Passage, Bethnal-Green-Road,—1st on the R in Charles-st. from op. Wilmot-sq.

Thomas-Pl. Bethnal-Green-R l. —a few doors on the L. in Abbey-st.

Thomas-Pl. Hampstead-Road, —from Henry-st. to Charles-street.

Thomas-Place, Crabtree-Row, Bethnal-Green,—R. side, a few doors from Hackney-rd.

Thomas-Pl. Old Nicols-St. Bethnal-Green,—3 doors W. of Nicols-row.

Thomas-Pl. Pell-St. Ratcliffe,— middle of the W side.

Thomas - Place, Parker's-Row, Dock-Head,—a few yards on the R. north from the Neckinger-turnpike.

Thomas-Pl. Deptford Lower-Road, Rotherhithe,—by Bedford-pl. near the E. end of Paradise-row.

Thomas's Rope-Walk, Queen-Street, Ratcliffe,—the last on the L. from Ratcliffe-cross.

Thomas-Row, Bethnal-Green-Road,—2d on the R. in Charles-st. from op. Wilmot-square.

Thomas-St. Bethnal-Green-Rd. —at 55, third on the R. near ¼ of a mile E. of the turn-pike.

Thomas-Street, Ducking-Pond-Lane,—op. Greyhound-lane, from 105, Whitechapel-road.

Thomas-Street, Mile-End New-Town,—the continuation of the last.

Thomas-St. Brick-Lane, Bethnal-Green,—at 120, 14 doors on the L. from 144, Church-street.

Thomas-St Curtain-Road,—4th on the L. from Worship st.

Thomas-St. Commercial-Road, —4th on the R. west of Cannon-st.-road.

Thomas-Street, Mary-St. Stepney, — 1st on the L. from Ocean-st. Cow-lane.

Thomas-Street, Prince's-Pl. St. George's East, — 1st on the L. from the New Road.

Thomas-St. Kent-Road, — 1st on the L. below the Bricklayers-arms.

Thomas-St. Poplar-Row, — 1st on the L. from the Kent-road.

Thomas-St. Lock's Fields, Walworth,—3d on the L. from Garmouth-row, Kent-road.

Thomas-St. Horselydown,—at 114, Shad-Thames, opposite George-stairs, extending to Three-Oak-lane.

St. Thomas's-Street, High-St. Boro.—at 43, 2d on the L. from London-bridge.

St. Thomas's Tents, Boro.—the E. continuation of the last.

Thomas's Wharf, Horselydown, —on the W. side of Horselydown New-stairs.

Thompson's-Pl. Wilmot-Street, Bethnal-Green,—near the S. end, towards Dog-row.

Thompson's Rents, Half-Moon-St.—3d on the L. from 170, Bishopsgate.

Thorney-St. Bloomsbury,—W. continuation of Hart-st. and Castle-st.

Thornhaugh-St. Bedford-Sq.— 1st on the R. in Francis-st. from op. Whitfield's chapel, Tottenham-court-road.

Thornhaugh-St. (Up.),—N. end of the last.

Thornton-Pl. Gloucester-Pl. — last on the R. from Portman-square.

Thorold-Sq. Church-St. Bethnal-Green, — at 92, nearly op. the church.

Thrawl-St. Brick-Lane, Spitalfields,—at 208, 2d on the L. from Whitechapel.

Threadneedle-St. Bishopsgate-Within,—from 116, to the N. side of the Royal-Exchange.

Three-Arrow-Court, Chancery-Lane,—at 97, three doors N. of Carey-st.

Three-Colts-Alley,—the continuation of King Edward-st. from 170, Wapping.

Three-Colts-Court, Worship-St. —at 7, the 1st on the L. from Paul-st.

Three-Colts-Court, Angel-Alley, Bishopsgate,—the continuation of Slade's-builds. on the R.

Three-Colts-Court,Three-Colts-St. Limehouse,—at 15, near Gun-lane.

Three-Colts-Lane, Hare-Street, Bethnal-Green,—at 80, first on the R. from 109, Brick-lane.

Three-Colts-Lane, Dog-Row, Bethnal-Green, — op. Duthie's nursery, leading to Wilmot-st.

Three-Colts-St. Limehouse, — on the E. side of the church.

Three-Colts-Yard, Mile-End-Road, — 2d on the L. below the Old Globe, ½ a mile E. of the turnpike.

Three-Compass-Court, Cow-Cross,—at 65, third on the L. from St. John-st.

Three-Crane-Court, Castle-Lane, Westminster,—middle of the S. side.

Three-Crane-Lane,Up.Thames-St.—at 75, four doors E. of Queen-st.

Three-Crane-Stairs,—bottom of Queen-st. Cheapside.

Three-Crane-Wharf, — by the last.

Three-Crane-Yard, High-St. Boro.—at 66, by St. Margaret's Hill.

Three-Crown-Court, Royal Hospital-Row, — at the E. end the Burying-ground.

Three-Crown-Court, White's-Alley, —1st on the R. from op. 77, Chancery-lane.

Three-Crown-Court, Garlick-Hill,—2 doors from 190, Up. Thames-st.

Three - Crown - Court, Foster-Lane,—20 doors on the L. from Cheapside.

Three-Crown-Court, Jewry-St. —12 doors on the R. from Aldgate.

Three-Crown-Court, High-St. Boro.—at 269, sixth on the R. from London-bridge.

Three-Cups-Alley, Shoreditch, —at 220, about 25 doors S. of Holywell-lane.

Three-Cups-Alley, Lower-Shadwell,—at 22, four doors W. of Gould's-hill.

Three-Cups-Court,—1st on the L. in the last, from 22, Lower Shadwell.

Three-Cups-Inn, Aldersgate-St. —at 88, twelve doors N. of Barbican.

Three-Cups-Yard, Bedford-St. Red-Lion-St. Holborn, — 6 doors W. of Bedford-row.

Three-Dagger-Court, Fore-St. Cripplegate,—at 110, nearly op. Wood-st.

Three-Falcon-Court, Fleet-St.— at 144, second W. of Shoe-lane.

Three-Falcon-Court, Fishmonger's-Alley, Boro.— 1st on the R. from 235, High-st.

Three-Fox-Court, Long-Lane, —12 doors on the L. from 67, W. Smithfield.

Three-Fox-Court, Narrow-St. Limehouse, — 2d on the L. from Ratcliffe-cross.

Three-Hammer-Alley, Glean-Alley,—S. end, on the L. from 218, Tooley-st.

Three-Hand-Court, Creechurch-Lane,—1st on the R. from 86, Leadenhall-st.

Three-Herrings-Court, Red-cross-St.—at 57, first on the L. from Barbican.

Three-Herrings-Court, Cree-Church-Lane,—1st on the R. from 87, Leadenhall-st.

Three Horseshoe-Court, St. Peter's-Lane, — 3d on the L. from Cow-Cross.

Three-Kings-Court, Chandos-St. Covent - Garden, — 6 doors from St. Martin's-lane.

Three-Kings-Court, Fleet-St.— at 150, op. Water-lane.

Three-Kings-Court, Whitecross-St.—at 90, 18 doors N. of Chiswell-st.

Three-Kings-Court, Lombard-St.—at 33, E. side Clement's lane.

Three-Kings-Court, Minories,— 10 doors on the L. from Aldgate.

Three-Kings Yard, Davies-St. Berkeley-Sq.—at 15, middle W. side.

Three-Legs-Court, Whitecross-Street, St. Luke's,—at 207, 3d on the left N. of Chiswell-st.

Three-Nuns-Inn, Aldgate, — 5 doors E. of the church.

Three-Oak-Lane, Horselydown, — the E. continuation of Freeschool-st. bearing to the left.

Three - Pigeons - Court, Angel-Alley, Bishopsgate,—1st on the L. from Long-alley.

Three-Pigeons-Court, Ray-St. Clerkenwell, — 2d on the L. from the Green.

Three - Tuns - Alley, Petticoat-Lane,—at 99, 2d S. of Wentworth-st.

Three-Tuns-Alley, Alderman-

B b

bury,—19 doors on the R. from Milk-st. Cheapside.

Three-Tuns-Court, Bunhill-Row, —at 100, middle of the W. side.

Three-Tuns-Court, Redcross-St. —at 53, nine doors on the L. from Barbican.

Three-Tuns-Court, Miles's Lane, —3 doors from 130, Up. Thames-st.

Three-Tuns-Court, Up. Thames-St.—3 doors on the R. from London-bridge.

Three-Tuns- Court, White-St. Boro.—at 18, fourth E. of St. George's church.

Three-Tuns-Inn, High-Street, Boro.—at 88, near St. Margaret's Hill.

Three-Tuns-Passage, Ivy-Lane, — 1st on the R. from 29, Newgate-st.

Throgmorton-St.—N. E. corner of the Bank of England.

Thurlow House, Hackney-Road, —about the middle of Thurlow-pl.

Thurlow-Pl. Hackney-Road,— part of the L. side, ¾ of a mile from Shoreditch.

Thurlow-Pl. Globe-St. Bethnal-Green, — between Globe-pl. and Pitt-st.

Thurlow-Pl. Apollo-Buildings, East-Lane, Walworth, — at 21, ⅓ of a mile on the L. from the Kent-road.

Thurlow-Street, York-St.—1st on the R. from Blackfriars-road.

Tidewaiters-Court,—the continuation of Chequer-sq. from 70, Aldgate.

Tiger-Court. See Tyger.

Tilney-Court, Old-St.—at 43, 2d W. of Bunhill-row.

Tilney-Street, South Audley-St. — 2d on the L. from Curzon-street.

Times Newspaper-Office, — on the E. side of Printing-house-square, Water-lane, Black-friars.

Tindall's-Court, Farmer-Street, Shadwell, — behind 65, towards Shakespear's Walk.

Tipping's Alley, New Way, Westr.—N. end, by the Almonry.

Titchborne-Court, High-Holborn,—at 280, W. side Gt. Turnstile.

Titchborne-St. Haymarket, — op. the N. end, from Piccadilly to Sherrard-st.

Titchfield-Chapel, Westmoreland-St. Marybone,—7 doors from 12, Gt. Marybone-st.

Titchfield-St. (Gt.), Marybone, —the continuation of Market-st. from 87, Oxford-st.

Titchfield-St. (Little), Marybone,—at 100, in the last, 6th on the L. from Oxford-street.

Titchfield-Street, Dean-St. Soho. —6 doors on the R. from 400, Oxford-st.

Tites-Alley, Narrow-St. Limehouse,—1st on the L. below Turner's Wharf.

Titmouse - Alley, Farmer - St. Shadwell,—at 54, middle of the E. side.

Tobacco-Roll-Court, Long - Alley,—3d on the L. from Moorfields.

Tobacco - Roll - Court, Gracechurch-St.—9 doors on the R. from Cornhill.

Tobit's Dog Coach-Office, St. Paul's Ch.-Yd.—2 doors on the R. from Ludgate-st.

Tobin's-Court, Broad-Street, St. Giles's,—at 10, op. the church.

Tokenhouse-Yard, Lothbury,—at 44, N. side the Bank of England.

Toms-Court, Duke-St. Grosvenor-Sq. — at 5, 2d on the L. from 277, Oxford-st.

Tonbridge-Pl. Sommers-Town, — op. Judd's-pl. near the Turnpike.

Tongue-Yard, Whitechapel-Rd. —at 247, 36 doors E. of the Church.

Tongue-Yard (Little),—10 doors W. of the last.

Took's-Court, Cursitor-St.—9 doors on the L. from 40, Chancery-lane.

Tooley-St. Boro.—1st on the L. from London-bridge.

Tooley's Gateway, Tooley-St. —at 63, nearly op. Bermondsey-st.

Topping's Rents, Ewer-St. Boro. —10 doors from Duke-st.

Topping's Wharf, Tooley-St.— 8 doors E. of London-bridge.

Torrington-Street, Keppel-St.— at 22, 1st on the R. from 30, Russell-sq.

Tothill-Court, Tothill-St. Westr. —3d on the R. from the Abbey.

Tothill-Fields, Westr.—W. side Milibank-walk.

Tothill-St. Westr.—from the Abbey to Queen-sq.

Tothill-St. (New),—1st on the L. in the last from the Abbey.

Tothill-St. Little Gray's-Inn-Lane,—1st on the R. from 72, Gray's-Inn-lane, Holborn.

Tottenham-Court, New-Road, —S. side, by Tottenham-court-road.

Tottenham-Court-Road,—from Oxford-st. St. Giles's, to the New-road.

Tottenham-Mews, Tottenham-St.—at 26, fourth on the R. from Tottenham-court-road.

Tottenham-Place, Tottenham-Court-Road,—8 doors S. of the New-road.

Tottenham-Pl. (Up.),—the continuation of the last.

Tottenham-St. Tottenham-Ct.-Road, — the continuation of Chapel-st. E. side the Chapel.

Totterburn Alley, Duke-Street, Boro.—2d on the L. from Queen-st.

Tower,—N. side the River, ⅓ of a mile below London-bridge.

Tower-Dock, Tower-Hill.—W. side the Tower, also 10 houses between Tower-st. and Lower Thames-st.

Tower-Hill (Great),—the open space, N. W. side the Tower.

Tower-Hill (Little),—the space on the E. side the Tower.

Tower-Royal, Watling-St.—at 50, ten doors E. of Queen-st.

Tower-Royal-Court, — E. side the last.

Tower-St. 7 Dials,—continuation of Little St. Martin's-lane, bearing to the L.

Tower-St. (Little),—the continuation of Little Eastcheap to Gt. Tower-st.

Tower-St. (Gt.),—the E. continuation of the last to Tower-hill.

Tower - Street, St. George's Fields,—4th on the R. from the Obelisk towards the Asylum.

Tower-Ward School, — at 91, Gt. Tower-st.

Town-Hall, Poplar High-St.—$\frac{1}{2}$ a mile on the R. from the Commercial-road.

Town-Hall, St. Margaret's Hill, Boro.—$\frac{1}{5}$ of a mile on the R. from London-bridge.

Townsend-Court, Queen-Street, Boro.—at 71, three doors W. of Little Guildford-st.

Townsend-St. Kent-Road,—3d on the R. below the Brick-layer's Arms.

Townsend's Yard, Charlotte-St. Portland-Pl.—3 doors from New Cavendish-st.

Trafalgar-Builds. Ebenezer-St. City-Road,—4 doors on the R. from Trafalgar-st.

Trafalgar-Mews, Carburton-St. Fitzroy-Sq.—6 doors E. of Up. Titchfield-st.

Trafalgar-Pl. New-Road, Mary-bone,—the E. end of Union-builds.

Trafalgar-Pl. Uxbridge-Road,—entrance about $\frac{1}{3}$ of a mile on the R. from Tyburn Turn-pike.

Trafalgar-Pl. Paul's-Alley, Crip-plegate,—3d on the L. from 17, Redcross-st.

Trafalgar-Pl. Hackney-Road,—part of the L. side, by Gt. Cambridge-st. $\frac{1}{2}$ a mile from Shoreditch.

Trafalgar-Pl. Pleasant-Pl. Step-ney,—behind 16, 1st on the L. from Redman's row.

Trafalgar-Pl. Lambeth,—S. end of Gibraltar-row, St. George's Fields.

Trafalgar-Place, Lock's Fields, Walworth,—the continuation of Garmouth-row, Kent-rd.

Trafalgar-Row, Green-Street, Bethnal-Green,—the E. continuation of it, $\frac{1}{2}$ a mile from the Green.

Trafalgar-Row, Walworth-Common, — by the Hour-glass, nearly op. Westmoreland-academy.

Trafalgar-Sq. White Horse-Lane, Stepney,—$\frac{1}{4}$ of a mile from the Church, towards Mile-End.

Trafalgar Stables-Yard, Mount-St. Berkeley-Sq.—32 doors on the R. from Davies-st.

Trafalgar-St. City-Road,—op. Fountain-pl. 4th on the R. north from Old-st.

Trafalgar - Street, Turville-St. Bethnal-Green,—4th on the L. from 37, Church-st.

Trafalgar-St. Walworth High-St.—1st S. parallel to East-lane.

Trafalgar-Terrace, Stepney,—the N. side of Cow-lane, by Ocean-st.

Trafalgar-Yd. Mount-St. Berke-ley-Sq. — at 33, middle N. side.

Trafalgar - Yard, Blackfriars-Road,—between the Obelisk and Circus.

Transport-Office. See Dorset-Sq. Cannon-Row, Westr.

Traveller Newspaper-Office,—at 151, Fleet-st. by Bolt-court.

Treasury, Whitehall, — a few yards on the R. from the

Horse-guards, towards the Abbey.

Trig's Court, Castle-St. Boro.—adjoins 14, Redcross-st.

Trig-Lane, Up. Thames-St.—at 33, op. Lambeth-hill.

Trig-Stairs and Wharf,—by the last.

Trinity Alms-Houses, Mile-End, — 12 doors on the L. below the turnpike.

Trinity-Court, Aldersgate-St.—at 171, op. Falcon-sq.

Trinity-Court, Little Trinity-Lane,—at 28, middle of the E. side.

Trinity-House, Trinity-Sq.—N. side, between Savage-gardens and Cooper's row.

Trinity-House (Old), Water-Lane,—4 doors from Tower-st.

Trinity-Lane (Gt.), Bread-St.—3d on the L. from 46, Cheapside.

Trinity-Lane (Little),—from the middle of the last to 199, Up. Thames-st.

Trinity-Pl. Charing-Cross,—6 doors on the L. from the Strand.

Trinity-Sq. — part of the N. side of Gt. Tower-hill.

Trinity-St. Rotherhithe,—the continuation of Lower Queen-st. leading to Russell-st. and Greenland-dock.

Tripe-Yard, Petticoat-Lane,—at 122, second on the R. from 41, Ald ate High-st.

Tripe-Yard, Petticoat-Lane,—4th N. of Wentworth-st.

Trotter's-Court, New Gravel-Lane,—at 60, second on the R. from Shadwell High-st.

Trotter's-Ways, Rotherhithe,—

E. side of Cherry-garden-stairs, $\frac{1}{4}$ of a mile above the church.

Trump-Court, Whitechapel-Rd. —at 43, a few doors on the L. below the church.

Trump-Street, King-St.—6 doors on the L. from 93, Cheapside.

Trundley's Lane, Deptford Lower-Road,—the 1st S. of the Halfway-house.

Truss-Society,—at 10, Grocers-hall-court, Poultry.

Tucker's-Row, Poplar,—nearly op. North-st.

Tudor-Street, New Bridge-St. Blackfriars, — at 15, second on the L. from the bridge.

Tuerena's Rents, Upper East-Smithfield, — behind 89, by Dock-st.

Tufton-Street, Wood-St. Westr. —3d street on the L. from 64, Millbank-st. extending to the Horseferry-road.

Tufton-St. (Little),—from 22, in the last, to St. John's Church.

Turk's-Head-Court, Bell-Alley, — 1st on the L. from 1, Golden-lane.

Turk's-Head-Court, Turnmill-St. Clerkenwell,—at 74, middle of the E. side.

Turk's-Head-Court, Oxford-St. —at 36, nearly op. the Pantheon.

Turk's-Head-Court, Golden-Lane,—at 120, sixth on the R. from Old-st.

Turk's-Head-Passage, New Gravel-Lane,—at 127, middle of the E. side.

Turk's Row, Chelsea,—extends from Lower Sloane-st. to the Hospital.

Turk-St. Bethnal-Green,—the continuation of Tyssen-st. op. Brick-lane, to Virginia-st.

Turn - Court, Camel-Builds.— 1st on the R. from 9, Orchard-st. Portman-sq.

Turnagain Lane, Fleet-Market, —at 36, N. end, leading to Skinner-st.

Turner's Builds. Poplar, — 2d on the L. from the Commercial-road.

Turner's-Builds. Christian - St. St. George's East,—last on the R. from Princes-pl. New-road.

Turner's Court,- St. Martin's-Lane, Charing-Cross,—at 37, N. side of Chandos-st.

Turner's Court,- Back Church-Lane, Whitechapel,- -1st on the R. from the Commercial-road.

Turner's Rents, Gravel-Lane, Boro.—op. George-st. from Blackfriars-road.

Turner-Sq. Whitechapel-Road, —at 219, 4 doors W. of Cannon-st.-road.

Turner-Sq. Hoxton, — op. the Hare, ⅓ of a mile on the L. from Old st.-road.

Turner-Street, Cartwright-St.— 3d on the L. from 32, Rose-mary-lane.

Turner's Wharf, Millbank-St. Westminster, — op. Vine-st. ⅓ of a mile above Westmr. bridge.

Turner's Wharf, Narrow - St. Limehouse,— ⅕ of a mile below Ratcliffe-cross.

Turnham - Pl. Curtain - Road, Shoreditch,—the R. side, ¼ of a mile from Old-st.-road.

Turnmill-St.—the continuation

of Cow-cross to the Sessions-house, Clerkenwell-green.

Turnstile (Gt.), High-Holborn, —at 282, E. side Lincoln's-inn-fields.

Turnstile. (Little), High - Holborn,—from 240, to Gate-st. Lincoln's-inn-fields.

Turnstile (New), High-Holborn, —at 232, eight doors W. of the last.

Turnstile, Gt. Saffron-Hill,—at 130, leading to Charles-st. Hatton-garden.

Turnwheel-Lane, Cannon-St.— from 6, to Dowgate-hill.

Turpentine-Lane, Neat-Houses, Chelsea,—1st on the R. from the bridge at Pimlico.

Turville-New - Builds. Turville-St.—12 doors on the R. from 38, Church - street, Bethnal-green.

Turville-Pl. Turville-St. Beth-nal-Green,— 3d on the L. from 37, Church-st.

Turville-Street, Church-Street, Bethnal-Green,—at 37, 4th on the L. from 65, Shoreditch.

Turville-Street (New), Bethnal-Green,— 4th on the R. in Cock-lane, from 65, Shore-ditch.

Tuson's Builds. Castle-Alley,— 1st on the L. from 124, Whitechapel.

Tutchey - Court, Strand, — at 137, W. side Somerset-pl.

Tweezers - Alley, Water-Street, Strand,—2d on the L. from 37, Arundel-st. leading to Milford-lane.

Twig-Folly, Green-St. Bethnal-Green,— ½ a mile on the R. east from the Green.

Twisden's-Builds.—at the bottom of Inner Temple-lane, from 16, Fleet-st.

Twisters-Alley, Bunhill-Row,— at 102, middle of the W. side.

Tyburn-Turnpike,—at the W. end of Oxford-st. by Edgware-road.

Tyers-Gateway, Bermondsey-St. — at 210, middle of the W. side.

Tyger-Court, Whitecross-St. Cripplegate,—7 doors S. of Beech-lane.

Tyler's-Court, Wardour-St. Soho,—at 82, six doors N. of Peter-st.

Tyler's-Court, Carnaby-Market, —at the N. W. corner, op. Tyler's-st.

Tyler's-Passage, King-Street,—5 doors on the L. from 323, Oxford-st.

Tyler's-Street, King-St.—at 30, 3d on the L. from 323, Oxford-st.

Type-Street, Chiswell-St. — 2d on the L. from Finsbury-sq.

Type-Court, Type-St.—2d on the R. from 24, Chiswell-st.

Tyrell-St. Bethnal-Green-Road, —N. E. corner of Thorold-square.

Tyse's-Court, Duke-Street, St. George's Fields,—N. end, the corner of Tower-st.

Tyson-Place, Kingsland-Road, —the L. side, ⅓ of a mile from Shoreditch, and op. the almshouses.

Tyssen-Street, Church-St. Bethnal-Green,—at 52, op. Bricklane, ¼ of a mile on the L. from 65, Shoreditch.

Tyssen-Street (New), Bethnal-Green, — 2d on the R. in

Satchwell's rents, from 32, Church-st.

Tyson's-Yard, Tooley-St. — at 181, op. Mill-lane.

UNANIMOUS-ROW, Queen-St. Mile-End New-Town,— a few yards behind 27, Church-st.

Unicorn-Court, Kent-St. Boro. —at 298, ten doors on the R. from St. George's church.

Unicorn-Passage, Vine-Yard, Tooley-St.--3d on the L. from 110, Tooley-st.

Unicorn-Yard, Oxford-St. — at 106, 5 doors W. of John-st.

Union-Bridge-Row, Boro. — W. end of the Grove, Great Guildford-st.

Unicorn-Yard, Tooley-St. — at 100,5 doors E. of Stoney-lane.

Unicorn-Passage, — 1st on the R. in the last, from Tooley-st.

Unicorn-Yard, Blackman-St. Boro.—at 61, op. the King's Bench.

Union-Bewery, Wapping-St. — ⅛ of a mile below Hermitagebridge.

Union-Brewery, Lambeth-Walk, —middle of the W. side, nearly op. Gray's Walk.

Union-Builds. New-Road, Marybone,—E. end of Alsop's buildings.

Union-Buildings, Leather-Lane, Holborn,—at 63, six doors S. of Portpool-lane.

Union-Builds. Union-St.—at 24, 1st on the R. from Hackneyroad.

Union - Builds. Hackney-Road,
—W. side of Somerset-builds.

Union-Builds. Kent - Road, —
adjoining Union-row.

Union-Chapel, Poplar,—op. the
Red lion.

Union-Court, Brunswick-Row,
Westr.—1st on the L. from
Bridewell.

Union-Court, Holborn-Hill, —
at 95, nearly op. St. An-
drew's church.

Union-Court (Up.),—the continuation of the last described.

Union-Court, Union-St. Middlesex-Hospital,—5 doors on the
R. from Norfolk-st.

Union-Court, Haymarket, — S.
side the Opera-house.

Union-Court, Old Broad-St.—
from 41, to Wormwood-st

Union-Court, Willow-St. — 2d
on the L. from Paul-st.

Union-Court, Hackney - Road,
—1st on the R. from Shoreditch-church.

Union-Court, Back-Lane, Poplar,—1st on the L. from the
Commercial-road.

Union-Court, New ' Gravel-
Lane,—12 doors on the L.
from 195, Wapping.

Union-Court, Kent-St. Boro.—
at 287, 20 doors on the R.
from St. George's church.

Union-Court, Maze, Boro. — 6
doors on the L. from 195,
Tooley-st.

Union - Court, Gibraltar - Row,
St. George's Fields,—1st on
the R. from Prospect-pl.

Union-Court, Tooley-St. — at
180, four doors W. of Bermondsey-st.

Union - Cour, Princes - Street,
St. George's Fields,—1st on
the L. from the London-rd.

Union-Court, Rotherhithe,—S.
side the church, by the Cha-
r ty school.

Union-Crescent, Union-Street,
Hackney-Road,—at 30, mid-
dle of the N. side.

Union-Crescent, Kent-Road,—
op. the Paragon.

Union Fire-Office, Cornhill,—
at 81, the corner of Finch-
lane.

Union Hall, Union-St. Boro.—
a few doors on the L. from
218, High-st.

Union-Mews, Union-St. Marybone,—at 38, three doors W.
of Suffolk-st.

Union-Mews,—at the N. end of
the Crescent, Minories.

Union-Gardens, Hackney - Rd.
—entrance by the N. end of
Union-walk.

Union-Pl. Orchard-St. Westr.—
at 47, op. New Tothill-st.

Union-Pl. Mill-Bank,—by the
New Ranelagh, S. side the
Spread-Eagle.

Union - Pl. Lower George - St.
Chelsea, — 4 doors on the L.
from Sloane-sq.

Union-Pl. Castle-Lane, Westr.
—1st on the R. from James-
street.

Union-Pl. Maiden-Lane, Battle-
Bridge, St. Pancras,—2d on
the L. from the Maiden-head.

Union-Pl. (Up.),—N. end of the
last.

Union-Pl. Collier-St. Pentonville,—1st E. of Cumming-
street.

Union - Pl. Curtain - Road, — a

few yards N. of Bateman's row.

Union-Pl. Stepney-Green,—2d on the R. from Mile-end.

Union-Pl. E. India Dock-Road, Poplar, — 1st W. from the Dock-gate, on the L.

Union-Pl. Garden-St. Poplar,— W. end of White-hart-place, Robinhood-lane.

Union-Pl. Lambeth,—W. continuation of Lambeth-terrace to Church-st.

Union-Pl. (Little),—middle of the last.

Union-Pl. Blackfriars-Road, — continuation of Edward-st.

Union - Pl. Union - Street, St. George's Fields,—2d on the R. from the London-road.

Union-Pl. Cross-St. Newington, —at the bottom of Collitch-place.

Union-Pl. Swan-Lane, Rotherhithe,—1st on the R. from Rotherhithe-street, towards Adam-st.

Union-Pl. Back-Hill, — 1st on the L. from Ray-st. towards Leather-lane.

Union-Pl. Jamaica - Pl. Limehouse,—1st on the R. from the Commercial-road.

Union-Pl. Ashton-St. Blackwall, —N. side, near the East-India-dock-gate.

Union-Pl. Ravel-Row,—N. side the King's Bench.

Union-Pl. Blackman-St. Boro. —at 42, middle of the E. side.

Union-Place, Three Oak-Lane, Horselydown,—entrance facing the E. end of Free-School-street.

Union-Row, George-St. Chel-

sea,—a few yards on the L. from the S. E. corner of Sloane-sq.

Union-Row, City-Road, — W. continuation of Fountain-pl. op. the Shepherd and Shepherdess-walk.

Union-Row, Essex-St. Kingsland-Road, — 2d on the R. from the said road.

Union-Row, Stepney-Green, — 1st on the R. in Union-pl. from the Green.

Union-Row, Bethnal-Green-Rd. —the continuation of the W. side of Wilmot-st.

Union-Row, Fashion-St. Spitalfields,—at 35, by Brick-lane.

Union-Row, White-Bear-Gardens, Hackney-Road. See Harris's Row.

Union-Row, Union-St. Whitechapel-Road, — facing Sionchapel.

Union - Row, Minories, — the corner of Rosemary-lane and Tower-hill.

Union-Row, Mile-End-Road,— part of the S. side, near the Plough, 2¼ miles from Aldgate.

Union-Row, Kent-Road, — 3d on the R. from the Elephant and Castle.

Union - Row, Snow's Fields, — 6th on the L. from 138, Bermondsey-st.

Union - Stairs, Wapping, — at 326, ⅙ of a mile below Hermitage-bridge, op. East-lane-stairs.

Union-St. Middlesex - Hospital, —last on the R. in Wells-st. from 63, Oxford-st.

Union-Street, New Bond-St.—

at 75, ten doors on the L. from Oxford-st.

Union-Street, Hill-St. — 3d on the L. from Berkeley-sq.

Union-Street, New Bridge-St. Blackfriars,—at 36, 3d on the L. from Ludgate-hill.

Union-St. Hackney-Road,—1st on the L. from Shoreditch-church.

Union-St. Bishopsgate-Without, —at 69, 5th on the R. north of the church.

Union-St. Whitechapel-Road,— at 281, 1st E. of the church.

Union-Street, Shadwell High-St.—at 227, op. New Gravel-lane.

Union-St. London-Road, — 2d on the R. from the Obelisk.

Union-St. Lambeth,—2d on the R. from the Stags towards Kennington.

Union-Street, Tower-St. — 2d on the L. from the Asylum.

Union-Street, Dover-St.—1st on the R. from Blackfriars-rd.

Union-Street, High-St. Boro.— at 218, 1st on the R. south from St. Margaret's Hill.

Union - Street, East - St. Walworth,—3d street on the L. from the High-st.

Union-St. Sommers-Town, — at the N. E. corner of Clarendon-sq.

Union-Street, Cornwall-Street, St. George's East,—op. Blue-gate-fields.

Union-Street, Lower Chapman-St.—E. end of it, and N. end of Duke-st.

Union-St. Bethnal-Green-Rd. —3 doors W. of the turnpike, ½ a mile on the L. from 65, Shoreditch.

Union - Wharf, St. Catherine's Dock, — on the E. side, by Little Thames-st.

Union-Walk, Union-St. Hackney-Road,—at 34, 1st on the L. from Kingsland-road.

Union - Yard, Tooley - St. See Unicorn-Yard.

United Society's School, Trinity-St. Rotherhithe, — at 46, op. Durand's wharf.

Upper-Ground-St. Blackfriars-Road,—1st on the R. from the bridge.

Upper - Turning, Shakespear's Walk, Shadwell.—at 54, 2d on the L. from 48, High-st.

Uxbridge-Road, — the continuation of Oxford-st. from Tyburn turnpike.

———

VACCINE - INSTITUTION. See Jennerian.

Vandermeulen's Pl. Newington, — E. side, between the Elephant and Castle and the ch.

Vain-St. Glean-Alley,—1st on the L. from 218, Tooley-st.

Valentine-Court, Webber-St.— 1st on the R. from Blackfriars-road.

Valentine-Pl. Blackfriars-Road, —W. side, op. Bennet's row.

Valentine-Row, Blackfriars-Rd. —from the S. end the last, to Webber-st.

Valentine - Row, Long - Lane, Bermondsey,—near the middle of the N. side.

Valiant Soldier-Alley, Bermondsey-St.—26 doors on the L. from Tooley-st.

Vauxhall, Lambeth,—at the W.

end of Up. Kennington-lane,
by the turnpike.

Vauxhall-Chapel, Vauxhall, —
adjoins the turnpike on the
W. side.

Vauxhall - Gardens, Up. Kennington-Lane,—⅓ of a mile on
the R. from Kennington-
cross.

Vauxhall-Pl. South Lambeth,—
1st row on the L. from the
turnpike.

Vauxhall - Road. See Upper
Kennington-Lane.

Vauxhall-Row, — the continuation of Princes-st. Lambeth.

Vauxhall-Sq.—at 10 in the last,
N.W. corner of the Gardens.

Vauxhall-Stairs, — ⅛ of a mile
from the turnpike towards
Lambeth.

Vauxhall-St. Up. Kennington-
Lane,—1st on the L. from
the Gardens.

Vauxhall - Terrace, Vauxhall-
Walk,—N. side of the Gar-
dens.

Vauxhall - Walk, — from Lambeth-Butts to the N. side the
Gardens.

St. Vedast's Church, Foster-
Lane,—on the R. from 147,
Cheapside.

Venetian-Row, Liquorpond-St.
— part of the N. side, by
Gray's-inn-lane.

Vere's Crescent, Lambeth-
Marsh,—E. end of James-st.

Vere-Street, Oxford-St.--at 151,
op. New Bond-st.

Vere-St. Clare-Market,—2d on
the R. in Princes-st. from
123, Drury-lane.

Vernon's Builds. St. Pancras,—

N. W. corner of the Small-
Pox-Hospital.

Verulam-Buildings, Gray's-Inn-
Lane,—op. 48, the 3d on the
L. from Holborn.

Vicar - General's Office, Doctors-Commons, — 1st house
on the L. in Bell-yard, from
10, Gt. Carter-lane.

Victory-Pl. Lock's Fields, Walworth,—1st on the L. from
Garmouth-row, Kent-road.

Victory-Row, Trafalgar-Square,
Stepney,--behind the N. side.

Victualling-Office, Somerset-Pl.
—centre of the R. side the
square from the Strand.

Victualling-Office (Army), Little
Thames-St.—adjoins Lower
East-Smithfield, near Burr-st.

Victualling-Office, Deptford,—
⅓ of a mile below Greenland-
dock.

Victualling - Office - Row,—the
continuation of Grove-st. W.
side the last.

Victualling - Office-Sq. Tower-
Hill,—E. side, by the New
Mint.

Vigo - Lane, Swallow-St. — at
149, 1st on the L. from 41,
Piccadilly.

Villa-Pl. Walworth - Common,
—by the Chapel and Paul's
place.

Villa-Row,—E. end of the last.

Villa-St. Walworth-Common,—
between Villa-row and Villa-
place.

Villiers - Court, Piccadilly,—at
166, leading into St. James's-
street.

Villier's St. Strand,—at 31, 4th
on the R. from Charing-cross.

Vincent's Court, Silver-St. Falcon-Sq.—2 doors from 81, Wood-st.

Vincent Row, City-Road,—part of the L. side, near a mile from Finsbury-sq.

Vincent-St. Bethnal-Green, — 4th on the R. in Cock-lane, from behind 65, Shoreditch.

Vine-Court, Bell-Alley, — 4th on the R. from 1, Golden-lane.

Vine-Court, Laystall-St. — at 14, 1st on the R. from Gray's inn-lane.

Vine-Court, Vine-St. — corner of Old Round-court, Strand.

Vine-Court, Vine - Yard - Gardens, Clerkenwell, — 1st on the R. from Bowling-green-lane.

Vine-Court, Golden-Lane, St. Luke's,— 4th on the R. from Barbican.

Vine-Court, Moor-Lane, Moor-fields,—2d on the R. from 86, Fore-st.

Vine-Court,—E. end of 3-Crane-wharf, Queen-st. Cheapside.

Vine-Court, Vine-Street, Spitalfields,—at 12, last on the R. from 23, Lamb-st.

Vine-Court, Vine-St. Minories, —on the W. side, by New-square.

Vine-Court, Broad-St. Ratcliffe, — behind 84, entrance by Vine-passage.

Vine-Court, Whitechapel-Road, —at 226, op. the Workhouse.

Vine-Court, Redcross-St. Upper East-Smithfield,—1st on the L. from 7, Nightingale-lane.

Vine-Court, Vine-St. Lambeth,

—1st on the L. from Narrow-wall.

Vine-Court, Blackman-St. Boro. —at 115, 2d on the R. from St. George's church.

Vine-Court, Vine-Yard,—1st on the L. from 109, Tooley-st.

Vine-Inn, Bishopsgate-Within, —at 70, 10 doors S. of the church.

Vine - Passage, Broad-St. Ratcliffe,—at 84, middle of the N. side.

Vine-Pl. Little Pearl-St. Spitalfields,—1st on the R. from 8, Gt. Pearl-st.

Vine-Pl. Vine-St. Lambeth,— 1st on the R. from Narrow-wall.

Vine-St. Westr.—at 43, Mill-bank-st. near Horseferry-rd.

Vine-Street (Little), Swallow-St. —6 doors on the R. from 45, Piccadilly.

Vine-St. Piccadilly,—the continuation of the last to Brewer-st.

Vine-Street, Chandos-St. Covent-Garden, — at 26, ten doors on the R. from 27, St. Martin's lane.

Vine-Street, Broad-St. Bloomsbury, — 12 doors on the R. from High-Holborn.

Vine-St. — the continuation of Bedford-st. from the N. end of Leather-lane, Holborn.

Vine-St. Hatton-Wall,—E. continuation of it to Mutton-lane.

Vine-Street, Lamb - St. Spitalfields,—at 24, 2d on the L. from Spital-sq.

Vine-Street, Phœnix-St. Spital-

VIN WAD

fields,—2d on the R. from 168, Brick-lane.

Vine-St. Minories,—1st on the L. in George-st. from 142, Minories.

Vine-St. (Little),—1st on the L. in the last from John-st.

Vine-St. Narrow-Wall, Lambeth,—1st on the R. from Westminster-bridge.

Vine-Yard, Vine-St. Piccadilly,—at 7, middle of the E. side.

Vine-Yard-Pl. Broad-St. Ratcliffe,—N. end of Vine-passage.

Vine-Yard, White-Horse-Street, Ratcliffe,—op. Butcher-row.

Vine-Yard, Tooley-St.—at 110, ⅛ of a mile on the L. from London-bridge.

Vine-Yard-Gardens, Bowling-Green-Lane, Clerkenwell,—2d on the L. from Coppice-row.

Vine-Yard-Walk,—the continuation of the last.

Vine-Yard, Aldersgate-St.—at 100, a few doors N. of Barbican.

Vinegar-Lane, St. George's E.—from Sun-Tavern-fields to White-horse-pl. Commercial-road.

Vinegar-Yard,—S. side Drury-lane theatre.

Vinegar-Yard, Clerkenwell,—the continuation of Eagle-court, from 5, St. John's lane.

Vinegar-Yard,—S. end of Darby-st. entering by 37, Rosemary-lane.

Vinegar-Yard, Parsons-St.—nearly op. Well-st. Wellclose-square.

Vinegar-Yard, Cannon-St. Boro.—the W. end of it.

Vinegar-Yard, Gravel-Lane, Boro.—nearly op. George-st.

Vinegar-Yard, Bermondsey-St.—at 210, N. side of Snow's fields.

Vinegar-Yard, Bow-Yard, St. Giles's,—1st on the L. from Broad-st.

Vintners-Alms-Houses, Mile-End,—⅛ of a mile on the L. below the turnpike.

Vintners-Hall, Up. Thames-St.—at 70, W. side of Queen-st. Cheapside.

Virgil-Pl. Bowling-Green-Builds. Marybone,—3d on the L. from the New-road.

Virgin's-Court, Well-Alley,—1st on the R. from 110, Wapping.

Virginia-Street, Parsons-St. Up. E.-Smithfield,—at 50, near Ratcliffe-highway.

Virginia-St. Bethnal-Green,—the continuation of Castle-st. behind Shoreditch church, to the Bird-cage.

WADE'S-PLACE, Mile-End-Road,—op. Bencroft's alms-houses.

Wade's Pl. Poplar,—op. the Green-Man and Dolphin-lane.

Wade's Fields,—W. side the last.

Waddel's Yard, Stacey-Street, St. Giles's,—N. end, by the church.

C c

Wadham's Court, Jacob-Street, Dock-Head,—last on the L. from Mill-st.

Wagstaff's Builds. Great Guildford-St. Boro.—N. end, by Maid-lane.

Wakefield's Pl. Bunhill-Row,— 1st on the R. from Old-st.

Wakefield's Rents, Old-St.—at 87, on the W. side the City-road.

Walbrook,—from the W.side the Mansion-house, to Cannon-st.

Walbrook-Pl. Hoxton,—¼ of a mile on the L. from Winkworth's builds. City-road.

Walbrook-School, Blue-Anchor-Alley,—a few yards on the R. from 108, Bunhill-row.

Walburge-Court, Walburge-St. —1st on the L. from Back-lane, St. George's East.

Walburge-Street, St. George's East,—1st E. of Cannon-st. turnpike.

Walcot-Pl. Lambeth, — both sides the high-road, ⅔ of a mile from Westr.-bridge.

Walker's Builds. Horse-Shoe-Alley, Moorfields, — E. end, from 14, Wilson-st.

Walker's Court, Berwick - St. Oxford-St. — S. continuation of it.

Walker's Court, Stoney-St. Boro. —W. side the Boro. market.

Walker's Yard, Rathbone - Pl. —at 29, op. Percy-st.

Waller-Pl. Lambeth - Road,— E. end of Durham-pl. by the Stags.

Wallis's Court, Mint-St. Boro.— 1st on the L. from op. St. George's church.

Wallis's Pl. Pimlico,—3d on the L. from Buckingham-gate.

Wallis's Yard, Worship - St. — 6 doors on the R. from 249, Shoreditch.

Walnut-Tree-Court, Globe-Alley, Limehouse,—the 1st on the R. from Fore-st.

Walnut-Tree-Walk, Walcot-Pl. Lambeth,—1st on the R. south of the Three Stags.

Walsh's Buildings, Curtain-Road, Shoreditch. See Mill's Court.

Walter's Alms-Houses, Old-St.-Road,—a few doors on the R. from Shoreditch church.

Walter's Ways, Rotherhithe,— by the entrance to the Surrey Canal.

Walton's Court, Cartwright-St. —3d on the R.from 32, Rosemary-lane.

Walton's Pl. Brook-St. Ratcliffe, —op. Stepney-causeway.

Walton's Wharf, Tooley-St.— E. side Battle-bridge-stairs, entering by Mill-lane.

Walworth,—a district in St. Mary's, Newington, from the Elephant and Castle towards Camberwell.

Walworth-Common,—the space on the S. side of East-lane, and from Surrey-sq. towards Camberwell.

Walworth-Pl. Walworth High-St.—part of the R. side, ⅔ of a mile from the Elephant and Castle.

Walworth-Workhouse,—on the S. side the entrance to the Montpelier.

Wapping-Charity-School, — adjoins Wapping-church, on the S. side.

Wapping-Dock-Stairs,—at 230, Wapping-st. near Old Gravel-lane.

Wapping-Dock-St.–op. the last.

Wapping-New-Stairs,—at 261, Wapping, near Red-Lion-st.

Wapping-Old-Stairs, — at 290, Wapping, W. side the church.

Wapping-St.—from Hermitage-bridge, where there are numbers 1 and 365, to New Gravel-lane.

Wapping-Wall,--the E. continuation of the last, by the side of the Thames.

War - Office, Horse - Guards, Whitehall,—1st door on the R. from St. James's Park.

Ward's Builds. Nottingham-St. Marybone, — middle of the S. side.

Ward's Court, Goswell-St.—at 42, op. Wilderness-row.

Ward's Row, Pimlico,—L. side, 10 doors from Buckingham-gate.

Ward's Row, Bethnal - Green-Road,—part of the L. side, between the turnpike and Pollard's row.

Warden's Court, Clerkenwell-Close,—W. side the church.

Wardour-Street, Oxford -St. — at 382, 4th on the L. from St. Giles's.

Wardour-Mews, Portland-St.—3 doors W. from 111, War-dour-st.

Wardrobe-Pl. Gt. Carter-Lane, Doctors' Commons, — 2d on the R. from Creed-lane.

Wardrobe-Terrace, Saint An-

drew's Hill,—S. side the ch. 1st on the R. from Earl-st.

Warner's Row, Walbrook-Place, Hoxton,—¼ of a mile on the left N. from Winkworth's buildings, City-road.

Warner-St. (Little),—the continuation of Ray-street, from Clerkenwell-green.

Warner-St. (Gt.),—the continuation of the last.

Warner's Yard, Mincing-Lane, — 8 doors on the R. from Fenchurch-st.

Warnford-Court, Throgmorton-St.—at 29, middle of the N. side.

Warren-Mews, Warren-Street, Fitzroy-Sq.—at 32, W. end.

Warren's Rents, Ropemakers-Fields, Limehouse, — at 20, middle of the S. side.

Warren-Row, Turner's Sq.—2d on the R. from Hoxton-town.

Warren-Square (Sir William's), Wapping,—at 181, W. side New Gravel-lane.

Warren-St. Fitzroy-Sq.--N. side, at 133, Tottenham-court-rd.

Warrant of Attorney's Office, Pump-Court, — entrance by the 1st on the L. in Middle Temple-lane, from 5, Fleet-st.

Warwick-Court, High Holborn, —39 doors W. of Gray's-inn-lane.

Warwick-Court, Warwick-Lane. See Warwick-Square.

Warwick-Lane, Newgate-St.—at 10, 1st on the R. from Snow-hill.

Warwick-Pl. Bedford-Row,—N. end of Brownlow-st. from 49, High-Holborn.

Warwick-Pl. Pimlico, — 2d on the R. in Princes-row, op. Arabella-row.

Warwick-Row, Pimlico, — 1st E. of the last.

Warwick-Row, Blackfriars-Rd. — E. side, between Bennet's row and Higlers-lane.

Warwick-Sq. Warwick-Lane, — 12 doors on the L. from Paternoster-row.

Warwick-St. Golden-Sq. — on the W. side, from Glasshouse-st. to Beak-st.

Warwick-Street, Cockspur-St. — 10 doors on the R. from Pall-mall.

Water-Lane, Fleet-St. — at 67, 3d on the L. from Fleet-market.

Water-Lane, Blackfriars, — 1st on the L. in Earl-st. from the bridge.

Water-Lane, Gt. Tower-St. — from 28, op. Mark-lane, to 61, Lower Thames-st.

Water-Lane, Jacob-St. Dock-Head, — 1st S. parallel to it, and the 1st N. to London-st.

Water-Street, Arundel-St. — 1st on the L. from 188, Strand.

Water-St. White-Friars, — 2d on the L. in Tudor-st. from 15, New Bridge-st.

Watermen's Alley, Boro. — the end of Pepper-alley, by London-bridge.

Watermen's Alley, White-Friars-Dock, — on the W. side, by the Rose and Crown.

Watermen's Hall, St. Mary's Hill, — at 18, three doors on the L. from op. Billingsgate.

Watermen's Row, St. George's East, — op. the N. end of

Well-alley, entering by 110, Wapping.

Watling-Street, Saint Paul's Church-Yd. — from 35, to Budge-row.

Watson's Buildings, Ducking-Pond-Row, Whitechapel, — 2d on the L. from North-st.

Watson's Builds. Poplar, — behind the Silver-lion, near North-st.

Watson's Wharf, Lower East-Smithfield, — on the E. side St. Catherine's Dock, by Little Thames-st.

Watts's Court, or Sq. See Chamber-Sq.

Watton-Pl. Blackfriars-Road, — W. side, by the Obelisk.

Waxchandler's Hall, — N. end of Gutter-lane, Cheapside.

Weatherhead's Gardens, Crabtree-Row, Bethnal-Green, — 2d on the R. from Hackney-road.

Weavers-Alley, Shoreditch, — at 188, six doors N. of Holywell-lane.

Weavers Alms-Houses, Hoxton, — the corner of Old-st.-road, and op. the Curtain-road.

Weavers Alms-Houses, Saint John-St. Bethnal-Green, — last on the R. from 105, Brick-lane.

Weavers Alms-Houses, — facing the N. end of Blossom-st. entering by 27, White-lion-st. Norton-Falgate.

Weavers-Arms-Court, Mile-End, — 40 doors E. of Stepney-green.

Weavers-Hall, Basinghall-St. — 22 doors on the R. from Cateaton-st.

Weavers-Lane, Tooley-St.—at 119, last on the L. from London-bridge.

Weavers-St. Bethnal-Green, or Spitalfields,—2d on the R. in Fleet-st.-hill, from St. John-street.

Webb's Builds. Hare-St. Bethnal-Green,—at 87, 1st on the R. from 100, Brick-lane.

Webb's Builds. Risby's Rope-Walk, Limehouse, — middle of the N. side.

Webb's Pl. Snows-Fields,— 2d on the L. from 236, Bermondsey-st.

Webb-Sq. Shoreditch,—behind 47, ¼ of a mile S. from the church.

Webb - Street, Bermondsey-St. —at 248, 1st on the R. from Tooley-st.

Webb - St. Bermondsey New-Road,—1st on the L. from Star-corner.

Webber-Row,—1st on the L. from behind the Magdalen-hospital, Blackfriars-road.

Webber-St. Blackfriars-Road,—by the last, 1st on the L. from the Obelisk.

Webster's Builds. Kennington-Green,—at 17, 2d on the R. from the Horns.

Webster's Wharf, Horselydown, — at the N. end of Freeman's lane, near the E. end of Tooley-st.

Weigh - House - Chapel, Little Eastcheap,—16 doors from Fish-st.-hill.

Weigh - House - Yard, — behind the last.

Weir's Passage, Chalton - St. Sommers-Town,—1st on the

R. from the road to Mary-bone.

Welbeck - Chapel, Westmoreland-St. — 7 doors from 12, Gt. Marybone-st.

Welbeck - Mews (Little), — N. side Little Welbeck-st.

Welbeck -St. Marybone, — 2d W. of Cavendish-sq.

Welbeck-St. (Little),—from 10, in the last, to 80, Wimpole-st.

Well-Alley, Minories, — at 22, that number on the L. from Aldgate.

Well-Alley (Up.), Wapping,— at 110, 15 doors below the London-docks.

Well-Alley (Lower),—the continuation of the last.

Well-Alley,Ropemakers-Fields, Limehouse, — at 63, middle of the N. side.

Well-Alley, Glean-Alley,—1st on the R. from 218, Tooley-street.

Well and Bucket-Court,Old-St. —at 32, 1st E. of Whitecross-street.

Well-Court,Queen-St.—8 doors on the R. from 69, Cheap-side.

Wells-Court, Wells-St.—at 63, 4th on the L. from Oxford-street.

Wells-Court, Hackney-Road,— of a mile on the R. from Shoreditch, and op. Middlesex-place.

Well-Court, Well-St. Mile-End New-Town,—at 36, W. side.

Well-Court, Well-St.Wellclose-Sq. — 1st on the R. from 84, Parsons-st.

Well-Court, Well-Alley, — 1st from Glean-alley, Tooley-st.

C c 3

Well-Court, Russell-St. Bermondsey,—2d on the R. east from Church-st.

Well-Court, Queen-St. Horselydown,—1st on the L. from 58, Gainsford-st.

Wells-Mews, Wells-St. — 25 doors on the R. from 63, Oxford-st.

Wells-Place, Pentonville-Road, Cold-Bath-Fields, — a few houses near Bagnigge-wells.

Wells-Street, Oxford-St.— at 63, the 6th on the R. from St. Giles's.

Wells-Street, St. James's,—the continuation of Eagle-street, from 212, Piccadilly.

Well-Street, Jewin-St. Cripplegate,—6 doors on the L. from Redcross-st.

Well-St. Mile-End New-Town, —the continuation of Montagu-st. from 55, Brick-lane.

Well-St. Wellclose-Sq.—1st on the R. in Cable-st. from Rosemary-lane.

Well-St. Robinhood-Lane,—2d on the L.from E.end of Poplar.

Well-Yard, Bainbridge-Street, St. Giles's, — 1st on the L. from Oxford-st.

Well-Yard, St. Bartholomew's Hospital,—1st on the R. from Little Britain, or from Duke-street.

Well-Yard, Hooper-Sq.—2d on the R. from 82, Lemon-st.

Well-Yard, Rosemary-Lane,— S. end of Peter's court.

Wellclose-Pl. New-Road, St. George's East, — 1st E. of Princes-sq.

Wellclose-Sq. — at 25, Cable-st. and at 72, Parsons-st.

Weller's-Pl. St. Pancras, — 2d from the Small-pox-hospital, towards the church.

Wellington-St. Blackfriars-Rd. —3d on the L. from Surrey-chapel towards the Obelisk.

Welsh's Builds. Royal-Hospital-Row, Chelsea, — 2 doors E. of White-lion-st.

Welsh's Builds. Curtain-Road, —entrance by the 2d on the R. from Old-st.-road.

Welsh-Chapel, — W. end Wilderness-row, Clerkenwell.

Welsh-Chapel,Little Guildford-St. Boro.—a few doors from 75, Queen-st.

Welsh-Charity-School, Gray's-Inn-Lane,—a few doors N. of Guildford-st.

Wenlock-Pl. City-Road, — N. side, between Windsor-terrace and Anderson's buildings.

Wenlock-St. Ironmongers-Row, St. Luke's, — 2d N. of the church.

Wentworth-Court, Wentworth-St.—at 28, op. Old Castle-st. Whitechapel.

Wentworth-Pl. Mile-End,—N. side, ⅓ of a mile below the turnpike, by Red-cow-lane.

Wentworth-St. Spitalfields, — 1st on the L. in Osborn-st. from op. the church, Whitechapel.

Weslake's Dock, Bermondsey-Wall, — W. side Fountain-stairs, nearly op. Farmer's rope-walk.

West-Ham Water-Works,Mile-End-Road,—N. side, 2 miles from Aldgate, and op. Ewing's builds.

West's Gardens, New Gravel-Lane, — at 87, three doors from 22, Shadwell High-st.

West-India-Docks,—E. end of Limehouse, extending to Blackwall.

West-India-Dock - Company's-Office,—N. W. corner Billiter-sq.

West-Lane, Walworth High-St. —op. East-lane, ½ a mile on the R. from the Elephant and Castle.

West-Lane, Bermondsey,—between Cherry-garden-st. and Mill-pond-bridge.

West-Pl. Bethnal-Green,—1st on the L. from Patriot-sq. towards the Hackney-road.

West-Pl. St. George's Fields,—by the Philanthropic-Reform.

West-Place, Ratcliffe-Row, St. Luke's, — N. side, between Pink's row and Nelson-st.

West-Row, Commercial-Road, Limehouse, — at the E. end of St. Ann's row.

West-Sq. St. George's Fields,—5th on the L. from the Elephant and Castle towards Lambeth.

West-St. Seven-Dials,—N. end of Little St. Martin's lane on the left.

West-St. W.-Smithfield,—at 87, the N. W. corner, leading to Chick-lane.

West-St. Sommers-Town,—2d on the R. from the turnpike, Battle-bridge, towards Marybone.

West-Street, Green-St. Bethnal-Green,—E. side of Green-pl. ⅓ of a mile on the R. from the Green.

West-Street, Crispin-St. Spital-fields,—at 10, leading to the W. side of Spitalfields-market.

West-Street, Prospect-Pl. St. George's Fields,—5th on the L. from the Elephant and Castle.

West's Warehouses,—at 7, Billiter-lane.

Westbourne-Pl. King's-Road,—adjoining the N. E. corner of Sloane-sq.

Westby's Alms-Houses, Hoxton,—N. end of Gloucester-terrace, and op. Brett's builds.

Western-Passage, Marman-St. —2d on the L. from the Commercial-road.

Western-Dispensary, — at 33, Charles-st. Westminster.

Westminster-Abbey,—W. side of Old Palace-yard.

Westminster-Bridge,—N. side the Abbey.

Westminster- Bridge - Road, — from the Obelisk towards the bridge.

Westminster Fire - Office, — at 27, King-st. Covent-garden.

Westminster General - Dispensary,—at 32, Gerrard-street, Soho.

Westminster-Hall,–S. side New Palace-yard, near the bridge.

Westminster-Hall-Court, Wentworth-St. Spitalfields,—at 44, 2d E. of Rose-lane.

Westminster-Hospital, or Public - Infirmary, — E. end of James-st.

Westminster-Library,--44, Jermyn-st.

Westminster - Journal-Newspaper-Office,—at 45, Old Bailey, the corner of Fleet-lane.

Westminster New Lying-Inn-Hospital,—⅛ of a mile on the L. from Westminster-bridge towards the Asylum.

Westmoreland-Academy, Walworth-Common,—¼ of a mile W. of Surrey-sq.

Westmoreland - Builds. Aldersgate-St.—at 159, 17 doors N. of Little Britain.

Westmoreland - Court, Falcon-Sq.—the corner of Silver-st. Wood-st.

Westmoreland-Mews, Gt. Marybone-St.—at 10, five doors W. of Wimpole-st.

Westmoreland - Pl. City-Road, —the continuation of Providence-st. nearly op. Fountain-place.

Westmoreland - Pl. Walworth-Common, — op. Westmoreland-row.

Westmoreland-Row, Walworth-Common,—from Surrey-sq. to Westmoreland-Academy.

Westmoreland-St. Great Marybone-St.—at 12, six doors W. of Wimpole-st.

Weston - Court, Weston - St. Boro.—1st on the R. from 35, Snow's fields.

Weston-Pl. Sommers-Town,—from the turnpike, Battle-bridge, towards St. Pancras.

Weston-St. — 1st in the last from the turnpike.

Weston-St. Pentonville,—nearly op. the Chapel, leading towards Clerkenwell.

Weston-St. Maze,—the continuation of it, entering by 195, Tooley-st.

Weymouth-Mews (Up.), Weymouth-St. — at 42, 1st W. from 51, Portland-pl.

Weymouth-Mews (Lower),—3 doors W. of the last.

Weymouth-Pl. Kent-Road,—adjoining Weymouth-st.

Weymouth-St. Kent-Road,—1st on the R. from the Elephant and Castle.

Weymouth-St. Marybone,—2d on the R. in Portland-road from the New-road.

Weymouth-Terrace, Hackney-Road,—by Alport's Nursery, ⅓ of a mile on the L. from Shoreditch.

Whalebone - Court, Throgmorton-St.—at 39, op. the N. E. corner of the Bank of England.

Whalebone - Court, Bell-Alley. —2d on the L. from 56, Coleman-st.

Wharton's Pl. Holborn, — entrance by 146, nearly op. Middle-row.

Wharton-Pl. Schoolhouse-Lane, Ratcliffe,—middle of the W. side.

Wheatsheaf-Alley, Up. Thames-St. — at 108, near London-bridge.

Wheatsheaf - Stone - Wharf, Wapping, — at 219, E. side King Edward's stairs.

Wheatsheaf- Yard, Fleet-Market,—at 22, 3d on the R. from Ludgate-hill.

Wheeler's Builds. George-Yard, — 1st on the R. from 87, Wentworth-st.

Wheeler - St. Spitalfields, —3d on the L. in Spital-sq. from 103, Bishopsgate.

Wheeler's Wharf, Saint Catherine's, — on the W. side of Hermitage-bridge, ¼ of a mile below the Tower.

Whetstone's Park,—1st on the R. in Gt. Turnstile from 282, High-Holborn.

Wheyman's Builds. Bermondsey-Spa,—nearly op. Augustus-row, W. side the Spa.

Whig (Independent) Newspaper-Office,—1st door on the L. in Warwick-sq. from Warwick-lane.

Whistlers - Court, Salters-Hall-Court,—2d on the L. from 82, Cannon-st.

Whisters-Ground, Gt. Peter-St. Westr.—3d on the L. from Gt. Smith-st.

Whitby-Wharf, Up. Thames-St. —entrance by 79, on the E. side of Three-crane-stairs.

Whitcomb-Court, Whitcomb-St. —1st on the R. from Coventry-st.

Whitcomb-St. Charing-Cross,— 1st on the R. from the Strand.

White's Alley, Chancery-Lane, —at 33, middle of the E. side.

White's Alley (Little), Bream's Builds. — near the E. end, bearing to the R. from 27, Chancery-lane.

White's Alley, Coleman-St.— at 60, 5th on the R. from Lothbury.

White's Alley, Long - Alley, Moorfields,— 1st on the L. from Worship-st. near the Curtain-road.

White - Bear - Alley, Aldgate-High-St.—at 18, ten doors E. of the church.

White-Bear-Alley, Princes- St. Lambeth, — 4th on the L. from Vauxhall.

White-Bear-Court, Shoreditch, —at 184, op. Church-st. leading to Foster's builds.

White - Bear - Court, Kent-St. Boro.—at 270, $\frac{1}{8}$ of a mile on the R. from St. George's ch.

White-Bear-Gardens,—the end of the last.

White - Bear - Gardens, Kingsland - Road, — entrance by Union-walk, Union-st.

White-Bear-Inn, Piccadilly, — E. end, near the Haymarket.

White-Bear-Inn, — at 31, Basinghall-st.

White-Bear -Yard, Eyre-St. — 1st on the R. from Leatherlane.

White-Bear-Yard, Bride-Lane, —1st on the R. from 9, New Bridge-st.

White's Builds. Rosemary-Lane. See Abel's Builds.

Whitechapel High-St.—the continuation of Aldgate, from Somerset-st. and Petticoatlane, to the church.

Whitechapel-Road, — from the church, where there are 1 and 281, to the turnpike.

Whitechapel-Workhouse,—$\frac{1}{4}$ of a mile on the L. below the church.

White's Court, Ropemakers-St. — 3d on the L. from the N. W. corner of Moorfields.

White's Court, Montagu - St. Spitalfields,—6 doors on the R. from 53, Brick-lane.

White's Court, Green-Bank,— 2d on the R. from Wapping-church.

White's Court, Vine - Yard,— 1st on the R. from 110, Tooley-st.

Whitecross-Pl. Wilson-St. — at 22, the 3d on the R. from Moorfields.

Whitecross-St. Cripplegate, — from 115, Fore-st. to nearly op. the church, Old-st.

Whitecross - Street, Queen-St. Boro.—at 96, 1st on the L. from Union-st.

Whitefriars,—N. side the river Thames, between New Bridge-st. and the Temple.

Whitefriars-Dock,—facing Water-lane, from 67, Fleet-st.

Whitefriars New Wharf, — on the E. side the Temple-gardens.

White's Grounds, Bethnal-Green-Road,—at 95, 1st on the R. east of the turnpike.

White's Grounds, Crucifix-Lane, —1st on the R. from 50, Bermondsey-st.

Whitehall, Charing-Cross,—the continuation of it, from the Admiralty to Parliament-st.

Whitehall - Court, Tower-Hill, —middle of the E. side, leading to St. Catherine's lane.

Whitehall-Court, Gascoigne-Pl. Bethnal-Green,—2d on the L. from 40, Castle-st.

Whitehall-Stairs,— entrance by Whitehall-yard.

Whitehall - Yard, Whitehall,— op. the Horse-guards.

Whitehall - Timber-Yard, — W. end of Cannon-row.

White - Hart Coach - Office, Strand,—at 296, 6 doors E. of the New Church.

White - Hart-Court, Windmill-St.—6 doors on the L. from 35, Tottenham-court-road.

White-Hart-Court, Castle - St. Leicester - Sq. — at 31, ten doors N. of Hemming's-row.

White-Hart-Court, Long-Lane,

W.-Smithfield,—at 17, 2d on the R. from 119, Aldersgate-street.

White - Hart - Court, Charter-House-Lane,—entrance by 6, 2d on the R. from St. John-street.

White - Hart - Court, Battle-Bridge, St. Pancras,—4 doors E. of the Maidenhead.

White - Hart - Court, Lombard-St.—from 41 to 28, Grace-church-st.

White-Hart-Court, Bishopsgate, --at 200, 2d N. of the church.

White-Hart-Court, Hoxton, — op. the Britannia, ¼ of a mile on the R. from Old-st.-road.

White-Hart-Court, Gascoigne-Pl.—1st on the L. from Castle-street, behind Shoreditch-church.

White-Hart-Court, Greenfield-St.—1st on the R. from Field-gate-st. Whitechapel.

White-Hart Court, Green-Bank, Wapping, — 2d on the R. from the church.

White-Hart - Court, Bermond-sey-St.—at 242, near Snow's fields.

White-Hart-Court, Walworth, —1st on the L. from the Elephant and Castle.

White-Hart-Fields, Kennington-Lane,—behind White-hart-pl.

White-Hart-Inn, St. John-Street, —at 120, ½ of a mile on the R. from Smithfield.

White-Hart-Inn, Boro.—at 62, near St. Margaret's hill.

White - Hart - Pl. Kennington-Lane, — L. side, from Kennington-cross towards Newington.

White - Hart - Pl. Robinhood-Lane, — 3 doors on the L. from the E. end of Poplar.

White-Hart-Row, Gravel-Lane, —E. end of George-st. Black-friars-road.

White-Hart-Row, Kennington-Lane, — 3d on the L. from Newington.

White-Hart-Row, Gray's-Inn-Lane, — N. end, adjoining Battle-bridge.

White-Hart-St. Warwick-Lane, —1st on the R. from Pater-noster-row.

White-Hart-Wharf, Lambeth,—op. Broad-st.

White-Hart-Yard, Tottenham-Court-Road,—at 197, op. Whitfield's chapel.

White-Hart-Yard, Titchborne-St.—12 doors on the R. from the Haymarket.

White-Hart-Yard, Drury-Lane, —at 82, 3d on the L. from the Strand.

White-Hart-Yard, Drury-Lane, —1st on the L. from Holborn.

White - Hart - Yard, Brook-St. Holborn,—at 20, op. Brook's Market.

White Hart Yard, London-Wall, —near the S. E. corner of Moorfields.

White-Hart Yard, Whitechapel, —10 doors E. of Somerset-st. Aldgate.

White-Hart-Yard, Lower East-Smithfield,—at 43, 1st on the L. from Butcher-row.

White-Hind-Alley, Maid-Lane, —op. Gt. Guildford-st.

White - Hind - Court, Bishops-gate-Without,— at 163, op. Widegate-st.

White-Horse-Alley, Cow-Cross, —2d on the R. from Saint John-st.

White-Horse-Alley, Turnmill-St. Clerkenwell,—at 35, mid-dle of the W. side.

White-Horse-Alley, Sharp's Al-ley, West-Smithfield,—1st on the L. from West-st.

White-Horse- Builds. Boot-St. Hoxton,—1st on the L. from Pitfield-st.

White - Horse - Cellar (New) Coach-Office, Piccadilly,—at 66, three doors W. of Albe-marle-st.

White - Horse - Cellar (Old) Coach-Office, Piccadilly,—at 159, two doors W. of Arling-ton-st.

White-Horse-Court, Windmill-St.—6 doors on the L. from Tottenham-court-road.

White -Horse- Court, Golden-Lane,—at 125, middle of the W. side.

White Horse Court, Whitecross-St. —at 93, 5th on the R. north of Chiswell-st.

White Horse-Court, Long-Lane, West-Smithfield,—a few doors on the R. from 118, Alders-gate-st.

White-Horse-Court, Wheeler St. Spitalfields,—at 16, 2d on the R. from Lamb-st.

White-Horse-Court, Rosemary-Lane,—3d on the L. from the Minories.

White-Horse-Court, High - St. Boro. — 8 doors on the L. from London-bridge.

White-Horse-Court, Kent - St. Boro.—at 293, the end of Royal Tents.

White-Horse-Court, Star-Corner, Bermondsey,—1st S. of Long-lane.

White-Horse-Inn, Fetter-Lane, —at 88, twelve doors on the R. from 32, Holborn-hill.

White-Horse-Inn, Friday-St.—30 doors on the R. from 36, Cheapside.

White-Horse-Inn, Cripplegate, —N. end of Wood-st. on the R. from 122, Cheapside.

White-Horse-Lane, Stepney. See Commercial-Road.

White-Horse-Lane, Mile-End, — op. the Old Globe, ½ a mile on the R. below the turnpike.

White-Horse-Mews, Coleman-St.—entrance by White-horse-yard.

White-Horse-Pl. Commercial-Road,—¼ of a mile E. of the Halfway-house.

White-Horse-St. Piccadilly,—1st W. of Halfmoon-st.

White-Horse-St. Ratcliffe,—the continuation of Butcher-row, Ratcliffe-cross.

White-Horse-Yard, Farm-St. Berkeley-Sq. — at 7, nearly op. John-st.

White-Horse-Yd. New Bond-St. —at 131, eight doors S. of Grosvenor-st.

White-Horse-Yd. Gt. Windmill-St. — 4 doors from the Haymarket.

White-Horse-Yard, Chapel-St. Westr.—6 doors on the R. from Tothill-st.

White-Horse-Yard, King-St. Westr.—5 doors S. of Charles-street.

White-Horse-Yard, George-St.

Bloomsbury,—2d on the I'. from 25, Broad-st.

White-Horse-Yd. St. Martin's Lane, Charing-Cross,—at 51, S. side New-st.

White-Horse-Yd. High-Holborn, — at 101, ten doors W. of Dean-st. Red-lion-sq.

White-Horse-Yd. Drury-Lane, —at 110, 5th on the R. from Wych-st.

White-Horse-Yard, Wood-St.—30 doors on the R. from Cheapside.

White-Horse-Yd. Coleman-St. —17 doors on the R. from London-wall.

White-Horse-Yd. Lincoln's-Inn-Fields,—op. E. end of Little-Wild-st.

White-Horse-Yd. London-Wal' — at 64, ditto, at 56, op. Bethlem-hospital.

White-Horse-Yard, Rood-Lane, Fenchurch-St.—op. the church.

White-Horse-Yd. Lower East-Smithfield,—at 44, 2d W. of Burr-st.

White-Horse-Yd. Blackman-St. Boro. — at 89, op. Union-place.

White-Horse-Yard, Kent-St. Boro.—at 124, ½ of a mile on the L. from Saint George's church.

Whitelands, King's Road, Chelsea, — by Colvill's Nursery, op. the Hospital.

White-Linen-Court, Bankside, Boro.—a few yards W. of Thames-st.

White-Lion-Court, Little Bell-Alley, — 1st on the L. fror London-wall.

White-Lion-Court, Birchin-

Lane,—at 21, 2d on the L. from Cornhill.

White-Lion-Court, Cornhill,— at 64, three doors from Bishopsgate-st.

White-Lion-Court, Throgmorton-St. — at 20, four doors from Broad-st.

White-Lion-Court, Bankside, Boro. — at 55, fourth W. of Thames-st.

White-Lion-Court, Bermondsey-St. — at 234, leading to Snow's fields.

White-Lion-Court, White-Lion-St. Seven-Dials, — 3 doors from Monmouth-st.

White-Lion-Court, Fleet-St.— at 76, five doors W. of Salisbury-court.

White-Lion-Court, or Builds. White-Lion-St. Pentonville,— 1st on the L. from Islington.

White-Lion-Court, Tower-St.— at 40, ten doors on the L. from Tower-hill.

White-Lion-Court, Charterhouse-Lane,—at 6, 2d on the L. from Charterhouse-sq.

White-Lion-Pl. Islington, — a few yards N. of White-lion-street.

White-Lion-Sq. Old Bethlem,— at 16, middle of the N. side.

White-Lion-St. Chelsea,—the continuation of Lower Sloane-st. to Royal Hospital-row.

White-Lion St. Norton-Falgate, —12 houses N. of Spital-sq.

White-Lion-St. Seven-Dials,— 1st on the L. in Monmouth-st. from Broad-st. St. Giles's.

White-Lion-St. (Little),—continuation of the last to Mercer-st. Long-acre.

White-Lion-St. Pentonville, — 1st on the L. in High-st. Islington, from the Angel-inn.

White-Lion-St. Whitechapel,— the continuation of Lemon-st. to 76, Rosemary-lane.

White - Lion - Wharf, Upper Thames-St.—at 19, op. Bennet's hill.

White-Lion-Yd. Vauxhall,—op. Vauxhall-stairs to the gardens.

White-Lion-Yd. Lambeth,—op. the church.

White-Lion-Yd. White-Lion-St. Norton-Falgate,—at 22, five doors E. of Blossom-st.

White-Lion-Yd. Whitecross-St. St. Luke's,—at 172, 5th on the R. from Old-st.

White-Lion-Yd. Oxford-St. — at 73, nearly op. the Pantheon.

White-Lion-Yd. Monmouth-St. Shadwell,—middle of the N. side.

White-Lion-Yd. Wych St. — 6 doors E. of Newcastle-st.

White's Rents, Wood-St. Westr. — 3d on the R. from 64, Millbank-st.

White's Rents, Fore-St. Limehouse, — at 86, 2d on the L. from Narrow-st.

White-Rose-Alley, Whitecross-St. Cripplegate,—at 58, 1st S. of Chiswell-st.

White - Rose - Court, Coleman-St.—at 30, op. Bell-alley.

White-Rose-Court, Widegate-St. — at 13, 2d on the R. from Bishopsgate.

White's Row, Baker's Row,— 1st on the R. from 94, Whitechapel-road.

D d

White-Row, Spitalfields, — the continuation of Fashion-st. from 194, Brick-lane.

White-St. Bethnal-Green-Rd.— at 72, 2d on the right E. of the turnpike.

White-Street, Cutler-St. — 2d on the R. from 114, Hounds-ditch.

White-Street, Church-St. Boro. —the continuation of it, on the L. from St. George's church.

White-St. Little Moorfields,— the last on the L. from 61, Fore-st.

White-Thorn-Court, King-St. St. George's East, — 1st on the L. from 29, New Gravel-lane.

White's Yard, Gt. Saffron-Hill, —at 23, nearly op. Charles-st. Hatton-garden.

White's Yard, Whitecross-St. St. Luke's, — at 155, 2d on the R. from Old-st.

White's Yard, Mile-End,—⅛ of a mile E. of Stepney green.

White's Yard,—from 58, Rose-mary-lane, to 97, Up. East-Smithfield.

Whitehead's Builds. Exeter-St. — 2d on the L. from 32, Sloane-st.

Whitfield-Street, Leonard-St.— 1st on the L. from Paul-st. towards the City-road.

Whiting's Rents, Hickman's Folly,—2d on the R. from Dock-head.

Whiting's Wharf, Broad-Street, Ratcliffe, — at 43, E. side Stone-stairs.

Whiting's Yard, Dog and Bear-

Yard,—1st on the R. from 127, Tooley-st.

Whittington's College, College-Hill,—by the church, middle of the E. side.

Whitley's Court, Brick-Lane, St. Luke's,—at 73, 2d on the R. from 113, Old-st.

Whitton's Folly, White-Hart-Row, Kennington, — 3d on the R. from Clayton-pl.

Wichelow's Warehouses, Lower Thames-St.—at 70, op. Bear-quay.

Wicher's Alms-Houses, Westr. — E. side the Blue-coat-school, near James-st.

Wickham-Court, Wych-Street, Drury-Lane,—at 23, 6 doors E. of Newcastle-st.

Widegate-St. Bishopsgate,— at 51, 3d on the right N. of the church.

Widnal's Pl. Vine-St. Mutton-Lane,—2d on the R. from Clerkenwell-green.

Wiggin's Quay, Lower Thames-St.—op. 80, E. side Billings-gate.

Wigmore-St. Cavendish-Sq. — from the N. W. corner, to Edward-st.

Wild-Court, Gt. Wild-St.—1st on the L. from 48, Great Queen-st.

Wild-Passage, Drury-Lane, — from 138, to Gt. Wild-st.

Wild-St.(Gt.),—1st on the R. in Gt. Queen-st. from 155, Drury-lane.

Wild-St. (Little), — 2d on the L. in the last, from Queen-street.

Wilderness-Lane, Dorset-St.

Salisbury-Sq.—at 59, 2d on the R. from 82, Fleet-st.

Wilderness-Row, Goswell-St.— nearly op. Old-st. leading to 54, St. John-st.

Wilderness-Row, Chelsea,—last on the R. in Royal Hospital-row, from the Hospital.

Wilkies-Court, Shoreditch,—at 101, 3d on the L. from the church.

Wilks Street, Quaker-St. Spital-fields,—2d on the L. from 173, Brick-lane, behind Hanbury's brewery.

Wilkinson's Builds. Edgeware-Road,—at 76, part of the E. side.

William's Buildings, Yeoman's Row, Brompton, — R. side, from Michael's pl.

Williams-Builds. French-Alley, —3d on the R. from 21, Goswell-st.

Williams's Builds. Three-Hammer - Alley, St. Thomas's, Southwark,— 1st on the R. from the Broadway.

Williams - Court, Maid - Lane, Boro.—nearly op. Gt. Guildford-st.

William's Court, William - St. Kent-Road,—1st on the R. from Pitt-st.

Williams's Court, New Gravel-Lane,— 8 doors on the R. from Shadwell High-st.

Williams-Mews, Devonshire-St. —5 doors E. of Portland-pl.

Williams's Mews, Adam-Street West, Portman-Sq.—5 doors on the right N. of Up. Berkeley-st.

Williams-Pl. Walworth,—part of the R. side, from the

Montpelier-gardens towards Camberwell.

William - St. Lisson - Green,— 2d E. of Little James-st.

William-Street, Henry-St.—1st on the R. from op. 91, Gray's-inn-lane.

William-Street, Lant-St. Boro. — 2d on the L from 108, Blackman-st.

William-St. Kennington - Common,—1st N. of the turnpike.

William-St. (Little),—1st N. of the last.

William-Street, Pitt - St.— 1st on the R. from the Kent-rd.

William-St. Blackfriars-Road,— 1st E of or behind Surrey-chapel.

William-Street, Union-St. Lambeth, — 1st on the L from Walcot-pl.

William-St. Marybone-Lane,— at 49, 3d on the L. from 158, Oxford-st.

William-Street, James - Street, Westr.—at 30, 1st on the R. from Buckingham-gate.

William-St. Adelphi, — at 64, Strand, ¼ of a mile on the R. from Charing-cross.

William-Street, New Bridge-St. Blackfriars, — at 21, 1st on the L. from the bridge.

William-St. Hampstead-Rd. — 5th on the R. from Tottenham-court.

William-Street, Cannon-St.-Rd. —2d on the R. south from the Commercial-road.

William-Street, Cannon-St.-Rd. —2d on the R. from Whitechapel.

William - St. Shoreditch, — at 137, 1st on the R. from the

church, extending to the Curtain-road.

William-St. Poplar-Row, — 2d on the R. from the Kent-road.

Willis's Court, Brackley-St.— 1st on the R. from 9, Golden-lane.

Willis's Builds. Bermondsey,— entrance by Calico-buildings, Printers-pl.

Willis's Rents, Bermondsey-St. — at 101, ten doors from Russell-st.

Willis's Rooms, King-Street, St. James's,—at 22, op. Duke-street.

Willow-Court, Seward-St.—1st on the L. from 80, Goswell-street.

Willow-Court, Willow-Street, Shoreditch, — 1st on the L. from Paul-st.

Willow-Row, Goswell-St. — at 50, 12 doors N. of Old-st.

Willow-Street, Paul-St.—2d on the R. north from Leonard-st.

Willow-St. Southwark,—continuation of Bankside to Holland-st. Blackfriars-bridge.

Willow-Walk, Westr. — from Rochester-row to the Neat Houses.

Willow-Walk, Hoxton,—2d on the left, N. from Haberdashers-alms-houses.

Willow-Walk, Curtain-Road,— the continuation of Susannah-row, bearing to the R.

Willow-Walk, Hackney-Road, —op. Middlesex-pl. ¼ of a mile on the R. from Shoreditch.

Willow-Walk, Bermondsey, — the last on the L. in Page's walk, from the Grange-road.

Willow-Tree-Court, Lower-Turning, Shadwell, — 2d on the L. from 76, Shakespear's walk.

Willow-Tree-Court, Newmarket-St.—10 doors on the L. from 157, Wapping.

Willsted-St. Sommers-Town,— 3d on the R. from the turnpike, Battle-bridge, towards Marybone.

Willsted-Court,—at 51, in the last, op. Phillips's builds.

Wilmot-Builds. White-St. Boro. —12 doors E. of St. George's church.

Wilmot's Folly, Bethnal-Green-Road, — N. end of Mary's row, entrance on the E. side of Wilmot-sq.

Wilmot's Grove, Bethnal-Green-Road,—N. side of Wilmot-square.

Wilmot-Sq. Bethnal-Green-Rd. —¾ of a mile on the L. from 65, Shoreditch.

Wilmot-St. Bethnal-Green-Rd. —last on the R. near a mile from Shoreditch.

Wilmot-Street, Bernard-St. — at 36, 1st on the R. from Brunswick-sq.

Wilson's Court, Duke-Street, St. George's Fields,—N. end, the corner of Tower-st.

Wilson's Court, Kent-St. Boro. —at 87, ⅓ of a mile on the L. from St. George's church.

Wilson-Court, Maid-Lane, Boro.—2d on the L. from Park-street.

Wilson's Place, Salmon's Lane, Limehouse,—1st on the L. from the Commercial-road.

Wilson's Court,—N. side the last.

Wilson-St. Moorfields, — near the middle of the N. side.

Wilton-St. Grosvenor-Pl. — at 43, fourth on the R. from Hyde-park-corner.

Wiltshire-Lane, Parsons-St. — at 40, 2d W. of Ratcliffe-highway.

Wimpole-Mews, Upper Devonshire-St.-between Up. Wimpole-st. and Beaumont-st.

Wimpole-Mews, Weymouth-St. —at 38, between Wimpole-st. and Harley-st.

Wimpole-St. Cavendish-Sq. — 1st W. of the square.

Wimpole-St. (Up.),—N. continuation of the last.

Winchester - Chapel, Parliament-Court, Artillery-Lane, Bishopsgate, on the W. side.

Winchester-Court, Monkwell-St.—6 doors on the R. from Falcon-sq.

Winchester-Court, Winchester-St. Pentonville,—8 doors N. of Collier-st.

Winchester-Gardens, Winchester-St. Pentonville,—at 32, 1st on the R. from the High-road.

Winchester-Pl. Pentonville, — R. side the road, ⅛ of a mile from Islington.

Winchester-Pl. Hackney-Road, —near the end of Willow-walk, or Green-gate-gardens.

Winchester-Pl. Pepper-St. Boro.—2d from the W. end of Queen-st.

Winchester-Row, Edgware-Rd. —at 81, near ½ a mile on the R. from Tyburn-turnpike.

Winchester-St. Pentonville, — 3d W. of the chapel.

Winchester-Street, Old Broad-St.—at 54, nearly op. the Excise-office.

Winchester-St. (Little),—1st in the last, from Old Broad-st.

Winchester-St. Boro.-Market, —N. side, by St. Saviour's church.

Winchester-St. (Little),—1st on the R. in the last from the church.

Winchester-Yd. Boro.-Market, —by Little Winchester-st.

Winchester - Wharf, Clink - St. Boro.—nearly op. Stoney-st.

Winckles-Buildings, Walworth-Common, — op. Phillips's builds.

Windle's Wharf,—at the bottom of Milford-lane, from 200, Strand.

Windmill-Court, Giltspur-St.— at 19, 4th on the R. from Newgate-st.

Windmill - Court, Rosemary-Lane, — at 54, three doors W. of White's yard.

Windmill-Inn, St. John-Street, —3d inn on the R. ⅛ of a mile from Smithfield.

Windmill-Lane, Deptford Lower-Road,—⅓ of a mile on the L. below the Halfway-house.

Windmill - Row, Kennington-Green, — W. side, near the Windmill-tavern.

Windmill-St. Tottenham-Court-Road,—at 45, op. Gt. Store-street.

Windmill-St. (Gt.) Haymarket, —op. the N. end of it, from Coventry-st. to Brewer-st.

Windmill-St. (Little),—the continuation of the last to Silver-street.

Windmill-St. City-Road,—a few yards bearing to the R. from the N. W. corner of Finsbury-sq.

Windsor-Court, Monkwell-St.— at 40, 1st on the L. from Falcon-sq.

Windsor-Court, Little Knight-Rider-St.—at 14, 1st on the R. from the Old Change.

Windsor-Court, Strand,—near 330, op. Somerset-pl.

Windsor-Pl. City-Road, — op. Windsor-terrace, ⅔ of a mile on the L. from Finsbury-square.

Windsor-Pl. Bird-St. Lambeth, —1st on the L. from Brook-street.

Windsor-Pl. Kent-Road, — S. side the Bricklayers-arms.

Windsor-Street, Widegate-St.— 1st on the R. from 51, Bishopsgate-st.

Windsor-Terrace, City-Rd.— W. side St. Luke's workhouse, ⅔ of a mile on the R. from Finsbury-sq.

Wine-Office-Court, Fleet St.— at 145, 3d W. of Shoe-lane.

Winford-Court, Wentworth-St. Spitalfields,—6 doors W. of Rose-lane.

Winkworth's Builds. City-Rd.— by Craven-builds. ⅓ of a mile on the R. from Finsbury-sq.

Winkworth's Wharf,—E. side of Broken-wharf, entering by 41, Up. Thames-st.

Winsley-Street, Oxford-St.—at 78, op. the Pantheon.

Winter's Court, Long-Lane, Bermondsey,—middle of the S. side.

Winter's Pl.—1st E. of the last.

Winter's Pl. Lambeth-Walk,— few doors on the L. from the New Chapel.

Wise-Court, Wheeler-St. — 1st on the L. from Spital-sq.

Wise-Court, Castle-St. Boro.— at 45, near Potts's Vinegar-ground.

Wither's Court, Whitecross-St. —at 140, 1st on the L. from Old-st.

Wittem's Builds. Old-St.-Road, — part of the N. side, adjoining the Vinegar-ground.

Woburn-Court, Duke-Street, Bloomsbury,—1st from 42, Gt. Russell-st.

Woburn-Mews, Little Guilford-St. Russell-Sq. — middle W. side.

Woburn-Pl. Russell-Sq.—from the N. E. corner to Tavistock-sq.

Woburn-Street, Gt. Russell-St. Bloomsbury,—at 39, middle of the S. side.

Woburn-Street, Brydges-Street, Covent-Garden,—at 23, S. side of Drury-lane-theatre.

Wolsingham-Pl. Lambeth, — from the Stags to the Asylum.

Wonder-What-Pl. New-Road, Sloane-St.—2d N. of Exeter-street.

Wood's Builds. George-Street, Chelsea, — 1st on the R. from Royal-Hospital-row.

Wood's Builds. St. Pancras,— E. side Paradise-row.

Wood's Builds. New-Inn-Yard, —last on the L. from 175, Shoreditch.

Wood's Builds. Whitechapel-

Road,—at 124, op. the London-hospital.

Wood's Builds. East - Lane, Walworth,—1st on the R. from the Kent-road.

Wood's Close, Church - Row, Bethnal - Green,—S. side the church, near Hare-st.

Wood's Court, George-Street, Westr,—2d on the L. from James-st.

Wood's Court, Oxford-St.—at 81, nearly op. the Pantheon.

Wood's Court, Norton-Falgate, —at 27, nearly op. White-lion-st.

Wood's Mews, Park-St. — at 82, 4th on the R. from 257, Oxford-st.

Wood's Pl. Bowling - Green-Lane, Clerkenwell,—1st on the R. from Coppice-row.

Wood's Pl. Chequer-Alley, — the 1st on the R. from 107, Whitecross-st.

Wood-Street, Millbank-Street, Westr.—at 64, 1st on the R. from Abingdon-st.

Wood-St. Spa-Pl. Spa-fields,— 6 doors E. of the turnpike, near the House of Correction.

Wood-St. Cheapside,—at 122, 3d on the L. from Newgate-street.

Wood-St. Spitalfields,—N. side the church to 8, Brown's lane.

Wood-St. Bethnal-Green,—last on the L. in Hare-st. from 110, Brick-lane.

Wood-Street, St. Agnes-le-Clair, —last on the L. in North-st. from the City-road.

Wood's Ways, Rotherhithe,— N. side of Rotherhithe-ch.

Wood's Wharf, Bridewell-Precinct,—1st W. of Blackfriars-bridge.

Wood's Yard, Phœnix-St. Spitalfields,—2d on the R. from 38, Wheeler-st.

Wood-Yard, Redcross-St. Boro. —at 74, 1st N. of Union-st.

Woodbridge - Street, St. John-St. Clerkenwell,— at 108, op. Compton-st.

Wooden-Bridge-Stairs, Westr. —N. E. corner of New Palace-yard.

Wooden-World-Court,—at the W. end of Bell-alley, Golden-lane.

Woodstock-Court, Woodstock-St.——1st on the R. from 302, Oxford-st.

Woodstock-Mews, Woodstock-St. Marybone,— behind 30, Weymouth-st.

Woodstock-St. (Little), Weymouth-St. Marybone,—at 30, 4 doors W. of 44, Wimpole-street.

Woodstock-Street, Paddington-St. Marybone,—10 doors on the R. from 70, High-st.

Woodstock-Street, Oxford-St. — at 303, 1st W. of New Bond-st.

Woodwards - Court, High - St. Marybone, — 1st on the R. from the New-road.

Wooldrich's Gardens, Fleet-St. Bethnal - Green, or Spitalfields, —a number of small houses at the E. end of it.

Woolford's Ways, Wapping-Wall,—E. side of King James's

stairs, op. Star-street, Shad-well.

Woolpack - Alley, Bermondsey-Street,—at 242, near Snow's fields.

Woolpack - Gardens, Goswell-St.-Road, — 1st on the R. from Islington.

Woolpack-Yard, Gravel-Lane, Boro.— op. George-st.

Woolpack-Yd. Dog and Bear-Yard,—1st on the L. from 127, Tooley-st.

Woolpack-Yd. Kent-St. Boro.— at 54, ¼ of a mile on the L. from St. George's church.

Woolmor-St. Robinhood-Lane, —3d on the L. from E. end of Poplar.

Wool - Staplers Alms - Houses, Gt. St. Ann's Street, Westr.—10 doors on the R. from Peter-st.

Worcester- Court, Worcester-St.—1st on the L. from Old Gravel-lane.

Worcester-Pl. Up. Thames-St. —at 67, op. Garlick-hill.

Worcester-St. Old Gravel-Lane, —at 143, 2d on the R. from Ratcliffe highway.

Worcester - Street, Queen - St. Boro. — 2d on the R. from Union-hall.

Works (Office of), Guildhall,— 2 doors on the R. from 75, Basinghall-st.

Workhouse- Alley, Limehouse. See Green-Dragon-Alley.

Workhouse-Lane, Hoxton,—op. the Queen's head, ½ a mile on the L. from Old-street-road.

Workhouse-Lane, Lambeth,—

the continuation of Lambeth-butts, towards Kennington.

World's End, Stepney, — near the N. E. corner of the Church-yard.

World's End-Court, Newington-Causeway,—N. side the turn-pike.

Worley's Court, Minories,—entrance by 79, op. the Crescent.

Wormwood-St. Bishopsgate, — at 65, S. side the church.

Worship-Court, Worship-St.— 4th on the L. from Paul-st.

Worship-Sq. Worship-St. — 3d on the L. from Paul-st. leading to Chapel-st.

Worship -St. Shoreditch, — 2d on the R. north from the N. E. corner of Finsbury-sq.

Wrestlers-Court, Camomile-St. —5 doors from Bishopsgate.

Wright's Builds. West-St. West-Smithfield, — 3d on the R. from 86, Smithfield.

Wright's Builds. Grange-Road, —4th on the R. from Bermondsey New-road towards Rotherhithe.

Wright's Passage, Tothill - St. Westr.—middle of the S. side.

Wright's Pl. Cotton-St. Poplar, —1st on the L. from the E.-India-dock-road.

Wright's Rents, Pell-St. Ratcliffe,—1st on the L. from 6, New-road.

Wright's Rents, Grange-Road, Bermondsey,—on the N. side Page's walk.

Wright's Yard, New Bond-St.— at 40, six doors S. of Maddox-st.

Wych-St. Drury-Lane,—1st on the R. from the New Church, Strand.

Wycomb-Pl. Kent-St. Boro.— at 70, ¼ of a mile on the L. from St. George's church.

Wynyatt-St. Islington-Road,— 5th on the R. from St. John-street.

Wynyatt-Pl. Wynyatt-St. — 3 doors on the R. from Goswell-st.-road.

———

Y AXLY-PLACE, Little Lant-St. Boro. — middle of the S. side.

Yeats-Court, Carey-St. Chance-ry-Lane,—at 23, 2d on the R. from Portugal-st.

Yeats - Court, Long - Alley, Moorfields, — 2d on the L. from 29, Sun-street, towards Moorfields.

Yeats-Rents, Clerkenwell-Close, —at 23, a few doors N. of the church.

Yeoman's Row, Brompton, — 5th on the L. from Knights-bridge.

Yerrway's Wharf, Earl-Street, Blackfriars, — 2d E. of the bridge.

Yoakley's Buildings, Mile-End-Green,— 9 doors E. from the London-hospital.

York-Builds. Grub-St. Westr.— middle of the E. side.

York-Builds. Adelphi,—the S. side of Duke-st.

York-Builds. Water-Works, — the bottom of Villiers-street, Strand.

York-Builds. New-Road, Marybone,—S. side, near Baker-st. Portman-sq.

York-Builds. York-St. Penton-ville, — 2d on the L. from Clarence-pl.

York-Builds. Bermondsey New-Road,—at the end of Kent-st.-road.

York-Builds. Chalton-St. Som-mers-Town,—at 48, middle of the W. side.

York-Builds. Hoxton-Fields,— ¼ of a mile on the L. from Winkworth's builds. City-rd. towards Kingsland.

York-Builds. York-Street, Wal-worth,—1st on the L. from the High-st.

York-Court, East-St. Manches-ter-Sq.—at 40, 12 doors on the L. from David-st.

York-Court, York-St. Penton-ville, — 1st on the L. from Clarence-pl.

York-Court, Paul-St. Finsbury-Sq.—at 14, leading into Castle-st.

York-Court, York-St. — 1st on the R. from the London-rd.

Yo k-Hospital, Ebury-St. Chel-sea,—at the W. end, by the Watch-house.

York-Mews South, Paddington-St. Marybone,—three doors from Baker-st.

York-Mews North, David -St. Marybone, — between York-pl. and East-st.

York-Mews (Gt.), York-Pl. Ma-rybone,—1st on the R. from the New-road.

York-Mews (Little), W. end of the last.

York-Pl. Marybone,—continuation of Baker-st. Portman-square.

York-Pl. (Little),—W. end of Gt. York-mews.

York-Pl. James-St. Westr.—E! en:d, op. the Blue-coat-school.

York-Pl. Pentonville, — from Clarence-pl. to the turnpike.

York-Pl. Banner-St.—at 27, 1st on the L. from 130, White-cross-st.

York-Pl. City-Road,—N. side, nearly op: Sidney-st. a mile from Finsbury-sq.

York-Pl. Lower Chapman-St.— 3d on the R. from Cannon-st.-road.

York-Pl. Cow-Lane, Stepney,— by the World's End public-house.

York-Pl. Mile-End-Road, — S. side, by Saville-pl. 2¼ miles from Aldgate.

York-Pl. York-St. — 1st on the L. from the Commercial-rd.

York-Pl. Lambeth,—op. the W. side of the Asylum.

York-Pl. Revel-Row,—N. side the King's Bench.

York-Pl. Walworth High-St.— the L. side, ⅓ of a mile from the Elephant and Castle.

York-Pl. Arnold-Pl. Walworth, —2d on the L. from Amelia-street.

York-Pl. Ossulston-St. Sommers-Town, — 1st on the L. north of Chapel-path.

York-Pl. Bird-St. Lambeth, — 2d on the L. from Brook-st.

York-Place, Kent-St. Road, — 1st on the R. from the Brick-layers-arms.

York-Pl. Walbrook-Pl. Hoxton, —¼ of a mile on the L. north from Winkworth's buildings, City-road.

York-Row, — at the N. end of the last.

York-Row, Hackney-Road, — R. side, ⅙ of a mile from Shoreditch-church.

York-Row, Kent-St.-Road,—N. end of York-terrace.

York-Row, Kennington-Road, —the continuation of Orange-row from the Plough and Harrow.

York-St. Hans-Pl. — 1st on the L. in Exeter-street, from 32, Sloane-st.

York-St. Westr.—the continuation of James-st. bearing to the L.

York-Street, St. James's Sq.— middle of the N. side, leading to the S. side of Saint James's church, Piccadilly.

York-St. Covent-Garden, — 2d on the L. along Catherine-st. from 343, Strand.

York-St. Marybone,—5th on the L. in Baker-st. from Portman-sq.

York-St. (Up.),— the continuation of the last.

York-St. Middlesex-Hospital, Marybone,—from 18, Union-st. to Foley-st.

York-Street, Castle-St.—1st on the R. from 60, Gt. Saffron-hill.

York-St. Pentonville, — 2d on the L. west of the chapel.

York-Street (Gt.), Church-St. Bethnal-Green,—at 185, 1st on the R. from 65, Shore-ditch.

York-Street (Little), Church-St. Bethnal-Green,—at 179, 2d

on the R. from 65, Shore-ditch.

York - St. Commercial - Road, Mild-End Old - Town, — 2d W. of Cannon-st.-road, extending to 45, Charlotte-st.

York-St. Walworth High-St.--3d on the L. from the Elephant and Castle.

York-St. Lock's Fields, Walworth,—2d on the L. in Pitt-st. from the Kent-road.

York-Street, Clarence-St.—1st on the R. from 303, Rotherhithe-st.

York-Street, High-St. Boro.—at 276, 1st on the R. from London-bridge.

York-St. London-Road, — 1st on the R. from the Elephant and Castle.

York-St. Blackfriars- Road,—1st N. of Surry-chapel.

York-Street (Lower), Bicknel's Row, Rotherhithe,—1st on the L. from Russell-st.

York-St. (Upper), — the continuation of the last.

York - Terrace, Kent-St.-Road, —the E. side, by the Bricklayers-arms.

York-Wharf, Fore-St. Lambeth, —20 doors S. of Broad-st.

Yorkshire-Crop-Yd. St. Peter's Lane, W.-Smithfield, — at 6, by St. John-st.

Yorkshire-Grey-Yd. Worship-Sq. —at the N. W. corner.

Yorkshire-Grey - Yard, Blackman-St. Boro.—at 107, by Lant-st.

Yorkshire-Stingo-Tavern, New-

Road, Marybone, — ½ of a mile on the R. from 82, Edgware-road.

Youl's Row, Kent-Road, — by Youl's nursery, East-lane.

Young's Builds. Horse-Shoe-Alley, Moorfields,—2d on the L. from 14, Wilson-st.

Young's Buildings, Nightingale-Lane, Limehouse,—2d on the L. from Ropemaker's fields.

Young's Builds. Old-St.—W. side of Whitecross-st. nearly op. the church.

Young's Builds. Paul's - Alley, Cripplegate, — 2d on the R. from 13, Redcross-st.

Young's Builds. Church-Alley, —1st on the R. from 70, Basinghall-st.

Young's Quay, Lower Thames-St.—at 24, E. side Billingsgate.

Yoxall's Wharf, — N. end of Mill-lane, bearing to the R. from 55, Tooley-st.

Yoxley's Builds. Raven - Row, Whitechapel,—8 doors E. of the London-hospital.

———

ZION-CHAPEL and Square. See Sion.

Zoar-Chapel, Ayliffe-St.—a few yards from Somerset-street, Aldgate.

Zoar-St. Gravel-Lane, Boro.—2d on the L. from Holland-st. Blackfriars-bridge.

THE END.

James Compton, Printer, Middle Street, Cloth Fair, London.

BOOKS
Printed for SHERWOOD, NEELY, and JONES.

MAVOR'S VOYAGES AND TRAVELS.
On the Firſt of November was publiſhed, price Six Shillings, in extra
boards, embelliſhed with Five Plates,
Volume the Firſt, of
A GENERAL COLLECTION of VOYAGES and
TRAVELS; including the moſt intereſting Records of Navigators and
Travellers, from the Diſcovery of America by Columbus, in the Year
1492, to the Travels of Lord Valentia.
By WILLIAM MAVOR, LL.D.
Author of the " Univerſal Hiſtory," &c. &c.

CONDITIONS.—For the convenience of the Public, this new and improved Edition of Dr. MAVOR's VOYAGES and TRAVELS will be publiſhed in Monthly Volumes, the Second Volume to appear on the Firſt
Day of December, and continued monthly till completed.—The Work
will be uniformly printed in Royal 18mo. and completed in Twenty-
eight handſome and cloſely-printed Volumes, each containing about
400 pages; the whole illuſtrated and embelliſhed with upwards of 150
Engravings and Maps.

This new and enlarged Work conſiſts partly of a Reprint of a ſimilar
Collection made by the ſame Author, which has for a conſiderable time
been out of print, and partly of new matter. In the Voyages, thoſe
of Anſon, Byron, Wallis, Carteret, and Cook, are copied, verbatim,
from the original editions; among the Travels, thoſe of Addiſon, Montagu, and Smollett, are entire; with abridgments of many valuable
works publiſhed ſubſequent to the appearance of the former Edition,
bringing the Collection down to the preſent time.

MAVOR'S UNIVERSAL HISTORY.
On the Firſt of November was publiſhed, cloſely printed in 18mo. embelliſhed with an Hiſtorical Frontiſpiece, deſigned by Burney, price
4s 6d in extra boards, or elegantly printed on fine Royal Paper, 6s;
Volume the Firſt, of
A UNIVERSAL HISTORY, Ancient and Modern;
comprehending a General View of the Tranſactions of every Nation,
Kingdom, and Empire, in the World, from the earlieſt Period to the
preſent Time.
By WILLIAM MAVOR, LL.D.
Vicar of Hurley in Berkſhire, &c. &c.

CONDITIONS.—This valuable Work will be uniformly printed in
demy 18mo. on good paper, and completed in 25 Volumes, (9 Ancient
and 16 Modern) price 4s 6d each; alſo a ſuperior Edition, printed uni-
form with Dr. Mavor's Voyages and Travels, on fine Royal Paper,
price 6s.—A Volume will be publiſhed regularly on the Firſt Day of
every Month, and will be illuſtrated with an Hiſtorical Frontiſpiece,
deſigned and engraved by an eminent Artiſt, repreſenting ſome principal
event; and the whole will be accompanied with a valuable Set of Maps.